BRIEF EDITION   SIXTH EDITION

Volume II: Since 1500

The Earth and Its Peoples

A Global History

Richard W. Bulliet
Columbia University

Pamela Kyle Crossley
Dartmouth College

Daniel R. Headrick
Roosevelt University

Steven W. Hirsch
Tufts University

Lyman L. Johnson
University of North Carolina–Charlotte

David Northrup
Boston College

CENGAGE
Learning·

Australia • Brazil • Mexico • Singapore • United Kingdom • United States

CENGAGE
Learning·

The Earth and Its Peoples: A Global History,
Brief Edition Sixth Edition
Volume II: Since 1500
Richard W. Bulliet, Pamela Kyle Crossley,
Daniel R. Headrick, Steven W. Hirsch, Lyman L.
Johnson, David Northrup

Product Director: Suzanne Jeans

Product Manager: Brooke Barbier

Senior Content Developer: Tonya Lobato

Content Coordinator: Cara Swan

Product Assistant: Katie Coaster

Media Developer: Kate MacLean

Marketing Brand Manager: Kyle Zimmerman

Senior Content Project Manager: Carol Newman

Senior Art Director: Cate Barr

Manufacturing Planner: Sandee Milewski

Senior Rights Acquisition Specialist: Jennifer
Meyer Dare

Production Service/Compositor: Lachina
Publishing Services

Text and Cover Designer: Dick Hannus, Hannus
Design Associates

Cover Image: Tile mural "Regresso de la Pesca"
on El Caminito Street in La Boca District.
Buenos Aires, Argentina, South America.
Richard Cummins/ Lonely Planet
Images/Getty Images

For product information and technology assistance, contact us at
Cengage Learning Customer & Sales Support, 1-800-354-9706

For permission to use material from this text or product,
submit all requests online at **www.cengage.com/permissions**.
Further permissions questions can be emailed to
permissionrequest@cengage.com.

Library of Congress Control Number: 2013946152

ISBN-13: 978-1-285-44553-3
ISBN-10: 1-285-44553-8

Cengage Learning
200 First Stamford Place, 4th Floor
Stamford, CT 06902
USA

Cengage Learning is a leading provider of customized learning solutions with office locations around the globe, including Singapore,
the United Kingdom, Australia, Mexico, Brazil and Japan. Locate your
local office at **international.cengage.com/region**.

Cengage Learning products are represented in Canada by Nelson
Education, Ltd.

For your course and learning solutions, visit **www.cengage.com**.

Purchase any of our products at your local college store or at our
preferred online store **www.cengagebrain.com**.

Instructors: Please visit **login.cengage.com** and log in to access
instructor-specific resources.

Printed in Canada
1 2 3 4 5 6 7 17 16 15 14 13

BRIEF CONTENTS

CONTENTS

PART SIX

Revolutions Reshape the World, 1750–1870 468

The New Power Balance, 1850–1900 564

The Crisis of the Imperial Order, 1900–1929 586

PART EIGHT
Perils and Promises of a Global Community, 1945 to the Present   654

New Challenges in a New Millennium   684

MAPS

FEATURES

ENVIRONMENT & TECHNOLOGY

ISSUES IN WORLD HISTORY

DIVERSITY & DOMINANCE

MATERIAL CULTURE

In preparing the sixth edition of this book, we examined the flow of topics from chapter to chapter and decided that certain rearrangements within chapters and in the order of chapters would accommodate the needs of instructors and students better than the template they had followed since the first edition. The first change was reversing the order of the third and fourth chapters to have early Mediterranean and Middle Eastern history directly follow the discussion of the origins of civilization in the Nile Valley and Mesopotamia.

The second change addressed the problem of when and how to discuss the history of pre-Columbian America. The time span to be covered, ranging from roughly 1500 B.C.E. to 1500 C.E., was too long to fit easily into the book's division into eight parts. The new structure we have adopted relocates the long pre-Aztec and pre-Inka narrative from Part Three, Growth and Interaction of Cultural Communities, to the end of Part Two, The Formation of New Cultural Communities. This change puts the status of the earliest civilizations in the Western Hemisphere on the same footing as the early civilizations of Greece, China, and South and Southeast Asia. It has the added benefit of making the history of East Asia in the Tang and Song periods directly precede the history of the Mongol empire, which allows instructors to have an uninterrupted focus on East Asia. The histories of the Aztecs and Inkas have been shifted to the chapter on tropical history located in Part Four, Interregional Patterns of Culture and Contact. This allows for a discussion of the overall influence of tropical environments and places them in close proximity to our treatment of the coming of Europeans to the New World.

A third structural change has shortened the length of the book by one chapter. To lessen the impression that Europe's domination of the world should always be the primary focus of student attention between the eighteenth and mid-twentieth centuries we have combined the two separate chapters on European imperialism, Chapters 22 and 24 in previous editions, into one. We feel that this change provides a better balance between the saga of European imperialism, accounts of resistance to imperialism, and the rise of independence movements in different parts of the world.

In a related change, we have relocated the chapter dealing with the histories of India, Latin America, and Africa in the first half of the twentieth century from after World War II, the former Chapter 27, to a position between the world wars. The aim of this largely new chapter, titled "Revolutions in Living," is to portray that period not only as a time of political change in parts of the world subjected to European imperialism, but also as one of transformation of daily lives of people in both the industrialized and nonindustrialized worlds. The added focus of the chapter fills a gap between discussion of the Industrial Revolution in the eighteenth and nineteenth centuries and the advent of major technological changes in the post-World War II era.

Finally in this new edition, contributor and East Asian specialist Michael Wert of Marquette University brought a fresh perspective to many of our chapters dealing with East Asia, helping ensure that our coverage is at the forefront of emerging scholarship.

The authors believe that these changes, along with myriad smaller changes detailed below, significantly enhance the overall goal of *The Earth and Its Peoples*, namely, to be a textbook that speaks not only for the past but also to today's student and teacher. Students and instructors alike should take away from this text a broad, and due to the changes, more flowing impression of human societies beginning as sparse and disconnected communities reacting creatively to local circumstances; experiencing ever more intensive stages of contact, interpenetration, and cultural expansion and amalgamation; and arriving at a twenty-first-century world in which people increasingly visualize a single global community.

Process, not progress, is the keynote of this book: a steady process of change over time, at first differently experienced in various regions, but eventually connecting peoples and traditions from all parts of the globe. Students should come away from this book with a sense that the problems and promises of their world are rooted in a past in which people of every sort, in every part of the world, confronted problems of a similar character and coped with them as best they could. We believe that our efforts will help students see where their world has come from and learn thereby something useful for their own lives.

Central Themes and Goals of the Text

We have subtitled *The Earth and Its Peoples* "A Global History" because the book explores the common challenges and experiences that unite the human past. Although the dispersal of early humans around the world resulted in many different economic, social, political, and cultural systems, all societies displayed analogous patterns in meeting their needs and exploiting their environments. Our challenge was to select the particular data and episodes that would best illuminate these global patterns of human experience.

To meet this challenge, we adopted two themes to serve as the spinal cord of our history: "technology and environment" and "diversity and dominance." The first theme represents the commonplace material bases of all human societies at all times. It grants no special favor to any cultural group even as it embraces subjects of the broadest topical, chronological, and geographical range. The second theme expresses the reality that every human society has constructed or inherited structures of domination. We examine practices and institutions of many sorts: military, economic, social, political, religious, and cultural, as well as those based on kinship, gender, and literacy. Simultaneously we recognize that alternative ways of life and visions of societal organization continually manifest themselves both within and in dialogue with every structure of domination.

With respect to the first theme, it is vital for students to understand that technology, in the broad sense of experience-based knowledge of the physical world, underlies all human activity. Writing is a technology, but so is oral transmission from generation to generation of lore about medicinal or poisonous plants. The magnetic compass is a navigational technology, but so is a Polynesian mariner's hard-won knowledge of winds, currents, and tides that made possible the settlement of the Pacific islands.

All technological development has come about in interaction with environments, both physical and human, and has, in turn, affected those environments. The story of how humanity has changed the face of the globe is an integral part of this central theme. Yet technology and the environment do not explain or underlie all important episodes of human experience. The theme of "Diversity and Dominance" informs all our discussions of politics, culture, and society. Thus, when narrating the histories of empires, we describe a range of human experiences within and beyond the imperial frontiers without assuming that the imperial institutions are a more suitable topic for discussion than the economic and social organization of pastoral nomads or the lives of peasant women. When religion and culture occupy our narrative, we focus not only on the dominant tradition but also on the diversity of alternative beliefs and practices.

Organization

The brief edition of *The Earth and Its Peoples*, sixth edition, retains the eight broad chronological divisions of previous editions to define its conceptual scheme of global historical development.

In **Part One: The Emergence of Human Communities, to 1500 B.C.E.**, we examine important patterns of human communal organization primarily in the Eastern Hemisphere. Small, dispersed human communities living by foraging spread to most parts of the world over tens of thousands of years. They responded to enormously diverse environmental conditions, at different times and in different ways discovering how to cultivate plants and utilize the products of domestic animals. On the basis of these new modes of sustenance, populations grew, permanent towns appeared, and political and religious authority, based on collection and control of agricultural surpluses, spread over extensive areas.

Part Two: The Formation of New Cultural Communities, from 1500 B.C.E. introduces the concept of a "cultural community," in the sense of a coherent pattern of activities and symbols pertaining to a specific human community. While all human communities develop distinctive cultures, including those discussed in Part One, historical development in this stage of global history prolonged and magnified the impact of some cultures more than others. In the geographically contiguous African-Eurasian landmass, as well as the Western Hemisphere, the cultures that proved to have the most enduring influence traced their roots to the second and first millennia B.C.E.

Part Three: Growth and Interaction of Cultural Communities, 300 B.C.E.–1200 C.E. deals with early episodes of technological, social, and cultural exchange and interaction on a continental scale both within and beyond the framework of imperial expansion. These are so different from earlier interactions arising from more limited conquests or extensions of political boundaries that they constitute a distinct era in world history, an era that set the world on the path of increasing global interaction and interdependence that it has been following ever since.

In **Part Four: Interregional Patterns of Culture and Contact, 1200–1550**, we take a look at the world during three centuries that saw both intensified cultural and commercial contact and increasingly confident self-definition of cultural communities in Europe, Asia, Africa, and the Americas. The Mongol conquest of a vast empire extending from the Pacific Ocean to eastern Europe greatly stimulated trade and interaction. In the West, strengthened European kingdoms began maritime expansion in the Atlantic, forging direct ties with sub-Saharan Africa and entering into conflict with the civilizations of the Western Hemisphere.

Part Five: The Globe Encompassed, 1500–1750 treats a period dominated by the global effects of European expansion and continued economic growth. European ships took over, expanded, and extended the maritime trade of the Indian Ocean, coastal Africa, and the Asian rim of the Pacific Ocean. This maritime commercial enterprise had its counterpart in European colonial empires in the Americas and a new Atlantic trading system. The contrasting capacities and fortunes of traditional land empires and new maritime empires, along with the exchange of domestic plants and animals between the hemispheres, underline the technological and environmental dimensions of this first era of complete global interaction.

In **Part Six: Revolutions Reshape the World, 1750–1870**, the word *revolution* is used in several senses: in the political sense of governmental overthrow, as in France and the Americas; in the metaphorical sense of radical transformative change,

as in the Industrial Revolution; and in the broadest sense of a perception of a profound change in circumstances and worldview. Technology and environment lie at the core of these developments. With the rapid ascendancy of the Western belief that science and technology could overcome all challenges, technology became not only an instrument of transformation but also an instrument of domination, to the point of threatening the integrity and autonomy of cultural traditions in nonindustrial lands and provoking strong movements of resistance.

Part Seven: Global Diversity and Dominance, 1850–1945, examines the development of a world arena in which people conceived of events on a global scale. Imperialism, international economic connections, and world-encompassing ideological tendencies, such as nationalism and socialism, present the picture of a globe becoming increasingly involved with European political and ideological concerns. Two world wars arising from European rivalries provide a climax to these developments, and European exhaustion affords other parts of the world new opportunities for independence and self-expression.

Part Eight: Perils and Promises of a Global Community, 1945 to the Present, divides at the turn of the millennium not because 2000 is a round number but because the terrorist attacks of 9/11 triggered, and now symbolize, so many changes in the world's political, economic, social, and ideological attitudes. Where the challenges of the Cold War and postcolonial nation building dominated the second half of the twentieth century, the promises and perils of globalization have been the hallmark of the twenty-first. Technology is a key topic in Part Eight because the threat of nuclear weapons and the urgency of supplying the growing world demand for oil overshadowed the late twentieth century, and the transformation of information technology has shaped the twenty-first, with worries about the impact of new technologies on the environment forming a constant and growing concern throughout the period.

The brief edition is produced in two formats: A complete edition covers the entire chronology from prehistory to the present, and a two-volume edition can be used for the two-semester survey. Volume I covers the period from prehistory to 1550, and Volume II covers 1500 to the present. There is a brief introduction to Volume II that orients students to the general political and social climate of the world before and up to 1500.

Changes in the Brief Sixth Edition

Several changes have been made to the organization of the text to make the narrative more logical and accessible. In Part One, Chapters 2 and 3 have been swapped for better continuity with Part Two. Chapter 3 now contains a substantial new section on pastoral nomadism in the Eurasian steppe. Additionally, descriptions of early civilizations in the Western Hemisphere have been shifted to Chapter 7 in order to facilitate a more unified discussion of Pre-Columbian America. The placement of Chapter 8 has been corrected in this edition, moving from Part Two to Part Three where it fits logically with the part focus on the growth and interaction of cultural communities.

Part Four features a new organization and contains heavily revised chapter material. Chapter 13 (formerly Chapter 14) has expanded coverage of eastern Europe and the Ottoman empire. A largely new Chapter 14 bears a new title, "Southern Empires, Southern Seas," and includes treatment of the Aztec and Inka empires that were previously covered much earlier in the book. Chapter 15 reflects new research on South Asian and Polynesian maritime cultures.

In Part Five, Chapter 18 has expanded to include the history of Russia, hence a new opening featuring a Russian popular hero and the change of title to "Territorial Empires Between Europe and China." Chapter 19 has a new discussion of Korean history and the Imjin War.

The organization of Part Six has been modified as well. Chapters 20 and 21 have been reversed in sequence to provide better continuity to discussions of revolutions in Europe and parallel changes in the Americas. Chapter 20 includes a new discussion of proto-industrialization as well as augmented discussions of the spread of industrialization to continental Europe and North America and the early career of Karl Marx. The section "Protest and Reform" has been broadly revised to include machine breaking in the textile sector and rural resistance to mechanization in the Captain Swing riots.

Part Seven has been the focus of our revision efforts and features a new organization highlighting global issues, much streamlined content, and one brand new chapter on culture and technology. The opening chapter of Part Seven now combines accounts of European imperialism that were previously contained in Chapters 22 and 24. Chapter 24 features a revised discussion of early Japanese industrialization as well as an expanded treatment of Marx and Marxism and a new discussion of Mikhail Bakunin and anarchism. Chapter 26 combines in a new chapter a discussion of technology and lifestyle changes that occurred between 1900 and 1945 with accounts of political movements in India, Latin America, and Africa that were previously located in Chapter 27.

The final Part Eight includes an updated discussion about the Cold War confrontation between West and East plus a revised discussion of apartheid and South Africa's struggle for independence. The final chapter updates world affairs through the first half of 2013.

Features and Pedagogical Aids

As with previous editions, the sixth edition offers a number of valuable features and pedagogical aids designed to pique student interest in specific world history topics and help them process and retain key information.

Our **Material Culture** feature calls particular attention to the many ways in which objects and processes of everyday life can help us understand human history on a broad scale. Thus essays like "Wine and Beer in the Ancient World" and "Cotton Clothing" are not only interesting in and of themselves but also suggestive of how today's world historians find meaning in the ordinary dimensions of human life.

The **Environment and Technology** feature, which has been a valuable resource in all prior editions of *The Earth and Its Peoples*, serves to illuminate the major theme of the text by demonstrating the shared material bases of all human societies across time.

Historical essays for each of the eight parts called ***Issues in World History*** were specifically designed to alert students to broad and recurring conceptual issues that are of great interest to contemporary historians; this feature has proved to be an instructor and student favorite.

Finally, **Diversity and Dominance**, also core to the theme of the text, is the primary source feature that brings a myriad of real historical voices to life in a common struggle for power and autonomy.

Pedagogical aids include the following:

Chapter Opening Focus Questions These questions are keyed to every major subdivision of the chapter through a system of color-coding and serve to help students focus on the core chapter concepts. The unique color-coded system helps students keep track of where they are in the text and easily identify which focus question corresponds to each section of the chapter. The color-coding carries through to the end of each chapter, where the focus questions for each section are answered and summarized.

Section Reviews Short bullet-point reviews appear at the end of each major section in every chapter and remind students of key information.

Chapter Conclusions Every chapter ends with a comparative conclusion that will help students synthesize chapter material and understand how it fits into the larger picture.

Key Terms with Definitions Students can handily find definitions for bolded key terms right on the page of the text where the term first appears.

Chapter Reviews Keyed to the chapter opening focus questions through a system of color-coding, the chapter reviews summarize the most important concepts addressed in the chapter, making studying more efficient and effective.

Pronunciation Guide Phonetic spellings for unfamiliar names and terms have been integrated into the text.

Supplements

A wide array of supplements accompany this text to assist students with different learning needs and to help instructors master today's various classroom challenges.

Instructor Resources

MindTap™ [ISBN: 9781285843056] The Personal Learning Experience. MindTap for *The Earth and Its Peoples* is a personalized, online digital learning platform providing students with *The Earth and Its Peoples* content and related interactive assignments and app services—while giving you a choice in the configuration of coursework and curriculum enhancement. Through a carefully designed chapter-based learning path, students can access the ebook (MindTap Reader, see description below); Aplia™ assignments developed for the most important concepts in each chapter (see Aplia description below); brief quizzes; and a set of web applications known as MindApps to help you create the most engaging course for your students. The MindApps range from ReadSpeaker (which reads the text out-loud to students) to Kaltura (allowing you to insert inline video and audio into your curriculum) to ConnectYard (allowing you to create digital "yards" through social media—all without "friending" your students). Mind-Tap for *The Earth and Its Peoples* goes well beyond an eBook, a homework solution/digital supplement, a resource center website, or a Learning Management System. It is truly a Personal Learning Experience that allows you to synchronize the text reading and engaging assignments and quizzes. To learn more, ask your Cengage Learning sales representative to demo it for you—or go to www.cengage.com/MindTap.

Aplia™ [ISBN: 9781285780382] is an online interactive learning solution that improves comprehension and outcomes by increasing student effort and engagement. Founded by a professor to enhance his own courses, Aplia provides automatically graded assignments with detailed, immediate explanations on every question. The interactive assignments have been developed to address the major concepts covered in *The Earth and Its Peoples* and are designed to promote critical thinking and engage students more fully in learning. Question types include questions built around animated maps, primary sources such as newspaper extracts, or imagined scenarios, like engaging in a conversation with a an historical figure or finding a diary and being asked to fill in some blanks; more in-depth primary source question sets address a major topic with a number of related primary sources and questions that promote deeper analysis of historical evidence. Many of the questions incorporate images, video clips, or audio clips. Students get immediate feedback on their work (not only what they got right or wrong, but why), and they can choose to see another set of related questions if they want more practice. A searchable eBook is available inside the course as well so that students can easily reference it as they work. Map-reading and writing tutorials are also available to get students off to a good start.

Aplia's simple-to-use course management interface allows instructors to post announcements, upload course materials, host student discussions, e-mail students, and manage the gradebook; a knowledgeable and friendly support team offers assistance and personalized support in customizing assignments to the instructor's course schedule. To learn more and view a demo for this book, visit www.aplia.com.

MindTap Reader for *The Earth and Its Peoples* is an eBook specifically designed to address the ways students assimilate content and media assets. MindTap Reader combines thoughtful navigation ergonomics, advanced student annotation, note-taking, and search tools, and embedded media assets such as video and MP3 chapter summaries, primary source documents with critical thinking questions, and interactive (zoomable) maps. Students can use the eBook as their primary text or as a multimedia companion to their printed book. The MindTap Reader eBook is available within the MindTap and Aplia online offerings found at www.cengagebrain.com.

Online PowerLecture with Cognero® [ISBN: 9781285455075] This PowerLecture is an all-in-one online multimedia resource for class preparation, presentation, and testing. Accessible through cengage.com/login with your faculty account, you will find available for download: book-specific Microsoft® PowerPoint® presentations; a Test Bank in both Microsoft® Word® and Cognero® formats; an Instructor Manual; Microsoft® PowerPoint® Image Slides; and a JPEG Image Library. The Test Bank, offered in Microsoft® Word® and Cognero® formats, contains multiple-choice and essay questions for each chapter. Cognero® is a flexible, online system that allows you to author, edit, and manage test bank content for *The Earth and Its People*, sixth edition. Create multiple test versions instantly and deliver through your LMS from your classroom, or wherever you may be, with no special installs or downloads required.

The **Instructor's Manual** contains for each chapter: an outline and summary; critical thinking questions; in-class activities; lecture launching suggestions; a list of key terms with definitions; and suggested readings and Web resources. The Microsoft® PowerPoint® presentations are ready-to-use, visual outlines of each chapter. These presentations are easily customized for your lectures and offered along with chapter-specific Microsoft® PowerPoint® Image Slides and JPEG Image Libraries. Access your Online PowerLecture at www.cengage.com/login.

CourseReader CourseReader is an online collection of primary and secondary sources that lets you create a customized electronic reader in minutes. With an easy-to-use interface and assessment tool, you can choose exactly what your students will be assigned—simply search or browse Cengage Learning's extensive document database to preview and select your customized collection of readings. In addition to print sources of all types (letters, diary entries, speeches, newspaper accounts, etc.), their collection includes a growing number of images and video and audio clips.

Each primary source document includes a descriptive headnote that puts the reading into context and is further supported by both critical thinking and multiple-choice questions designed to reinforce key points. For more information visit www.cengage.com/coursereader.

Cengagebrain.com Save your students time and money. Direct them to www.cengagebrain.com for choice in formats and savings and a better chance to succeed in your class. Cengagebrain.com, Cengage Learning's online store, is a single destination for more than 10,000 new textbooks, eTextbooks, eChapters, study tools, and audio supplements. Students have the freedom to purchase a-la-carte exactly what they need when they need it. Students can save 50% on the electronic textbook, and can pay as little as $1.99 for an individual eChapter.

Reader Program Cengage Learning publishes a number of readers, some containing exclusively primary sources, others a combination of primary and secondary sources, and some designed to guide students through the process of historical inquiry. Visit Cengage.com/history for a complete list of readers.

Custom Options Nobody knows your students like you, so why not give them a text that is tailor-fit to their needs? Cengage Learning offers custom solutions for your course—whether it's making a small modification to *The Earth and Its Peoples* to match your syllabus or combining multiple sources to create something truly unique. You can pick and choose chapters, include your own material, and add additional map exercises along with the Rand McNally Atlas to create a text that fits the way you teach. Ensure that your students get the most out of their textbook dollar by giving them exactly what they need. Contact your Cengage Learning representative to explore custom solutions for your course.

Student Resources

***Writing for College History*, First Edition [ISBN: 9780618306039]** Prepared by Robert M. Frakes, Clarion University. This brief handbook for survey courses in American history, Western Civilization/European history, and world civilization guides students through the various types of writing assignments they encounter in a history class. Providing examples of student writing and candid assessments of student work, this text focuses on the rules and conventions of writing for the college history course.

***The History Handbook*, Second Edition [ISBN: 9780495906766]** Prepared by Carol Berkin of Baruch College, City University of New York and Betty Anderson of Boston University. This book teaches students both basic and history-specific study skills such as how to read primary sources, research historical topics, and correctly cite sources. Substantially less expensive than comparable skill-building texts, The History Handbook also offers tips for Internet research and evaluating online sources.

***Doing History: Research and Writing in the Digital Age*, Second Edition [ISBN: 9781133587880]** Prepared by Michael J. Galgano, J. Chris Arndt, and Raymond M. Hyser of James Madison University. Whether you're starting down the path as a history major, or simply looking for a straightforward and systematic guide to writing a successful paper, you'll find this text to be an indispensible handbook to historical research. This text's "soup to nuts" approach to researching and writing about history addresses every step of the process, from locating your sources and gathering information, to writing clearly and making proper use of various citation styles to avoid plagiarism. You'll also learn how to make the most of every tool available to you—especially the technology that helps you conduct the process efficiently and effectively.

***The Modern Researcher*, Sixth Edition [ISBN: 9780495318705]** Prepared by Jacques Barzun and Henry F. Graff of Columbia University. This classic introduction to the techniques of research and the art of expression is used widely in history courses, but is also appropriate for writing and research methods courses in other departments. Barzun and Graff thoroughly cover every aspect of research, from the selection of a topic through the gathering, analysis, writing, revision, and publication of findings, presenting the process not as a set of rules but through actual cases that put the subtleties of research in a useful context. Part One covers the principles and methods of research; Part Two covers writing, speaking, and getting one's work published.

***Rand McNally Historical Atlas of the World*, Second Edition [ISBN: 9780618841912]** This valuable resource features over 70 maps that portray the rich panoply of the world's history from preliterate times to the present. They show how cultures and civilization were linked and how they interacted. The maps make it clear that history is not static. Rather, it is about change and movement across time. The maps show change by presenting the dynamics of expansion, cooperation, and conflict. This atlas includes maps that display the world from the beginning of civilization; the political development of all major areas of the world; expanded coverage of Africa, Latin America, and the Middle East; the current Islamic World; and the world population change in 1900 and 2000.

Acknowledgments

In preparing the sixth edition, we benefited from the critical readings of many colleagues. Our sincere thanks go in particular to contributor Michael Wert of Marquette University who lent his fresh perspective to our coverage of East Asia. We thank Beatrice

Manz of the History Department at Tufts University who provided guidance on the new Pastoral Nomads section in Part One. We are also indebted to the following instructors who lent their insight over various editions: Hedrick Alixopuilos, Santa Rosa Junior College; Hayden Bellenoit, U.S. Naval Academy; Dusty Bender, Central Baptist College; Cory Crawford, Ohio University; Adrian De Gifis, Loyola University New Orleans; Peter de Rosa, Bridgewater State University; Aaron Gulyas, Mott Community College; Darlene Hall, Lake Erie College; Vic Jagos, Scottsdale Community College; Adrien Ivan, Vernon College; Andrew Muldoon, Metropolitan State College of Denver; Percy Murray, Shaw University; Dave Price, Santa Fe College; Anthony Steinhoff, University of Tennessee-Chattanooga; Anara Tabyshalieva, Marshal University; Susan Autry, Central Piedmont Community College; Anna Collins, Arkansas Tech University; William Connell, Christopher Newport University; Gregory Crider, Winthrop University; Shawn Dry, Oakland Community College; Nancy Fitch, California State University, Fullerton; Christine Haynes, University of North Carolina at Charlotte; Mark Herman, Edison College; Ellen J. Jenkins, Arkansas Tech University; Frank Karpiel, The Citadel; Ken Koons, Virginia Military Institute; David Longfellow, Baylor University; Heather Lucas, Georgia Perimeter College; Jeff Pardue, Gainesville State College; Craig Patton, Alabama A & M University; Linda Scherr, Mercer County Community College; Robert Sherwood, Georgia Military College; Brett Shufelt, Copiah-Lincoln Community College; Kristen Walton, Salisbury University; Christopher Ward, Clayton State University; William Wood, Point Loma Nazarene University.

When textbook authors set out on a project, they are inclined to believe that 90 percent of the effort will be theirs and 10 percent that of various editors and production specialists employed by their publisher. How very naïve. This book would never have seen the light of day had it not been for the unstinting labors of the great team of professionals who turned the authors' words into beautifully presented print. Our debt to the staff of Cengage Learning remains undiminished in the sixth edition. Brooke Barbier, product manager, has offered us firm but sympathetic guidance throughout the revision process. Tonya Lobato, senior product developer, offered astute and sympathetic assistance as the authors worked to incorporate many new ideas and subjects into the text. Carol Newman, senior content project manager, moved the work through the production stages to meet a challenging schedule. Abbey Stebing did an outstanding job of photo research.

We thank also the many students whose questions and concerns, expressed directly or through their instructors, shaped much of this revision. We continue to welcome all readers' suggestions, queries, and criticisms. Please contact us at our respective institutions.

ABOUT THE AUTHORS

RICHARD W. BULLIET Professor of Middle Eastern History at Columbia University, Richard W. Bulliet received his Ph.D. from Harvard University. He has written scholarly works on a number of topics: the social and economic history of medieval Iran (The Patricians of Nishapur and Cotton, Climate, and Camels in Early Islamic Iran), the history of human-animal relations (The Camel and the Wheel and Hunters, Herders, and Hamburgers), the process of conversion to Islam (Conversion to Islam in the Medieval Period), and the overall course of Islamic social history (Islam: The View from the Edge and The Case for Islamo-Christian Civilization). He is the editor of the Columbia History of the Twentieth Century. He has published four novels, coedited The Encyclopedia of the Modern Middle East, and hosted an educational television series on the Middle East. He was awarded a fellowship by the John Simon Guggenheim Memorial Foundation and was named a Carnegie Corporation Scholar.

PAMELA KYLE CROSSLEY Pamela Kyle Crossley received her Ph.D. in Modern Chinese History from Yale University. She is currently the Robert and Barbara Black Professor of History at Dartmouth College. Her books include The Wobbling Pivot: An Interpretive History of China Since 1800; What Is Global History?; A Translucent Mirror: History and Identity in Qing Imperial Ideology; The Manchus; Orphan Warriors: Three Manchu Generations and the End of the Qing World; and (with Lynn Hollen Lees and John W. Servos) Global Society: The World Since 1900.

DANIEL R. HEADRICK Daniel R. Headrick received his Ph.D. in History from Princeton University. Professor of History and Social Science, Emeritus, at Roosevelt University in Chicago, he is the author of several books on the history of technology, imperialism, and international relations, including The Tools of Empire: Technology and European Imperialism in the Nineteenth Century; The Tentacles of Progress: Technology Transfer in the Age of Imperialism; The Invisible Weapon: Telecommunications and International Politics; Technology: A World History; Power Over Peoples: Technology, Environments and Western Imperialism, 1400 to the Present; and When Information Came of Age: Technologies of Knowledge in the Age of Reason and Revolution, 1700–1850. His articles have appeared in the Journal of World History and the Journal of Modern History, and he has been awarded fellowships by the National Endowment for the Humanities, the John Simon Guggenheim Memorial Foundation, and the Alfred P. Sloan Foundation.

STEVEN W. HIRSCH Steven W. Hirsch holds a Ph.D. in Classics from Stanford University and is currently Associate Professor of Classics and History at Tufts University. He has received grants from the National Endowment for the Humanities and the Massachusetts Foundation for Humanities and Public Policy. His research and publications include The Friendship of the Barbarians: Xenophon and the Persian Empire, as well as articles and reviews in the Classical Journal, the American Journal of Philology, and the Journal of Interdisciplinary History. He is currently completing a comparative study of ancient Greco-Roman and Chinese civilizations.

LYMAN L. JOHNSON Professor Emeritus of History at the University of North Carolina at Charlotte, Lyman L. Johnson earned his Ph.D. in Latin American History from the University of Connecticut. A two-time Senior Fulbright-Hays Lecturer, he also has received fellowships from the Tinker Foundation, the Social Science Research Council, the National Endowment for the Humanities, and the American Philosophical Society. His recent books include Workshop of Revolution: Plebeian Buenos Aires and the Atlantic World, 1776-1810; Death, Dismemberment, and Memory; The Faces of Honor (with Sonya Lipsett-Rivera); Aftershocks: Earthquakes and Popular Politics in Latin America (with Jürgen Buchenau); Essays on the Price History of Eighteenth-Century Latin America (with Enrique Tandeter); and Colonial Latin America (with Mark A. Burkholder). He also has published in journals, including the Hispanic American Historical Review, the Journal of Latin American Studies, the International Review of Social History, Social History, and Desarrollo Económico. He has served as president of the Conference on Latin American History.

DAVID NORTHRUP David Northrup earned his Ph.D. in African and European History from the University of California, Los Angeles. He has published scholarly works on African, Atlantic, and world history. His most recent books are How English Became the Global Language, the third edition of Africa's Discovery of Europe, 1450–1850, and the Diary of Antera Duke, an Eighteenth-Century African Slave Trader. He taught at a rural secondary school on Nigeria, Tuskegee Institute in Alabama, Boston College, and Venice International University and is a past president of the World History Association.

NOTE ON SPELLING AND USAGE

Where necessary for clarity, dates are followed by the letters C.E. or B.C.E. The abbreviation C.E. stands for "Common Era" and is equivalent to A.D. (anno Domini, Latin for "in the year of the Lord"). The abbreviation B.C.E. stands for "before the Common Era" and means the same as B.C. ("before Christ"). In keeping with our goal of approaching world history without special concentration on one culture or another, we chose these neutral abbreviations as appropriate to our enterprise. Because many readers will be more familiar with English than with metric measurements, however, units of measure are generally given in the English system, with metric equivalents following in parentheses.

In general, Chinese has been Romanized according to the pinyin method. Exceptions include proper names well established in English (e.g., Canton, Chiang Kaishek) and a few English words borrowed from Chinese (e.g., kowtow). Spellings of Arabic, Ottoman Turkish, Persian, Mongolian, Manchu, Japanese, and Korean names and terms avoid special diacritical marks for letters that are pronounced only slightly differently in English. An apostrophe is used to indicate when two Chinese syllables are pronounced separately (e.g., Chang'an).

For words transliterated from languages that use the Arabic script—Arabic, Ottoman Turkish, Persian, Urdu—the apostrophe indicating separately pronounced syllables may represent either of two special consonants, the hamza or the ain. Because most English-speakers do not hear the distinction between these two, they have not been distinguished in transliteration and are not indicated when they occur at the beginning or end of a word. As with Chinese, some words and commonly used place-names from these languages are given familiar English spellings (e.g., Quran instead of Qur'an, Cairo instead of al-Qahira). Arabic romanization has normally been used for terms relating to Islam, even where the context justifies slightly different Turkish or Persian forms, again for ease of comprehension.

Before 1492 the inhabitants of the Western Hemisphere had no single name for themselves. They had neither a racial consciousness nor a racial identity. Identity was derived from kin groups, language, cultural practices, and political structures. There was no sense that physical similarities created a shared identity. America's original inhabitants had racial consciousness and racial identity imposed on them by conquest and the occupation of their lands by Europeans after 1492. All of the collective terms for these first American peoples are tainted by this history. Indians, Native Americans, Amerindians, First Peoples, and Indigenous Peoples are among the terms in common usage. In this book the names of individual cultures and states are used wherever possible. Amerindian and other terms that suggest transcultural identity and experience are used most commonly for the period after 1492.

There is an ongoing debate about how best to render Amerindian words in English. It has been common for authors writing in English to follow Mexican usage for Nahuatl and Yucatec Maya words and place-names. In this style, for example, the capital of the Aztec state is spelled Tenochtitlán, and the important late Maya city-state is spelled Chichén Itzá. Although these forms are still common even in the specialist literature, we have chosen to follow the scholarship that sees these accents as unnecessary. The exceptions are modern place-names, such as Mérida and Yucatán, which are accented. A similar problem exists for the spelling of Quechua and Aymara words from the Andean region of South America. Although there is significant disagreement among scholars, we follow the emerging consensus and use the spellings khipu (not quipu), Tiwanaku (not Tiahuanaco), and Wari (not Huari). In this edition we have introduced the now common spelling Inka (not Inca) but keep Cuzco for the capital city (not Cusco), since this spelling facilitates locating this still-important city on maps.

The World Before 1500

ANTIQUITY: HUMANS, CULTURES, AND CONQUESTS, TO 400 C.E.

GROWTH AND INTERACTION, 400–1200

INTERREGIONAL CONQUESTS AND EXCHANGES, 1200–1500

History occurs in a continuous stream. Because new events are the products of their past, each historical period is intimately linked to what preceded it. As a Roman historian put it, "History doesn't make leaps." Nevertheless, modern historians find it useful to divide the past into eras or ages to make sense of the sweep of history. The longest historical eras are antiquity, the Middle Ages, and modern times. Volume II of *The Earth and Its Peoples* is devoted to the third of these—modern world history, the five centuries since about 1500.

World historians largely agree that the intensity of interaction around the world during the modern period distinguishes it from all earlier times. European maritime exploration opened up or intensified these contacts. The modern era is also characterized by the steady expansion of European political, economic, and cultural leadership in every part of the world.

How and when different parts of the world felt the impact of the West varied. By 1500 parts of the Americas were already reeling under the impact of their first contacts with Europeans, but in most other parts of the world the West did not make a big difference until the century after 1750 or even later. Thus, while in hindsight Western ascendancy seems to be a defining theme of modern history, for the people of Asia, Africa, and elsewhere the modern era was a time in which the internal patterns of historical change only gradually became altered by the growing influence of Westerners and by their own reactions to these influences.

In order to explain how the modern era came into being, the first chapter of Volume II of *The Earth and Its Peoples* (Chapter 15) begins in about 1450. To help the reader understand the broader sweep of history, this Introduction provides an overview of earlier eras. The Introduction reviews three periods of decreasing temporal length. The first is the very long period from human origins until the end of ancient history in about 400 C.E. Next comes the early medieval period down to about 1200; and, finally, the three hundred years immediately preceding 1500. Because the centuries after 1200 were most important for shaping the transition to the modern era, they receive the most detailed treatment.

ANTIQUITY: HUMANS, CULTURES, AND CONQUESTS, TO 400 C.E.

All historical periods were shaped by natural environment and human technology (whether simple tools, techniques, or complex machines). The paramount role played by environmental forces is apparent when historians seek to explain how human beings—and thus history—began. Like all other living creatures, early humans were products of biological adjustments to changing environments. Over millions of years, our ancestors in eastern and southern Africa evolved biologically to enhance their chances for survival. The evolution of an upright posture enabled early people to walk and run on two legs, thereby freeing their hands for tool making. The evolution of larger brains gave them the capacity to learn and understand all sorts of new things and devise techniques for putting them to use. Finally, evolutionary changes in the throat gave humans the capacity for speech, which, as language developed, had the dual effect of making complex social relations easier and fostering the development of intellectual culture.

With these physical traits in place, humans were able to develop in a direction taken by no other creature. Instead of relying on the glacially slow process of biological evolution to adapt their bodies to new environments, our ancestors used their minds to devise technologies for transforming nature to suit their needs. By the standards of today, these early technologies may seem crude—stone tools for cutting and chopping, clothing made from plants and animal skins, shelters in caves and huts—but they were sufficient to enable humans to survive environmental changes in their homelands. They also enabled bands of humans to migrate to new environments in every part of the world. Through trial and error Stone Age people learned what could safely be eaten in new environments. Other primates acted primarily by instinct; humans acted according to the dictates of culture. The capacity to create and change material and intellectual culture marked the beginning of human history.

Agricultural Civilizations

Beginning about 10,000 years ago, the transition from food gathering to food production marked a major turning point in history. Human communities in many different parts of the world learned to alter the natural food supply. Some people promoted the growth of foods they liked by scattering seeds on good soils and restricting the growth of competing plants.

Scene from the Egyptian Book of the Dead, ca. 1300 B.C.E.   The mummy of a royal scribe named Hunefar is approached by members of his household before being placed in the tomb. Behind Hunefar is jackel-headed Anubis, the god who will conduct the spirit of the deceased to the afterlife. The Book of the Dead provided Egyptians with the instructions they needed to complete this arduous journey and gain a blessed existence in the afterlife.

In time some people became full-time farmers. Other communities tamed wild animals whose meat, milk, fur, and hides they desired, and they controlled their breeding to produce animals with the most desired characteristics. Promoted by a warmer world climate, these agricultural revolutions slowly spread from the Middle East around the Mediterranean. People in South and East Asia, Africa, and the Americas domesticated other wild plants and animals for their use. Just as humans had ceased to rely on evolution to enable them to adjust to new surroundings, so too they had bypassed evolution in bringing new species of plants and animals into existence (see Map I.1).

The agricultural revolutions greatly enhanced people's chances for survival in two ways. One was a rapid increase in population fostered by the ability to grow and store more food (see Issues in World History: Climate and Population, to 1500). A second change was taking place in the composition of human communities. The earliest communities consisted of small bands of biologically related people and their spouses from other bands. However, more complex societies made their first appearances as more and more unrelated people concentrated in lush river valleys, where the soils, temperatures, and potential to irrigate with river water produced conditions suitable for farming.

In the Fertile Crescent of the Middle East, Egypt, India, and China the existence of a regular food surplus enabled a few people to develop highly specialized talents and tools that were not tied to food production. Some talented military leaders became rulers of large areas and headed government with specialized administrators. Specialists constructed elaborate irrigation systems, monumental palaces, and temples. Others made special metal tools and weapons, first of bronze, then of iron. Because of the value of their talents these specialists acquired privileges. It was grandest to be a king, queen, or head priest. For the average person, life was harder in complex societies than in parts of the world where such specialization had not yet occurred.

Culture and Civilization

Complex and populous agricultural societies developed specialists who dealt with abstract and unseen forces. This development was not entirely new. For tens of thousands of years before the first settled societies, humans had used their minds to think about the meaning of life. The remains of elaborate burials and sites of worship suggest that some early societies had clear beliefs in an afterlife and in spiritual forces that controlled their lives. Many cultures believed the sun, moon, and nature had supernatural powers.

Another form of intellectual activity was the collection of technical knowledge about the environment. Cultural communities learned what plants were best for food, clothing, or building materials and passed this knowledge along to later generations. Most specialized was the knowledge of how to make medicines and poisons. Assigning names for all these facilitated the transmission of this knowledge. In the absence of written records, very little specific information about these early treasuries of knowledge exists, but the elaborate and beautiful paintings in caves dating to tens of thousands of years before the emergence of early agricultural societies provide the clearest evidence of the cultural sophistication of early humans.

Cultural change surged as settled agricultural communities became more specialized. Temple priests devised elaborate rituals and prayers for the gods who protected the community, and they studied the movements of stars, planets, and the moon for signs of the progress of the seasons or the will of the gods. In Mesopotamia, Egypt, and elsewhere a new class of scribes used written symbols to preserve administrative and commercial records, laws, and bodies of specialized knowledge. Thoughtful people recorded the myths and legends passed down orally from earlier days, systematizing them and often adapting them to new social conditions, as well as creating new literary forms. Communications could now be sent unchanged over long distances. Some of these works were lost for millennia only to be rediscovered in recent times, allowing us to know much more about the lives, thoughts, and values of ancient peoples.

Empires and Regional Communication

In time governments weakened or fell victim to conquest. Egypt, for example, fell to Nubians from up the Nile then to the Assyrians from Mesopotamia. Some conquerors created vast new empires. Late in the fourth century B.C.E., Alexander the Great brought everything from the eastern Mediterranean to India and

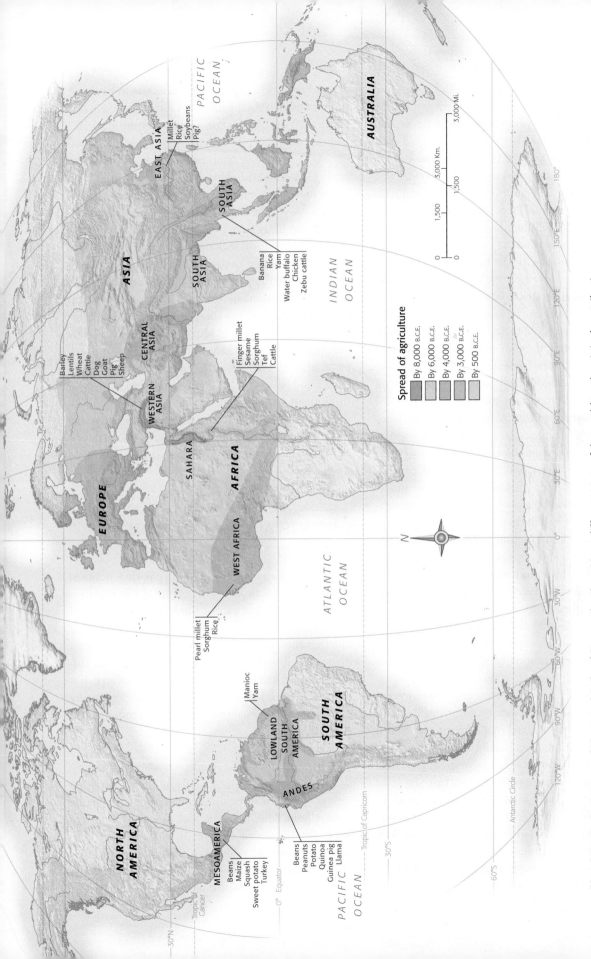

Map I.1 Early Centers of Plant and Animal Domestication Many different parts of the world made original contributions to domestication during the Agricultural Revolutions that began about 10,000 years ago. Later interactions helped spread these domesticated animals and plants to new locations. In lands less suitable for crop cultivation, pastoralism and hunting remained more important for supplying food. © Cengage Learning

Spread of agriculture

- By 8,000 B.C.E.
- By 6,000 B.C.E.
- By 4,000 B.C.E.
- By 3,000 B.C.E.
- By 500 B.C.E.

EAST ASIA
Millet
Rice
Soybeans
Pig?

SOUTH ASIA
Banana
Rice
Yam
Water buffalo
Chicken
Zebu cattle

WESTERN ASIA
Barley
Lentils
Wheat
Cattle
Dog
Goat
Pig
Sheep

CENTRAL ASIA / Finger millet
Finger millet
Sesame
Sorghum
Tef
Cattle

WEST AFRICA
Pearl millet
Sorghum
Rice

LOWLAND SOUTH AMERICA
Manioc
Yam

MESOAMERICA
Beans
Maize
Squash
Sweet potato
Turkey

ANDES
Beans
Peanuts
Potato
Quinoa
Guinea pig
Llama

PACIFIC OCEAN
ATLANTIC OCEAN
INDIAN OCEAN

NORTH AMERICA
SOUTH AMERICA
EUROPE
ASIA
AFRICA
AUSTRALIA
SAHARA

Tropic of Cancer
Equator
Tropic of Capricorn
Antarctic Circle

0 1,500 3,000 Km.
0 1,500 3,000 Mi.

Egypt under his sway, spreading Greek culture and language. After the collapse of Alexander's empire, the first of a series of Indian empires arose. In the second and first centuries B.C.E., Latin-speakers spread their rule, language, and culture throughout the Roman Empire, which encompassed the Mediterranean and reached across the Alps into Gaul (France) and Britain. At much the same time, the Han consolidated control over the densely populated lands of China, and successive rulers extended the sway of imperial China over much of East Asia. In the isolated continents of the Americas, advanced agricultural societies were also building larger states in late antiquity.

Essential to empire formation was the significant enhancement of old technologies and the development of new ones. In many parts of the world iron replaced bronze as the preferred metal for tools and weapons. In the Middle East and China soldiers on horseback played important military roles. In most places there were advances in the fighting techniques and in defensive strategies and fortifications.

Empires encouraged the growth of cities to serve as administrative, economic, and cultural centers. Temples, palaces, monuments, markets, and public amenities advertised the glory of these imperial centers. Large states regularly mobilized large pools of labor for massive construction projects. By late antiquity, a few cities had populations in the hundreds of thousands—Alexandria in Egypt, Rome in Italy, Chang'an in China, Pataliputra in India—though such large numbers strained cities' capacities to supply food and water and dispose of waste. Such architectural monuments established "classical" styles that were frequently imitated and affected wide areas even after the empires were gone.

Other imperial building projects were more practical. The Roman and Chinese governments built thousands of miles of paved roads for moving troops and communication; long barrier walls and strings of forts defended frontier areas from invasion. Trade often flourished on these political frontiers, and good roads further encouraged trade. Improvements in shipping also encouraged the movement of goods over long distances and allowed transport of bulkier goods. Much long-distance trade in antiquity was in luxury goods for the privileged classes in urban civilizations. The search for exotic items tied remote

parts of the world together and gave rise to new specialists both within the urban civilizations and in less stratified parts of the world. Gold, ivory, animal pelts, and exotic feathers from inner Africa reached Egypt. Phoenician mariners marketed lumber, papyrus (for paper), wine, and fish around the Mediterranean Sea. Other merchants carried silk from China across arid Central Asia to the Middle East and lands to the west. The advent of coinage in the first millennium B.C.E. stimulated local and regional economies.

The routes that carried goods also helped spread religions, inventions, and ideas. The Zoroastrian religion of the Persians became one of the great ethical creeds of antiquity. The diaspora of Jews from Palestine after their southern kingdom was destroyed by the Neo-Babylonian Empire in the seventh century B.C.E. also helped spread monotheistic beliefs. The beliefs and culture of the Greeks and Romans spread throughout their empires, largely because many of their subjects saw the advantages in adopting the ways of the ruling elite. Similarly, Indian traders introduced Hinduism and Buddhism to Southeast Asia.

GROWTH AND INTERACTION, 400–1200

During the Early Middle Ages expanding political and commercial links drew regions closer together. In addition, the growth of interregional trade and the spread of new world religions helped unite and redefine the boundaries of cultural regions, though divisions within religions undercut some of this cultural unity. All of these factors were interrelated, but let's begin with the one that left the most enduring impression on the course of history: the spread of world religions.

World Religions   The first religious tradition to experience widespread growth in this period was Buddhism, which spread from the Indian homeland where it had arisen around 500 B.C.E. One direction of growth was eastward into Southeast Asia. After 500 C.E. there were particular strongholds of the faith on the large islands of Ceylon, Sumatra, and Java, whose kings supported the growth

Armored Knights in Battle   This painting from around 1135 shows the armament of knights at the time of the Crusades. Chain mail, a helmet, and a shield carried on the left side protect the rider. The lance carried underarm and the sword are the primary weapons. Notice that riders about to make contact with lances have their legs straight and braced in the stirrups, while riders with swords and in flight have bent legs.

Pierpont Morgan Library/ Art Resource, NY

when the western half of the empire collapsed under the onslaught of "barbarian" invasions in the late fifth century, the Latin Church had to shoulder alone the tasks of converting these peoples to Christianity and preserving the intellectual, political, and cultural heritage of Roman antiquity. In its religious mission the Latin Church was quite successful. One by one Frankish, German, English, Irish, Hungarian, and other leaders were converted, and their subjects gradually followed suit. Preserving other Roman achievements was more difficult. The church continued to use the Latin language and Roman law, and Christian monasteries preserved manuscripts of many ancient works. But the trading economy and urban life that had been the heart blood of ancient Rome became only a memory in most of the Latin West.

In the eastern Mediterranean, Byzantine Roman emperors continued to rule, and the Greek-speaking Christian church continued to enjoy political protection. Greek monks were also active Christian missionaries among the Slavic peoples of eastern Europe. The conversion of the Russian rulers in the tenth century was a notable achievement. However, by the middle of the next century, cultural, linguistic, and theological differences led to a deep rift between Greek and Russian Christians in the east and Latin Christians in the west.

Meanwhile, prophetic religion founded by Muhammad in the seventh century was spreading like a whirlwind out of its Arabian homeland. With great fervor Arab armies introduced Islam and an accompanying state system into the Middle East, across North Africa, and into the Iberian Peninsula. Over time most Middle Eastern and African Christians and members of other religions chose to adopt the new faith. Muslim merchants helped spread the faith along trade routes into sub-Saharan Africa and across southern Asia. Like Christianity, Islam

of schools and monasteries and constructed temple complexes. Traders also carried Buddhism to China and from there to Korea, Japan, and Tibet. In some places Buddhism's growing strength led to political reactions. In China the Tang emperors reduced the influence of the monasteries in 840 by taking away their tax exemption and by promoting traditional Confucian values. A similar effort by the Tibetan royal family to curtail Buddhism failed, and Buddhist monks established their political dominance in mountainous Tibet. In India, however, Buddhism gradually lost support during this period and by 1200 had practically disappeared from the land of its origin.

Meanwhile, people in western Eurasia were embracing two newer religious systems. In the fourth century, Christianity became the official religion of the Roman Empire, adding new followers all around the Mediterranean to this once persecuted faith. But eventually split along cultural, theological, and political lines as it expanded. Beginning in 1095, Latin Christians launched military Crusades against Muslim dominance of Christian holy places in Palestine. In later Crusades, political and commercial ends became more important than religious goals, and the boundaries between Christianity and Islam changed little.

Commercial and Political Contacts

In many other parts of the world empires played a fundamental role in defining and unifying cultural areas. Under the Tang and Song dynasties (618–1279) China continued to have stability and exhibited periods of remarkable economic growth and technological creativity. Ghana, the first notable empire in sub-Saharan Africa, emerged to control one end of the trans-Saharan trade. In the isolated continents of the Americas a series of cultural complexes formed in the Andes, among the Maya of the Yucatán, along the Mississippi, and in the arid North American southwest. But despite efforts by Christian northern Europeans to create a loosely centralized "Holy Roman Empire," a very decentralized political system prevailed in most of western Europe. In Japan development was moving in a similar direction.

Political and religious expansion helped stimulate regional and long-distance trade. The challenge of moving growing quantities of goods over long distances produced some important innovations in land and sea travel. Two of the most important land-based, long-distance routes in this period depended on pack animals, especially the camel. One was the Silk Road, a caravan route across Central Asia. On the other trade route, between sub-Saharan Africa and North Africa, camels carried goods across the Sahara, the world's largest desert.

The Silk Road took its name from the silk textiles that were carried from eastern China to the Mediterranean Sea. In return, the Chinese received horses and other goods from the West. In existence since about 250 B.C.E., this series of roads nearly 6,000 miles (9,000 kilometers) in length passed through arid lands whose pastoral populations provided guides, food, and fresh camels (specially bred for caravan work).

After 900 C.E. the Silk Road declined for a time. By coincidence, the trans-Saharan caravan routes were growing more important during the period from 700 to 1200. Here, too, horses were an important trade purchased by African rulers to the south in return for gold, slaves, and other goods. The pastoralists who controlled the Saharan oases became essential guides for the camel caravans.

Since ancient times sea travel had been important in moving goods over relatively short distances, usually within sight of land, as around the Mediterranean Sea, the Red Sea, the Persian Gulf, and among the islands of the East Indies. During this period the water links around and through the Indian Ocean were increasing enough to make it an alternative to moving goods from China to the Middle East. Shipments went from port to port and were exchanged many times. Special ships known as dhows made use of the seasonal shifts in the winds across the Indian Ocean to plan their voyages in each direction. These centuries also saw remarkable maritime voyages in the Pacific (see Chapter 15).

INTERREGIONAL CONQUESTS AND EXCHANGES, 1200–1500

Between 1200 and 1500, cultural and commercial contacts grew rapidly across wide expanses of Eurasia, Africa, the Americas, and the Indian Ocean. In part, the increased contacts were the product of an unprecedented era of empire building around the world. The Mongols conquered a vast empire spanning Eurasia from the Pacific to eastern Europe. Muslim peoples created new empires in India, the Middle East, and sub- Saharan Africa. Amerindian empires united extensive regions of the Americas. Most of Europe continued to lack political unity, but unusually powerful European kingdoms were expanding their frontiers.

Empires stimulated commercial exchanges. The Mongol conquests revived the Silk Road across Central Asia, while a complex maritime network centered on the Indian Ocean stretched around southern Eurasia from the South China Sea to the North Atlantic, with overland connections in all directions (see Map I.2). Trade in the Americas and Africa also expanded. In the fifteenth century, Portuguese and Spanish

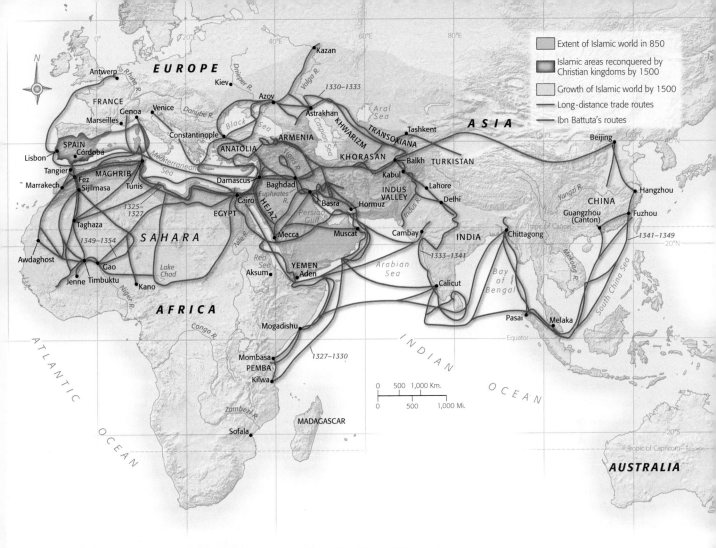

Map I.2 Arteries of Trade and Travel in the Islamic World, to 1500 Ibn Battuta's journeys across Africa and Asia made use of land and sea routes along which Muslim traders and the Islamic faith had long traveled. © Cengage Learning

explorers began an expansion southward along the Atlantic coast of Africa that by 1500 had opened a new all-water route to the riches of the Indian Ocean and set the stage for transoceanic routes that for the first time were to span the globe.

Mongol, Muslim, and European expansion promoted the spread of technologies. Printing, compasses, crossbows, gunpowder, and firearms—all East Asian inventions found broader applications and new uses in western Eurasia. Both the Ottomans and the kingdoms of western Europe made extensive use of gunpowder technologies. However, the highly competitive and increasingly literate peoples of the Latin West surpassed all others of this period in their use of technologies that they borrowed from elsewhere or devised themselves. Europeans mined and refined more metals, produced more books, built more kinds of ships, and made more weapons than did people in any other comparable place on earth.

Why was so much change taking place all at once? Historians attribute many of the changes in South and Central Asia directly or indirectly to the empire building of the Mongols. But other changes took place far from that area. The role of simple coincidence, of course, should never be overlooked in history. And some historians believe that larger environmental factors were also at work—changes in climate that promoted population growth, trade, and empire building.

Mongols and Turks

The earliest and largest of the new empires was the work of the Mongols of northeastern Asia. Using their extraordinary command of horses and refinements in traditional forms of military and social organization, Mongols and allied groups united under Genghis Khan overran northern China in the early thirteenth century and spread their control westward across Central Asia to eastern Europe. By the later part of the century, the Mongol Empire stretched from Korea to Poland. It was ruled initially in four separate khanates: one in Russia, one in Iran, one in Central Asia, and one in China.

By ensuring traders protection from robbers and excessive tolls, the Mongol Empire revitalized the Silk Road. Never before had there been such a volume of commercial exchanges between eastern and western Eurasia. Easier travel also helped Islam and Buddhism spread to new parts of Central Asia.

The strains of holding such vast territories together caused the Mongol Empire to disintegrate over the course of the fourteenth and early fifteenth centuries. The Ming rulers of China overthrew Mongol rule in 1368 and began an expansionist foreign policy to reestablish China's predominance and prestige. Their armies repeatedly invaded Mongolia, reestablished dominion over Korea, and occupied northern Vietnam (Annam). One by one the other khanates collapsed.

The Mongols left a formidable legacy, but it was not Mongolian. Instead, Mongol rulers tended to adopt and promote the political systems, agricultural practices, and local customs of the peoples they ruled. Their encouragement of local languages helped later literary movements to flower. The political influence of the administrations the Mongols established in China, Iran, and Russia lingered even after locals had overthrown their rule, creating the basis for new national regimes.

At about the same time as the early Mongol expansion, Turkic war leaders from what is now Afghanistan were surging through the Khyber Pass and established a Muslim empire centered at Delhi. In short order, they overwhelmed the several Hindu states of north and central India and established a large empire ruled from the city of Delhi. The subsequent migration of large numbers of Muslims into India and the prestige and power of the Muslim ruling class brought India into the Islamic world. After their conquests in the Middle East, Mongols had recruited other Turkic-speaking Muslims from Central Asia to serve as their agents. In the decades after 1250, a large Turkic community in Anatolia (now Turkey) known as Ottomans took advantage of the weakness of the Byzantine Empire to extend their base in Anatolia. They then crossed into the Balkan Peninsula of southeastern Europe.

Genghis Khan (c. 1162–1227) in Battle, from a book by Rashid-al-Din (1247–1318) (gouache), Persian School, (14th century)/Bibliotheque Nationale, Paris, France/The Bridgeman Art Library

Steppe Warfare in the Mongol Era These helmeted steppe warriors wear chain mail hauberks under their tunics and carry small round shields. Their horses are unarmored and thus more maneuverable than the charger of a heavily armored European knight. Swords and lances serve for close combat, but the bows in holsters on their thighs were a devastating long-distance weapon. Ethnicity varied more than armament. The man thrusting his sword and the man above and behind him have red facial hair while the two on the far right look East Asian.

In the late 1300s, the Central Asian conqueror Timur (Tamerlane) shattered the Delhi Sultanate and stopped the expansion of the Ottoman Empire. The conquest and pillage of Timur's armies left the Delhi Sultanate a shadow of its former self, but the Ottoman Turks were able to reconstitute their empire in the fifteenth century. Ottoman conquerors swept deep into southeastern Europe (taking Constantinople, the last surviving remnant of the Byzantine Empire, in 1453) and southward into the Middle East, establishing a stable presence that was to endure into the twentieth century.

Indian Ocean Exchanges

In the wake of the Mongol Empire's collapse, the Indian Ocean assumed greater importance in the movement of goods across Eurasia. Alliances among Muslim merchants of many nationalities made these routes the world's richest trading area. Merchant dhows sailed among the trading ports, carrying cotton textiles, leather goods, grains, pepper, jewelry, carpets, horses, ivory, and many other goods. Chinese silk and porcelain and Indonesian spices entered from the east, meeting Middle Eastern and European goods from the west. It is important to note that Muslim merchant networks were almost completely independent of the giant Muslim land empires.

As a consequence of the Islamic world's political and commercial expansion, the number of adherents to the Muslim faith also grew. By 1500 Islam had replaced Buddhism as the second most important faith in India and was on its way to displacing Hinduism and Buddhism in Southeast Asia. The faith was also spreading in the Balkans. Meanwhile, raids by Arab pastoralists undermined ancient Christian states along Africa's upper Nile, leaving Ethiopia as the only Christian-ruled state in Africa. In the trading cities below the Sahara and along the Indian Ocean coast where Islam had established itself well before 1200, the strength and sophistication of Islamic religious practice was growing.

Mediterranean Exchanges

The Mediterranean Sea, which since antiquity had been a focus of commerce and cultural exchange for the peoples of Europe, the Middle East, and Africa, saw increased activity in the later Middle Ages. Part of the Mediterranean's importance derived from its trading links to the Indian Ocean by land and water routes. Another area that contributed to expanded trade was northern Africa. Camel caravans brought great quantities of gold and large numbers of slaves to the Mediterranean from the lands below the Sahara. This trade facilitated the growth of the powerful empire of Mali, which controlled some of the main gold-producing regions of West Africa. The rulers of Mali became rich and Muslim. Their wars and those of other states produced the captives that were sold north. In the fourteenth century the disruption of supplies of slaves from the eastern Mediterranean led to more slaves being purchased in southern Europe.

Another part of the expansion of Mediterranean trade was tied to the revival of western Europe. In 1204 the Italian city-state of Venice had shown its determination to be a dominant player in the eastern Mediterranean by attacking the Greek city of Constantinople and ensuring access to the Black Sea. Trade routes from the Mediterranean spread northward to the Netherlands and connected by sea to the British Isles, the Baltic Sea, and the Atlantic. The growth of trade in Europe accompanied a revival of urban life and culture. Both the cities and the countryside saw increased use of energy, minerals, and technologies from printing to gunpowder. Despite a high level of warfare among European states and devastating population losses in the fourteenth century, much of Europe was exhibiting cultural and economic vitality that was to have great consequences for the entire world in the centuries that followed.

The Aztecs and Inca

In the continents of the Western Hemisphere, American peoples were also creating important empires in the period from 1200 to 1500, although they had more limited resources with which to do so. For thousands of years their cultures had developed in isolation from the rest of humanity and thus had been unable to borrow any plants, animals, or technologies. Amerindian conquests were made without the aid of riding animals like the Mongols' horses, without the iron weapons all Old World empire builders had been using for many centuries, and without the new gunpowder weaponry that some Eurasians were employing in their conquests in this period.

In the wake of the collapse of the Toltec Empire, a martial people known as the Aztecs pushed southward into the rich agricultural lands of central Mexico. At first the Aztecs placed themselves at the service of strong indigenous residents, but after 1300 they began to build their own empire. Relying on their military skills, members of the Aztec warrior elite were able to conquer territories and reduce peasants to their service. The growth of a servile class at the bottom of society was paralleled by the growth of a powerful ruling class housed in well-constructed two-story dwellings in the Aztec capital cities. The servile laborers supplied the food needs of the growing cities and were impressed into building elaborate canals and land reclamation projects. Underpinning the power of the Aztec rulers were religious rituals that emphasized human sacrifice, mostly captives of the armies. By 1500 the Aztecs ruled a densely populated empire of subject and allied peoples.

Meanwhile, in the Andean highlands of western South America another powerful Amerindian empire was forming. Like central Mexico this region already had a rich agricultural base and a dense population when, in the fifteenth century, the Inca began using military skills to expand from a chiefdom into an empire. The Inca rulers, like the Aztecs, built impressive cities, promoted irrigation projects, and relied on religious rituals to bolster their authority. Tribute in goods and labor from their subject peoples supported their projects, and a network of mountain roads tied together the pieces of an empire that stretched for more than 3,000 miles (nearly 5,000 kilometers) north to south.

Both empires were cultural and commercial centers as well as political ones. In the Aztec Empire, well-armed private merchants controlled a long-distance trade in luxuries for the elites, including gold, jewels, feathered garments, and animal skins. There was also a network of local markets, large and small, that supplied the needs of more ordinary folks. State direction featured more prominently in Inca-ruled areas and promoted a vast exchange of specialized goods and a huge variety of foodstuffs grown at different altitudes.

The Maritime Revolution

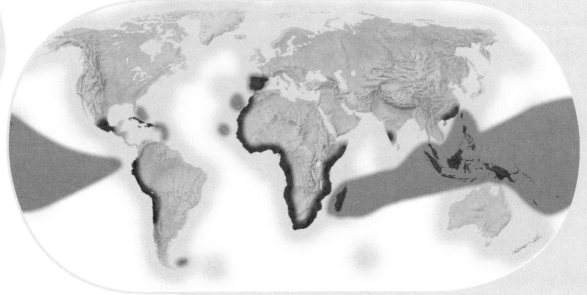

© Cengage Learning

In 1511 young Ferdinand Magellan sailed from Europe around the southern tip of Africa and eastward across the Indian Ocean as a member of the first Portuguese expedition to explore the East Indies (maritime Southeast Asia). Eight years later, this time in the service of Spain, he led an expedition that sought to reach the East Indies by sailing westward. By the middle of 1521 Magellan's expedition had achieved its goal by sailing across the Atlantic, rounding the southern tip of South America, and crossing the Pacific Ocean—but at a high price.

Of the five ships that had set out from Spain in 1519, only three made the long passage across the vast Pacific. Dozens of sailors died from starvation and disease during the voyage. In the Philippines, Magellan, having survived numerous mutinies during the voyage, died in battle on April 27, 1521, while aiding a local ruler who had promised to become a Christian.

To consolidate their dwindling resources, the expedition's survivors burned the least seaworthy of their remaining three ships and consolidated men and supplies. In the end only the *Victoria* made it home across the Indian Ocean and back to Europe. Nevertheless, the *Victoria*'s return to Spain on September 8, 1522, was a crowning example of Europeans' determination to make themselves masters of the oceans. A century of daring and dangerous voyages backed by the Portuguese crown had opened new routes through the South Atlantic to Africa, Brazil, and the rich trade of the Indian Ocean. Rival voyages sponsored by Spain since 1492 opened new contacts with the American continents. A maritime revolution was under way that would change the course of history.

This new maritime era marked the end of a long period when Asia had been the source of the most useful technologies and the most influential systems of belief. It was also home to the most powerful states and the richest overland and maritime trading networks. The success of European voyages of exploration in the following century would redirect the world's center of power, wealth, and innovation to the West.

This maritime revolution broadened and deepened contacts, alliances, and conflicts across ancient cultural boundaries. Some of these contacts ended tragically for individuals like Magellan. Some proved disastrous for entire populations: Amerindians, for instance, suffered conquest, colonization, and a rapid decline in numbers. And sometimes the results were mixed: Asians and Africans found both risks and opportunities in their new relations with Europe.

GLOBAL MARITIME EXPANSION BEFORE 1450

■ *What were the objectives and major accomplishments of the voyages of exploration undertaken by Chinese, Polynesians, and other non-Western peoples?*

By 1450 daring mariners had discovered and settled most of the islands of the Pacific, the Atlantic, and the Indian Ocean, and a great trading system united the peoples around the Indian Ocean. But no one had yet crossed the Pacific in either direction. Even the smaller Atlantic remained a barrier to contact between the Americas, Europe, and Africa. The inhabitants of Australia were also nearly cut off from contact with the rest of humanity. All this was about to change.

The Indian Ocean   Connected through trade, the archipelagos and coastal regions of Southeast Asia were divided politically, culturally, and religiously, but their languages all originated from a common Austronesian root. Scholars often use the term *Malayo Indonesians* or *Malay* to describe the early peoples of this maritime realm.

The region's sailors were highly skilled navigators, ship builders, and sail makers who influenced Chinese and Arab maritime advances. They discovered two direct sea routes between Sri Lanka and the South China Sea through the Straits of Malacca and Sunda, thus opening a profitable link to China's silk markets, and they also used the seasonal monsoon winds of the Indian Ocean to extend their voyages for thousands of miles, ultimately reaching East Africa and settling in Madagascar (see Chapter 8).

By the first century C.E. India and Southeast Asia were trading across the region for spices, gold, and aromatic woods, even sending spices as far west as Rome through Mediterranean intermediaries (see

Chapter 5). Their success attracted African, Arab, and Chinese merchants, creating a large, integrated, and highly profitable market in the centuries that followed. By 1000 the dhows (dow) of Arabs and Africans as well as Malay *jongs* and Chinese junks came together in the region's harbors for commerce.

The rise of Islam (see Chapter 9) gave Indian Ocean trade an important boost. The great Muslim cities of the Middle East provided a demand for valuable commodities, and networks of Muslim traders who shared a common language, ethic, and law actively spread their religion to distant trading cities. By 1400 there were Muslim trading communities all around the Indian Ocean. Chinese merchant communities were present as well.

Indian Ocean traders operated independently of the empires and states they served, but when Ming rulers overthrew Mongol rule in China, they became interested in these wealthy ports and reestablishing China's predominance and prestige abroad. The Ming moved to establish direct contacts with the peoples around the Indian Ocean, sending out seven imperial fleets between 1405 and 1433. Admiral Zheng He (jung huh) (1371–1435) commanded the expeditions. A Chinese Muslim with ancestral connections to the Persian Gulf, Zheng was a fitting emissary to the increasingly Muslim-dominated Indian Ocean Basin (see Chapter 14).

The enormous size of these expeditions, far larger than needed for exploration or promoting trade, indicates that the Ming sought to inspire awe. The first consisted of sixty-two specially built "treasure ships," large Chinese junks each about 300 feet long by 150 feet wide (90 by 45 meters). There were also at least a hundred smaller vessels. Each treasure ship had nine masts, twelve sails, many decks, and a carrying capacity of 3,000 tons (six times the capacity of Columbus's entire fleet). One expedition carried over 27,000 individuals, including infantry and cavalry troops. The ships were armed with small cannon, but highly accurate crossbows dominated most Chinese sea battles.

One Chinese-Arabic interpreter kept a journal recording local customs and beliefs. He observed new flora and fauna, noting exotic animals such as the black panther of Malaya and the tapir of Sumatra. In India he described the division of the coastal population into five classes, which correspond to the four Hindu varna and a separate Muslim class, and the fact that traders in the Indian port of Calicut (KAL-ih-kut) could perform error-free calculations by

Chinese Junk This modern drawing shows how much larger the Chinese ships were compared to one of Vasco da Gama's vessels. Watertight interior bulkheads made junks the most seaworthy large ships of the fifteenth century. Sails made of pleated bamboo matting hung from the junk's masts, and a stern rudder provided steering. European ships of exploration, though smaller, were faster and more maneuverable.

Chronology

	Pacific Ocean	Atlantic Ocean	Indian Ocean
Pre-1400	**300 B.C.E.–1200 C.E.** Polynesian settlement of Pacific islands **By 1000** Sporadic Polynesian contacts with American mainland **1200–1300** Polynesian societies in Hawaii, Tonga, and elsewhere develop clear class structures with hereditary chiefs	**770–1200** Viking voyages **1300s** Settlement of Madeira, Azores, Canaries **Early 1300s** Mali voyages	
1400		**1418–1460** Voyages of Henry the Navigator **1440s** Slaves from West Africa **1482** Portuguese at Gold Coast and Kongo **1486** Portuguese at Benin **1488** Bartolomeu Dias reaches Indian Ocean **1492** Columbus reaches Caribbean **1492–1500** Spanish conquer Hispaniola **1493** Columbus returns to Caribbean (second voyage) **1498** Columbus reaches mainland of South America (third voyage)	**1405–1433** Voyages of Zheng He **1497–1498** Vasco da Gama reaches India
1500	**1518** Smallpox arrives in Caribbean **1519–1522** Magellan expedition	**1500** Cabral reaches Brazil **1519–1521** Cortés conquers Aztec Empire **1531–1533** Pizarro conquers Inka Empire **1536** Rebellion of Inka in Peru	**1505** Portuguese bombard Swahili Coast cities **1510** Portuguese take Goa **1511** Portuguese take Malacca **1515** Portuguese take Hormuz **1535** Portuguese take Diu **1538** Portuguese defeat Ottoman fleet **1539** Portuguese aid Ethiopia

counting on their fingers and toes rather than using the Chinese abacus. After his return, the interpreter went on tour in China, telling of these exotic places and "how far the majestic virtue of [China's] imperial dynasty extended."[1]

---

[1]Ma Huan, *Ying-yai Sheng-lan: "The Overall Survey of the Ocean's Shores,"* ed. Feng Ch'eng-Chün, trans. J. V. G. Mills (Cambridge, England: Cambridge University Press, 1970), 180.

While curiosity about the region was likely one motive, the fact that the fleets visited major commercial ports suggests that expanding China's trade was an objective as well, and it appears that China's lavish gifts to local rulers stimulated the Swahili market for silk and porcelain. But interest in new contacts was not limited to the Chinese. At least three trading cities on the Swahili (swah-HEE-lee) Coast of East Africa sent delegations to China between 1415 and 1416.

Delegates from Malindi presented the Chinese emperor with a giraffe, creating quite a stir among normally reserved imperial officials. These African delegations may have encouraged more contacts because the next three of Zheng's voyages reached the African coast. Unfortunately, no documents record how Africans and Chinese reacted to each other.

Later Ming emperors would focus their attention on internal matters, facing opposition to the expeditions from some Chinese officials who opposed increased contact with peoples they regarded as barbarians incapable of making contributions to China. Such opposition caused a suspension in the voyages from 1424 to 1431. The final Chinese expedition sailed between 1432 and 1433. But long-established Chinese merchant communities continued as major participants in Indian Ocean trade. As the sultan of Malacca, one of the most prosperous trade centers (see Chapter 14), described the era in 1468, "We have learned that to master the blue oceans people must engage in commerce and trade. All the lands within the seas are united in one body. Life has never been so affluent in preceding generations as it is today."[2]

The Pacific Ocean

Around 3000 B.C.E. Austronesian-speaking seafarers from Southeast Asia reached the island of New Guinea. Contact with the island's original population eventually forged a new cultural identity between these peoples, called *Lapita* by archaeologists. Lapita settlers colonized the island chains of Melanesia (mel-uh-NEE-zhuh), reaching Tonga, Fiji, and Samoa around 1000 B.C.E. By 500 B.C.E. a linguistically and culturally distinct Polynesian culture had emerged from this Lapita origin.

While European sailors were still staying close to shore, Polynesians had mastered long-distance maritime exploration. Pushing east from Tonga, Samoa, and Fiji, they colonized the Marquesas (mar-KAY-suhs) and the Cook and Society archipelagos by approximately 300 B.C.E. Before 500 C.E. Polynesian colonies were established on the Hawaiian Islands 2,200 miles (3,541 kilometers) away. Colonists also

settled Easter Island, 2,300 miles (3,702 kilometers) to the southeast, by 800 C.E., and finally, New Zealand by 1200 C.E. Polynesian voyagers even made periodic contact with the mainland of South America after 1000 C.E., passing on the domesticated Asian chicken and returning with the sweet potato.

Both DNA and linguistic evidence make clear that the Polynesian settlement of the islands of the eastern Pacific was no accident, but rather part of a systematic cultural drive to discover new lands. Following voyages of reconnaissance, Polynesian mariners carried out colonizing expeditions in fleets of large double-hulled canoes that relied on scores of paddlers as well as sails. Their largest canoes reached 120 feet (37 meters) in length and carried crews of fifty. A wide platform connected the two hulls and permitted the transportation of animals and plants crucial to the success of distant and isolated settlements. Long-range expeditions took pigs, dogs, and chickens with them as well as domesticated plants such as taro, bananas, yams, and breadfruit. Their success depended upon reliably navigating thousands of miles of ocean using careful observation of the currents and stars as the crews searched for evidence of land (see Map 15.1).

While all Polynesian societies descended from the same culture and most depended on farming and fishing, differences in geography and climate led to varying colonization experiences. In Hawaii low-lying native forests were converted to farmland using controlled burns, and fishponds were built to increase fish yields. As a result, the Polynesian communities of Hawaii thrived into the era of European expansion. However, in Easter Island, among the most isolated of the Polynesian colonies, population growth led to total deforestation, soil erosion, intense resource competition, and, ultimately, a brutal cycle of warfare that drastically reduced the population. The hierarchical social and political structures that are in evidence throughout the Polynesian archipelagos and New Zealand around 1200–1300 led to chronic warfare elsewhere as well, as hereditary chiefs competed for resources.

The Atlantic Ocean

From the early Middle Ages, Viking raiders used their small, open ships to attack northern Europe's coastal settlements. Like the Polynesians, the Vikings

---

[2]Quotation in Craig A. Lockard, "'The Sea Common to All': Maritime Frontiers, Port Cities, and Chinese Traders in the Southeast Asian Age of Commerce, ca. 1400–1750," *Journal of World History* 21, no. 2 (2010): 228.

navigated by their knowledge of the heavens and the seas rather than by maps and other navigational devices. They first settled Iceland in 770, established a colony on Greenland in 982, and sighted North America in 986. Fifteen years later Leif Ericsson established a short-lived Viking settlement on the island of Newfoundland, which he called *Vinland*. When the climate turned colder after 1200, the settlements in Greenland declined and Vinland was abandoned.

Some southern Europeans applied their Mediterranean experience to Atlantic exploration. In the fourteenth century, Genoese and Portuguese expeditions settled the islands of Madeira (muh-DEER-uh), the Azores (A-zorz), and the Canaries.

There is some evidence that Africans also explored the Atlantic in this period. The Syrian geographer al-Umari (1301–1349) relates that when Mansa Kankan Musa (MAHN-suh KAHN-kahn MOO-suh), the ruler of the West African empire of Mali, passed through Egypt on his lavish pilgrimage to Mecca in 1324 (see Chapter 14), he told of Atlantic voyages undertaken by his predecessor, Mansa Muhammad. Muhammad had sent out four hundred vessels with men and supplies, telling them, "Do not return until you have reached the other side of the ocean or if you have exhausted your food or water." After a long time one canoe returned, reporting that the others were lost in a "violent current in the middle of the sea." Muhammad himself then set out at the head of a second, even larger, expedition, from which no one returned.

On the other side of the Atlantic, Amerindian voyagers from the Caribbean coast of South America colonized the West Indies. By the year 1000 the **Arawak** (AR-uh-wahk) (also called *Taino*) had followed the small islands of the Lesser Antilles (Barbados, Martinique, and Guadeloupe) to the Greater Antilles (Cuba, Hispaniola, Jamaica, and Puerto Rico) as well as to the Bahamas. The Carib followed the same route in later centuries, and by the late fifteenth century they had overrun most Arawak settlements in the Lesser Antilles and were raiding parts of the Greater Antilles. Both Arawak and Carib peoples also made contact with the North American mainland.

The transfer of maize cultivation to South America after its domestication in Mesoamerica suggests contact among Amerindian peoples, including the use of boats along the Pacific coast. After 100, mari-

SECTION REVIEW

- Polynesians explored and settled the eastern Pacific from the Marquesas to Hawaii and Easter Island.
- The Indian Ocean became a center of commerce and cultural exchange. Between 1405 and 1433 Chinese admiral Zheng He's seven expeditions established contacts with South Asian and African peoples.
- Vikings, Amerindians, and Africans also pursued long-distance explorations and settlement.

ners in two-masted balsa rafts as long as 36 feet (11 meters) were sailing north from the coast of Ecuador bringing pottery, jewelry made of copper as well as gold and silver, and textiles. The rafts could carry over 20 metric tons and ten or more crew members. Favorable winds and Pacific currents facilitated travel north, but these crafts were also capable of returning south, often with cargos of spondylus shells (a spiny bivalve considered sacred by ancient peoples). Through such contact metallurgy was introduced to Mesoamerica around 650.

EUROPEAN EXPANSION, 1400–1550

■ *In this era of long-distance exploration, did Europeans have any special advantages over other cultural regions?*

While the pace and intensity of maritime contacts increased in many parts of the world before 1450, it was the epic sea voyages sponsored by the European kingdoms of Portugal and Spain that launched the maritime revolution that would profoundly alter world history, ending the isolation of the Americas and increasing global interaction.

Overseas expansion arose from two related phenomena. First, Portuguese and Spanish rulers had strong economic, religious, and political motives to expand their influence. And second, improvements in maritime and military technologies gave them the means to master treacherous and unfamiliar ocean environments, seize control of existing maritime trade routes, and conquer new lands.

Arawak Amerindian peoples who inhabited the Greater Antilles of the Caribbean at the time of Columbus.

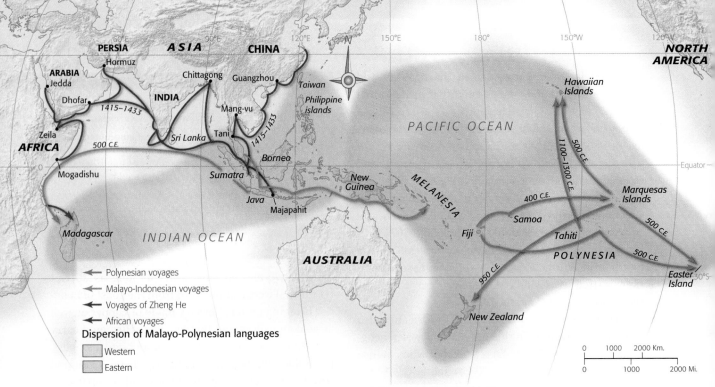

Map 15.1 Exploration and Settlement in the Indian and Pacific Oceans Before 1500 Over many centuries, mariners originating in Southeast Asia gradually colonized the islands of the Pacific and Indian Oceans. The Chinese voyages led by Zheng He in the fifteenth century were lavish official expeditions. © Cengage Learning

Motives for Exploration

The immediate cause of the voyages in the fifteenth century was the ambitions and adventurous personalities of the rulers of Portugal and Spain, but the underlying causes were four trends evident in the countries of western Europe since about the year 1000: (1) the revival of urban life and trade, (2) the unique alliance between merchants and rulers, (3) a struggle with Islamic powers for dominance of the Mediterranean that mixed religious motives with the desire for trade, and (4) growing intellectual curiosity about the outside world.

By 1450 the city-states of northern Italy had well-established trade links to northern Europe, the Indian Ocean, and the Black Sea, and their merchant princes had also sponsored an intellectual and artistic Renaissance. The Italian trading states of Venice and Genoa maintained commercial ties in the Mediterranean that depended on lucrative alliances with Muslims from the East. Even after the expansion of the Ottoman Empire disrupted this trade, these cities did not take the lead in exploring the Atlantic. However, many individual Italians played leading roles in the Atlantic explorations.

In contrast, the Iberian kingdoms had been engaging in anti-Muslim warfare since the eighth century. By 1250 the Iberian kingdoms of Portugal, Castile, and Aragon had reconquered all the Muslim lands except the kingdom of Granada (see Chapter 13). The dynastic marriage of Isabella of Castile and Ferdinand of Aragon in 1469 facilitated the conquest of Granada in 1492 and the formation of Spain, sixteenth-century Europe's most powerful state.

Christian militancy continued to drive Portugal and Spain in their overseas ventures. But the Iberian rulers and their adventurous subjects also sought material returns. Their modest share of the Mediterranean trade made them more willing than the Italians to seek new routes to Africa and Asia via the Atlantic. Both kingdoms participated in the shipbuilding and the gunpowder revolutions that were under way in Atlantic Europe, and both were especially open to new geographical knowledge.

Portuguese Voyages

When the Muslim government of Morocco in northwestern Africa weakened in the fifteenth century, the Portuguese attacked, conquering the city of Ceuta (say-OO-tuh) in 1415. Despite the capture of several more ports along Morocco's Atlantic coast, they could not push inland and gain direct access to the gold trade. So they sought contact with the gold producers by sailing down the African coast.

Prince Henry (1394–1460), third son of the king of Portugal, had led the attack on Ceuta. Because from 1418 on he devoted the rest of his life to promoting exploration, he is known as **Henry the Navigator**. His official biographer emphasized Henry's desire to convert Africans to Christianity, make contact with Christian rulers in Africa, and launch joint crusades with them against the Ottomans. Profit also figured in his dreams. His initial explorations focused on Africa, but reaching India became the eventual goal of Portuguese explorers. While called "the Navigator," Henry himself never ventured far from home. Instead, he founded a research center at Sagres (SAH-gresh) to study navigation built on the pioneering efforts of Italian merchants and fourteenth-century Jewish cartographers, and to improve navigational instruments, including the magnetic compass, first developed in China, and the astrolabe, an instrument of Arab or Greek invention that enabled mariners to determine their latitude at sea by measuring the position of the sun or the stars. This center collected geographical information from sailors and travelers and sponsored new expeditions to explore the Atlantic. Henry's ships established permanent contact with the islands of Madeira in 1418 and with the Azores in 1439.

The Portuguese also developed a new type of long-distance sailing vessel. Large crews of oarsmen prevented Mediterranean galleys from carrying enough supplies for long voyages, and the square-rigged vessels of northern Europe could not sail into the wind. The Portuguese **caravel** (KAR-uh-vel) solved both problems. Much smaller than either the largest European ships or the Chinese junks, it could enter shallow coastal waters and explore upriver and yet also had the strength to weather ocean storms. When equipped with triangular lateen sails, caravels had great maneuverability and could sail at greater speeds into the wind. The addition of small cannon made them good fighting ships as well. The caravels' economy, speed, agility, and power justified a con-

temporary's claim that they were "the best ships that sailed the seas."[3]

Pioneering captains had to overcome the common fear that South Atlantic waters were boiling hot or contained ocean currents that would prevent any ship entering them from ever returning home. It took Prince Henry from 1420 to 1434 to coax an expedition to venture beyond southern Morocco (see Map 15.2). It would ultimately take the Portuguese four decades to cover the 1,500 miles (2,400 kilometers) from Lisbon to Sierra Leone (see-ER-uh lee-OWN); it then took only three additional decades to explore the remaining 4,000 miles (6,400 kilometers) to the southern tip of the African continent. With experience, navigators learned to return home speedily by sailing northwest into the Atlantic to the latitude of the Azores, where they picked up prevailing westerly winds. The knowledge that ocean winds tend to form large circular patterns helped later explorers discover many other ocean routes.

During the 1440s Portuguese raiders on the northwest coast of Africa and the Canary Islands began to return with slaves, finding a profitable market in an Iberia still recovering from the population losses of the Black Death. The total number of Africans captured or purchased on voyages exceeded eighty thousand by the end of the century and rose steadily thereafter. However, gold quickly became more important once the Portuguese contacted the trading networks that flourished in West Africa and reached across the Sahara. By 1457 enough African gold was coming back to Portugal for the kingdom to issue a new gold coin bearing a large cross and called the *cruzado*, another reminder of how deeply the Portuguese entwined religious and secular motives.

---

[3]Alvise da Cadamosto in *The Voyages of Cadamosto and Other Documents*, ed. and trans. G. R. Crone (London: Hakluyt Society, 1937), 2.

Henry the Navigator Portuguese prince who promoted the study of navigation and directed voyages of exploration down the western coast of Africa in the fifteenth century.

caravel A small, highly maneuverable three-masted ship used by the Portuguese and Spanish in the exploration of the Atlantic.

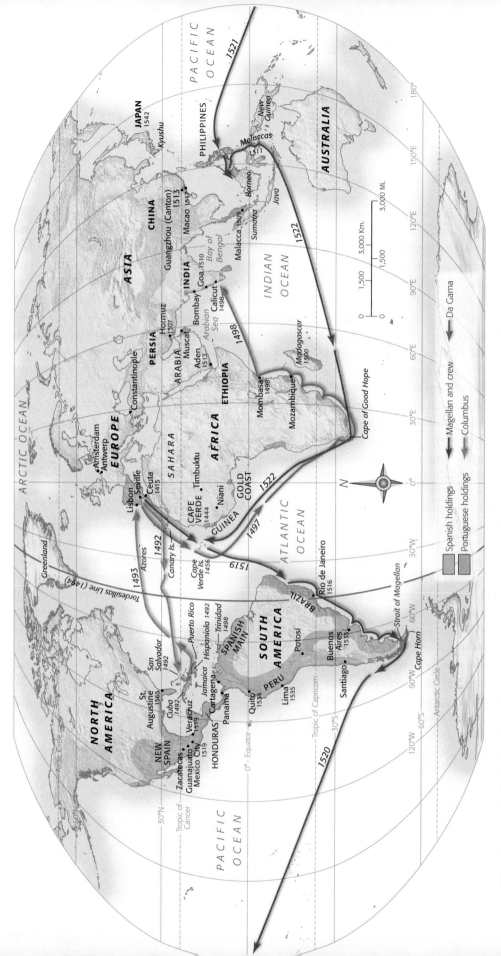

Map 15.2 European Exploration, 1420–1542 Portuguese and Spanish explorers showed the possibility and practicality of inter-continental maritime trade. Before 1540 European trade with Africa and Asia was much more important than that with the Americas, but after the Spanish conquest of the Aztec and Inka Empires, transatlantic trade began to increase. Notice the Tordesillas line, which in theory separated the Spanish and Portuguese spheres of activity. © Cengage Learning

Royal sponsorship continued, but private commercial interests accelerated the pace of exploration. In 1469 a Lisbon merchant named Fernão Gomes purchased from the Crown the privilege of exploring 350 miles (550 kilometers) of African coast in return for a trade monopoly. He discovered the uninhabited island of São Tomé (sow toh-MAY) on the equator and following the example of the Venetians in the eastern Mediterranean converted it into a major producer of sugar dependent on slave labor. In the next century the island would serve as a model for the sugar plantations of Brazil and the Caribbean. Gomes also explored the **Gold Coast**, which became the headquarters of Portugal's West African trade.

The desire to find a passage around Africa to the rich spice trade of the Indian Ocean spurred the final thrust down the African coast. In 1488 **Bartolomeu Dias** rounded the southern tip of Africa and entered the Indian Ocean, and in 1497–1498 **Vasco da Gama** sailed around Africa and reached India. Then, in 1500, ships under the command of Pedro Alvares Cabral (kah-BRAHL) sailed too far west and accidentally reached the South American mainland, establishing Portugal's claim to Brazil. The gamble that Prince Henry had begun eight decades earlier was about to pay off handsomely.

Spanish Voyages

Spain's early discoveries owed more to haste and blind luck than to careful planning. Only in the last decade of the fifteenth century did the Spanish monarchs turn their attention from the conquest and organization of previously Muslim territories to overseas exploration. By that time, the Portuguese had already found their route to the India.

The leader of the overseas mission was **Christopher Columbus** (1451–1506), a Genoese mariner. His four voyages between 1492 and 1504 established the existence of a vast new world across the Atlantic. But Columbus refused to accept this momentous discovery, insisting he had found a shorter route to the Indian Ocean.

As a young man Columbus participated in Portuguese explorations along the African coast, but he dreamed of a shorter way to the riches of the East. By his reckoning (based on a serious misreading of a ninth-century Arab authority), the Canaries were a mere 2,400 nautical miles (4,450 kilometers) from Japan. The actual distance was five times greater.

It was not easy for Columbus to find a sponsor to underwrite his theory that Asia could be reached by sailing west. The Portuguese twice rejected his plan, and a Castilian commission questioned his geographical assumptions. Though more sympathetic, Queen Isabella rejected it, too. But his persistence paid off, and in 1492, the queen and her husband, King Ferdinand of Aragon, agreed to fund a modest expedition.

Columbus recorded in his log that he and his crew of ninety men "departed Friday the third day of August of the year 1492" toward "the regions of India." Their mission, the royal contract stated, was "to discover and acquire certain islands and mainland in the Ocean Sea." He carried letters of introduction from the Spanish sovereigns to Eastern rulers, including one to the "Grand Khan" (meaning the Chinese emperor), and brought along an Arabic interpreter. The expedition traveled in three small ships, the *Santa María*, the *Niña*, and the *Pinta*. The *Niña* and the *Pinta* were caravels.

Unfavorable headwinds had impeded other attempts to explore the Atlantic west of the Azores, but Columbus chose a southern route because he had learned in his earlier voyages along the African coast that there were west-blowing winds at the latitude of the Canaries. In October 1492 the expedition reached the islands of the Caribbean. Columbus called the inhabitants Indians because he believed he had reached the East Indies. His second voyage to the Caribbean in 1493 did nothing to change his mind. Even when, two months after Vasco da Gama reached India in 1498, Columbus first sighted the mainland of

Gold Coast Region of the Atlantic coast of West Africa occupied by modern Ghana; named for its gold exports to Europe from the 1470s onward.

Bartolomeu Dias Portuguese explorer who in 1488 led the first expedition to sail around the southern tip of Africa from the Atlantic and sight the Indian Ocean.

Vasco da Gama Portuguese explorer. In 1497–1498 he led the first naval expedition from Europe to sail to India, opening an important commercial sea route.

Christopher Columbus Genoese mariner who in the service of Spain led expeditions across the Atlantic, reestablishing contact between the peoples of the Americas and the Old World and opening the way to Spanish conquest and colonization.

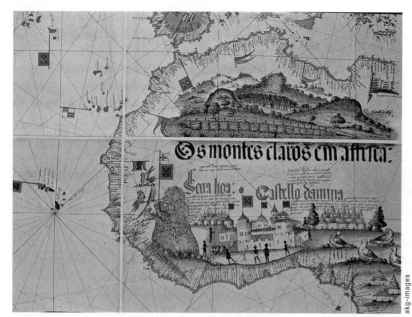

Portuguese Map of Western Africa, 1502 This map shows in great detail a section of African coastline that Portuguese explorers charted and named in the fifteenth century. The cartographer illustrated the African interior, which was almost completely unknown to Europeans, with drawings of birds and views of coastal sights: Sierra Leone (Serra lioa), named for a mountain shaped like a lion, and the Portuguese Castle of the Mine (Castello damina) on the Gold Coast.

akg-images

South America on his third voyage, he insisted it was part of Asia. But by then other Europeans were convinced that he had discovered islands and continents previously unknown to the Old World. Amerigo Vespucci's explorations, first on behalf of Spain and then for Portugal, led mapmakers to name the new continents "America," after him.

To prevent disputes about exploiting these lands and spreading Christianity among their peoples, Spain and Portugal agreed to split the world between them. The Treaty of Tordesillas (tor-duh-SEE-yuhs), negotiated by the pope in 1494, drew an imaginary line down the middle of the Atlantic Ocean. Lands east of the line in Africa and southern Asia were Portugal's to exploit; lands to the west in the Americas were reserved for Spain. Cabral's discovery of Brazil, however, gave Portugal a valid claim to the part of South America located east of the line.

Where would Spain's and Portugal's spheres of influence divide in the East? Given Europeans' ignorance of the earth's true size in 1494, it was not clear whether the Moluccas (muh-LOO-kuhz), the source of valuable spices in the East Indies, were on Portugal's or Spain's side of the Tordesillas line extended around the globe. The size of the Pacific Ocean would determine the boundary. In the end, the Moluccas turned out to lie well within Portugal's sphere, as Spain formally acknowledged in 1529.

In 1519 **Ferdinand Magellan** (ca. 1480–1521) sought to complete Columbus's interrupted westward voyage by sailing around the Americas and across the Pacific. Despite his death during this voyage on behalf of the king of Spain, Magellan was considered the first person to encircle the globe because a decade earlier he had sailed from Europe to the East Indies on an expedition sponsored by his native Portugal. His two voyages took him across the Tordesillas line and through the separate spheres claimed by Portugal and Spain; they also established the basis for Spanish colonization of the Philippines after 1564.

Columbus and those who followed in his wake laid the foundation for the colonial empires of Spain and other European nations. In turn, these empires promoted a major new trading network whose importance rivaled and eventually surpassed that of the Indian Ocean. Portugal's entry into the Indian Ocean led quickly to a major European presence and profit. Both the eastward and the westward voyages of exploration marked a tremendous expansion of Europe's role in world history.

Ferdinand Magellan Portuguese navigator who led the Spanish expedition of 1519–1522 that was the first to sail around the world.

SECTION REVIEW

- Portugal and Spain initiated oversees explorations to expand Christianity and gain new markets.
- Portugal, aided by Prince Henry the Navigator, created a trading empire in Africa and the Indian Ocean.
- Columbus first revealed the Americas to Europe, and other Spanish explorers reached Asia by crossing the Pacific.

ENCOUNTERS WITH EUROPE, 1450–1550

■ *What were the different outcomes of European interactions with Africa, India, and the Americas?*

European actions alone did not determine the global consequences of these new contacts. The ways in which Africans, Asians, and Amerindians perceived these visitors and interacted with them influenced developments as well. Everywhere indigenous peoples evaluated the Europeans as potential allies or enemies. In general,

Africans and Asians recognized the benefits and dangers of European contact. However, the long isolation of the Amerindians from the rest of the world made them vulnerable to European diseases, limiting their ability to resist European settlement.

Western Africa   Many Africans welcomed trade with the Portuguese, since it offered new markets for exports and access to imports cheaper than those transported overland from the Mediterranean. Miners in the hinterland, which the Portuguese had first visited in 1471, had long sold their gold to merchants from trading cities along the southern edge of the Sahara for transshipment to North Africa. Recognizing the possibility of more favorable terms, coastal Africans negotiated with the royal representative of Portugal, who arrived in 1482 seeking permission to erect a trading fort.

This Portuguese noble and his officers (likely including the young Christopher Columbus) were eager to make a proper impression. They dressed in their best clothes, erected a reception platform, celebrated a Catholic Mass, and signaled the start of negotiations with trumpets, tambourines, and drums. The African king, Caramansa, staged his entrance with equal ceremony, arriving with a large retinue of attendants and musicians. Through an African interpreter, the two leaders exchanged flowery speeches pledging goodwill and mutual benefit.

Caramansa then gave permission for a small trading fort, assured, he said, by the appearance of the royal delegate that they were honorable persons, unlike the "few, foul, and vile" Portuguese visitors of the previous decade.

Neither side made a show of force, but Caramansa warned that if the Portuguese acted aggressively, he and his people would move away, depriving their fort of food and trade. Trade at the post of Saint George of Elmina (the Arabic word for "seaport") enriched both sides. The Portuguese crown had soon purchased gold equal to one-tenth of the world's production at the time. In return, Africans received shiploads of

Bronze Figure of Benin Ruler Both this prince and his horse are protected by chain mail introduced in the fifteenth century to Benin by Portuguese merchants. Antenna Gallery Dakar Senegal/ G.Dagli Orti/The Art Archive

goods brought by the Portuguese from Asia, Europe, and other parts of Africa.

After a century of aggressive expansion, the kingdom of Benin in the Niger Delta was near the peak of its power when it first encountered the Portuguese. Its oba (king) presided over an elaborate bureaucracy from a spacious palace in his large capital city, also known as Benin. In response to a Portuguese visit in 1486, the oba sent an ambassador to Portugal to learn more about these strangers. He then established a royal monopoly on Portuguese trade, selling pepper and ivory tusks (for export to Portugal) as well as stone beads, textiles, and prisoners of war (for resale at Elmina). In return, Portuguese merchants provided Benin with copper and brass, fine textiles, glass beads, and a horse for the king's royal procession. In the early sixteenth century, as the demand for slaves for the Portuguese sugar plantations on the nearby island of São Tomé grew, the oba first raised the price of slaves and then imposed restrictions that limited their sale.

Early contacts generally involved a mix of commercial, military, and religious exchanges. Some African rulers appreciated the advantage of European firearms. Because African religions were generally not exclusive, coastal rulers were also willing to test the value of the Christian practices promoted by the Portuguese. The rulers of Benin and Kongo, the two largest coastal kingdoms, accepted Portuguese missionaries and soldiers as allies in battle to determine the efficacy of the religion and the weaponry.

However, Portuguese efforts to persuade the king and nobles of Benin to accept the Catholic faith ultimately failed. Early kings showed some interest, but after 1538 rulers declined to receive more missionaries. They also closed the market in male slaves for the rest of the sixteenth century. We do not know why Benin chose to limit its contacts with the Portuguese, but the result makes clear that these rulers had the power to control their contacts with Europeans.

Farther south, on the lower Congo River, the manikongo (mah-NEE-KONG-goh) (king of Kongo) also sent delegates to Portugal, established a royal monopoly on trade, and expressed interest in missionary teachings. But here the royal family made Catholicism the kingdom's official faith. Lacking ivory and pepper, Kongo sold more slaves to acquire the goods brought by the Portuguese and to pay missionary expenses. Soon the royal trade monopoly broke down. In 1526 the Christian manikongo, Afonso I (r. 1506–ca. 1540), wrote to his royal "brother," the king of Portugal, begging for his help in stopping the trade because unauthorized Kongolese were kidnapping and selling people, even members of good families (see Diversity and Dominance: Kongo's Christian King). Alfonso received no reply from Portugal, whose interests were now concentrated in the Indian Ocean. Soon rebellion and the relocation of the slave trade from his kingdom to the south weakened the manikongo's authority.

Eastern Africa

Different still were the reactions of the Muslim rulers of the coastal trading states of eastern Africa. As Vasco da Gama's fleet sailed up the coast in 1498, most rulers gave the Portuguese a cool reception, suspicious of the painted crusaders' crosses on their sails. The ruler of Malindi, however, saw the Portuguese as an ally who could help him expand Malindi's trade, and he provided da Gama with a pilot to guide him to India. The suspicions of the other rulers were proven correct seven years later when a Portuguese war fleet bombarded and looted most of the coastal cities of eastern Africa in the name of Christ and commerce, while sparing Malindi.

Christian Ethiopia also saw the benefit of an alliance with the Portuguese. In the fourteenth and fifteenth centuries, Ethiopian conflicts with Muslim states along the Red Sea Increased. After the Ottoman Turks conquered Egypt and launched a fleet in the Indian Ocean to counter the Portuguese in 1517, the warlord of the Muslim state of Adal (now Djibouti) attacked Ethiopia. A decisive victory in 1529 put the Christian kingdom in jeopardy, making Portuguese support crucial.

For decades, delegations from Portugal and Ethiopia had explored a Christian alliance. Queen Helena of Ethiopia, who acted as regent for her young sons after her husband's death in 1478, sent a letter in 1509 to "our very dear and well-beloved brother," the king of Portugal, along with a gift of two tiny crucifixes said to be made of wood from the cross on which Christ was crucified. She proposed joining forces—her army and Portugal's fleet—to fight the Ottomans;

however, Helena's death in 1522 occurred before the alliance could be arranged. Ethiopia's situation then grew more desperate.

Finally, a small Portuguese force commanded by Vasco da Gama's son Christopher arrived to aid Ethiopia in 1539. With Portuguese help, another queen rallied the Ethiopians. Muslim forces captured and tortured to death Christopher da Gama, but they retreated when their own leader fell in battle. Portuguese aid helped save the Ethiopian kingdom from extinction, but a permanent alliance faltered because Ethiopian rulers refused to transfer their Christian affiliation from the patriarch of Alexandria to the Latin patriarch of Rome (the pope).

As these examples illustrate, African encounters with the Portuguese before 1550 varied considerably. Africans and Portuguese might become royal brothers, bitter opponents, or partners in a mutually profitable trade, but Europeans remained a minor presence in most of Africa in 1550. By then the Portuguese had become far more interested in the Indian Ocean trade.

Indian Ocean States

Vasco da Gama's arrival on the Malabar Coast of India in May 1498 did not impress the citizens of Calicut. The Chinese fleets of gigantic junks that had called at Calicut sixty-five years earlier dwarfed his four small ships, which were no larger than many of the dhows already filling the harbor. The samorin (ruler) of Calicut and his Muslim officials showed mild interest, but the gifts da Gama brought provoked derisive laughter: twelve pieces of fairly ordinary striped cloth, four scarlet hoods, six hats, and six wash basins. When da Gama tried to defend his gifts as those of an explorer, not a merchant, the samorin cut him short, asking whether he had come to discover men or stones: "If he had come to discover men, as he said, why had he brought nothing?"

Coastal rulers soon discovered that the Portuguese had no intention of remaining poor competitors in the Indian Ocean trade. Upon da Gama's return to Portugal in 1499, the jubilant King Manuel styled himself "Lord of the Conquest, Navigation, and Commerce of Ethiopia, Arabia, Persia, and India." Previously the Indian Ocean had been an open sea, used by merchants (and pirates) of all the surrounding coasts. Now the Portuguese crown intended to make it Portugal's sea, to be used on Portuguese terms alone.

Portugal's hope of controlling the Indian Ocean stemmed from the superiority of its ships and weapons, especially over the lightly armed merchant dhows. In 1505 a Portuguese fleet of eighty-one ships and some seven thousand men bombarded Swahili Coast cities. Indian ports were the next targets. Goa, on the west coast of India, fell to a well-armed fleet in 1510, becoming the base from which the Portuguese menaced the trading cities of Gujarat (goo-juh-RAHT) to the north and Calicut and other Malabar Coast cities to the south. The port of Hormuz, controlling entry to the Persian Gulf, fell in 1515. Aden, at the entrance to the Red Sea, successfully resisted, but the capture of the Gujarati port of Diu in 1535 consolidated Portuguese dominance of the western Indian Ocean.

Meanwhile, Portuguese explorers had reconnoitered the Bay of Bengal and the waters farther east. The city of Malacca (muh-LAH-kuh) on the strait between the Malay Peninsula and Sumatra became the focus of their attention. During the fifteenth century, Malacca had become the main entrepôt for the trade from China, Japan, India, the Southeast Asian mainland, and the Moluccas. The city's more than 100,000 residents spoke eighty-four different languages, including those of merchants from Cairo, Ethiopia, and the Swahili Coast. Many non-Muslim residents supported letting the Portuguese join its cosmopolitan trading community, perhaps hoping to offset the growing solidarity of Muslim traders. In 1511, however, the Portuguese seized Malacca with a force of a thousand fighting men, including three hundred recruited in southern India.

Force was not always necessary. On the China coast, local officials and merchants persuaded the imperial government to allow the Portuguese to establish a trading post at Macao (muh-COW) in 1557. Subsequently, Portuguese ships nearly monopolized trade between China and Japan.

Control of major port cities enabled the Portuguese to enforce their demands that all spices be carried in Portuguese ships, as well as goods on the major ocean routes such as between Goa and Macao. The Portuguese also tried to control and tax other Indian Ocean trade. Merchant ships entering and leaving their ports had to carry a Portuguese passport and

Diversity & Dominance

Kongo's Christian King

The new overseas voyages brought conquest to some and opportunities for fruitful borrowings and exchanges to others. The decision of the ruler of the kingdom of Kongo to adopt Christianity in 1491 added cultural diversity to Kongolese society and in some ways strengthened the hand of the king. From then on Kongolese rulers sought to introduce Christian beliefs and rituals while at the same time Africanizing Christianity to make it more intelligible to their subjects. In addition, the kings of Kongo sought a variety of more secular aid from Portugal, including schools and medicine. Trade with the Portuguese introduced new social and political tensions, especially in the case of the export trade in slaves for the Portuguese sugar plantations on the island of São Tomé to the north.

Two letters sent to King João (zhwao) III of Portugal in 1526 illustrate how King Afonso of Kongo saw his kingdom's new relationship with Portugal and the problems that resulted from it. (Afonso adopted that name when baptized as a young prince.) After the death of his father in 1506, Afonso successfully claimed the throne and ruled until 1542. His son Henrique became the first Catholic bishop of the Kongo in 1521.

These letters were written in Portuguese and penned by the king's secretary João Teixera (tay-SHER-uh), a Kongo Christian, who, like Afonso, had been educated by Portuguese missionaries.

6 July 1526

To the very powerful and excellent prince Dom João, our brother:

On the 20th of June just past, we received word that a trading ship from your highness had just come to our port of Sonyo. We were greatly pleased by that arrival for it had been many days since a ship had come to our kingdom, for by it we would get news of your highness, which many times we had desired to know, . . . and likewise as there was a great and dire need for wine and flour for the holy sacrament; and of this we had had no great hope for we have the same need frequently. And that, sir, arises from the great negligence of your highness's officials toward us and toward shipping us those things. . . .

Sir, your highness should know how our kingdom is being lost in so many ways that we will need to provide the needed cure, since this is caused by the excessive license given by your agents and officials to the men and merchants who come to this kingdom to set up shops with goods and many things which have been prohibited by us, and which they spread throughout our kingdoms and domains in such abundance that many of our vassals, whose submission we could once rely on, now act independently so as to get the things in greater abundance than we ourselves; whom we had formerly held content and submissive and under our vassalage and jurisdiction, so it is doing a great harm not only to the service of God, but also to the security and peace of our kingdoms and state.

And we cannot reckon how great the damage is, since every day the mentioned merchants are taking our people, sons of the land and the sons of our noblemen and vassals and our relatives, because the thieves and men of bad conscience grab them so as to have the things and wares of this kingdom that they crave; they grab them and bring them to be sold. In such a manner, sir, has been the corruption and deprivation that our land is becoming completely depopulated, and your highness should not deem this good nor in your service. And to avoid this we need from these kingdoms [of yours] no more than priests and a few people to teach in schools, and no other goods except wine and flour for the holy sacrament, which is why we beg of your highness to help and assist us in this matter. Order your agents to send here neither merchants nor wares, because it is our will that in these kingdoms there should not be any dealing in slaves nor outlet for them, for the reasons stated above. Again we beg your highness's agreement, since otherwise we cannot cure such manifest harm. May Our Lord in His mercy have your highness always under His protection and may you always do the things of His holy service. I kiss your hands many times.

From our city of Kongo. . . .

The King, Dom Afonso ▶

18 October 1526

Very high and very powerful prince King of Portugal, our brother,

Sir, your highness has been so good as to promise us that anything we need we should ask for in our letters, and that everything will be provided. And so that there may be peace and health of our kingdoms, by God's will, in our lifetime. And as there are among us old folks and people who have lived for many days, many and different diseases happen so often that we are pushed to the ultimate extremes. And the same happens to our children, relatives, and people, because this country lacks physicians and surgeons who might know the proper cures for such diseases, as well as pharmacies and drugs to make them better. And for this reason many of those who had been already confirmed and instructed in the things of the holy faith of Our Lord Jesus Christ perish and die. And the rest of the people for the most part cure themselves with herbs and sticks and other ancient methods, so that they live putting all their faith in these herbs and ceremonies, and die believing that they are saved; and this serves God poorly.

And to avoid such a great error, I think, and inconvenience, since it is from God and from your highness that all the good and the drugs and medicines have come to us for our salvation, we ask your merciful highness to send us two physicians and two pharmacists and one surgeon, so that they may come with their pharmacies and necessary things to be in our kingdoms, for we have extreme need of each and every one of them. We will be very good and merciful to them, since sent by your highness, their work and coming should be for good. We ask your highness as a great favor to do this for us, because besides being good in itself it is in the service of God as we have said above.

Moreover, sir, in our kingdoms there is another great inconvenience which is of little service to God, and this is that many of our people, out of great desire for the wares and things of your kingdoms, which are brought here by your people, and in order to satisfy their disordered appetite, seize many of our people, freed and exempt men. And many times noblemen and the sons of noblemen, and our relatives are stolen, and they take them to be sold to the white men who are in our kingdoms and take them hidden or by night, so that they are not recognized. And as soon as they are taken by the white men, they are immediately ironed and branded with fire. And when they are carried off to be embarked, if they are caught by our guards, the whites allege that they have bought them and cannot say

from whom, so that it is our duty to do justice and to restore to the free their freedom. And so they went away offended.

And to avoid such a great evil we passed a law so that every white man living in our kingdoms and wanting to purchase slaves by whatever means should first inform three of our noblemen and officials of our court on whom we rely in this matter, namely Dom Pedro Manipunzo and Dom Manuel Manissaba, our head bailiff, and Gonçalo Pires, our chief supplier, who should investigate if the said slaves are captives or free men, and, if cleared with them, there will be no further doubt nor embargo and they can be taken and embarked. And if they reach the opposite conclusion, they will lose the aforementioned slaves. Whatever favor and license we give them [the white men] for the sake of your highness in this case is because we know that it is in your service too that these slaves are taken from our kingdom; otherwise we should not consent to this for the reasons stated above that we make known completely to your highness so that no one could say the contrary, as they said in many other cases to your highness, so that the care and remembrance that we and this kingdom have should not be withdrawn. . . .

We kiss your hands of your highness many times.

From our city of Kongo, the 18th day of October,

The King, Dom Afonso

QUESTIONS FOR ANALYSIS

1. What sorts of things does King Afonso desire from the Portuguese?
2. What is he willing and unwilling to do in return?
3. What problem with his own people has the slave trade created, and what has King Afonso done about it?
4. Does King Afonso see himself as an equal to King João or his subordinate? Do you agree with that analysis?

Source: From António Brásio, ed., *Monumenta Missionaria Africana: Africa Ocidental (1471–1531)* (Lisbon: Agência Geral do Ultramar, 1952), I: 468, 470–471, 488–491. Translated by David Northrup.

Portuguese in India In the sixteenth century Portuguese men moved to the Indian Ocean Basin to work as administrators and traders. This Indo-Portuguese drawing from about 1540 shows a Portuguese man speaking to an Indian woman, perhaps making a proposal of marriage.

Album/Art Resource, NY

pay customs duties. Portuguese patrols seized vessels that did not comply, confiscated their cargoes, and either killed the captain and crew or sentenced them to forced labor.

Reactions to this power grab varied. Like the emperors of China, the Mughal (MOO-gahl) emperors of India largely ignored Portugal's maritime intrusions. The Ottomans confronted the Christian intruders more aggressively. They supported Egypt's defensive efforts in 1501 and 1509 and then sent their own fleet into the Indian Ocean in 1538. However, Ottoman galleys proved no match for the faster, better-armed Portuguese vessels in the open ocean. They retained their advantage only in the Red Sea and Persian Gulf, where they controlled many ports.

Smaller trading states also could not challenge the Portuguese because their mutual rivalry kept them from forming a common front. Some cooperated with the Portuguese to safeguard their prosperity and security, while others engaged in evasion and resistance. When the merchants of Calicut put up sustained resistance, the Portuguese embargoed all trade with Aden, Calicut's principal trading partner, and centered their trade on the port of Cochin, which had once been a dependency of Calicut. Some Calicut merchants evaded their patrols, but Calicut's impor-

tance shrank as Cochin gradually became the major pepper-exporting port on the Malabar Coast.

Farther north, Gujarat initially resisted Portuguese attempts at monopoly and in 1509 joined Egypt's futile effort to sweep the Portuguese from the Arabian Sea. But in 1535, finding his state weakened by Mughal attacks, the ruler allowed the Portuguese to build a fort at Diu in return for their support. Once established, the Portuguese gradually extended their control, and by midcentury they were licensing and taxing all Gujarati ships. Even after the Mughals took control of Gujarat in 1572, the Mughal emperor Akbar permitted the Portuguese to continue their maritime monopoly in return for allowing one pilgrim ship a year to travel to Mecca without paying a fee.

The Portuguese never gained complete control of the Indian Ocean trade, but their domination of key ports and trade routes brought them considerable profits from spices and other luxury goods. The Portuguese broke the trading monopoly of Venice and Genoa by selling pepper at much lower prices.

The consequences flowing from these events were dramatic. The Portuguese were able to fund an aggressive colonization of Brazil, while Asian and East African traders were at the mercy of their warships. But because the Portuguese concentrated on maritime trade routes in Asia and Africa, Portugal had little impact on the Asian and African mainlands, in sharp contrast to what was occurring in the Americas.

The Americas

The Spanish and Portuguese monarchies had similar motives for expansion and used identical ships and weapons, but the Spanish established a territorial rather than a trading empire in the Americas. The outcomes had little to do with differences between the two kingdoms. Rather, the isolation of the Amerindian peoples was key, making their responses to outside contacts different from those of African and Indian Ocean peoples. Isolation had slowed the development of metallurgy and other militarily useful technologies in the Americas and also made these large populations more susceptible to new diseases. It was the spread of deadly new diseases, especially smallpox, among Amerindians after 1518 that weakened their ability to resist and facilitated Spanish and Portuguese occupation.

The first Amerindians to encounter Columbus were the Arawak of Hispaniola (modern Haiti and the Dominican Republic) in the Greater Antilles and the Bahamas to the north (see Map 15.2). They cultivated maize (corn), cassava (yuca), sweet potatoes, and hot peppers, as well as cotton and tobacco. Although the islands did not have large gold deposits and, unlike West Africans, the Arawak had not previously traded gold over long distances, the natives were skilled at working gold. They extended a cautious welcome, but they soon learned to tell exaggerated stories about gold in other places to persuade the Spanish to move on.

Columbus brought several hundred settlers, as well as missionaries, on his second trip to Hispaniola in 1493. The settlers provoked the Arawak by demanding indigenous labor to look for gold, stealing gold ornaments and food, and sexually assaulting native women. The Arawak rebelled in 1495 but were slaughtered by the tens of thousands, no match for Spanish horses, body armor, and steel swords. Thousands more were forced to labor for the Spanish. Meanwhile, cattle, pigs, and goats introduced by the settlers devoured the Arawaks' food crops, causing deaths from famine and disease, particularly smallpox. A governor appointed by the Spanish crown in 1502 institutionalized these demands by forcing the surviving Arawak to become laborers under the control of Spanish settlers.

The actions of the Spanish in the Antilles were similar to those used by the Spanish against the Muslims in previous centuries: they sought to serve God by defeating, controlling, and converting nonbelievers and to become rich in the process. Individual **conquistadors** (kon-KEY-stuh-dor) (conquerors) extended that pattern around the Caribbean. Some raided the Bahamas for gold and labor as both became scarce on Hispaniola. New expeditions searched for gold and Amerindian laborers across the Caribbean region, capturing thousands of Amerindians and relocating them to Hispaniola as slaves. The island of Borinquen (Puerto Rico) was conquered in 1508 and Cuba between 1510 and 1511.

An ambitious and ruthless nobleman, **Hernán Cortés** (kor-TEZ) (1485–1547) undertook a new expedition to the mainland. Cortés left Cuba in 1519 with six hundred fighting men to assault the Mexican mainland in search of slaves and trade. After learning of the rich Aztec Empire in central Mexico, he expanded the exploitation and conquest carried out in the Greater Antilles.

Many subject peoples resented the tribute payments, forced labor, and large-scale human sacrifices demanded by the Aztecs. Consequently, some embraced the Spanish as allies. The Aztecs also had powerful native enemies, including the Tlaxcalans (thlash-KAH-lans), who became crucial allies of Cortés. Individual Amerindians also calculated the potential benefit or threat represented by these strange visitors. Malintzin (mah-LEENT-zeen) (also called Malinche), a native woman given to Cortés shortly after his arrival in the Maya region, became his translator, key source of intelligence, and mistress. As peoples and as individuals, native allies were crucial to the Spanish campaign.

While the emperor **Moctezuma II** (mock-teh-ZOO-ma) (r. 1502–1520) hesitated to use force and

conquistadors Early-sixteenth-century Spanish adventurers who conquered Mexico, Central America, and Peru.

Hernán Cortés Spanish explorer and conquistador who led the conquest of Aztec Mexico in 1519–1521 for Spain.

Moctezuma II Aztec emperor who died while in custody of the Spanish conquistador Hernán Cortés.

Montezuma wearing on his back the royal standard of green Quetzal bird feathers, copied from a native artist (colour litho)/Private Collection/Peter Newark American Pictures/The Bridgeman Art Library

Coronation of Emperor Moctezuma This painting by an unnamed Aztec artist depicts the Aztec ruler's coronation. Moctezuma, his nose pierced by a bone, receives the crown from a prince in the palace at Tenochtitlan.

attempted diplomacy instead, Cortés pushed toward the Aztec capital of Tenochtitlan (teh-noch-TIT-lan). Spanish forces overcame opposition with firearms, cavalry tactics, and steel swords. As the Spanish approached his island capital, the emperor went out in a great procession, dressed in his finery, to welcome Cortés.

Despite Cortés's initial pledge of friendship, Moctezuma was quickly imprisoned. The Spanish looted his treasury, interfered with the city's religious rituals, and eventually massacred hundreds during a festival. The Aztecs rebelled, killing half the Spanish force and four thousand of Cortés's native allies. In the confusion Moctezuma also lost his life, either killed by the Spanish or in the Aztec attack.

The survivors, strengthened by Spanish reinforcements and aided by the Tlaxcalans, renewed their attack and captured Tenochtitlan in 1521. Their victory was aided by a smallpox epidemic that killed more of the city's defenders than did the fighting. One source remembered that the disease "spread over the people as a great destruction." Many Amerindians as well as Europeans blamed the devastating spread of this disease on supernatural forces. Cortés and other Spanish leaders then led expeditions to the north and south accompanied by the Tlaxcalans and other indigenous allies. Everywhere epidemic disease, especially smallpox, helped crush indigenous resistance.

Meanwhile, Spanish settlers in Panama began hearing of another empire to the south. The Inka Empire stretched nearly 3,000 miles (5,000 kilometers) south of the equator along the Pacific coast (see Chapter 14). During its expansion, it had enforced labor demands and taxes on conquered peoples and exiled rebellious populations. When the Inka ruler Huayna Capac (WHY-nah KAH-pak) died in 1525, a civil war ensued as his sons fought for the throne. **Atahuallpa** (ah-tuh-WAHL-puh) (r. 1531–1533), the candidate of the northern army, defeated Huascar, the candidate of the royal court at Cuzco, but political leadership was weakened and the military

Atahuallpa Last ruling Inka emperor of Peru. He was executed by the Spanish.

Francisco Pizarro Spanish explorer who led the conquest of the Inka Empire of Peru in 1531–1533.

decimated. At this critical time **Francisco Pizarro** (pih-ZAHR-oh) (ca. 1478–1541) and his force of 180 men, thirty-seven horses, and two cannon entered the region.

Pizarro had come to the Americas in 1502 at the age of twenty-five to seek his fortune. He had participated in the conquest of Hispaniola and in Balboa's expedition across the Isthmus of Panama to the Pacific. In the 1520s he gambled his fortune on exploring the Pacific coast south of the equator, where he learned of the riches of the Inka. With a license from the king of Spain, he set out from Panama in 1531 to conquer them.

Having seen signs of the civil war after landing, Pizarro arranged to meet the Inka emperor, Atahuallpa, near the Andean city of Cajamarca (kah-hah-MAHR-kah) in November 1532. With supreme boldness and brutality, Pizarro's small band of armed men attacked Atahuallpa and his followers as they entered an enclosed courtyard. Though surrounded by an Inka army of at least forty thousand, the Spaniards were able to use their cannon to create confusion while their swords brought down thousands of the emperor's lightly armed retainers and servants.

Atahuallpa attempted to purchase his freedom. Noting the glee with which the Spaniards seized gold and silver, Atahuallpa offered what he thought would satisfy even the greediest among them: rooms filled to shoulder height with gold and silver. But after receiving 13,400 pounds (6,000 kilograms) of gold and 26,000 pounds (12,000 kilograms) of silver, the Spaniards still executed Atahuallpa. His death broke the unity of an empire already battered by civil war.

The Execution of Inka Ruler Atahuallpa

Felipe Guaman Poma de Ayala, a native Andean from the area of Huamanga in Peru, drew this representation of the execution. While Pizarro sentenced Atahuallpa to death by strangulation, not beheading, Guaman Poma's illustration forcefully made the point that Spain had imposed an arbitrary and violent government on the Andean people.

SECTION REVIEW

- African kingdoms reacted in various ways to the opportunities and threats created by the arrival of the Portuguese, but only Kongo embraced Christianity and accepted a large Portuguese military presence in the sixteenth century.

- The Portuguese used military force to consolidate a trade empire in the Indian Ocean.

- After the Spanish occupied the Caribbean, Cortés led an expedition that conquered the Aztecs, who were weakened by disease.

- The Spanish under Pizarro conquered the Inka Empire, already suffering from civil war, and then fell on each other; but surviving conquistadors continued to explore the Americas.

In 1533, the Spanish had taken Cuzco, but in 1536 Pizarro had to put down another massive native rebellion. The remaining Inka now retreated, creating a small kingdom in the mountains that lasted until 1572. In 1541, Pizarro himself met a violent death at the hands of Spanish rivals, but the conquest of the mainland continued. Incited by the fabulous wealth of the Aztecs and Inka, conquistadors extended Spanish conquest and exploration in South and North America, dreaming of new treasures.

CONCLUSION

The rapid expansion of European empires and the projection of European military power around the world, one of the most important events in world history, would have seemed unlikely in 1492. No European power matched the military and economic strength of China, and few could rival the Ottomans. Spain lacked strong national institutions and Portugal had a small population; both had limited resources. Because of these limitations, the monarchs of Spain and Portugal allowed their subjects greater initiative. While royal sponsorship was often crucial in the Portuguese contacts with Africa and the first voyages to Asia, many of the commercial and military expeditions were effectively organized and financed as private companies. Very often the kings of Spain and Portugal struggled to catch up with their restless and ambitious subjects, sometimes taking decades to establish royal control in new colonies.

The pace and character of European expansion in Africa and Asia were different than in the Americas. In Africa local rulers were generally able to limit European military power to coastal outposts and to control European trade. Only in the Kongo were the Portuguese able to project their power inland. When the Europeans arrived in the Indian Ocean, mature markets and specialized production for distant consumers already existed. Here Portuguese (and later Dutch and British) naval power allowed Europeans to harvest large profits and influence regional commercial patterns, but most indigenous populations continued to enjoy effective autonomy for centuries.

In the Americas, however, the terrible effects of epidemic disease and the destructiveness of the Spanish conquests led to the rapid creation of European settlements and the subordination of the surviving indigenous population. As we shall see in Chapter 16, American gold, silver, and sugar eventually produced great wealth but only through the introduction of new technologies, the imposition of oppressive forms of labor, most notably slavery, and the development of new roads and ports.

What gave the European maritime revolution unprecedented importance had more to do with what happened after 1550 than what happened prior. The overseas empires of the Europeans would endure longer than the Mongols' and would continue to expand for three centuries after 1600. Unlike the Chinese, the Europeans did not turn their backs on the world after an initial burst of exploration. Not content with dominance in the Indian Ocean trade, Europeans opened an Atlantic maritime network that grew to rival the Indian Ocean network in the wealth of its trade; they also pioneered trade across the Pacific. The maritime expansion, begun in the period from 1450 to 1550, marked the beginning of a new age of global interaction.

CHAPTER REVIEW

GLOBAL MARITIME EXPANSION BEFORE 1450

■ *What were the objectives and major accomplishments of the voyages of exploration undertaken by Chinese, Polynesians, and other non-Western peoples?* (page 355)

The voyages of exploration undertaken by the Malays, Chinese, and Polynesians pursued diverse objectives. Malay voyagers were crucial participants in the development of the rich and varied commerce of Southeast Asia and initiated connections between these markets and Arabia and Africa. The great voyages of the Chinese in the early fifteenth century were motivated by an interest in trade, curiosity, and the desire to project imperial power. For the Polynesians, the discovery and settlement of new lands was a recurring objective because most of the islands that were settled were too small to support large populations. The Vikings, Africans, and Amerindians all undertook long-distance explorations as well, although with fewer lasting consequences.

EUROPEAN EXPANSION, 1400–1550

■ *In this era of long-distance exploration, did Europeans have any special advantages over other cultural regions?* (page 359)

This projection of European influence between 1450 and 1550 was in some ways similar to that of other cultural regions in that it expanded commercial linkages, increased cross-cultural contacts, and served the ambitions of political leaders. But in the aftermath of several centuries of Spanish and Portuguese combat against Muslim kingdoms in Iberia, it was driven by unusually powerful urges to fight Muslims, acquire their riches, and spread Christianity. During those years European explorers opened new long-distance trade routes across the world's three major oceans, for the first time establishing regular contact among all the continents.

ENCOUNTERS WITH EUROPE, 1450–1550

■ *What were the different outcomes of European interactions with Africa, India, and the Americas?* (page 365)

Europeans created colonial empires in the Americas quite rapidly, while their progress in Africa and Asia was much slower. Many Amerindians welcomed the Spanish settlers at first, only to have the Spanish tax their labors, steal their food, introduce disease and warfare, and eventually subjugate them. In contrast, Portuguese visitors to Africa remained a minor presence in 1550. In some regions, the Portuguese were welcomed as trading partners; in others they were regarded as potential political and military allies. The real focus of the Portuguese was to capture the rich trade of the Indian Ocean. While they never gained complete control, they used their superior military strength to dominate key ports and major trade routes.

Key Terms

Arawak (p. 359)
Henry the Navigator (p. 361)
caravel (p. 361)
Gold Coast (p. 363)
Bartolomeu Dias (p. 363)
Vasco da Gama (p. 363)
Christopher Columbus (p. 363)
Ferdinand Magellan (p. 364)
conquistadors (p. 371)
Hernán Cortés (p. 371)
Moctezuma II (p. 371)
Atahuallpa (p. 372)
Francisco Pizarro (p. 372)

Climate and Population to 1500

During the millennia before 1500, human populations expanded in three momentous surges. The first occurred after 50,000 B.C.E. when humans emigrated from their African homeland to all of the inhabitable continents. After that, the global population remained steady for many millennia. During the second expansion, between about 5000 and 500 B.C.E., population rose from about 5 million to 100 million as agricultural societies spread around the world (see Figure 1). Population growth then slowed for several centuries before a third surge took world population to over 350 million by 1200 C.E. (Figure 2 shows population in China and Europe.)

For a long time historians tended to attribute these population surges to cultural and technological advances. Indeed, a great many changes in culture and technology are associated with adaptation to different climates and food supplies in the first surge and with the domestication of plants and animals in the second. However, historians have not found a cultural or technological change to explain the third surge, nor can they explain why creativity would have stagnated for long periods between the surges. Something else must have been at work.

Recently historians have begun to pay more attention to the impact of long-term variations in

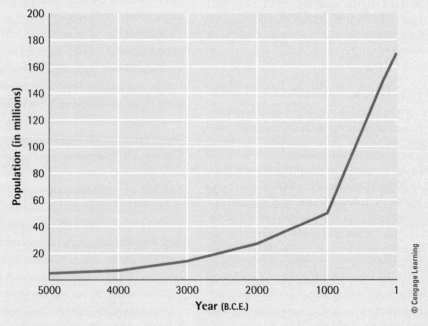

Figure 1 World Population, 5000–1 B.C.E.

global climate. By examining ice cores drilled out of glaciers, scientists have been able to compile records of thousands of years of climate change. The comparative width of tree rings from ancient forests has provided additional data on periods of favorable and unfavorable growth. Such evidence shows that cycles of population growth and stagnation followed changes in global climate.

Historians now believe that global temperatures were above normal for extended periods from the late 1100s to the late 1200s C.E. In the temperate lands where most of the world's people lived, above-normal temperatures meant a longer growing season, more bountiful harvests, and thus a more adequate and reliable food supply. The ways in which societies responded to the Medieval Warm Period (see Chapter 13) and the simultaneous cooling of the Middle East are as important as the climate change, but it is unlikely that human agency alone would have produced Europe's medieval surge. One notable response was that of the Vikings, who increased the size and range of their settlements in the North Atlantic, although their raids also caused death and destruction.

Some of the complexities involved in the interaction of human agency, climate, and other natural factors are also evident in the demographic changes that followed the Medieval Warm Period. During the 1200s the Mongol invasions caused death and disruption of agriculture across Eurasia. China's population, which had been over 100 million in 1200, declined by a third or more by 1300. The Mongol invasions did not cause harm west of Russia, but climate changes in the 1300s resulted in population losses in Europe. Unusually heavy rains caused crop failures and a prolonged famine in northern Europe from 1315 to 1319.

The freer movement of merchants within the Mongol Empire also facilitated the spread of disease across Eurasia, culminating in the great pandemic known as the Black Death in Europe. The demographic recovery under way in China was reversed. The even larger population losses in Europe may have been affected by the decrease in global temperatures to their lowest point in many millennia between 1350 and 1375. After 1400 improving economic conditions enabled population to recover more rapidly in Europe than in China, where the conditions of rural life remained harsh.

Because many other historical circumstances interact with changing weather patterns, historians have a long way to go in deciphering the role of climate in history. Nevertheless, it is a factor that can no longer be ignored.

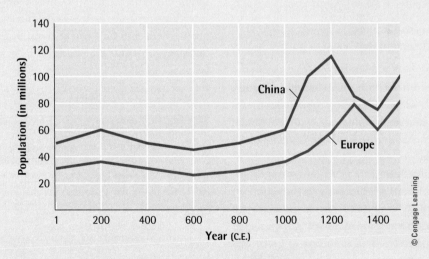

Figure 2 Population in China and Europe, 1–1500 C.E.

Part Five

The Globe Encompassed, 1500–1750

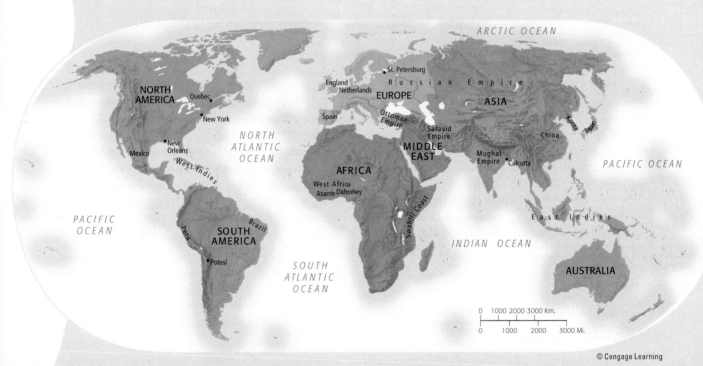

© Cengage Learning

	1500	1550	1600	1650
AMERICAS	• **1500** Portuguese discover Brazil	• **1540** Viceroyalty of Peru • **1535** Viceroyalty of Mexico • **1545** Silver discovered at Potosí, Bolivia	Brazil is world's main source of sugar **1600** •	Dutch bring sugar and slavery to West Indies **1640s** • **1607–1640** England and France found colonies
EUROPE	**1500–1600** Spain's golden century • **1519** Protestant Reformation begins	• **1545** Catholic Reformation begins • **1550** Scientific Revolution begins	• **1588** English defeat Spanish Armada **1600–1700** Netherlands' golden century	**1618–1648** Thirty Years War
AFRICA	• **1505** Portuguese begin assault on Swahili cities		• **1591** Morocco conquers Songhai Empire Expansion of transatlantic slave trade **1640's** •	
MIDDLE EAST		**1520–1566** Reign of Ottoman sultan Suleiman the Magnificent	• **1571** Ottoman defeat at Lepanto **1588–1629** Reign of Safavid shah Abbas the Great	• **1622** Iranians expel Portuguese from Hormuz
ASIA AND OCEANIA		• **1526** Mughal Empire founded in India **1556–1605** Reign of Mughal emperor Akbar	• **1582** Russia conquers Sibir Khanate • **1603** Tokugawa Shogunate founded in Japan "Closing" of Japan **1639** • Qing Empire begins in China **1644** •	

The decades between 1500 and 1800 witnessed a tremendous expansion of commercial, cultural, and biological exchanges around the world. New long-distance sea routes linked Europe with sub-Saharan Africa and the already established maritime networks of the Indian Ocean and East Asia. Spanish and Portuguese voyages ended the isolation of the Americas and created new webs of exchange in the Atlantic and Pacific. Overland expansion of Muslim, Russian, and Chinese empires also expanded global interaction.

These expanding contacts brought significant change. New agriculture transformed the diets of the Old World and the Americas, particularly with domesticated animals from Europe and such Amerindian crops as the potato. European diseases devastated the Amerindian population, facilitating the establishment of large Spanish, Portuguese, French, and British empires. Europe introduced enslaved Africans to relieve the labor shortage. With colonial empires Europe's cities grew richer, and its economies gained strength. But Spain, France, and England faced stiff competition from the Dutch, who introduced innovative economic institutions.

In Asia and Africa, unlike the Americas, the most important changes owed more to internal forces than to European actions. The Portuguese seized control of some important trading ports and networks in the Indian Ocean and pioneered new contacts with China and Japan, and in time the Dutch, French, and English expanded these profitable connections; but in 1750 Europeans were still primarily a maritime force. Asians and Africans generally retained control of their lands and participated freely in overseas trade.

The Islamic world saw the dramatic expansion of the Ottoman Empire in the Middle East and the establishment of the Safavid Empire in Iran and the Mughal Empire in South Asia. In East Asia, China acquired vast new territories and populations, while a new national government in Japan promoted economic development and resisted foreign influence.

	1700	1750	1800
• **1660** English take Jamaica	• **1700** West Indies are world's main source of sugar	**1754–1763** French and Indian War; British take Canada	
	• **1718** French found New Orleans	**1780–1782** Revolt of Tupac Armaru in Peru	
1667–1697 Wars of Louis XIV	• **1712** Peter the Great founds St. Petersburg	**1772–1795** Poland partitioned	
England's Glorious Revolution **1688** •	**1700–1800** The Enlightenment		
	1701–1714 War of the Spanish Succession		
• **1680s** Rise of Asante kingdom	• **1720s** Rise of kingdom of Dahomey		
		1750–1800 Growing slave trade reduces population	
• **1683** Last Ottoman siege of Vienna	**1718–1730** Tulip Period of Ottoman Empire; Ottoman military decline		
Fall of Safavid Empire **1722** •	**1736–1747** Nadir Shah reunites Iran		
• **1689** Treaty of Nerchinsk			
• **1691** British found trading post at Calcutta	**1736–1799** Reign of Qing emperor Qianlong		

CHAPTER 16

1500–1750

Transformations in Europe

© Cengage Learning

CHAPTER PREVIEW

CULTURE AND IDEAS

- How did the interplay of traditional beliefs and revolutionary ideas influence the cultural history of early modern Europe?

SOCIAL AND ECONOMIC LIFE

- What factors contributed to the wealth of some Europeans and the great poverty of others in this period?

POLITICAL INNOVATIONS

- How did differing policies in the areas of religion, foreign relations, and economics determine the very different experiences of early modern European states?

Conclusion

ENVIRONMENT + TECHNOLOGY:
Mapping the World

In the late sixteenth century Dutch cities grew rich from long-distance trade in the Baltic and Mediterranean and in the newly opened markets of South Asia, Africa, and the Americas. Prosperity allowed merchants, ship owners, and even artisans to consume extravagant luxuries previously limited to nobles. They built substantial houses, wore rich clothing, and developed a taste for exotic goods.

The new prosperity also brought the risk of speculation. By the 1570s tulips, introduced by the Ottomans, were avidly collected by Dutch enthusiasts. Scarce and expensive, they became a sign of sophistication and wealth. The collectors and botanists who originally purchased tulips were joined by thousands of eager consumers who recognized potential profit in a rare commodity. As prices surged in the 1620s and 1630s, a speculative market developed and the ownership of tulip bulbs became a form of investment. Confident that prices would continue upward, individuals and partnerships paid extravagant amounts for bulbs. Between December 1636 and February 1637, for example, one of the most popular tulip varieties increased twelve times in value. At the peak of this frenzy the rarest bulbs sold for three times the annual income of a skilled carpenter. Then, in February 1637, the tulip market crashed as panicked investors rushed to unload their bulbs. If some had been made rich in this extraordinary trade, many of those who entered the market at the height of Tulipmania were financially ruined. Such speculative bubbles roiled European economies throughout the early modern period.

The introduction of commercial and financial innovations, such as stock markets, commercial insurance, and expanded property right protections, was part of a dramatic commercial and manufacturing expansion spurred by European exploration and conquest and dynamic social change. By 1750 Europe had brought much of the world under its control. At the same time, wealthy merchants, investors, and manufacturers grew in power relative to Europe's hereditary nobility, cities grew in population relative to the countryside, and secular political and economic institutions grew relative to a church challenged by the Protestant Reformation, religious wars, and the Scientific Revolution.

CULTURE AND IDEAS

■ *How did the interplay of traditional beliefs and revolutionary ideas influence the cultural history of early modern Europe?*

During the Reformation, theological controversies broke the religious unity of the Latin Church and contributed to long and violent wars. While the influence of classical ideas from Greco-Roman antiquity increased among better-educated Europeans, some bold thinkers challenged the authority of the ancients. They introduced new ideas about the motion of the planets and the natural world, encouraging others to challenge traditional social and political systems. Once in place, these new ideas would influence revolutionary political and social movements in the period after 1750. Each of these events had its own causes, but the impact of all of them was broadened by the technology of the printing press.

Early Reformation

In 1500 the **papacy**, the central government of Latin Christianity, held an unrivaled position as Europe's preeminent religious and intellectual authority, although lax clerical standards and corruption were endemic. Recovered from a period when competing popes supported by rival secular rulers disputed control of the church, the papacy now exercised greater power that was funded by larger donations and by income from its enormous real estate holdings. The construction of fifty-four new churches and other buildings in Rome demonstrated the church's power and showcased the artistic Renaissance then under way. The unprecedented size and splendor of the magnificent new Saint Peter's Basilica in Rome was intended to glorify God and enhance the standing of the papacy, but the vast expense of its construction and rich decoration also caused scandal.

The skillful overseer of the design and financing of the Saint Peter's Basilica was Pope Leo X

papacy The central administration of the Roman Catholic Church, of which the pope is the head.

(r. 1513–1521), a member of the wealthy Medici (MED-ih-chee) family of Florence, famous for its patronage of the arts. Pope Leo's artistic taste was superb and his personal life free from scandal, but he was more a man of action than a spiritual leader. During his papacy the church aggressively raised funds through the sale of **indulgences**—absolutions for past sins.

A young professor of sacred scripture, Martin Luther (1483–1546), saw this practice and other excesses as intolerably corrupt. Having forsaken money and marriage for a monastic life of prayer, self-denial, and study, Luther found personal consolation in a passage in Saint Paul's Epistle to the Romans stating

Private Collection/The Bridgeman Art Library

Luther and the Reformation This sixteenth-century woodcut of Martin Luther shows him writing his demands for religious reform with a symbolically oversized quill pen on the door of All Saints Church in Wittenberg, Germany.

that salvation resulted from religious faith, not from "doing certain things." That passage led Luther to object to the way preachers emphasized giving money to the church more than they emphasized faith. He complained to Pope Leo and challenged preachers to debate the theology of indulgences.

Theology aside, Pope Leo regarded Luther's letter as a challenge to papal power and moved to silence him. During a debate in 1519, a papal representative led Luther into open disagreement with church doctrines, for which the papacy condemned him. Unable to reform the church from within, Luther burned the papal bull (document) of condemnation, rejected the pope's authority, and began the movement known as the **Protestant Reformation**.

Accusing those whom he called "Romanists" (Roman Catholics) of relying on "good works," Luther insisted that the only way to salvation was through faith in Jesus Christ. He further declared that Christian belief should be based on the word of God in the Bible and on Christian tradition, not on the authority of the pope. Luther's use of the printing press to spread his ideas won him the support of powerful Germans, who responded to his nationalist portrayal

of an Italian pope seeking to beautify Rome with German funds.

Luther's denunciation of the ostentation and corruption of the church led others to call for a return to what they saw as authentic Christian practices and beliefs. John Calvin (1509–1564), a Frenchman who abandoned law for theology, became an influential Protestant leader. Calvin also exalted faith over works, but unlike Luther he denied that human faith alone could merit salvation. Salvation, Calvin believed, was a gift God gave to those he "predestined." Calvin also went beyond Luther in curtailing the power of the clergy and simplifying religious rituals. Calvinist congregations elected their governing

indulgence The forgiveness of the punishment due for past sins, granted by the Catholic Church authorities as a reward for a pious act. Martin Luther's protest against the sale of indulgences is often seen as touching off the Protestant Reformation.

Protestant Reformation Religious reform movement within the Latin Christian Church beginning in 1519. It resulted in the "protesters" forming several new Christian denominations, including the Lutheran and Reformed Churches and the Church of England.

Chronology

	Politics, Economy, and Culture	Environment and Technology	Warfare
1500	**1500s** Spain's golden century **1519** Protestant Reformation begins **1545** Catholic Reformation begins **Late 1500s** Witch-hunts increase	**1590s** Dutch develop flyboats; Little Ice Age begins	**1529** Ottoman siege of Vienna fails **1546–1555** German Wars of Religion **1566–1648** Netherlands Revolt
1600	**1600s** Holland's golden century **1602** East India Company stocks exchanged in Amsterdam **1620s–1637** Tulip bubble in Netherlands	**1600s** Depletion of forests growing **1609** Galileo's astronomical telescope **1682** Canal du Midi completed	**1618–1648** Thirty Years' War **1642–1649** English Civil War **1652–1678** Anglo-Dutch Wars
1700	**1700s** The Enlightenment begins **1720** Mississippi Company bubble bursts in France	**1720** South Sea Company bubble peaks in England **1750** English mine nearly 5 million tons of coal a year	**1701–1714** War of the Spanish Succession

committees and in time created regional and national synods (councils) to regulate doctrinal issues. Calvinists also wore simple black clothes and avoided ostentation, stripping churches of statues, most musical instruments, stained-glass windows, incense, and vestments.

The reformers appealed to genuine religious sentiments, but their successes and failures were also due to political conditions. It was no coincidence that German-born Luther had his greatest success among German speakers and linguistically related Scandinavians. Nor was it surprising that peasants and urban laborers sometimes defied their masters by adopting a different faith. Protestants were no more inclined than Roman Catholics to question male dominance in the church and the family, but most Protestants rejected the medieval tradition of celibate priests and nuns and advocated Christian marriage for all adults.

Shaken by the Protestant attack, the Catholic Church initiated internal reforms. A church council meeting in Trent in northern Italy between 1545 and 1563 sought to distinguish Catholic doctrines from Protestant "errors." Bishops allied with the pope dominated the council and reaffirmed the supremacy of the pope and the ecclesiastical authorities in interpreting scriptures, as well as the importance of confession and salvation through both faith and good works. But the council did call for some reform: bishops were to reside in their dioceses, for example, and maintain a theological seminary to train priests.

The creation in 1540 of a new religious order, the Society of Jesus, or "Jesuits," by a Spanish nobleman, Ignatius of Loyola (1491–1556), was among the most important events of the **Catholic Reformation**. Well-educated Jesuits helped stem the Protestant tide by their teaching and preaching (see Map 16.1) and became missionaries overseas (see Chapters 15 and 19).

Catholic Reformation Religious reform movement within the Latin Christian Church, begun in response to the Protestant Reformation. It clarified Catholic theology and reformed clerical training and discipline.

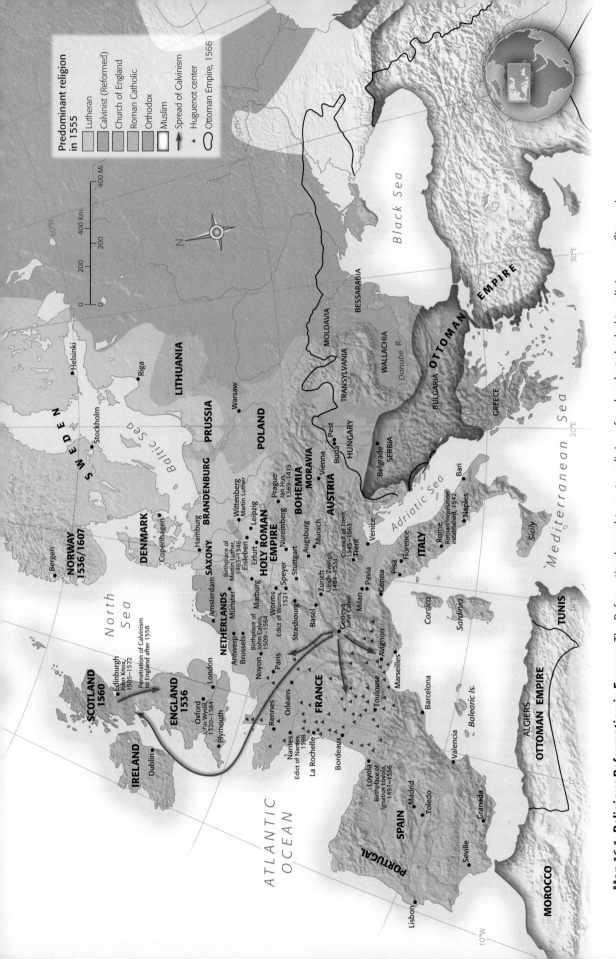

Map 16.1 Religious Reformation in Europe The Reformation brought greater religious freedom but also led to religious conflict and persecution. In many places the Reformation accelerated the trend toward state control of religion and added religious differences to the motives for wars among Europeans. © Cengage Learning

Legend

Predominant religion in 1555

- Lutheran
- Calvinist (Reformed)
- Church of England
- Roman Catholic
- Orthodox
- Muslim

→ Spread of Calvinism

▲ Huguenot center

◯ Ottoman Empire, 1566

Map Labels

ATLANTIC OCEAN

North Sea

Baltic Sea

Mediterranean Sea

Adriatic Sea

Black Sea

NORWAY 1536/1607

SWEDEN

DENMARK

SCOTLAND 1560

ENGLAND 1536

IRELAND

NETHERLANDS

FRANCE

SPAIN

PORTUGAL

HOLY ROMAN EMPIRE

SAXONY

BRANDENBURG

PRUSSIA

LITHUANIA

POLAND

BOHEMIA

MORAVIA

AUSTRIA

HUNGARY

TRANSYLVANIA

WALLACHIA

MOLDAVIA

BESSARABIA

BULGARIA

SERBIA

GREECE

ITALY

OTTOMAN EMPIRE

MOROCCO

ALGIERS OTTOMAN EMPIRE

TUNIS

Corsica

Sardinia

Sicily

Balearic Is.

Danube R.

Cities and places

Bergen

Helsinki

Riga

Stockholm

Copenhagen

Hamburg

Warsaw

Amsterdam

Brussels

Antwerp

Münster

Birthplace of Martin Luther, 1483–1546

Eisleben

Wittenberg Martin Luther

Erfurt

Leipzig

Marburg

Birthplace of John Calvin, 1509–1564

Worms Edict of Worms 1521

Speyer

Nuremberg

Augsburg

Munich

Stuttgart

Strasbourg

Basel

Zurich Ulrich Zwingli, 1484–1531

Geneva John Calvin

Noyon

Paris

Rennes

Orléans

Nantes Edict of Nantes, 1598

La Rochelle

Bordeaux

Toulouse

Marseilles

Avignon

Milan

Pavia

Genoa

Pisa

Florence

Venice

Council of Trent, 1545–1563 Trent

Rome Roman Inquisition established, 1542

Naples

Bari

Vienna

Prague Jan Hus, 1369–1415

Budapest

Pest

Belgrade

Dublin

Oxford John Wyclif, 1320–1384

London

Plymouth

Edinburgh John Knox, 1505–1572

Penetration of Calvinism to England after 1558

Loyola Birthplace of Ignatius Loyola, 1491–1556

Madrid

Toledo

Seville

Granada

Barcelona

Valencia

Lisbon

Scale

400 Mi.

400 km.

200

0

Art Resource, NY

Death to Witches This woodcut from 1574 depicts three women convicted of witchcraft being burned alive in Baden, Switzerland. The scene on the left illustrates the purported witchcraft practiced by the three condemned women.

Given the intense emotions stirred by the Protestant Reformation, it is not surprising that both sides persecuted and sometimes executed those of differing views. Bitter "wars of religion" would continue in parts of western Europe until 1648.

Traditional Thinking and Witch-Hunts

Religious differences continued to generate animosity long after the first generation of reformers, but for both the Protestant north and the Catholic south the widespread **witch-hunts** that Protestants and Catholics undertook in early modern Europe were less about religious doctrine than they were about prevailing European ideas about the natural world. These views blended two distinct traditions. One was an enduring belief in magic and spirits passed down orally from pre-Christian times. The second was the biblical teachings about miracles, saints, and devils heard in church and read by growing numbers in vernacular translations. These Christian teachings coincided easily with beliefs about magic, sorcery, and witchcraft rooted in the distant past.

While traditional folk beliefs were more common in small towns and villages, these beliefs and fears would not have had such deadly consequences if many educated and powerful city dwellers did not believe in the Devil's power to affect society broadly.

It was widely assumed that special powers could be derived from occult knowledge or, in some cases, from a compact with the Devil. In its benign version, practitioners could heal the sick, cause love to flourish, or guarantee good fortune. They could also solve disputes with masters or employers or punish enemies. The malevolent version could cause infertility, illness, or death of loved ones and neighbors, cause crops or businesses to fail, or even provoke epidemics or droughts. The vigor of these local religious traditions ebbed and flowed, and some theologians and jurists questioned the intellectual and religious underpinnings of these assumptions before the mid-sixteenth century. Nevertheless, the fear of witches that swept across Europe in the late sixteenth and seventeenth centuries was testimony to the endurance of these beliefs.

Before this hysteria ended, secular and church authorities had tried approximately 100,000 people and executed 60,000—some three-fourths of them women—for practicing witchcraft. Trial records make it clear that both the accusers and the accused believed that it was possible for individuals to use black magic in concert with the Devil to cause injury to others. Apparently many admitted to having occult powers, though the common use of torture explains most of the confessions of accused witches.

The trials and executions transcended national and religious boundaries, but there were significant

witch-hunt The pursuit of people suspected of witchcraft, especially in northern Europe in the late sixteenth and seventeenth centuries.

differences in regional and national practice. The death toll was highest in German states like Wurzburg and Bamberg, which executed 900 and 600, respectively, between 1626 and 1631, including scores of children. Protestant Scotland also convicted 120 witches who were burned at the stake in 1661 and 1662 alone. But Protestant England and more egalitarian Holland were reluctant to prosecute witches. The relatively strong Catholic states of France and Spain also had low numbers of executions. In Spain the Inquisition limited arrests as early as 1526.

No single reason can explain the witchcraft hysteria in early modern Europe, but these events coincided with rising social tensions, growing rural poverty, and environmental strains. They also coincided with the violent wars of the Reformation period. Far from being an aberration, witch-hunts reflected the tension between popular beliefs and the ambitions of aggressive new religious and political institutions. The Reformation's focus on the Devil—the enemy of God—as the source of evil and the Catholic Counter-Reformation's effort to enforce orthodoxy both helped to propel the brutal persecutions of this period.

The Scientific Revolution

Beginning in the sixteenth century, European understanding of the natural world shifted away from the physics of the classical Aristotle, who taught that everything on earth was reducible to four elements: earth and water on the surface and air and fire floating above the ground. Experimentation, careful observation, and mathematical calculations challenged the thinking of classical antiquity, newly discovered by Renaissance scholars. Most intellectuals of the **Scientific Revolution** were committed Christians (both Catholic and Protestant) who sought to use science to reinforce religious beliefs. Nevertheless, as this movement gained momentum, European intellectual life became more secular and independent.

Nicholas Copernicus (1473–1543), a Polish monk and mathematician, helped initiate the new era when he proposed that the sun, not the earth, was the center of the universe (see Chapter 12). To escape controversy, Copernicus delayed the publication of his heliocentric (sun-centered) theory until the end of his life. Once disseminated, his research began a

Maritime Museum Kronberg Castle Denmark/ G.Dagli Orti/The Art Archive

Tycho Brahe at Work   Between 1576 and 1597, on the island of Ven between Denmark and Sweden, Tycho built the best observatory in Europe and set a new standard for accurate celestial observations before the invention of the telescope. This contemporary hand-colored engraving shows the Danish astronomer at work.

revolution in the way human beings understood the structure of the heavens.

Other astronomers, including the Danish Tycho Brahe (1546–1601) and his German assistant Johannes Kepler (1571–1630), improved on Copernicus's model, showing that planets actually move in elliptical, not circular, orbits. The most brilliant of the Copernicans was the Italian Galileo Galilei (gal-uh-LAY-oh gal-uh-LAY-ee) (1564–1642). In 1609 Galileo built a telescope through which he took a closer look at the heavens, thus confirming the speculations of other astronomers.

At first, the Copernicans faced formidable resistance because they directly challenged classical and biblical authorities. Many intellectual and religious

Scientific Revolution The intellectual movement in Europe, initially associated with planetary motion and other aspects of physics, that by the seventeenth century had laid the groundwork for modern science.

leaders sought to suppress the new ideas. Following the lead of Martin Luther, most Protestant leaders condemned the heliocentric universe as contrary to the Bible. Catholic authorities did not react immediately, but, when they did act, they more effectively suppressed the new science.

Copernicus died before his book was deemed heretical by Catholic authorities in 1616 and placed on the index of prohibited books. Yet his discoveries helped lead to a more accurate calendar issued in 1582 by Pope Gregory XIII and still used today. Galileo's defense of the heliocentric theory led to a confrontation with the Inquisition. Galileo argued that the Bible was an inspired text, but, when science had established a demonstrable fact, the Bible should be interpreted to coincide with the evidence, since it could not be God's intention to mislead. Despite the controversial nature of his opinions, he continued to publish, pressing for a reliance on physical evidence and accurate measurement. Ordered before the Inquisition in 1633, Galileo was forced to sign a formal renunciation of his research. An apparent victory for tradition, this action put the Catholic Church in untenable opposition to a key early achievement of the new science.

Despite opposition, printed books spread the new scientific ideas across Europe, influencing, among others, the French philosopher and mathematician René Descartes (1595–1650). Descartes played a key role in the development of physics and calculus when he demonstrated the usefulness of algebra to geometry, but the Inquisition's condemnation of Galileo influenced Descartes to delay publication of a potentially controversial work on optics and astronomy in 1633.

In England, Robert Boyle (1627–1691) advocated tirelessly for the use of experimental methods. One of the founders of modern chemistry, he was among the first to publish the details of experiments, including his failures, and demonstrate that air was necessary for the transmission of sound. In 1662 he was also instrumental in founding the Royal Society, whose motto "Nullius in Verba" (nothing in words) was a rallying cry demanding that science be based on experiments alone.

Another Englishman, the mathematician Isaac Newton (1642–1727), began his work in optics and mathematics by building on the work of Boyle and Descartes. Carrying Galileo's demonstration that the heavens and earth share a common physics to its logical conclusion, he formulated mathematical laws that all physical objects obeyed. His Law of Gravity and his role in developing the calculus made him the most famous and influential man of his era, serving as president of the Royal Society from 1703 until his death.

Although Galileo and Descartes, both Catholics, as well as the Protestant Boyle, were convinced that scientific discoveries and revealed religion could be reconciled, most religious and intellectual leaders viewed the new science with suspicion or hostility because it challenged long-established ways of thought. These principal pioneers of the Scientific Revolution showed that the ideas of the Aristotelians and biblical writers were unsupportable in the face of scientific discovery. Using reason to challenge a broader range of unquestioned traditions and superstitions, they changed the world of ideas forever.

The Early Enlightenment

Advances in scientific thought inspired some to question the reasonableness of everything from agricultural methods to laws, religion, and social hierarchies. Their belief that they could apply the scientific method to economics, politics, and social organization to devise the best policies energized a movement known as the **Enlightenment**. Like the Scientific Revolution, this movement was the work of a few "enlightened" individuals, who often faced bitter opposition. Leading Enlightenment thinkers became accustomed to having their books banned and spending long periods in exile to escape persecution.

Influences besides the Scientific Revolution affected the Enlightenment. The religious warfare and intolerance associated with the struggle between Catholicism and Protestantism undermined the authority of religion for many, as did the killing of suspected witches. Church efforts to impugn the breakthroughs of science also pushed European intellectuals in a secular direction. The leading French thinker Voltaire (1694–1778) declared: "No opinion is worth burning your neighbor for."

Enlightenment A philosophical movement in eighteenth-century Europe that fostered the belief that one could reform society by discovering rational laws that governed social behavior and were just as scientific as the laws of physics.

Although many circumstances shaped "enlightened" thinking, new scientific methods and discoveries provided the clearest model for changing European society. Voltaire linked the prestige of the newly ascendant scientific method with his generation's mounting political and social concerns in these terms: "It would be very peculiar that all nature, all the planets, should obey eternal laws" but a human being, "in contempt of these laws, could act as he pleased solely according to his caprice." The English poet Alexander Pope (1688–1774) made a similar point in verse: "Nature and Nature's laws lay hidden in night; / God said, 'Let Newton be' and all was light."

The Enlightenment was more a frame of mind than a coherent movement. Its proponents were clearer about what they disliked than about what changes were necessary. Nearly all were optimistic that—at least in the long run—human beliefs and institutions could be improved. This faith in progress would help foster political and social revolutions after 1750, as Chapter 21 recounts.

While the Catholic Church and many Protestant clergymen opposed the Enlightenment, European monarchs, ambitious to increase power, found anticlerical intellectuals useful allies against church power and wealth. Monarchs and their reforming advisers discovered justification for the expansion of royal authority and modern tax systems. Europe in 1750 was a place where political and religious divisions, growing literacy, and the printing press made it possible for these controversial and exciting new ideas to thrive in the face of opposition from ancient and powerful institutions.

SECTION REVIEW

- Outraged by corrupt church practices, reformers like Luther and Calvin challenged papal authority and traditional Catholic theology.
- In response to the Protestant reformers, the Catholic Church launched a Counter-Reformation.
- Both Protestants and Catholics, seeking to enforce orthodoxy, sanctioned widespread witch-hunts.
- The thinkers of the Scientific Revolution challenged traditional biblical and classical Greco-Roman conceptions of the cosmos.
- The advances in science prompted Enlightenment thinkers to question many conventional ideas and practices.

SOCIAL AND ECONOMIC LIFE

■ *What factors contributed to the wealth of some Europeans and the great poverty of others in this period?*

There were large and important differences in the social structures of the major European nations, but there were many shared characteristics as well. European society was dominated by a small number of noble families who monopolized church, government, and military offices and enjoyed many privileges, often including exemption from taxation. Below them was a much larger class of prosperous commoners that included many clergy, bureaucrats, professionals, and military officers as well as merchants, some artisans, and rural landowners. The vast majority of men and women were very poor. Laborers, journeymen, apprentices, and rural laborers struggled to earn their daily bread and often faced unemployment and privation. The poorest members of society lived truly desperate lives, surviving only through guile, begging, or crime. Women remained subordinated to men.

Some social mobility did occur, however. The principal engine of social change was an economy stimulated by long-distance trade and by access to the gold and silver of the Americas. Because cities enjoyed most of this new wealth, they became the centers of opportunity and upward mobility.

The Bourgeoisie Europe's cities grew in response to expanding trade and rising commercial profits. In 1500 Paris was the only northern European city with over 100,000 inhabitants. By 1700 both Paris and London had populations over 500,000, and eleven other European cities contained over 100,000 people.

Urban wealth came from manufacturing and finance, but especially from trade, both within Europe and overseas. The French called the urban class that dominated these activities the **bourgeoisie** (boor-zhwah-ZEE) (burghers, town dwellers). Members of the bourgeoisie poured much of their profits back into their businesses or into new ventures. Even so, most had enough money to live comfortably in

bourgeoisie In early modern Europe, the class of well-off town dwellers whose wealth came from manufacturing, finance, commerce, and allied professions.

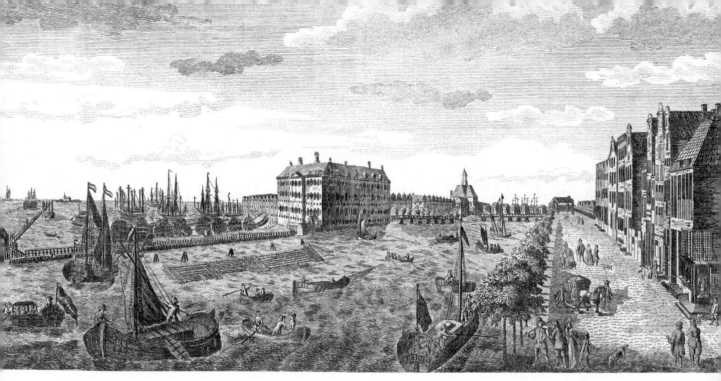

Port of Amsterdam Ships, barges, and boats of all types are visible in this busy seventeenth-century scene. The large building in the center is the Admiralty House, the headquarters of the Dutch East India Company. Mansell/TimeLife Pictures/Getty Images

large houses, and some had servants. In the seventeenth and eighteenth centuries wealthier consumers could buy exotic luxuries imported from the far corners of the earth—Caribbean and Brazilian sugar and rum, Mexican chocolate, Virginia tobacco, North American furs, East Indian cotton textiles and spices, and Chinese tea.

The Netherlands provides one of the best examples of this new bourgeois reality. The Dutch Republic was the most egalitarian European country in the early modern period. While it retained an aristocracy, wealthy commoners dominated its economy and politics. Manufacturers and craftsmen turned out a great variety of goods in their factories and workshops. The highly successful textile industry concentrated on the profitable weaving, finishing, and printing of cloth, leaving the spinning to low-paid workers elsewhere. Along with fine woolens and linens, the Dutch made cheaper textiles for mass markets. Other factories in Holland refined West Indian sugar, brewed beer from Baltic grain, cut Virginia tobacco, and made imitations of Chinese ceramics. Free from the censorship and religious persecution imposed in neighboring countries, Holland's intellectuals were active in the Scientific Revolution and early Enlightenment. Its

printers published books in many languages, including manuals with the latest advances in machinery, metallurgy, and agriculture. For a small nation that lacked timber and other natural resources, this was a remarkable achievement.

With a population of 200,000 in 1700, Amsterdam was Holland's largest city and Europe's major port. Huge commercial fleets supported this growth and dominated sea trade in Europe and overseas using ship designs like the *fluit*, or "flyboat," a large-capacity cargo ship developed in the 1590s that was inexpensive to build and required only a small crew, and the heavily armed "East Indiaman" that helped the Dutch establish their supremacy in the Indian Ocean. By one estimate, more than half of all the oceangoing commercial shipping occurred on Dutch ships. Dutch mapmaking supported these distant commercial connections (see Environment and Technology: Mapping the World).

Amsterdam also served as Europe's financial center. Seventeenth-century Dutch banks had such a reputation for security that wealthy individuals and governments from all over western Europe entrusted them with their money. The banks in turn invested these funds in real estate, loaned money to factory

environment & technology

Mapping the World

In 1602 Matteo Ricci, a Jesuit missionary in China, printed an elaborate map of the world (see Chapter 19). Working from maps produced in Europe and incorporating the latest knowledge gathered by European maritime explorers, Ricci introduced two changes to make the map more appealing to his Chinese hosts. He labeled it in Chinese characters, and he split his map down the middle of the Atlantic so that China lay in the center. This version pleased the Chinese elite, who considered China the "Middle Kingdom" surrounded by lesser states. A copy of Ricci's map in six large panels adorned the emperor's Beijing palace.

The stunningly beautiful maps and globes of sixteenth-century Europe were the most complete, detailed, and useful representations of the earth that any society had ever produced. The best mapmaker of the century was Gerhard Kremer, who is remembered as Mercator (the merchant) because his maps were so useful to European ocean traders. By incorporating the latest discoveries and scientific measurements, Mercator could depict the outlines of the major continents in painstaking detail, even if their interiors were still largely unknown to outsiders.

To represent the spherical globe on a flat map, Mercator drew the lines of longitude as parallel lines. Because such lines actually meet at the poles, Mercator's projection greatly exaggerated the size of every landmass and body of water distant from the equator. However, Mercator's rendering offered a very practical advantage: sailors could plot their course by drawing a straight line between their point of departure and their destination. Because of this useful feature, the Mercator projection of the world remained in common use until quite recently. To some extent, its popularity came from the exaggerated size this projection gave to Europe. Like the Chinese, Europeans liked to think of themselves as being at the center of things. Yet Europeans also understood their true geographical position better than people in any other part of the world.

Dutch World Map, 1641
It is easy to see why the Chinese would not have liked to see their empire at the far right edge of this widely printed map. Besides the distortions caused by the Mercator projection, geographical ignorance exaggerates the size of North America and Antarctica.

owners and governments, and provided capital for big business operations overseas. Individuals seeking higher returns than those provided by banks could purchase shares in a **joint-stock company**, a sixteenth-century forerunner of the modern corporation. Individuals bought and sold shares in specialized financial markets called **stock exchanges**, an Italian innovation transferred to the cities of northwestern Europe in the sixteenth century. The Amsterdam Exchange, founded in 1602, became the greatest stock market in the seventeenth and eighteenth centuries.

The Dutch government played a direct role in this process by pioneering the creation of commercial enterprises like the Dutch East and West India Companies, which were granted trade monopolies with the East and West Indies. France and England soon chartered monopoly trading companies of their own. These companies then sold shares to individuals to raise large sums for overseas enterprises while spreading the risks (and profits) among many investors (see Chapter 17). In this same era large insurance companies were developed to insure long-distance voyages against loss, and by 1700 purchasing insurance had become standard commercial practice. Governments also sought to promote trade by investing in canals to speed transport, lower costs, and drain the lowlands for agriculture. Other governments financed canals as well, including systems of locks to raise barges up over hills. One of the most important was the 150-mile (240-kilometer) Canal du Midi built by the French government between 1661 and 1682 to link the Atlantic and the Mediterranean.

Successful bourgeois merchants in England and France traded wealth for social status. By retiring from their businesses and buying country estates, they could become members of the **gentry**. They loaned money to impoverished peasants and to members of the nobility and in time increased their land ownership. Some sought aristocratic husbands for their daughters. The old nobility found such alliances attractive because of the large dowries that the bourgeoisie provided. Even in colonial settings, some families purchased titles of nobility. While satisfying the desire for status, this move out of the bourgeoisie also removed capital from commerce and production.

Peasants and Laborers

At the other end of society, serfdom, which bound men and women to land owned by a local lord, declined in western Europe after the great plague of the mid-fourteenth century. As the population recovered, competition for work exerted a downward pressure on wages, reducing the usefulness of serfdom to landowners. In eastern Europe, however, large-scale landowners required serfs to make grain production profitable. Slavery expanded briefly around 1500 in southern Europe, but after 1600 Europeans shipped nearly all African slaves to the Americas. Thus western Europe's dependence on unfree labor was kept at a distance rather than at home (see Chapters 15 and 17).

Legal freedom did not make a peasant's life more secure. Agricultural efficiency had improved little since 1300. As a result, bad years brought famine; good ones provided only small surpluses. The material conditions experienced by the poor in western Europe may have worsened between 1500 and 1750 as the result of warfare, environmental degradation, and economic contractions. Europeans also felt the effects of a century of relatively cool climate that began in the 1590s. During this **Little Ice Age** average temperatures fell only a few degrees, but the effects were startling (see Issues in World History: The Little Ice Age on page 466).

By 1700 high-yielding new crops from the Americas were helping the rural poor avoid starvation. Potatoes sustained life in northeastern and central Europe and in Ireland, while poor peasants in Italy subsisted on maize. Ironically, all of these lands were major exporters of wheat, but agricultural workers could not afford to eat it.

Other rural residents made their living as miners, lumberacks, and charcoal makers. The expanding

---

joint-stock company A business, often backed by a government charter, that sold shares to individuals to raise money for its trading enterprises and to spread the risks (and profits) among many investors.

stock exchange A place where shares in a company or business enterprise are bought and sold.

gentry In England, the class of landholding families below the aristocracy.

Little Ice Age A century-long period of cool climate that began in the 1590s. Its ill effects on agriculture in northern Europe were notable.

iron industry in England provided work for all three, but the high consumption of wood fuel caused serious **deforestation**. One early-seventeenth-century observer lamented: "Within man's memory, it was held impossible to have any want of wood in England. But . . . at present, through the great consuming of wood . . . and the neglect of planting of woods, there is a great scarcity of wood throughout the whole kingdom."[1] Eventually, the high price of wood and charcoal encouraged smelters to use coal as an alternative fuel. England's coal mining increased twelvefold, from 210,000 tons in 1550 to 2,500,000 tons in 1700 and nearly 5 million tons by 1750.

France was more forested than England, but deforestation there prompted Jean Baptiste Colbert, France's minister of finance, to predict that "France will perish for lack of wood." By the late eighteenth century deforestation had become an issue even in Sweden and Russia, where iron production had become a major industry.

Even in the prosperous Dutch towns, half of the population lived in acute poverty. Authorities estimated that permanent city residents who were too poor to tax, the "deserving poor," made up 10 to 20 percent of the population. This left out the large numbers of "unworthy poor"—recent migrants, peddlers traveling from place to place, and beggars (many with horrible deformities and sores) who tried to survive on charity. The pervasive poverty of rural and urban Europe shocked those who were not hardened to it. Around 1580 the mayor of the French city of Bordeaux (bor-DOH) asked a group of visiting Amerindian chiefs what impressed them most about European cities. The chiefs are said to have expressed astonishment at the disparity between the fat, well-fed people and the poor, half-starved men and women in rags. Why, the visitors wondered, did the poor not grab the rich by the throat or set fire to their homes?[2]

In fact, misery provoked many rebellions in early modern Europe. For example, in 1525 peasant rebels in the Alps attacked both nobles and the clergy as representatives of the privileged and landowning classes. They had no love for merchants either, whom they denounced for lending at interest and charging high prices. Rebellions multiplied as rural conditions worsened. In southwestern France alone, some 450 uprisings occurred between 1590 and 1715, many set off by food shortages and tax increases. A rebellion in southern France in 1670 began when a mob of townswomen attacked the tax collector. It quickly spread to the country, where peasant leaders cried, "Death to the people's oppressors!" Authorities dealt severely with such revolts and executed or maimed their leaders.

Women and the Family

A woman's status was closely tied to her husband's. In some nations a woman could inherit a throne (see Table 16.1 for examples)—in the absence of a male heir. These rare exceptions do not negate the rule that women everywhere ranked below men. Nevertheless, class and wealth defined a woman's position in life more than her sex. The wife or daughter of a rich man, for example, had a materially better life than any poor man. Sometimes a single woman might secure a position of responsibility, as in the case of women from good families who headed convents in Catholic countries. But unmarried women were routinely controlled by fathers and married women by husbands. Some widows controlled property and other assets.

Men and women often chose their own spouses. Privileged families were more likely to arrange marriages than poor ones. Royal and noble families carefully plotted their children's marriages to further family interests. Bourgeois parents were less likely to force their children into arranged marriages, but nearly all found spouses within their own social class, suggesting that the bourgeoisie promoted marriages that buttressed business alliances.

Europeans also married later than people in the rest of the world. While people in other regions usually married in their teens, the sons of Europeans often put off marriage until they could live on their own. Young women worked helping their parents, as domestic

[1]Quoted by Carlo M. Cipolla, "Introduction," *The Fontana Economic History of Europe*, vol. 2, *The Sixteenth and Seventeenth Centuries* (Glasgow: Collins/Fontana Books, 1976), 11–12.

[2]Michel de Montaigne, *Essais* (1588), ch. 31, "Des Cannibales."

deforestation The removal of trees faster than forests can replace themselves.

The Fishwife, 1572
Women were essential partners in most Dutch family businesses. This scene by the Dutch artist Adriaen van Ostade shows a woman preparing fish for retail sale.

Iberfoto/The Image Works

servants, or in some other capacity to save money for their dowry: the money and household goods—the amount varied by social class—that enabled a young couple to begin marriage independent of their parents. The typical groom in western and central Europe could not hope to marry before his late twenties, and his bride would be a few years younger.

The late age of marriage held down the birthrate and thus limited family size. Even so, about one-tenth of urban births were to unmarried women, often servants. Such newborns were generally left on the doorsteps of churches, convents, or rich households. Many perished. Delayed marriage and poverty helped force unfortunate young women newly arrived from the countryside into brothels.

SECTION REVIEW

- Early modern European society was more fluid than it appeared, with an expanding economy and improved education promoting some mobility.

- The urban bourgeoisie created much of Europe's wealth through trade, manufacture, finance, and technological innovation.

- Governments sought lucrative alliances with the bourgeoisie, whose wealth afforded them political and social advancement as well as revenue.

- Oppressed by economic and environmental trends, peasants and laborers generally lived in poverty, and their misery often provoked rebellion.

- Although women remained subordinate to men, class and wealth were the main determinants of their positions in life.

POLITICAL INNOVATIONS

■ *How did differing policies in the areas of religion, foreign relations, and economics determine the very different experiences of early modern European states?*

The monarchs of early modern Europe occupied the apex of the social order, arbitrated intellectual and religious conflicts, and influenced economic life. In addition, royal political agendas introduced new elements of conflict and change.

Though no unified European empire emerged, political centralization increased in separate kingdoms. Frequent civil and international conflicts sometimes promoted cooperation and often encouraged innovation. Leadership in Europe passed from Spain to the Netherlands and then to England and France.

State Development

Political diversity abounded. City-states, principalities, and a small number of republics existed either independently or bound together in federations, of which the **Holy Roman Empire** of the German heartland was the foremost example. In western Europe strong monarchies emerged and developed national identities.

Dynastic ambitions and historical circumstances combined to favor and then block the creation of an integrated European empire in the early sixteenth century. In 1519, electors of the Holy Roman Empire chose Charles V, the King of Spain, to be emperor. Like his predecessors for three generations, Charles belonged to the powerful **Habsburg** (HABZ-berg) family of Austria, but he had recently inherited the Spanish kingdoms of Castile and Aragon. With these vast resources, Charles hoped to centralize his imperial power and turn back the advance of the Ottoman Empire on Europe's Mediterranean flank while contending with France for dominance of Italy.

Charles and his allies did stop the Ottomans at the gates of Vienna in 1529, but Ottoman attacks continued on and off until 1697. King Francis I of France, who had lost to Charles in the imperial election, worked tirelessly to defeat Charles's ambitions, openly supporting the Ottomans (whom the Europeans called Turks). In addition, German princes swayed by Luther's appeals to German nationalism and the Reformation opposed Charles's defense of Catholic doctrine. These disputes led to open warfare in 1546 (the German Wars of Religion), which drained Charles's treasury and forced him to accept a stalemate in the Mediterranean with the Ottomans.

In the end the ambitions of Charles V were overwhelmed by the scale of his challenges, despite his enormous resources. In the Peace of Augsburg (1555) he recognized the German princes' right to choose either Catholicism or Lutheranism as their state religion and allowed them to keep any church lands

they had seized. This triumph of religious diversity put off German political unification for three centuries. Charles abdicated the Holy Roman and Spanish thrones and retired to a monastery in 1556.

Charles V's son, Philip II, inherited his father's European territories in the low countries and Italy, where quelling unrest would drain his resources for decades, but he also inherited the Spanish throne with its rich American empire. In 1580 Philip inherited the throne of Portugal as well, adding Brazil and Portuguese colonies in Africa and Asia to his Spanish possessions. With this great wealth, he aggressively pursued the geopolitical policies that had thwarted his father.

But the American bullion that enriched Europe brought inflation (rising prices) to Spain, and Philip's effort to seal Spain off from the Protestant Reformation and the Scientific Revolution also imposed economic costs. Spanish guilds and merchants lost ground at a time when technological innovation and commercial expansion grew across northern Europe. Manufactured goods in France, Italy, or other European countries were now cheaper than goods made in Spain, and most goods imported to Spanish colonies were of foreign origin.

Though Philip was ruler of the sixteenth century's mightiest state, his wars against the Ottomans, northern European Protestants, and rebellious Dutch subjects squandered his Iberian wealth, leading to four bankruptcies during his reign and a Spain unprepared to maintain its early domination of the Atlantic when faced by sustained challenges from the English, Dutch, and French.

The Monarchies of England and France

Although the rulers of Spain, France, and England all enjoyed some success in promoting national political unification and religious unity, the stormy process led to diverse outcomes. Over the course of the seventeenth century, the

Holy Roman Empire Loose federation of mostly German states and principalities, headed by an emperor elected by the princes. It lasted from 962 to 1806.

Habsburg A powerful European family that provided many Holy Roman Emperors, founded the Austrian (later Austro-Hungarian) Empire, and ruled sixteenth- and seventeenth-century Spain.

TABLE 16.1	Rulers in Early Modern Western Europe	
Spain	**France**	**England/Great Britain**
Habsburg Dynasty	**Valois Dynasty**	**Tudor Dynasty**
Charles 1 (1516–1556) (Holy Roman Emperor Charles V) Philip II (1556–1598)	Francis I (1515–1547) Henry II (1547–1559) Francis II (1559–1560) Charles IX (1560–1574) Henry III (1574–1589)	Henry VIII (1509–1547) Edward VI (1547–1553) Mary I (1553–1558) Elizabeth I (1558–1603)
	Bourbon Dynasty	**Stuart Dynasty**
Philip III (1598–1621) Philip IV (1621–1665) Charles II (1665–1700)	Henry IV (1589–1610)[a] Louis XIII (1610–1643) Louis XIV (1643–1715)	James I (1603–1625) Charles I (1625–1649)[a,b] (Puritan Republic, 1649–1660) Charles II (1660–1685) James II (1685–1688)[b] William III (1689–1702) and Mary II (1689–1694) Anne (1702–1714)
Bourbon Dynasty		**Hanoverian Dynasty**
Philip V (1700–1746) Ferdinand VI (1746–1759)	Louis XV (1715–1774)	George I (1714–1727) George II (1727–1760)

[a] Died a violent death. [b] Was overthrown.

© Cengage Learning

monarchs of England and France faced intense conflict with powerful rivals. Religion was never absent as an issue in these struggles, but the very different constitutional outcomes they produced in these two countries were of more significance in the long run.

To evade any check on his power, King Charles I of England (see Table 16.1) ruled for eleven years without summoning Parliament, his kingdom's representative body. Lacking Parliament's consent to new taxes, he raised funds by coercing "loans" from wealthy subjects and applying existing tax laws more broadly. But in 1640 a rebellion in Scotland forced him to summon Parliament to approve new taxes to pay for an army. Noblemen and churchmen sat in the House of Lords while representatives from towns and counties sat in the House of Commons. Before it would authorize new taxes, Parliament insisted on strict guarantees that the king would never again ignore the body's traditional rights. Charles refused and in 1642 attempted to arrest his critics in the House of Commons, plunging the kingdom into the **English Civil War**.

Militarily defeated in 1648, Charles still refused to compromise. A year later a "Rump" Parliament purged of his supporters ordered his execution. Parliament replaced the monarchy with a republic under Oliver Cromwell, a Puritan general who ruled until his death in 1658. Cromwell expanded England's presence overseas and imposed firm control over Ireland and Scotland, but he was also unwilling to share power with Parliament. Two years after his death, Parliament restored the Stuart line, making it unclear, for a time, which side had won the war.

King James II clarified matters when he refused to respect Parliament's rights by baptizing his heir as a Roman Catholic. Parliament responded by forcing James into exile in the bloodless Glorious Revolution

English Civil War (1642–1649) A conflict over royal versus parliamentary rights, caused by King Charles I's arrest of his parliamentary critics and ending with his execution. Its outcome checked the growth of royal absolutism and, with the Glorious Revolution of 1688 and the English Bill of Rights of 1689, ensured that England would be a constitutional monarchy.

Versailles Constructed during the reign of Louis XIV of France, the palace of Versailles could house ten thousand people. Surrounded by elaborately landscaped grounds and parks, it became an effective symbol of royal absolutism.

Erich Lessing/Art Resource, NY

of 1688. The Bill of Rights of 1689 formalized this new constitutional order by requiring the king to call Parliament frequently to consent to changes in laws or to raise an army in peacetime. Another law reaffirmed the official status of the Church of England but extended religious toleration to dissenting Puritans.

In France the Estates General, like the English Parliament, represented the traditional rights of the clergy, the nobility, and the towns (that is, the bourgeoisie). The Estates General had asserted its rights during the sixteenth-century French Wars of Religion, when the monarchy was weak. Thereafter France's Bourbon monarchs generally ruled without calling it into session. They put off financial crises by more efficient tax collection and by selling appointments to high government offices, but by 1700 French debt levels challenged traditional fiscal practice. While some historians have used the term *absolutism* to describe the power of French monarchs in this era, even the most powerful, Louis XIV, carefully negotiated his policies with both the nobility and city authorities. While the king's power grew, long-established ways of governing, such as the sale of offices and reliance on patronage networks and personal relationships, continued to frame decision making.

Louis XIV moved his court to a gigantic new palace at **Versailles** (vuhr-SIGH) in 1682. Capable of housing ten thousand people and surrounded by elaborately landscaped grounds and parks, the palace became an effective symbol of growing royal grandeur and power and an arena where the high nobility and ecclesiastical hierarchy interacted with the monarch in a dense cycle of rituals and ceremonies that emphasized royal power.

Most European rulers admired and imitated the centralized powers and apparent absolutist authority of the French monarch until well after 1750. The English model of balanced powers would be widely admired in later times, gaining a favorable press with the beginnings of the Enlightenment. In his influential *Second Treatise of Civil Government* (1690), the English political philosopher John Locke (1632–1704) disputed monarchial claims to absolute authority by divine right. He argued that rulers derived their authority from the consent of the governed and were

Versailles The huge palace built for French king Louis XIV south of Paris. The palace symbolized both French power and the triumph of royal authority over the French nobility.

subject to the law. If monarchs overstepped the law, citizens had the right and the duty to rebel.

Warfare and Diplomacy

In addition to their bitter civil wars, European monarchies engaged in numerous international conflicts provoked in part by efforts to protect or extend colonial empires. Warfare was almost constant (see the Chronology at the beginning of the chapter). As the geographic scope of warfare and the size of armies and navies grew, monarchs expended ever-larger sums of money and caused widespread devastation and death. The worst of the international conflicts, the Thirty Years' War (1618–1648), caused long-lasting depopulation and economic decline in much of the Holy Roman Empire.

Not surprisingly, war-making skills and weaponry improved dramatically, making European armed forces the most powerful in the world. The numbers of men in arms increased steadily. French forces, for example, grew from 88 regiments of infantry and 72 of cavalry in 1691 to 238 regiments of infantry and 94 of cavalry in 1714. Even smaller European states built up impressive armies. Sweden, with under a million people, had one of the finest and best-armed military forces in the seventeenth century. Prussia, a country with fewer than 2 million inhabitants in 1700, had a large, well-disciplined army that made it a major power.

Larger armies required better command structures. The officer corps of the major powers was largely drawn from the nobility, and patronage, not skill, guided promotion and advancement. Training and battlefield control were marginally improved through more frequent drilling for professional troops and the introduction of new signaling techniques, but battlefields remained chaotic. Fortifications were expanded and improved in Europe and in colonial possessions, and even Spain, facing a deep fiscal crisis, borrowed to fortify Cartagena on its Mediterranean coast and Havana. Paying for larger and better-armed fleets proved similarly expensive, but in the face of an intensifying competition for colonial wealth that stretched from the East Indies to the Caribbean and South Atlantic, no great power could afford to cut back.

Safe from the threat of direct invasion, England alone did not maintain a standing army. Its power depended on the navy begun under King Henry VIII, who had spent heavily on ships and promoted a domestic iron industry to supply cannon. The Royal Navy also copied innovative ship designs from the Dutch. The crushing defeat of the Spanish Armada in 1588 by Henry's daughter, Elizabeth I, demonstrated the usefulness of these decisions and accelerated Spain's decline under Philip II. By the early eighteenth century, the Royal Navy surpassed the rival French fleet in numbers. By then, England had merged with Scotland to become Great Britain, annexed Ireland, and built a North American empire.

Although France was Europe's most powerful state, Louis XIV's efforts to expand were increasingly frustrated by a coalition of other powers. In a series of costly eighteenth-century wars beginning with the War of the Spanish Succession (1701–1714), the combination of Britain's naval strength and the land armies of Austria and Prussia blocked French expansionist efforts and prevented the Bourbons from uniting the thrones of France and Spain. France's defeat illustrates the principle of **balance of power** in international relations: the major European states formed temporary alliances to prevent any one state from becoming too powerful (see Map 16.2). These pragmatic alliances were the first successful efforts at international peacekeeping.

Paying the Piper

European nations struggled to pay for their wars. But the obstacles were formidable, particularly the tax exemptions enjoyed by the nobility and clergy, since they controlled most of Europe's wealth. In Spain, for example, 97 percent of the land was owned by the 3 percent of the population that constituted the nobility. To raise revenue, regressive new taxes were imposed on the peasants and commerce. To collect them governments turned to **tax farmers**, private individuals who advanced the government a fixed sum of money, typically less than 50 percent of the estimated tax

---

balance of power The policy in international relations by which, beginning in the eighteenth century, the major European states acted together to prevent any one of them from becoming too powerful.

tax farmers Private individuals or small partnerships who were given contracts to collect taxes for the government. In return tax farmers could keep whatever money they were able to collect above their tax obligation to the government.

Map 16.2 Europe in 1740 By the middle of the eighteenth century, the great powers of Europe adhering to four different branches of Christianity—Catholic France and Austria, Anglican Britain, Lutheran Prussia, and Orthodox Russia—maintained an effective balance of power by shifting their alliances for geopolitical rather than religious reasons. Spain, the Holy Roman Empire, and the Ottoman Empire were far weaker in 1740 than they had been two centuries earlier. © Cengage Learning

obligation, for the right to collect the tax. In return they could keep whatever money they were able to collect from taxpayers. This allowed governments to avoid creating expensive new bureaucracies, but the system guaranteed corruption and limited revenue growth.

Desperate governments began to find dangerous short-term fiscal expedients attractive, including currency debasement and cynical defaults on debts like Philip II's four bankruptcies. It was inevitable that early capitalism's innovations, such as joint-stock companies and stock markets, would draw governments thwarted by the tax intransigence of the elite to look to these highly speculative novelties to solve fiscal problems. Eventually, markets would grow stronger, but two nearly simultaneous speculative bubbles attached to the French Mississippi Company and the English South Sea Company resulted in spectacularly visible flaws that would force governments to turn to the taxation of reluctant citizens to pay their debts (see Chapter 21).

In 1716 the French government granted John Law, a fugitive Scottish nobleman, a license to create a bank and issue paper money based on the promise to exchange for coins at par. To everyone's surprise, the notes issued by Law's bank not only maintained their value but also were preferred to coins. The value of shares in the bank increased dramatically. Then in 1717 the French government allowed Law to create a monopoly company for development along the Mississippi, a region erroneously believed to have rich mines. The value of the initial shares soared, with prices rising 10 or 20 percent in the course of a few hours. Stories of once-poor servants buying mansions and marrying their children into noble families abounded. As the frenzy mounted, the French government used Law's bank to print more paper money rather than collect taxes. Law then satisfied the public clamor for Mississippi Company shares by imitating this irresponsible behavior. When a nervous French public began to hoard coins and avoid paper currency, Law got the government to discount gold and silver coins against the paper currency and then to restrict individual possession of coins. The subsequent panicked selling of shares in both the bank and the Mississippi Company in 1720 forced Law to run for his life. Paper wealth disappeared in a matter of days, leaving the French government to face its fiscal crisis.

In a similar scheme, the English lord treasurer in 1711 granted exclusive rights to the South Sea Company to trade with the Spanish colonies in the Americas to reduce the British government's huge wartime debt. Holders of war debts were forced to accept shares in the company as payment. Once in possession of the government bonds, the company borrowed new funds based on the supposed security of government debt. At first, the large annual interest payments from the government and a monopoly right to trade slaves to the Spanish colonies made the South Sea Company seem like a profitable investment. With news of the Mississippi Company's success, the government used the South Sea Company to transform another £30,000,000 in debt into shares. When South Sea shares issued at £300 rose to £325, the company issued more stock, even though it had almost no income from its commercial ventures. In January 1720 share prices reached £1,050. With the inevitable crash, thousands of investors were ruined. Among the investors was the scientist Isaac Newton, who said, "I can calculate the motions of the heavenly bodies but not the madness of people."

The rise of the Netherlands as an economic power stemmed from very different policies. The Spanish crown had acquired these resource-poor but commercially successful provinces as part of Charles V's inheritance. But King Philip II's decision to impose Spain's ruinously heavy sales tax and to enforce Catholic orthodoxy drove the Dutch to revolt in 1566 and again in 1572. If successful, those measures would have discouraged business and driven away the Calvinists, Jews, and other key contributors to Dutch prosperity. The Dutch fought with skill and ingenuity, raising and training an army and a navy that were among the most effective in Europe. Unable to bear the military costs any longer, Spain accepted a truce that recognized autonomy in the northern Netherlands in 1609. Finally, in 1648, the independence of the seven United Provinces of the Free Netherlands (their full name) became final.

Rather than being ruined by the long war, the Netherlands emerged as the world's greatest trading nation. This economic success owed much to a decentralized government. During the struggle against Spain, the provinces united around the Prince of Orange, their sovereign and commander-in-chief. But in economic matters each province was free to pursue its own interests. The maritime province of Holland grew rich by favoring commercial interests.

After 1650 the Dutch faced growing competition from England, where business was also allied with government. In a series of wars (1652–1678) England naval might broke Dutch dominance in overseas trade. With government support, the English merchant fleet doubled between 1660 and 1700, and foreign trade rose by 50 percent. State revenue from customs duties tripled. During the eighteenth century Britain's trading position strengthened still more.

The debts run up by the Anglo-Dutch Wars persuaded the English monarchy to enlarge the government's role in managing the economy. The outcome has been called a "financial revolution." The government increased revenues by taxing the formerly exempt landed estates of the aristocrats and by collecting taxes directly instead of relying on tax farmers. To secure cash quickly for warfare and other emergencies and to reduce the burden of debts from earlier wars, England imitated the Dutch by creating a central bank that could issue long-term loans at low rates.

The French government also developed its national economy, especially under the royal adviser Jean Baptiste Colbert. Colbert streamlined tax collection, promoted French manufacturing and shipping by imposing taxes on foreign goods, and improved transportation. Yet the power of the wealthy aristocrats kept the French government from following England's lead in taxing wealthy landowners, collecting taxes directly, and securing low-cost loans. Nor did France succeed in managing its debt as efficiently as England.

CONCLUSION

European historians have used the word *revolution* to describe many different changes taking place in Europe between 1500 and 1750. The expansion of trade has been called a *commercial revolution*, the reform of state spending a *financial revolution*, and the changes in weapons and warfare a *military revolution*. We have also encountered a scientific revolution and the religious revolution of the Reformation.

Yet the years from 1500 to 1750 were not simply—perhaps not even primarily—an age of progress for Europe. For many, the ferocious competition of European armies, merchants, and ideas was a wrenching experience. The growth of powerful states exacted a terrible price in death, destruction, and misery. While the Reformation brought greater individual choice in religion, it also brought widespread persecution. And while the expanding economy benefited the emerging merchant elite and their political allies, most Europeans became worse off as prices rose faster than wages. Finally, new scientific and enlightened ideas ignited controversies long before yielding any tangible results.

The historical significance of this period of European history is clearer when viewed in a global context. What stands out are the powerful and efficient European armies, economies, and governments. From a global perspective, the balance of political and economic power was shifting slowly, but inexorably, in the Europeans' favor. In 1500 the Ottomans threatened Europe. By 1750, Europeans had brought the world's seas and a growing portion of its lands and peoples under their control.

SECTION REVIEW

- Greater political centralization enabled early modern monarchs to exert increased influence on economic, religious, and social life.

- While the Holy Roman Empire fragmented along religious and political lines, Spain, France, and England achieved greater centralization and religious unity.

- In both England and France, monarchs struggled with rivals over the limits of royal authority.

- Armies grew larger and more sophisticated while European powers strove to maintain a balance of power.

- High military costs drove the European powers to attempt a variety of tax and financial policies, the most successful being those of England and the Netherlands.

CHAPTER REVIEW

CULTURE AND IDEAS

■ *How did the interplay of traditional beliefs and revolutionary ideas influence the cultural history of early modern Europe?* (page 381)

Early modern Europe underwent the Scientific Revolution as well as the fragmentation of the Catholic Church. Traditional antifeminist beliefs and pagan folklore about witchcraft fed a witch-hunting craze that took thousands of lives. Supporting the belief in witchcraft was a more fundamental idea that human misfortune could be blamed on supernatural forces, but this idea was powerfully challenged by pioneers of the Scientific Revolution such as Copernicus and Newton, who showed that the workings of the physical universe could be explained in natural terms. These scientists did not see any conflict between science and religion, and they paved the way for influential figures of the Enlightenment, who believed that human reason was capable of discovering laws that govern social behavior.

SOCIAL AND ECONOMIC LIFE

■ *What factors contributed to the wealth of some Europeans and the great poverty of others in this period?* (page 388)

Thanks to foreign and domestic trade, European cities in this period experienced rapid growth and the rise of a wealthy commercial class. It was also an era of growing speculative risk and market bubbles like Tulipmania and the South Sea bubble. The Netherlands in particular prospered from expanded manufacturing and trade: with the formation of joint-stock companies and a powerful stock market, Amsterdam became Europe's major port and financial center. For peasants and laborers, however, life did not improve much, although serfdom had all but ended in western Europe. Rural poverty, coupled with the exemption from taxation enjoyed by wealthy landowners, sparked numerous armed rebellions.

POLITICAL INNOVATIONS

■ *How did differing policies in the areas of religion, foreign relations, and economics determine the very different experiences of early modern European states?* (page 393)

Differing policies in the areas of religion, foreign relations, and economics explain the different histories of Europe's early modern states. Charles V, unable to reconcile the diverse interests of his Catholic and Protestant territories and their powerful local rulers, failed to create a unified Holy Roman Empire. Power struggles in England during this period led to a stronger Parliament, while in France a stronger monarchy emerged, symbolized by Louis XIV's construction of the palace at Versailles. Spain dominated Europe in the sixteenth century, but its failure to suppress revolts in the Netherlands and the costs of other wars led to bankruptcy and decline. In the seventeenth century the Netherlands became the dominant commercial power on the continent. However, the growth of English naval power led to the defeat of the Dutch in the Anglo-Dutch Wars and of France in the early eighteenth century when it attempted to expand its own empire through a union with Spain. Unlike Spain and France, which maintained aristocrats' traditional exemption from taxation, England began to tax their estates, and this policy—together with the establishment of direct taxation and the creation of a central bank from which it could secure low-cost loans—gave England a stronger financial foundation than its rivals enjoyed.

Key Terms

papacy (p. 381)

indulgence (p. 382)

Protestant Reformation (p. 382)

Catholic Reformation (p. 383)

witch-hunt (p. 385)

Scientific Revolution (p. 386)

Enlightenment (p. 387)

bourgeoisie (p. 388)

joint-stock company (p. 391)

stock exchange (p. 391)

gentry (p. 391)

Little Ice Age (p. 391)

deforestation (p. 392)

Holy Roman Empire (p. 394)

Habsburg (p. 394)

English Civil War (p. 395)

Versailles (p. 396)

balance of power (p. 397)

tax farmers (p. 397)

The Americas, the Atlantic, and Africa

© Cengage Learning

After 1600, Spain became increasingly impoverished and had difficulty protecting its American empire from pirates, privateers, and the rising powers of Europe: the Netherlands, France, and Britain. These nations, like Spain before them, benefited from the advantage that diseases gave to their people in their encounters with Native Americans. As with Spanish colonies before them, the development of English and French colonies in North America in the seventeenth century led to similar patterns of contagion and mortality. In 1616 and 1617 epidemics nearly exterminated New England's indigenous groups, while French fur traders transmitted measles, smallpox, and other diseases as far as Hudson Bay and the Great Lakes.

Although there is very little evidence that Europeans consciously used disease as a tool of empire, they inadvertently increased the rate of contagion by making Native Americans live in denser concentrations. The deadly results of contact with Europeans undermined the ability of native peoples to resist European settlement, and Europeans and their African slaves occupied these depopulated lands. Transformed biologically and culturally, the Americas were subjected to Europeans' political and economic demands.

The colonies of the Americas were crucial pieces of a booming new **Atlantic system**, a network of trading links that moved goods and wealth, as well as peoples and cultures, around the Atlantic. The Atlantic system also affected Africa but less severely than the Americas. Despite the loss of millions to the slave trade, Africa did not suffer population loss due to epidemics as in the Americas. On the contrary, the diseases prevalent in Africa—especially malaria and yellow fever—killed most of the Europeans who visited that continent. As a result, Africans remained in control of their land, except for small enclaves on the coast.

Amerindians, Europeans, and Africans all contributed to the creation of new cultures in the Americas. The societies that arose reflected each colony's mix of native peoples, its connections to the slave trade, and the policies of its European rulers.

SPANISH AMERICA AND BRAZIL

■ *What role did forced labor play in the main industries of Spanish America and Brazil?*

Within one hundred years of Columbus's first voyage to the Western Hemisphere, the Spanish Empire in America included most of the islands of the Caribbean and a vast area that stretched from northern Mexico to the plains of the Rio de la Plata region (a region that includes the modern nations of Argentina, Uruguay, and Paraguay). Portuguese settlement developed more slowly, but before the end of the sixteenth century, Portugal had occupied most of the Brazilian coast.

Early settlers from Spain and Portugal sought to create colonial societies based on the institutions and customs of their homelands. They viewed society as a vertical hierarchy of estates (classes of society), as uniformly Catholic, and as an arrangement of patriarchal extended-family networks. But despite the imposition of European religious, social, and administrative institutions and the massive loss of life caused by epidemics, indigenous peoples exercised a powerful influence on the development of colonial societies. Aztec and Inka elite families sought to protect their traditional privileges and rights through marriage or less formal alliances with Spanish settlers. They also used colonial courts to defend their claims to land. Nearly everywhere, Amerindian religious beliefs and practices survived beneath the surface of an imposed Christianity. Amerindian languages, cuisines, medical practices, and agricultural techniques also survived the conquest and influenced the development of Latin American culture.

The African slave trade added a third cultural stream to colonial Latin American society. At first, African slaves were concentrated in plantation regions of Brazil and the Caribbean, but by the end of the colonial era, Africans and their descendants were living throughout Latin America, enriching the agricultural practices, music, religious beliefs, cuisine, and social customs of colonial societies.

Atlantic system The network of trading links after 1500 that moved goods, wealth, people, and cultures around the Atlantic Basin.

State and Church   The Spanish crown moved quickly to curb the independent power of the conquistadors and to establish royal authority over both defeated native populations and European settlers. As a result, the highest-ranking Spanish officials in the colonies, the viceroys of New Spain and Peru, enjoyed broad power, but they also faced obstacles to their authority in the vast territories they sought to control. Created in 1535, the Viceroyalty of New Spain, with its capital in Mexico City, included Mexico, the southwest of what is now the United States, Central America, and the islands of the Caribbean. Created five years later, the Viceroyalty of Peru, with its capital in Lima, governed Spanish South America (see Map 17.1). Until the seventeenth century, most colonial officials were born in Spain, but fiscal mismanagement eventually forced the Crown to sell appointments, and later, local-born members of the colonial elite gained many offices.

In the sixteenth century Portugal concentrated its resources and energies on Asia and Africa, because early settlers found neither mineral wealth nor rich native empires in Brazil. Finally, the king appointed a governor-general in 1549 and made Salvador Brazil's capital. In 1720 the king named the first viceroy of Brazil.

The colonial bureaucracies imposed Spanish and Portuguese oversight (and heavy tax burdens) on the silver and gold mines in Spanish America and the sugar plantations in Brazil, justifying their American conquests by assuming an obligation to convert native populations to Christianity. This effort to convert America's native peoples expanded Christianity on a scale similar to its earlier expansion in Europe at the time of Constantine in the fourth century. The Catholic Church undertook the conversion of Amerindians, ministered to the spiritual needs of European settlers, and promoted intellectual life through the introduction of the printing press and the founding of schools and universities. Together, the Spanish and Portuguese colonial governments and the efforts of the Catholic Church brought European language and a more unified culture to the Iberian Americas than would be found in North American settlements.

Although European clergy had arrived in the Americas with the intention of transmitting Catholic Christian belief and ritual without alteration, the linguistic diversity of Amerindian populations and their geographic dispersal over a vast landscape defeated this ambition. Initially, Franciscan missionaries in Mexico tried to extend their reach by creating a seminary to train members of the indigenous elite to become priests. These efforts were abandoned when church authorities discovered that many converts were secretly observing old beliefs and rituals. Although priests at times resorted to forced conversion and the violent repression of native religions, including torture among the Maya in the 1560s, these practices repelled the church hierarchy and were outlawed. Despite European disapproval, Amerindians blended Catholic Christian belief with important elements of traditional native cosmology and ritual that are now embedded in such celebration as saints' days or Catholic rituals associated with the Virgin Mary.

Despite its failures, the Catholic clergy did provide native peoples with some protections against the abuse and exploitation of Spanish settlers. **Bartolomé de Las Casas** (1474–1566), who had arrived in Hispaniola in 1502 and initially lived from the forced labor of Amerindians, was deeply moved by the deaths of so many Amerindians and by the misdeeds of the Spanish. He entered the Dominican Order, becoming the first bishop of Chiapas, in southern Mexico, and spent the remainder of his long life as an advocate for native peoples. His most important achievement was the enactment of the New Laws of 1542, which outlawed the enslavement of Amerindians and limited other forms of forced labor.

After 1600 the terrible loss of Amerindian populations caused by epidemics and resistance to conversion led the Catholic Church to redirect its resources from native regions in the countryside to growing colonial cities and towns with large European populations. This altered mission included the founding of universities and secondary schools, which stimulated urban intellectual life. Over time, the church became the richest institution in the Spanish colonies, controlling ranches, plantations, and vineyards as well as serving as the society's banker.

Bartolomé de Las Casas First bishop of Chiapas, in southern Mexico. He devoted most of his life to protecting Amerindian peoples from exploitation. His major achievement was the New Laws of 1542, which limited the ability of Spanish settlers to compel Amerindians to labor for them.

Chronology

	Spanish America	Brazil	British America	French America
1500	**1518** Smallpox arrives in Caribbean **1535** Creation of Viceroyalty of New Spain **1540** Creation of Viceroyalty of Peru **1542** New Laws attempt to outlaw Amerindian enslavement **1545** Silver discovered at Potosí, Bolivia	**1549** Appointment of first Portuguese governor-general of Brazil **1540–1600** Era of Amerindian slavery **After 1540** Sugar begins to dominate the economy		
1600		**By 1620** African slave trade provides majority of plantation workers **1630s** Quilombo of Palmares founded	**1607** Jamestown founded **1620** Plymouth founded **1660–1756** Rapid growth of slavery in Virginia **1664** English take New York from Dutch	**1608** Quebec founded **1699** Louisiana founded
1700	**1713** Beginning of Bourbon dynasty in Spain	**1750–1777** Reforms in Brazil and Spanish America	**1754–1763** French and Indian War	**1760** English take Canada

Colonial Economies

The silver mines of Peru and Mexico and the sugar plantations of Brazil dominated the colonial economy and fueled the early development of European capitalism. Profits also promoted the growth of colonial cities, concentrated scarce investment capital and labor resources, and stimulated the livestock industry. Mineral and agricultural exports remain an enduring legacy in Latin America. Silver generated the most wealth and exercised the greatest economic influence in the Spanish colonies, though gold mines were also productive. In 1545, the single richest silver deposit in the Americas was discovered at **Potosí** (poh-toh-SEE) in what is now Bolivia.

Silver mining also altered the environment. Within a short time, wasteful use of forest resources to fuel furnaces for smelting ore led to deforestation near the mining centers. Faced with rising fuel costs, Mexican miners developed an efficient method of chemical extraction that relied on mixing mercury with the silver ore. Silver yields and profits increased, but since mercury is a poison, its use contaminated the environment and sickened the Amerindian workforce.

Indigenous populations had been compelled to provide labor for European settlers in the Americas since Columbus. Until the 1540s Amerindians were divided among settlers in the Spanish colonies and forced to provide labor or goods. This form of forced labor was called **encomienda** (in-co-mee-EN-dah). The discovery of silver in Peru led to use of the *mita*

Potosí Located in Bolivia, one of the richest silver mining centers and most populous cities in colonial Spanish America.

encomienda A grant of authority over a population of Amerindians in the Spanish colonies. It provided the grant holder with a supply of cheap labor and periodic payments of goods by the Amerindians. It obliged the grant holder to Christianize the Amerindians.

Map 17.1 Colonial Latin America in the Eighteenth Century Spain and Portugal controlled most of the Western Hemisphere in the eighteenth century. In the sixteenth century they had created new administrative jurisdictions—viceroyalties—to defend their respective colonies against European rivals. Taxes assessed on colonial products helped pay for this extension of governmental authority. © Cengage Learning

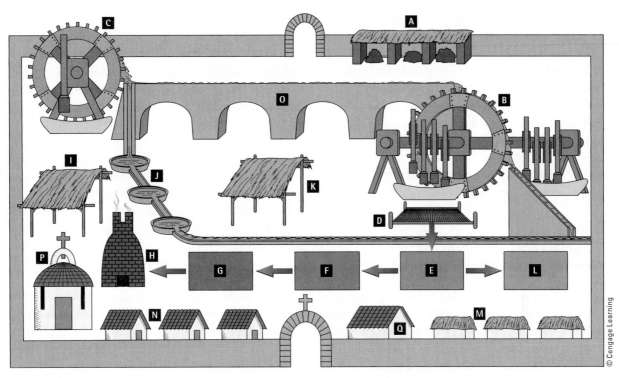

Legend

(A) Storage sheds for ore
(B) Two water-driven stamping mills to crush ore
(C) Additional stamping mill
(D) Screen to sort ore
(E) Ore packed in mixing box

(F) Mercury and catalysts added to ore
(G) Amalgamation occurs
(H) Ore dried in furnace
(I) Mercury removed
(J) Refined ore washed
(K) Ore assayed

(L) Poor quality ore remixed with catalysts
(M) Housing
(N) Offices and sheds
(O) Aquaduct
(P) Chapel
(Q) Mill owner's house

A Bolivian Silver Refinery, 1700 The silver refineries of Spanish America were among the largest industrial establishments in the Western Hemisphere.

(MEE-tah) system of compulsory labor (see Chapters 7 and 14). Under this system, one-seventh of adult male Amerindians were compelled to work for two to four months each year in mines, farms, or textile factories. As the Amerindian population declined with new epidemics, villages began to shorten the period between mita obligations. Instead of serving every seven years, many men returned to the mines after only a year or two, and thousands abandoned traditional agriculture and moved permanently to Spanish mines and farms as paid laborers to avoid mita service and other taxes, weakening Amerindian village life and promoting Amerindian assimilation into Spanish-speaking Catholic colonial society.

The Portuguese had developed sugar plantations using African slave labor on the Atlantic islands of Madeira, the Azores, the Cape Verdes, and São Tomé,

and they quickly transferred this system to Brazil. From roughly 1540 onward sugar dominated the Brazilian economy. Between then and 1600, the Portuguese sugar planters enslaved Amerindians, but as epidemics decimated the Amerindian workforce, planters eventually came to rely more on African slaves. Imports of African slaves rose from an average of two thousand per year in the late sixteenth century to approximately seven thousand per year a century later, outstripping the immigration of free Portuguese settlers.

The mining centers of Latin America exercised global economic influence. American silver increased the European money supply, promoting commercial expansion. Large amounts of silver also flowed to Asia, exchanged for spices, silk, and porcelain. As a result, both Europe and Latin America ran chronic trade deficits with Asia. The sugar plantations of Brazil played a similar role in integrating the economy of the South Atlantic region. Both Spain and Portugal attempted to control the trade of their American colonies, but monopoly commerce and convoy shipping slowed the flow of Europeans goods to the colonies and kept prices high. Frustrated, colonial populations established illegal trade with the English, French, and Dutch. By the middle of the seventeenth century, a majority of European imports were arriving in Latin America illegally.

Society in Colonial Latin America

With the exception of some early viceroys, few members of Spain's nobility came to the New World. *Hidalgos* (ee-DAHL-goes)—lesser nobles—were well represented, as were Spanish merchants, artisans, miners, priests, and lawyers. Small numbers of criminals, beggars, and prostitutes also found their way to the colonies. Spanish settlers, however, were always a tiny minority in a colonial society numerically dominated by Amerindians and rapidly growing populations of Africans, **creoles** (whites born in America to European parents), and people of mixed ancestry.

Conquistadors and early settlers who received from the Crown grants of labor and tribute goods (*encomienda*) from Amerindian communities as rewards for service to Spain sought to create a hereditary social and political class comparable to the European nobility. But their position was undermined by their abuse of Amerindian communities, the catastrophic effects of the epidemics of the sixteenth century, and the growing power of colonial officials, the clergy, and the richest merchants. The elite of Spanish America included both European immigrants and creoles. Europeans controlled the highest levels of the church and government as well as commerce, while wealthy creoles commonly controlled colonial agriculture and mining. Although tensions between Spaniards and creoles were inevitable, most elite families included both groups.

Before the Europeans arrived in the Americas, the native peoples were members of a large number of distinct cultural and linguistic groups. Cultural diversity and class distinctions were present even in the highly centralized Aztec and Inka Empires. This rich

social and cultural complexity was undermined by the effects of conquest and epidemics, and the imposition of Catholic Christianity. The broad application of the racial label *Indian* to all Amerindians helped organize the tribute and labor demands imposed on native peoples while erasing long-standing class and ethnic differences.

Indigenous Amerindian elites struggled to survive. Hereditary native elites established political alliances with colonial administrations and gained some security by becoming their intermediaries with the indigenous masses, collecting Spanish taxes and organizing the labor of their dependents. Some elite Amerindian women married colonists, but over time, these family ties diminished. Indigenous commoners suffered the heaviest burdens of tribute, forced labor, and the loss of native lands. Survivors adapted by embracing elements of colonial culture or entering the market economies of the cities.

Thousands of blacks participated in the conquest and settlement of Spanish America, and the opening of a direct slave trade with Africa added millions more. African slaves arrived in the colonies with different languages, religious beliefs, and cultural practices. European settlers viewed these differences as signs of inferiority that served as a justification for slavery. However, slaves still had an impact on Spanish America beyond serving as a source of labor. Exposure to Iberian culture in West-Central Africa, where many slaves originated, facilitated African influence on the emerging colonial cultures of Latin America. Over time, elements from many African traditions blended and mixed with European (and in some cases Amerindian) languages and beliefs to forge distinct local cultures.

African slaves became skilled artisans, musicians, servants, artists, cowboys, and even soldiers. However, the vast majority worked in agriculture. To escape harsh discipline and backbreaking labor, many slaves rebelled or ran away. Communities of runaways, called *quilombos* (key-LOM-bos) in Brazil and *palenques* (pah-LEN-kays) in Spanish colonies, were common. The largest quilombo was Palmares,

creoles In colonial Spanish America, the term used to describe someone of European descent born in the New World. Elsewhere in the Americas, the term is used to describe all nonnative peoples.

where thousands of slaves defended themselves against Brazilian authorities for sixty years until they were finally overthrown in 1694.

Brazil attracted smaller numbers of European immigrants than did Spanish America, and its native populations were smaller and less urbanized than the Aztecs or Inka. Brazil also came to depend on African slave labor earlier than any other American colony, and by the early seventeenth century, Africans and their American-born descendants were by far the largest racial group in that country. As a result, Brazilian colonial society (unlike Spanish Mexico and Peru) was more influenced by African culture than by Amerindian culture.

SECTION REVIEW

- Colonial governments were created to rule distant colonies.
- The Catholic Church led conversion of Amerindian peoples and spread European cultures and languages.
- Silver mining and sugar production dominated colonial Latin American economies.
- Spanish and Portuguese colonies relied on forced labor of Amerindians and African slaves.
- New peoples and new cultures resulted from colonial contacts among Amerindians, Europeans, and Africans.
- Colonial reforms disrupted colonial economic and political accommodations and led to rebellion and resistance.

Imperial Reform and Resistance

Spain's Habsburg dynasty ended when Charles II died without an heir in 1700, and Philip of Bourbon, grandson of Louis XIV of France, secured the throne after thirteen years of costly war involving the major European powers and factions within Spain. To replenish revenue, Philip V looked to the remarkable economic expansion and population growth of Spanish America in the eighteenth century. Silver production in Mexico and Peru rose steadily, and agricultural exports also expanded: tobacco, dyes, hides, chocolate, cotton, and sugar joined the flow of goods to Europe. Spain instituted reforms during this period, reorganizing colonial administration and tax collection to force colonial populations to pay a larger share of the costs of administration and defense. Portugal followed suit, as gold was discovered in Brazil in the 1690s and diamonds after 1720.

Both Spain and Portugal also sought to reduce the power of the Catholic Church in their colonies and to transfer some church wealth to their treasuries. These

Sir Henry Chamberlain, *Views and Costumes of the City and Neighborhoods of Rio de Janeiro*, London, 1822

Market in Rio de Janeiro In many of the cities of colonial Latin America, female slaves and black free women dominated retail markets. In this scene from late colonial Brazil, Afro-Brazilian women sell a variety of foods and crafts.

efforts led to a succession of confrontations between colonial officials and the church hierarchy. In the eighteenth century, the clergy could no longer be relied on to support the colonial state, and many colonists saw the reforms as an abuse of power. In the 1770s tax rebellions, urban riots, and Amerindian uprisings tied to these reforms began in Spanish America, and open warfare occurred between "sons of the soil" and "outsiders" in São Paolo, Brazil. A more unified colonial culture had begun to assert itself against the will of distant monarchs.

ENGLISH AND FRENCH COLONIES IN NORTH AMERICA

■ *What were the differences between the English and the French colonies of North America?*

The North American empires of England and France had much in common with those of Spain and Portugal. They hoped to find precious metals or great indigenous empires like those of the Aztecs and Inka, and their settlers responded to native peoples with a mixture of diplomacy and violence. They also imported large numbers of African slaves.

There were also important differences. The English and French colonies were founded nearly a century after Cortés's conquest of Mexico and the initial Portuguese settlement of Brazil. By the time England and France secured a foothold, trade had increased the integration of world cultural regions. Distracted by ventures elsewhere, neither England nor France imitated the large and expensive colonial bureaucracies that Spain and Portugal established. Instead, private companies and individual proprietors pioneered development. The Protestant Reformation had also helped frame the character of English and French settlement in the Americas. Greater variety in economic activity, political institutions and culture, and social structure was evident here compared with Latin American colonies.

The South

London investors organized as the Virginia Company took up the challenge of colonizing Virginia in 1607 and 1608. However, 80 percent of the settlers at Jamestown died of disease or Amerindian attack. After the English crown dissolved the Virginia Company because of its mismanagement in 1624, colonists were free to move from the swampy unhealthy Jamestown deeper into the interior, developing a sustainable economy based on furs, timber, and, increasingly, tobacco. The profits from tobacco soon attracted new immigrants and new capital. Along the shoreline of Chesapeake Bay and the rivers that fed it, settlers spread out, developing plantations and farms.

Indentured servants eventually accounted for approximately 80 percent of all English immigration to the Chesapeake Bay region. Young European men and women racially and religiously indistinguishable from free settlers paid for their transportation to America by accepting indentures (contracts) that bound them to a term ranging from four to seven years of labor and that provided, at the end of the contract, a small parcel of land, some tools, and clothes. During the seventeenth century, approximately 1,500 indentured servants—mostly male—arrived each year. Initially, high mortality rates among slaves made indentured servants more economical than slaves. But as life expectancy improved, planters calculated that the higher initial cost of buying a slave, who would be owned for life, would contribute to greater profits. As a result, Virginia's slave population grew from 950 in 1660 to 120,000 by 1756.

Ironically, increased dependence on slavery occurred along with the expansion in colonial liberties and political rights. At first, colonial government had been administered by a Crown-appointed governor and by representatives of towns meeting together as the **House of Burgesses**. When elected representatives began to meet alone as a deliberative body, they initiated a form of democratic representation that distinguished the English colonies of North America from the colonies of other European powers. The intertwined evolution of American freedom and slavery gave England's southern colonies a unique and conflicted political character.

---

indentured servant A migrant to British colonies in the Americas who paid for passage by agreeing to work for a set term ranging from four to seven years.

House of Burgesses Elected assembly in colonial Virginia, created in 1618.

Colonial South Carolina was the most hierarchical society in British North America. Settled first by planters from Barbados in 1670, this colony developed an economy based on plantations and slavery in imitation of the colonies of the Caribbean and Brazil. The richest maintained households in both the countryside and Charleston, the largest city in the southern colonies. Small farmers, cattlemen, artisans, merchants, and fur traders held an intermediate but clearly subordinate social position. At the bottom were the slaves on whom South Carolina depended. African slaves had been present from the founding of Charleston and were instrumental in introducing irrigated rice agriculture and in developing plantations of indigo (a plant that produced a blue dye). Although native peoples remained influential participants in colonial society through commercial contracts and alliances, they were increasingly marginalized.

New England

New England was colonized by two separate groups of Protestant dissenters. The **Pilgrims** established the coastal colony of Plymouth in present-day Massachusetts in 1620. Although nearly half of the settlers died during the first winter, the colony survived. In 1691, Plymouth was absorbed into the larger Massachusetts Bay Colony of the **Puritans**. By 1643 more than twenty thousand Puritans had settled in the Bay Colony.

Unlike in the southern colonies, most newcomers to Massachusetts arrived with their families. A normal gender balance and a healthy climate resulted in a rapid increase in population. Massachusetts also was more homogeneous and less hierarchical than the southern colonies.

Political institutions evolved from the terms of the Puritans' royal charter. A governor was elected, along with a council of magistrates drawn from the board of directors of the Massachusetts Bay Company. Disagreements between this council and elected representatives of the towns led, by 1650, to the creation of a lower legislative house that selected its own speaker and developed procedures and rules similar to those of the House of Commons in England.

Economically, agriculture met basic needs, but the poor soils and harsh climate did not favor cash crops like tobacco or rice. To pay for imported tools, textiles, and other essentials, the colonists provided commercial and shipping services to the southern colonies, the Caribbean islands, Africa, and Europe. In contrast to Latin America's heavily capitalized monopolies, New England merchants depended on market intelligence, flexibility, and streamlined organization. By 1740, Boston, with 16,000 inhabitants, was the largest city in British North America.

The Middle Atlantic Region

The rapid economic development and cultural diversity of the Middle Atlantic colonies added to the success of English-speaking North America. The **Iroquois Confederacy**—an alliance among the Mohawk, Oneida, Onondaga, Cayuga, and Seneca peoples—established treaties and trading relationships with the Dutch. When confronted by an English military expedition in 1664, the Dutch surrendered without a fight. James, duke of York and later King James II of England, renamed the colony *New York*. Located at the mouth of the Hudson River, New York City developed as a commercial and shipping center, playing an essential role in connecting the region's grain farmers to the booming markets of the Caribbean and southern Europe. By the early eighteenth century, this colony had a diverse population that included English, Dutch, German, and Swedish settlers as well as a large slave community.

Pennsylvania began as a proprietary colony in 1682 and as a refuge for Quakers, a persecuted religious minority. The founder, William Penn, quickly lost control of the colony's political life, but the colony enjoyed remarkable success. By 1700, Pennsylvania had a population of more than 21,000, and Philadelphia, its capital, soon overtook Boston to become the largest city in the British colonies. Healthy climate,

Pilgrims Group of English Protestant dissenters who established Plymouth Colony in Massachusetts in 1620 to seek religious freedom after having lived briefly in the Netherlands.

Puritans English Protestant dissenters who believed that God predestined souls to Heaven or Hell before birth. They founded Massachusetts Bay Colony in 1629.

Iroquois Confederacy An alliance of five northeastern Amerindian peoples (six after 1722) that made decisions on military and diplomatic issues through a council of representatives. Allied first with the Dutch and later with the English, the Confederacy dominated the area from western New England to the Great Lakes.

"Johnson Hall," by E. L. Henry. Courtesy, Albany Institute of History and Art

The Home of Sir William Johnson, British Superintendent for Indian Affairs, Northern District As the colonial era drew to a close, the British attempted to limit the cost of colonial defense by negotiating land settlements with native peoples, but the growing tide of western migration doomed these agreements. William Johnson (1715–1774) maintained a fragile peace along the northern frontier by building strong personal relations with influential leaders of the Mohawk and other members of the Iroquois Confederacy. His home in present-day Johnstown, New York, shows the mixed nature of the frontier—the relative opulence of the main house offset by the two defensive blockhouses built for protection.

excellent land, and relatively peaceful relations with native peoples attracted free workers without reproducing South Carolina's hierarchical and repressive social order based on slavery. By the early eighteenth century, however, a rich merchant elite was in place and the prosperous city of Philadelphia had a large population of black slaves, servants, and skilled tradesmen.

Reform and Reorganization in British America

After the period of Cromwell's Puritan Republic (see Chapter 16), the restored Stuart king, Charles II, undertook an ambitious campaign to establish greater control over the colonies. Between 1651 and 1673 a series of Navigation Acts sought to severely limit colonial trade and production that competed directly with English manufacturers. Because the king viewed the New England colonies as centers of smuggling, he temporarily suspended their elected assemblies while appointing colonial governors and granting them new fiscal and legislative powers.

During the eighteenth century the English colonies experienced renewed economic growth and attracted a new wave of European immigration, but social divisions were increasingly evident. The colonial population in 1770 was more urban, more clearly divided by class and race, and more vulnerable to economic downturns. Crises were provoked when imperial wars with France and Spain disrupted trade in the Atlantic, increased tax burdens, forced military mobilizations, and incited frontier conflicts with Amerindians.

French America

French settlement patterns more closely resembled those of Spain and Portugal than of England. The French were committed to missionary activity among Amerindian peoples and emphasized the extraction of natural resources—in this case furs.

Coming to Canada after spending years in the West Indies, Samuel de Champlain founded the colony of **New France** at Quebec (kwuh-BEC), on the banks of the St. Lawrence River, in 1608. The European market

New France French colony in North America, with a capital in Quebec, founded in 1608. New France fell to the British in 1763.

for fur, especially beaver, fueled French settlement. Young Frenchmen were sent to live among native peoples to master their languages and customs, and these men and their children by native women organized the fur trade and led French expansion to the west and south. Amerindians actively participated in the trade because they came to depend on the goods they received in exchange for furs—firearms, metal tools, textiles, and alcohol.

The Iroquois Confederacy responded to the increased military strength of France's Algonquin allies by forging commercial and military links with Dutch and later English settlements along the Hudson River. Now well armed, the Iroquois Confederacy nearly eradicated the Huron in 1649 and inflicted a series of humiliating defeats on the French. At the high point of their power in the early 1680s, Iroquois hunters and military forces gained control of much of the Great Lakes region and the Ohio River Valley. A large French military expedition and a relentless attack focused on Iroquois villages and agriculture finally checked Iroquois power in 1701.

In French Canada, the Jesuits led the effort to convert native peoples to Christianity. Building on evangelical efforts in Brazil and Paraguay, French Catholic missionaries mastered native languages,

SECTION REVIEW

- In contrast to Spanish colonies, the development of British and French colonies was shaped by private companies and individuals.
- North American colonies developed strong regional characters and strong local political traditions. British colonies attracted large numbers of free immigrants, but indentured servitude and slavery were crucial to economic development.
- The southern colonies' dependence on forced labor and plantation agriculture led to a society that was more hierarchical and less democratic that those found in the colonies of New England and the Middle Atlantic region.
- The development of French America was shaped by missionary activity and the fur trade, which was dependent on Amerindian participation.
- Eventually England defeated France and gained control of North America east of the Mississippi.

created boarding schools for young boys and girls, and set up model agricultural communities for converts. Their greatest successes coincided with a destructive wave of epidemics and renewed warfare among native peoples in the 1630s. Nevertheless, native culture persisted.

Although the fur trade flourished, population growth was slow. Founded at about the same time,

Canadian Fur Traders The fur trade provided the economic foundation of early Canadian settlement. Fur traders were cultural intermediaries. They brought European technologies and products like firearms and machine-made textiles to native peoples and native technologies and products like canoes and furs to European settlers. This canoe with sixteen paddlers was adapted from the native craft by fur traders to transport large cargoes. Frances Anne Hopkins, "Shooting the Rapids," Library and Archives Canada, Ref. # C-2774

Choctaw Village in Louisiana at Time of French Colonial Rule This scene of village life illustrates the integration of the Choctaw in the colonial economy. The painting places a young African slave and European trade goods in a scene where the Choctaw pursue traditional tasks. © President and Fellows of Harvard College, Peabody Museum of Archaeology and Ethnology, 41–72–10/20

Virginia had twenty times more European residents by 1627. Canada's small settler population and the fur trade's dependence on Amerindians allowed indigenous peoples to retain greater independence and more control over their encounters with new religious, technological, and market realities. Nevertheless, the French aggressively expanded and in 1699 founded Louisiana, which was also dependent on the fur trade with Amerindians.

France's North American colonies were ultimately threatened by a series of wars with England and the neighboring English colonies. The "French and Indian War" (also known as the Seven Years' War, 1756–1763) proved to be the final contest for the North American empire. England committed a larger military force to the struggle and, despite early defeats, took the French capital of Quebec in 1759. The peace agreement signed the next year forced France to yield Canada to the English and cede Louisiana to Spain.

PLANTATIONS IN THE WEST INDIES

■ *What factors contributed to the development of plantations in the West Indies?*

The West Indies was the first place in the Americas reached by Columbus and the first region where native populations collapsed, smallpox arriving in 1518. It took a long time to repopulate these islands

and forge economic links with other parts of the Atlantic. But after 1650 sugar plantations, African slaves, and European capital made these islands a major center of the Atlantic economy.

Spanish settlers introduced sugar-cane cultivation into the West Indies shortly after 1500, but these colonies soon fell into neglect as attention shifted to colonizing the American mainland. After 1600 the West Indies revived as a focus of colonization, this time by northern Europeans interested in growing tobacco and other crops. The islands' value mushroomed after the Dutch reintroduced sugar cultivation from Brazil in the 1640s and supplied the African slaves and European capital necessary to create a new economy.

Sugar and Slaves The English colony of Barbados illustrates the dramatic transformation that sugar brought to the seventeenth-century Caribbean. In 1640, Barbados's economy depended largely on tobacco, mostly grown by European settlers, both free and indentured. By the 1680s, sugar had become the colony's principal crop, and enslaved Africans were three times as numerous as Europeans. Exporting up to 15,000 tons of sugar a year, Barbados had become the wealthiest and most populous of England's American colonies. By 1700, the West Indian colonies had collectively surpassed Brazil as the world's principal source of sugar.

Plantation Scene, Antigua, British West Indies The sugar made at the mill in the background was sealed in barrels and loaded on carts that oxen and horses drew to the beach. By means of a succession of vessels the barrels were taken to the ship that hauled the cargo to Europe. The importance of African labor is evident from the fact that only one white person appears in the painting.

British Library Board

The expansion of sugar plantations in the West Indies required a sharp increase in the volume of the slave trade from Africa. During the first half of the seventeenth century about ten thousand slaves a year had arrived from Africa, most destined for Brazil and the mainland Spanish colonies. In the second half of the century, the trade averaged twenty thousand slaves annually. More than half were intended for the English, French, and Dutch West Indies and most of the rest for Brazil. A century later, the volume of the Atlantic slave trade was three times larger.

What produced this shift in favor of African slaves? Recent scholarship has cast doubts on the once common assertion that Africans were more suited than Europeans to field labor; in fact, both died in large numbers in the American tropics. The West Indian historian Eric Williams has also refuted the idea that the rise of African slave labor was primarily motivated by prejudice. Citing the West Indian colonies' prior use of enslaved Amerindians and indentured Europeans, along with European convicts and prisoners of war, he argued, "Slavery was not born out of racism: rather, racism was the consequence of slavery."[1] Williams suggested that the shift was due to the lower cost of African labor.

Cash-short tobacco planters in the seventeenth century preferred indentured Europeans to African slaves because they cost half as much. However, as the cultivation of sugar spread after 1750, speculators drove land prices in the West Indies so high that the parcel of land promised as part of the payment for indentured servants became expensive. Without the promise of land, wages would have to be raised to attract European laborers. Caribbean sugar planters switched to slaves, and indentured servitude moved to Britain's North American colonies instead, where there was still cheap land.

Rising sugar prices helped West Indian sugar planters afford the higher cost of African slaves. The fact that slaves lived seven years on average after their arrival, while the typical indentured labor contract was for only three or four years, also made slaves a better investment. Dutch and other traders could be relied upon to supply new slaves to meet the demands of expanding plantations. Responding to rising demand, slave prices rose throughout the eighteenth century. These high labor costs were one more factor favoring large plantations over smaller operations.

To find more land for sugar plantations, France and England founded new Caribbean colonies. In 1655 the English wrested the island of Jamaica from the Spanish (see Map 17.1), and in the 1670s the French seized the western half of the large Spanish island of

---

[1] Eric Williams, *Capitalism and Slavery* (Charlotte: University of North Carolina Press, 1944), 7.

Hispaniola. During the eighteenth century this new French colony of Saint Domingue (san doh-MANGH) (present-day Haiti) became the greatest producer of sugar in the Atlantic world, while Jamaica surpassed Barbados as England's most important sugar colony. Later, Spanish Cuba became a major sugar producer.

Technology and Environment

What made the sugar plantation a complex investment was that it had to be a factory as well as a farm. Fresh-cut cane needed to be crushed within a few hours to extract the sugary sap. Thus for maximum efficiency, each plantation needed its own expensive crushing and processing equipment.

At the heart of the sugar works was the mill where canes were crushed between heavy rollers. From the mill, lead-lined wooden troughs carried cane juice to a series of large copper kettles in the boiling shed, where excess water was boiled off, leaving thick syrup. Workers poured the syrup into conical molds in the drying shed. The sugar crystals that formed in the molds were packed in wooden barrels for shipment to Europe.

To make the operation more efficient and profitable, investors gradually increased the size of the typical West Indian plantation from around 100 acres (40 hectares) in the seventeenth century to at least twice that size in the eighteenth century. A plantation became a huge investment. One source estimated that a planter had to invest nearly £20,000 ($100,000) to acquire a Jamaican plantation of 600 acres (250 hectares) in 1774: a third for the land, a quarter for equipment, and £8,000 for 200 slaves. Jamaica specialized so heavily in sugar production that the island had to import most of its food. Saint Domingue was more diverse in its economy.

In some ways, the mature plantation was environmentally responsible. The crushing mill was powered by water, wind, or animals, not fossil fuels. The boilers were largely fueled by burning crushed cane, and the fields were fertilized by cattle manure. In two respects, however, the plantation was very damaging to the environment: soil exhaustion and deforestation. Instead of rotating sugar with other crops to restore the nutrients naturally, planters found it more profitable to clear new lands when yields declined in the old fields. When land close to the sea was exhausted, planters moved on to new islands. Many of the English who first settled Jamaica were from Barbados, and the pioneer planters on Saint Domingue came from older French sugar colonies. Everywhere in the Caribbean, forests were cleared. By the end of the eighteenth century, deforestation was so complete that only land in the interior of the islands retained dense forests.

The most tragic and dramatic transformation of the West Indies was demographic. During the eighteenth century West Indian plantation colonies

Caribbean Sugar Mill The windmill crushes sugar cane, whose juice is boiled down in the smoking building next door. The Crusher Squeezes Juice from the Cane, Antigua, 1823 (print), Clark, William (fl.1823)/British Library, London, UK/© British Library Board. All Rights Reserved/The Bridgeman Art Library

were the world's most polarized societies. On most islands, 90 percent or more of the inhabitants were slaves. A small number of very rich men owned most of the slaves and most of the land as well. A few estate managers and government officials existed between master and slave, but it is only a slight simplification to describe eighteenth-century Caribbean society as being made up of a large, abject class of slaves and a small, powerful class of masters.

The profitability of a Caribbean plantation depended on extracting as much work as possible from the slaves through the threat and use of force. On a typical Jamaican plantation, about 80 percent of the slaves actively engaged in productive tasks; the only exceptions were infants, the seriously ill, and the very old. Slave labor was organized by age, sex, and ability. Only 2 or 3 percent of the slaves were house servants. About 70 percent of the able-bodied slaves worked in the fields, generally in one of three labor gangs. Women formed the majority of the field laborers, even in the "great gang" made up of the strongest slaves. A second gang of youths, elders, and less fit slaves did somewhat lighter work. A "grass gang," composed of children under the supervision of an elderly slave, did simple work, such as weeding or collecting grass for the animals. A little over half of adult males did nongang work, tending livestock or serving as blacksmiths and carpenters. The most important artisan slave was the head boiler, who oversaw the delicate process of reducing the cane sap to crystallized sugar and molasses.

Planters often rewarded skilled slaves with food and clothing or time off, but most slaves were compelled to work hard to avoid the lash. Slave gangs were led by a privileged male slave, appropriately called the **driver**, whose job was to ensure that the gang completed its work. Production quotas were high, and slaves toiled in the fields from sunup to sunset, except for meal breaks. Those who fell behind due to fatigue or illness soon felt the sting of the whip. Openly rebellious slaves who refused to work, disobeyed orders, or tried to escape were punished with floggings, confinement in irons, or mutilation.

The harsh conditions of plantation life played a major role in shortening slaves' lives, but the greatest killer was disease. The very young were carried off by dysentery caused by contaminated food and water.

Slaves newly arrived from Africa went through a period of adjustment to a new environment known as **seasoning**, during which one-third, on average, died of unfamiliar diseases. Slaves also suffered from diseases brought with them, including malaria. On one plantation, for example, more than half of the slaves incapacitated by illness had yaws, a painful and debilitating skin disease common in Africa.

Such high mortality greatly added to the volume of the Atlantic slave trade, since plantations had to purchase new slaves every year or two to replace those who died. The additional imports of slaves to permit expansion of the sugar plantations meant that the majority of slaves on most West Indian plantations were African-born. As a result, African religious beliefs, patterns of speech, styles of dress and adornment, and music were prominent parts of West Indian life.

Given the harsh conditions of their lives, it is not surprising that slaves in the West Indies often sought to gain their freedom. Individual slaves often ran away, hoping to elude the men and dogs that would track them. Sometimes large groups of plantation slaves rose in rebellion against their bondage and abuse. For example, a large rebellion in Jamaica in 1760 was led by a slave named Tacky, who had been a chief on the Gold Coast of Africa. One night, his followers broke into a fort and armed themselves. Joined by slaves from nearby plantations, they stormed several plantations, setting them on fire and killing the planter families. Tacky died in the fighting, and three of his lieutenants stoically endured cruel deaths by torture meant to deter others from rebellion.

Because European planters believed that slaves with the strongest African heritage led rebellions, they tried to curtail African cultural traditions. They required slaves to learn the colonial language and discouraged the use of African languages by deliberately mixing slaves from different parts of Africa. In French and Portuguese colonies, slaves were encouraged to adopt Catholic religious practices, though

driver A privileged male slave whose job was to ensure that a slave gang did its work on a plantation.

seasoning An often difficult period of adjustment to new climates, disease environments, and work routines, such as that experienced by slaves newly arrived in the Americas.

African deities, beliefs, and practices survived. In the British West Indies, where only Quaker slave owners encouraged Christianity among their slaves before 1800, African herbal medicine remained strong, as did African beliefs concerning nature spirits and witchcraft.

As in Latin America, slavery provoked flight. In the Caribbean, runaways were known as **maroons**. Maroon communities were especially numerous in the mountainous interiors of Jamaica and Hispaniola, as well as in the inland parts of the Guianas (guy-AHN-uhs). The Jamaican maroons, after withstanding several attacks by the colony's militia, signed a treaty in 1738 that recognized their independence in return for their cooperation in stopping new runaways and suppressing slave revolts. Unable to win decisive victories, colonial authorities in Spanish, Dutch, and Portuguese colonies signed similar treaties with runaway leaders.

CREATING THE ATLANTIC ECONOMY

■ *What was the relationship between private investors and European governments in the development of the Atlantic economy?*

The West Indian plantation colonies played a crucial role in the emerging Atlantic economy. At once archaic in its cruel system of slavery and oddly modern in its specialization in a single product, the plantation system profitably dominated a broad region from the Chesapeake to the Caribbean and then to South America and Brazil. African slaves made the plantation economies possible, and profits from the exports of plantation products helped finance commercial and manufacturing expansion. Three other elements went into the creation of a new Atlantic economy: new economic institutions, new partnerships between private investors and governments in Europe, and new working relationships between European and African merchants. This new trading system is a prime example of how European capitalist relationships were reshaping the world.

The Spanish and Portuguese voyages of exploration in the fifteenth and sixteenth centuries were government ventures, and both countries tried to keep their overseas trade with colonies royal monopolies (see Chapters 15). Monopoly control, however, proved both expensive and inefficient. The success of the Atlantic economy in the seventeenth and eighteenth centuries owed much to private enterprise, which made trade more efficient and profitable.

Two European innovations, capitalism and mercantilism, enabled private investors to fund the rapid growth of the Atlantic economy. **Capitalism** was a system of large financial institutions—banks, stock exchanges, and chartered trading companies—that enabled wealthy investors to reduce risks and increase profits (see Chapter 16). Early capitalism was buttressed by **mercantilism**, policies adopted by European states to promote their citizens' overseas trade and defend it, by armed force when necessary.

maroon A slave who ran away from his or her master. Often a member of a community of runaway slaves in the West Indies and South America.

capitalism The economic system of large financial institutions—banks, stock exchanges, investment companies—that first developed in early modern Europe. *Commercial capitalism*, the trading system of the early modern economy, is often distinguished from *industrial capitalism*, the system based on machine production.

mercantilism European government policies of the sixteenth, seventeenth, and eighteenth centuries designed to promote overseas trade between a country and its colonies and accumulate precious metals by requiring colonies to trade only with their motherland country. The British system was defined by the Navigation Acts, the French system by laws known as the *Exclusif*.

Chartered companies were one of the first examples of mercantilist capitalism. A charter issued by the government of the Netherlands In 1602 gave the Dutch East India Company a legal monopoly over all Dutch trade in the Indian Ocean. This privilege encouraged private investors to buy shares in the company. They were amply rewarded when the Dutch East India Company captured control of long-distance trade in the Indian Ocean from the Portuguese (see Chapter 16). A sister firm, the **Dutch West India Company**, was chartered in 1621 to engage in the Atlantic trade by seizing sugar-producing areas in Brazil and African slaving ports from the Portuguese.

Such successes inspired other governments to set up their own chartered companies. In 1672, a royal charter placed all English trade with West Africa in the hands of the new **Royal African Company** (RAC), which established its headquarters at Cape Coast Castle, just east of Elmina on the Gold Coast. The French government also chartered East India and West India companies to reduce French dependence on Dutch and English traders. The Spanish and Portuguese governments imitated this model.

French and English governments used military force in pursuit of commercial dominance, especially to break the trading advantages of the Dutch in the Americas. Restrictions on Dutch access to French and English colonies provoked a series of wars with the Netherlands between 1652 and 1678, during which the larger English and French navies defeated the Dutch and drove the Dutch West India Company into bankruptcy.

With Dutch competition in the Atlantic reduced, the French and English limited the privileges of their chartered companies. England opened trade in Africa to any English subject in 1698 on the grounds that ending monopolies would be "highly beneficial and advantageous to this kingdom." It was hoped that such competition would also cut the cost of slaves to West Indian planters, though the demand for slaves soon drove the prices up again.

Such new mercantilist policies fostered competition among the nation's own citizens while using high tariffs and restrictions to exclude foreigners. In the 1660s, England had passes a series of Navigation Acts that confined trade with its colonies to English ships and cargoes. The French called their mercantil-

SECTION REVIEW

- Capitalism and mercantilism encouraged private funding of the Atlantic economy.
- These systems often worked through chartered companies and military force.
- Mercantilism promoted competition among a country's citizens while blocking foreign competition.

ist legislation, first codified in 1698, the *Exclusif* (ek-skloo-SEEF), highlighting its exclusionary intentions. Other mercantilist laws defended manufacturing and processing interests in Europe against competition from the colonies, imposing prohibitively high taxes on their manufactured goods and products like refined sugar.

As a result of these mercantilist measures, the Atlantic became Britain, France, and Portugal's most important overseas trading area. The value of imports from West Indian colonies alone accounted for over one-fifth the value of total British imports. The French West Indian colonies played an even larger role in France's overseas trade. Only the Dutch, closed out of much of the American trade, depended more heavily on Asian trade. Profits from the Atlantic economy, in turn, promoted further economic expansion and increased the revenues of European governments.

AFRICA AND THE ATLANTIC

■ *How was the effect of slavery on Africa different under the Atlantic system?*

The Atlantic system took a terrible toll in African lives. Many died while being marched to African ports for sale. The overall effects on Africa of these losses and of other aspects of the slave trade have been the subject of considerable historical debate. It is clear

chartered companies Groups of private investors who paid an annual fee to France and England in exchange for a monopoly over trade to the West Indies colonies.

Dutch West India Company Trading company chartered by the Dutch government to conduct its merchants' trade in the Americas and Africa.

Royal African Company A trading company chartered by the English government in 1672 to conduct its merchants' trade on the Atlantic coast of Africa.

that the trade's impact depended on the intensity and terms of involvement in different African regions.

Any assessment of the Atlantic system's effects in Africa must also take into consideration the fact that slavery had existed in Africa long before the Atlantic system. Some Africans profited from the trade, marching slaves to the coast chained together or bound to forked sticks, then bartering them to the European slavers for trade goods.

The Gold Coast and the Slave Coast

The transition to slave trading was not sudden. Even as slaves were becoming Atlantic Africa's most valuable export, goods such as gold, ivory, and timber remained important. For example, during its eight decades of operation from 1672 to 1752, the Royal African Company made 40 percent of its profits from gold, ivory, and forest products. In some parts of West Africa, such non-slave exports remained predominant even at the peak of the Atlantic trade.

African merchants were very discriminating about merchandise they took in exchange for slaves or goods. A ship that arrived with goods of low quality or not suited to local tastes found it hard to purchase a cargo at a profitable price. Textiles, hardware, and guns were in high demand. Of the goods the Royal African Company traded in West Africa in the 1680s, over 60 percent were Indian and European textiles and 30 percent were hardware and weaponry. In the eighteenth century, tobacco and rum from the Americas became welcome imports.

Both Europeans and Africans attempted to drive the best bargain for themselves and sometimes engaged in deceitful practices. The strength of the African bargaining position, however, may be inferred from the fact that as the demand for slaves rose, so too did their price in Africa. In the course of the eighteenth century the value of goods needed to purchase a slave on the Gold Coast doubled and in some places tripled or quadrupled.

African governments on the Gold and Slave Coasts forced Europeans to observe African trading customs and prevented them from taking control of African territory. Rivalry among European nations, each of which established its own trading "castles" along the Gold Coast, also reduced bargaining strength.

How did African kings and merchants obtain slaves for sale? Most accounts agree that prisoners of war were the greatest source of slaves. It is harder to prove that capturing slaves for export was a main cause of wars. An early-nineteenth-century king of Asante stated, "I cannot make war to catch slaves in the bush, like a thief. My ancestors never did so. But if I fight a king, and kill him when he is insolent, then certainly I must have his gold, and his slaves, and his people are mine too. Do not the white kings act like this?"[2] English rulers had indeed sentenced seventeenth-century Scottish and Irish prisoners to forced labor in the West Indies.

The Bight of Biafra and Angola

In the eighteenth century the slave trade expanded eastward to the Bight (bite) of Biafra. In contrast to the Gold and Slave Coasts, where strong kingdoms predominated, the densely populated interior of the Bight of Biafra contained no large states. Even so, powerful merchant princes of the coastal ports made European traders give them rich presents.

As the volume of the Atlantic trade along the Bight of Biafra expanded in the late eighteenth century, some inland markets evolved into giant fairs, with different sections specializing in slaves and imported goods. In the 1780s an English ship's doctor reported that slaves were "bought by the black traders at fairs, which are held for that purpose, at a distance of upwards of two hundred miles from the sea coast." He reported seeing from twelve hundred to fifteen hundred enslaved men and women arriving at the coast from a single fair.[3]

Angola, south of the Congo estuary, was the greatest source of slaves for the Atlantic trade. This was also the one place along the Atlantic coast where a single European nation, Portugal, controlled a significant amount of territory. Portuguese residents of the main ports served as middlemen between the caravans that arrived from the interior and the ships from Brazil. Many of the slaves sold at Angolan markets were prisoners of war captured by expanding

---

[2]King Osei Bonsu, quoted in David Northrup, ed., *The Atlantic Slave Trade* (Boston: Houghton Mifflin, 2001), 93.

[3]Alexander Falconbridge, *Account of the Slave Trade on the Coast of Africa* (London: J. Phillips, 1788), 12.

African states. As elsewhere in Africa, such prisoners seem to have been a byproduct of African wars, rather than the objective of the warring parties.

Research has linked other enslavement with environmental crisis in the hinterlands of Angola. During the eighteenth century, these southern grasslands periodically suffered severe droughts, which drove famished refugees to better-watered areas. Powerful African leaders gained control of many refugees and sold the adult males because they were more likely than women and children to escape or challenge the ruler's authority. The most successful of these inland Angolan leaders became heads of powerful new states, stabilizing areas devastated by war and drought and repopulating them with the refugees and prisoners they retained. The slave frontier then moved farther inland. This cruel system worked to the benefit of a few African rulers and merchants at the expense of the many thousands of Africans who were sent to death or perpetual bondage in the Americas.

European and Islamic Slavery

The ways in which sub-Saharan Africans established new contacts with Europe paralleled their much older pattern of relations with the Islamic world. Africans ceded very little territory to Europeans, and local African rulers kept close tabs on the European trading posts and collected lucrative rents and fees. The size of Africa's slave trade to the Islamic north also seems to have been substantial, if smaller than the transatlantic trade at its peak. Between 1600 and 1800 slave traders sent about 850,000 slaves to Muslim North Africa, and a nearly equal number of slaves from sub-Saharan Africa entered the Islamic Middle East and India by way of the Red Sea and the Indian Ocean.

In contrast to the plantation slavery of the Americas, most African slaves in the Islamic world were soldiers and servants. In the late seventeenth and eighteenth centuries Morocco's rulers employed an army of 150,000 African slaves, trusting their loyalty more than that of recruits from their own lands. Moroccans also used slaves on sugar plantations, as servants, and as artisans. Unlike in the Americas, the majority of African slaves in the Islamic world were women who served wealthy households as concubines, servants, and entertainers. The trans-Saharan slave trade also included a much higher proportion of children than the Atlantic trade.

Like Christians of this period, Muslims saw no moral impediment to owning or trading in slaves. Indeed, Islam considered enslaving "pagans" to be a meritorious act because it brought them into the faith, and it encouraged manumission Although Islam forbade the enslavement of Muslims, Muslim rulers were not strict observers of that rule (see Diversity and Dominance: Slavery in West Africa and the Americas).

While Muslims and Europeans obtained slaves from sub-Saharan Africa, the European trade was larger. The Atlantic trade carried about 8 million Africans to the Americas between 1550 and 1800. During this period the Islamic trade to North Africa and the Middle East transported perhaps 2 million African captives. Scholars generally agree on three points: (1) even at the peak of the trade in the 1700s, sub-Saharan Africa's overall population remained very large; (2) localities that contributed heavily to the slave trade, such as lands near the Slave Coast, suffered acute losses; (3) the ability of a population to recover from losses was related to the proportion of fertile women who were shipped away. The fact that Africans sold fewer women than men into the larger Atlantic trade somewhat reduced the long-term effects of this larger trade.

The slave trade had a mixed impact on sub-Saharan economies. Africans were very particular about what they received in exchange for slaves, and the limited volume of manufactured imports could not overwhelm established African weavers, metalworkers, and other producers. Some imported products like textiles and metal bars stimulated the local production of tools and clothing. While both African and European states benefited by taxing this trade, most of the economic benefits went to European nations and their American colonies, just as the profits from transporting and selling slaves mostly went to European merchants and ship owners. The American colonies were the major beneficiaries of the African slave trade. With the Amerindian population diminished by epidemics and European immigration inadequate to develop American resources, it was the forced labor of African slaves that made possible the enormous wealth produced in a vast region that spread from the

Diversity & Dominance

Slavery in West Africa and the Americas

Social diversity was common in Africa, and the domination of masters over slaves was a feature of many societies. Ahmad Baba (1556–1627) was an outstanding Islamic scholar in the city of Timbuktu. In about 1615 he replied to some questions that had been sent to him. His answers reveal a great deal about the official and unofficial condition of slavery in the Sudan of West Africa, especially in the Hausa states of Kano and Katsina.

You asked: What have you to say concerning the slaves imported from the lands of the Sudan whose people are acknowledged to be Muslims, such as Bornu, . . . Kano, Goa, Songhay, Katsina and others among whom Islam is widespread? Is it permissible to possess them [as slaves] or not?

Know—may God grant us and you success—that these lands, as you have stated are Muslim. . . . But close to each of them are lands in which are unbelievers whom the Muslim inhabitants of these lands raid. Some of these unbelievers are under the Muslims' protection and pay them [taxes]. . . . Sometimes there is war between the Muslim sultans of some of these lands and one attacks the other, taking as many prisoners as he can and selling the captive though he is a free-born Muslim. . . . This is a common practice among them in Hausaland; Katsina raids Kano, as do others, though their language is one and their situations parallel; the only difference they recognize among themselves is that so-and-so is a born Muslim and so-and-so is a born unbeliever. . . .

Whoever is taken prisoner in a state of unbelief may become someone's property, whoever he is, as opposed to those who have become Muslims of their own free will . . . and may not be possessed at all.

A little over a century later another African provided information about enslavement practices in the Western Sudan. Ayuba Suleiman Diallo (ah-YOO-bah SOO-lay-mahn JAH-loh) (1701–?), of the state of Bondu some 200 miles from the Gambia River, was enslaved and transported to Maryland, where he was a slave from 1731 to 1733. When an Englishman learned of Ayuba's literacy in Arabic, he recorded his life story, anglicizing his name to Job Solomon. According to the account, slaves in Bondu did much of the hard work, while men of Ayuba's class were free to devote themselves to the study of Islamic texts.

In February, 1730, Job's father hearing of an English ship at Gambia River, sent him, with two servants to attend him, to sell two Negroes, and to buy paper, and some other necessaries; but desired him not to venture over the river, because the country of the Mandingoes, who are enemies to the people of Futa, lies on the other side. Job not agreeing with Captain Pike (who commanded the ship, lying then at Gambia, in the service of Captain Henry Hunt, brother to Mr. William Hunt, merchant, in Little Tower-street, London) sent back the two servants to acquaint his father with it, and to let him know that he intended to go no farther. Accordingly . . . he crossed the River Gambia, and disposed of his Negroes for some cows. As he was returning home, he stopped for some refreshment at the house of an old acquaintance; and the weather being hot, he hung up his arms in the house, while he refreshed himself. . . . It happened that a company of the Mandingoes, . . . passing by at that time, and observing him unarmed, rushed in, to the number of seven or eight at once, at a back door, and pinioned Job, before he could get his arms, together with his interpreter, who is a slave in Maryland still. They then shaved their heads and beards, which Job and his man resented as the highest indignity; tho' the Mandingoes meant no more by it, than to make them appear like slaves taken in war. On the 27th of February, 1730, they carried them to Captain Pike at Gambia, who purchased them; and on the first of March they were put on board. Soon after Job found means to acquaint Captain Pike that he was the same person that came to trade with him a few days before, and after what manner he had been taken. Upon this Captain Pike gave him free leave to redeem himself and his man; and Job sent to an acquaintance of his father's, near Gambia, who promised to send to Job's father, to inform him of what had happened, that he might take some course to have him set at liberty. But it being a fortnight's [two weeks'] journey between that friend's house and his father's, and the ship sailing in about a week after, Job was brought with the rest of the slaves to Annapolis in Maryland, and delivered to Mr. Vachell Denton. . . .

➤

Mr. Vachell Denton sold Job to one Mr. Tolsey in Kent Island in Maryland, who put him to work in making tobacco; but he was soon convinced that Job had never been used to such labour. He every day showed more and more uneasiness under this exercise, and at last grew sick, being no way able to bear it; so his master was obliged to find easier work for him, and therefore put him to tend the cattle. Job would often leave the cattle, and withdraw into the woods to pray; but a white boy frequently watched him, and whilst he was at his devotion would mock him and throw dirt in his face. This very much disturbed Job, and added considerably to his other misfortunes; all which were increased by his ignorance of the English language, which prevented his complaining, or telling his case to any person about him. Grown in some measure desperate, by reason of his present hardships, he resolved to travel at a venture; thinking he might possibly be taken up by some master, who would use him better, or otherwise meet with some lucky accident, to divert or abate his grief. Accordingly, he travelled thro' the woods, till he came to the County of Kent, upon Delaware Bay. . . . There is a law in force, throughout the [mid-Atlantic] colonies . . . as far as Boston in New England, viz. that any Negroe, or white servant who is not known in the county, or has no pass, may be secured by any person, and kept in the common [jail], till the master of such servant shall fetch him. Therefore Job being able to give no account of himself, was put in prison there.

This happened about the beginning of June 1731, when I, who was attending the courts there, and heard of Job, went with several gentlemen to the [jailer's] house, being a tavern, and desired to see him. He was brought into the tavern to us, but could not speak one word of English. Upon our talking and making signs to him, he wrote a line to two before us, and when he read it, pronounced the words Allah and Mahommed; by which, and his refusing a glass of wine we offered him, we perceived he was a Mahometan [Muslim], but could not imagine of what country he was, or how he got thither; for by his affable carriage, and the easy composure of his countenance, we could perceive he was no common slave.

When Job had been some time confined, an old Negroe man, who lived in that neighborhood, and could speak the Jalloff [Wolof] language, which Job also understood, went to him, and conversed with him. By this Negroe the keeper was informed to whom Job belonged, and what was the cause of his leaving his master. The keeper thereupon wrote to his master, who soon after fetched him home, and was much kinder to him than before; allowing him place to pray in, and in some other conveniences, in order to make his slavery as easy as possible. Yet slavery and confinement was by no means agreeable to Job, who had never been used to it; he therefore wrote a letter in Arabick to his father, acquainting him with his misfortunes,

Ayuba Suleiman Diallo (1701–?) Portrait of Ayuba Suleiman Diallo, 1733 (oil on canvas), Hoare, William, of Bath (1707–92)/Private Collection/Photo © Christie's Images/The Bridgeman Art Library

hoping he might yet find means to redeem him. . . . It happened that this letter was seen by James Oglethorpe, Esq. [founder of the colony of Georgia and director of the Royal African Company]; who, according to his usual goodness and generosity, took compassion on Job, and [bought him from his master]; his master being very willing to part with him, as finding him no ways fit for his business.

In spring 1733 Job's benefactors took him to England, teaching him passable English during the voyage, and introduced him to the English gentry. Job attracted such attention that local men took up a collection to buy his freedom and pay his debts, and they also introduced him at the royal court. In 1735 Job returned to Gambia in a Royal African Company ship, richly clothed and accompanied by many gifts.

QUESTIONS FOR ANALYSIS

1. Since Ahmad Baba points out that Islamic law permitted a Muslim to raid and enslave non-Muslims, do you think that the non-Muslim Mandinka (Mandingoes) would have considered it justifiable to enslave Ayuba, since he was a Muslim?

2. Which aspects of Ayuba Suleiman's experiences of enslavement were normal, and which unusual?

3. How different might Ayuba's experiences of slavery have been had he been sold in Jamaica rather than Maryland?

4. How strictly was the ban against enslaving Muslims observed in Hausaland?

Source: Thomas Hodgkin, ed., *Nigerian Perspectives: An Historical Anthology*, 2d ed. (London: Oxford University Press, 1975), 154–156; Thomas Bluett, *Some Memoirs of the Life of Job, the Son of Solomon the High Priest of Boonda in Africa* (London: Richard Ford, 1734), 16–24.

- African trade and cultural relations with European nations paralleled already established relations with Muslim regions.

- Most slaves exported to the Western Hemisphere were prisoners of war.

- In contrast to the plantation slavery of the Americas, most African slaves sent to the Islamic world served as soldiers or servants.

- The wealth created by the labor of African slaves in the Americas significantly expanded capitalism in the seventeenth and eighteenth centuries.

Chesapeake to the Río de la Plata. This wealth accelerated the rapid expansion of Western capitalism in the seventeenth and eighteenth centuries.

CONCLUSION

The colonial empires of Spain, Portugal, France, and England had many characteristics in common. All subjugated Amerindian peoples, introduced large numbers of enslaved Africans, and transformed the natural environment. Each of the New World empires also reflected the distinctive cultural and institutional heritages of its colonizing power.

Spain's discovery of mineral wealth allowed it to develop the largest and most centralized colonial government. Portugal and France pursued similar objectives, but neither Brazil's agricultural economy, based on sugar, nor France's Canadian fur trade produced the level of centralized control achieved by Spain. There was greater cultural and religious diversity in British North

America, and the British colonial government was less centralized and in some cases more responsive to local interests.

From the seventeenth century onward, European powers expanded and created new colonies in the Caribbean. Spain's early control of the region was lost as settlers moved to the mainland once gold and silver were discovered. The British, French, and Dutch also established colonies. While tobacco initially dominated these economies, sugar eventually made these once-isolated islands part of a dynamic trading system controlled from Europe and dependent on slave labor.

European merchants and investors played a central role in the creation of the Atlantic system. By the seventeenth century an adventurous European investor class aggressively promoted colonial production and long-distance trade. The development of banks, stock exchanges, maritime insurance, and chartered companies supported these new ambitions, and the development of the Atlantic system showed their ability to move beyond capturing the benefits of existing trading systems to creating a major new trading network.

The new Atlantic system, a milestone in trade, had great importance in world history as a model of the kind of highly interactive economy that became global in later centuries. However, its transformations were destructive as well as creative, victimizing Amerindians and African slaves while benefiting European commercial and manufacturing interests. Africa played an essential role in the Atlantic system, importing trade goods and exporting slaves to the Americas. However, it was less dominated by the Atlantic system than were Europe's American colonies. Africans remained in control of their continent and interacted culturally and politically more with the Islamic world than with the Atlantic.

CHAPTER REVIEW

SPANISH AMERICA AND BRAZIL

■ *What role did forced labor play in the main industries of Spanish America and Brazil?* (page 403)

The development of the Spanish colonies was promoted by the discovery of rich gold and silver mines and by the *encomienda* and *mita*, which forced tens of thousands

of indigenous laborers to work in mines, farms, and factories. The sugar industry was crucial to Brazil. At first the enslavement of Amerindians provided labor for the sugar plantations, but eventually Brazil depended on the African slave trade, importing nearly 2 million slaves in the eighteenth century.

ENGLISH AND FRENCH COLONIES IN NORTH AMERICA

■ *What were the differences between the English and the French colonies of North America?* (page 410)

While French Canada was founded with the hope of mineral wealth, it survived on the modest profits of the fur trade. Like the Spanish and Portuguese, the French also tried to convert the Amerindian peoples. Population grew slowly, and France relied on alliances with native peoples to exploit the fur trade and protect its North American colony. First created by groups of private investors or by religious minorities, the English colonies of North America followed a different path. Because England never established centralized political control over its colonies, settlers exercised more political power. In the northern colonies, a greater gender balance led to a larger population increase than in either the French colonies or the southern colonies. Britain's North American colonies were also economically more diverse than those of France, which relied solely on the fur trade. The northern colonies attracted large numbers of free immigrants, while southern colonies relied on plantation slavery to generate wealth.

PLANTATIONS IN THE WEST INDIES

■ *What factors contributed to the development of plantations in the West Indies?* (page 414)

The islands of the West Indies were divided among a number of European powers. After devastating epidemics eliminated the indigenous populations, settlers relied heavily on slavery to produce a range of export crops. When settlers and European investors realized sugar's profitability, they were willing to finance the forced transfer of hundreds of thousands of Africans to work the Caribbean plantations. Since Africans and their American-born descendants outnumbered the Europeans across the area, African culture took root and served as an important basis for these new American societies.

CREATING THE ATLANTIC ECONOMY

■ *What was the relationship between private investors and European governments in the development of the Atlantic economy?* (page 418)

European merchants and investors played a central role in the creation of the Atlantic system. In the century before Columbus they traded over longer distances and introduced new credit mechanisms. By the seventeenth century a more confident and adventurous European investor class was ready to promote colonial production and long-distance trade in a much more aggressive way. The development of banks, stock exchanges, and chartered companies supported these new ambitions.

AFRICA AND THE ATLANTIC

■ *How was the effect of slavery on Africa different under the Atlantic system?* (page 419)

The Atlantic slave trade that began in the late fifteenth century grew spectacularly after the introduction of sugar to the Caribbean islands. The slave trade provided kingdoms on the coast of West and equatorial Africa with weapons for waging war against the peoples of the interior. These kingdoms then sold their captives to European traders as they had to Islamic traders, but the plantation slavery of the Americas was more brutal and mortality was high. The Atlantic system also had a greater effect on Africa because it enslaved many more Africans than did the Islamic trade. Ultimately, the biggest economic benefit went to European slave merchants and colonies in the Americas, where forced labor created wealth that promoted a capitalist economic system.

Key Terms

Atlantic system (p. 403)
Bartolomé de Las Casas (p. 404)
Potosí (p. 405)
encomienda (p. 405)
creoles (p. 408)
indentured servant (p. 410)
House of Burgesses (p. 410)
Pilgrims (p. 411)
Puritans (p. 411)
Iroquois Confederacy (p. 411)
New France (p. 412)
driver (p. 417)
seasoning (p. 417)
maroon (p. 418)
capitalism (p. 418)
mercantilism (p. 418)
chartered companies (p. 419)
Dutch West India Company (p. 419)
Royal African Company (p. 419)

Territorial Empires Between Europe and China

© Cengage Learning

CHAPTER PREVIEW

THE OTTOMAN EMPIRE, TO 1750

- *How did the Ottoman Empire rise to power, and what factors contributed to its transformation?*

THE SAFAVID EMPIRE, 1502–1722

- *How did the Safavid Empire both resemble and differ from its neighbors?*

THE MUGHAL EMPIRE, 1526–1761

- *How did the Mughal Empire combine Muslim and Hindu elements into an effective state?*

THE RUSSIAN EMPIRE, 1500–1762

- *What were the similarities between the Christian Russian Empire and the Muslim Ottoman, Safavid, and Mughal Empires to the south?*

THE MARITIME WORLDS OF ISLAM, 1500–1750

- *What role does maritime history play in the political and economic life of this period?*

Conclusion

ENVIRONMENT & TECHNOLOGY:
Tobacco and Waterpipes

In 1667, Stenka Razin, the leader of a robber band camped on a tributary of the Don River in southern Russia, pillaged a rich convoy of government and merchant barges on the Volga River and sailed southward toward the trading city of Astrakhan. The city's governor was unable to stop his progress, and his band established a new camp by the Caspian Sea at the mouth of the Ural River. From there Razin raided across the sea and down into Iran, defeating both Iranian and Russian armies. In 1670, his forces swollen to 20,000, Razin moved up the Volga, threatening to take Moscow and overthrow the tsar. There a tsarist army finally stopped him, and he was executed in the following year.

Razin's followers were Cossacks, people of various ethnic origins who made their way to southern Russia, many of them escaping serfdom in the north, to live as social equals in societies with minimal government and the power to maintain their independence. Modern Russian culture has glorified Razin in music and poetry as a defender of the poor and foe of noble privilege. A famous folksong portrays him sacrificing his bride for the sake of leading his warriors.

> So that peace may reign forever
> In this band so free and brave
> Volga, Volga, Mother Volga
> Make this lovely girl a grave.

A less lurid historical understanding of his revolt focuses on the unsettled state of the lands north of the Caspian Sea that had once been the center of the Mongol Golden Horde (see Chapter 12). Muslim Tatars, Buddhist Kalmyks from western Mongolia, and Orthodox Christian Ukrainians and Russians mingled in the sparsely populated frontier between the tsars, the Ottoman sultans, and the Iranian shahs.

A new trading axis was in the process of opening, one that built on the old Silk Road and linked the Ottoman, Safavid, and Mughal Empires to the south with a growing Russian Empire to the north. Russia imported cotton and silk textiles from Iran and India and exported furs, leather goods, walrus tusks, and some woolens. While few Russian merchants traveled beyond the tsarist frontiers, Indian and Armenian traders abounded, and Indian family firms resembled the Italian merchant enterprises of the Renaissance era. Twenty-seven Indians resided on the outskirts of Moscow in 1684, along with various Armenian, Iranian, and Bukharan merchants. Ten times that number lived in Astrakhan, which Ivan "the Terrible" had added to his domains in 1556 and defended against Ottoman attack in 1569.

Thus a pattern was set that would last into the twentieth century: while western Europe maintained rigid religious boundaries with very few Muslims living under Christian monarchs, Russia more closely resembled the Muslim empires to its south in tolerating the ethnic and religious diversity that had been a hallmark of Mongol rule.

In the domain of maritime trade, the European powers held a dominant position, but this did not prevent various muslim rulers from carving out their own domains.

THE OTTOMAN EMPIRE, TO 1750

■ *How did the Ottoman Empire rise to power, and what factors contributed to its transformation?*

The most durable of the post-Mongol Muslim realms was the **Ottoman Empire** (see Map 18.1), founded around 1300. By extending Islamic conquests into eastern Europe starting in the late fourteenth century, and by taking Syria and Egypt from the Mamluk rulers in the early sixteenth century, the Ottomans seemed to re-create the might of the medieval Islamic caliphate. However, the empire actually resembled the new centralized monarchies of Europe (see Chapter 16) more than any medieval model.

Enduring until 1922, the Ottoman Empire survived several periods of wrenching change, some caused by economic and political problems and others by military innovations. These periods of change reveal the problems faced by the land-based empires situated between Europe and China.

Ottoman Empire Islamic state founded by Osman in northwestern Anatolia around 1300. After the fall of the Byzantine Empire, the Ottoman Empire was based at Istanbul (formerly Constantinople) from 1453 to 1922. It encompassed lands in the Middle East, North Africa, the Caucasus, and eastern Europe.

Aya Sofya Mosque in Istanbul
Originally a Byzantine cathedral, Aya Sofya (in Greek, Hagia Sophia) was transformed into a mosque after 1453, and four minarets were added. It then became a model for subsequent Ottoman mosques. To the right behind it is the Bosporus strait dividing Europe and Asia, to the left the Golden Horn inlet separating the old city of Istanbul from the newer parts. The gate to the Ottoman sultan's palace is to the right of the mosque. The pointed tower to the left of the dome is part of the palace.

mozcann/iStockphoto.com

Expansion and Frontiers

The Ottoman Empire grew from a tiny state in northwestern Anatolia because of three factors: (1) the shrewdness of its founder, Osman (from which the name *Ottoman* comes), and his descendants, (2) control of a strategic link between Europe and Asia on the Dardanelles strait, and (3) the creation of an army that took advantage of the traditional skills of the Turkish cavalryman and the new military possibilities presented by gunpowder.

Ottoman armies attacked Christian enemies in Greece and the Balkans before conquering neighboring Muslim principalities. In 1389 a strong Serbian kingdom was defeated at the Battle of Kosovo (KO-so-vo), and by 1402 the sultans ruled much of southeastern Europe and Anatolia. In 1453, Sultan Mehmed II, "the Conqueror," laid siege to Constantinople. His forces used enormous cannon to crush the city's walls, dragged warships over a high hill from the Bosporus strait to the city's inner harbor to get around its sea defenses, and finally overcame the city's land walls with direct infantry assaults. The fall of Constantinople—henceforward commonly known as Istanbul—brought to an end over eleven hundred years of Byzantine rule and made the Ottomans seem invincible.

Selim (seh-LEEM) I, "the Grim," conquered Egypt and Syria in 1516 and 1517, making the Red Sea the Ottomans' southern frontier. His son, **Suleiman** (SOO-lay-man) **the Magnificent** (r. 1520–1566), presided over the greatest Ottoman assault on Christian Europe. Seemingly unstoppable, he conquered Belgrade in 1521, expelled the Knights of the Hospital of St. John

from the island of Rhodes the following year, and laid siege to Vienna in 1529. Vienna was saved by the need to retreat before the onset of winter more than by military action. Later Ottoman historians looked back on the reign of Suleiman as the period when the imperial system worked to perfection, and they spoke of it as the golden age of Ottoman greatness.

While Ottoman armies pressed deeper and deeper into eastern Europe, the sultans also sought to control the Mediterranean. Between 1453 and 1502, the Ottomans fought the opening rounds of a two-century war with Venice, the most powerful of Italy's commercial city-states. The initial fighting left Venice in control of its lucrative islands like Crete and Cyprus for another century. But it also left Venice a reduced military power compelled to pay tribute to the Ottomans.

In the early sixteenth century, merchants from southern India and Sumatra sent emissaries to Istanbul requesting naval support against the Portuguese. The Ottomans responded to Portuguese threats close to their territories, such as at Aden at the southern entrance to the Red Sea, but the flow of eastern luxury products to Ottoman markets was not threatened by Portuguese coastal strongholds, and by century's end the Ottomans had pulled back from maritime commitments outside the Mediterranean Sea to concentrate on defending territory in Europe.

Suleiman the Magnificent   The most illustrious sultan of the Ottoman Empire (r. 1520–1566); also known as Suleiman Kanuni, "The Lawgiver." He significantly expanded the empire in the Balkans and eastern Mediterranean.

Chronology

	Ottoman Empire	Safavid Empire	Mughal Empire	Russian Empire
1500	**1516–1517** Selim I conquers Egypt and Syria **1520–1566** Reign of Suleiman the Magnificent; peak of Ottoman Empire **1529** First Ottoman siege of Vienna **1571** Ottoman naval defeat at Lepanto	**1502–1524** Shah Ismail establishes Safavid rule in Iran **1587–1629** Reign of Shah Abbas the Great; peak of Safavid Empire	**1526** Babur defeats last sultan of Delhi **1556–1605** Akbar rules in Agra; peak of Mughal Empire	**1547** Ivan IV adopts title of *tsar* **1582** Russians conquer Khanate of Sibir
1600	**1610** End of Anatolian revolts		**1658–1707** Aurangzeb imposes conservative Islamic regime	**1613–1645** Rule of Mikhail, the first Romanov tsar **1649** Subordination of serfs complete
1700	**1730** Janissary revolt begins period of Ottoman conservatism	**1722** Afghan invaders topple last Safavid shah **1736–1747** Nadir Shah temporarily reunites Iran; invades India (1739)	**1739** Iranians under Nadir Shah sack Delhi	**1689–1725** Rule of Peter the Great **1712** St. Petersburg becomes Russian capital

Central Institutions

By the 1520s, the Ottoman Empire was the most powerful and best-organized state in either Europe or the Islamic world. Its military was balanced between cavalry archers, primarily Turks, and military slaves known as **Janissaries** (JAN-nih-say-rees) [*yeni cheri* in Turkish], who had originated as Christian prisoners of war and been converted to Islam. These new troops gave the Ottomans unusual military flexibility. Since horseback riding and bowmanship were not part of their cultural backgrounds, they readily accepted the idea of fighting on foot and learning to use guns, which at that time were still too heavy and awkward for a horseman to load and fire. The Janissaries lived in barracks and trained all year round.

The recruitment of Janissaries from prisoners changed early in the fifteenth century, when a new system imposed a levy of male children on Christian villages in the Balkans and occasionally elsewhere. Selected children were placed with Turkish families for language learning and then sent to Istanbul for an education that included instruction in Islam, military training, and, for the top 10 percent, skills that could be used in government administration. Senior military commanders and heads of government departments up to the rank of grand vizier were commonly drawn from among the chosen few who received special training.

The cavalrymen were supported by land grants and administered most rural areas in Anatolia and the Balkans. They maintained order, collected taxes, and reported for each summer's campaign with their horses, retainers, and supplies, all paid for from the

Janissaries Infantry, originally of slave origin, armed with firearms and constituting the elite of the Ottoman army from the fifteenth century until the corps was abolished in 1826.

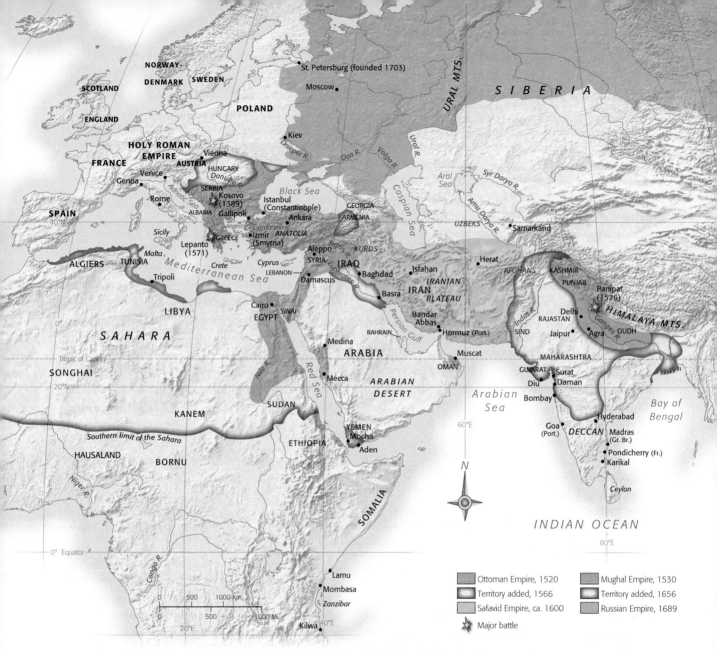

Map 18.1 Muslim Empires in the Sixteenth and Seventeenth Centuries Iran, a Shi'ite state flanked by Sunni Ottomans on the west and Sunni Mughals on the east, had the least exposure to European influences. Ottoman expansion across the southern Mediterranean Sea intensified European fears of Islam. The areas of strongest Mughal control dictated that Islam's spread into Southeast Asia would be heavily influenced by merchants and religious figures from Gujarat instead of from eastern India. © Cengage Learning

taxes they collected. When not campaigning, they stayed at home.

A galley-equipped navy was manned by Greek, Turkish, Algerian, and Tunisian sailors, usually under the command of an admiral from one of the North African ports. The balance of the Ottoman land forces brought success to Ottoman arms in recurrent wars with the Safavids of Iran, who were slower to adopt firearms, and in the inexorable conquest of

the Balkans. Expansion by sea was less dramatic. A major expedition against Malta in the western Mediterranean failed in 1565. Combined Christian forces also achieved a massive naval victory at the Battle of Lepanto, off Greece, in 1571. But the Ottomans' resources were so extensive that in a year's time they had replaced all of the galleys sunk in that battle.

The Ottoman Empire became cosmopolitan in character. The sophisticated court language,

Osmanli (os-MAHN-lih) (the Turkish form of *Ottoman*), shared basic grammar and vocabulary with Turkish, but Arabic and Persian elements made it distinct from the Turkish spoken by Anatolia's nomads and villagers. Everyone who served in the military or the bureaucracy and conversed in Osmanli was considered to belong to the *askeri* (AS-keh-ree), or "military," class. Members of this class were exempt from taxes and owed their positions to the sultan.

The Ottomans saw the sultan as providing justice for his "flock of sheep" (*raya* [RAH-yah]) and military forces to protect them. In return, the raya paid the taxes that supported both the sultan and the military. In reality, the sultan's government remained comparatively isolated from the lives of most subjects. As Islam gradually became the majority religion in some Balkan regions, Islamic law (the Shari'a [sha-REE-ah]) conditioned urban institutions and social life. Local customs prevailed among non-Muslims and in many rural areas, while non-Muslims looked to their own religious leaders for guidance in family and spiritual matters.

Crisis of the Military State, 1585–1650

As military technology evolved, cannon and lighter-weight firearms played an ever-larger role on the battlefield. Accordingly, the size of the Janissary corps—and its cost to the government—grew steadily, and the role of the Turkish cavalry diminished. To pay the Janissaries, the sultan started reducing the number of landholding cavalrymen and diverting revenues previously spent on their living expenses and military equipment to the imperial treasury. As inflation caused by a flood of cheap silver from the New World bankrupted many of the remaining landholders, who were restricted by law to collecting a fixed amount of taxes, their land returned to the state. Displaced cavalrymen, armed and unhappy, became a restive element in rural Anatolia.

This complicated situation, exacerbated after 1600 by the climatic deterioration known as the Little Ice Age (see Issues in World History: The Little Ice Age on page 466), resulted in revolts that devastated Anatolia between 1590 and 1610. Former landholding cavalrymen, short-term soldiers released at the end of the campaign season, peasants overburdened by emergency taxes, and even impoverished students of religion formed bands of marauders. Anatolia experienced the worst of the rebellions and suffered greatly from emigration and the loss of agricultural production. But an increase in banditry, made worse by the government's inability to stem the spread of muskets among the general public, beset other parts of the empire as well.

In the meantime, the Janissaries took advantage of their growing influence to gain relief from prohibitions on their marrying and engaging in business. Janissaries who involved themselves in commerce lessened the burden on the state budget, and married Janissaries who enrolled sons or relatives in the corps made it possible in the seventeenth century for the government to save state funds by abolishing forced recruitment. These savings, however, were more than offset by the increase in the total number of Janissaries and in their steady deterioration as a military force, which necessitated the hiring of more and more supplemental troops.

Economic Change and Growing Weakness

A very different Ottoman Empire emerged from this crisis. Sultans once had led armies. Now they mostly resided in palaces, and the affairs of government were overseen more and more by the chief administrators—the grand viziers. Janissaries, now a hereditary class, became a powerful faction in urban politics, sometimes controlling the tax farms that had replaced land grants as payment for military service (see Chapters 12 and 16). Tax farmers paid specific taxes, such as customs duties, in advance in return for the privilege of collecting a greater amount from the actual taxpayers.

Rural administration, already disrupted by the rebellions, suffered from the transition to tax farms. The former military landholders had kept order on their lands in order to maintain their incomes. Tax farmers were less likely to live on the land. The imperial government therefore faced greater administrative burdens and came to rely heavily on powerful provincial governors or on wealthy men who purchased lifelong tax collection rights and behaved more or less like private landowners.

Military power slowly ebbed. The ill-trained Janissaries sometimes resorted to hiring substitutes to go on campaign, and the sultans relied on partially trained seasonal recruits and on armies raised by the governors of frontier provinces. A second mighty siege of Vienna failed in 1683, and by the middle of the eighteenth century it was obvious to the Austrians and Russians that the Ottoman Empire was weakening. On the eastern front, however, Ottoman exhaustion after many wars was matched by the demise in 1722 of their perennial adversary, the Safavid state of Iran.

Although the Ottoman Empire lacked the wealth of western Europe, it remained much more prosperous than the Russian Empire. As political disorder in Safavid Iran cut deeply into Iranian silk production, overland trade from the East dwindled, but new products also came into vogue. Farmers in Greece, Macedonia, Bulgaria, and Anatolia grew mild-flavored, low-nicotine tobacco (see Environment and Technology: Tobacco and Waterpipes); and coffee, a Yemeni product, rose from obscurity in the fifteenth century to become the rage first in the Ottoman Empire and then in Europe. By 1770, however, Muslim merchants trading in the Yemeni port of Mocha (MOH-kuh) (literally "the coffee place") were charged 15 percent in duties and fees, while European traders, benefiting from long-standing trade agreements with the Ottoman Empire, paid little more than 3 percent.

Such trade agreements, called capitulations (from Latin *capitula*, or "chapter"), were first granted as favors by powerful sultans, but they eventually led to European domination of Ottoman seaborne trade. Nevertheless, the Europeans did not control strategic ports in the eastern and southern Mediterranean comparable to Malacca in the Indian Ocean and Hormuz on the Persian Gulf, so their economic power stopped short of colonial settlement or direct control in Ottoman territories.

A few astute Ottoman statesmen observed the growing disarray of the empire and advised the sultans to reestablish the land grant system and the recruitment of the Janissary corps. Most people, however, did not feel the threat or see Europe as the enemy that would eventually dismantle the empire. The Istanbul elite experimented with European clothing and furniture styles and purchased printed books from the empire's first (and short-lived) press. Ottoman historians named the period between 1718 and 1730 when European fashions were in favor the **Tulip Period** because of the craze for high-priced tulip bulbs that swept Ottoman ruling circles. The craze echoed a Dutch tulip mania that had begun in the mid-sixteenth century, when the flower was intro-

duced into Holland from Istanbul (see Chapter 16), and peaked in 1636 with particularly rare bulbs going for 2,500 florins apiece—the value of twenty-two oxen.

In 1730, however, gala soirees at which guests watched turtles with candles on their backs wander in the dark through massive tulip beds gave way to a conservative Janissary revolt with strong religious overtones. Sultan Ahmed III abdicated, and the leader of the revolt, Patrona Halil (pa-TROH-nuh ha-LEEL), an Albanian former seaman and stoker of the public baths, swaggered around the capital for several months dictating government policies before he was seized and executed.

The Patrona Halil rebellion confirmed the perceptions of a few that the Ottoman Empire was facing severe difficulties. Yet decay at the center spelled benefit elsewhere. In the provinces, ambitious and competent governors, wealthy landholders, urban notables, and nomad chieftains took advantage, and by the middle of the eighteenth century Mamluks had regained a dominant position in Egypt. Though Selim I had defeated the Mamluk sultanate in the early sixteenth century, the practice of buying slaves in the Caucasus and training them as soldiers reappeared by the end of the century in several Arab cities. In Baghdad, Janissary commanders and Georgian Mamluks competed for power, with the

---

Tulip Period Last years of the reign of Ottoman sultan Ahmed III (1718–1730), during which European styles and attitudes became briefly popular in Istanbul.

SECTION REVIEW

- The Ottoman Empire grew through the skill of its founding rulers, control of strategic territory, and military power.

- The empire expanded into southern and eastern Europe, the Middle East, and Africa, reaching its height under Suleiman the Magnificent.

- Unwilling to build a strong navy, the Ottomans never adapted to developments in the Indian Ocean.

- The empire rested on the military led by the sultan, and changes in military structure ultimately weakened the state.

- As the imperial economy reoriented toward Europe, the central government weakened, permitting the rise of local powers.

environment & technology

Tobacco and Waterpipes

Tobacco, a plant native to the Western Hemisphere, may have been introduced into Ottoman Syria as early as 1570 and was certainly known in Istanbul by 1600. In Iran, one historian noted that when an Uzbek ruler entered the northeast province of Khurasan in 1612 and called for tobacco, it was quickly provided for him, while a Spanish diplomat remarked just a few years later that Shah Abbas, who had banned smoking as a sinful practice, nevertheless permitted an envoy from the Mughal sultan to indulge. European traders initially brought tobacco by sea, but it quickly became a cultivated crop in Mughal India, whence it was exported to Iran. By the middle of the seventeenth century, however, it had also become a significant crop in Ottoman and Safavid territories.

The waterpipe became a distinctive means of smoking in the Islamic world, but when the device came into use is disputed. Iranian historians assert that it was invented in Iran, where one reference in poetry goes back to before 1550. This early date suggests that waterpipes may have been used for smoking some other substance before tobacco became known. Straight pipes of clay or wood were also used, especially in Turkish areas and among poorer people.

The Persian word for a waterpipe, *qalyan*, comes from an Arabic verb meaning "to boil, or bubble." Arabic has two common words: *nargila*, which derives ultimately from the Sanskrit word for "coconut," and *shisha*, which means "glass" in Persian. In India, where coconuts were often used to contain the water, the usual term was *hookah*, meaning "jar." The absence of a clear linguistic indication of the country of origin enhances the possibility that waterpipes evolved and spread before the introduction of tobacco.

All levels of society took to smoking, with women enjoying it as much as men. The leisurely ceremony of preparing and lighting the waterpipe made it an ideal pastime in coffeehouses, which became popular in both the Ottoman and Safavid Empires. In other settings, the size and fragility of

From Rudi Matthee, *The Pursuit of Pleasure: Drugs and Stimulants in Iranian History, 1500—1900* (Princeton: Princeton University Press) p. 125

Iranian Waterpipe *Moistened tobacco is placed in cup A, and a glowing coal is put on top of it to make it smolder. When the smoker draws on the stem sticking out to the side, the smoke bubbles up from beneath the water, which cools and filters it. The sophisticated manufacture shown in this drawing, which was rendered in 1622, supports the theory that the waterpipe went through a lengthy period of development before the seventeenth century.*

the waterpipe could cause inconvenience. When traveling, wealthy Iranian men sometimes had a pipe carrier in their entourage who carried the *qalyan* in his hand and had a small pot containing hot coals dangling from his saddle in case his master should wish to light up on the road.

latter emerging triumphant by the mid-eighteenth century. In Aleppo and Damascus, however, the Janissaries came out on top. Meanwhile, in central Arabia, a puritanical Sunni movement inspired by

Muhammad ibn Abd al-Wahhab began a remarkable rise beyond the reach of Ottoman power. Although no region declared full independence, the sultan's power was slipping away in all parts of the empire while the Ottoman economy was reorienting itself toward Europe.

THE SAFAVID EMPIRE, 1502–1722

■ *How did the Safavid Empire both resemble and differ from its neighbors?*

The **Safavid Empire** of Iran (see Map 18.1) resembled its long-time Ottoman foe in many ways: it initially relied militarily on cavalry paid through land grants, and its population spoke several languages and included many non-Muslims. It also had distinct qualities that to this day set Iran off from its neighbors: it derived part of its legitimacy from the pre-Islamic dynasties of ancient Iran, and it adopted the Shi'ite form of Islam.

Safavid Society and Religion

The ultimate victor in a complicated struggle for power among Turkish chieftains east of the Ottoman lands was Ismail (IS-ma-eel), a boy of Kurdish, Iranian, and Greek ancestry. In 1502, at age sixteen, Ismail proclaimed himself shah of Iran and declared that from that time forward his realm would be devoted to **Shi'ite** Islam, which revered the family of Muhammad's cousin and son-in-law Ali (see Chapter 9). Although Ismail's reasons for compelling Iran's conversion to Shi'ism are unknown, the effect of this radical act was to create a deep chasm between Iran and its Sunni Muslim neighbors. Iran became a truly separate country for the first time since its incorporation into the Islamic caliphate in the seventh century.

The imposition of Shi'ite belief confirmed differences between Iran and its neighbors that had been long in the making. Persian, written in the Arabic script from the tenth century onward, had emerged as the second language of Islam. Iranian scholars and writers normally read Arabic as well as Persian and sprinkled their writings with Arabic phrases, but their Arab counterparts were much less inclined to learn Persian. After the Mongols destroyed Baghdad, the capital of the Islamic caliphate, in 1258, Iran developed largely on its own, having more extensive contacts with India—where Muslim rulers favored the Persian language—than with the Arabs.

In the post-Mongol period, artistic styles in Iran, Afghanistan, and Central Asia also went their own

way. Painted and molded tiles and tile mosaics, often in vivid turquoise blue, became the standard exterior decoration of mosques in Iran but were never used in Syria and Egypt. Persian poets raised verse to peaks of perfection that had no counterpart in Arabic poetry, generally considered to be in a state of decline.

To be sure, Islam itself provided a tradition of belief, learning, and law that crossed ethnic and linguistic borders, but Shah Ismail's imposition of Shi'ism set Iran significantly apart. Shi'ite doctrine says that all temporal rulers, regardless of title, are temporary stand-ins for the **Hidden Imam**, the twelfth descendant of Ali, the Prophet Mohammad's cousin and son-in-law who disappeared as a child in the ninth century. Some Shi'ite scholars taught the faithful to calmly accept the world as it was and wait quietly for the Hidden Imam's return. Others maintained that they themselves should play a stronger role in political affairs because they were best qualified to know the Hidden Imam's wishes. These two positions, which still play a role in Iranian Shi'ism, enhanced the self-image of religious scholars as independent of imperial authority and stood in the way of their becoming subordinate government functionaries, as happened in the Ottoman Empire.

Shi'ism also affected popular psychology. Annual commemoration of the martyrdom of Imam Husayn (d. 680), Ali's son and third Imam, regularized an emotional outpouring with no parallel in Sunni lands. Day after day for two weeks, preachers recited the woeful tale to crowds of weeping believers, and elaborate street processions, often organized by craft guilds, paraded chanting and self-flagellating men past crowds of reverent onlookers. Of course, Shi'ites elsewhere observed rites of mourning for Imam Husayn, but the impact of these rites was especially great in Iran, where 90 percent of the population was

---

Safavid Empire Iranian kingdom (1502–1722) established by Ismail Safavi, who declared Iran a Shi'ite state.

Shi'ites Muslims belonging to the branch of Islam believing that God vests leadership of the community in a descendant of Muhammad's son-in-law Ali. Shi'ism is the state religion of Iran.

Hidden Imam Last in a series of twelve descendants of Muhammad's son-in-law Ali, whom Shi'ites consider divinely appointed leaders of the Muslim community. In occlusion since around 873, he is expected to return as a messiah at the end of time.

Shi'ite. Over time, the subjects of the Safavid shahs came to feel more than ever a people apart.

A Tale of Two Cities: Isfahan and Istanbul

Outwardly, Ottoman Istanbul looked quite different from Isfahan (is-fah-HAHN), which became Iran's capital in 1598 by decree of **Shah Abbas I** (r. 1587–1629). Built on seven hills beside the narrow Golden Horn inlet, Istanbul boasted a skyline punctuated by the gray stone domes and thin, pointed minarets of the great imperial mosques. The mosques surrounding the royal plaza in Isfahan, in contrast, had unobtrusive minarets and brightly tiled domes. High walls surrounded the sultan's palace in Istanbul. Shah Abbas in Isfahan focused his capital on the giant royal plaza, which was large enough for his army to play polo, and he used an airy palace overlooking the plaza to receive dignitaries and review his troops.

Istanbul's harbor teemed with sailing ships and smaller craft, many of them belonging to a colony of European merchants perched on a hilltop on the other side of the Golden Horn. Isfahan, far from the sea, was only occasionally visited by Europeans. Trade was mostly in the hands of Jews, Hindus, and Jains from India, and especially a colony of Armenian Christians brought in by Shah Abbas.

Beneath these superficial differences, the two capitals had much in common. Wheeled vehicles were scarce in Istanbul and nonexistent in Isfahan. Both cities were built for walking and, aside from the royal plaza in Isfahan, lacked the open spaces common in contemporary European cities. Streets were narrow and irregular. Houses crowded against each other in dead-end lanes. Residents enjoyed their privacy in interior courtyards. Artisans and merchants organized themselves into guilds that had strong social and religious bonds. Shops adjoined one another in the markets.

Women seldom appeared in public, even in Istanbul's mazelike covered market or in Isfahan's long, serpentine bazaar. At home, the women's quarters—called *anderun* (an-deh-ROON), or "interior," in Iran and *harem*, or "forbidden area," in Istanbul—were separate from the public rooms where the men of the family received visitors. In both areas, low cushions, charcoal braziers for warmth, carpets, and small tables constituted most of the furnishings.

SuperStock/Glow Images, Inc.

Mughal Emperor Jahangir Embracing the Safavid Shah Abbas Painted by the Mughal artist Abu al-Hasan around 1620, this miniature shows the artist's patron, Jahangir, on the right standing on a lion, dominating the diminutive Shah Abbas, standing on a sheep. Though this may accurately reflect Jahangir's view of their relationship, in fact Shah Abbas was a powerful rival for control of Afghanistan, the gateway to India and the meeting point of the lion and the sheep. The globe the monarchs stand on reflects the spread of accurate geographical ideas into the Muslim world.

The private side of family life has left few traces, but women's society—consisting of wives, children, female servants, and sometimes one or more eunuchs—was not entirely cut off from the outside world. Ottoman court records reveal that women, using male agents, were very active in the urban real estate market. Often they were selling inherited shares of their father's estate, but some both bought and sold real estate on a regular basis and even established

Shah Abbas I The fifth and most renowned ruler of the Safavid dynasty in Iran (r. 1587–1629). Abbas moved the royal capital to Isfahan in 1598.

religious endowments for pious purposes. The fact that Islamic law, unlike European codes, permitted a wife to retain her property after marriage gave some women a stake in the general economy and a degree of independence from their spouses. Women also appeared in other types of court cases, where they often testified for themselves, for Islamic courts did not recognize the role of attorney. Although comparable Safavid court records do not survive, historians assume that a parallel situation prevailed in Iran.

European travelers commented on the veiling of women outside the home, but the norm for both sexes was complete coverage of arms, legs, and hair. Miniature paintings indicate that ordinary female garb consisted of a long, ample dress with a scarf or shawl pulled tight over the forehead to conceal the hair. Lightweight baggy trousers were worn under the dress. This mode of dress differed little from that of men. Poor men wore light trousers, a long shirt, a jacket, and a hat or turban. Wealthier men wore over their trousers ankle-length caftans, often closely fitted around the chest.

Public life was a male domain. Poetry and art, both more elegantly developed in Isfahan than in Istanbul, were as likely to extol the charms of beardless boys as pretty women. Despite religious disapproval of homosexuality, attachments to adolescent boys were neither unusual nor hidden. Women who appeared in public—aside from non-Muslims, the aged, and the very poor—were usually slaves. Miniature paintings frequently depict female dancers,

Austrian National Library, picture archive

Istanbul Family on the Way to a Bath House Public baths, an important feature of Islamic cities, set different hours for men and women. Young boys, such as the lad in the turban shown here, went with their mothers and sisters. Notice that the children wear the same styles as the adults.

musicians, and even acrobats in attitudes and costumes that range from decorous to decidedly erotic.

Despite social similarities, the overall flavors of Isfahan and Istanbul were not the same. Isfahan had its prosperous Armenian quarter across the river from the city's center, but it was not as cosmopolitan as Istanbul. Shah Abbas located his capital toward the center of his domain away from any unstable frontier. Istanbul, in contrast, was a great seaport and a crossroads located on the straits separating the sultan's European and Asian possessions. People of all sorts

Royal Square in Isfahan Built by the order of Shah Abbas over a period of twenty years starting in 1598, the open space is as long as five football fields (555 by 172 yards). At the right end, not shown in this photograph, is the entrance to the covered bazaar. The dominating structure is the immense Royal Mosque at the left-hand end. The seven-story "High Porte" pavilion overlooking the far side of the reflecting pool was the entrance to an extensive palace complex, now mostly gone. Its richly painted rooms were used for entertaining guests. Opposite it is a smaller mosque without minarets used only by the ruler and his household. Georg Gerster/Photo Researchers, Inc.

lived or spent time in Istanbul: Venetians, Genoese, Arabs, Turks, Greeks, Armenians, Albanians, Serbs, Jews, Bulgarians, and more. In this respect, Istanbul conveyed the cosmopolitan character of major seaports from Venice to Canton (Guangzhou), though its prosperity rested on the vast reach of the sultan's territories rather than on the voyages of merchants.

Economic Crisis and Political Collapse

The silk fabrics of northern Iran were the mainstay of the Safavid Empire's foreign trade. However, the product that eventually became associated with Iran was the deep-pile carpet made by knotting colored yarns around stretched warp threads, work often done by women and girls. Different cities produced distinctive carpet designs.

Overall, Iran's manufacturing sector was neither large nor notably productive. Most of the shah's subjects, whether Iranians, Turks, Kurds, or Arabs, lived by subsistence farming or herding. Neither area of activity recorded significant technological advances during the Safavid period.

The Safavids, like the Ottomans, had difficulty finding the money to pay troops armed with firearms. The crisis occurred somewhat later in Iran because of its geographic distance from Europe. By the end of the sixteenth century, it was evident that a more systematic adoption of cannon and firearms in the Safavid Empire would be needed to hold off the Ottomans and the Uzbeks (UHZ-bex), Turkish rulers who had succeeded the Timurids on Iran's Central Asian frontier (see Map 18.1). Like the Ottoman cavalry a century earlier, warriors from nomadic groups were not inclined to trade their bows for firearms. Shah Abbas responded by establishing a slave corps of year-round soldiers and arming them with guns. The Christian converts to Islam who initially provided the manpower for the new corps were mostly captives taken in raids on Georgia in the Caucasus (CAW-kuh-suhs).

In the late sixteenth century, the inflation caused by cheap silver spread into Iran; then overland trade through Safavid territory declined because of mismanagement of the silk monopoly after Shah Abbas's death in 1629. As a result, the later shahs could not afford to pay their army and bureaucracy. Trying to unseat the nomads from their lands to regain control of taxes was

SECTION REVIEW

- The rise of the Shi'ite Safavid Empire completed the long-growing split between Iran and its neighbors.
- Despite significant differences, Istanbul and Isfahan reflected some cultural similarities between the Ottoman and Safavid Empires.
- Silks and carpets were important manufactures, but most Safavid subjects made a living by farming or herding.
- High military costs, inflation, and decline of overland trade weakened the state, which fell to Afghan invaders in 1722.

more difficult and more disruptive militarily than the piecemeal dismantlement of the land-grant system in the Ottoman Empire. The nomads remained cohesive military forces, and pressure from the center simply caused them to withdraw to their mountain pastures. By 1722, the government had become so weak and commanded so little support from the nomadic groups that an army of marauding Afghans was able to capture Isfahan and effectively end Safavid rule.

THE MUGHAL EMPIRE, 1526–1761

■ *How did the Mughal Empire combine Muslim and Hindu elements into an effective state?*

What distinguished the Indian empire of the Mughal (MOH-guhl) sultans from the empires of the Ottomans and Safavids was the fact that India was a land of Hindus ruled by a Muslim minority. Muslim domain was established by repeated military campaigns from the early eleventh century onward, and even five centuries later Hindus still resented the Muslims. Thus, the challenge facing the Mughals was not just conquering and organizing a large territorial state but also finding a formula for Hindu-Muslim coexistence.

Political Foundations

Babur (BAH-bur) (1483–1530), the founder of the **Mughal Empire**, was a Muslim descendant of both Timur and Chinggis Khan (*Mughal* is

Mughal Empire Muslim state (1526–1857) exercising dominion over most of India in the sixteenth and seventeenth centuries. Fragmentation of power and growth of English imperial strength marked the subsequent period.

Persian for "Mongol"). Invading from Central Asia, Babur defeated the last Muslim sultan of Delhi (DEL-ee) in 1526. Babur's grandson **Akbar** (r. 1556–1605) established the central administration of the expanding state. Under him and his three successors—the last of whom died in 1707—all but the southern tip of India fell under Mughal rule, administered first from Agra and then from Delhi.

Akbar, a brilliant but mercurial man, granted land revenues to military officers and government officials in return for their service. Assignments of land revenue, called *mansabs* (MAN-sab), some large and some small, determined their holders ranks. As in the other Islamic empires, revenue grants were not considered hereditary, and the central government kept careful track of them.

With a population of 100 million, a thriving trade in cotton cloth, and a generally efficient administration, India under Akbar was the most prosperous empire of the sixteenth century. He and his successors faced few external threats and experienced generally peaceful conditions in their northern Indian heartland.

European trade boomed at the port of Surat in the northwest, but merchants from Multan, today on the Indus River in Pakistan, did more business overland with Iran and Russia. Lacking a regular navy, the rulers saw the Europeans—after Akbar's time, primarily Dutch and English, the Portuguese having lost most of their Indian ports—less as enemies than as shipmasters whose support could be procured as needed in return for trading privileges.

Hindus and Muslims

The Mughal state inherited traditions of religious tolerance from both the Islamic caliphate and the Mongols. Seventy percent of the *mansabdars* (man-sab-DAHRZ) (officials holding land revenues) appointed under Akbar were Muslim soldiers born outside India, but 15 percent were Hindus. Most of the Hindu appointees were warriors from the north called **Rajputs** (RAHJ-putz), one of whom rose to be a powerful revenue minister.

Akbar, the most Illustrious ruler of his dynasty, differed from his Ottoman and Safavid counterparts—Suleiman the Magnificent and Shah Abbas the Great—in his striving for social harmony and not just for

territory and revenue. His marriage to a Rajput princess encouraged reconciliation and even intermarriage between Muslims and Hindus. The birth of a son in 1569 ensured that future rulers would have both Muslim and Hindu ancestry.

Akbar ruled that in legal disputes between two Hindus, decisions would be made according to village custom or Hindu law as interpreted by local Hindu scholars. Shari'a law was for Muslims. Akbar made himself the legal court of last resort.

Akbar also made himself the center of a new "Divine Faith" incorporating Muslim, Hindu, Zoroastrian, Sikh (sick), and Christian beliefs. He liked Sufi ideas, which permeated the religious rituals he instituted at court. To promote serious consideration of his religious doctrines, he personally oversaw, from an elevated catwalk, debates among scholars of all religions assembled in his octagonal audience chamber. When courtiers uttered the Muslim exclamation "Allahu Akbar"—"God is great"—they also understood it in its second grammatical meaning: "God is Akbar."

Akbar's religious views did not survive him, but the court culture he fostered, reflecting a mixture of Muslim and Hindu traditions, flourished until his zealous great-grandson Aurangzeb (ow-rang-ZEB) (r. 1658–1707) reinstituted many restrictions on Hindus. Mughal and Rajput miniature paintings reveled in realistic portraits of political figures and depictions of scantily clad women, even though they brought frowns to the faces of pious Muslims, who deplored the representation of human beings. Most of the leading painters were Hindus. In addition to the florid style of Persian verse favored at court, a new taste developed for poetry and prose in the popular language of the Delhi region. The modern descendant of this language is called *Urdu* in Pakistan and *Hindi* in India.

Akbar Most illustrious sultan of the Mughal Empire in India (r. 1556–1605). He expanded the empire and pursued a policy of conciliation with Hindus.

mansabs In India, grants of land given in return for service by rulers of the Mughal Empire.

Rajputs Members of a mainly Hindu warrior caste from northwest India. The Mughal emperors drew most of their Hindu officials from this caste, and Akbar married a Rajput princess.

Akbar Tames the Savage Elephant, Hawa'i, Outside the Red Fort at Agra, miniature from the Akbarnama of Abul Fazl, c. 1590 (left-hand side of double page miniature, see 4042) (gouache on paper), Basawan and Chatai (fl.1590)/British Museum, London, UK/The Bridgeman Art Library

Elephants Breaking Bridge of Boats This illustration of an incident in the life of Akbar illustrates the ability of Mughal miniature painters to depict unconventional action scenes. Because the flow of rivers in India and the Middle East varied greatly from dry season to wet season, boat bridges were much more common than permanent constructions.

Central Decay and Regional Challenges Mughal power did not long survive Aurangzeb's death in 1707. Some historians consider the land-grant system a central element in the rapid decline of imperial authority, but other factors were at play as well. Aurangzeb's additions to Mughal territory in southern India were not all well integrated into the imperial structure, and strong regional powers arose to challenge Mughal military supremacy. A climax came in 1739 when Nadir Shah, a warlord who had seized power in Iran after the fall of the Safavids, invaded the Mughal capital and carried off to Iran the "peacock throne," the priceless jewel-encrusted symbol of Mughal grandeur. Another throne was found for the later Mughals

to sit on; but their empire, which survived in name to 1857, was finished.

In 1723, Nizam al-Mulk (nee-ZAHM al-MULK), the sultan's powerful vizier, gave up on the central government and established his own nearly independent state at Hyderabad in the eastern Deccan. Other officials bearing the title *nawab* (nah-WAHB) became similarly independent in Bengal and Oudh (OW-ad) in the northeast, as did the militant Marathas in the center. In the northwest, simultaneous Iranian and Mughal weakness allowed the Afghans to establish an independent kingdom.

Some of the new regional powers were prosperous and benefited from the removal of the sultan's heavy hand. Linguistic and religious communities, freed from Aurangzeb's religious intolerance, similarly enjoyed greater opportunity for political expression. However, this disintegration of central power favored the intrusion of European adventurers.

In 1741 Joseph François Dupleix (doo-PLAY) took over the presidency of the French stronghold of Pondicherry (pon-dih-CHER-ree), thus beginning a new phase of European involvement in India. He captured the English trading center of Madras and used his small contingent of European and European-trained Indian troops to become a power broker in southern India. Though offered the title *nawab*, Dupleix preferred to operate behind the scenes, using Indian princes as puppets. His career ended in 1754 when he was called home. Deeply involved in European wars, the French government declined further adventures in India. Dupleix's departure opened the way for the British, whose exploits in India are described in Chapter 23.

SECTION REVIEW

- Founded by Babur, the Mughal Empire grew under Akbar and his successors to encompass most of India.

- The empire prospered through trade and granted trade privileges to Europeans in exchange for naval support.

- Akbar included both Muslims and Hindus in his government, respected Hindu customs, and strove for religious harmony.

- A hybrid culture flourished, but Aurangzeb practiced Muslim intolerance.

- After Aurangzeb's death, the empire declined through foreign invasion, the rise of regional powers, and European encroachment.

THE RUSSIAN EMPIRE, 1500–1762

■ *What were the similarities between the Christian Russian Empire and the Muslim Ottoman, Safavid, and Mughal Empires to the south?*

Before 1500, the Russian principalities had been dominated by steppe nomads (see Chapter 12). During the next three centuries, however, the rulers of **Muscovy** (MUSS-koe-vee), the principality based on Moscow (a forest zone north of the steppe), forged an empire that stretched from eastern Europe across northern Asia and into North America. Moving against the Mongol Golden Horde (also known as *Tatars*), the princes of Muscovy ruthlessly annexed the territories of the neighboring Russian state of Novgorod, which lay on the Volga River, in 1478. Prince Ivan IV (r. 1533–1584), known as "the Terrible" (meaning the fearsome), pushed Muscovy's conquests further along the Volga River east and south at the expense of the Tatar khanates of Kazan and Astrakhan.

The Russian church called Moscow the "third Rome" and the successor to Constantinople, which the Ottomans took in 1453, and in 1547 the Russian ruler formally took the title **tsar** (zahr), a title based on the Roman imperial title *caesar* that had been previously reserved for such foreign rulers as the Mongols. Despite these grand titles, in 1600 the empire was poor, backward, and landlocked. Only one seaport—Arkhangelsk near the Arctic circle—connected Russia to the world's oceans. The Crimean Tatars to the south were powerful enough to sack Moscow in 1571, just as Stenka Razin's Cossacks from a nearby region threatened to do a century later. Beyond them, the Ottoman Empire controlled access to the Black Sea, while trade with India had to go through Iran. The kingdoms of Sweden and Poland-Lithuania to the west similarly blocked Russian access to the Baltic Sea.

The one route open to expansion, **Siberia**, turned out to be Russia's version of the New World, an immense northern region of little-known peoples and untapped resources. Particularly prized was the soft, dense fur of sables and other forest animals who were able to survive the long winters. Foragers, reindeer herders, and the Khanate of Sibir were no match for the rifles of Russian troops hired to protect explorers and fur trappers who moved through the frozen forests by river. After reaching the Pacific Ocean during the seventeenth century, the Russians crossed over into Alaska. The Khanate of Sibir fell in 1582, but Russian political control followed more slowly. Beginning in the early seventeenth century, the tsars used Siberia as a penal colony. In the 1640s Russian settlers began to grow grain in the Amur River Valley east of Mongolia, where they came into contact with Chinese authorities (see Chapter 19).

Russian Society and Politics to 1725

As the empire expanded, it incorporated people with different languages, religious beliefs, and ethnic identities. Orthodox missionaries strove to Christianize the peoples of Siberia, but among the relatively more populous steppe peoples, Islam prevailed as the dominant religion. Differences in how people outside of cities made their living were equally fundamental. Russians tended to live as farmers and hunters, while the peoples newly incorporated into the empire were either herders and caravan workers or hunters and fishers living along the Siberian rivers.

Diversity prevailed even among Russian speakers of Orthodox faith. The name *Cossack*, referring to bands of people living on the steppes between Moscovy and the Caspian and Black Seas, probably comes from a Turkish word for a warrior or mercenary soldier. Actually, Cossacks had diverse origins and beliefs, but they all belonged to close-knit bands, fought superbly from the saddle, and terrified both villagers and legal authorities. Cossack allegiances with rulers were temporary; loyalty to the chiefs of their bands was paramount.

Muscovy The Russian principality that emerged gradually during the era of Mongol domination. The muscovite dynasty ruled without interruption from 1276 to 1598.

tsar (czar) From Latin *caesar*, this Russian title for a monarch was first used in reference to a Russian ruler by Ivan III (r. 1462–1505).

Siberia The extreme northeastern sector of Asia, including the Kamchatka Peninsula and the present Russian coast of the Arctic Ocean, the Bering Strait, and the Sea of Okhotsk.

Cossacks Peoples of the Russian Empire who lived outside the farming villages, often as herders, mercenaries, or outlaws. Cossacks led the expansion into Siberia in the sixteenth and seventeenth centuries.

Cossacks provided most of the soldiers employed by the early fur traders, and they founded every major town in Russian Siberia. They also manned the Russian camps on the Amur River and protected settlers. West of the Urals the Cossacks defended Russia against Swedish and Ottoman incursions, but they also preserved their political autonomy (as discussed at the beginning of this chapter).

In the early seventeenth century, a "Time of Troubles" that coincided with the beginning of the Little Ice Age (see Issues in World History, page 466) and that was marked by famine and warfare ended the old line of Muscovite rulers. On separate occasions, Swedish and Polish forces occupied Moscow. Russian aristocrats (boyars [BOY-ars]) responded to this period of internal disorder by electing a new tsar, Mikhail Romanov (ROH-man-off or roh-MAN-off) (r. 1613–1645). Mikhail defended Russia from neighboring powers and inaugurated a new Romanov dynasty, characterizing the Turkish steppe peoples as "infidels" and "barbarians" and Russians as "civilized "and "Christian." Despite this rhetoric, there were many similarities between the Russian Empire and its Muslim neighbors to the south.

Like the sultans and shahs, Moscovy rulers rewarded the military service of nobles with land grants. Peasants were obliged to work for the lord, and the rising commercialization of agriculture raised the value of these labor obligations. Law and custom permitted peasants to change masters during a two-week period each year, which encouraged lords to treat their peasants well, but warfare in the late sixteenth and early seventeenth centuries disrupted peasant life, and many fled to the Cossacks or into Siberia. Those who stayed sold themselves into slavery to keep from starving.

When peace returned, landlords sought to recover the runaways and bind them more tightly to their land. A law change in 1649 eliminated the period when peasants could change masters and ordered runaways to return to their masters, transforming peasants into **serfs**. Like slavery, serfdom was hereditary. In theory the serf was tied to a piece of land, not owned by a master. In practice, strict laws narrowed the difference between serf and slave. In the Russian census of 1795, serfs made up over half the population; landowners made up only 2 percent.

Peter the Great

The greatest of the Romanov tsars, **Peter the Great** (r. 1689–1725), came to the throne a century or so later than the eminent Muslim potentates Suleiman the Magnificent, the Safavid shah Abbas, and the Mughal sultan Akbar. Whereas Suleiman fought wars with Europeans, and Abbas and Akbar knew Europeans as merchant adventurers, Peter was aware that Europe's wealth and military power had increased enormously. The "Tulip Period" that coincided with Peter's reign reveals Ottoman awareness of Europe, but no Muslim notable could safely sojourn in Christian Europe long enough to master the new techniques of ruling and acquiring power.

When Peter ascended the throne, there were already hundreds of foreign merchants in Moscow, as there were in Istanbul. Military officers from western Europe introduced new weapons and techniques, and Italian builders influenced church and palace architecture. Peter accelerated these tendencies in unprecedented fashion. While his half-sister Sophia governed as regent for him and her sickly brother Ivan, he lived on an estate near the foreigners' quarter outside Moscow, gaining practical skills in blacksmithing, carpentry, shipbuilding, and the arts of war. When Princess Sophia tried to take complete control of the government in 1689, Peter rallied enough support to send her to a monastery, secure the abdication of Ivan, and take charge of Russia. He was still in his teens.

To secure a port on the Black Sea, Peter constructed a small but formidable navy. Describing his wars with the Ottoman Empire as a new crusade to liberate Constantinople from the Muslim sultans, Peter fancied himself the legal protector of Orthodox Christians living under Ottoman rule. His forces seized the port of Azov in 1696 but lost it again in 1713, thus calling a halt to southward expansion.

In the winter of 1697–1698, after his Black Sea campaign, Peter traveled in disguise across Europe

serf In medieval Europe, an agricultural laborer legally bound to a lord's property and obligated to perform set services for the lord. In Russia some serfs worked as artisans and in factories; serfdom was not abolished there until 1861.

Peter the Great Russian tsar (r. 1689–1725). He enthusiastically introduced Western languages and technologies to the Russian elite and moved the capital from Moscow to the new city of St. Petersburg.

to discover how western European societies were becoming so powerful and wealthy. He paid special attention to ships and weapons, even working for a time as a ship's carpenter in the Netherlands. Upon his return to Russia, Peter resolved to expand and reform his vast but backward empire.

In the long and costly Great Northern War (1700–1721), Peter's modernized armies broke Swedish control of the Baltic Sea, making possible more direct contacts between Russia and Europe. This victory forced the European powers for the first time to recognize Russia as a major power. Then, Peter captured from Sweden the eastern end of the Baltic and built St. Petersburg, his window on the West. In 1712 the city became Russia's capital. To demonstrate Russia's new sophistication, Peter ordered architects to build St. Petersburg's houses and public buildings in the baroque style then fashionable in France.

Peter also pushed the Russian elite to imitate European fashions. He personally shaved off some of his noblemen's long beards to conform to Western styles. To end the traditional seclusion of upper-class Russian women, Peter required officials, military officers, and merchants to bring their wives to the social gatherings he organized in the capital. He also directed the nobles to educate their children.

A decree of 1716 proclaimed that the tsar "is not obliged to answer to anyone in the world for his doings, but possesses power and authority over his kingdom and land, to rule them at his will and pleasure as a Christian ruler." Under this expansive definition of his role, Peter sharply reduced the traditional roles of the boyars in government and the army, brought the Russian Orthodox Church more firmly under state control, built factories and foundries to provide supplies for the military, increased taxes, and imposed more forced labor on the serfs. Peter was an absolutist ruler of the sort then common in western Europe (see Chapter 16), but he is equally comparable to the most authoritarian rulers in the contemporary Muslim empires.

SECTION REVIEW

- Russia grew vastly by colonizing Siberia.
- Lacking seaports, Russia relied on overland trade with European and Muslim neighbors.
- Peter the Great copied western European military and economic techniques and imposed a complete autocracy on his subjects.

THE MARITIME WORLDS OF ISLAM, 1500–1750

■ *What role does maritime history play in the political and economic life of this period?*

As land powers, the Mughal, Safavid, Ottoman, and Russian Empires faced similar problems in the seventeenth and eighteenth centuries. Complex changes in military technology and in the world economy, along with the increasing difficulty of basing an extensive land empire on military forces paid through land grants, affected them all adversely.

The new pressures faced by land powers were less important to seafaring countries intent on turning trade networks into maritime empires. Improvements in ship design, navigation accuracy, and the use of

The Fontanka Canal in St. Petersburg in 1753 The Russian capital continued to grow as a commercial and administrative center. As in Amsterdam, canals were the city's major arteries. On the right is a new summer palace built by Peter's successor.

View of the Fontanka River from the grotto and the Guest Palace, etched by Grigory Anikievich Kachalov (1711/12-1759), 1753 (etching with engraving), Makhaev, Mikhail Ivanovich (c.1718-1770) (after) / Hermitage, St. Petersburg, Russia/The Bridgeman Art Library

cannon gave an ever-increasing edge to European powers competing with local seafaring peoples. Moreover, the development of joint-stock companies, in which many merchants pooled their capital, provided a flexible and efficient financial instrument for exploiting new possibilities. The English East India Company was founded in 1600, the Dutch East India Company in 1602.

The Ottomans, Safavids, and Mughals did not effectively contest the growth of Portuguese and then Dutch, English, and French maritime power. Muslim shipbuilders, captains, sailors, and traders—and sizable groups of Armenian, Jewish, and Hindu traders—remained aloof from the Europeans. The presence in every port of Muslims following the same legal traditions and practicing their faith in similar ways cemented the Muslims' trading network. Conversion to Islam encouraged the growth of coastal Muslim communities.

Although European missionaries, particularly the Jesuits, tried to extend Christianity into Asia and Africa (see Chapters 15 and 19), most Europeans, the Portuguese excepted, did not treat local converts or the offspring of mixed marriages as full members of their communities. Islam was generally more welcoming. As a consequence, Islam spread extensively into East Africa and Southeast Asia during precisely the same time as rapid European commercial expansion.

Muslims in Southeast Asia

Historians disagree about the chronology and manner of Islam's spread in Southeast Asia. Arab traders appeared in southern China as early as the eighth century, so Muslims probably reached the East Indies (the island portions of Southeast Asia) at a similarly early date. Nevertheless, the continuing dominance of Indian cultural influences in the area indicates that early Muslim visitors had little impact on local beliefs. Clearer indications of the formation of Muslim communities date from roughly the fourteenth century, with the strongest overseas linkage being to the port of Cambay in India (see Map 18.2) rather than to the Arab world. Islam first took root in port cities and in some royal courts and spread inland only slowly, possibly transmitted by itinerant Sufis.

Although appeals to the Ottoman sultan for support against the Europeans ultimately proved futile, Islam strengthened resistance to Portuguese, Spanish, and Dutch intruders. When the Spaniards conquered the Philippines during the decades following the establishment of their first fort in 1565, they encountered Muslims on the southern island of Mindanao (min-duh-NOW) and the nearby Sulu archipelago. They called them "Moros," the Spanish term for their old enemies, the Muslims of North Africa. In the ensuing Moro wars, the Spaniards portrayed the Moros as greedy pirates who raided non-Muslim territories for slaves. In fact, they were political, religious, and commercial competitors whose perseverance enabled them to establish the Sulu Empire based in the southern Philippines, one of the strongest states in Southeast Asia from 1768 to 1848.

Other local kingdoms that looked on Islam as a force to counter the aggressive Christianity of the Europeans included the actively proselytizing Brunei (BROO-neye) Sultanate in northern Borneo and the **Acheh** (AH-cheh) **Sultanate** in northern Sumatra. At its peak in the early seventeenth century, Acheh succeeded Malacca as the main center of Islamic expansion in Southeast Asia. It prospered by trading pepper for cotton cloth from Gujarat in India. Acheh declined after the Dutch seized Malacca from Portugal in 1641.

How well Islam was understood in these Muslim kingdoms is open to question. In Acheh, for example, a series of women ruled between 1641 and 1699. This practice ended when local Muslim scholars obtained a ruling from scholars in Mecca and Medina that Islam did not approve of female rulers. After this ruling, scholarly understandings of Islam gained greater prominence in the East Indies.

Historians have looked at merchants, Sufi preachers, or both as the first propagators of Islam in Southeast Asia. The scholarly vision of Islam, however, took root in the sixteenth century by way of pilgrims returning from years of study in Mecca and Medina. Islam promoted the dissemination of writing in the region. Some of the returning pilgrims wrote in Arabic, others in Malay or Javanese using Arabic script. As Islam continued to spread, *adat* ("custom"),

Acheh Sultanate Muslim kingdom in northern Sumatra. Main center of Islamic expansion in Southeast Asia in the early seventeenth century, it declined after the Dutch seized Malacca from Portugal in 1641.

Map 18.2 European Colonization in the Indian Ocean, to 1750 Since Portuguese explorers were the first Europeans to reach India by rounding Africa, Portugal gained a strong foothold in both areas. Rival Spain was barred from colonizing the region by the Treaty of Tordesillas in 1494, which limited Spanish efforts to lands west of a line drawn through the mid-Atlantic Ocean. The line carried around the globe provided justification of Spanish colonization in the Philippines. French, British, and Dutch colonies date from after 1600, when joint-stock companies provided a new stimulus for overseas commerce. © Cengage Learning

a form of Islam rooted in pre-Muslim religious and social practices, retained its preeminence in rural areas over practices centered on the Shari'a, the religious law. But the royal courts in the port cities began to heed the views of the pilgrim teachers.

Muslims in Coastal Africa

Muslim rulers also governed the East African ports that the Portuguese began to visit in

the fifteenth century (see Map 18.2). People living in the millet and rice lands of the Swahili Coast—from the Arabic *sawahil* (suh-WAH-hil) meaning "coasts"—had little contact with those in the dry hinterlands. Throughout this period, the East African lakes region and the highlands of Kenya witnessed unprecedented migration and relocation of peoples because of drought conditions that persisted from the late sixteenth through most of the seventeenth century.

Cooperation among the trading ports of Kilwa, Mombasa, and Malindi was hindered by the thick bush country that separated the cultivated tracts of coastal land and by the fact that the ports competed with one another in the export of ivory; ambergris (AM-ber-grees) (a whale byproduct used in perfumes); and forest products such as beeswax, copal tree resin, and wood. Kilwa also exported gold. In the eighteenth century slave trading, primarily to Arabian ports but also to India, increased in importance. Because Europeans—the only peoples who kept consistent records of slave-trading activities—played a minor role in this slave trade, few records have survived to indicate its extent. Perhaps the best estimate is that 2.1 million slaves were exported between 1500 and 1890, a little over 12.5 percent of the total traffic in African slaves during that period (see Chapter 17).

Initially, the Portuguese favored the port of Malindi, which caused the decline of Kilwa and Mombasa. Repeatedly plagued by local rebellion, Portuguese power suffered severe blows when the Arabs of **Oman** in southeastern Arabia captured their south Arabian stronghold at Musqat (1650) and then went on to seize Mombasa (1698), which had become the Portuguese capital in East Africa. The Portuguese briefly retook Mombasa but lost control permanently in 1729. From then on, the Portuguese had to content themselves with Mozambique in East Africa and a few remaining ports in India (Goa) and farther east (Macao and Timor).

The Omanis created a maritime empire of their own, one that worked in greater cooperation with the African populations. The Bantu language of the coast, broadened by the absorption of Arabic, Persian, and Portuguese loanwords, developed into **Swahili** (swah-HEE-lee), which was spoken throughout the region. Arabs and other Muslims who settled in the area intermarried with local families, giving rise to a mixed population that played an important role in developing a distinctive Swahili culture.

In Northwest Africa the seizure by Portugal and Spain of coastal strongholds in Morocco provoked a militant response. The Sa'adi family, which claimed descent from the Prophet Muhammad, led a resistance to Portuguese aggression that climaxed in victory at the battle of al-Qasr al-Kabir (Ksar el Kebir)

in 1578. The triumphant Moroccan sultan, Ahmad al-Mansur, restored his country's strength and independence. By the early seventeenth century naval expeditions from the port of Salé, referred to in British records as "the Sally Rovers," raided European shipping as far as Britain itself.

Corsairs, or sea raiders, working out of Algerian, Tunisian, and Libyan ports brought the same sort of warfare to the Mediterranean. European governments called these Muslim raiders pirates and slave-takers, and they leveled the same charges against other Muslim mariners in the Persian Gulf and the Sulu Sea. But there was little distinction between the actions of the Muslims and of their European adversaries.

European Powers in Southern Seas

Through their well-organized Dutch East India Company, the Dutch played a major role in driving the Portuguese from their possessions in the East Indies. Just as the Portuguese had tried to dominate the trade in spices, so the Dutch concentrated at first on the spice-producing islands of Southeast Asia. The Portuguese had seized Malacca, a strategic town on the narrow strait at the end of the Malay Peninsula, from a local Malay ruler in 1511 (see Chapter 15). The Dutch took it away from them in 1641, leaving Portugal little foothold in the East Indies except the islands of Ambon (am-BOHN) and Timor (see Map 18.2).

Although the United Netherlands was one of the least autocratic countries of Europe, the governors-general appointed by the Dutch East India Company deployed almost unlimited powers in their efforts to maintain their trade monopoly. They could even order the execution of their own employees for "smuggling"—that is, trading on their own. Under strong governors-general, the Dutch fought a series of wars against Acheh and other local kingdoms on Sumatra and Java. In 1628 and

Oman Arab state based in Musqat, the main port in the southeast region of the Arabian peninsula. Oman succeeded Portugal as a power in the western Indian Ocean in the eighteenth century.

Swahili Bantu language with Arabic loanwords spoken in coastal regions of East Africa.

- The majority of non-European shipbuilders, captains, sailors, and traders in the Indian Ocean were Muslim.

- A number of local kingdoms in Southeast Asia took on Islam as a force to resist the aggressive Christianity of the Europeans.

- Muslims in coastal Africa intermarried locally, creating a mixed population and helping to form a distinctive Swahili culture.

- Over time the successes of European trading companies changed the balance of power in the southern seas, but local merchants never completely disappeared from the commercial scene.

1629 their new capital at **Batavia**, now the city of Jakarta on Java, was besieged by a fleet of fifty ships belonging to the sultan of Mataram (MAH-tah-ram), a Javanese kingdom. The Dutch held out with difficulty and eventually prevailed when the sultan was unable to get effective help from the English.

In the course of the eighteenth century, the Dutch gradually turned from being middlemen between Southeast Asian producers and European buyers to producing crops in areas they controlled, notably in Java. Javanese teak forests yielded high-quality lumber, and coffee, transplanted from Yemen, grew well in the western hilly regions. In this new phase of colonial export production, Batavia developed from being the headquarters town of a far-flung enterprise to being the administrative capital of a conquered land.

CONCLUSION

The complex changes in military technology and economic organization that were under way in smaller European countries in the seventeenth and eighteenth centuries affected the Ottoman, Safavid, and Mughal Empires adversely. Only Russia, by virtue of a single ruler who was able to learn western European techniques at first hand, found success in adopting some of the changes. By western European standards, however, Russia was still poor and backward when Peter's reign ended in 1762, while the Muslims ruled rich lands that were ripe for European exploitation.

Improvements in ship design, navigation accuracy, and the use of cannon gave an ever-increasing edge to European powers competing with local seafaring peoples. In contrast to the age-old Eurasian belief that imperial wealth came from controlling broad expanses of land, western European rulers promoted joint-stock companies and luxuriated in the prosperity gained from their ever-increasing control of Indian Ocean commerce. Eighteenth-century European observers marveled no less at the riches and industry of these eastern lands than at the fundamental weakness of their political and military systems.

Batavia Fort established around 1619 as headquarters of Dutch East India Company operations in Indonesia; today the city of Jakarta.

CHAPTER REVIEW

THE OTTOMAN EMPIRE, TO 1750
■ *How did the Ottoman Empire rise to power, and what factors contributed to its transformation?* (page 427)

Strategic location and a centralized army well balanced between mounted bowmen and an infantry armed with gunpowder weapons were key to Ottoman success during the empire's first two centuries. With territorial growth, however, the borders became too distant from the capital for the efficient deployment of a centralized army, and economic pressures, notably those associated with a flood of cheap silver from the New World, forced modifications in the ruling system. Military, and increasingly political, power devolved to commanders and governors in provincial capitals and border districts, while new fiscal arrangements captured more tax revenue for the central government and the Istanbul elite.

THE SAFAVID EMPIRE, 1502–1722

■ *How did the Safavid Empire both resemble and differ from its neighbors?* (page 434)

The Safavid Empire embodied some of the same Turkish tribal traditions and Islamic governing institutions that were found among the Ottomans, but the formal adoption of Shi'ism as the state religion at the beginning of the sixteenth century created such a gulf between them that these similarities were seldom recognized. In some respects, such as their practice of using Christian prisoners of war as infantry, the Safavids followed the Ottoman lead. By contrast, the Mughals drew military forces from Central Asia and Afghanistan and adopted Persian as the language of government but never enjoyed the religious and cultural homogeneity that was a hallmark of Safavid Iran.

THE MUGHAL EMPIRE, 1526–1761

■ *How did the Mughal Empire combine Muslim and Hindu elements into an effective state?* (page 437)

Dealing with the Hindu majority in their domain was a continuing problem for the Mughal rulers. Akbar took the path of accommodation by appointing Hindu officials and trying to harmonize religious differences. Aurangzeb, his great-grandson, took the opposite path of persecuting Hindus and exalting Islam. Both rulers enjoyed military success against various Indian adversaries, but neither hit on a formula that would permanently bridge the gap between the Muslim ruling minority and the non-Muslim majority. Nevertheless, by comparison with earlier Indian states, and measured by the problems and successes of the contemporary Ottoman and Safavid realms, Mughal rule must be deemed effective.

THE RUSSIAN EMPIRE, 1500–1762

■ *What were the similarities between the Christian Russian Empire and the Muslim Ottoman, Safavid, and Mughal Empires to the south?* (page 440)

Like the Ottoman, Safavid, and Mughal Empires, Russia gave land grants for military service. This practice reinforced a system of serfdom, akin to slavery, whereby peasants tilled the land for distant landlords. The absolutist rule of Peter the Great was influenced by absolutist philosophies in western Europe but also resembled the form of rule practiced by the shahs and sultans of the Ottoman, Safavid, and Mughal Empires. Despite fiery rhetoric about "Christians" and "infidels," the Russian Empire closely resembled the Muslim empires to its south in tolerating the ethnic and religious diversity that had also been a hallmark of Mongol rule.

THE MARITIME WORLDS OF ISLAM, 1500–1750

■ *What role does maritime history play in the political and economic life of this period?* (page 442)

Muslim rulers who saw greater opportunities and dangers along imperial land frontiers than at sea saw nothing threatening in the vigorous commercial activity of the non-Muslim merchants in their realms—Jews, Christians, and Hindus—or even European trading companies. To be sure, the Ottoman navy was a formidable military force in the Mediterranean, and Muslim rulers in Morocco, Oman, and Southeast Asia sometimes reacted effectively to European maritime pressure. But the greatest battles were fought on land, and acquisition or loss of territory was taken by Muslims and non-Muslims alike as a more important sign of an empire's strength than its command of maritime trade routes. European domination of maritime trade, however, eventually outpaced the power of the land-based empires even as it incorporated locals in the maritime trade and in the manufacture of goods like Indian cotton for export.

Key Terms

Ottoman Empire (p. 427)
Suleiman the Magnificent (p. 428)
Janissaries (p. 429)
Tulip Period (p. 432)
Safavid Empire (p. 434)
Shi'ites (p. 434)
Hidden Imam (p. 434)
Shah Abbas I (p. 435)
Mughal Empire (p. 437)
Akbar (p. 438)
mansabs (p. 438)
Rajputs (p. 438)
Muscovy (p. 440)
tsar (p. 440)
Siberia (p. 440)
Cossacks (p. 440)
serf (p. 441)
Peter the Great (p. 441)
Acheh Sultanate (p. 443)
Oman (p. 445)
Swahili (p. 445)
Batavia (p. 446)

East Asia in Global Perspective

© Cengage Learning

In the sixteenth century Ming China became a driving force in the first truly global economy, one that joined together Asia, Europe, the Americas, and, to a lesser extent, Africa. To meet China's skyrocketing demand for silver, European traders imported American silver and in return shipped silk, spices, tea, and other precious goods back to Europe. Christian missionaries joined European merchants as intellectual middlemen in this global interaction.

At century's end, however, from 1592 to 1598, the Imjin War, a conflict surpassed in violence only by the wars of the nineteenth and twentieth century, embroiled Korea, Japan, and China. After attempting to conquer China, the Japanese finally returned to their islands, leaving the weakened Ming to face other foes. Korea, the devastated battleground, did not recover for centuries.

In the seventeenth century, **Manchu** armies from Manchuria on China's northeast frontier succeeded where Japan had failed. The Ming emperor had slashed the government payroll to pay the army defending Beijing (bay-JING). Among those losing his job was an apprentice ironworker named Li Zicheng (lee ZUH-cheng). By 1630 Li Zicheng had found work as a soldier, but he and his fellow soldiers mutinied when the government failed to provide needed supplies. A natural leader, Li soon headed several thousand Chinese rebels, and in 1635 he and other rebel leaders gained control over much of north-central China.

Wedged between the rebels and the Manchu armies to the north, the Ming government tottered. Li Zicheng's forces moved on Beijing, promising an end to Ming abuses and a restoration of peace and prosperity. In April 1644 Li's forces took the city without a fight. The last Ming emperor hanged himself in the palace garden, bringing to an end the dynasty that had ruled China since 1368.

Li's victory was short-lived, however. Preferring the Manchus to an uneducated warlord, the Ming general Wu Sangui and his new northern allies retook Beijing in June. Li's forces scattered, and a year later he was dead, either a suicide or beaten to death by peasants whose food he tried to steal.[1] Now the new masters of China, the Manchus installed their young sovereign as emperor, declared the beginning of a new dynasty called "Qing" (ching), and over the next two decades hunted down the last of the Ming loyalists and heirs to the throne.

The causes of the changes in governance that affected East Asia in this period differed from those that disrupted the empires discussed in the previous chapter, but the impacts were similarly far-reaching. By the late eighteenth century, China, Korea, and Japan were very different than they had been in 1500.

EAST ASIA AND EUROPE

■ *How did the West and East Asia affect each other commercially and intellectually?*

European merchants who made their way from Southeast Asia to East Asia in the sixteenth century helped build thriving trade networks. Because of changes in the Ming fiscal system that required taxes to be paid in cash, China had developed an urgent need for silver, consuming as much as 30 percent of the world's total silver output. After 1500, the Americas replaced Japan as China's silver supplier (see Chapter 17), and European ships transported the bullion along Asian trade routes, sometimes operating as middlemen and sometimes as privateers and even pirates.

Trading Companies and Missionaries

For European merchants, the China trade was second in importance only to the spice trade of Southeast Asia. China's vast population and manufacturing skills drew a steady stream of ships from western Europe, but enthusiasm for trade developed only slowly at the Ming court (see Chapter 12).

[1]Adapted from Jonathan D. Spence, *The Search for Modern China* (New York: W. W. Norton, 1990), 21–25.

Manchu Federation of Northeast Asian peoples who founded the Qing Empire.

In late 1513 a Portuguese ship reached China but was not permitted to trade. Four years later a formal Portuguese embassy got bogged down in Chinese protocol and procrastination, and in 1522 China expelled the Portuguese. The Portuguese finally gained permission to trade from a base in Macao (muh-KOW) on the southern coast in 1557. Spain's China trade was conducted from Manila in the Philippines, where silver-laden galleons arrived from South America. For a time, the Spanish and the Dutch both maintained trading outposts on the island of Taiwan, but in 1662 they were forced to concede control to the Qing, who for the first time incorporated Taiwan into China.

By then, the Dutch East India Company (VOC for Vereenigde Oost-Indische Compagnie) (see Chapter 17) had displaced the Portuguese as the paramount European traders in the Indian Ocean and was establishing itself as the main European trader in East Asia. VOC representatives courted official favor in China by acknowledging the moral superiority of the emperor. This meant performing the ritual kowtow (in which the visitor knocked his head on the floor while crawling toward the throne) to the Ming emperor.

Catholic missionaries accompanied the Portuguese and Spanish merchants to East Asia. The Franciscans and Dominicans pioneered a missionary approach that focused on the poor and low-born. The Jesuits' appeal to the intellectual and political elite was more successful in gaining converts. The outstanding Jesuit of late Ming China, Matteo Ricci (mah-TAY-oh REE-chee) (1552–1610), who resided in Beijing from 1601, became expert in the Chinese language and a scholar of the Confucian classics, and under Ricci's leadership, the Jesuits adapted Catholicism to Chinese cultural traditions. Most importantly, they tolerated Confucian ancestor worship—a move that created a fevered controversy with not only Franciscan and Dominican rivals but also the pope. In 1690 the Chinese emperor wrote to Rome supporting the Jesuit position. When the dispute continued, the Chinese emperor ordered the expulsion of all missionaries who refused to sign a certificate accepting his position. The Jesuit presence in China declined in the eighteenth century. Later Chinese emperors would persecute Christians rather than naming them to high office.

Chinese Influences on Europe

The exchange of information between Chinese and Europeans went both ways. The Jesuits had introduced the Chinese to the latest European science and technology. Jesuits had also helped create maps in the European style as practical guides to newly conquered regions and as symbols of Qing dominance. One Chinese emperor, Kangxi (KAHNG-shee) (r. 1662–1722) (discussed later in this chapter), considered introducing the European calendar, but protests from the Confucian elite caused him to drop the plan. When Kangxi fell ill with malaria in the 1690s, Jesuit medical treatment (in this case, South American quinine) aided his recovery, and Kangxi ordered the creation of illustrated books in Manchu detailing European anatomical and pharmaceutical knowledge. While the Jesuits brought forward new knowledge of anatomy, the Chinese demonstrated an early form of inoculation, called "variolation," that had helped curtail smallpox after the conquest of Beijing. The technique inspired Europeans to develop other vaccines.

Having learned about China from Jesuit writings, European admiration for China created a demand for Chinese things among the wealthy and aspiring middle classes, including cloisonné jewelry, jade, lacquered and jeweled room dividers, painted fans, and carved ivory (which originated in Africa and was finished in China). Silk, porcelain, and tea were avidly sought. Wallpaper, which began as an adaptation of the Chinese practice of covering walls with enormous loose-hanging watercolors or calligraphy scrolls, was by the mid-1700s exported from special workshops throughout China.

Chinese political philosophy impressed Europeans, too. In the late 1770s poems supposedly written by Emperor Qianlong (chee-YEN-loong) (r. 1736–1796) (discussed later in this chapter) were translated into French and disseminated in intellectual circles. In them the Chinese emperors rule as benevolent despots campaigning against superstition and ignorance, curbing aristocratic excesses, and patronizing science and the arts. This image of a practical, secular, compassionate ruler impressed the French thinker Voltaire, who proclaimed that Chinese emperors were model philosopher-kings and advocated such rulership as a protection against the growth of aristocratic privilege.

Chronology

	Korea and Japan	China and Central Asia
1500	**1543** First Portuguese contacts **1592** Japanese invasion of Korea	**1517** Portuguese embassy to China
1600	**1603** Tokugawa Shogunate formed **1633–1639** Edicts close down trade with Europe	**1601** Matteo Ricci allowed to reside in Beijing **1644** Qing conquest of Beijing **1662–1722** Rule of Emperor Kangxi **1689** Treaty of Nerchinsk with Russia **1691** Qing control of Inner Mongolia
1700	**1702** Trial of the Forty-Seven Ronin **1792** Macartney Mission dispatched from Britain	**1736–1796** Rule of Emperor Qianlong

Japan and the Europeans

Europeans also traveled to Japan. Within thirty years of the arrival of the first Portuguese in 1543, warlords known as **_daimyo_** (DIE-mee-oh) were fighting with Western-style firearms, copied and improved upon by Japanese armorers.

The Japanese welcomed but closely regulated traders from Portugal, Spain, the Netherlands, and England. Aside from a brief boom in porcelain exports in the seventeenth century, few Japanese goods went to Europe, and not much from Europe found a market in Japan. The Japanese sold the Dutch copper and silver, which the Dutch exchanged in China for silks that they then resold in Japan. The Japanese, of course, had their own trade with China.

Portuguese and Spanish merchant ships also brought Catholic missionaries. One of the first, Francis Xavier, went to India in the mid-sixteenth century looking for converts and later traveled throughout Southeast and East Asia. He spent two years in Japan, where he died in 1552, hoping to gain entry to China. Japanese responses to Xavier and other Jesuits were mixed. Many ordinary Japanese found the new faith deeply meaningful, but the Japanese elite more often opposed it as disruptive and foreign. By 1580 more than 100,000 Japanese had become Christians, and one daimyo gave Jesuit missionaries the port city of Nagasaki (NAH-guh-SAHK-kee). In 1613 Date Masamune (DAH-tay mah-suh-MOO-nay), the fierce and independent daimyo of northern Honshu (HOHN-shoo), sent his own embassy to the Vatican by way of the Philippines (where there were significant communities of Japanese merchants and pirates) and Mexico City. Some daimyo converts ordered their subjects to become Christians as well.

By the early seventeenth century there were some 300,000 Japanese Christians and even some Japanese priests. However, suspicions about the intentions of the Europeans turned the samurai regime against Christianity. A decree issued in 1614 banned Christianity and charged its adherents with seeking to overthrow true doctrine, change the government, and seize the country. Some missionaries left Japan; others worked underground. The government began persecutions in earnest in 1617, and the beheadings, crucifixions, and forced recantations over the next several decades destroyed almost the entire Christian community.

To keep Christianity from resurfacing, a series of decrees issued between 1633 and 1639 sharply curtailed trade with Europe. Europeans who entered the

> **_daimyo_** Literally, "great name(s)." Japanese warlords and great landowners, whose armed samurai gave them control of the Japanese islands from the eighth to the later nineteenth century. Under the Tokugawa Shogunate they were subordinated to the imperial government.

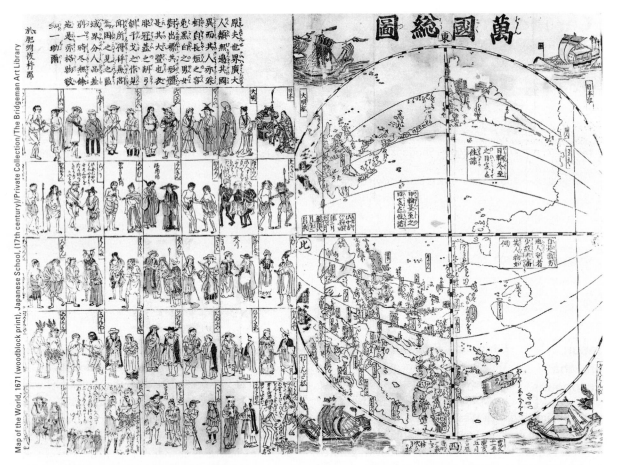

Map of the World, 1671 (woodblock print), Japanese School, (17th century)/Private Collection/The Bridgeman Art Library

Comprehensive Map of the Myriad Nations   Thanks to the "Dutch studies" scholars and to overseas contacts, many Japanese were well informed about the cultures, technologies, and political systems of various parts of the world. This combination map and ethnographic text of 1671 enthusiastically explores the differences among the many peoples living or traveling in Asia. The map of the Pacific hemisphere has the north pole on the left and the south pole on the extreme right of the drawing.

country illegally faced the death penalty, and Japanese subjects were required to produce certificates from Buddhist temples attesting to their religious

SECTION REVIEW

- European merchants pursued trade contacts with China despite official resistance, and missionaries worked successfully until the eighteenth century.

- The Qing and Europeans engaged in productive exchanges of ideas, and Chinese producers supplied growing European consumer markets.

- The Japanese engaged in regulated trade with Europeans, but rising suspicions caused the Japanese to restrict foreign contacts.

orthodoxy and loyalty to the regime. However, the exclusion of Europe was not total. A few Dutch were permitted to reside on a small artificial island in Nagasaki's harbor, and a few Japanese were licensed to supply their needs. What these intermediaries learned about European weapons technology, shipbuilding, mathematics and astronomy, anatomy and medicine, and geography was termed "Dutch studies."

Japanese restrictions on the number of Chinese ships that could trade in Japan were harder to enforce. Regional lords in northern and southern Japan not only pursued overseas trade and piracy but also claimed dominion over islands between Japan and Korea and southward toward Taiwan, including present-day Okinawa.

JAPANESE UNIFICATION AND THE IMJIN WAR

■ *What was the effect of Japanese unification on Korea and China?*

The Imjin War, the largest pre-twentieth-century conflict in East Asian history, had no European involvement. *Imjin* is the Korean term for the year of the water dragon, but Chinese sources refer to this war by many names, including "the Korean campaign." In Japan today, it is called "Hideyoshi's invasions." Seven years long (1592–1598), the war had lasting effects in Korea, facilitated the demise of the Ming dynasty in China, and produced bad feelings between Japan and Korea that have lasted down to the present.

Japanese Unification

Japan changed in three different dimensions between 1500 and 1800: internal and external military conflicts, political growth and strengthening, and expanded commercial and cultural contacts. Along with its relatively homogeneous population and natural boundaries, Japan's smaller size made political unification more achievable than in the great empire of China.

The Ashikaga Shogunate had weakened after the Onin War (see Chapter 12), opening opportunities for daimyo across Japan to fight for land and influence. The daimyo pledged a loose allegiance to the Japanese emperor residing in the capital city of Kyoto (KYOH-toh) and to the shogun, the hereditary chief of the imperial government and armies. But neither wielded significant political power. Each daimyo had a castle town, a small bureaucracy, and a band of warriors, his *samurai*. Warfare among the different daimyo was common, and in the late 1500s it culminated in a prolonged civil war. The warlord to emerge victorious was Hideyoshi (HEE-duh-YOH-shi), a lowly peasant who had risen through military ranks.

The Invasion of Korea

In 1592, buoyed with his success in unifying Japan, the supremely confident Hideyoshi sent a 160,000-man force to the Asian mainland. Various reasons are given for his decision to invade: to impress domestic rivals, to keep major daimyo busy fighting outside of Japan so they could not rebel, to push out Christian daimyo (who made up a sizable force in Korea), to dominate East Asian trade networks. However, even as he was consolidating his control over Japan, Hideyoshi was planning to invade Korea in order to conquer China.

Several centuries of peace and court factionalism had left the Koreans ill prepared to handle the battle-tested samurai-led armies. At the beginning of the war, the Koreans did not have large-scale muskets, though they did possess some cannon, and they suffered disastrous defeats. But although daimyo armies were skilled at land-based fighting, the Japanese navy was unprepared for serious combat. The Koreans deployed ingenious covered warships, or "turtle ships," to intercept a portion of the Japanese fleet and won some twenty-three consecutive naval battles. On land, the Koreans called upon China for help.

Regarding Korea as one of its client states, China obliged, eventually sending 100,000 Chinese troops. After Hideyoshi revoked the short peace China had negotiated, Japanese forces invaded again in 1597, employing brutal punitive measures as they advanced through the Korean peninsula. However, many daimyo were now more interested in securing a few provinces in southern Korea than in supporting Hideyoshi's dream of defeating China. Hideyoshi, in poor health, gave an order to withdraw all troops from Korea, which occurred after his death in 1598. It still took many years for Japan to conclude peace with Korea. Formal relations did not resume until 1617.

The invasion devastated Korea. In the turmoil after the Japanese withdrawal, the Korean *yangban* (ruling class of nobles) laid claim to so much taxpaying land that royal revenues plunged. China also suffered dire consequences. Fighting in Korea depleted the Ming coffers at a time when the empire was also battling peoples to the north. The emperor established a new tax to recover revenue, but this led to protests in the provinces. The battles in Manchuria weakened the Chinese garrisons there, permitting Manchu opposition to consolidate. Manchu forces invaded Korea in the 1620s and eventually compelled Korea to become a tributary state. The Manchus would be in possession of Beijing, China's capital, by 1644.

> **samurai** Literally "those who serve," the hereditary military elite of the Tokugawa Shogunate.

Korean Turtle Boats This painting shows a fleet of Korean warships under the command of Admiral Yi SunShin, who repelled numerous attacks by the Japanese in the last decade of the sixteenth century. Admiral Yi is celebrated for his use of the "turtle boats," vessels whose covered decks, possibly made of iron plate, are shown in gray.

SECTION REVIEW

- A weakened Ashikaga Shogunate led to civil war among the daimyo, from which emerged Hideyoshi, who, as supreme warlord, invaded Korea as a step toward conquering China.

- Although Korean naval victories and the dispatch of Chinese armies to Korea blunted the Japanese invasion, Korea suffered long-lasting devastation.

- The war also weakened the Ming, leading to the dynasty's fall.

TOKUGAWA JAPAN AND CHOSON KOREA, TO 1800

■ *How did Japan respond to unification and domestic peace, and Korea to the ravages of the Imjin War?*

Japanese Reunification and Economic Growth

Despite wartime losses, Japan flourished after Hideyoshi's death. Tokugawa Ieyasu (TOH-koo-GAH-wah ee-ay-YAH-soo) (1543–1616) asserted his domination over other daimyo and in 1603 established a new military regime known as the **Tokugawa Shogunate**. More inward-looking, this shogunal family concentrated on economic revitalization. Trade from the new administrative capital at Edo (EH-doh) (now Tokyo) along the well-maintained road to the imperial capital of Kyoto promoted the development of the Japanese economy and the formation of other trading centers.

Although the Tokugawa Shogunate gave Japan more political unity than the islands had seen in centuries, the regionally based daimyo retained a great deal of power and autonomy. Economic integration proved to be a more important feature of Tokugawa Japan than political centralization. Because the shoguns required the daimyo to visit Edo frequently, good pedestrian roads and maritime transport linked the city to the castle towns on three of Japan's four main islands. Commercial traffic developed along these routes. Lords received their incomes locally in rice, and they paid their followers in rice. Recipients converted much of this rice into cash, a practice that led to the development of rice exchanges at Edo and at Osaka (OH-sah-kah), where merchants speculated in rice prices. By the late seventeenth century Edo was one of the largest cities in the world, with nearly a million inhabitants.

Tokugawa Shogunate The last of the three shogunates of Japan.

The domestic peace of the Tokugawa era forced the warrior class to adapt to the growing bureaucratic needs of the state. As the samurai became better educated and more attuned to the tastes of the civil elite, they became important customers for merchants dealing in silks, *sake* (SAH-kay) (rice wine), fans, porcelain, lacquer ware, books, and moneylending. The state attempted—unsuccessfully—to curb the independence of the merchants when the economic well-being of the samurai was threatened by low rice prices or high interest rates.

The 1600s and 1700s were centuries of high achievement in artisanship. Japanese skills in steel making, lacquer ware, and pottery were joined by excellence in the production of porcelain, thanks in no small part to Korean experts brought back to Japan after Hideyoshi's invasions, whose advanced skills transformed the Japanese pottery industry. In the early 1600s manufacturers and merchants amassed enormous family fortunes. Several of the most important industrial and financial enterprises—for instance, the Mitsui (MIT-sue-ee) companies—had their origins in sake breweries of the early Tokugawa period and then branched out into manufacturing, finance, and transport.

Wealthy merchants weakened the Tokugawa policy of controlling commerce by cultivating close alliances with their regional daimyo and, when possible, with the shogun himself. By the end of the 1700s the merchant families of Tokugawa Japan held the key to future modernization and the development of heavy industry.

Japanese Elite Decline and Social Crisis

During the 1700s population growth put a great strain on the well-developed lands of central Japan. In more remote provinces, where the lords promoted new settlements and agricultural expansion, the rate of economic growth was significantly greater.

Also troubling the Tokugawa government in the 1700s was the shogunate's inability to stabilize rice prices and halt the economic decline of the samurai. The Tokugawa government realized that the rice brokers could manipulate prices and interest rates to enrich themselves at the expense of the samurai, who had to convert their rice allotments into cash.

Early Tokugawa laws designed to regulate interest and prices were later supplemented by laws requiring moneylenders to forgive samurai debts. But these laws were not always enforced. By the early 1700s many lords and samurai were dependent on the willingness of merchants to provide credit.

The legitimacy of the Tokugawa shoguns rested on their ability to reward and protect the interests of the lords and samurai who had supported their rise to power. Moreover, the Tokugawa government, like the governments of China, Korea, and Vietnam, accepted the Confucian idea that agriculture should be the basis of state wealth and that merchants, who were considered morally weak, should occupy lowly positions in society. Tokugawa decentralization, however, not only failed to hinder but actually stimulated the growth of commercial activities. From the founding of the Tokugawa Shogunate in 1603 until 1800, the economy grew faster than the population. Household amenities and cultural resources that in China appeared only in the cities were common in the Japanese countryside. Despite official disapproval, merchants enjoyed relative freedom and influence in eighteenth-century Japan. They produced a vivid culture of their own, fostering the development of *kabuki* theater, colorful woodblock prints and silk-screened fabrics, and restaurants.

The "Forty-Seven Ronin" (ROH-neen) incident of 1701–1703 exemplified the ideological and social crisis of Japan's transformation from a military to a civil society. A senior minister provoked a young daimyo into drawing his sword at the shogun's court. For this offense the young lord was sentenced to commit *seppuku* (SEP-poo-koo), the ritual suicide of the samurai. His own followers then became *ronin*, "masterless samurai," obliged by the traditional code of the warrior to avenge their deceased master. They broke into the house of the senior minister and killed him and others in his household. Then they withdrew to a temple in Edo and notified the shogun of what they had done out of loyalty to their lord and to avenge his death.

A legal debate ensued. To deny the righteousness of the ronin would be to deny samurai values. But to approve their actions would create social chaos, undermine laws against murder, and deny the shogunal government the right to try cases of samurai violence. The shogun ruled that the ronin had to die but would be permitted to die honorably by committing seppuku. Traditional samurai values had to surrender to the supremacy of law. The purity of purpose of the ronin is still celebrated in Japan, but since then Japanese writers, historians, and teachers have recognized that the self-sacrifice of the ronin for the sake of upholding civil law was necessary.

Choson Korea

Despite the Imjin War, the Choson dynasty (1392–1910), established after Mongol rule (see Chapter 12), proved to be the longest-lasting state in East Asian history. The dominant influence on Korean culture had long been China, to which Korean rulers generally paid tribute, and the Choson dynasty aligned itself with the Ming. Even though the Korean and Japanese languages are closely related, Korean printing continued to use Chinese characters for its writing system into the fifteenth century.

In many ways the Choson dynasty was a model Confucian state. The government was staffed by men who passed the civil examination system, modeled on the Chinese institution of the same name. But there was one important difference. In theory, if not in practice, anyone could sit for the civil examinations in China, but by the sixteenth century in Choson Korea, one had to be born into the *yangban* (YAHNG-bahn) class to take an examination and work in any position of real influence in government. Only occasionally was social mobility possible for commoners who tested into the military yangban group, a status typically disdained by the civil yangban.

The yangban, literally "two orders," were a hereditary status group who dominated the civil and military examinations, filling nearly all of the official positions in the national and local governments. Unlike the majority, commoner population, they did not have to pay a household tax, nor did they have to serve in the military (unless they were military yangban). As mentioned in the previous section, the yangban increased their landholdings after the Imjin War, making more land tax-exempt. Revenues fell by two-thirds, preventing Choson Korea from recovering quickly from the war.

The yangban also owned most of Korea's slaves, which at one point made up nearly 30 percent of the population. In addition to privately owned slaves,

SECTION REVIEW

• After Hideyoshi's death, the Tokugawa Shogunate unified Japan and moved the capital to Edo (Tokyo).
• Economic growth nourished a new merchant-class culture in Japan.
• Under economic and social pressures, the position of the samurai deteriorated.
• Choson Korea survived Hideyoshi's invasion and modeled itself on the Confucian government of Ming China.
• However, the Korean noble class paid no taxes and laid claim to more land, stifling recovery from wartime devastation.

local governments maintained slaves for a variety of clerical and labor jobs. Even Buddhist temples owned slaves. The slave population dropped to about 10 percent in the eighteenth century, when runaway slaves increased and the poor economy meant that most yangban simply hired poor commoners to work in agriculture.

FROM MING TO QING

■ *How did China deal with military and political challenges both inside and outside its borders?*

The internal and external forces at work in China were different from those in Japan and operated on a much larger scale, but they led in similar directions. By 1800 China had a greatly enhanced empire, an expanding economy, and growing doubts about the importance of European trade and Christianity.

Ming Economic Growth, 1500–1644

The economic and cultural achievements of the early Ming Empire (see Chapter 12) continued during the 1500s. But this productive period was followed by many decades of political weakness, warfare, and rural woes until a new dynasty, the Qing from Manchuria, guided China back to peace and prosperity.

European accounts from the early sixteenth century express astonishment at the power, exquisite manufactures, and vast population of the Ming. Ming cities had long been culturally and commercially vibrant (see Material Culture: Four-Wheeled

Vehicles). Many large landowners and absentee landlords lived in town, as did officials, artists, and rich merchants who had purchased ranks or prepared their sons for the examinations. The elite classes had created a brilliant culture in which novels, operas, poetry, porcelain, and painting were closely interwoven. Catering to these urban elites were small businesses that prospered through printing, tailoring, running restaurants, or selling paper, ink, ink-stones, and writing brushes. The imperial government operated factories for the production of ceramics and silks, and enormous government complexes at Jingdezhen and elsewhere invented assembly-line techniques and produced large quantities of high-quality ceramics for sale in China and abroad.

Despite these achievements, serious problems developed that left the Ming Empire economically and politically exhausted. There is evidence that the climate changes known as the Little Ice Age in seventeenth-century Europe affected the climate in China as well (see Issues in World History: The Little Ice Age on page 466). Annual temperatures dropped, reached a low point about 1645, and remained low until the early 1700s. The resulting agricultural distress and famine fueled large uprisings that sped the end of the Ming Empire.

The rapid urban growth and business speculation that were part of the burgeoning trading economy also produced problems. Some provinces suffered from price inflation caused by the flood of silver. In contrast to the growing involvement of European governments in promoting economic growth, the Ming government pursued some policies that hindered growth. Ming governments persisted, despite earlier failed experiments, in issuing new paper money and copper coinage, even after silver had won the approval of the markets. Corruption compounded government problems. Disorder and inefficiency came to plague the imperial factories, touching off strikes in the late sixteenth and seventeenth centuries. During a labor protest at Jingdezhen in 1601, workers threw themselves into the kilns to protest working conditions.

Yet the urban and industrial sectors of later Ming society fared much better than the agricultural sector. Despite knowledge of new African and American crops gained from European traders, farmers were slow to change their ways. Neither the rice-growing regions in southern China nor the wheat-growing regions in northern China experienced a meaningful increase in productivity under the later Ming. After 1500 economic depression in the countryside, combined with recurring epidemics in central and southern China, kept rural population growth in check.

Ming Collapse and the Rise of the Qing

Environmental, economic, and administrative problems aside, the primary reasons for the fall of the Ming Empire were internal rebellion and threats on the borders. Ming frontiers had long been under pressure from the powerful Mongol federations of the north and west. In the late 1500s large numbers of Mongols were unified by their devotion to the Dalai Lama (DAH-lie LAH-mah), or universal teacher of Tibetan Buddhism. Building on this spiritual unity, a brilliant leader named Galdan restored Mongolia as a regional military power around 1600. At the same time, the Manchus, an agricultural people who controlled the region north of Korea, grew stronger in the northeast.

In the southwest, native peoples repeatedly resisted the immigration of Chinese farmers. Pirates based in Okinawa and Taiwan, many of them Japanese, frequently looted the southeast coast. Ming military resources, concentrated against the Mongols and the Manchus in the north, could not be deployed to defend the coasts. As a result, many southern Chinese migrated to Southeast Asia to profit from the sea-trading networks of the Indian Ocean.

The Imjin War had prompted the Ming to seek the assistance of Manchu troops that they were then unable to restrain. With the rebel leader Li Zicheng in possession of Beijing (see the beginning of this chapter) and the emperor dead by his own hand, a Ming general joined forces with the Manchu leaders in the summer of 1644. Instead of restoring the Ming, however, the Manchus claimed China for their own and began a forty-year conquest of the remaining Ming territories, as well as Taiwan and parts of Mongolia and Central Asia (see Map 19.1).

Qing Empire Empire established in China by Manchus who overthrew the Ming Empire in 1644. At various times the Qing also controlled Manchuria, Mongolia, Turkestan, and Tibet. The last Qing emperor was overthrown in 1911.

A Manchu family headed the new **Qing Empire**, and Manchu generals commanded the military forces. But Manchus made up a very small portion of the population. Most Qing officials, soldiers, merchants, and farmers were ethnic Chinese. Like other successful invaders of China, the Qing soon adopted Chinese institutions and policies.

Emperor Kangxi

The seventeenth and eighteenth centuries—particularly the reigns of the **Kangxi** (KAHNG-shee) (r. 1662–1722) and Qianlong (chee-YEN-loong) (r. 1736–1796) emperors—saw renewed economic, military, and cultural achievement in China. Roads and waterworks were repaired, transit taxes lowered, rents and interest rates cut, and incentives established for resettling areas devastated by peasant rebellions. Foreign trade was encouraged. Vietnam, Burma, and Nepal sent embassies to the Qing tribute court and carried the latest Chinese fashions back home. Overland routes from Korea to Central Asia revived.

Kangxi Qing emperor (r. 1662–1722). He oversaw the greatest expansion of the Qing Empire.

Map 19.1 The Qing Empire, 1644–1783 The Qing Empire began in Manchuria and captured north China in 1644. Between 1644 and 1783 the Qing conquered all the former Ming territories and added Taiwan, the lower Amur River basin, Inner Mongolia, eastern Turkestan, and Tibet. The resulting state was more than twice the size of the Ming Empire.

© Cengage Learning

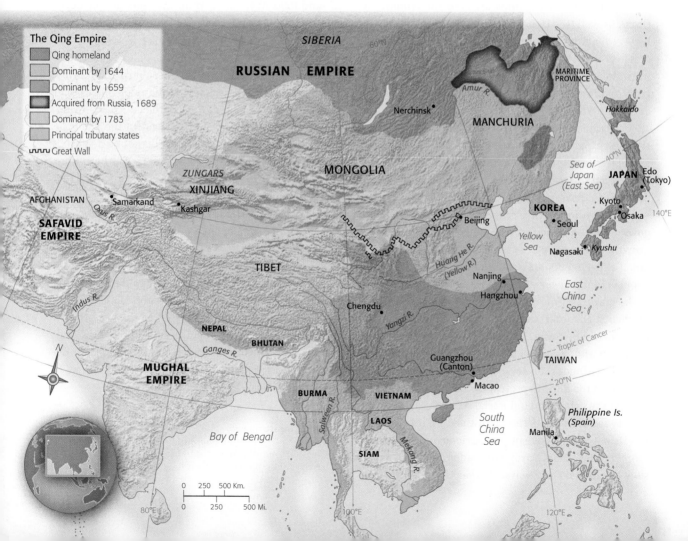

The Manchu aristocrats who led the conquest of Beijing and north China dominated the first Qing emperor and served as regents for his young son, who was declared emperor in 1662. This child-emperor, Kangxi, sparred politically with the regents until 1669, when at age sixteen he executed the chief regent and thereby gained real control of the government. An intellectual prodigy who had mastered classical Chinese, Manchu, and Mongolian and memorized the Chinese classics, Kangxi guided imperial expansion and maintained stability until his death in 1722.

Contact with Russia

In the north, the Qing rulers feared an alliance between Galdan's Mongol state and the expanding Russian presence along the **Amur** (AH-moor) **River**. In the 1680s Qing forces attacked the wooden forts built by hardy Russian scouts on the river's northern bank. Neither empire sent large forces into the Amur territories, so the contest was partly a struggle for the goodwill of the local peoples. The Qing emperor emphasized the importance of treading lightly in the struggle:

> Upon reaching the lands of the Evenks and the Dagurs you will send to announce that you have come to hunt deer. Meanwhile, keep a careful record of the distance and go, while hunting, along the northern bank of the Amur until you come by the shortest route to the town of Russian settlement at Albazin. Thoroughly reconnoiter its location and situation. I don't think the Russians will take a chance on attacking you. If they offer you food, accept it and show your gratitude. If they do attack you, don't fight back. In that case, lead your people and withdraw into our own territories.[2]

Qing forces twice attacked Albazin. The Qing were worried about Russian alliances with other frontier peoples, while Russia wished to protect its access to the furs, timber, and metals concentrated in Siberia and Manchuria (see Chapter 18). The Qing and Russians were also rivals for control of northern Asia's Pacific coast. Seeing little benefit in continued

Wu Chingteng/Xinhua/Photoshot/Newscom

Emperor Kangxi In a portrait from about 1690, the young Manchu ruler is portrayed as a refined scholar in the Confucian tradition. He was a scholar and had great intellectual curiosity, but this portrait would not suggest that he was also capable of leading troops in battle.

conflict, in 1689 the two empires negotiated the Treaty of Nerchinsk, using Jesuit missionaries as interpreters. The treaty fixed the border along the Amur River and regulated trade across it. Although this was a thinly settled area, the treaty proved important, and the frontier it demarcated has long endured.

[2]Adapted from G. V. Melikhov, "Manzhou Penetration into the Basin of the Upper Amur in the 1680s," in *Manzhou Rule in China*, ed. S. L. Tikhvinshii (Moscow: Progress Publishers, 1983).

Amur River This river valley was a contested frontier between northern China and eastern Russia until the settlement arranged in the Treaty of Nerchinsk (1689).

Material Culture

Four-Wheeled Vehicles

Most modern motor transport is based on the principle of the four-wheeled vehicle. Yet prior to the spread of European technologies and tastes in the age of imperialism, four-wheeled vehicles were rarely seen outside of Europe. The wheeled transport of India, East Asia, and Southeast Asia was almost exclusively of the two-wheeled cart variety, though even carts were rare in Japan.

Economically, the two-wheeled cart was generally superior to the four-wheeled wagon throughout the era of animal-drawn transport. The power a team of oxen or horses could exert did not change with the number of wheels. But each added axle, that is, each additional pair of wheels, increased the friction the animals had to overcome in pulling and also added weight to the vehicle. So even though a wagon might have more space than a cart, the weight that could be loaded was invariably smaller.

Four-wheeled vehicles had the additional disadvantage of being difficult to steer. Paved roads were rare, and rutted dirt tracks made for a bumpy ride unless the wheels were of great diameter. Three feet (1 meter) was a common size. However, such large wheels could not turn very far when the front axle pivoted because they hit the frame of the wagon, and raising the wagon-bed more than 3 feet above the ground made the vehicle unstable. Limited to a turning radius of only a few degrees, or more often being constrained by a nonpivoting axle, four-wheeled vehicles could not readily operate in towns and other places where sharp turns were required. Yet making the front wheels smaller so they could turn underneath the wagon-bed made the vehicle difficult to use on rough roads.

Despite these limitations, archaeological evidence shows that both four-wheeled and two-wheeled vehicles were used in Europe, Central Asia, and the Middle East from the fourth millennium B.C.E. onward. By the later days of the Roman Empire, the two-wheeled chariot, formerly the vehicle of warriors, had disappeared, and noblemen had taken to riding horseback. Eventually wagons disappeared in North Africa and the Middle East, but they continued to be used in Europe.

The reasons for European persistence in an inefficient mode of transport are not clear. However, ancient and medieval images suggest that four-wheeled wagons were used primarily for passengers from the upper classes. More specifically, many images show groups of female passengers. Wagons had advantages as conveyances for elite

Nineteenth-Century Children's Carriage *This nineteenth-century children's carriage shows the essential changes that defined the coach. The small front wheels turn under the body of the carriage when the front axle pivots in the center. The back wheels are much larger. And the passenger compartment is suspended on springs that run from the front to the back of the vehicle.*

women. They could easily be enclosed for privacy, and they could hold a noblewoman and her female attendants, thus eliminating the dangers of traveling with only a male driver.

Increased comfort probably played a role in a series of technological improvements that began around the thirteenth century. The word *coach*, of Hungarian origin, signaled the new designs. Pivoting front axles became common, while better paving, particularly in towns, accommodated the required smaller wheels. To reduce jolting, the passenger cabin was first suspended on chains or leather straps and later on springs. Efficient harnessing techniques that had first appeared centuries earlier made possible larger teams of animals, heavier vehicles, and faster speeds. And brakes were developed to help manage the heavier loads.

Coach and carriage designs, particularly associated with the upper classes, became more sophisticated over the following centuries. Charles Darwin's grandfather, Erasmus Darwin, was the first to design a steering system of the type used today on automobiles in which each front wheel turns separately while the axle remains fixed. The four-wheeled coach became the basis for steam locomotives and railway carriages, and eventually for the automobile. Other parts of the world adopted European transport designs as symbols of modernity.

However, the question remains: Why did the Europeans stick with inefficient four-wheeled wagons for over four thousand years when other parts of the world opted exclusively for the two-wheeled alternative? It is unlikely that providing a private traveling compartment for groups of elite women was the sole reason. But the fact that such traveling accommodations became available may offer a technological clue as to why upper-class women in the Middle East, China, India, and other non-European lands were so often prohibited from leaving the house whereas European women enjoyed relatively greater freedom of movement.

QUESTIONS FOR ANALYSIS

1. Why did most societies prefer two-wheeled transportation?
2. How do different societies solve the problem of providing privacy and safety to women who are traveling?
3. Which is more important in the technological development of transport vehicles, social status or gender?

Martyn Vickery/Alamy

The next step was to settle the Mongolian frontier. Kangxi personally led troops in the great campaigns that defeated Galdan and brought Inner Mongolia under Qing control by 1691.

Tea and Diplomacy

To maintain control over trade, facilitate tax collection, and suppress piracy, the Qing permitted only one market point for each foreign sector. Thus Europeans could trade only at Canton.

This system worked well enough until the late 1700s, when Britain became worried about its massive trade deficit with China. From bases in India and Singapore, British traders moved eastward and by the early 1700s dominated European trading in Canton, displacing the Dutch. The directors of the East India Company (EIC) anticipated limitless profits from China's gigantic markets and advanced technologies.

In medieval times, tea from China, carried overland to Russia, Central Asia, and the Middle East, had become a prized import. Consumers knew it by its northern Chinese name, *cha*—as did the Portuguese.

Great Pagoda at Kew Gardens A testament to Europeans' fascination with Chinese culture is the towering Pagoda at the Royal Botanic Gardens in London. Completed in 1762, it was designed by Sir William Chambers as the principal ornament in the pleasure grounds of the White House at Kew, residence of Augusta, the mother of King George III.

Other western Europeans acquired tea from the sea routes and with it the name used in the Fujian province of coastal China and Taiwan: *te*. In much of Europe, tea competed with chocolate and coffee as a fashionable drink by the mid-1600s.

British tea importers accumulated great fortunes. However, the Qing Empire took payment in silver and rarely bought anything from Britain. With domestic revenues declining in the later 1700s, the Qing government needed the silver and was disinclined to loosen import restrictions. To make matters worse, the East India Company had managed its worldwide holdings badly. As it teetered on bankruptcy, its attempts to manipulate Parliament became increasingly intrusive. In 1792 the British government dispatched Lord George Macartney, a well-connected peer with practical experience in Russia and India, to China. Staffed by scientists, artists, and translators as well as guards and diplomats, the **Macartney mission** showed Britain's great interest in the Qing Empire as well as the EIC's desire to revise the trade system.

To fit Chinese traditions, Macartney portrayed himself as a "tribute emissary" come to salute the Qianlong emperor's eightieth birthday. However, he refused to perform the kowtow, though he did agree to bow on one knee as he would to King George III. The Qianlong emperor received Macartney courteously in September 1793 but refused to alter the Canton trading system, open new ports of trade, or allow the British to establish a permanent mission in Beijing. The emperor sent a letter to King George explaining that China had no need to increase its foreign trade, had no use for Britain's ingenious devices and manufactures, and set no value on closer diplomatic ties.

Dutch, French, and Russian missions also failed. European frustration mounted and admiration for China faded. The Qing court would not communicate with foreign envoys or observe the simplest rules of the European diplomatic system. In Macartney's view, China was like a venerable old warship, well maintained and splendid to look at, but obsolete and no longer up to the task.

Population Growth and Environmental Stress

The Chinese who escorted Macartney and his entourage in 1792–1793 took them through China's prosperous cities and productive farmland. They did not see the economic and environmental decline that had set in during the last decades of the 1700s.

Population growth—a tripling in size since 1500—had intensified demand for food and for more intensive agriculture. With an estimated 350 million people in the late 1700s, China had twice the population of all of Europe. Despite efficient farming and the gradual adoption of New World crops like corn and sweet potatoes, population pressure touched off social and environmental problems. As increased demand for building materials and firewood shrank woodlands, the deforestation, in turn, accelerated wind and water erosion and increased flooding. Dams and dikes were not maintained, and silted-up river channels were not dredged. By the end of the eighteenth century parts of the thousand-year-old Grand Canal linking the rivers of north and south China were nearly unusable, and the towns that bordered it were starved for commerce.

Some interior districts responded to this misery by increasing their output of export goods like tea, cotton, and silk. Some peasants sought seasonal jobs in better-off agricultural areas or worked in low-status jobs as barge pullers, charcoal burners, or night soil (human waste) carriers. Begging, prostitution, and theft increased in the cities, and rebellions broke out in flood-ravaged central and southwestern China. Indigenous peoples concentrated in the less fertile lands in the south and in the northern and western borderlands of the empire often joined in revolts.

The Qing government was not up to controlling its vast empire. It was twice the size of the Ming geographically, but it employed about the same number of officials. The government's dependence on working

Macartney mission The unsuccessful attempt by the British Empire to establish diplomatic relations with the Qing Empire.

- After the year 1500, financial, environmental, and administrative problems weakened the Ming Empire, and it fell to the Manchus.
- Kangxi expanded the Qing Empire's borders, subdued or contained rival powers, and presided over a flourishing economy and culture.
- The one-sided Qing trade system prompted the Macartney mission and other European embassies to the Qing court, but the Qing refused all requests for more equitable trading conditions.
- By the late eighteenth century, population growth had created social and environmental problems that the Qing could not control.

alliances with local elites had led to widespread corruption and shrinking government revenues. The Qing's spectacular rise had ended, and decline had set in.

CONCLUSION

It would be a mistake to think of early modern East Asia as three strictly defined countries filled with people who invariably acted on behalf of their homelands in trade or warfare. During the Imjin War, some Japanese, tired of fighting in Korea, decided to join the Ming military and were promoted to high posts by the Chinese. Similarly, some Chinese troops remained in Korea, married local women, and became part of local Korean communities.

Trade and warfare also presented opportunities for groups of people who did not identify with any one country. As a case in point, the Ming-Qing transition and growth in sea trade spurred an increase in piracy during the seventeenth century. The Zheng family dominated piracy in East Asia, defeated the Dutch bases in Taiwan, and eventually worked for the Ming regime to battle the Manchus. The founder of this pirate family, Zheng Zhilong, worked alongside the Dutch and the Portuguese. He was baptized a Catholic and given the name Nicholas Iquan. He married a Japanese woman, and their son, Zheng Chenggong, continued to expand the Zheng enterprise. He is better known as Koxinga, the Portuguese pronunciation for an official title given to him by the Ming. Zheng even pursued state-building activities

such as establishing an office to collect tax and regulating trade in the South China Sea.

Already a vast empire under the Ming, China doubled in size under the Qing, mostly through westward expansion into less densely populated areas. China was land based, just like the Russian, Safavid, Ottoman, and Mughal Empires, with the strengths and problems of administrative control and tax collection that size entailed. The expansion of China incorporated not just new lands but also new peoples. Chinese society had long been diverse, and its geographical, occupational, linguistic, and religious differences grew as the Qing expanded. China had also long used Confucian models, imperial customs, and a common system of writing to transcend such differences and to assimilate elites.

Japan was different. Though nominally headed by an emperor, real power lay with the successive shoguns. However, Japan lacked a centralizing, common political philosophy like China's Confucianism, vast conquered territories, and ethnic diversity. Tokugawa Japan was similar in size and population to France, the most powerful state of western Europe, but its political system was much more decentralized. Japan's efforts to add colonies on the East Asian mainland had failed.

By the late eighteenth century, the weaknesses in China and Japan were becoming more evident and would ultimately make these countries vulnerable to Western aggression. China had once led the world in military innovation, including the first uses of gunpowder, but Chinese armies continued to depend on superior numbers and tactics for their success, rather than on new technology. Infantrymen armed with guns served alongside others armed with bows and arrows, swords, and spears.

The military forces of Japan underwent more innovative changes than those of China and Korea, in part through Western contacts. In the course of its sixteenth-century wars of unification, Japan produced its own gunpowder revolution but thereafter lacked the motivation and the means to stay abreast of the world's most advanced military technology. The samurai preferred swords.

Finally, neither China nor Japan developed navies commensurate with their size and coastlines. Korea had a small but effective navy during the Imjin War, but it could not match China's in strength or size. China's defenses against pirates and other sea invaders were left to the small war junks of its maritime provinces. Japan's naval capacity was similarly decentralized.

CHAPTER REVIEW

EAST ASIA AND EUROPE

■ *How did the West and East Asia affect each other commercially and intellectually?* (page 449)

Missionaries and merchants brought European culture to East Asia, and information about Asia traveled back to an interested Europe. Europeans demanded Chinese silk, porcelain, and tea, as well as jewelry, jade, lacquered screens, painted fans, and wallpaper. European political philosophy was influenced by the idea of the Confucian emperor as a philosopher-king. Ideas about weaponry, medicine and anatomy, mapmaking, and astronomy attracted Asian elites. Silver flowed from the new world via European merchant ships in exchange for Chinese consumer goods, but suspicions arose on both sides. European merchants were tightly regulated, and European adaptations to Asian culture erupted in controversy when the Franciscans and Dominicans opposed Jesuit acceptance of ancestor worship. Ultimately Christians were expelled from China and Japan and were later persecuted.

JAPANESE UNIFICATION AND THE IMJIN WAR

■ *What was the effect of Japanese unification on Korea and China?* (page 453)

After a period of daimyo rivalry and civil war, Hideyoshi emerged victorious. The unification of Japan had seasoned his war forces and inflated his ambitions, and he set his sights on China. Korea became the battleground for the bloody Imjin War. A superior naval strategy helped Korea defend itself against the Japanese, but the experienced Japanese land forces devastated the population. China, which regarded Korea as a tribute state, responded to appeals for help. Hideyoshi never reached China, and the military stalemate eventually caused Japan to withdraw, but only after the Japanese had laid waste to Korea's infrastructure and agriculture. The war also depleted Ming resources, and new taxes for recovery created internal unrest. A depleted military left vulnerable borders elsewhere. After setting out to conquer the Ming, Hideyoshi facilitated its fall, and other foes would emerge as China's next rulers.

TOKUGAWA JAPAN AND CHOSON KOREA, TO 1800

■ *How did Japan respond to unification and domestic peace, and Korea to the ravages of the Imjin War?* (page 454)

The unification of Japan under the Tokugawa Shogunate ushered in a long period of relative peace. Commerce and craft industries flourished with sake brewing becoming a particularly profitable business. Merchants as a class commanded little respect, but their ability to manipulate interest rates and rice prices worsened the economic status of the samurai, the military elite.

In the aftermath of the Imjin War, Korean nobles strengthened their position at the expense of the country's recovery. Although aligned with Chinese Confucian culture, Korea's civil service examinations were open only to a hereditary noble class. Nobles filled all government posts and were exempt from taxes and military service. In addition, they were able to expand their landholdings after the war, making more land tax-exempt. At one point, 30 percent of the population were slaves. Royal revenues needed to rebuild fell by an estimated two-thirds.

FROM MING TO QING

■ *How did China deal with military and political challenges both inside and outside its borders?* (page 456)

China's history illustrates a complex interplay of internal and external forces. During the final days of the Ming dynasty, China suffered from internal rebellions caused by deteriorating economic conditions, to which the Ming responded ineffectively. When Japan invaded, the Ming sought help from the Manchus, who then turned on them and established the Qing Empire. The Qing's settlement of the Amur frontier with Russia illustrates how diplomacy and compromise could serve mutual interests. Finally, the Chinese added new European customers to already extensive internal and external markets and developed both positive and problematic cultural relations with the Jesuits and some other Europeans. From a Chinese perspective, European contacts could be useful but were neither essential nor of great importance.

Key Terms

Manchu (p. 449)

daimyo (p. 451)

samurai (p. 453)

Tokugawa Shogunate (p. 454)

Qing Empire (p. 457)

Kangxi (p. 458)

Amur River (p. 459)

Macartney mission (p. 462)

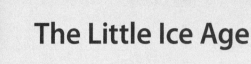

The Little Ice Age

A giant volcanic eruption in the Peruvian Andes in 1600 affected the weather in many parts of the world for several years. When volcanic ash from the eruption of Mount Huanyaputina (hoo-AHN-yah-poo-TEE-nuh) shot into the upper atmosphere and spread around the world, it screened out sunlight. As a result, the summer of 1601 was the coldest in two hundred years in the Northern Hemisphere.

Archaeologist Brian Fagan has pointed out that Mount Huanyaputina's chilling effects were a spectacular event in a much longer pattern of climate change that has been called the Little Ice Age.[1] Although global climate had been cooling since the late 1200s, in the northern temperate regions the 1590s had been exceptionally cold. Temperatures remained cooler than normal throughout the seventeenth century.

The most detailed information on the Little Ice Age comes from Europe. Glaciers in the Alps grew much larger. Trade became difficult when rivers and canals that had once been navigable in winter froze solid from bank to bank. In the coldest years, the growing season in some places was as much as two months shorter than normal. Unexpectedly late frosts withered the tender shoots of newly planted crops in spring. Wheat and barley ripened more slowly during cooler summers and were often damaged by early fall frosts.

People could survive a smaller-than-average harvest in one year by drawing on food reserves, but when cold weather damaged crops in two or more successive years, the consequences were devastating. Deaths due to malnutrition and cold increased sharply when summer temperatures in northern Europe registered 2.7°F (1.5°C) lower than average in 1674 and 1675 and again in 1694 and 1695. The cold spell of 1694 and 1695 caused a famine in Finland that carried off a quarter to a third of the population.

At the time people had no idea what was causing the unusual cold of the Little Ice Age. Advances in climate history make it clear that the cause was not a single terrestrial event such as the eruption of Mount Huanyaputina. Nor was the Little Ice Age the product of human actions, unlike some climate changes such as today's global warming.

Ultimately, the earth's weather is governed by the sun. In the seventeenth century astronomers in Europe reported seeing fewer sunspots, dark spots on the sun's surface that are indicative of solar activity and thus the sun's warming power. Diminished activity in the sun was primarily responsible for the Little Ice Age.

If the sun was the root cause, the effects of global cooling should not have been confined to northern Europe. Although contemporary accounts are much scarcer in other parts of the world, there is evidence of climate changes around the world in this period. Observations of sunspots in China, Korea, and Japan drop to zero between 1639 and 1700. China experienced unusually cool weather in the seventeenth century, but the warfare and disruption accompanying the fall of the Ming and the rise of the Qing probably were much more to blame for the famines and rural distress of that period.

By itself, a relatively slight decrease in average annual temperature would not have a significant effect on human life outside the northern temperate areas. However, evidence suggests that there was also a significant rise in humidity in this period in other parts of the world. Ice cores drilled into ancient glaciers in the Arctic and Antarctic show increased snowfall. Information compiled by historian James L. A. Webb, Jr., shows that lands south of the Sahara received more rainfall between 1550 and 1750 than they had during the previous era.[2] Increased rainfall would have been favorable for pastoral people, whose herds found new pasture in what had once been desert, and for the farmers farther south whose crops got more rain.

In the eighteenth century the sun's activity began to return to normal. Rising temperatures led to milder winters and better harvests in northern Eurasia. Falling rainfall allowed the Sahara to advance southward, forcing the agricultural frontier to retreat.

---

[1] Brian Fagan, *The Littlest Ice Age: How Climate Made History, 1300–1850* (New York: Basic Books, 2000).

[2] James L. A. Webb, Jr., *Desert Frontier: Ecological Change Along the Western Sahel, 1600–1850* (Madison: University of Wisconsin Press, 1995).

Part Six

Revolutions Reshape the World, 1750–1870

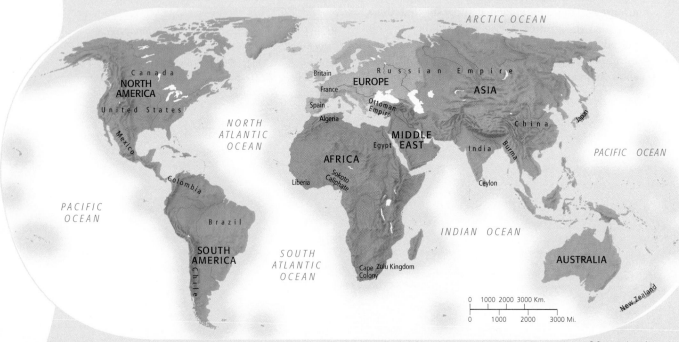

© Cengage Learning

	1750	1775	1800
AMERICAS	**1754–1763** French and Indian War	• **1776** U.S. Declaration of Independence • **1789** U.S. Constitution ratified	• **1791** Slaves revolt in Haiti	• **1803** Louisiana Purchase **1809–1825** Wars for independence in Spanish America
EUROPE	• **ca. 1750** Industrial Revolution begins in Britain **1756–1763** Seven Years War		**1789–1799** French Revolution **1799–1815** Rule of Napoleon in France	**1814–1815** Congress of Vienna
AFRICA	**1750–1800** Growing slave trade reduces population		• **1795** Britain takes Cape Colony	•**1809** Sokoto Caliphate founded Shaka founds Zulu kingdom **1818** •
MIDDLE EAST		**1769–1772** High point of restored Mamluk influence in Egypt	**1789–1807** Reign of Ottoman sultan Selim III • **1798** Napoleon invades Egypt Muhammad Ali founds dynasty in Egypt **1805** •	
ASIA AND OCEANIA	• **1755** Qing conquest of Turkestan	**1769–1778** Captain Cook's exploration of Australia, New Zealand • **1765** East India Company rule of Bengal begins	**1796–1804** White Lotus Rebellion in China	East India Company creates Bombay presidency **1818** •

468

CHAPTER 20
Industrial Revolution and Global Impact, 1760–1851

CHAPTER 21
Revolutionary Changes in the Atlantic World,
1750–1850

CHAPTER 22
Land Empires in the Age of Imperialism, 1800–1870

Between 1750 and 1870, nearly every part of the world experienced dramatic political, economic, and social change. The beginnings of industrialization, the American, French, and Haitian Revolutions, as well as the struggles for independence in Latin America, transformed political and economic life. European nations expanded into Africa, Asia, and the Middle East while Russia and the United States acquired vast new territories.

The Industrial Revolution introduced new technologies and patterns of work that made these societies wealthier and militarily more powerful. Western intellectual life became more secular. The Atlantic slave trade and later slavery itself were abolished, and the first efforts to improve the status of women were made.

The Industrial Revolution led to a new wave of imperialism. France conquered Algeria, and Great Britain expanded its colonial rule in India and established colonies in Australia and New Zealand. European political and economic influence also expanded in Africa and Asia. The Ottoman Empire and the Qing Empire met this challenge by implementing reform programs that preserved traditional structures while adopting elements of Western technology and organization. Though lagging behind western Europe in transforming its economy and political institutions, Russia attempted modernization efforts, including the abolition of serfdom.

The economic, political, and social revolutions that began in the mid-eighteenth century shook the foundations of European culture and led to the expansion of Western power around the globe. Some of the nations of Asia, Africa, and Latin America reformed and strengthened their own institutions and economies, while others pushed for more radical change. After 1870 Western imperialism became more aggressive, and few parts of the world were able to resist it.

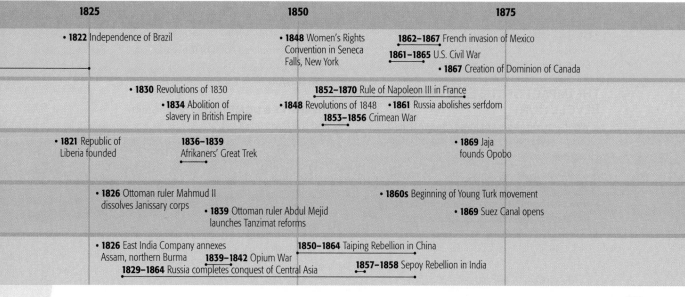

1825	1850	1875
• **1822** Independence of Brazil	• **1848** Women's Rights Convention in Seneca Falls, New York	**1862–1867** French invasion of Mexico
		1861–1865 U.S. Civil War
		• **1867** Creation of Dominion of Canada
• **1830** Revolutions of 1830	**1852–1870** Rule of Napoleon III in France	
• **1834** Abolition of slavery in British Empire	•**1848** Revolutions of 1848 • **1861** Russia abolishes serfdom	
	1853–1856 Crimean War	
• **1821** Republic of Liberia founded	**1836–1839** Afrikaners' Great Trek	• **1869** Jaja founds Opobo
• **1826** Ottoman ruler Mahmud II dissolves Janissary corps	• **1839** Ottoman ruler Abdul Mejid launches Tanzimat reforms	• **1860s** Beginning of Young Turk movement
		• **1869** Suez Canal opens
• **1826** East India Company annexes Assam, northern Burma **1839–1842** Opium War	**1850–1864** Taiping Rebellion in China	
1829–1864 Russia completes conquest of Central Asia	**1857–1858** Sepoy Rebellion in India	

CHAPTER 20

1760–1851

Industrial Revolution and Global Impact

© Cengage Learning

Manchester was just a small town in northern England in the early eighteenth century. A hundred years later, it had turned into the fastest-growing city in history. To contemporaries, it was both a marvel and a horror. Prosperous cotton mills were interspersed with workers' housing, built as cheaply as possible. The economist Nassau Senior described these workers' quarters:

> But when I went through their habitations . . . my only wonder was that tolerable health could be maintained by the inmates of such houses. These towns . . . have been erected by small speculators with an utter disregard to everything except immediate profit. . . . Not a house in this street escaped cholera. . . . the streets are unpaved, with a dunghill or a pond in the middle; the houses built back to back, without ventilation or drainage, and whole families occupy each a corner of a cellar or of a garret.[1]

Not everyone deplored the living conditions in the new industrial city. Friedrich Engels, both a factory owner and critic of capitalism, recounted a meeting with a well-to-do citizen:

> One day I walked with one of these middle-class gentlemen into Manchester. I spoke to him about the disgraceful unhealthy slums and drew his attention to the disgusting condition of that part of the town in which the factory workers lived. I declared that I had never seen so badly built a town in my life. He listened patiently and at the corner of the street at which we parted company, he remarked: "And yet there is a great deal of money made here. Good morning, Sir!"[2]

---

[1]Nassau W. Senior, *Letters on the Factory Act, as it affects the cotton manufacture, addressed to the Right Honourable, the President of the Board of Trade*, 2d ed. (London: Fellows, 1844), 20.

[2]Friedrich Engels, *Condition of the Working Class in England*, trans. and ed. by W. O. Henderson and W. H. Chaloner (Oxford: Blackwell, 1958), 312.

Manchester's rise as a large, industrial city was a result of what historians call the **Industrial Revolution**, the most profound transformation in human life since the beginnings of agriculture. This revolution involved dramatic innovations in manufacturing, mining, transportation, and communications and equally rapid changes in society and commerce. New relationships between social groups created an environment that was conducive to technical innovation and economic growth. The introduction of new technologies and new social and economic arrangements allowed the industrializing countries—first Britain, then western Europe and the United States—to unleash massive increases in production and productivity, exploit the world's natural resources as never before, and transform the environment and human life in unprecedented ways.

Industrialization widened the gap between rich and poor. Those who owned and controlled the innovations amassed wealth and power and lived in spectacular luxury. The middle class of industrializing nations grew rapidly, exercising increased influence in politics and culture. But workers, including children, worked long hours in dangerous factories and lived crowded together in unsanitary tenements.

The effect of the Industrial Revolution around the world was also very uneven. The first countries to industrialize grew rich and powerful, facilitating a second great wave of European imperialism in the nineteenth century. In Egypt and India, the economic and military power of Europe stifled the tentative beginnings of industrialization. The disparity between the industrial and the developing countries that exists today has its origins in the early nineteenth century.

Industrial Revolution The transformation of the economy, the environment, and living conditions, occurring first in England in the eighteenth century, that resulted from the use of steam engines, the mechanization of manufacturing in factories, and innovations in transportation and communication.

Manchester from Kersal Moor, 1852 (w/c with bodycolour and gum arabic on paper), Wyld, William (1806–89)/The Royal Collection © 2011 Her Majesty Queen Elizabeth II/The Bridgeman Art Library

Manchester, the First Industrial City The first cotton mills, built on the banks of the River Irwell in northern England, transformed Manchester from a country town into a booming industrial city. The use of chemicals to bleach and dye the cloth and the introduction of steam engines in the early nineteenth century to power the spinning and weaving machines made Manchester, for a time, the most polluted city on earth.

CAUSES OF THE INDUSTRIAL REVOLUTION

■ *What caused the Industrial Revolution?*

What caused the Industrial Revolution, and why did it develop so rapidly in England in the eighteenth century? The basic preconditions of this momentous event seem to have been population growth, an agricultural revolution, the expansion of trade, and an openness to innovation.

Preconditions for Industrialization

Population growth fueled the Industrial Revolution by increasing consumer demand and lowering labor costs. Between 1650 and 1850 Europe's population grew from 100 million to 266 million, and the number of city dwellers more than doubled. In England and Wales, for example, the population increased from about 6 million in 1700 to 9 million in 1800 and 18 million by 1850—increases never before experienced in European history. As the pace of manufacturing mounted in the eighteenth century, rural laborers and their families moved to cities in hope of higher earnings and better lives.

The population explosion and urbanization resulted from more widespread resistance to disease and an **agricultural revolution** that provided food for city dwellers and forced poorer peasants off the land. Long before the eighteenth century, the acceptance of the potato and maize from the Americas had increased food supplies in Europe. In the cool and humid regions of Europe, potatoes yielded two or three times more calories per acre than grain. Maize (American corn) was also grown across Europe from northern Iberia to the Balkans.

Prosperous landowners tried new methods and new crops, draining marshes to improve the soil, breeding better livestock whose manure was used to improve fertilizer, and introducing crop rotation. Some "enclosed" their land—that is, consolidated their holdings, including commons that in the past had been open to all. The "enclosure movement" turned the rural poor into tenants and sharecroppers into landless farm laborers. Many moved to the cities to seek work; others became vagrants; still others emigrated to Canada, Australia, and the United States.

Expanding domestic and foreign demand for textiles also led to innovation in Europe. Traditionally, European textiles were produced by skilled artisans organized in guilds using centuries-old technologies, an expensive process that took years. But a system called *proto-industrialization* replaced expensive

agricultural revolution The transformation of farming that resulted in the eighteenth century from the spread of new crops, improvements in cultivation techniques and livestock breeding, and the consolidation of small holdings into large farms from which tenants and sharecroppers were forcibly expelled.

Chronology

	Technology	Economy, Society, and Politics
1750	1702–1712 Thomas Newcomen builds first steam engine 1759 Josiah Wedgwood opens pottery factory 1764 Spinning jenny 1769 Water frame introduced; James Watt patents steam engine 1779 First iron bridge 1785 Samuel Crompton's mule 1794 Eli Whitney's cotton gin	1 776 Adam Smith's *Wealth of Nations* 1776–1783 American Revolution 1789–1799 French Revolution
1800	1800 Alessandro Volta's battery 1807 Robert Fulton's *North River* 1837 Wheatstone and Cooke's telegraph; Morse's code 1838 First ships steam across the Atlantic 1840 *Nemesis* sails to China 1840s Telegraphs cross eastern U.S., western Europe	1804–1815 Napoleonic Wars 1820s U.S. cotton industry begins 1833 Factory Act in Britain 1834 Robert Owen's Grand National Consolidated Trade Union 1847–1848 Irish famine 1848 Collapse of Chartist movement; revolutions in Europe; publication of *Communist Manifesto*
1850	1851 Crystal Palace opens in London	1854 First cotton mill in India

artisans who typically earned daily wages with proto-industrial workers who were only paid for what they produced. Raw materials and simple machinery, like looms and spinning wheels, were delivered to the homes of farm families and rural jobbers who organized groups of laborers. Complex tasks were subdivided into simple procedures easily mastered by rural workers. Chronic problems with quality control and inefficiencies that resulted from the dispersal of production were offset by increased cloth production and lowered labor costs. (See Diversity and Dominance: Adam Smith and the Division of Labor).

Trade also stimulated a growing interest in technology and innovation among educated people throughout Europe and the America, as well as a much deeper engagement of colonial possessions with foreign markets. Nearly all the European powers profited from plantation colonies in the Americas. But there was also a dramatic expansion of European commerce with markets in Africa and Asia. Europeans of even modest means consumed ever-growing quantities of sugar to sweeten their tea, coffee, cocoa, pastries, and candies, and the demand for manufactures like porcelain cups and dinnerware increased as well. At the same time Caribbean planters imported a steeply rising volume of cotton textiles to clothe themselves and their slaves. Initially, these cotton textiles were imported from Asia, but increasing demand led to the creation of domestic cotton textile industries, the first truly modern mechanized industry.

European governments played a key role in this economic expansion. During the eighteenth century the French, Spanish, and British governments sent expeditions around the world to collect plants that could profitably be grown domestically or in their colonies. They offered prizes for scientific discoveries, like determining the longitude of a ship at sea and the accurate measurement of the earth's circumference, and created royal manufacturers that produced fine china, silks, and carpets. As the volume of commerce increased, canal building boomed. Governments also sponsored improvements in road networks, but maintenance was often inadequate. In Britain this neglect

Diversity & Dominance

Adam Smith and the Division of Labor

*A*dam Smith (1723–1790), a Scottish philosopher, is famous for his book An Inquiry into the Nature and Causes of the Wealth of Nations, *first published in 1776. It was the first work to explain the economy of a nation as a system. Smith criticized the notion, common in the eighteenth century, that a nation's wealth was synonymous with the amount of gold and silver in the government's coffers. Instead, he defined wealth as the amount of goods and services produced by a nation's people. By this definition, labor and its products are an essential element in a nation's prosperity.*

In the passage that follows, Smith contrasts two methods of making pins. In one a team of workers divided up the job of making pins and produced a great many every day; in the other pin workers "wrought separately and independently" and produced very few pins per day. It is clear that the division of labor produces more pins per worker per day. But who benefits? Left unsaid is that a pin factory had to be owned and operated by a manufacturer who hired workers and assigned a task to each one.

The illustration shows a pin-maker's workshop in late-eighteenth-century France. Each worker is performing a specific task on a few pins at once, and all the energy comes from human muscles. These are the characteristics of a proto-industrial workshop.

To take an example, therefore, from a very trifling manufacture—but one in which the division of labour has been very often taken notice of—the trade of the pin-maker: a workman not educated to this business (which the division of labour has rendered a distinct trade), nor acquainted with the use of machinery employed in it (to the invention of which the same division of labour has probably given occasion), could scarce, perhaps, with his utmost industry, make one pin in a day, and certainly could not make twenty. But in the way in which this business is now carried on, not only the whole work is a peculiar trade, but it is divided into a number of branches, of which the greater part are likewise peculiar trades. One man draws out the wire, another straights it, a third cuts it, a fourth points it, a fifth grinds it at the top for receiving the head; to make the head requires two or three distinct operations, to put it on, is a peculiar business, to whiten the pins is another; it is even a trade by itself to put them into the paper; and the important business of making a pin is, in this manner, divided into about eighteen distinct operations, which, in some manufactories, are all performed ➤

A Pin-Maker's Workshop *The man in the middle (Fig. 2) is pulling wire off a spindle (G) and through a series of posts. This ensures that the wire will be perfectly straight. The worker seated on the lower right (Fig. 3) takes the long pieces of straightened wire and cuts them into shorter lengths. The man in the lower left-hand corner (Fig. 5) sharpens twelve to fifteen wires at a time by holding them against a grindstone turned by the worker in Fig. 6. The men in Figs. 4 and 7 put the finishing touches on the points. Other operations—such as forming the wire to the proper thickness, cleaning and coating it with tin, and attaching the heads—are depicted in other engravings in the same encyclopedia.*

by distinct hands, though in others the same man will sometimes perform two or three of them. I have seen a small manufactory of this kind where ten men only were employed, and where some of them, consequently, performed two or three distinct operations. But though they were very poor, and therefore but indifferently accommodated with the necessary machinery, they could, when they exerted themselves, make among them about twelve pounds of pins in a day.

There are in a pound upwards of four thousand pins of a middling size. Those ten persons, therefore, could make among them upwards of forty-eight thousand pins in a day. Each person, therefore, making a tenth part of forty-eight thousand pins, might be considered as making four thousand eight hundred pins a day. But if they had all wrought separately and independently, and without any of them having been educated to this peculiar business, they certainly could not each of them have made twenty, perhaps not one pin in a day; that is, certainly, not the two hundred and fortieth, perhaps not the four thousand eight hundredth part of what they are at present capable of performing, in consequence of a proper division and combination of their different operations.

QUESTIONS FOR ANALYSIS

1. Why does dividing the job of pin-making into ten or more operations result in the production of more pins per worker? How much more productive are these workers than if each one made complete pins from start to finish?

2. How closely does the picture of a pin-maker's workshop illustrate Smith's verbal description?

3. What disadvantage would there be to working in a pin factory where the job was divided as in Smith's example, compared to making entire pins from start to finish?

4. What other examples can you think of, from Adam Smith's day or from more recent times, of the advantages of the division of labor?

Source: Adam Smith, *An Inquiry into the Nature and Causes of the Wealth of Nations*, ed. Edward Gibbon Wakefield (London: Charles Knight and Co., 1843), 7–9.

led to the formation of private "turnpike trusts" that built numerous toll roads. Authorities in England, France, Prussia, and Spain, among other European nations, recruited skilled artisans from rival nations, subsidized periodicals that disseminated new technologies, and expanded their navies to better protect foreign trade.

Britain's Advantages

These changes were widespread, but Britain in the eighteenth century had the fastest-growing population, food supply, and overseas trade. Already the world's leading exporter of tools, guns, hardware, clocks, and other manufactured goods (see Map 20.1), Britain took the lead in introducing new technologies and maintained its place as Europe's foremost industrial power to the end of the nineteenth century. After developing machines that multiplied the productive capacities of individual workers in the eighteenth century, British inventors developed efficient steam engines in the nineteenth century that replaced wind, water, and animal power as the source of energy for industrial machinery. Prosperity from good harvests and a booming overseas trade fueled a rising standard of living that stimulated consumption and led to innovation in manufacturing. More important still, Britain had abundant supplies of coal and iron ore, two key ingredients in the Industrial Revolution. Britain's mining and metal industries employed engineers with a tradition of experimentation and innovation, its strong craft tradition trained a large number of skilled mechanics, and its patent system offered inventors the hope of rich rewards by protecting their intellectual property rights. Examples of men who became wealthy and respected for their inventions stimulated others to experiment.

Britain had other advantages as well. At the dawn of the industrial age, it had one of the most fluid societies in Europe. With the exception of the Netherlands, British political power was not as centralized as elsewhere in Europe; its court was less ostentatious, its aristocracy was less powerful, there were fewer obstacles to commerce and manufacturing, and the lines separating the social classes were not as sharply drawn. British commercial culture had long enjoyed the benefits of strong banks, joint-stock companies,

- The Industrial Revolution arose from population growth, an agricultural revolution, increased trade, and an interest in innovation.

- Britain industrialized first, thanks to its fluid political structures, transportation infrastructure, inventiveness, and a society open to talented and enterprising people.

- On the European continent, greater industrial growth followed political movements that swept away the restrictions of the old aristocratic regimes.

a stock market, and commercial insurance. At a time when overland transportation was costly, Britain also had good water transportation thanks to its long coastline, navigable rivers, and a growing network of canals, with none of the duties and tolls that goods had to pay every few miles in France or Spain.

In contrast to Britain, the economies of continental Europe were hampered by high transportation costs, misguided government regulations, and rigid social structures. Once revolutions had swept away Europe's old regimes (see Chapter 21), both private investors and European governments—acutely aware of Britain's head start—recruited British engineers and artisans, created technical schools, eliminated internal tariff barriers, tolls, and other hindrances to trade, and encouraged the formation of joint-stock companies and banks to channel private savings into industrial investments. Rich in coal and iron-ore deposits, first Belgium, and then Germany after 1850, enjoyed industrial booms based on iron, cotton, steam engines, and railroads. The United States was well established as a major industrial power by 1860, having quickly adopted textile and metallurgical technologies developed first in Great Britain. Without abundant coal, France retained a more traditional manufacturing economy until the introduction of electricity late in the nineteenth century.

THE TECHNOLOGICAL REVOLUTION

■ *What were the key innovations that increased productivity and drove industrialization?*

Five innovations spurred industrialization: (1) mass production through the division of labor, (2) new machines and mechanization, (3) a great increase in the manufacture of iron, (4) the steam engine, and (5) the electric telegraph. While the full realization of these innovations occurred first in Great Britain and then spread to the United States and continental Europe in the nineteenth century, China had achieved the first three during the Song dynasty (960–1279) (see Chapter 11). But China did not develop the steam engine or electricity, innovations that dramatically increased human productivity. The transformation of Western economies through industrialization depended on the application of these new forms of energy to the process of mechanical innovation.

Mass Production and Mechanization

Before the mid-eighteenth century, only the wealthy could afford fine china, but in 1759, **Josiah Wedgwood**, the son of a potter, started his own pottery business to satisfy the demand from more and more Europeans who wanted to drink their tea, cocoa, and coffee from porcelain because it would not spoil their flavor. He subdivided the work into simple repetitive tasks, such as unloading the clay, mixing it, pressing flat pieces, dipping the pieces in glaze, putting handles on cups, packing kilns, and carrying things from one part of his plant to another. He also used molds instead of the potter's wheel wherever possible, a change that saved labor and created uniform plates and bowls that could be stacked. Wedgwood's china production is a case in point for how **mass production** and the **division of labor** affected traditional industries: workers became more productive and, requiring fewer skills, were paid less. Wedgwood was able to lower the cost of his products while improving their quality, and to offer his wares for sale at lower prices.

Josiah Wedgwood English industrialist whose pottery works were the first to produce fine-quality pottery by industrial methods.

mass production The manufacture of many identical products by the division of labor into many small repetitive tasks. This method was introduced into the manufacture of pottery and into the spinning of cotton thread.

division of labor A manufacturing technique that breaks down a craft into many simple and repetitive tasks that can be performed by unskilled workers. Pioneered in the manufacture of pottery and in other eighteenth-century factories, it greatly increased the productivity of labor and lowered the cost of manufactured goods.

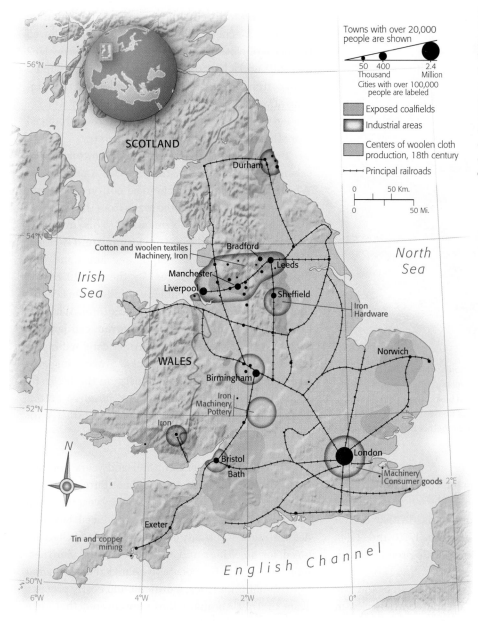

Towns with over 20,000
people are shown

50   400   2.4
Thousand   Million
Cities with over 100,000
people are labeled

Exposed coalfields

Industrial areas

Centers of woolen cloth
production, 18th century

Principal railroads

0   50 Km.

0   50 Mi.

Map 20.1 The Industrial Revolution in Britain, ca. 1850 The first industries arose in northern and western England. These regions had abundant coal and iron-ore deposits for the iron industry, as well as moist climate and fast-flowing rivers, factors important for the cotton textile industry.

© Cengage Learning

The cotton industry, the largest in this period, illustrates the role of **mechanization**, the use of machines to do work previously done by hand. The cotton plant did not grow in England, but the cloth was so much cooler, softer, and cleaner than wool that wealthy Europeans developed a liking for the costly import. When the powerful English woolen industry persuaded Parliament to forbid the import of cotton cloth, it stimulated attempts to import cotton fiber and make the cloth domestically. Here was an opportunity for enterprising inventors to reduce costs with laborsaving machinery.

Beginning in the 1760s a series of inventions—the spinning jenny, the water frame, and the mule—

mechanization The application of machinery to manufacturing and other activities. Among the first processes to be mechanized were the spinning of cotton thread and the weaving of cloth in late-eighteenth- and early-nineteenth-century England.

Wedgwood's Potteries In Staffordshire, England, Josiah Wedgwood established a factory to mass-produce beautiful and inexpensive china. The bottle-shaped buildings are kilns in which thousands of pieces of china could be fired at one time. Kilns, factories, and housing were all mixed together in pottery towns, and smoke from burning coal filled the air.

managers often hired children to tend the spinning machines. Mechanization and cheap labor allowed the price of cloth to fall by 90 percent between 1782 and 1812, and it kept on dropping. Machinery adapted from cotton production quickly transformed the spinning of wool as well. In Belgium in 1810, only 5 of 144 woolen factories were mechanized, but they produced more than 50 percent of total production.

Britain's industrialization made cotton America's most valuable crop. In 1794 the American Eli Whitney patented his mechanical cotton gin, a simple device that separated the seeds from the fiber and made cotton growing economical. This invention permitted the spread of cotton farming into Georgia, then into Alabama, Mississippi, and Louisiana, and finally as far west as Texas. By the late 1850s the southern states were producing a million tons of cotton a year, five-sixths of the world's total. With the help of British immigrants who introduced jennies, mules, and power looms (and Americans willing to ignore the British patent rights), Americans also developed their own cotton industry in the 1820s. By 1840 the United States had twelve hundred cotton mills that served the booming domestic market, two-thirds of them in New England.

revolutionized the spinning of cotton thread and allowed British industry to undersell high-quality handmade cotton cloth from India. British cotton output increased tenfold between 1770 and 1790, despite the fact that these large-scale producers still depended on water power.

When the boom in thread production and the soaring demand for cloth created bottlenecks in weaving, inventors rose to the challenge with power looms, carding machines, chlorine bleach, and cylindrical printing presses. By the 1830s, large English textile mills powered by steam engines were turning raw cotton into printed cloth. This was a far cry from the cottage industries of the previous century.

Mechanization offered two advantages: increased productivity for the manufacturer and lower prices for the consumer. Whereas in India it took five hundred hours to spin a pound of cotton, the improved, self-regulating mule of 1830 required only eighty minutes. Cotton mills needed few skilled workers, and

The Iron Industry

For over two thousand years iron had been used throughout Eurasia, Africa, and China for tools, weapons, and household items. Wherever it was produced, however, deforestation eventually drove up the cost of charcoal (used for smelting) and restricted output. Furthermore, iron had to be repeatedly heated and hammered to drive out impurities, a difficult and costly process. Then in 1709 Abraham Darby discovered that coke (coal that has had the impurities removed) could be used in place of charcoal. The resulting metal was of lower quality than charcoal iron but much cheaper to produce, for coal was plentiful. In 1784 British inventor Henry Cort found a way to remove some of the impurities in coke-iron by puddling—stirring the molten iron with long rods—prior to rolling the iron into bars. Cort's process made it possible to produce wrought iron (a soft and malleable form of iron) very cheaply.

By 1790 four-fifths of Britain's iron was made with coke, while other countries still used charcoal. Coke-iron allowed a great expansion in the size of

Pit Head of a Coal Mine This is a small coal mine. In the center of this picture stands a Newcomen engine used to pump water. The work of hauling coal out of the mine was still done by horses and mules. The smoke coming out of the smokestack is a trademark of the early industrial era.

Walker Art Gallery, National Museums Liverpool/The Bridgeman Art Library

individual blast furnaces, substantially reducing the cost of iron production. There seemed almost no limit to the quantity of iron that could be produced with coke. Britain's iron production rose fast, from 17,000 tons in 1740 to 3 million tons in 1844, as much as in the rest of the world put together.

In turn, there seemed no limit to the amount of iron that an industrializing society would purchase or the novel applications for this cheap and useful material. In 1779 Abraham Darby III (grandson of the first Abraham Darby) built a bridge of iron across the Severn River. In 1851 Londoners marveled at the **Crystal Palace**, a huge exhibition hall made entirely of iron and glass that showcased British industry but also included exhibits from the colonies and other nations.

The availability of cheap iron made the mass production of objects such as guns, hardware, and tools appealing. However, fitting together the parts of these products required a great deal of labor. To reduce labor costs, manufacturers like the Americans Eli Whitney (firearms) and Eli Terry (clocks) contributed to the development of standardized interchangeable parts that did not require high levels of crasftsmanship. By the mid-nineteenth century, interchangeable parts had been widely adopted in the manufacture of firearms, farm equipment, and sewing machines, and Europeans, who still relied on

skilled artisans, had begun to call this the "American system of manufactures" because it was a distinctively American response to a shortage of skilled craftsmen in its immigrant population.

The Steam Engine

The first machine to transform fossil fuel into mechanical energy was the **steam engine**, a device that set the Industrial Revolution apart from all previous periods of growth and innovation.

Before the eighteenth century, deep mines filled with water faster than horses could pump it out. Scientists understood the concept of atmospheric pressure and had created experimental devices to turn heat into motion, but they had not found a way to put the principles involved to practical use. Then, between 1702 and 1712, Thomas Newcomen developed the first practical steam engine, a huge but

Crystal Palace Building erected in Hyde Park, London, for the Great Exhibition of 1851. Made of iron and glass, like a gigantic greenhouse, it was a symbol of the industrial age.

steam engine A machine that turns the energy released by burning fuel into motion. Thomas Newcomen built the first crude but workable steam engine in 1712. James Watt vastly improved his device in the 1760s and 1770s. Steam power was later applied to operating machinery in factories and to propelling ships and locomotives.

The *De Witt Clinton* Locomotive, 1835–1840 The *De Witt Clinton* was the first steam locomotive built in the United States. The high smokestack let the hot cinders cool so they would not set fire to nearby trees, an important consideration at a time when eastern North America was still covered with forest. The three passenger cars are clearly horse carriages fitted with railroad wheels.

Bettmann/Corbis

effective device that could clear water from mines much faster than earlier pumps.

The Newcomen engine's voracious appetite for fuel mattered little in coal mines, where fuel was cheap, but it made the engine too costly for other uses. In 1764 **James Watt**, an instrument maker at Glasgow University in Scotland, was asked to repair the university's model Newcomen engine. Watt realized that the engine wasted fuel because the cylinder had to be alternately heated and cooled. He developed a separate condenser—a vessel into which the steam was allowed to escape, leaving the cylinder always hot and the condenser always cold. Watt patented his idea in 1769 and enlisted the help of the iron manufacturer Matthew Boulton to turn his invention into a commercial product. Their first engines were used to pump water out of copper and tin mines, where fuel was too costly for Newcomen engines. In 1781 Watt invented the sun-and-planet gear, which turned the back-and-forth action of the piston into rotary motion. This allowed steam engines to power machinery in flour and cotton mills, pottery manufactures, and other industries.

Watt's steam engine was the most celebrated invention of the eighteenth century. Because coal supplies seemed unlimited, steam-generated energy appeared to be an inexhaustible source of power that could be used where animal, wind, and water power were lacking. Inspired by the success of Watt's

engine, several inventors put steam engines on boats. The first commercially successful steamboat was Robert Fulton's *North River*, which sailed the Hudson River between New York City and Albany, New York, in 1807. Soon steamboats were launched on the Ohio and the Mississippi, gateways to the Midwest. By 1830 some three hundred steamboats plied the Mississippi and its tributaries. The United States was fast becoming a nation that moved by water.

Oceangoing steam-powered ships were much more difficult to build than river boats, for the first steam engines used so much coal that no ship could carry more than a few days' supply. The *Savannah*, which crossed the Atlantic in 1819, was a sailing ship with an auxiliary steam engine that was used for only ninety hours of its twenty-nine-day trip. Engineers soon developed more efficient engines, and in 1838 two steamers, the *Great Western* and the *Sirius*, crossed the Atlantic on steam power alone.

Railroads Steam engines were initially too heavy and weak to pull any weight. After Watt's patent expired in 1800, however, inventors experimented with lighter, more powerful

James Watt Scot who invented the condenser and other improvements that made the steam engine a practical source of power for industry and transportation. The watt, an electrical measurement, is named after him.

high-pressure engines. In the early 1800s they built several steam-powered vehicles able to travel on roads or rails. Between 1830 and 1850, a railroad-building mania swept Britain. The first lines linked towns and mines with the nearest harbor or waterway. As passenger traffic soared, entrepreneurs built lines between the major cities and even to small towns. Railroads were far cheaper, faster, and more comfortable than stagecoaches.

Railroads had their most transformative effects in the United States. By the 1840s, 6,000 miles (10,000 kilometers) of track radiated from Boston, New York, Philadelphia, and Baltimore. In the 1850s, 21,000 miles (34,000 kilometers) of additional track were laid, much of it westward across the Appalachians to Memphis, St. Louis, and Chicago. The trip from New York to Chicago, which once took three weeks by boat and on horseback, could be made in forty-eight hours. The railroads opened up the Midwest, dispersing the waves of immigrants, turning the vast prairie into farms to feed the industrial cities of the eastern United States, and creating a prodigious internal market for manufactures.

Railways also accelerated the industrialization of Europe. Belgium, independent since 1830, quickly copied the British. In France and Prussia, construction in the mid-1840s not only satisfied the long-standing need for transportation but also stimulated the iron, machinery, and construction industries. By 1850 Germany had built 3,639 miles (5,856 kilometers) of railroad line and France 1,811 miles (2,915 kilometers).

Communication over Wires

After the Italian scientist Alessandro Volta invented the battery in 1800, making it possible to produce an electric current, many inventors tried to apply electricity to communication. The first practical **electric telegraph** systems were developed almost simultaneously in England and America. In 1837 in England, Charles Wheatstone and William Cooke introduced a five-wire telegraph, while the American Samuel Morse introduced a code of dots and dashes that could be transmitted with a single wire.

By the late 1840s telegraph wires crisscrossed the eastern United States and western Europe. In 1851 the first submarine telegraph cable was laid across the English Channel from England to France (cutting the transmission of news from up to four days to minutes). Thus began a network that eventually connected the entire globe. The world was rapidly shrinking, to the applause of Europeans and Americans, for whom speed was a clear measure of progress. No longer was the movement of information limited to the speed of a sailing ship, a galloping horse, or a fast-moving train.

THE IMPACT OF THE EARLY INDUSTRIAL REVOLUTION

■ What was the impact of these changes on the society and environment of the industrializing countries?

The Industrial Revolution led to profound changes in society, politics, and the economy. Early changes—smoky cities, slum neighborhoods, polluted water, child labor in mines and textile mills—were being alleviated by the mid-nineteenth century. But by then national or even international problems were replacing those local ones: business cycles, labor conflicts, and the degradation of entire regions into industrial landscapes.

electric telegraph A device for rapid, long-distance transmission of information over an electric wire. It was introduced in England and North America in the 1830s and 1840s and replaced telegraph systems that utilized visual signals such as semaphores.

SECTION REVIEW

- The technological revolution involved the development of cost-saving machines and processes, such as mass production through the division of labor.

- Beginning in the 1760s a series of inventions mechanized the British cotton industry and stimulated cotton farming in the United States, while American manufacturers pioneered processes involving interchangeable parts.

- Innovations in processing transformed the British iron industry, making cheap iron widely available for various applications.

- With the perfection of the steam engine, steamboats and railroads proliferated, the latter spurring the industrialization of Europe.

- Practical electric telegraphs appeared in England and America and quickly spread.

The New Industrial Cities

The most dramatic environmental changes occurred in the towns. Never before had towns grown so fast. London, one of the largest cities in Europe in 1700 with 500,000 inhabitants, grew to 1,117,000 by 1800 and to 2,685,000 by 1850, making it the largest city in the world. New York City, already 100,000 strong in 1815, reached 600,000 (including Brooklyn) in 1850. In some areas, towns merged and formed megalopolises, such as Greater London, the English Midlands, central Belgium, and the Ruhr district of Germany.

A great deal of money went into the building of fine homes, churches, museums, and theaters. Yet, by all accounts, the industrial cities grew much too fast. As poor migrants streamed in from the countryside, developers built cheap, shoddy row houses for them to rent. These tenements were dangerously overcrowded, with several families often living in one room. Moreover, town dwellers recently arrived from the country brought country ways with them. People threw their sewage and trash out the windows to be washed down the gutters in the streets. The poor kept pigs and chickens; the rich kept horses; and pedestrians stepped into the street at their own risk. Air pollution from burning coal got steadily worse, and people drank water drawn from wells and rivers contaminated by sewage and industrial runoff. The River Irwell, which ran through Manchester, was, in the words of one visitor, "considerably less a river than a flood of liquid manure."[3]

To the long list of preindustrial diseases (such as smallpox, dysentery, and tuberculosis), industrialization added new ailments. Rickets, a bone disease caused by lack of sunshine, became endemic in dark and smoky industrial cities. Steamships brought cholera from India, causing great epidemics that struck poor neighborhoods especially hard. In the 1850s, the average life expectancy in England was forty years. In Manchester's poorest neighborhoods, it was around seventeen. Shocking reports of slum life eventually led to municipal reforms, such as garbage removal, water and sewage systems, and parks and schools. These measures began to alleviate the ills of urban life after the mid-nineteenth century.

---

[3]Quoted in Lewis Mumford, *The City in History* (New York: Harcourt Brace, 1961), 460.

Rural Environments

Long before the Industrial Revolution, wilderness areas had largely disappeared in Britain and much of western Europe. Almost every piece of land was covered with fields, pastures, or towns. The most serious problem was deforestation. People cut timber to build ships and houses, to heat homes, and to manufacture bricks, iron, glass, beer, bread, and many other items.

Americans transformed their environment on a vast scale. Settlers viewed forests not as a valuable resource but as a hindrance to development. In their haste to "open up the wilderness," pioneers felled trees and burned them, built houses and abandoned them when they moved on. The cultivation of cotton was especially harmful. Planters cut down forests, grew cotton for a few years until the soil was depleted, and then moved west, abandoning the land to scrub pines.

In industrializing Europe, raw materials once grown on the land—such as wood, hay, and wool—were replaced by materials found underground, like iron ore and coal, or obtained overseas, like cotton. Across Europe the expansion of coal and iron mining had dramatic effects on the environment. As the population increased and land grew scarcer, the cost of growing feed for horses rose, creating incentives to find new, less land-hungry means of transportation. Likewise, iron became cheaper and wood more expensive. Canal building boomed in Britain, France, and the low countries. The marvels of canal construction—deep-cut tunnels and even aqueducts—were then applied to the railroads. Soon, rattling trains pulled by puffing, smoke-belching locomotives invaded long-isolated districts.

Working Conditions

Most industrial jobs were unskilled, repetitive, and boring. Factory work did not vary with the seasons or the time of day but began and ended by the clock. Factories used the invention of gas lighting to expand the working day past sunset. Workdays were long, there were few breaks, and foremen watched constantly. Workers who performed one simple task over and over had little sense of achievement or connection to the final product. Industrial accidents were common and could ruin a family. Unlike even the poorest

An Industrial Canal In the late eighteenth and early nineteenth centuries, before railroads were introduced, many canals were constructed in England so that barges could transport heavy materials cheaply, such as coal for industrial works and steam engines, stone and bricks for buildings, clay for pottery works, and ores for metal foundries. Canals such as this one, which ran alongside a copper foundry, contributed greatly to Britain's industrial development.

preindustrial farmer or artisan, factory workers had no control over their tools, jobs, or working hours.

Industrial work also had a major impact on women and family life. Women who could not afford servants had always worked, but mostly within the family: spinning and weaving, sewing hats and clothes, preparing food, washing, and doing a myriad other household chores. In rural areas, women also did farm work, especially caring for gardens and small animals. However, factory work was never the main occupation of working women. Most young women who sought paid employment became domestic servants in spite of the low pay, drudgery, and risk of sexual abuse. Other women with small children tried hard to find work they could do at home, such as laundry, sewing, embroidery, millinery, or taking in lodgers.

Those who worked in factories were concentrated in textile mills, because textile work required less strength than metalworking, construction, or hauling. On average, women earned one-third to one-half as much as men. Young unmarried women worked to support themselves or to save for marriage, while married women took factory jobs when their husbands were unable to support the family. Mothers of infants faced a hard choice: whether to leave their babies with wet nurses at great expense or bring them to the factory and keep them quiet with opiates. Rather than working together as a family, husbands and wives increasingly worked in different places.

Even with both parents working, poor families found it hard to make ends meet. As in preindustrial societies, parents thought children should contribute to their upkeep as soon as they were able to. The first generation of industrial workers brought children as young as five or six with them to the factories and mines, since there were no public schools or day-care centers. Employers preferred child workers because they were cheaper and more docile than adults and because they were better able to tie broken threads or crawl under machines to sweep the dust. Mine operators used children to pull coal carts along the low passageways from the coal face to the mine shaft.

Some manufacturers tried to provide more humane environments. When Francis Cabot Lowell built a cotton mill in Massachusetts, he hired the unmarried daughters of New England farmers, promising them decent wages and housing in dormitories under careful moral supervision. Other manufacturers eager to combine profits with morality followed his example. But soon the profit motive won out, and manufacturers imposed longer hours, harsher working conditions, and lower wages. When young women in New England factories went on strike, the mill owners replaced them with Irish immigrants willing to accept lower pay and worse conditions.

Rising demand for cotton also reinforced and expanded the institution of slavery in the Americas. In the 1790s, there were 700,000 slaves of African descent in the United States. As the "Cotton Kingdom" expanded, the number of slaves increased to 3.2 million by 1850, 60 percent located in the cotton region. Similarly, European demand for sugar prolonged plantation slavery in the West Indies and spread it to the coffee-growing regions of southern Brazil. Slavery was an integral part of both commercial capitalism and the Industrial Revolution, not, as some maintained at the time, a consequence of biological differences or biblical injunctions.

Changes in Society

Industrialization accentuated the polarization of society and disparities of income. In Britain the worst-off were those who clung to an obsolete skill or craft. Even by working more hours, handloom weavers could not compete with power looms and were reduced to destitution. The standard of living of factory workers did not decline steadily like those of handloom weavers but fluctuated wildly with the cycles of economic growth and contraction. During the war years 1792 to 1815, the poor suffered widespread hardship when the price of food rose faster than wages. Then, in the 1820s, real wages and public health began to improve, as industrial production grew at over 3 percent a year, pulling the rest of the economy along. Prices for food, housing, and clothing fell so that even the poor could afford comfortable, washable cotton clothes. Hard times returned in the "hungry forties" when, in 1847–1848, the potato crop failed in Ireland and one-quarter of the Irish population died.

Overall, the benefits of industrialization—cheaper food, clothing, and utensils—did not improve workers' standard of living until the 1850s.

SECTION REVIEW

- The Industrial Revolution spurred rapid urbanization, causing severe pollution, overcrowding, and myriad health and hygiene problems.

- Industrialization hastened deforestation and brought pollution to rural environments.

- Industrial working conditions were harsh and dangerous, especially for children, until Britain passed child-labor laws.

- Working-class women faced difficult choices between factory work and family obligations, and slavery persisted because of industrialization.

- Industrialization benefited owners more quickly than workers, the former often being able to rise in society, while the cult of domesticity shaped middle class women's lives.

The real beneficiaries of the early Industrial Revolution were the middle class. Most were the sons of middling shopkeepers, craftsmen, or farmers who had a little capital to start a cotton-spinning or machine-building business. Many tried and some succeeded, largely plowing their profits back into the business. A generation later, in the nineteenth century, some newly rich industrialists bought their way into high society. With industrialization came a "cult of domesticity" that removed middle-class women from contact with the business world and left them responsible for the home, the servants, the education of children, and the family's social life.

NEW ECONOMIC AND POLITICAL IDEAS

■ *How did the Industrial Revolution influence the rise of new economic and political ideas?*

Changes as profound as the Industrial Revolution triggered political ferment and ideological conflict. So many wars and revolutions took place during those years that we cannot neatly separate out the consequences of industrialization from the rest (see Chapter 21). But it is clear that the Industrial Revolution strengthened the ideas of laissez faire (LAY-say fair) and socialism and sparked workers' protests.

Laissez Faire

The most celebrated exponent of **laissez faire** ("let them do [as they will]") was Adam Smith (1723–1790), a Scottish economist. In *The Wealth of Nations* (1776) Smith argued that if individuals were allowed to seek personal gain, the effect, as though guided by an "invisible hand," would be to increase the general welfare (see Diversity and Dominance: Adam Smith and the Division of Labor). Except to protect private property, the government should refrain from interfering in business; it should even allow duty-free trade with foreign countries.

Although it was true that governments at the time were incompetent at regulating their national economies, it was becoming obvious that industrialization was not improving the general welfare but was causing great misery for some segments of society. Some thinkers blamed the workers' plight on the population boom, which outstripped the food supply and led to falling wages. The workers' poverty, they claimed, was as much a result of "natural law" as was the wealth of successful businessmen, and the only way for the working class to avoid mass famine was to delay marriage and practice self-restraint and sexual abstinence.

Laissez faire provided an ideological justification for a special kind of capitalism: banks, stock markets, and chartered companies allowed investors to obtain profits with reasonable risks but with much less government control and interference than in the past. But not everyone accepted the grim conclusions of the "dismal science," as economics was then termed. Jeremy Bentham (1748–1832) believed that it was possible to maximize "the greatest happiness of the greatest number," if only a Parliament of enlightened reformers would study the social problems of the day and pass appropriate legislation. His philosophy became known as utilitarianism.

Positivism and Marxism

Some French social thinkers, moved by sincere concern for the poor, offered a more radically new vision of a just civilization. Espousing a philosophy called **positivism**, the Count of Saint-Simon (1760–1825) argued that the scientific method could solve social as well as technical problems. He recommended that the poor, guided by scientists and artists,

form workers' communities under the protection of benevolent business leaders. Instead of attracting workers, these ideas found enthusiastic support from bankers and entrepreneurs, who were inspired by them to invest in railroads, canals, and other symbols of modernity. Positivism also influenced the political elites of Brazil and Mexico, who pursued a top-down program of economic development reinforced by harsh police controls and the manipulation of political institutions. Its chief tenets are emblazed on the Brazilian flag: Order and Progress.

Numerous protest organizations formed across Europe, the most prominent of which—calling themselves *communists*—were led by two German-born intellectuals, Karl Marx (1818–1883) and his long-time collaborator and benefactor Friedrich Engels (1820–1895). They argued that the concentration of wealth and power associated with industrialization had led to the unbearable oppression of industrial workers (whom they called the **proletariat**), that history was dominated by class struggle, and that proletarians would inevitably come together to overthrow the bourgeoisie, the modern class that controlled industry. The final words of *The Communist Manifesto*, published in 1848 with Engels, urged revolutionary action with the challenge "Proletarians of all countries unite!"

Protests and Reforms

Workers benefited little from the ideas of these middle-class philosophers. Instead, they resisted harsh working conditions in their own ways. They changed jobs frequently and were often absent, especially on Mondays. Periodically, workers rioted, went

laissez faire The idea that government should refrain from interfering in economic affairs. The classic exposition of laissez-faire principles is Adam Smith's *Wealth of Nations* (1776).

positivism A philosophy developed by the French Count of Saint-Simon. Positivists believed that social and economic problems could be solved by application of the scientific method, leading to continuous progress. Their ideas became popular in France and Latin America in the nineteenth century.

proletariat Industrial workers whose oppression was an example of how, according to *The Communist Manifesto*, history was dominated by class struggle between the workers who sold their labor for survival and those who owned the mills, factories, mines, or other means of industrial production and wealth (the bourgeoisie).

on strike, or violently resisted the introduction of new technologies, believing that mechanized production would diminish the value of their skills and force them into poverty. As early as 1767, disgruntled textile workers mobilized to destroy the spinning jenny. In 1779 workers destroyed the machines driven by water power in Blackburn, England, and in 1811 angry lace and stocking workers calling themselves *Luddites* attacked more than one hundred businesses and destroyed nearly every machine in the district.

In the late 1770s, French workers organized protests against "foreign" innovations, attacking British craftsmen and destroying the new machines. In the early stages of the French Revolution (see Chapter 21), popular revolutionary sentiment reinforced the resistance of workers to new machinery and undermined the ability of the government to protect factories. The result was that French artisans retained traditional control of production and France fell decades behind Britain in industrializing.

When wealthy farmers began to introduce reapers and other machines, the rural poor set fires, threatened landlords, demanded higher wages, and broke the machines. This popular movement culminated after 1830 when widespread rural riots forced the British government to mobilize troops and militia in defense of property. In the end, thousands of protestors were arrested and either imprisoned in Britain or transported to Australia as convict laborers.

These violent efforts to block innovation and protect long-established customs in manufacturing and agriculture were superseded by laboring-class organizations focused on workplace reform, higher wages, and expanded political rights. Gradually, workers formed benevolent societies and organized to demand universal male suffrage and shorter workdays. In 1834 Robert Owen founded the Grand National Consolidated Trade Union to lobby for an eight-hour workday; it quickly gained half a million members but collapsed a few months later in the face of government prosecution of trade union activities. The Chartist movement had more success, gathering petitions by the thousands to present to Parliament. Although Chartism collapsed in 1848, it left a legacy of labor organizing.

SECTION REVIEW

- Industrialization reinforced Adam Smith's laissez-faire, free-market theories even in the face of conditions that prompted competing ideas such as utilitarianism. Many people sought explanations and proposed solutions for the changes in society and the economy.

- Positivists deplored the hardships caused by industrialization but asserted that they could be ameliorated by technological advances and wise policies, while communists advocated revolutionary action.

- Agitation by workers led politicians to investigate the working conditions in mines and factories, especially the work of women and children.

Eventually, mass movements persuaded the British Parliament to investigate conditions in factories and mines and initiate some reforms. The Factory Act of 1833 prohibited the employment of children younger than nine in textile mills and limited the working hours of children between the ages of nine and thirteen to eight hours a day and of fourteen- to eighteen-year-olds to twelve hours. The Mines Act of 1842 prohibited the employment of women and boys under age ten underground. On the European continent, in contrast, the revolutions of 1848 revealed widespread discontent with repressive governments but failed to soften the hardships of industrialization (see Chapter 21).

THE LIMITS OF INDUSTRIALIZATION OUTSIDE THE WEST

■ *How did the Industrial Revolution affect the relations between the industrialized and the nonindustrialized parts of the world?*

The spread of the Industrial Revolution in the early nineteenth century transformed the relations of western Europe and North America with the rest of the world. In Egypt and India, cheap industrial imports, backed by the power of Great Britain, delayed industrialization for a century or more, and China was defeated by the products of industrial manufacture. In these three cases, we can discern outlines of the Western domination that has characterized the history of the world since the late nineteenth century.

A Railroad Bridge Across the Nile In the second half of the nineteenth century, industrialized nations, especially Great Britain, sent engineers and equipment to build railroads in less industrialized parts of the world, such as India, South Africa, Latin America, and the Middle East. One such railway connected Cairo and Alexandria in Egypt. Here a railroad bridge crosses the Nile at Benha near the pyramids. Corbis

Egypt, strongly influenced by European ideas since the French invasion of 1798, began to industrialize in the early nineteenth century. The driving force was its ruler, Muhammad Ali (1769–1849), a man who was to play a major role in the history of the Middle East and East Africa (see Chapter 22). Wanting to build up the Egyptian economy and military in order to become less dependent on the Ottoman sultan, his nominal overlord, Muhammad Ali imported advisers and technicians from Europe and built cotton mills, foundries, shipyards, weapons factories, and other industrial enterprises. To pay for all this, he made the peasants grow wheat and cotton, which the government bought at a low price and exported at a profit. He also imposed high tariffs on imported goods to force the pace of industrialization.

Muhammad Ali's efforts fell afoul of the British, who did not want a powerful country threatening to interrupt the flow of travelers and mail across Egypt, the shortest route between Europe and India. When Egypt went to war against the Ottoman Empire in 1839, Britain intervened and forced Muhammad Ali to eliminate all import duties in the name of free trade. Unprotected, Egypt's fledgling industries could not compete with the flood of cheap British products. Thereafter, Egypt exported raw cotton, imported manufactured goods, and became an economic dependency of Britain.

Until the late eighteenth century, India had been the world's largest producer and exporter of cotton textiles, handmade by skilled spinners and weavers. The British East India Company took over large parts of India just as the Industrial Revolution was beginning in Britain. It allowed cheap British factory-made yarn and cloth to flood the Indian market duty-free, putting spinners and handloom weavers out of work. Unlike Britain, India had no factories where displaced handicraft workers could work. Most of them became landless peasants, eking out a precarious living.

Like other tropical regions, India became an exporter of raw materials and an importer of British industrial goods. To hasten the process, British entrepreneurs and colonial officials introduced railroads into the subcontinent. The construction of India's railroad network began in the mid-1850s, along with coal mining to fuel the locomotives and the installation of telegraph lines to connect the major cities.

Some Indian entrepreneurs saw opportunities in the atmosphere of change that the British created. In 1854 the Bombay merchant Cowasjee Nanabhoy Davar imported an engineer, four skilled workers, and several textile machines from Britain and started India's first textile mill. This was the beginning of India's mechanized cotton industry. Despite many gifted entrepreneurs, however, India's industrialization proceeded at a snail's pace, for the government was in British hands and the British did nothing to encourage Indian industry.

Having benefited from a long period of relative political stability, population growth, and commercial expansion, the Qing dynasty saw little reason to focus on foreign trade or promote the new machine technologies that had rapidly transformed the European economy in the first half of the nineteenth century. China continued to play a major role in the major markets of Asia even as European power grew, maintaining a favorable balance of trade that Europe paid for in silver (see Chapter 19). Moreover, China remained an agrarian empire with a conservative elite and a growing peasant population. As such, China focused on the production and distribution of food, rather than on trade, as an effective guarantee of social peace.

This situation was about to change. In January 1840 a shipyard in Britain launched a radically new ship whose iron hull and flat bottom allowed it to navigate in shallow waters, with a steam engine to power it upriver and against the wind. In November the *Nemesis* arrived off the coast of China, heavily armed and ready to reverse the steep trade imbalance long enjoyed by China. Though ships from Europe had been sailing to China for three hundred years, the *Nemesis* was the first steam-powered iron gunboat in Asian waters. It was soon joined by other steam-powered warships that collectively established European control of Chinese rivers, bombarding forts and cities and transporting troops and supplies from place to place along the coast and up the rivers far

more quickly than Chinese soldiers could move on foot. With this new weapon, Britain, a small island nation half a world away, compelled China to recognize the economic and military transformations wrought by industrial innovation in Europe and defeated the largest and most populated country in the world (see Chapter 22).

CONCLUSION

The Industrial Revolution was the most momentous transformation in history since the beginning of agriculture. The steam engine and other new machines greatly lowered the cost and increased the production of goods like cotton and iron and the speed of transportation and communication.

However, the process caused social upheavals and environmental problems. Many entrepreneurs and businesspeople became very wealthy, while industrial workers—many of them children—worked under appalling conditions and lived in overcrowded tenements in badly polluted cities. Economists and philosophers proposed many theories and offered many solutions to the radical problems of industrial societies.

Industrialization had political consequences on a global scale. A small number of industrializing nations—first Great Britain, then those of western Europe and North America—grew more powerful. Other parts of the world were left behind to become political or economic dependencies of these powerful nations.

Eventually the industrial nations learned to alleviate their social problems, but the disparity between the rich and poor nations persisted for two centuries or more, and the environmental effects of industrialization have changed from local to global.

SECTION REVIEW

- Industrialization contributed to Europe's and North America's domination of large parts of the world.

- Britain snuffed out the incipient industrialization in Egypt and India and turned these countries intro producers of raw materials.

- Steam-powered iron warships enabled Britain to defeat China.

CHAPTER REVIEW

CAUSES OF THE INDUSTRIAL REVOLUTION
■ *What caused the Industrial Revolution?* (page 472)

The Industrial Revolution arose from a combination of factors in European society in the eighteenth and early nineteenth centuries. The population grew, but so did the food supply, thanks to improvements in agriculture. Among upper- and middle-class Europeans, practical subjects like business, science, and technology became fashionable. Great Britain had a particularly fluid society open to talents and enterprise.

THE TECHNOLOGICAL REVOLUTION
■ *What were the key innovations that increased productivity and drove industrialization?* (page 476)

A series of technological and organizational innovations transformed the manufacture of many products, reducing their costs and increasing their productivity. New machines, assembled in mills, mass-produced cotton thread and cloth. Work formerly done by skilled craftsmen was divided into many simple tasks assigned to workers in factories. New techniques also made iron cheap and abundant. Steam engines provided power to factories, ships, and railroads, while electricity found its first practical application in telegraphy.

THE IMPACT OF THE EARLY INDUSTRIAL REVOLUTION
■ *What was the impact of these changes on the society and environment of the industrializing countries?* (page 481)

The Industrial Revolution changed people's lives and the environments in which they lived. Cities grew huge, and for most of their inhabitants, unsightly and unhealthy. While middle-class women were consigned to caring for the home and children, working-class women and children as well as men were obliged to earn their living in mines and factories. Rural environments were also transformed as roads, canals, and railroads crisscrossed open land.

NEW ECONOMIC AND POLITICAL IDEAS
■ *How did the Industrial Revolution influence the rise of new economic and political ideas?* (page 484)

Some thinkers defended the growing disparities between rich and poor in the name of laissez faire. Government and businesspeople eagerly adopted many of the free-market capitalist views of Adam Smith. Others, such as positivists and utopian socialists, criticized the injustices caused by industrialization and offered a new vision of just communities. Still others, like communists, called for revolution. Workers created labor unions, leading political leaders to reexamine the working conditions of factories and mines, especially as they concerned women and children. However, not until the mid-nineteenth century did industrialization begin to raise living standards in the industrialized countries.

THE LIMITS OF INDUSTRIALIZATION OUTSIDE THE WEST
■ *How did the Industrial Revolution affect the relations between the industrialized and the nonindustrialized parts of the world?* (page 486)

The Industrial Revolution changed life around the world because it gave the newly industrial nations of the West new powers to coerce non-Western societies. In particular, incipient industrialization in Egypt and India was actively thwarted or intentionally ignored, and those countries turned into producers of raw materials and consumers of British goods. British steam-powered gunboats forced China to open its doors to unequal trade.

Key Terms

Industrial Revolution (p. 471)	Crystal Palace (p. 479)
agricultural revolution (p. 472)	steam engine (p. 479)
Josiah Wedgwood (p. 476)	James Watt (p. 480)
mass production (p. 476)	electric telegraph (p. 481)
division of labor (p. 476)	laissez faire (p. 485)
mechanization (p. 477)	positivism (p. 485)
	proletariat (p. 485)

Revolutionary Changes in the Atlantic World

© Cengage Learning

In August 1791 slaves and free blacks began an insurrection in the plantation district of northern Saint Domingue (san doe-MANG) (present-day Haiti). During the following decade and a half, Haitian revolutionaries abolished slavery; defeated military forces from Britain and France; and achieved independence.

News and rumors about revolutionary events in France had helped move the island's slave community to rebel. These same events had divided the island's white population into royalists (supporters of France's King Louis XVI) and republicans (who sought an end to monarchy). The large free mixed-race population secured some political rights from the French Assembly but were forced into rebellion by the violent resistance of the slave-owning elite.

Among those planning the insurrection was Toussaint L'Ouverture (too-SAN loo-ver-CHORE), a black freedman. This remarkable revolutionary organized the rebels militarily, negotiated with the island's competing factions and with representatives of Britain and France, and wrote his nation's first constitution. Commonly portrayed as a fiend by slave owners, Toussaint became a towering symbol of resistance to oppression to slaves everywhere.

The Haitian slave rebellion was an important event in the political and cultural transformation of the Western world. Profound changes to the economy, politics, and intellectual life occurred as well. The Industrial Revolution (see Chapter 20) increased manufacturing productivity and led to greater global interdependence, new patterns of consumerism, and altered social structures. At the same time, intellectuals questioned the traditional place of monarchy and religion in society. Merchants, professionals, and manufacturers provided an audience for the new intellectual currents and pressed for a larger political role.

This revolutionary era turned the Western world "upside down." The *ancien régime* (ahn-see-EN ray-ZHEEM), the French term for Europe's old order, rested on medieval principles: politics dominated by powerful monarchs, intellectual and cultural life dominated by religion, and economics dominated by hereditary agricultural elites. In the West's new order, commoners entered political life; science took the place of religion in intellectual life; and economies opened to competition.

Revolutionary steps forward were often matched by reactionary steps backward. Imperial powers resisted the loss of colonies; monarchs and nobles struggled to retain their ancient privileges; and church authorities fought against the claims of science. While the liberal and nationalist ideals of the eighteenth-century revolutionary movements were sometimes thwarted in Europe and the Americas, belief in national self-determination and universal suffrage and a passion for social justice continued to animate reformers into the twentieth century.

PRELUDE TO REVOLUTION: THE EIGHTEENTH-CENTURY CRISIS

■ *How did the costs of imperial wars and the Enlightenment challenge the established authority of monarchs in Europe and the American colonies?*

The cost of wars fought among Europe's major powers over colonies and trade helped precipitate the revolutionary era that began in 1775 with the American Revolution. The struggles of Britain, France, and Spain for political preeminence in western Europe and overseas produced violent conflicts in the eighteenth century. In the Seven Years' War (1756–1763)—known as the French and Indian War in America—Britain gained dominance in North America and India. The enormous cost of these conflicts distinguished them from earlier wars.

However, the intellectual environment transformed by the **Enlightenment** made people much more critical of any effort to extend the power of a monarch or impose new taxes, and it also raised questions about the rights of individuals, applying the methods and questions of the Scientific Revolution to the study of human society (see Chapter 16). Some thinkers challenged long-established religious and political institutions. They argued that if scientists

Enlightenment A philosophical movement in eighteenth-century Europe that fostered the belief that one could reform society by discovering rational laws that governed social behavior and were just as scientific as the laws of physics.

could understand the laws of nature, then surely similar forms of disciplined investigation might reveal laws of human nature. The most radical wondered whether society and government could be better regulated and more productive if guided by reason rather than by hereditary rulers and the church.

These new perspectives and the intellectual optimism that fed them helped guide the English political philosopher John Locke (1632–1704). Locke argued in 1690 that governments were created to protect life, liberty, and property and that the people had a right to rebel when a monarch violated these natural rights. In *The Social Contract*, published in 1762, the French-Swiss intellectual Jean-Jacques Rousseau (zhan-zhock roo-SOE) (1712–1778) asserted that the will of the people was sacred and that the legitimacy of monarchs depended on the consent of the people. Although both men believed that government rested on the will of the people, Locke emphasized the importance of the individual, while Rousseau envisioned the people acting collectively because of their shared historical experience.

The Enlightenment is commonly associated with hostility toward religion and monarchy, but Voltaire (1694–1778), one of the Enlightenment's most critical intellects, believed that Europe's monarchs were likely agents of political and economic reform, and he wrote favorably of China's Qing emperors (see Chapter 19). Indeed, sympathetic members of the nobility and reforming European monarchs in Spain, Russia, and Prussia actively sponsored and promoted the dissemination of new ideas, providing patronage for many intellectuals. They recognized that elements of the Enlightenment buttressed their own efforts to expand royal authority at the expense of religious institutions, the nobility, and regional autonomy. Monarchs also understood that the era's passion for science and technology held the potential of fattening national treasuries and improving economic performance.

Women were instrumental in the dissemination of these new ideas. In England large numbers of educated middle-class women purchased and discussed books and pamphlets. Some were important contributors to intellectual life, raising arguments for the rights of women. In Paris wealthy women made their homes centers of debate, intellectual speculation, and free inquiry. Their salons brought together

The Art Archive

Beer Street (1751) William Hogarth's engraving shows an idealized London street scene where beer drinking is associated with manly strength, good humor, and prosperity. The self-satisfied corpulent figure in the left foreground reads a copy of the king's speech to Parliament. We can imagine him offering a running commentary to his drinking companions as he reads.

philosophers, social critics, artists, members of the aristocracy, and the commercial elite.

The intellectual ferment of the era deeply influenced the expanding middle class, who were eager consumers of the widely available books and inexpensive newspapers and journals. This broadening of the intellectual audience overwhelmed traditional institutions of censorship. New public venues like the thousands of coffeehouses and teashops of cities and market towns also became locations to discuss scientific discoveries, new technologies, and controversial works on human nature and politics, expanding the Enlightenment's influence beyond the literate minority.

The Western Hemisphere shared in Europe's intellectual ferment. Among peoples compelled to accept the dependence and inferiority explicit in colonial rule, the idea that government authority rested on the consent of the governed proved explosive. The efforts of ordinary men and women to resist the growth of government power and the imposition

Chronology

	The Americas	Europe
1750	1756–1763 French and Indian War 1770 Boston Massacre 1776 American Declaration of Independence 1778 U.S. alliance with France 1781 British surrender at Yorktown 1783 Treaty of Paris ends American Revolution 1791 Slaves revolt in Saint Domingue (Haiti) 1798 Toussaint L'Ouverture defeats British in Haiti	1756–1763 Seven Years' War 1778 Death of Voltaire and Rousseau 1789 Storming of Bastille begins French Revolution; Declaration of Rights of Man and of the Citizen in France 1793–1794 Reign of Terror in France 1795–1799 The Directory rules France 1799 Napoleon overthrows the Directory
1800	1804 Haitians defeat French invasion and declare independence 1808–1809 Revolutions for independence begin in Spanish South America 1810–1821 Mexican movement for independence 1822 Brazil gains independence 1838 Slavery abolished in British colonies 1848 Women's Rights Convention in Seneca Falls, New York; slavery abolished in French colonies	1804 Napoleon crowns himself emperor 1804–1814 Napoleon occupies most of Europe 1812 Napoleon fails to conquer Russia 1814 Napoleon abdicates; Congress of Vienna opens 1830 Greece gains independence; revolution in France 1848 Revolutions in France, Austria, Germany, Hungary, and Italy
1850	1861–1865 U.S. Civil War; 1863 Emancipation Proclamation; 1865 Thirteenth Amendment abolishes slavery in United States 1873 Puerto Rico abolishes slavery 1886 Cuba abolishes slavery 1888 Brazil abolishes slavery	

of new cultural forms provided an important political undercurrent to much of the revolutionary agitation and conflict between 1750 and 1850. But spontaneous popular uprisings gained revolutionary potential only when they coincided with ideological division and conflict within the governing class.

SECTION REVIEW

- Wars fought to protect colonies and trade routes overwhelmed the fiscal resources of European powers.
- Also important were the ideas and critical spirit of the Enlightenment, particularly the political ideas of Locke and Rousseau.
- These new ideas received the support of reformist nobles and monarchs.
- Progressive intellectual debate spread to the colonial societies of the Western Hemisphere.

THE AMERICAN REVOLUTION, 1775–1800

■ What were the direct causes of the American Revolution?

After defeating the French in 1763, the British government faced two related problems in its North American colonies. One was the likelihood of armed conflict with Amerindian peoples as settlers quickly pushed west of the Appalachian Mountains across the Ohio River. Already burdened with war debts, Britain desperately wanted to avoid additional expenditures for frontier defense. The other problem was how to get colonists to shoulder more of the costs of colonial defense and administration. Every effort to impose new taxes or prevent new settlements sparked bitter resentment and protest and ultimately led to violent rebellion.

Frontiers and Taxes   The British government's Proclamation of 1763, which sought to establish an effective western limit for settlement, threw into question the claims of thousands of established farmers without effectively protecting Amerindian land. The Quebec Act of 1774 annexed disputed lands to the province of Quebec, thus denying eastern colonies the authority to distribute lands claimed on the basis of original charters. Colonists saw the Quebec Act as tyrannical, and the Amerindian peoples received no relief from the continuous assault on their lands.

In comparison with the French, Spanish, and Portuguese colonies of the Americas, the settlers of the British colonies enjoyed substantial political autonomy. Metropolitan producers and merchants grew rich on colonial consumption of British cloth, porcelains, tea, and other imports, and these goods played a key role in forging a unified colonial culture. When new commercial regulations threatened New England's profitable trade with Spanish and French Caribbean sugar colonies, women from prominent colonial families organized boycotts of British goods. The Stamp Act of 1765, a tax on all legal documents, newspapers, pamphlets, and nearly all printed material, led to angry protests and more boycotts. Although this combination of protest and boycott forced the repeal of the Stamp Act, Britain imposed new taxes and duties in 1767. Parliament also sent British troops to quell colonial riots. Unable to control the streets of Boston, British authorities reacted by threatening colonial liberties, dissolving the colonial legislature of Massachusetts, and dispatching a warship and two regiments of soldiers. Support for a complete break with Britain grew in 1770 when British soldiers fired at an angry Boston crowd, killing five civilians. The "Boston Massacre," which seemed to expose the naked force on which colonial rule rested, radicalized public opinion throughout the colonies.

Parliament attempted to calm colonial opinion by repealing some taxes and duties, then stumbled into another crisis when it granted the East India Company a monopoly for importing tea to the colonies, raising anew the constitutional issue of Parliament's right to tax the colonies. The monopoly also offended wealthy colonial merchants, who were excluded from this profitable commerce. The crisis

The Tarring and Feathering of a British Official, 1774 British periodicals responded to the rising tide of colonial protest by focusing on mob violence and the breakdown of public order. This illustration portrayed the brutal treatment given John Malcomb, commissioner of customs at Boston. For many in Britain, colonial demands for liberty were little more than an excuse for mob violence.

came to a head in the already politically tense port of Boston when protesters dumped tea worth £10,000 into Boston harbor.

The Course of Revolution   As the crisis mounted, patriots created new governing bodies, effectively deposed many British governors and other officials, passed laws, appointed judges, and even took control of colonial militias. Simultaneously, radical leaders organized crowds to intimidate loyalists—people who were pro-British—and to enforce the boycott of British goods. Few thought compromise possible. Elected representatives, meeting in Philadelphia as the Continental

Congress of 1775, now assumed the powers of government, creating a currency and organizing an army. **George Washington** (1732–1799), a Virginia planter who had served in the French and Indian War, was named commander. On July 4, 1776, Congress approved the Declaration of Independence, the document that proved to be the most enduring statement of the revolutionary era's ideology:

> We hold these truths to be self evident: That all men are created equal; that they are endowed by their creator with certain unalienable rights; that among these are life, liberty and the pursuit of happiness; that, to secure these rights, governments are instituted among men, deriving their just powers from the consent of the governed.

This affirmation of popular sovereignty and individual rights influenced the language of revolution and popular protest around the world.

To shore up British authority, Great Britain sent more than 400 ships, 50,000 soldiers, and 30,000 German mercenaries. But this military commitment proved futile. Although British forces won most of the battles, Washington slowly built a competent Continental army and civilian support networks that provided supplies and financial resources. In the final decisive battle, fought at Yorktown, Virginia, an American army, supported by French soldiers, who had allied with the Continentals in 1778, besieged a British army led by General Charles Cornwallis. With escape cut off by a French fleet, Cornwallis surrendered to Washington as the British military band played "The World Turned Upside-Down."

New Republican Institutions

Ignoring the British example of an unwritten constitution, representatives in each of the newly independent states drafted formal charters and submitted the results to voters for ratification. Europeans were fascinated by these written constitutions and by their formal ratification by the people. Here was the social contract of Locke and Rousseau made manifest. The state constitutions also placed severe limits on executive authority and granted broad powers to legislatures. Many state constitutions included bills of rights to provide further protection against tyranny.

SECTION REVIEW

- The American Revolution grew from British settlement and tax policies after the French and Indian War.
- New taxes and commercial policies provoked colonial protest and riots in the colonies.
- Armed conflict between British troops and colonists led to the calling of the Continental Congress and the Declaration of Independence.
- French support for the American Revolution proved crucial.
- The American states developed republican institutions and procedures on the state and national levels.
- Although the new government was quite democratic, only a minority of adults gained full rights.

It proved more difficult to frame a national constitution. The Articles of Confederation—the first constitution of the United States—were not accepted until 1781. With the coming of peace in 1783, there was an effort to fashion a new convention. Debate at the **Constitutional Convention**, which began meeting in May 1787, focused on several issues: representation, electoral procedures, executive powers, and the relationship between the federal government and the states. The final compromise provided for a two-house legislature: the lower house (the House of Representatives) to be elected directly by voters and the upper house (the Senate) to be elected by state legislatures. The chief executive—the president—was to be elected indirectly by "electors" selected by ballot in the states (each state had a number of electors equal to the number of its representatives and senators).

Although the U.S. Constitution created the most democratic government of the era, only a minority of the adult population had full political rights. Southern leaders were able to protect the institution of slavery by counting three-fifths of the slave population to allocate the number of congressional representatives. Although women had led prewar boycotts and organized charitable relief during the war, they also were denied political rights in the new republic.

George Washington Military commander of the American Revolution. He was the first elected president of the United States (1789–1797).

Constitutional Convention Meeting in 1787 of the elected representatives of the thirteen original states to write the Constitution of the United States.

THE FRENCH REVOLUTION, 1789–1815

■ *What were the origins and accomplishments of the French Revolution?*

The French Revolution confronted the entrenched privileges of an established church, monarchy, and aristocracy more directly than the American Revolution did. It also expanded mass participation in political life and radicalized the democratic tradition. But in the end, the passions unleashed in France by revolutionary events could not be sustained.

French Society and Fiscal Crisis

French society was divided into three estates. The clergy, called the First Estate, numbered about 130,000 in a nation of 28 million. The Catholic Church owned about 10 percent of the nation's land and extracted substantial amounts of wealth from the economy in the form of tithes and ecclesiastical fees. Despite its substantial wealth, the church was exempted from nearly all taxes.

The 300,000 members of the nobility, the Second Estate, controlled about 30 percent of the land and retained ancient rights on much of the rest. Nobles held the vast majority of high administrative, judicial, military, and church positions. Though traditionally barred from some types of commercial activity, nobles were also important participants in wholesale trade, banking, manufacturing, and mining.

The Third Estate included everyone else. There were three times as many members of the bourgeoisie (boor-zhwah-ZEE) in 1774, when Louis XVI took the throne, as there had been in 1715, at the end of Louis XIV's reign. Peasants accounted for 80 percent of the French population. They owned some property and lived decently when crops were good and prices stable. By 1780, however, poor harvests had decreased their incomes.

The nation's poor were a large, growing, and troubling sector. Urban streets swarmed with beggars and prostitutes. Unable to afford decent housing, obtain steady employment, or protect their children, the poor periodically erupted in violent protest and rage. In the countryside, violence was often the reaction to increased dues and fees. In towns and cities, an increase in the price of bread often provided the spark.

Private Collection

Parisian Stocking Mender The poor lived very difficult lives. This woman uses a discarded wine barrel as a shop where she mends socks.

These explosive episodes, however, were not revolutionary in character. The remedies sought were conventional and immediate rather than structural and long term. That was to change when the Crown tried to solve its fiscal crisis by imposing new taxes on the nobility and other groups that in the past had enjoyed exemptions. The effort failed in the face of widespread protests and the refusal of the Parlement of Paris, an appeals court, to register the new tax. Frustrated by these actions, French authorities exiled the members of the Parlement and pushed through a series of unpopular fiscal measures.

Despite the worsening fiscal crisis, the French government took on the heavy burden of supporting the American Revolution, delaying financial collapse by borrowing enormous sums. By the end of the war with Britain, more than half of France's national budget was required to service the debt alone. In 1787, the desperate king called an Assembly of Notables to approve a radical and comprehensive reform of economic and fiscal policy. Despite the fact that the king's advisers selected this assembly from the high nobility, the judiciary, and the clergy, these representatives of France's most privileged classes proved unwilling to support the proposed reforms and new taxes. Instead, they sought to protect their interests by questioning the competence of the king and his ministers to supervise the nation's affairs, thus creating the conditions for political revolution.

Protest Turns to Revolution

The refusal of the elite to grant needed tax concessions forced the king to call the **Estates General**, a customary consultative body representing the three estates that had not met since 1614. Traditionally, the three estates met separately, and a positive vote by two of the three was required for action. Tradition, however, was quickly overturned when the Third Estate—mostly men of substantial property, including some who were inclined toward constitutional monarchy—refused to conduct business until the king ordered the other two estates to sit with it in a single body. During a six-week period of stalemate, sympathetic clergy, and eventually nobles, joined the debates of the Third Estate, beginning a transition toward an assembly that could claim to represent the nation.

When this expanded Third Estate declared itself the **National Assembly**, the king realized the reformers intended to force him to accept a constitutional monarchy. Louis's agenda for fiscal reform was being displaced by the central ideas of the era: that the people are sovereign and the legitimacy of rulers depends on their fulfilling the people's will. Louis prepared for a confrontation with the National Assembly by moving military forces to Versailles.

A succession of bad harvests beginning in 1785 had propelled bread prices upward throughout France and provoked an economic depression. By the time the Estates General met, nearly a third of

the Parisian workforce was unemployed. Hunger and anger marched hand in hand through working-class neighborhoods. When the people of Paris heard that the king was massing troops to arrest the representatives, crowds of common people began to seize arms and mobilize. On July 14, 1789, a crowd attacked the Bastille (bass-TEEL), a medieval fortress used as a prison. The futile defense of the Bastille cost ninety-eight lives before its garrison surrendered. Enraged, the attackers hacked the commander to death and then paraded through the city with his head and that of Paris's chief magistrate stuck on pikes.

These events coincided with uprisings by peasants in the country. Peasants sacked manor houses, destroyed documents that recorded their traditional obligations, refused to pay taxes and dues to landowners, and seized common lands. Forced to recognize the fury raging through rural areas, the National

The Siege of the Bastille, 1789 (gouache on card), Cholat, Claude (18th–19th century) / Musee de la Ville de Paris, Musee Carnavalet, Paris, France / Giraudon / The Bridgeman Art Library

Parisians Storm the Bastille An eyewitness to the storming of the Bastille on July 14, 1789, painted this representation of this epochal event, still celebrated by the French as a national holiday.

Estates General France's traditional national assembly with representatives of the three estates, or classes, in French society: the clergy, nobility, and commoners. The calling of the Estates General in 1789 led to the French Revolution.

National Assembly French Revolutionary assembly (1789–1791). The Estates General gave itself this title when it came together and demanded radical change. In 1789 it passed the Declaration of the Rights of Man and of the Citizen.

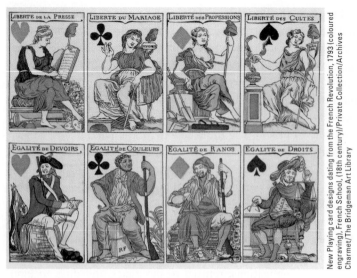

New Playing card designs dating from the French Revolution, 1793 (coloured engraving), French School, (18th century)/Private Collection/Archives Charmet/The Bridgeman Art Library

Playing Cards from the French Revolution Even playing cards could be used to attack the aristocracy and Catholic Church. In this pack of cards, "Equality" and "Liberty" replaced kings and queens.

Assembly voted to end traditional obligations and the privileges of the nobility and church, essentially ending the feudal system. Having won this victory, peasants ceased their revolt.

These popular uprisings strengthened the hand of the National Assembly in its dealings with the king and led to passage of the **Declaration of the Rights of Man and of the Citizen**, which was more sweeping in its language than the American Declaration of Independence. Among the enumerated natural rights were "liberty, property, security, and resistance to oppression." The Declaration of the Rights of Man and of the Citizen also guaranteed free expression of ideas, equality before the law, and representative government.

While delegates debated political issues in Versailles, the economic crisis worsened in Paris. The anger of the working women of Paris, struggling to feed their families in the face of high food prices, had a hard edge. On October 5, thousands of women marched the 12 miles (19 kilometers) to Versailles and forced their way into the National Assembly to demand action: "the point is that we want bread," they shouted. The crowd then entered the royal apartments, killed some of the king's guards, and searched for Queen Marie Antoinette (ann-twah-NET), whom they hated as a symbol of extravagance. They then forced the royal family to relocate to Paris.

In the next two years, the National Assembly achieved a radically restructured French society. It passed a new constitution that dramatically lim-

ited monarchial power and abolished the nobility as a hereditary class. Economic reforms swept away monopolies and trade barriers within France. This body was eventually renamed the Legislative Assembly. Its legislators seized church lands to use as collateral for a new paper currency and mandated that priests, who were to be elected, be placed on the public payroll. When the Assembly forced priests to take a loyalty oath, however, many Catholics joined a growing counter-revolutionary movement.

At first, many European monarchs welcomed the weakening of the French king, but by 1791 Austria and Prussia were threatening to intervene in support of the monarchy. The Legislative Assembly responded by declaring war. Although the war went badly at first for French forces, people across France responded patriotically to foreign invasions, forming huge new volunteer armies and mobilizing national resources to meet the challenge. By the end of 1792, French armies had gained the upper hand everywhere.

In this period of national crisis and foreign threat, the French Revolution entered its most radical phase. A failed effort by the king and queen to escape from Paris cost the king his remaining popular support. As foreign armies crossed into France, his behavior was seen as treasonous. In August 1792, the Legislative Assembly suspended his authority and ordered his imprisonment, calling for the formation of a new National Convention to be elected by all men. Swept along by popular passion, the newly elected National Convention convicted Louis XVI of treason, sentenced him to death, and proclaimed France a republic.

Declaration of the Rights of Man and of the Citizen Statement of fundamental political rights adopted by the French National Assembly at the beginning of the French Revolution.

The Guillotine

No machine more powerfully symbolizes the revolutionary era than the guillotine. The machine immortalizes Joseph Ignace Guillotin (1738–1814), a physician and member of the French Constituent Assembly. In 1789 Guillotin recommended that executions be made more humane by use of a beheading device. He sought to replace hangings, used for commoners, and beheadings by axe, used for the nobility. Both forms of execution were often conducted with little skill, leading to gruesome and painful deaths. Guillotin believed that a properly designed machine would produce predictable, nearly painless deaths and remove the social distinction between commoners and nobles, embarrassing in a more egalitarian age.

After 1791 execution by beheading became the common sentence for all capital crimes. Another physician, Antoine Louis, secretary of the College of Surgeons, designed the actual machine. Once directed to produce a suitable device, Louis, in many ways a typical technician of his time, systematically examined devices used elsewhere and experimented until satisfied with his results. Praised by contemporaries because it seemed to remove human agency, and therefore revenge, from the death penalty, the guillotine became the physical symbol of the Terror.

The Art Archive

The Guillotine *The guillotine, introduced as a more humane and democratic alternative to traditional executions, came to symbolize the arbitrary violence of the French Revolution. In this contemporary cartoon Robespierre, the architect of the Terror, serves as executioner while surrounded by guillotines.*

The guillotine ended the king's life in January 1793. Invented in the spirit of the era as a more humane way to execute the condemned, this machine was to become the bloody symbol of the Revolution (see Environment and Technology: The Guillotine). During this period of repression, called the Reign of Terror (1793–1794), competing factions used rumors of counter-revolutionary plots to justify the use of violence. Approximately 40,000 people were executed or died in prison. This radical phase ended in July 1794 when the Terror's leaders were themselves executed by guillotine.

Reaction and Dictatorship

Purged of the radicals, the National Convention began to undo the radical reforms. It removed emergency economic controls that held down prices and protected the working class. Gone also was toleration for violent popular demonstrations. When the Paris working class rose in protest in 1795, the Convention reacted with overwhelming military force. It allowed the Catholic Church to regain much of its former influence, but it did not return the church's confiscated wealth. Finally, it ratified a more conservative constitution that protected property, established a voting process that reduced the power of the masses, and created a new executive authority, the Directory.

After losing the election of 1797, the Directory refused to give up power, effectively ending the republican phase of the Revolution. Political authority now depended on coercive force rather than elections. Two years later, a brilliant young general in the French army, **Napoleon Bonaparte** (1769–1821), seized power. Just as the American and French Revolutions had been the start of the modern democratic tradition, the military intervention that brought Napoleon to power in 1799 marked the advent of another modern form of government: popular authoritarianism.

In contrast to the National Convention, Napoleon proved capable of realizing France's dream of dominating Europe and providing effective protection for persons and property at home. Negotiations with the Catholic Church led to the Concordat of 1801, which gave French Catholics the right to practice their religion freely. Napoleon's Civil Code of 1804 asserted two basic principles inherited from the moderate first stage of the French Revolution: equality in law and protection of property. Even some members of the nobility were won over when Napoleon declared himself emperor and France an empire in 1804.

While it reestablished order, the Napoleonic system denied or restricted many individual rights. The Civil Code denied women basic political rights (a process that had begun under the Terror) and only allowed them to participate in the economy with the guidance and supervision of fathers and husbands. Free speech was limited. Criticism of the government, viewed as subversive, was proscribed, and most opposition newspapers disappeared.

Ultimately, the Napoleonic system depended on the success of French arms (see Map 21.1). From Napoleon's assumption of power until his fall, no single European state could defeat the French military. Austria and Prussia were forced to become allies of France. Only Britain, protected by its powerful navy,

remained able to thwart Napoleon's plans to dominate Europe. In June 1812, Napoleon made the fateful decision to invade Russia with 600,000 men, the largest army ever assembled in Europe. Five weeks after occupying Moscow, he was forced to retreat, his army destroyed by the brutal Russian winter and attacks by Russian forces. A broken and battered remnant of 30,000 men made it back to France.

After the debacle in Russia, Austria and Prussia deserted Napoleon and entered an alliance with England and Russia. Unable to defend Paris, Napoleon abdicated the throne in April 1814 and was exiled to the island of Elba off the coast of Italy.

Retrenchment, Reform, and Revolution

The French Revolution and Napoleon's imperial ambitions had threatened the survival of the old European order by overturning ancient monarchies and tossing aside long-established political institutions. The very existence of the nobility and church had seemed at risk. Under the leadership of the Austrian foreign minister, Prince Klemens von Metternich (MET-uhr-nik) (1773–1859), Britain, Russia, Austria, and Prussia, along with representatives from other countries, worked together in Vienna to create a comprehensive peace settlement that would safeguard the conservative order. Because the participants in the **Congress of Vienna** believed that a strong and stable France was the best guarantee of future peace, the French monarchy was reestablished, and Metternich sought to offset French strength with a balance of power.

Despite the power of the conservative monarchs, popular support for national self-determination and democratic reform grew throughout Europe. In 1821 Greek patriots launched a movement for independence from Ottoman control, and in 1830 Russia, France, and Great Britain forced the Ottoman Empire to recognize Greek independence. That same year,

Napoleon Bonaparte General who overthrew the French Directory in 1799 and became emperor of the French in 1804. Failed to defeat Great Britain and abdicated in 1814. Returned to power briefly in 1815 but was defeated and died in exile.

Congress of Vienna Meeting of representatives of European monarchs called to reestablish the old order after the defeat of Napoleon I.

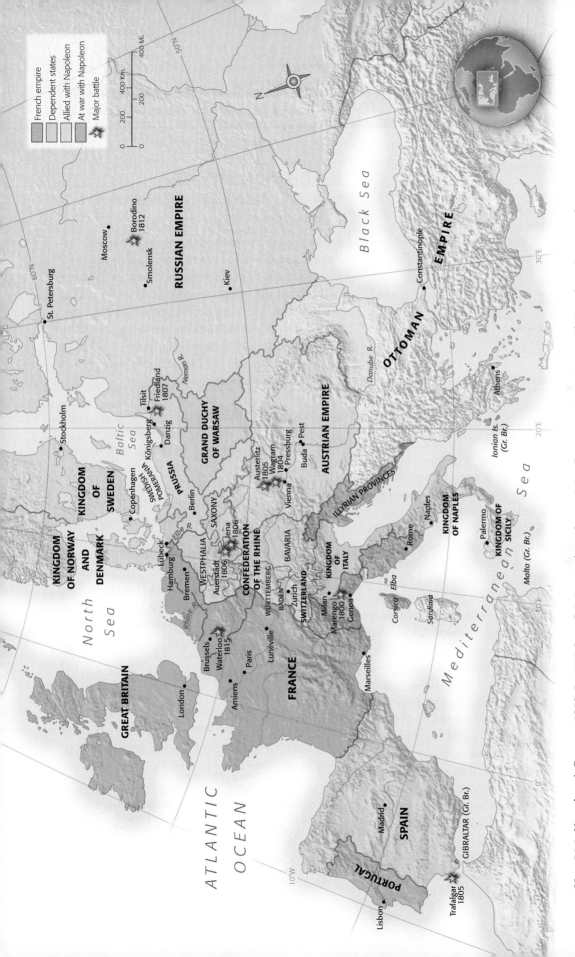

Map 21.1 Napoleon's Europe, 1810 By 1810 Great Britain was the only remaining European power at war with Napoleon. Because of the loss of the French fleet at the Battle of Trafalgar in 1805, Napoleon was unable to threaten Britain with invasion, and Britain was able to assist the resistance movements in Spain and Portugal, thereby helping weaken French power. © Cengage Learning

French empire
Dependent states
Allied with Napoleon
At war with Napoleon
Major battle

ATLANTIC OCEAN

North Sea

GREAT BRITAIN
London

FRANCE
Paris
Amiens
Lunéville
Brussels
Waterloo 1815
Marseilles

SPAIN
Madrid
PORTUGAL
Lisbon
Trafalgar 1805
GIBRALTAR (Gr. Br.)

KINGDOM OF NORWAY AND DENMARK
Copenhagen
Hamburg
Bremen
Lübeck

KINGDOM OF SWEDEN
Stockholm

Baltic Sea
SWEDISH POMERANIA
PRUSSIA
Berlin
Königsberg
Danzig
Tilsit
Friedland 1807

WESTPHALIA
Auerstädt 1806
Jena 1806
SAXONY
CONFEDERATION OF THE RHINE
Elbe R.
Rhine R.
Neman R.

GRAND DUCHY OF WARSAW

WÜRTTEMBERG
BADEN
Zurich
SWITZERLAND
BAVARIA

KINGDOM OF ITALY
Milan
Marengo 1800
Genoa

Corsica
Sardinia
Elba
Rome

KINGDOM OF NAPLES
Naples
Palermo
KINGDOM OF SICILY
Malta (Gr. Br.)

Mediterranean Sea

AUSTRIAN EMPIRE
Vienna
Austerlitz 1805
Wagram 1804
Pressburg
Buda
Pest
Danube R.
ILLYRIAN PROVINCES

RUSSIAN EMPIRE
St. Petersburg
Moscow
Borodino 1812
Smolensk
Kiev

Black Sea

OTTOMAN EMPIRE
Constantinople
Athens
Ionian Is. (Gr. Br.)

50°N
60°N
10°W
0°
10°E
20°E
30°E

400 Mi.
400 Km.
200
0

the people of Paris rose up and forced King Charles X to abdicate. His successor, Louis Philippe (loo-EE fee-LEEP) (r. 1830–1848), reestablished the constitution and extended voting privileges.

Despite limited political reform, conservatives continued to hold the upper hand in Europe. Finally, in 1848, the desire for democratic reform and national self-determination and the frustrations of urban workers led to upheavals across Europe. The **Revolutions of 1848** began in Paris, where members of the middle class and workers united to overthrow the regime of Louis Philippe and create the Second French Republic. Adult men were given voting rights, slavery was abolished in French colonies, the death penalty was ended, and a ten-hour workday was legislated for Paris. But Parisian workers' demands for programs to reduce unemployment and lower prices provoked conflicts with the middle class, which wanted to protect property rights. Desiring the reestablishment of order, the French elected Louis Napoleon, a nephew of the former emperor, president in December 1848. Three years later, he overturned the constitution and, after ruling briefly as dictator, proclaimed himself Emperor Napoleon III. He remained in power until 1871. Despite the heroism of the 1848 revolutionaries in Vienna, Rome, and Berlin, they failed to gain either their nationalist or republican objectives. Metternich, the symbol of reaction, fled Vienna in disguise, but little lasting change occurred. Monarchs retained the support not only of aristocrats but also of professional militaries, largely recruited from among peasants who had little sympathy for urban workers.

REVOLUTION SPREADS

■ *How did revolution in one country help incite revolutions elsewhere?*

In the Americas the legacies of the American and French Revolutions led to a new round of struggles for independence. News of revolutionary events in France destabilized the colonial regime in Saint Domingue (present-day Haiti) and helped initiate the first successful slave rebellion. The same economic and political forces that had undermined British rule in the colonies that became the United States were present in Spanish America and Brazil.

The Haitian Revolution

The French colony of Saint Domingue produced two-thirds of France's tropical imports and generated nearly one-third of all French foreign trade. This impressive wealth depended on a brutal slave regime. The harsh punishments and high mortality rate inflicted on the slaves of Saint Domingue were notorious throughout the Caribbean.

In 1789, when news of the meeting of the Estates General arrived on the island, wealthy white planters sent a delegation to Paris to seek more home rule and greater economic freedom. The **gens de couleur** (zhahn deh koo-LUHR), the large mixed-race population of free black planters and urban merchants who owned slaves, also sent representatives. They sought political rights and a limit to racial discrimination, not an end to slavery.

The political turmoil in France weakened the colonial authority, permitting rich planters, poor whites, *gens de couleur*, and slaves to pursue their narrow interests in an increasingly bitter and

Revolutions of 1848 Democratic and nationalist revolutions that swept across Europe. The monarchy in France was briefly overthrown. In Germany, Austria, Italy, and Hungary the revolutions failed.

gens de couleur Free men and women of color in Haiti. They sought greater political rights and later supported the Haitian Revolution.

Burning of the town of Cap-Francais, Saint-Domingue (Haiti), 1795 (colour engraving), French School, (18th century)/Private Collection/Archives Charmet/The Bridgeman Art Library

Burning of Cap Français, Saint Domingue, in 1793 In 1791, the slaves of Saint Domingue, France's richest colony, began a rebellion that, after years of struggle, ended slavery and created the Western Hemisphere's second independent nation, Haiti.

confrontational struggle. By 1791 whites and the *gens de couleur* were engaged in open warfare. This breach between the two groups of slave owners gave slaves an opening. Their rebellion began on the plantations of the north and spread through the colony. Rebelling slaves destroyed plantations, killed masters and overseers, and burned crops.

A leadership emerged that relied on elements of African political practice and revolutionary ideology from France to mobilize and direct the rebelling slaves. **Toussaint L'Ouverture** (discussed at the beginning of this chapter), a former domestic slave, swept aside his local rivals, defeated the British expeditionary force in 1798, and then led an invasion of the neighboring Spanish colony of Santo Domingo, freeing slaves there. While Toussaint asserted his loyalty to France, he gave the French government no effective role in local affairs.

In 1802, Napoleon sent a large military force to Saint Domingue as well as Guadeloupe to reestablish both French colonial authority and slavery. At first, French forces were successful, capturing Toussaint and sending him to France, where he died in prison. Eventually, however, the loss of thousands of lives to yellow fever and the resistance of the revolutionaries turned the tide. In 1804 Toussaint's successors declared independence, and the free republic of Haiti

joined the United States as the second independent nation in the Western Hemisphere, but the economy was now in ruins.

Latin American Revolutions

Revolutionary documents like the American Declaration of Independence and the French Declaration of the Rights of Man and of the Citizen circulated widely in Latin America as well. But it was Napoleon's decision to invade Portugal (1807) and Spain (1808), not revolutionary ideas, that ignited Latin America's struggle for independence.

As a French army neared Lisbon in 1808, the Portuguese royal family fled to Brazil. Once arrived, King John VI maintained his court there for over a decade. In Spain, by contrast, Napoleon forced King Ferdinand VII to abdicate and placed his own brother, Joseph Bonaparte, on the throne. When Spanish patriots fighting against the French created a new political body, the Junta (HUN-tah) Central, they claimed authority over Spain's colonies. A vocal minority of powerful colonists objected.

Toussaint L'Ouverture Leader of the Haitian Revolution. He freed the slaves and gained effective independence for Haiti despite military interventions by the British and French.

In 1808 and 1809, popular movements overthrew Spanish colonial officials in Venezuela, Mexico, and Bolivia and created local juntas. In each case, Spanish repression strengthened the resolve for independence. By 1810 Spanish colonial authorities were facing a new round of revolutions.

In Caracas (the capital city of modern Venezuela), a revolutionary junta led by creoles (colonial-born whites) declared independence in 1811. Its leaders were landowners whose aim was to expand their own privileges by eliminating Spaniards from the upper levels of government and the church. They defended slavery and opposed full citizenship for the black and mixed-race majority. The junta's narrow agenda spurred Spanish loyalists to rally thousands of free blacks and slaves to defend the Spanish Empire.

In response, the revolutionary movement placed total political authority in the hands of its military leader **Simón Bolívar** (see-MOAN bow-LEE-varh) (1783–1830), the son of wealthy Venezuelan planters. Bolívar had traveled in Europe and studied the works of the Enlightenment. He was charismatic and effective in mobilizing support, successfully adapting his objectives and policies to attract new allies and build coalitions. He agreed to support emancipation in order to draw slaves and freemen to his cause and to gain military supplies from Haiti.

Military advantage shifted back and forth, but in 1820 a revolt in Spain distracted Spanish forces and swung momentum to Bolivar. After liberating present-day Venezuela, he also liberated Colombia, Ecuador, Bolivia, and finally Peru in 1824. But Bolívar's attempts to draw the former Spanish colonies into a formal confederation failed (see Map 21.2).

Buenos Aires (the capital city of modern Argentina and after Caracas the second important center of revolutionary activity in Spanish South America) declared independence as the United Provinces of the Río de la Plata in 1816. In the south, this coalition of militia commanders, merchants, and ranchers sought to retain control over the territory of the Viceroyalty of Río de la Plata, but a separatist movement defeated these ambitions and Argentina descended into chaos. However, a mixed force of Chileans and Argentines, led by José de San Martín (hoe-SAY deh san mar-TEEN) (1778–1850), liberated Chile in 1820.

The arrival of the Portuguese royal family in Brazil in 1808 had helped to maintain the loyalty of the colonial elite, but with Napoleon's defeat, King John VI returned to Portugal in 1821, leaving his son Pedro in Brazil as regent. By then, some of the Spanish colonies along Brazil's borders had gained independence, and Brazilians began to talk openly of independence. To hold on to Brazil, Pedro aligned himself with rising separatist sentiment, and in 1822 he declared Brazilian independence. Unlike its neighbors, which became constitutional republics, Brazil thus gained independence as a constitutional monarchy with Pedro I, son of the king of Portugal, as emperor. However, Pedro I ran afoul of the dominant slave-owning class because he opposed slavery, and he became unpopular when he used military force to control neighboring Uruguay. The constitutional monarchy was overthrown by republicans in 1889.

Mexico

In 1810 Mexico was Spain's wealthiest and most populous colony. The first stage of the revolution against Spain occurred in central Mexico, where ranchers and farmers had aggressively forced Amerindian communities from their traditional agricultural lands. Crop failures and epidemics further afflicted the region's rural poor.

On September 16, 1810, the parish priest of the small town of Dolores, **Miguel Hidalgo y Costilla** (mee-GEHL ee-DAHL-go ee cos-TEE-ah), rang the church bells and attracted thousands. In a fiery speech he urged the crowd to rise up against the oppression of Spanish officials. Tens of thousands of the rural and urban poor soon joined his movement. The Spanish as well as the wealthy Mexicans who owned the ranches and mines recognized the threat posed by the angry masses following Hidalgo, and Spanish forces captured and executed him in 1811.

Although insurgents continued to wage war, colonial rule seemed secure, but in 1821 Colonel Agustín de Iturbide (ah-goos-TEEN deh ee-tur-BEE-deh) and

Simón Bolívar The most important military leader in the struggle for independence in South America. Born in Venezuela, he led military forces there and in Colombia, Ecuador, Peru, and Bolivia.

Miguel Hidalgo y Costilla Mexican priest who led the first stage of the Mexican independence war in 1810. He was captured and executed in 1811.

OREGON
COUNTRY
(Joint U.S.-British
occupation)

BRITISH NORTH AMERICA
(CANADA)
(Gr. Br.)

Mississippi R.

Colorado R.

New York

UNITED STATES

Philadelphia
Washington, D.C.

40°N

N

*ATLANTIC
OCEAN*

40°W

**MEXICO
1821**

Rio Grande

San
Antonio

New Orleans

Charleston

Gulf of Mexico

Mexico City

Veracruz

Havana

CUBA
(Spain)

BAHAMA IS.
(Gr. Br.)

HAITI 1804

20°N

PUERTO RICO (Spain)

BRITISH
HONDURAS (Gr. Br.)

GUATEMALA
Guatemala City

JAMAICA
(Gr. Br.)

Caribbean Sea

TRINIDAD (Gr. Br.)

BR. GUIANA (Gr. Br.)

**UNITED PROVINCES OF
CENTRAL AMERICA
1823–1839**

Panama

Caracas

VENEZUELA

DUTCH GUIANA (Neth.)

FRENCH GUIANA (France)

Magdalena R.

Orinoco R.

Socorro

Bogotá

**GRAN COLOMBIA
1819–1830**

Quito

ECUADOR

*Galápagos
Islands*

Amazon R.

Equator   0°

*PACIFIC
OCEAN*

Lima

**PERU
1824**

**EMPIRE OF BRAZIL
1822**

Salvador

**BOLIVIA
1825**

La Paz

Sucre

Paraná R.

20°S

**PARAGUAY
1811**

São Paulo

Rio de Janeiro

**CHILE
1817**

**UNITED
PROVINCES OF
THE RIO DE
LA PLATA
1816**

**URUGUAY
1828**

Valparaíso

Santiago

ARGENTINA

Buenos Aires

Montevideo

Bahía
Blanca

**Map 21.2 Latin America by
1830** By 1830 patriot forces
had overturned the Spanish and
Portuguese Empires of the Western
Hemisphere. Regional conflicts,
local wars, and foreign interventions challenged the survival of
many of these new nations following independence. © Cengage Learning

PATAGONIA
(Disputed between
Argentina and Chile)

*Islas Malvinas
(Falkland Islands)*

80°W

60°W

0   500   1000 Km.

0   500   1000 Mi.

1811 Year independence gained

Colony

505

SECTION REVIEW

- Revolutionary events in France prompted Saint Domingue's whites and *gens de couleur* to demand reforms.

- The French invasion of Portugal and Spain created a political crisis in their American colonies that in turn led to independence movements.

- Under the leadership of Simón Bolívar, several South American countries gained independence.

- Led by the son of the Portuguese king, Brazil gained independence as a monarchy.

- Mexico gained independence after a long and destructive war.

Schaalkwijk/Art Resource, NY

Miguel Hidalgo y Costilla Padre Miguel Hidalgo y Costilla led the first stage of Mexico's revolution for independence by rallying the rural masses. His defeat, trial, and execution made him one of Mexico's most important political martyrs.

other loyalist commanders forged an alliance with insurgents to declare Mexico's independence. The conservative origins of Mexico's independence were made clear by the decision to create a monarchial government and crown Iturbide emperor. In early 1823, however, the army overthrew Iturbide and Mexico became a republic.

ECONOMIC AND SOCIAL LIBERATION MOVEMENTS

■ *What economic and social liberation movements rose during the nineteenth century?*

The newly independent nations of the Western Hemisphere struggled to realize the Enlightenment ideals of freedom and individual liberty that had helped ignite the revolutions for independence. In both the United States and Latin America, strong antislavery sentiments were expressed during the struggles for independence. But in nearly all the new nations of the Western Hemisphere, revolutionary leaders asserted universal ideals of freedom and citizenship that contrasted sharply with the reality of slavery. Two groups denied full rights under the Constitution, women and free African Americans, played important roles in the abolition of slavery. By century's end, reform movements had made significant progress, but much remained to be done.

The Abolition of Slavery In regions where the export of plantation products was most important—such as the United States, Brazil, and Cuba—the abolition of slavery was achieved with great difficulty. Those who sought to end slavery as an institution were called **abolitionists**. Despite their efforts, slavery survived in most of the hemisphere until the 1850s.

In the United States, some northern states had abolished slavery after the Revolution, and Congress banned the importation of new slaves in 1808. But the expansion of cotton agriculture stalled further progress. In Spanish America tens of thousands of slaves gained freedom by joining revolutionary armies during the wars for independence. After independence,

abolitionists Men and women who agitated for a complete end to slavery. Abolitionist pressure ended the British transatlantic slave trade in 1808 and slavery in British colonies in 1834. In the United States the activities of abolitionists were one factor leading to the Civil War (1861–1865).

most Spanish American republics prohibited the slave trade, but growing international demand for sugar and coffee slowed the achievement of abolition. As prices rose for plantation products, Brazil and Cuba increased their imports of slaves.

After Britain ended its participation in the slave trade in 1807, it negotiated treaties with Spain, Brazil, and other importers of slaves to eliminate the slave trade to the Americas. But enforcement proved difficult. In the Caribbean, where almost 40 percent of all African slaves were shipped, the slave rebellion in Saint Domingue struck terror in the hearts of slave owners and convinced many that any effort to overthrow colonial rule would unleash new insurrections. As a result, there was little local support for abolition in the Caribbean. In these colonies abolition would result from decisions made in Europe by imperial governments.

Abolition in British colonies occurred in 1834, but "freed" slaves were compelled to remain with former masters as "apprentices." Abuses by planters and resistance to apprenticeship by former slaves led to complete abolition in 1838. France abolished slavery in its colonies a decade later. The decision to abolish slavery in the Dutch Empire in 1863 freed 33,000 slaves in Surinam and 12,000 in the Antilles.

During the long struggle to end slavery in the United States, American abolitionists argued that slavery offended both morality and the universal rights asserted in the Declaration of Independence. Southern leaders sought to protect slavery, however, by expanding into new territories in Louisiana and the West. While territorial expansion redrew the map of the United States, it also forced a national debate about slavery that contributed to the election of Abraham Lincoln as president in 1860.

After the election of Lincoln, who was committed to checking the spread of slavery, the southern states where slavery was legal seceded from the United States to form a new nation, the Confederate States of America. During the Civil War (1861–1865) that broke out between the northern states of the Union and the Confederacy, pressure for emancipation rose. Tens of thousands of black freemen and escaped slaves joined the Union army, while hundreds of thousands of slaves fled their masters' plantations and farms for the protection of advancing northern armies. President Lincoln began the abolition of slavery in 1863 by issuing the Emancipation Proclamation, which ended slavery in rebel states not occupied by the Union army. Up to 750,000 lives were lost before the Confederacy surrendered in 1865, making the U.S. Civil War the most destructive conflict in the history of the Western Hemisphere. Also in 1865 the Thirteenth Amendment to the Constitution abolished slavery completely.

After abolition in the United States, slavery continued to survive in Brazil, Puerto Rico, and Cuba. Reformers secured abolition in Puerto Rico in 1873, but in sugar-rich Cuba, abolition was more gradual, with Spain finally abolishing slavery in 1886. In Brazil, however, it was patriotism that won slaves their emancipation. Large numbers of slaves joined the Brazilian army in exchange for freedom during a war with Paraguay (1865–1870), and Brazil abolished slavery in 1888.

Equal Rights for Women and Blacks

Two groups denied full rights under the Constitution, women and free African Americans, played important roles in the abolition of slavery. Women were among the leaders of the American Anti-Slavery Society and produced effective propaganda against slavery. Eventually, thousands of women joined the abolitionist cause. When social conservatives attacked their highly visible public role, many women became public advocates of female suffrage as well.

In 1848 a group of women angered by their exclusion from an international antislavery meeting issued a call for a conference to discuss women's rights. The resulting **Women's Rights Convention** at Seneca Falls, New York, issued a statement that said, in part, "We hold these truths to be self-evident: that all men and women are equal." While moderates focused on the issues of economic independence and legal rights, increasing numbers of women demanded the right to vote. Others lobbied to gain better conditions for women working outside the home, especially in textile factories.

Women's Rights Convention An 1848 gathering of women angered by their exclusion from an international antislavery meeting. They met at Seneca Falls, New York, to discuss women's rights.

Progress toward equality between men and women was equally slow in Canada and in Latin America. Canada's first women doctors received their training in the United States because women could not receive medical degrees until 1895. Argentina and Uruguay were among the first Latin American nations to provide public education for women, and both nations introduced coeducation in the 1870s. Chilean women gained access to some careers in medicine and law in the 1870s. In Brazil, where many women were in the abolitionist movement, four women graduated in medicine by 1882. Throughout the hemisphere more rapid progress occurred in lower-status careers that threatened male economic power less directly, and, by the end of the century, women dominated elementary school teaching.

From Canada to Argentina and Chile, the majority of working-class women, although having no direct involvement in reform movements, succeeded in transforming gender relations in their daily lives. By the end of the nineteenth century, large numbers of poor women worked outside the home on farms, in markets, and, increasingly, in factories.

Throughout the hemisphere, there was little progress toward eliminating racial discrimination. Blacks were denied the vote throughout the southern United States and were subjected to the indignity of segregation—consigned to separate schools, hotels, restaurants, seats in public transportation, and even water fountains. Racial discrimination against men and women of African descent was also common in Latin America, though seldom spelled out in legal codes. Latin Americans tended to view racial identity across a continuum of physical characteristics rather than in the narrow terms of black and white that defined race relations in the United States.

SECTION REVIEW

- Following independence, American nations eventually abolished the slave trade and slavery.
- The long struggle to achieve women's rights and end racial and ethnic discrimination altered the Western Hemisphere's political culture.

CONCLUSION

The last decades of the eighteenth century began a long period of revolutionary upheaval in the Atlantic world. Costly wars in Europe and along Europe's colonial frontiers in the Americas and Asia helped to provoke change, forcing European monarchs to impose new and unpopular taxes. The American Revolution initiated these transformations. Having defeated Britain, the citizens of this new American republic created the most democratic government of the time. While full rights were limited and slavery persisted, many Europeans saw this experiment as demonstrating the efficacy of the Enlightenment's most revolutionary political ideas. In the end, however, the compromises over slavery that had made a new Constitution possible in 1787 failed, and the new nation nearly disintegrated after 1860.

The French Revolution led temporarily to a more radical formulation of representative democracy, but it also led to the Terror, which cost tens of thousands of lives, the militarization of western Europe, and a destructive cycle of wars. Yet, despite these terrible costs, the French Revolution propelled the idea of democracy and the ideal of equality far beyond the boundaries established by the American Revolution. The Haitian Revolution, set in motion by events in France, not only created the second independent nation of the Western Hemisphere but also delivered a powerful blow to the institution of slavery. In Europe the excesses of the French Revolution and the wars that followed in its wake promoted the political ascent of Napoleon Bonaparte and democracy's modern nemesis, popular authoritarianism.

Each revolution had its own character. The revolutions in France and Haiti proved to be more violent and destructive than the American Revolution. American revolutionaries defeated Great Britain and established independence without overturning a colonial social and political order that depended on slavery in most of the southern colonies. Revolutionaries in France and Haiti faced more strongly entrenched and more powerful oppositions as well as greater social inequalities than American revolutionaries, and the resistance of privileged elites led inexorably to greater violence. Both French and Haitian revolutionaries also faced powerful foreign interventions that intensified the bloodshed and destructiveness of these revolutions.

The conservative retrenchment that followed the defeat of Napoleon succeeded in the short term. Monarchy, multinational empires, and the established church retained the loyalty of millions of Europeans and could count on the support of many of Europe's wealthiest and most powerful individuals. But liberalism and nationalism continued to stir revolutionary sentiment. The contest between adherents of the old order and partisans of change was to continue well into the nineteenth century. In the end, the nation-state, the Enlightenment legacy of rational inquiry, broadened political participation, and secular intellectual culture prevailed. This outcome was determined in large measure by the old order's inability to satisfy the demands of new social classes tied to an emerging industrial economy. The narrow confines of a hereditary social system could not contain the material transformations generated by industrial capitalism, and the doctrines of traditional religion could not contain the rapid expansion of scientific learning.

These revolutions began the transformation of Western society, but they did not complete it. Only a minority gained full political rights. Women did not achieve full political rights until the twentieth century. Democratic institutions, as in revolutionary France, often failed. Moreover, slavery endured in the Americas past the mid-1800s despite the revolutionary era's enthusiasm for individual liberty, leaving a legacy of racism and discrimination across the Americas.

CHAPTER REVIEW

PRELUDE TO REVOLUTION: THE EIGHTEENTH-CENTURY CRISIS

■ *How did the costs of imperial wars and the Enlightenment challenge the established authority of monarchs in Europe and the American colonies?* (page 491)

This era of revolution was, in large measure, the product of a long period of costly warfare among the imperial nations of Europe. Britain and France in particular faced fiscal crises as a result of colonial wars. Using taxes and institutions inherited from the past, they found it increasingly difficult to fund distant wars in the Americas or in Asia. In the British case, the costs of the French and Indian War led the government to attempt to impose unpopular taxes on its colonies. France faced an even more dire fiscal emergency as a result of its aid to the American revolutionaries. The refusal of powerful French interests to accept new taxes forced the king to call the Estates General and ultimately led to the French Revolution.

    Meanwhile, the spread of literacy and the greater availability of books helped create an Enlightenment culture more open to reform and to the revolutionary change of existing institutions in Europe and in the Americas. But there were many distinct, even contradictory, currents in the Enlightenment. Nevertheless, the intellectual ferment of the era gave educated men and women the tools to criticize existing political institutions and the confidence to design new ones. The language of liberty and equality, even if poorly realized in the actions of revolutionary governments, proved a powerful solvent when applied to hierarchy and privilege.

THE AMERICAN REVOLUTION, 1775–1800

■ *What were the direct causes of the American Revolution?* (page 493)

The American Revolution grew from British colonial policy after the French and Indian War. To avoid new military costs, Britain tried unsuccessfully through the Quebec Act to restrict western settlement and thus reduce conflict with the Amerindians. To pay its war debt, Britain imposed new taxes, duties, and commercial regulations on the colonies, including the Stamp Act. These acts led to violent unrest that culminated with the "Boston Massacre." Parliament repealed some of these acts but then gave the British East India Company a tea monopoly, thus provoking more violence. Colonial patriots met in the Continental Congress, assumed government powers, raised an army, and issued the Declaration of Independence.

THE FRENCH REVOLUTION, 1789–1815

■ *What were the origins and accomplishments of the French Revolution?* (page 496)

The French Revolution erupted from the crises provoked by France's archaic social and tax system, financial collapse, urban unrest, and division between the monarchy and aristocracy. The immediate cause was the crisis within the Estates General, during which the Third Estate broke away and declared itself the National Assembly. Uprisings in Paris and the countryside strengthened the Assembly position, enabling it to press reforms embodied in the Declaration of the Rights of Man and of the Citizen. Further reforms restructured France's society and economy. However, foreign intervention pushed the Legislative Assembly to radical extremes that culminated with the execution of Louis XVI and the Reign of Terror.

Reaction against the Terror resulted in the conservative Directory and in the even more repressive dictatorship of Napoleon Bonaparte. Napoleon's military adventures ultimately led to his fall, and the Congress of Vienna sought to reestablish a conservative balance of power. Despite this retrenchment, revolutionary struggles continued, especially in France, where the 1830 uprising replaced Charles X with Louis-Philippe. In 1848 nationalist and republican revolutions flared throughout Europe. These won few lasting gains, however, and in France they resulted in the imperial rule of Napoleon III.

REVOLUTION SPREADS

■ *How did revolution in one country help incite revolutions elsewhere?* (page 502)

Though very different in its root causes, the French Revolution was affected by the political ideas of the American Revolution. Those ideas expressed in Paris in turn encouraged Haitians to seek independence. Though the French Republic descended into dictatorship, Napoleon's occupation of Portugal and Spain had repercussions in the Western Hemisphere. The Portuguese king took refuge in Brazil, and after his return to Portugal the Brazilians supported a constitutional monarchy under his son. Different Spanish colonies saw the rise of revolutionary movements, some of which resulted in new independent countries. Each of these movements reflected some of the same rivalries among economic interests and between religious conservatives and champions of Enlightenment ideas.

ECONOMIC AND SOCIAL LIBERATION MOVEMENTS

■ *What economic and social liberation movements rose during the nineteenth century?* (page 506)

In the newly independent nations of the Americas, the persistence of slavery and gender inequality clashed with the Enlightenment ideals that had fostered their revolutions. Rising demand for export crops after 1800 strengthened slavery in the southern United States and part of Latin America. Although Lincoln issued the Emancipation Proclamation during the Civil War, final abolition did not come until the Thirteenth Amendment passed in 1865. Britain ceased to participate in the slave trade in 1807 and worked to end the Atlantic trade through treaties with slave importers. Although Britain's navy forced compliance on Latin American importers, slavery continued in Brazil, Cuba, and Puerto Rico until late in the nineteenth century. Many women and free blacks were important abolitionists, and a movement for equal rights for these groups emerged. In the United States, women declared equal rights at the Seneca Falls Women's Rights Convention, but progress on gender equality and the elimination of racial discrimination was slow throughout the Western Hemisphere. Racial discrimination was legalized in the southern United States. It also persisted in Latin America without formal codification.

Key Terms

Enlightenment (p. 491)

George Washington (p. 495)

Constitutional Convention (p. 495)

Estates General (p. 497)

National Assembly (p. 497)

Declaration of the Rights of Man and of the Citizen (p. 498)

Napoleon Bonaparte (p. 500)

Congress of Vienna (p. 500)

Revolutions of 1848 (p. 502)

gens de couleur (p. 502)

Toussaint L'Ouverture (p. 503)

Simón Bolívar (p. 504)

Miguel Hidalgo y Costilla (p. 504)

abolitionists (p. 506)

Women's Rights Convention (p. 507)

CHAPTER 22

1800–1870

Land Empires in the Age of Imperialism

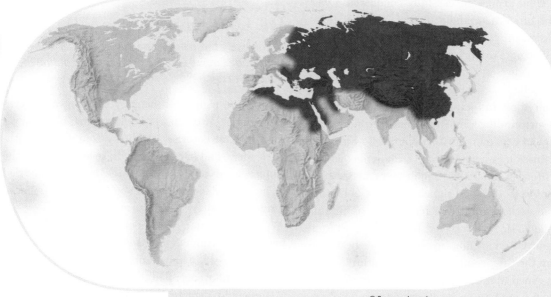

© Cengage Learning

During the late 1860s, a little-known warlord named Yaqub Beg (ya-KOOB Bek) unified several Muslim uprisings in Inner Asia against a foreign Qing occupier. Only a hundred years earlier, in 1759, Qing armies successfully conquered a vast region of Inner Asia and called it Xinjiang (shin-JYAHNG), meaning "new territory" (see Chapter 19). Despite attempts to work with local leaders, tensions between locals and Chinese never eased, and the natives rebelled.

Yaqub took full diplomatic advantage of the empires surrounding him. To his south lay India, controlled by an expanding British Empire. To his north was the Russian Empire, Britain's rival in the quest to gain territory in Inner Asia. Yaqub sent emissaries to both empires in 1868 and signed commercial treaties in 1872 in exchange for their recognition of his rule over Xinjiang. He even received military support from the distant Ottoman Empire, whose ruler bestowed upon him the title "commander of the faithful." For a time it seemed that the Qing might not try to retake Xinjiang. It would be an expensive venture for a government that preferred to spend its money modernizing its army and navy. But fears that Russia might take over neighboring Mongolia drove the Chinese back into Xinjiang, and Yaqub's regime collapsed in 1877.

Yaqub's story illustrates the challenges facing Eurasian empires: old and inefficient ways of governing and an international climate dominated by European dependence on colonial wealth. During the early 1800s rapid population growth and slow agricultural growth affected much of Eurasia. In addition, earlier military expansion had left the land-based empires vulnerable to European military pressure (see Chapter 19). Responses to this pressure varied, with reform gaining headway in some lands, while tradition was reasserted in others. In the long run, attempts to meet western Europe's economic and political demands resulted in an increased foreign debt that further stressed the economies of Eurasian empires.

This chapter contrasts the experiences of the Qing Empire with those of the Russian and Ottoman Empires. Whereas the Qing opted for resistance, the others made varying attempts to adapt and reform. Russia eventually became part of Europe, while the Ottomans and the Qing became subject to ever-greater imperialist pressure. These different responses raise the question of the role of culture in shaping western Europe's relations with the rest of the world in the nineteenth century.

THE OTTOMAN EMPIRE

■ *What were the benefits and the drawbacks to the Ottoman Empire of the reforms adopted during the Tanzimat period?*

During the eighteenth century the central government of the Ottoman Empire lost much of its power to provincial governors, military commanders, ethnic leaders, and bandit chiefs. In several parts of the empire local officials and large landholders tried to increase their independence and divert imperial funds into their own coffers.

This Ottoman weakness allowed Muhammad ibn Abd al-Wahhab (moo-HAH-muhd ib-uhn ab-dahl-wa-HAHB), a puritanical fundamentalist from Arabia, to take control of the holy cities of Mecca and Medina and deprive the sultan of organizing the annual pilgrimage. Mamluk slave-soldiers, who as a military class that ruled Egypt between 1260 and 1517, reemerged as a military force; and the Ottoman Janissaries, who had evolved into a hereditary military class of that in some provincial areas came into conflict with the mamluks (see Chapter 18), used their Istanbul power base to force Sultan Selim III to abandon efforts to train a modern, European-style army. For the sultans, the outlook was bleak, but the situation unexpectedly changed when France invaded Egypt.

Egypt and the Napoleonic Example

Napoleon Bonaparte and an invasion force of 36,000 men and four hundred ships invaded Egypt in May 1798. The French quickly defeated the mamluk army. Fifteen months later, after being stopped by Ottoman land and British naval forces in an attempted invasion of Syria, Napoleon secretly left Cairo and returned to France. Three months later he seized power and made himself emperor.

Chronology

	Ottoman Empire	Russian Empire	Qing Empire
1800			1794–1804 White Lotus Rebellion
		1801–1825 Reign of Alexander I	
	1805–1849 Muhammad Ali governs Egypt		
	1808–1839 Rule of Mahmud II	1812 Napoleon's retreat from Moscow	
	1826 Janissary corps dissolved	1825 Decembrist revolt	
	1830 Greek independence	1825–1855 Reign of Nicholas I	
	1839 Abdul Mejid begins Tanzimat reforms		1839–1842 Opium War
1850	1853–1856 Crimean War	1853–1856 Crimean War	1850–1864 Taiping Rebellion
		1855–1881 Reign of Alexander II	1856–1860 Arrow War
		1861 Emancipation of the serfs	
	1876 First constitution by an Islamic governmen		

Back in Egypt, his generals were cut off from France by British ships in the Mediterranean and had little hope of remaining in power. They agreed to withdraw in 1801. For the second time in three years, a collapse of military power produced a power vacuum in Egypt. The winner of the ensuing contest was **Muhammad Ali** (moo-HAM-mad AH-lee), whom the sultan had sent with a contingent of Albanian soldiers to restore imperial control. By 1805 he had taken the place of the official Ottoman governor, and by 1811 he had dispossessed the mamluks of their lands and privileges.

Muhammad Ali's rise to power coincided with the meteoric career of Emperor Napoleon I. It is not surprising, therefore, that he adopted many French practices in rebuilding the Egyptian state. Militarily, he established special schools for training artillery and cavalry officers, army surgeons, military bandmasters, and others. The curricula of these schools featured European skills and sciences, and Muhammad Ali began to send promising officer trainees to France for education. In 1824 he started a gazette devoted to official affairs, the first newspaper in the Islamic world. As discussed in Chapter 20, Muhammad Ali built various sorts of factories to outfit his new army. These did not prove efficient enough to survive, but they showed a determination to achieve independence and parity with the European powers.

In the 1830s Muhammad Ali's son Ibrahim invaded Syria and instituted some of the changes already under way in Egypt. The improved quality of the new Egyptian army had been proven during the Greek war of independence (discussed later in this chapter), when Ibrahim had commanded an expeditionary force to help the sultan. In response, the sultan embarked on building his own new army in 1826. The two modernized forces met when Ibrahim invaded Anatolia in 1839 and defeated the Ottoman sultan's army. The road to Istanbul seemed open until the European powers intervened and forced a withdrawal to Egypt. Muhammad Ali remained Egypt's ruler, under the suzerainty of the sultan, until his death in 1849, and his family continued to rule the country until 1952. But his dream of making Egypt a mighty country capable of standing up to Europe faded. What survived was the example he had set for the sultans in Istanbul.

Muhammad Ali Leader of Egyptian modernization in the early nineteenth century. He ruled Egypt as an Ottoman governor but had imperial ambitions. His descendants ruled Egypt until overthrown in 1952.

From Ignatius Mouradgea d'Ohsson, *Tableau General de l'Empire Ottoman,* large folio edition, Paris, 1787–1820, pl. 178, following p. 340

Interior of the Ottoman Financial Bureau This engraving from the eighteenth century depicts the governing style of the Ottoman Empire before the era of westernizing reforms. By the end of the Tanzimat period in 1876, government offices and the costumes of officials looked much more like those in contemporary European capitals.

Ottoman Reform and the European Model, 1807–1853

At the end of the eighteenth century, Sultan Selim (seh-LEEM) III (r. 1789–1807), a forward-looking ruler who stayed abreast of events in Europe, introduced reforms to create European-style military units, bring provincial governors under central government control, and standardize taxation. The rise in government expenditures to implement the reforms was supposed to be offset by taxes on selected items, primarily tobacco and coffee. The Janissary military corps preserved their own economic privileges and power by violently resisting the creation of new military units, and the reforms ultimately failed on political rather than economic grounds.

At times, Janissary power produced military uprisings. In the Ottoman territory of **Serbia**, local residents intensely resented the control exercised by Janissary

governors. The Orthodox Christians claimed that the Janissaries abused them. In response, Selim threatened to reassign the Janissaries to Istanbul. Suspecting that the sultan wanted to curb their political power, in 1805 the Janissaries revolted and massacred Christians in Serbia. Unable to reestablish central Ottoman rule over Serbia, the sultan had to rely on the ruler of Bosnia, another Balkan province, who joined his troops with the peasants of Serbia to suppress the Janissary uprising. When the threat of Russian intervention prevented the Ottomans from disarming the victorious Serbians, Serbia became effectively independent.

Other opponents of reform included ulama, or Muslim religious scholars, who distrusted the

Serbia The Ottoman province in the Balkans that rose up against Janissary control in the early 1800s. After World War II the central province of Yugoslavia.

From Edward William Lane, *The Manners and Customs of the Modern Egyptians* (London: J. M. D & Co. 1860)

Street Scene in Cairo This engraving from Edward William Lane's influential travel book, *Account of the Manners and Customs of the Modern Egyptians Written in Egypt During the Years 1833–1835*, conveys the image of narrow lanes and small stores that became stock features of European thinking about Middle Eastern cities.

secularization of law and taxation that Selim proposed. In the face of widespread rejection of his reforms, Selim suspended his program in 1806. Nevertheless, a massive military uprising occurred at Istanbul, and the sultan was deposed and imprisoned. Reform forces recaptured the capital, but not before Selim had been executed. Selim's cousin, Sultan Mahmud (mah-MOOD) II (r. 1808–1839), cautiously revived Selim's program, but he realized that reforms needed to be more systematic and imposed more forcefully. The effectiveness of radical reform in Muhammad Ali's Egypt drove this lesson home,

as did the insurrection in Greece, during which the Egyptian military outperformed the main Ottoman army.

Greek independence in 1830 had dramatic international significance. A combination of Greek nationalist organizations and interlopers from Albania powered the independence movement. Europe's interest in the classical age of Greece and Rome led many Europeans to consider the Greeks' struggle for independence a campaign to recapture their classical glory from Muslim oppression. Some—including English poet Lord Byron, who lost his life in the war— went to Greece to fight as volunteers. When the combined squadrons of the British, French, and Russian fleets, under orders to observe but not intervene in the war, made an unauthorized attack that sank the Ottoman fleet at the Battle of Navarino, Greek victory was assured (see Map 22.1).

Mahmud II concurred with the pro-Greek Europeans in viewing Ottoman military reversals in Greece as a sign of profound weakness. The sultan capitalized on popular outrage over the military setbacks by announcing the creation of a new artillery unit—one he had secretly been training. When the Janissaries revolted in 1826, he bombarded their barracks. The Janissary corps was officially dissolved.

Like Muhammad Ali, Mahmud felt he could not implement major changes without reducing the political power of the religious elite. But Ibrahim attacked from Syria in 1839 before he could restructure the bureaucracy and the educational and legal systems, where ulama power was strongest. Battlefield defeat, the decision of the rebuilt Ottoman navy to switch sides and support Egypt, and the death of Mahmud, all in the same year, left the empire completely dependent on the European powers for survival.

Mahmud's reforming ideas received their widest expression in the **Tanzimat** (TAHNZ-ee-maht) ("reorganization"), a series of reforms begun under his sixteen-year-old son and successor, Abdul Mejid (abdul meh-JEED), in 1839 and strongly endorsed by the European ambassadors. One proclamation called for

Tanzimat Restructuring reforms by the nineteenth-century Ottoman rulers, intended to move civil law away from the control of religious elites and make the military and the bureaucracy more efficient.

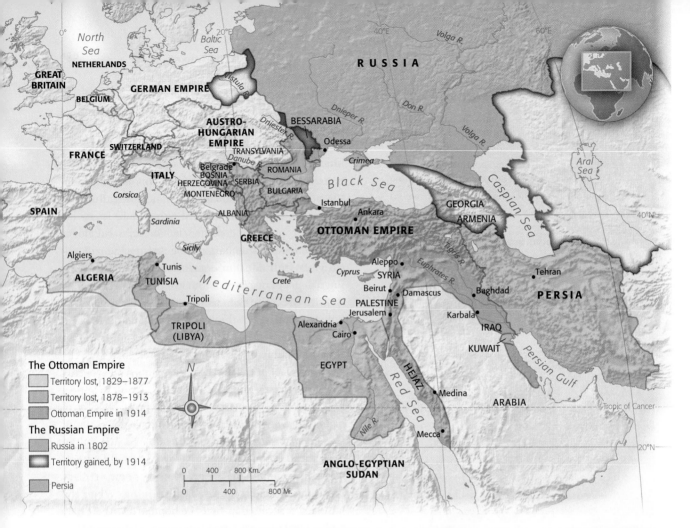

Map 22.1 The Ottoman and Russian Empires, 1829–1914 At its height the Ottoman Empire controlled most of the perimeter of the Mediterranean Sea. But in the 1800s Ottoman territory shrank as many countries gained their independence. The Black Sea, where the Turkish coast was vulnerable to assault, became a weak spot as Russian naval power grew. Russian challenges to the Ottomans at the eastern end of the Black Sea and to the Persians east and west of the Caspian aroused fears in Europe that Russia was trying to reach the Indian Ocean. © Cengage Learning

public trials and equal protection under the law for all, whether Muslim, Christian, or Jew. It also guaranteed some rights of privacy, equalized the eligibility of men for conscription into the army (a practice copied from Egypt), and provided for a new, formalized method of tax collection that legally ended tax farming in the Ottoman Empire. It took many years and strenuous efforts by reforming bureaucrats, known as the "men of the Tanzimat," to give substance to these reforms.

Over time, one legal code after another—commercial, criminal, civil procedure—was introduced to take the place of the corresponding areas of religious legal jurisdiction. All the codes were modeled closely on those of Europe. The Shari'a, or Islamic law,

gradually became restricted to matters of family law such as marriage and inheritance. As the Shari'a was displaced, job opportunities for the ulama shrank.

European observers praised the reforms for their noble principles and rejection of religious influence. Ottoman citizens were more divided; the Christians and Jews, for whom the Europeans showed the greatest concern, were generally more enthusiastic than the Muslims. Many historians see the Tanzimat as the dawn of modern thought and enlightened government in the Middle East. Others point out that removing the religious elite from influence in government also removed the one remaining check on authoritarian rule.

Modernized Ottoman Troops This photograph of a contingent of Imperial Guards in the late nineteenth century shows them equipped and uniformed much like any other European army of the time. The only distinctive feature is the fez, a brimless hat adopted earlier in the century as a symbol of reform.

From one of the original photographic albums of Sultan Abdul Hamid II, 1842–1918/Library of Congress

Like Muhammad Ali, Sultan Mahmud sent military cadets to France and the German states for training. In the 1830s an Ottoman imperial school of military sciences, later to become Istanbul University, was established. Instructors from western Europe taught chemistry, engineering, mathematics, and physics in addition to military history. Military education became the model for more general educational reforms. In 1838 the first medical school was established to train army doctors and surgeons. Later, a national system of preparatory schools was created to feed graduates into the military schools. The subjects that were taught and many of the teachers were foreign, raising the issue of whether Turkish should be a language of instruction. Because it was easier to import and use foreign textbooks than to write new ones in Turkish, French became the preferred language in all advanced professional and scientific training. However, the great majority of students still learned to read and write in Quran schools down to the twentieth century.

In the capital city of Istanbul, the reforms stimulated the growth of a small but cosmopolitan milieu embracing European language and culture. The first Turkish newspaper, a government gazette modeled on that of Muhammad Ali, appeared in 1831. Other newspapers followed, many written in French. Travel to Europe—particularly to England and France—became popular among wealthy Turks. Interest in importing European military, industrial, and communications technology remained strong through the 1800s.

Changes in military practice had unforeseen cultural and social effects. Accepting the European notion that modern weapons and drill required modern military dress, beards were deemed unhygienic and, in artillery units, a fire hazard. Military headgear also became controversial. European military caps, which had leather bills on the front to protect against the glare of the sun, were not acceptable because they interfered with Muslim soldiers' touching their foreheads to the ground in prayer. The compromise was the brimless cap now called the *fez*, which was adopted by the military and then by Ottoman civil officials in the early years of Mahmud II's reign.

The empire's new orientation spread beyond the military. Government ministries that normally recruited from traditional bureaucratic families and relied on on-the-job training were gradually transformed into formal civil services hiring men educated in the new schools. Among self-consciously progressive men, particularly those in government service, European dress became the fashion in the Ottoman cities of the later 1800s, while traditional dress became a symbol of the religious, the rural, and the parochial.

Secularization of the legal code particularly affected non-Muslim Ottoman subjects. Islamic law had required non-Muslims to pay a special head tax that was sometimes explained as a substitute for military service. Under the Tanzimat, the tax was abolished and non-Muslims became liable for military service—unless they bought their way out by paying a new military exemption tax. The new law codes gave all subjects equal access to the civil courts, while the operations of the Islamic law courts shrank. What enhanced the status of non-Muslims most, however, was the strong concern for their welfare consistently expressed by the European powers. The Ottoman Empire became a rich field of operation for Christian missionaries and European supporters of Jewish community life in the Muslim world.

The public rights and political participation granted during the Tanzimat applied specifically to men. Private life, including everything connected to marriage and divorce, remained within the sphere of religious law, and at no time was there a question of political participation or reformed education for women. Indeed, the reforms may have decreased the influence of women. The political changes ran parallel to economic changes that also narrowed women's opportunities.

After silver from the Americas began to flood the empire in the 1600s, workers were increasingly paid in cash rather than in goods, and businesses associated with banking and finance developed. But women were barred from the early industrial jobs and the professions, and traditional "woman's work" such as weaving was increasingly mechanized and done by men.

Nevertheless, in the early 1800s women retained considerable power in the management and disposal of their own property, gained mostly through fixed shares of inheritance. After marriage a woman was often pressured to convert her landholdings to cash in order to transfer her personal wealth to her husband's family, with whom she and her husband would reside. However, this was not a requirement, since men were legally obligated to support their families single-handedly. Until the 1820s many wealthy women retained their say in the distribution of property through the creation of charitable trusts for their offspring. Because these trusts were set up in the religious courts, they could be designed to conform to the wishes of family members. Then, in the 1820s and 1830s the secularizing reforms of Mahmud II transferred jurisdiction over the charitable trusts from religious courts to the state and ended women's control over this form of property.

The Crimean War and Its Aftermath

Since the reign of Peter the Great (r. 1689–1725), the Russian Empire had been attempting to expand southward at the Ottomans' expense (also discussed later in this chapter in the section on Russia and Asia). His successor, Catherine the Great (r. 1762–1796), had captured control of the north shore of the Black Sea by 1783; by 1815 Russia had pried the Georgian region of the Caucasus away from the Ottomans, and the threat of Russian intervention had prevented the Ottomans from crushing Serbian independence. When Muhammad Ali's Egyptian army invaded Syria in 1833, Russia signed a treaty in support of the Ottomans. In return, the sultan recognized Russia's claim to being the protector of all of the empire's Orthodox subjects. This set the stage for an obscure dispute that resulted in war.

Bowing to British and French pressure, in 1852 the sultan named France Protector of the Holy Sepulchre in Jerusalem. Russia protested, but the sultan held firm. So Russia invaded Ottoman territories in what is today Romania, and Britain and France went to war as allies of the sultan. The real causes of the war went beyond church quarrels in Jerusalem and involved diplomatic maneuvering among European powers over whether the Ottoman Empire should continue to exist and, if not, who should take over its territory. The *Eastern Question* was the simple name given to this complex issue. Though the powers, including Russia, had agreed to save the empire in 1839, Britain subsequently became suspicious of Russian ambitions. Prominent anti-Russian politicians in Britain feared that Russia would threaten the British hold on India.

Between 1853 and 1856 the **Crimean** (cry-ME-uhn) **War** raged in Romania, on the Black Sea, and on the Crimean peninsula. Britain, France, and the Italian kingdom of Sardinia-Piedmont sided with the Ottomans. Britain and France trapped the Russian fleet in the Black Sea, where its commanders decided to sink the ships to protect the approaches to Sevastopol, their main base in Crimea. An army largely made up of British and French troops landed and laid siege to the city. Official corruption and lack of railways hampered the Russians' attempts to supply their forces. On the Romanian front, the Ottomans resisted effectively. At Sevastopol, the Russians were outmatched militarily and suffered badly from disease. Tsar Nicholas died as defeat loomed, leaving his successor, Alexander II (r. 1855–1881), to sue for peace when Sevastopol finally fell three months later.

The Crimean War brought significant changes to all the combatants. The tsar and his government, already beset by demands for the reform of serfdom, education, and the military, were further discredited. In Britain and France, the conflict was accompanied by massive propaganda campaigns. For the first time newspapers effectively mobilized public support for a war. British press accounts so glamorized British participation that the false impression has lingered that Ottoman troops played a negligible role in the conflict. At the time, however, British and French commanders noted the massive losses among Turkish troops in particular. The French press, dominant in Istanbul, promoted a sense of unity between Turkish and French society that continued to influence many aspects of Turkish urban culture.

The larger significance of the Crimean War was that it marked the transition from traditional to modern warfare (see Environment and Technology: The Web of War). All the combatants had previously prided themselves on the use of highly trained cavalry to smash through the front lines of infantry. Cavalry coexisted with firearms until the early 1800s, primarily because early rifles were awkward to load and not very accurate. Cavalry could attack during the intervals between volleys. Then in the 1830s and 1840s percussion caps that did away with pouring gunpowder into the barrel of a musket came into use. In Crimean War battles many cavalry units were destroyed by the rapid fire of rifles that loaded at the breech rather than down the barrel. That was the fate of the famed British Light Brigade, which was sent to relieve an Ottoman unit surrounded by Russian troops.

After the Crimean War, the Ottoman Empire increased its involvement with European commerce. The Ottoman imperial bank was founded in 1840, and a few years later currency reform pegged the value of Ottoman gold coins to the British pound. Sweeping changes in the 1850s expedited the creation of banks, insurance companies, and legal firms throughout the empire. Bustling trade also encouraged a migration from country to city between about 1850 and 1880. Many of the major cities of the empire—Istanbul, Damascus, Beirut, Alexandria, Cairo—expanded. A small but influential urban professional class emerged, as did a considerable class of wage laborers.

However, commercial vigor and urbanization could not make up for declining revenues and the chronic insolvency and corruption of the imperial government. From the conclusion of the Crimean War in 1856 on, the Ottoman government became heavily dependent on foreign loans. In return it lowered tariffs to favor European imports and allowed European banks to open in Ottoman cities. Europeans living in Istanbul and other commercial centers enjoyed **extraterritoriality**, the right to be subject to their own laws and exempt from Ottoman jurisdiction.

As the result of these measures, imported goods multiplied, but—apart from tobacco and the Turkish opium that American traders took to China to compete against British opium from India—Anatolia produced few exports. As foreign debt grew, so did inflationary trends that left urban populations in a precarious position. By contrast, Egyptian cotton exports soared during the American Civil War, when American cotton exports plummeted; but the profits benefited Muhammad Ali's descendants, who had become the hereditary governors of Egypt, rather

Crimean War Conflict between the Russian and Ottoman Empires fought primarily in the Crimean peninsula. To prevent Russian expansion, Britain and France sent troops to support the Ottomans.

extraterritoriality The right of foreign residents in a country to live under the laws of their native country and disregard the laws of the host country. In the nineteenth and early twentieth centuries, European and American nationals living in certain areas of Chinese and Ottoman cities were granted this right.

The Web of War

The lethal military technologies of the mid-nineteenth century that were used on battlefields in the United States, Russia, India, and China were rapidly transmitted from one conflict to the next. This dissemination was due not only to the rapid development of communications but also to the existence of a new international network of soldiers who moved from one trouble spot to another, bringing expertise in the use of new techniques.

General Charles Gordon (1833–1885), for instance, was commissioned in the British army in 1852 and then served in the Crimean War after Britain entered on the side of the Ottomans. In 1860 he was dispatched to China, where he served with British forces during the Arrow War and took part in the sack of Beijing. Afterward, he stayed in China and was assigned to the Qing imperial government until the suppression of the Taipings in 1864, earning himself the nickname "Chinese" Gordon. Gordon later served the Ottoman rulers of Egypt as governor of territory along the Nile. He was killed in Egyptian-ruled Sudan in 1885 while leading his Egyptian troops in defense of the city of Khartoum against an uprising by the Sudanese religious leader, the Mahdi.

Journalism played an important part in the developing web of telegraph communications that sped orders to and from the battlefields. Readers in London could learn details of the drama occurring in the Crimea or in China within a week—or in some cases days—after they occurred. Print and, later, photographic journalism created new "stars" from these war experiences. Charles Gordon was one. Florence Nightingale was another.

In the great wars of the 1800s, the vast majority of deaths resulted from infection or excessive bleeding, not from the wounds themselves. Florence Nightingale (1820–1910), while still a young woman, became interested in hospital management and nursing and went to Prussia and France to study advanced techniques. Before the outbreak of the Crimean War she was credited with bringing about marked improvement in British health care. When the public reacted to news reports of the suffering in the Crimea, the British government sent Nightingale to the region. Within a year of her arrival the death rate in the military hospitals there dropped from 45 percent to under 5 percent. Her techniques for preventing septicemia and dysentery, essentially sanitary measures like washing bed linens after a death and emptying toilet buckets outside, were quickly adopted by those working for and with her. On her return to London, Nightingale established institutes for nursing that soon were recognized as leaders around the world. She herself was lionized by the British public and received the Order of Merit in 1907, three years before her death.

The importance of Nightingale's innovations in public hygiene is underscored by the life of her contemporary, Mary Seacole (1805–1881). A Jamaican woman who volunteered to nurse British troops in the Crimean War, Seacole was repeatedly excluded from nursing service by British authorities. She eventually went to Crimea and used her own funds to run a hospital there, bankrupting herself in the process. The drama of the Crimean War moved the British public to support Seacole after her sacrifices were publicized. She was awarded medals by the British, French, and Turkish governments and today is recognized with her contemporary Florence Nightingale as an innovative field nurse and a champion of public hygiene in peacetime.

Private Collection/The Stapleton Collection/The Bridgeman Art Library

Florence Nightingale During Crimean War *This 1856 lithograph shows Florence Nightingale supervising nursing care in a hospital in Scutari (Üsküdar) across the Bosphorus strait from Istanbul. Though the artist may have exaggerated the neatness and cleanliness of the ward, sanitary measures proved the key to Nightingale's raising of the survival rate of sick and wounded soldiers.*

than the Ottoman government. The Suez Canal, which was partly financed by cotton profits, opened in 1869, and Cairo was redesigned and beautified. Eventually overexpenditure on such projects plunged Egypt into the same debt crisis that plagued the empire as a whole.

The decline of Ottoman power and prosperity had a strong impact on a group of well-educated young urban men who aspired to wealth and influence. They doubted that the empire's rulers and the Tanzimat officials who worked for them would ever stand up to European domination. Though lacking a sophisticated organization, these **Young Ottomans** (sometimes called Young Turks, though that term properly applies to a later movement) promoted a mixture of liberal ideas derived from Europe, national pride in Ottoman independence, and modernist views of Islam. Prominent Young Ottomans helped draft a constitution that was promulgated in 1876 by a new and as yet untried sultan, Abdul Hamid II. This apparent triumph of liberal reform was short-lived. With war against Russia again threatening in the Balkans in 1877, Abdul Hamid suspended the constitution and the parliament that had been elected that year. Though he ruthlessly opposed further political reforms, the Tanzimat programs of extending modern schooling, utilizing European military practices and advisers, and making the government bureaucracy more orderly continued during his reign.

SECTION REVIEW

- After French withdrawal from Egypt, Muhammad Ali seized control and began a French-influenced modernization program.

- His successors continued the program and attacked the Ottoman Empire, but they were thwarted by the European powers.

- The Greek insurrection, European intervention, and Egyptian attack drove the westernizing reform efforts of Mahmud II and his successors.

- The most comprehensive reform initiative was Abdul Mejid's Tanzimat program.

- The Crimean War marked the transition from traditional to modern warfare and drew the Ottoman Empire into greater involvement with European commerce.

- Declining power and prosperity led to the rise of the Young Ottomans.

THE RUSSIAN EMPIRE

■ How did the Russian Empire maintain its status as both a European power and a great Asian land empire?

In 1812, when Napoleon's march on Moscow ended in a disastrous retreat, the European image of Russia changed. Just as Napoleon's withdrawal from Egypt led to Muhammad Ali briefly becoming a political power, so his withdrawal from Russia conferred status on Tsar Alexander I (r. 1801–1825). Conservative Europeans still saw Russia as alien, backward, and oppressive, but they acknowledged its immensity and potential and included the tsar in efforts to suppress revolutionary tendencies throughout Europe.

In several important respects Russia resembled the Ottoman Empire more than the conservative kingdoms of Europe whose autocratic practices it so staunchly supported. Socially dominated by nobles whose country estates were worked by unfree serfs, Russia had almost no middle class. Industry was still at the threshold of development by the standards of the rapidly industrializing European powers, though it was somewhat more dynamic than Ottoman industry. Like Egypt and the Ottoman Empire, Russia engaged in reforms from the top down under Alexander I, but when his conservative brother Nicholas I (r. 1825–1855) succeeded to the throne, iron discipline and suspicion of modern ideas took priority over reform.

Russia and Europe   In 1700 only three Russians out of a hundred lived in cities, two-thirds of them in Moscow alone. By the mid-1800s the town population had grown tenfold, though it still accounted for only 6 percent of the total because the territories of the tsars had grown greatly through wars and colonization (see Chapter 18). These figures demonstrate that, like the Ottoman Empire, Russia was an overwhelmingly agricultural land. However, it had poorer transportation than the Ottoman Empire, since many Ottoman cities were

Young Ottomans Movement of young intellectuals to institute liberal reforms and build a feeling of national identity in the Ottoman Empire in the second half of the nineteenth century.

seaports. Both empires encompassed peoples speaking many different languages.

Well-engineered roads did not begin to appear until 1817, and steam navigation commenced on the Volga in 1843. Tsar Nicholas I built the first railroad from St. Petersburg, the Russian capital, to his summer palace in 1837. A few years later his commitment to strict discipline led him to insist that the trunk line from St. Petersburg to Moscow run in a perfectly straight line. Industrialization projects depended heavily on foreign expertise. While American engineers oversaw the laying of track and built locomotive workshops, British engineers set up the textile mills that gave woolens and cottons a prominent place among Russia's industries.

Until the late nineteenth century the Russian government's interest in industry was limited. An industrial revolution required educated and independent-minded artisans and entrepreneurs, but Nicholas feared the spread of literacy and modern education—especially anything smacking of liberalism, socialism, or revolution—beyond the minimum needed to train the officer corps and the bureaucracy. He preferred serfs to factory workers, and he paid for imported industrial goods with exports of grain and timber.

Like Egypt and the Ottoman Empire, Russia aspired to Western-style economic development. But when France and Britain entered the Crimean War, they faced a Russian army equipped with obsolete weapons and bogged down by lack of transportation. At a time when European engineers were making major breakthroughs in loading cannon through an opening at the breech end, muzzle-loading artillery remained the Russian standard.

Yet in some ways Russia bore a closer resemblance to other European countries than the Ottoman Empire did. From the point of view of the French and the British, the Cyrillic alphabet and the Russian Orthodox form of Christianity seemed foreign, but they were not nearly as foreign as the Arabic alphabet and the Muslim faith. Britain and France feared Russia as a rival for power in the east, but they increasingly accepted Tsar Nicholas's view of the Ottoman Empire as "the sick man of Europe," capable of surviving only so long as the European powers permitted.

From the Russian point of view, kinship with western Europe was of questionable value. Westernizers, like the men of the Tanzimat in the Ottoman Empire, put their trust in technical advances and governmental reform. Opposing them were intellectuals known as **Slavophiles**, who considered the Orthodox faith, the solidity of peasant life, and the tsar's absolute rule to be the proper bases of Russian civilization. After Russia's humiliation in the Crimea, the Slavophile tendency gave rise to **Pan-Slavism**, a militant political doctrine advocating unity of all the Slavic peoples, including those living under Austrian and Ottoman rule.

On the diplomatic front, the tsar's inclusion as a major European ruler contrasted sharply with the sultan's exclusion. However, this did not prevent a powerful sense of Russophobia from developing in the West. Britain in particular saw Russia as a threat to India and despised the subjection of the serfs, who gained their freedom from Tsar Alexander II only in 1861, twenty-seven years after the British had abolished slavery. The passions generated by the Crimean War and its outcome affected the relations of Russia, Europe, and the Ottoman Empire for the remainder of the nineteenth century.

Russia and Asia

The Russian drive to the east in the eighteenth century brought the tsar's empire to the Pacific Ocean and the frontiers of China (see Map 19.1) by century's end. In the nineteenth century Russian expansionism focused on the south. There the backwardness of the Russian military did not matter since the peoples they faced were even less industrialized and technologically advanced. In 1860 Russia established a military outpost on the Pacific coast that would eventually grow into the great naval port of Vladivostok. In Central Asia the steppelands of the Kazakh nomads came under Russian control early in the century, setting the stage for a confrontation with three Uzbek states farther south. They succumbed one by one, beginning

Slavophiles Russian intellectuals in the early nineteenth century who favored resisting western European influences and taking pride in the traditional peasant values and institutions of the Slavic peoples.

Pan-Slavism Movement among Russian intellectuals in the second half of the nineteenth century to identify culturally and politically with the Slavic peoples of eastern Europe.

in 1865, giving rise to the new province of Turkestan, with its capital at Tashkent in present-day Uzbekistan. In the region of the Caucasus Mountains, the third area of southward expansion, Russia first took over Christian Georgia (1786), Muslim Azerbaijan (ah-zer-by-JAHN) (1801), and Christian Armenia (1813) before gobbling up the many small principalities in the heart of the mountains. Between 1829 and 1864 Dagestan, Chechnya (CHECH-nee-yah), and Abkhazia (ab-KAH-zee-yah) became parts of the Russian Empire.

The drive to the south intensified political friction with Russia's new neighbors: Qing China and Japan in the east, Iran on the Central Asian and Caucasus frontiers, and the Ottoman Empire at the eastern end of the Black Sea. In the latter two instances, Muslim refugees from the territories newly absorbed by Russia spread anti-Russian feelings, though some brought with them modern skills and ideas gained from exposure to Russian administration and education.

The Russian drive to the south added a new element to the Eastern Question. Many British statesmen and strategists reckoned that a warlike Russia would press on until it had conquered all the lands separating it from British India, a prospect that made them shudder, given India's enormous contribution to Britain's prosperity. The competition that ensued over which power would control southern Central Asia resulted in a standoff in Afghanistan, which became a buffer zone under the control of neither. In Iran, the standoff between the powers helped preserve the weak Qajar dynasty of shahs.

Cultural Trends

Unlike Egypt and the Ottoman Empire, which began to send students to Europe for training only in the nineteenth century, Russia had been in cultural contact with western Europe since the time of Peter the Great (r. 1689–1725). Members of the Russian court knew Western languages, and the tsars employed officials and advisers from Western countries. Peter had also enlisted the well-educated Ukrainian clerics who headed the Russian Orthodox Church to help spread a Western spirit of education. As a result, Alexander I's reforms met a more positive reception than those of Muhammad Ali and Mahmud II. However, his reforms promised more on paper than they brought about in practice. It took many years to develop a sufficient pool of trained bureaucrats to make the reforms effective.

Ironically, much of the opposition to Alexander's reforms came from well-established families that were not at all unfriendly to Western ideas. Their fear was that the new government bureaucrats, who often came from humbler social origins, would act as agents of imperial tyranny. Individuals favoring more liberal reforms, including military officers who had served in western Europe, intellectuals who read Western political tracts, and members of Masonic lodges who exchanged views with Freemasons in the West, formed secret societies of opposition. Some placed their highest priority on freeing the serfs; others advocated a constitution and a republican form of government. When Alexander I died in December 1825, confusion over who was to succeed him encouraged a group of reform-minded army officers to try to take over the government and provoke an uprising. This so-called **Decembrist revolt** failed, and many of the participants were severely punished. These events ensured that the new tsar, Nicholas I, would pay little heed to calls for reform over the next thirty years. His conservative reign realized the liberals' worst fears in the same way that the Tanzimat-inspired bureaucracy of the Ottoman Empire served the despotic purposes of Sultan Abdul Hamid II after 1877.

The great powers meeting in Paris to settle the Crimean War in 1856 forced Russia to return land to the Ottomans in both Europe and Asia. This humiliation spurred Nicholas's son and successor, Alexander II (r. 1855–1881), to institute major new reforms to reinvigorate the country. The greatest of his reforms was the emancipation of the serfs in 1861. He also authorized new joint-stock companies, projected a railroad network to tie the country together, and modernized the legal and administrative arms of government.

Earlier intellectual and cultural trends flourished under Alexander II. More and more people became involved in intellectual, artistic, and professional life. Most prominent intellectuals received some amount of instruction at Moscow University or some German university. Universities also appeared

Decembrist revolt Abortive attempt by army officers to take control of the Russian government upon the death of Tsar Alexander I in 1825.

Raising of the Alexander Monument in St. Petersburg The death of Alexander I in 1825 brought to power his conservative brother Nicholas I. Yet Alexander remained a heroic figure for his resistance to Napoleon. This monument in Winter Palace Square was erected in 1829.

Visual Connection Archive

in provincial cities like Kharkov in Ukraine and Kazan on the Volga River. Student clubs, along with Masonic lodges, became places for discussing new ideas. As Russian scholars and scientists began to achieve recognition for their contributions to European thought, scholarly careers attracted young men from clerical families, who in turn helped stimulate reforms in religious education.

Just as the Tanzimat reforms of the Ottoman Empire preceded the emergence of the Young Ottomans as a new and assertive political and intellectual force in the second half of the nineteenth century,

so the initially ineffective reforms of Alexander I set in motion cultural currents that would make Russia a dynamic center of intellectual, artistic, and political life under his nephew Alexander II. Thus Russia belonged to two different spheres of development. It entered the nineteenth century a recognized force in European politics, but in other ways it resembled the Ottoman Empire. Rulers in both empires instituted reforms, overcame opposition, and increased the power of their governments. These activities stimulated intellectual and political trends that would ultimately work against the absolute rule of tsar and sultan. Yet Russia would eventually develop much closer relations with western Europe and become an arena for every sort of European intellectual, artistic, and political tendency, while the Ottoman Empire would ultimately succumb to European imperialism.

SECTION REVIEW

- Russian society resembled Ottoman society, but Alexander I undertook top-down westernizing reforms.

- Nicholas I's suspicion of Western ideas stalled reform and slowed industrial development.

- Slavophiles opposed westernizers and, after the Crimean War, embraced Pan-Slavism, contributing to Russophobia in the West.

- Russian expansion southward and eastward added vast territories to the empire and caused friction with China, Japan, Iran, and the Ottoman Empire.

- Resistance to Alexander I's bureaucratic reforms sparked the Decembrist revolt, which stiffened Nicholas I's hostility to Western ideas.

- The humiliation of the Crimean War drove Alexander II's reforms, including emancipation of the serfs.

THE QING EMPIRE

■ *How did the impact of European imperialism on China differ from its impact on Russia and the Ottoman Empire?*

In 1800 the Qing Empire faced many problems, but no reform movement of the kind initiated by Sultan Selim III emerged in China. Unlike the Ottomans, the Qing did not know that Europeans were making enormous fortunes in the early 1800s or that illegal Chinese trade in opium was helping finance the

Trade Warehouse in Guangzhou A European merchant enters in the background while Chinese workers pack tea and porcelain.

industrial transformation of England and the United States. China viewed its most serious crises as domestic, not foreign. The Qing emperors had skillfully countered Russian expansion in the 1600s, and instead of facing a Napoleonic threat, they enjoyed the admiration of Jesuit priests, who likened them to enlightened philosopher-kings. So they brushed aside European complaints about the restrictions of the "Canton system" by which the Qing limited and controlled foreign trade, and they rebuffed the British Macartney mission sent to improve trade relations in 1792 (see Chapter 19). Instead, China focused on quelling rebellions and protests, little realizing the significance of European opinion turning against it.

Economic and Social Disorder

Early Qing successes and territorial expansion sowed the seeds of the domestic and political chaos of the later period. The early emperors encouraged the recovery of farmland, the opening of previously uncultivated areas, and the restoration and expansion of the road and canal systems. These measures expanded the agricultural base and supported a doubling of the population between about 1650 and 1800. Enormous numbers of farmers, merchants, and day laborers migrated in search of less crowded conditions, and a permanent floating population of the unemployed and homeless emerged. By 1800 population strain had caused serious environmental damage in some parts of central and western China.

While farmers tried to cope with agricultural deterioration, other groups vented grievances against the government: minority peoples in central and southwestern China complained about being driven off their lands during the boom of the 1700s, and Mongols resented appropriation of their grazing lands and the displacement of their traditional elites. In some regions, village vigilante organizations took over policing and governing functions from Qing officials who had lost control. Growing numbers of people mistrusted the government, suspecting that all officials were corrupt. The increasing presence of foreign merchants and missionaries in Canton and in the Portuguese colony of Macao aggravated discontent in neighboring districts.

In some parts of China the Qing were hated as foreign conquerors and were suspected of sympathy with the Europeans. In 1794 the White Lotus Rebellion—partly inspired by a messianic ideology that predicted the restoration of the Chinese Ming dynasty and the coming of the Buddha—raged across central China and was not suppressed until 1804. It initiated a series of internal conflicts that continued through the 1800s. Ignited by deepening social instabilities, these movements were sometimes intensified by local ethnic conflicts and by unapproved religions. The ability of some village militias to defend themselves and attack others intensified the conflicts, though the same techniques proved useful to southern coastal populations attempting to fend off British invasion.

The Opium War and Its Aftermath, 1839–1850

Only slowly did Qing officials become aware of British colonies in India that grew and exported opium and of the major naval base at Singapore through which British opium reached East Asia. The first Qing law banning opium imports had been promulgated in 1729. By 1800, however, opium smuggling had swelled to as many as four thousand chests per year. Though British merchants had pioneered this profitable trade, Chinese merchants likewise profited from distributing the drugs. A price war in the early 1820s stemming from competition between British and American importers raised demand so sharply that as many as thirty thousand chests were being imported by the 1830s. Addiction spread to all levels of Qing society, including high-ranking officials. The Qing emperor and his officials debated whether to legalize and tax opium or to enforce the existing ban more strictly. Having decided to root out the use and importation of opium, in 1839 they sent a high official to Canton to deal with the matter.

Britain considered the ban on opium importation an intolerable limitation on trade, a direct threat to Britain's economic health, and a cause for war. British naval and marine forces arrived on the south China coast in late 1839. The **Opium War** (1839–1842) broke out when negotiations between the Qing official and British representatives reached a stalemate. The war exposed the fact that the traditional, hereditary soldiers of the Qing Empire—the **Bannermen**—were, like the Janissaries of the Ottoman Empire, hopelessly obsolete. As in the Crimean War, the British excelled at sea, where they deployed superior technology. British ships landed marines who pillaged coastal cities and then sailed to new destinations (see Map 22.2). Qing sea forces were no match for Britain's powerful navy. Even in land engagements, Qing resources proved woefully inadequate. The British could quickly transport their troops by sea along the coast, whereas Qing soldiers moved primarily on foot. Moving Qing reinforcements from central to eastern China took more than three months; and when the defense forces arrived, they were exhausted and basically without weapons.

The Bannermen used the few muskets the Qing had imported during the 1700s. The weapons were matchlocks, which required the soldiers to ignite the load of gunpowder in them by hand. Firing the weapons was dangerous, and the canisters of gunpowder that each musketeer carried on his belt were likely to explode if a fire broke out nearby—a frequent occurrence in encounters with British artillery. Most of the

Opium War War between Britain and the Qing Empire that was, in the British view, occasioned by the Qing government's refusal to permit the importation of opium into its territories. The victorious British imposed the one-sided Treaty of Nanking on China.

Bannermen Hereditary military servants of the Qing Empire, in large part descendants of peoples of various origins who had fought for the founders of the empire.

Bannermen, however, had no guns at all and fought with swords, knives, spears, and clubs. Soldiers under British command—many of them Indians—carried percussion-cap rifles, which were far quicker, safer, and more accurate than the matchlocks. In addition, the long-range British artillery could be moved from place to place and proved deadly in the cities and villages of eastern China.

Assuming that British gunboats rode so low in the water that they could not sail up the Chinese rivers, Qing commanders evacuated the coastal areas to counter the British threat. But the British deployed new gunboats for shallow waters and moved without difficulty up the Yangzi River (see Chapter 20).

When the invaders approached Nanjing, the former Ming capital, the Qing decided to negotiate. The

Map 22.2 Conflicts in the Qing Empire, 1839–1870 In both the Opium War of 1839–1842 and the Arrow War of 1856–1860, the seacoasts saw most of the action. Since the Qing had a weak navy, the well-armed British ships encountered little resistance as they shelled the southern coasts. In inland conflicts, such as the Taiping Rebellion, the opposing armies were massive and slow moving. Battles on land were often prolonged attempts by one side to starve out the other side before making a major assault. © Cengage Learning

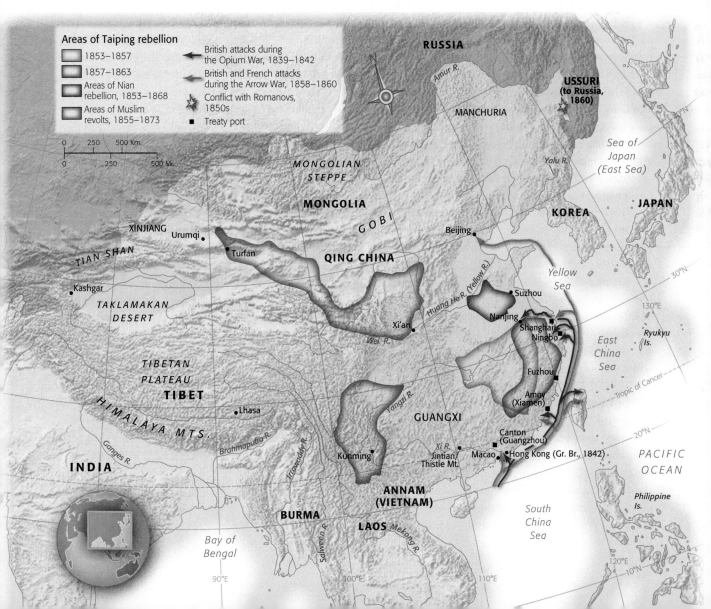

Treaty of Nanking (the British name for Nanjing) dismantled the old Canton system. The number of **treaty ports**—cities opened to foreign residents—increased from one (Canton) to five (Canton, Xiamen, Fuzhou, Ningbo, and Shanghai [shahng-high]). The island of Hong Kong became a British colony, and British residents in China gained extraterritorial rights. The Qing government agreed to set a low tariff of 5 percent on imports and to pay Britain an indemnity of 21 million ounces of silver as a penalty for having started the war. A supplementary treaty the following year guaranteed Britain **most-favored-nation status**: any privileges that China granted to another country would be automatically extended to Britain as well. This provision effectively prevented the colonization of China, because giving land to one country would have necessitated giving it to all.

With each round of treaties came a new round of privileges for foreigners. In 1860 a new treaty legalized their right to import opium. Later, French treaties established the rights of foreign missionaries to travel in the Chinese countryside and preach their religion. The number of treaty ports grew, too; by 1900 they numbered more than ninety. The treaty system and the principle of extraterritoriality resulted in the colonization of small pockets of Qing territory, where foreign merchants lived at ease.

Greater territorial losses resulted when outlying regions gained independence or were ceded to neighboring countries. Districts north and south of the Amur River in the northeast fell to Russia by treaty in 1858 and 1860; parts of modern Kazakhstan and Kyrgyzstan in the northwest met the same fate in 1864. From 1865 onward the British gradually gained control of territories on China's Indian frontier. In the late 1800s France forced the court of Vietnam to end its tribute relationship to the Qing, while Britain encouraged Tibetan independence.

In Canton, Shanghai, and other coastal cities, Europeans and Americans maintained offices and factories that employed local Chinese as menial laborers. The foreigners built comfortable housing in zones where Chinese were not permitted to live, and they entertained themselves in exclusive restaurants and bars. Around the foreign establishments, gambling and prostitution offered employment to part of the local urban population.

Whether in town or in the countryside, Christian missionaries whose congregations sponsored hospitals, shelters, and soup kitchens or gave stipends to Chinese who attended church enjoyed a good reputation. But just as often the missionaries themselves were regarded as another evil. They seemed to subvert Confucian beliefs by condemning ancestor worship, pressured poor families to put their children into orphanages, and fulminated against footbinding. The growing numbers of foreigners, and their growing privileges, became targets of resentment for a deeply dissatisfied, daily more impoverished, and increasingly militarized society.

The Taiping Rebellion, 1850–1864

The inflammatory mixture of social unhappiness and foreign intrusion exploded in the great civil war usually called the **Taiping** (tie-PING) **Rebellion**. In Guangxi, where the Taiping movement originated, entrenched social problems had been generating disorders for half a century. Agriculture in the region was unstable, and many people made their living from arduous and despised trades such as disposing of human waste, making charcoal, and mining. Ethnic divisions complicated economic distress. The lowliest trades frequently involved a minority group, the Hakkas, and tensions between them and the majority were rising. Problems may have been intensified by sharp fluctuations in the opium trade and reactions to the cultural and economic impact of the Europeans and Americans in Canton.

Hong Xiuquan (hoong shee-OH-chew-an), the founder of the Taiping movement, experienced all of these influences. Hong came from a humble Hakka

Treaty of Nanking The treaty that concluded the Opium War. It awarded Britain a large indemnity from the Qing Empire, denied the Qing government tariff control over some of its own borders, opened additional ports of residence to Britons, and ceded the island of Hong Kong to Britain.

treaty ports Cities opened to foreign residents as a result of the forced treaties between the Qing Empire and foreign signatories. In the treaty ports, foreigners enjoyed extraterritoriality.

most-favored-nation status A clause in a commercial treaty that awards to any later signatories all the privileges previously granted to the original signatories.

Taiping Rebellion A Christian-inspired rural rebellion that threatened to topple the Qing Empire.

background. After years of study, he competed in the provincial Confucian examinations, hoping for a post in government. He failed the examinations repeatedly, and it appears that he suffered a nervous breakdown in his late thirties. Afterward he spent some time in Canton, where he met both Chinese and American Protestant missionaries, who inspired him with their teachings. Hong had his own interpretation of the Christian message. He saw himself as the younger brother of Jesus, commissioned by God to found a new kingdom on earth and drive the Manchu conquerors, the Qing, out of China. The result would be universal peace. Hong called his new religious movement the "Heavenly Kingdom of Great Peace."

Hong quickly attracted a community of believers, primarily Hakkas like himself. They believed in the prophecy of dreams and claimed they could walk on air. Hong and his rivals for leadership in the movement went in and out of ecstatic trances and denounced the Manchus as creatures of Satan. After news of the sect reached the government, Qing troops arrived to arrest the Taiping leaders but were soundly repelled. Local loyalty to the Taipings spread quickly; their numbers multiplied; and they began to enlarge their domain.

The Taipings relied at first on Hakka sympathy and the charismatic appeal of their religious doctrine to attract followers. But as their numbers and power grew, they altered their methods of preaching and governing, replacing the anti-Chinese appeals used to enlist Hakkas with anti-Manchu rhetoric designed to enlist Chinese. They also forced captured villages to join their movement. Once people were absorbed, the Taipings strictly monitored their activities, segregating men and women and organizing them into work and military teams. Women were forbidden to bind their feet (the Hakkas had never practiced footbinding) and participated fully in farming and labor. Brigades of women soldiers took to the field against Qing forces.

As the movement grew, it began to move toward eastern and northern China (see Map 22.2). Panic preceded the Taipings. Villagers feared being forced into Taiping units, and Confucian elites recoiled in horror from the bizarre ideology of foreign gods, totalitarian rule, and walking, working, warring women. But the huge numbers the Taipings were able to muster over-whelmed attempts at local defense. The tremendous growth in the number of Taiping followers required the movement to establish a permanent base. When the rebel army conquered Nanjing in 1853, the Taiping leaders decided to settle there and make it the capital of the new "Heavenly Kingdom of Great Peace."

Qing forces attempting to defend north China became more successful as problems of organization and growing numbers slowed Taiping momentum. Increasing Qing military successes resulted mainly from the flexibility of the imperial military commanders in the face of an unprecedented challenge. In addition, the military commanders received strong backing from a group of civilian provincial governors who had studied the techniques developed by local militias for self-defense. Certain provincial governors combined their knowledge of civilian self-defense and local terrain with more efficient organization and the use of modern weaponry. The result was the formation of new military units in which many of the Bannermen voluntarily served under civilian governors. The Qing court agreed to special taxes to fund the new armies and acknowledged the new combined leadership.

When the Taipings settled into Nanjing, the new Qing armies surrounded the city, hoping to starve out the rebels. The Taipings, however, had provisioned themselves well. They also had the services of several brilliant young military commanders, who mobilized enormous campaigns in nearby parts of eastern China, scavenging supplies and attempting to break the encirclement of Nanjing. For more than a decade the Taiping leadership remained ensconced at Nanjing, and the "Heavenly Kingdom" endured.

In 1856 Britain and France, freed from their preoccupation with the Crimean War, turned their attention to China. European and American missionaries had visited Nanjing, but their reports were discouraging. Hong Xiuquan and the other leaders appeared to lead lives of indulgence and abandon, and more than one missionary accused them of homosexuality. The British and French surveyed the situation without fear of quashing a pious Christian movement. Though the Taipings were not going to topple the Qing, rebellious Nian ("Bands") in northern China added a new threat in the 1850s. A series of simultaneous large insurrections might indeed

Nanjing Encircled For a decade the Taipings held the city of Nanjing as their capital. For years Qing and international troops attempted to break the Taiping hold. By the summer of 1864, Qing forces had built tunnels leading to the foundations of Nanjing's city walls and had planted explosives. The detonation of the explosives signaled the final Qing assault on the rebel capital. As shown here, the common people of the city, along with their starving livestock, were caught in the crossfire. Many of the Taiping leaders escaped the debacle at Nanjing, but nearly all were hunted down and executed.

destroy the empire. Moreover, since the Qing had not observed all the provisions of the treaties signed after the Opium War, Britain and France were now considering renewing war on the Qing themselves.

In 1856 the British and French launched a series of swift, brutal coastal attacks—a second opium war, called the Arrow War (1856–1860)—which culminated in the sacking of the Beijing Summer Palace in 1860. A new round of treaties punished the Qing for not enacting all the provisions of the Treaty of Nanking. Having secured their principal objective, the British and French forces then joined the Qing campaign against the Taipings. Attempts to coordinate the international forces were sometimes riotous and sometimes tragic, but the injection of European weaponry and money helped quell both the Taiping and the Nian rebellions during the 1860s.

The Taiping Rebellion ranks as the world's bloodiest civil war and the greatest armed conflict before the twentieth century. Estimates of deaths range from 20 million to 30 million, caused primarily by starvation and disease. Military engagement consisted of surrounding fortified cities and waiting until the enemy forces died, surrendered, or became too weak to defend themselves. Many sieges continued for months. Reports of people eating grass, leather, hemp, and human flesh were widespread. The dead were rarely buried properly, and epidemic disease was common.

The area of early Taiping fighting was close to the regions of southwest China in which bubonic plague had been lingering for centuries. When the rebellion was suppressed, many Taiping followers sought safety in the highlands of Laos and Vietnam, which soon showed infestation by plague. Within a few years the disease reached Hong Kong. From there it spread to Singapore, San Francisco, Calcutta, and London. In the late 1800s Chinese immigrants were regarded as likely carriers, and apprehension over the possibility of a worldwide outbreak contributed to the passage of discriminatory immigration bans on Chinese in the United States in 1882.

The Taiping Rebellion devastated the agricultural centers of China. Many of the most intensely cultivated regions of central and eastern China were depopulated. Some were still uninhabited decades later, and major portions of the country did not recover until the twentieth century.

Cities, too, were hard hit. Shanghai, a treaty port of modest size before the rebellion, saw its population multiplied many times by the arrival of refugees from war-blasted neighboring provinces. The city then endured months of siege by the Taipings. Major cultural centers in eastern China lost masterpieces of art and architecture; imperial libraries were burned or their collections exposed to the weather; and the printing blocks used to make books were destroyed. While the empire faced the mountainous challenge of dealing with the material and cultural destruction of the war, it also was burdened by a major ecological disaster in the north. The Yellow River changed course in 1855, flooding the southern part of impoverished Shandong province and initiating decades of water shortage along the former riverbed in northern Shandong.

Decentralization at the End of the Qing Empire, 1864–1875

The Qing government emerged from the 1850s with no hope of achieving solvency. The corruption of the 1700s, attempts in the very early 1800s to restore waterworks and roads, and declining yields from land taxes had bankrupted the treasury. By 1850, before the Taiping Rebellion, Qing government expenditures were ten times revenues. The indemnities demanded by Europeans after the Opium and Arrow Wars compounded the problem. Vast stretches of formerly productive rice land were devastated, and the population was dispersed. Refugees pleaded for relief, and the imperial, volunteer, foreign, and mercenary troops that had suppressed the Taipings demanded unpaid wages.

Britain and France became active participants in the period of recovery that followed the rebellion. To ensure repayment of the debt to Britain, Robert Hart was installed as inspector-general of a newly created Imperial Maritime Customs Service. Britain and the Qing split the revenues he collected. Britons and Americans worked with the Qing government as advisers and ambassadors, attempting to smooth communications between the Qing, Europe, and the United States.

The real work of the recovery, however, was managed by provincial governors who had come to the forefront in the struggle against the Taipings. To prosecute the war, they had won the right to levy their own taxes, raise their own troops, and run their own bureaucracies. These special powers were not entirely canceled when the war ended. Chief among these governors was Zeng Guofan (zung gwoh-FAHN), who—looking to the United States rather than Britain for models and aid—oversaw programs to restore agriculture, communications, education, and publishing, as well as efforts to reform the military and industrialize armaments manufacture. He hired American advisers and sponsored a daring program in which promising Chinese boys were sent to Hartford, Connecticut, a center of missionary activity, to learn English, science, mathematics, engineering, and history. They returned to China to assume positions previously held by foreign advisers. Though he did not advocate for a public role for women, Zeng was convinced by Confucian principles that educated mothers were needed more than ever and provided an advanced classical education for his own daughters. With Zeng's death in 1872, China lost a major force for reform.

A coalition of aristocrats supported the reform and recovery programs after 1850, marking a fundamental structural change in the Qing Empire. Without provincial governors like Zeng Guofan, the empire might have evaporated within a generation. A crucial member of this alliance was Cixi (TSUH-shee), who was known as the "Empress Dowager" after the 1880s. Later observers, both Chinese and foreign, reviled her as a monster of corruption and arrogance. But in the 1860s and 1870s Cixi supported the provincial governors, some of whom became so powerful that they were managing Qing foreign policy as well as domestic affairs.

Cixi's Allies In the 1860s and 1870s, Cixi was a supporter of reform. In later years she was widely regarded as corrupt and self-centered and as an obstacle to reform. Her greatest allies were the court eunuchs. Introduced to palace life in early China as managers of the imperial harems, eunuchs became powerful political parties at court. The first Qing emperors refused to allow the eunuchs any political influence, but by Cixi's time the eunuchs once again were a political factor.

Tz'u His (1835–1908) Empress Dowager of China 1903 (b/w photo), French Photographer, (20th century)/Private Collection/The Bridgeman Art Library

No longer a conquest regime dominated by a Manchu military caste and its Chinese civilian appointees, the empire now came under the control of a group of reformist aristocrats and military men, independently powerful civilian governors, and a small number of foreign advisers. Without a strong, central, unified leadership, the Qing could not recover their powers of taxation, legislation, and military command. From the 1860s forward, China disintegrated into a number of large power zones. The Qing court's role now was to ritually legitimate the control of provincial governors.

CONCLUSION

The Ottoman, Qing, and Russian Empires shared several characteristics both in their early successes and late-stage challenges. All three maintained a flexible approach when incorporating a diverse group of peoples and cultures into their growing empires. Around the mid-eighteenth century, however, the need to maintain order and increase tax revenues pushed rulers to differentiate groups of people, creating stricter hierarchies within each empire and leading to conflict between the rulers and the ruled. The population growth that began in the sixteenth century throughout Eurasia, and that had been sustainable, and beneficial, in the expanding territories of Russia and the Qing, eventually became unsupportable. By the nineteenth century, even the Qing Empire, the largest and most advanced Eurasian empire in terms of commercial economy and efficient bureaucratic structures, could no longer effectively deal with the increasing demographic pressures, regional conflict, and political dysfunctions.

Most of the subjects of the Ottoman, Russian, and Qing rulers did not think of European pressure or competition as determining factors in their lives during the

SECTION REVIEW

- Social unrest grew in Qing China through a combination of discontent among the poor and displaced indigenous peoples and resentment of growing European influence.
- Qing attempts to ban opium imports provoked the Opium War with Britain, which exposed Qing military inferiority.
- The Treaty of Nanking gave extraterritoriality and other privileges to Britain and led to further losses to other Western powers.
- Social resentment and foreign intrusion ignited the Taiping Rebellion, which, after the Arrow War, the Qing quelled with British and French aid.
- The rebellion encouraged epidemics, devastated agriculture, produced overcrowded cities filled with refugees, and coincided with environmental disasters.
- The rebellion and China's recovery afterward resulted in a process of decentralization led by reformist aristocrats.

first half of the nineteenth century. They continued to live according to the social and economic institutions they inherited from previous generations. By the 1870s, however, the challenge of Europe had become widely realized. The Crimean War, where European allies achieved a hollow victory for the Ottomans and then pressured the sultan for more reforms, confirmed both Ottoman and Russian military weakness. The Opium War did the same for China. But China, unlike the other empires, was also stricken by rampaging civil war and regional uprisings.

In analyzing the crises of the three empires, historians today stress European economic pressures and observe that all three empires ultimately became insolvent and saw the overthrow of their ruling dynasties. However, at the time what most impressed the Ottomans, Russians, and Chinese was European military superiority, as demonstrated in the Greek war of independence, the Crimean War, and the Opium War. Thus for all three empires, dealing with military emergency took priority over deeper reforms throughout most of the time period of this chapter.

CHAPTER REVIEW

THE OTTOMAN EMPIRE

■ *What were the benefits and the drawbacks to the Ottoman Empire of the reforms adopted during the Tanzimat period?* (page 512)

Although the Tanzimat period began with the sultan declaring in 1839 a measure of equality for all Ottoman citizens, improving military performance was the center of the reforming effort. This reform enhanced the role of the military while other administrative changes reduced the social role and governmental influence of the religious elite. The result was an unbalanced reform effort that eventually led to a military takeover of the country.

THE RUSSIAN EMPIRE

■ *How did the Russian Empire maintain its status as both a European power and a great Asian land empire?* (page 521)

For Russians, defeat in the Crimean War and the revelation that Russian arms were no match for modern European weaponry were counterbalanced by the comparative weakness of the peoples in the east and south into whose territories they aggressively expanded. Thus, while lagging far behind in industrialization and having an inefficient government, Russia, like the other European states, engaged in imperialist expansion.

THE QING EMPIRE

■ *How did the impact of European imperialism on China differ from its impact on Russia and the Ottoman Empire?* (page 524)

The course of Russian expansion into Asia made it a neighbor of Qing China, but other European powers were seen as greater threats. Britain, France, and the United States used every means available to gain the freedom to exploit China economically. With respect to the Russian and Ottoman empires nearer to home, however, European imperialists—the United States had minimal involvement—considered financial investment to be somewhat less important than limiting Russian expansion or weakening the Ottoman state and improving the lives of its Christian and Jewish populations.

Key Terms

Muhammad Ali (p. 513)	Decembrist revolt (p. 523)
Serbia (p. 514)	Opium War (p. 526)
Tanzimat (p. 515)	Bannermen (p. 526)
Crimean War (p. 519)	Treaty of Nanking (p. 528)
extraterritoriality (p. 519)	treaty ports (p. 528)
Young Ottomans (p. 521)	most-favored-nation status (p. 528)
Slavophiles (p. 522)	
Pan-Slavism (p. 522)	Taiping Rebellion (p. 528)

State Power, the Census, and the Question of Identity

Between the American Revolution and the last decades of the nineteenth century, new ways of organizing political, economic, and intellectual life transformed Europe and the Americas. One of the less heralded but enduringly significant changes was the expansion of government statistical services.

Bureaucratic departments that depended on reliable statistics to measure the nation's achievements and discover its failures accompanied the rise of the nation-state. Mobilizing resources on a previously unimaginable scale, as exemplified by the modernization of militaries, the internal improvements such as railroads, and the growth in state revenues, became a hallmark of the nation-state. Historians have recently begun examining a less visible but equally important manifestation of growing state power: census taking.

Counting people or estimating their numbers was nothing new. Our best assessments of the Amerindian population of the Western Hemisphere in 1500 rest almost entirely on what were little more than missionary guesses about the numbers they baptized. Spanish and Portuguese kings were eager to count native populations, since "indios" (adult male Amerindians) were subject to labor obligations and tribute payments. So, from the mid-sixteenth century onward, imperial officials conducted regular censuses of Amerindians, adapting practices already in place in Europe.

In the last decades of the eighteenth century, however, the Enlightenment belief that scientific method could be applied to human society attracted both political radicals, like the French Revolutionaries, and reforming monarchs like Maria Theresa of Austria. A science of government, they maintained, could remove the inefficiencies and irrationalities that stood in the way of prosperity and happiness. The French intellectual Condorcet wrote in 1782:

Those sciences, created almost in our own days, the object of which is man himself, the direct goal of which is the happiness of man, will enjoy a progress no less sure than that of the physical sciences.... In meditating on the nature of the moral sciences [what we now call the social sciences], one cannot help seeing that, as they are based like the physical sciences on the observation of fact, they must follow the method, acquire a language equally exact and precise, attaining the same degree of certainty.[1]

As confidence in this new "science" grew, governments and practitioners abandoned the term previously used to describe the collection of numbers about society, political arithmetic, in favor of statistics, a term that suggests its close ties to the "state." The new objectives set out by Condorcet and others led to both the formal university training of statisticians and the creation of government statistical services.

The new nation-states self-consciously sought to transform society, sponsoring economic development, education, and improvements in health and welfare. Statistics allowed them to measure the effectiveness of their policies so they counted practically everything: taverns, urban buildings, births and deaths, and arrests and convictions. They also counted their populations with unprecedented thoroughness. Improved statistical reporting allowed governments to measure not only their own progress but also that of their neighbors and rivals.

The revolutionary governments of France modernized the census practices of the overthrown monarchy by spending more money, hiring more census takers, and improving the training of the staff that designed censuses and analyzed results. Great Britain had an official census in 1801, but established a special administrative structure only in the 1830s. In the Western Hemisphere most independent nations provided for "scientific" censuses. The United States Constitution stipulated a census every ten years. Latin American nations, often torn by civil war, took censuses less regularly; but even the poorest nations took censuses when they could. The census itself seemingly confirmed the existence of the government, demonstrating its modernity and seriousness.

Until recently, historians asked few questions about the politics of census design. What could be more objective than rows of numbers? But census managers were uninhibited in proclaiming the usefulness of reliable numbers to the governments that employed them. At the 1860 International Statistical Congress held in London one speaker said, "I think the true meaning to be attached to 'statistics' is not every collection of figures, but figures collected with the sole purpose of applying the principles deduced from them to questions of importance to the state."[2] The desire to be useful meant that statistics might not be fully objective.

Subjectivity was an unavoidable problem. Censuses that identified citizens and foreign residents by place of residence, sex, age, and family relationships within households, as well as specifying profession and literacy, often undercounted the poor and those living in rural areas.

Moreover, because census takers were determined to be politically useful, they were necessarily concerned with issues of nationality and, in the Americas, with race because these characteristics commonly determined political rights and citizenship. The assessment of nationality and race would prove to be among the most politically dubious objectives of the new social sciences.

Though traditional monarchies commonly disregarded nationality, nation-states could not. A country's strength was assumed to depend in large measure on the growth of its national population, a standard that suggested that the growth of minority populations was dangerous. Who was French? Who was Austrian or Hungarian? European statisticians relied on language of use and mother tongue as proxies for nationality, the first term being flexible enough to recognize the assimilation of minorities, the second suggesting a permanent identity based on a person's birth language. Both terms forced bilingual populations to simplify complex identities. Ethnic minorities were sometimes excluded from military careers,

university admission, or other benefits of citizenship. In parts of Spanish America language was a proxy for race. Spanish speakers were citizens in the full sense, even if they were indistinguishable from Amerindians in appearance. Those who spoke indigenous languages were "indios" and therefore subject to special taxes and labor obligations and effectively denied the right to vote.

Beyond justifying discrimination, census categories compressed and distorted the complexity and variety of human society to fit political preconceptions. Large percentages of the residents of Mexico, Peru, and Bolivia, among other parts of the Americas, were descended from both Europeans and Amerindians and, in the Caribbean region, from Europeans and Africans. Census categories could not capture the complexities of these biological and cultural mixtures. We now know that the poor were often identified as "indios" or "blacks" and the better-off were often called something else, "Americanos," "criollos" (creoles), or even whites. Since this process flattened and streamlined the complexities of identity, censuses on their own could not truly reflect the distribution of ethnicity and race in a population.

In Europe the issue of nationality similarly perplexed the census takers and endangered minorities. Politically dominant national majorities usually lived alongside ethnic minorities: Jewish and Polish minorities in areas controlled by German speakers, German speakers among the French, and Serbo-Croatian speakers among Hungarians, for example. The frontiers between these minority populations and their neighbors were always porous. Sexual unions and marriages were common, and two or more generations of a family often lived together in the same household, with the elder members speaking one language and the younger members another. Who was what? In a very real sense, nationality, like race in the Americas, was ultimately fixed by the census process, where the nation-state forced a limited array of politically utilitarian categories onto the rich diversity of ethnicity and culture.

1.   Quoted in James C. Scott, *Seeing like a State. How Certain Schemes to Improve the Human Condition Have Failed* (New Haven: Yale University Press, 1998), 91.
2.   This discussion relies heavily on Eliza Johnson (now Ablovatski), "Counting and Categorizing: The Hungarian Gypsy Census of 1893" (M.A. Thesis, Columbia University, 1996), especially Chapter III. She quotes from the *Proceedings of the Sixth International Statistical Congress Held in London, 1860*, 379.

Part Seven

Global Diversity and Dominance, 1850–1945

© Cengage Learning

		1850		1870		1890	
AMERICAS			**1861–1865** U.S. Civil War	• **1867** Creation of Dominion of Canada		• **1880s** British build railroads in Brazil and Argentina	• **1898** Spanish-American War
						1880–1914 Immigration from southern and eastern Europe surges	
EUROPE		• **1851** Majority of British population living in cities	• **1856** Transformation of steel and chemical industries begins	**1870–1914** Era of the New Imperialism			
				• **1871** Unification of Germany, Italy		**1894–1906** Dreyfus affair in France	
AFRICA			End of transatlantic slave trade **1867** •	West Africa conquered by France and Britain **1880s** •	**1884–1885** Berlin Africa Conference	• **1896** Ethiopians defeat Italian army at Adowa	
					Nigeria becomes British protectorate **1899** •		
MIDDLE EAST			**1863–1879** Ismail westernizes Egypt		• **1882** British occupy Egypt		
				• **1869** Suez Canal opens	• **1878** Ottoman Empire loses most of its European territories		
ASIA AND OCEANIA		• **1858** Direct British rule in India	• **1868** Meiji Restoration in Japan	First Indian National Congress **1885** •		• **1894** Sino-Japanese War	
			• **1862** French conquer Indochina		**1884–1887** Russia conquers Central Asia	Boxer Rebellion in China **1900** •	

536

In 1850, the world embraced a huge diversity of societies and cultures, but a preceding century of European imperialist adventures had imposed a common theme on many parts of the globe. During the century that followed, Europe, the United States, and Japan dominated much of the world and tried to convert other peoples to their own cultures and ways of life.

In Europe, mounting tensions led to the Great War of 1914–1918. Russia and China erupted in revolution. Soon after, the heartland of the Ottoman Empire became modern Turkey, while its Arab provinces were taken over by France and Britain.

In the 1930s, amidst a worldwide transformation of lifestyles brought on by new technologies, the political and economic system the European pow-

ers crafted after the war fell apart. While the capitalist nations fell into a depression, the Soviet Union industrialized at breakneck speed. In Germany and Japan, extremists sought to solve their countries' grievances by military conquest.

Nationalists in India yearning for independence, as well as nationalists in Latin America seeking an end to foreign military interventions, increased global economic and political tensions as World War II loomed.

The war caused the death of millions of people and the destruction of countless cities. It also weakened Europe's overseas empires. India gained its independence in 1947. Two years later, Mao Zedong led the Chinese communists to victory. Of all the once great powers, only the United States and the Soviet Union remained to compete for global dominance.

1910	1930	1950
1906–1914 U.S. builds Panama Canal	**1929** U.S. stock market crash leads to Great Depression	**1938** Mexico nationalizes oil industry	**1946** Juan Perón becomes president of Argentina
1917 U.S. enters World War I			
1911–1920 Mexican Revolution			
1905 Revolution of 1905 in Russia	**1922–1945** Fascism in Italy		
1917 Russian Revolutions	**1933** Hitler takes power in Germany		
1914–1918 World War I	**1939–1945** World War II		
1908 Congo annexed by Belgium		**1939–1945** A million Africans serve in World War II	
1909 African National Congress founded			
Balfour Declaration **1917**	**1922–1938** Atatürk secularizes Turkey	**1948** State of Israel founded	
1904 Young Turk reforms in Ottoman Empire	**1918** Breakup of Ottoman Empire		
1915–1918 Arab Revolt against Ottomans			
1904–1905 Russo-Japanese War	**1910** Korea annexed by Japan	**1931** Japanese invasion of Manchuria	**1945** U.S. atomic bombs force Japanese surrender
	1911 Overthrow of Qing dynasty in China	**1941** Japan attacks U.S.	**1947** India and Pakistan win independence
			1949 Communists take power in China

Varieties of Imperialism in Africa, India, Southeast Asia, and Latin America

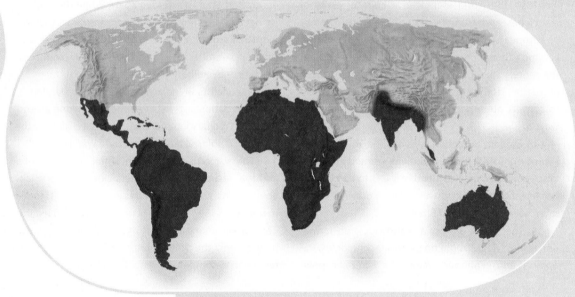

© Cengage Learning

Like many regions that looked to be coherent countries on the maps drawn by imperialism, Algeria was not a unified realm in 1830 when France landed 35,000 troops outside of Algiers. Five days later, at a cost of 6,000 dead and wounded Frenchmen, the dey of Algiers, an autonomous governor ruling under Ottoman suzerainty, surrendered the city. French nationalists called the invasion a defense of French honor because three years earlier the dey had struck a French diplomat with a fly whisk during an argument over debts lingering from the Napoleonic wars, which had ended more than a decade earlier. Actually the invasion plan had been drawn up by Napoleon himself in 1808 in response to commercial interests in southern France that sought to acquire new land in North Africa.

Control of Algiers, however, did not prevent the king of Morocco from pressing a claim to rule Algeria's western region, nor did it fit the political interests of the country's five major Sufi brotherhoods, which had earlier staged revolts against Ottoman imperialism. The brotherhood that would prove the hardest for the French to defeat was the Qadiriya, which waged a fifteen-year *jihad* (holy war) that only ended in 1847 with the surrender of its leader Abd al-Qadir.

Abd al-Qadir (AHB-dahl-KAH-deer) was only twenty-five when he took over from his father as head of the brotherhood in 1832. The key to Abd al-Qadir's success was a network of religious centers (*zawiyas*) that trained judges and administrators and disseminated his vision of an egalitarian society that would observe Islamic law and be dominated by neither Ottoman officials nor French generals. Other Sufi brotherhoods fought separately against the French, but not as successfully.

Though Abd al-Qadir was allowed to settle in Damascus after his defeat and there pursued an eminent career as a leader of the Muslim community, his historical image is primarily one of resistance to imperialism. Like most movements elsewhere opposing imperialist aggression, Abd al-Qadir's Sufi followers could not prevail against European firepower but laid the groundwork for anticolonial movements that would gain momentum after World War II.

Defenders of imperialism often cite the benefits of European rule in terms of railroad construction, orderly governance, integration of local production with currents of international trade, and similar economic and administrative factors. But the reputations or legends of leaders like Abd al-Qadir would eventually eclipse the memory of some of the generals and administrators who oversaw a massive increase in European imperialism starting in the late eighteenth century.

CHANGES AND EXCHANGES IN AFRICA

■ *Why were imperialists interested in conquering Africa, and how did their presence on that continent change the environment?*

In the century before 1870 Africa underwent dynamic political changes and a great expansion of foreign trade. While a few indigenous African leaders held out against European imperialism, maps of Africa became tinted with pink and green, the conventional colors of British and French colonies, respectively. The slave trade died under British pressure, and trade in other goods grew sharply. Africans consumed large quantities of imported machine-made textiles, and those rulers who retained a measure of independence purchased European firearms.

Southern Africa For many centuries the Nguni (ng-GOO-nee) peoples had farmed and raised cattle in the fertile coast-lands of southeastern Africa (see Map 23.1). When drought hit the region at the beginning of the nineteenth century, an upstart military leader named Shaka (r. 1818–1828) created the **Zulu** kingdom in 1818. Strict military discipline and courage soon made the Zulu the most powerful and most feared fighters in southern Africa. Shaka expanded his kingdom by raiding his African neighbors, seizing their cattle, and capturing their women and children. Although Shaka ruled for little more than a decade, he left behind a

Zulu A people of modern South Africa whom King Shaka united in 1818.

Eileen Tweedy/The At Archive/Art Resource, NY

Zulu in Battle Dress, 1834 Elaborate costumes helped impress opponents with the Zulus' strength. Shown here are long-handled spears and thick leather shields.

Africa and were beginning to refer to themselves as **Afrikaners** (af-rih-KAHN-uhr). Firearms enabled the Afrikaners to win some important battles against the Zulu and other Africans, but they were still a tiny minority surrounded by the populous and powerful independent African kingdoms. The British prohibited further expansion because it invariably led to wars with indigenous Africans; this decision alienated many Afrikaners who had left the British-ruled Cape Colony between 1836 and 1839 to go north in what is called the "Great Trek."

After diamonds were discovered in 1868, Great Britain annexed the diamond area in 1871, further angering Afrikaners. Once in the interior, the British came into conflict first with the Xhosa (KOH-sah) people in 1877 and 1878, and then in 1879 they confronted the Zulu, militarily the most powerful of the African peoples in the region.

The Zulu, led by their king Cetshwayo (set-SHWAH-yo), resented their encirclement by Afrikaners and British. A growing sense of nationalism and their proud military tradition led them into a war with the British in 1879. They defeated the British at Isandlwana (ee-sawn-dull-WAH-nuh), but a few months later they were in turn defeated. Cetshwayo was captured and sent into exile, and the Zulu lands were given to white ranchers.

Relations between the British and the Afrikaners, already tense as a result of British encroachment, took a turn for the worse when gold was discovered in the Afrikaner republic of Transvaal (trans-VAHL) in 1886. In the gold rush that ensued, the British soon outnumbered the Afrikaners.

new national identity destined to clash with European colonial designs.

Southern Africa attracted European settlers first because of its good pastures and farmlands and later because of the discovery of phenomenal deposits of diamonds, gold, and copper, as well as coal and iron ore. The Cape Colony, a Dutch possession that came definitively under British rule after 1806, flourished because of Cape Town's strategic importance as a supply station for ships making the long voyages between Europe and India. With the port city came some twenty thousand descendants of Dutch and French settlers who occupied farms and ranches in the fertile high *veld* (plateau) in the north that two decades of Zulu wars had depopulated.

Despite their European origins, these people thought of themselves as permanent residents of

Afrikaners South Africans descended from Dutch and French settlers of the seventeenth century. Their Great Trek founded new settler colonies in the nineteenth century. Though a minority among South Africans, they held political power after 1910, imposing a system of racial segregation called apartheid after 1949.

Chronology

	Slavery	Africa	India and Southeast Asia	Latin America
1750			**1756** Black Hole of Calcutta	
		1795–1802 Britain takes control of Dutch Cape Colony; **1806** British possession becomes permanent	**1765** East India Company (EIC) rule of Bengal begins	
1800	**1807** Britain outlaws slave trade	**1808** Britain takes over Sierra Leone **1809** Sokoto Caliphate founded		
		1818 Shaka founds Zulu kingdom **1821** Foundation of Liberia	**1818** EIC creates Bombay Presidency **1826** EIC conquers Assam and northern Burmaco	
	1834 Britain frees slaves in its colonies. Indentured labor migrations begin **1848** France abolishes slaves in its colonies	**1831–1847** Algerians resist French takeover **1836–1839** Afrikaners' Great Trek **1840** Omani sultan moves capital to Zanzibar	**1828** Brahmo Samaj founded	
1850	**1867** End of Atlantic slave trade		**1857–1858** Sepoy Rebellion leads to end of EIC rule **1877** Queen Victoria becomes Empress of India **1885** Indian National Congress formed **1898** Spanish-American War. U.S. takes over Philippines	**1876–1910** Porfirio Díaz, dictator of Mexico **1898** Spanish-American War. U.S. takes over Cuba
1900		**1899–1902** South African (Boer) War **1900s** Railroads connect ports to the interior		**1910** Mexican Revolution begins **1917** New constitution proclaimed in Mexico

Britain's invasion of southern Africa was driven in part by the ambition of **Cecil Rhodes** (1853–1902), who once declared that he would "annex the stars" if he could. Rhodes made his fortune in the diamond fields, founding De Beers Consolidated, a company

Cecil Rhodes (1853–1902) British entrepreneur and politician involved in the expansion of the British Empire from South Africa into Central Africa. The colonies of Southern Rhodesia (now Zimbabwe) and Northern Rhodesia (now Zambia) were named after him.

Map 23.1 Africa in the Nineteenth Century Expanding trade drew much of Africa into global networks, but foreign colonies in 1870 were largely confined to Algeria and southern Africa. Growing trade, Islamic reform movements, and other internal forces created important new states throughout the continent. © Cengage Learning

Map legend:

- Zanzibari trading post
- Nguni/Ngoni states
- Reformist Muslim states
- Nyamwezi states
- Ethiopia, 1880
- Ethiopia, 1900
- Other states
- European colonies
- → Migrations of the Nguni/Ngoni
- → The Great Trek
- → Trade routes
- 1857 External slave trade and date of suppression

that has dominated the world's diamond trade ever since. He then turned to politics. He encouraged a concession company, the British South Africa Company, to push north into Central Africa, where he named two new colonies after himself: Southern Rhodesia (now Zimbabwe) and Northern Rhodesia (now Zambia). The Ndebele (en-duh-BELL-ay) and Shona peoples, who inhabited the region, resisted this invasion, but the machine guns of the British finally defeated them.

The inflow of English-speaking whites into the gold- and diamond-mining areas and British attempts to annex the two Afrikaner republics, Transvaal and

ish government expected European settlers in Africa to manage their own affairs, as they were doing in Canada, Australia, and New Zealand. Thus, in 1910 the European settlers created the Union of South Africa, in which the Afrikaners eventually emerged as the ruling element.

Unlike Canada, Australia, and New Zealand, South Africa had a majority of indigenous inhabitants and substantial numbers of Indians and "Cape Coloureds" (people of mixed ancestry). Yet the Europeans were both numerous enough to demand self-rule and powerful enough to deny the vote and other civil rights to the majority. In 1913 the South African parliament passed the Natives Land Act, assigning Africans to reservations and forbidding them to own land elsewhere. This and other racial policies turned South Africa into a land of segregation and oppression.

Simultaneous with the formation of Shaka's Zulu kingdom, Islamic reform movements were creating another cluster of powerful states in the savannas of West Africa. The reformers followed a classic Muslim pattern: a *jihad* (holy war) added new lands, spreading Islamic beliefs and laws among conquered peoples. The largest reform movement was led by Usuman dan Fodio (OO-soo-mahn dahn FOH-dee-oh) (1745–1817), whose armed supporters conquered and combined the older Hausa (HOW-suh) states into a new empire ruled by a caliph in the city of Sokoto. The **Sokoto Caliphate** (1809–1906) was the largest state in West Africa since the sixteenth century (see Map 23.1).

In coastal West Africa, however, the French, who had maintained a foothold in Senegal for centuries,

Gardiner F. Williams/NGS Image Collection

South African Diamond Mine When diamonds were found in Kimberley, South Africa, in 1868, the discovery precipitated a rush of prospectors from Europe and America. As soon as surface deposits were exhausted, their claims were bought by large companies that could afford the heavy equipment needed to mine deep underground. By the early twentieth century, diamonds came from major industrial mines like the Premier Mine shown here.

Orange Free State, led to the South African or Boer War, which lasted from 1899 to 1902. At first the Afrikaners had the upper hand, for they were highly motivated, possessed modern rifles, and knew the land. In 1901, however, Great Britain brought in 450,000 troops and crushed the Afrikaner armies. Ironically, the Afrikaners' defeat in 1902 led to their ultimate victory. Wary of costly commitments overseas, the Brit-

Sokoto Caliphate   A large Muslim state founded in 1809 in what is now northern Nigeria.

envisioned building a railroad from the upper Senegal River to the upper Niger to open the interior to French merchants. This in turn led the French military to undertake the conquest of the interior. Sokoto remained independent, but after 1890 it was embattled both by neighboring rulers and European encroachment. In 1906 the empire came to an end, with France, Britain, and Germany gobbling up various portions.

Farther south, **King Leopold II** of Belgium, following the advice of an American journalist and explorer, Henry Morton Stanley, invested his personal fortune in "opening up"—that is, occupying—the Congo Basin, an enormous forested region in the heart of equatorial Africa. With Leopold's money, Stanley returned to Africa from 1879 to 1884 to establish trading posts along the southern bank of the Congo River. At the same time Savorgnan de Brazza, an Italian officer serving in the French army, obtained from an African ruler living on the opposite bank a treaty that placed that area under the "protection" of France.

These events sparked a flurry of diplomatic activity. German chancellor Bismarck called the **Berlin Conference** on Africa of 1884 and 1885. There the major powers agreed that henceforth "effective occupation" would replace the former trading relations between Africans and Europeans. Every country with colonial ambitions had to send troops into Africa and participate in the division of the spoils. As a reward for triggering the "scramble" for Africa, Leopold II acquired a personal domain under the name *Congo Free State*, while France and Portugal took most of the rest of equatorial Africa. In this manner, the European powers and King Leopold managed to divide Africa among themselves, at least on paper.

Except in Kenya, Northern Rhodesia, and South Africa, where Europeans found the land and climate to their liking and forced Africans to become squatters, sharecroppers, or ranch hands on land they had farmed for generations, the colonial rulers declared any land that was not farmed to be "vacant" and gave it to private concession companies. In the Gold Coast (now Ghana), British trading companies bought the cocoa grown by African farmers at low prices and resold it for large profits. The interior of French West Africa lagged behind. Although the region could produce cotton, peanuts, and other crops, the difficulties of transportation limited its development before 1914.

Compared to West Africa, equatorial Africa had few inhabitants and little trade. Rather than try to govern these vast territories directly, authorities in the Congo Free State, the French Congo, and the Portuguese colonies of Angola and Mozambique granted huge pieces of land to private concession companies, offering them monopolies on the natural resources and trade of their territories and the right to employ soldiers and impose taxes.

Freed from outside supervision, the companies forced the African inhabitants at gunpoint to produce cash crops and carry them, on their heads or backs, to the nearest railroad or navigable river. The worst abuses took place in the Congo Free State, where a rubber boom made it profitable for private companies to brutalize Africans collecting latex from vines that grew in the forests. After 1906 the British press began publicizing the horrors. The public outcry that followed, coinciding with the end of the rubber boom, convinced the Belgian government to take over Leopold's private empire in 1908. (See Diversity and Dominance: Two Africans Recall the Arrival of the Europeans.)

Modernization in Egypt and Ethiopia

While colonial states were arising elsewhere, in northeastern Africa Egypt and Ethiopia retained their independence and experimented with **modernization**. Muhammad Ali, who ruled Egypt from 1805 to 1849, began a series of reforms aimed at creating a modern Egypt (see Chapter 22). European pressure sharply curtailed these efforts after 1839, but by the end of his reign Egypt's population had nearly doubled; trade with Europe had expanded

---

King Leopold II (1835–1909) King of Belgium (r. 1865–1909). He was active in encouraging the exploration of Central Africa and became the ruler of the Congo Free State (to 1908).

Berlin Conference (1884–1885) Conference that German chancellor Otto von Bismarck called to set rules for the partition of Africa. It led to the creation of the Congo Free State under King Leopold II of Belgium.

modernization The process of reforming political, military, economic, social, and cultural traditions in imitation of the early success of Western societies, often with little regard for accommodating local traditions in non-Western societies.

by almost 600 percent; and a new class of educated Egyptians was beginning to wield some influence.

Muhammad Ali's grandson Ismail (is-mah-EEL) (r. 1863–1879) placed emphasis on westernizing Egypt. "My country is no longer in Africa," Ismail declared, "it is in Europe."[1] Massive cotton exports during the American Civil War helped finance a network of new irrigation canals, 800 miles (1,300 kilometers) of railroads, a postal service, and dazzling changes in the capital city of Cairo. Once cotton prices returned to normal after 1865, other sources of revenue were needed to finance such projects as the **Suez Canal**, which opened in 1869 and was the greatest construction project of the century. The canal allowed ships to travel between Europe and India in less than two weeks—much less than the month or longer consumed by sailing around Africa and across the Indian Ocean. Ismail even tried to make Egypt the center of an empire reaching into Sudan and Ethiopia.

Instead of making Egypt powerful and independent, ambitious projects like the Suez Canal forced Egypt to borrow from European creditors at high interest rates. Half the Suez Canal was financed by the French; the other half by Egypt. By 1876 foreign debt had risen to £100 million sterling, and the interest payments alone consumed one-third of Egypt's foreign export earnings. To avoid bankruptcy, the Egyptian government sold its shares in the Suez Canal to Great Britain and accepted foreign oversight. When high taxes caused hardship and popular discontent, the French and British persuaded the Ottoman sultan to depose Ismail. This foreign intervention provoked a military uprising under the Egyptian army colonel Arabi Pasha, which threatened the Suez Canal.

Fearing for their investments, the British sent an army into Egypt in 1882. So important was the Suez Canal to Britain's maritime supremacy that they stayed for seventy years. During those years the British ruled Egypt "indirectly"—that is, they maintained the Egyptian government and the fiction of Egyptian sovereignty but retained real power in their own hands.

Eager to develop Egyptian cotton production, the British brought in engineers and contractors to build the first dam across the Nile, at Aswan in Upper Egypt. When completed in 1902, it captured the annual Nile flood and released its waters throughout the year, allowing farmers to grow two, sometimes three, crops a year. The economic development of Egypt by the British enriched a small elite of landowners and merchants, many of them foreigners. Egyptian peasants got little relief from the heavy taxes collected to pay for their country's crushing foreign debt and the expenses of the British army of occupation. Most Egyptians found British rule more onerous than that of the Ottomans. By the 1890s Egyptian politicians and intellectuals were demanding that the British leave.

Beginning in the 1840s, Christian Ethiopia was also modernizing its state, purchasing weapons from European sources and creating strong armies loyal to the ruler. Emperor Téwodros (tay-WOH-druhs) II (r. 1833–1868) and his successor, Yohannes (yoh-HAHN-nehs) IV (r. 1872–1889), brought back under imperial rule large areas of ancient Ethiopia. When King Menelik II (MEN-uh-lik) of Shoa succeeded Yohannes as emperor in 1889, the merger of their separate realms created the modern boundaries of Ethiopia.

Transition from the Slave Trade

Trade between Africa and the other Atlantic continents more than doubled between the 1730s and the 1780s, then doubled again by 1870.[2] Before about 1825, the slave trade accounted for most of that increase. Western criticism of slavery was rising, however. Once the world's greatest slave traders, the British became the most aggressive abolitionists. During the half century after 1815, Britain spent some $60 million (£12 million) in its efforts to end the slave

> **Suez Canal** Ship canal dug across the Isthmus of Suez in Egypt, designed by Ferdinand de Lesseps. It opened to shipping in 1869 and shortened the sea voyage between Europe and Asia. Its strategic importance led to the British occupation of Egypt in 1882.

[1] Quoted in P. J. Vatikiotis, *The History of Modern Egypt: From Muhammad Ali to Mubarak*, 4th ed. (Baltimore: Johns Hopkins University Press, 1991), 74.

[2] David Eltis, "Precolonial Western Africa and the Atlantic Economy," in *Slavery and the Rise of the Atlantic Economy*, ed. Barbara Solow (New York: Cambridge University Press, 1991), table 1.

Diversity & Dominance

Two Africans Recall the Arrival of the Europeans

We know a great deal about the arrival of the Europeans into the interior of Africa from the perspective of the conquerors, but very little about how the events were experienced by Africans. Here are two accounts by African women, one from northern Nigeria whose land was occupied by the British, the other from the Congo Free State, a colony of King Leopold II of Belgium. They show not only how Africans experienced European colonial dominance but also how diverse these African experiences were.

Baba of Karo, a Nigerian Woman, Remembers Her Childhood

When I was a maiden the Europeans first arrived. Ever since we were quite small the *malams* had been saying that the Europeans would come with a thing called a train, they would come with a thing called a motor-car, in them you would go and come back in a trice. They would stop wars, they would repair the world, they would stop oppression and lawlessness, we should live at peace with them. We used to go and sit quietly and listen to the prophecies.

I remember when a European came to Karo on a horse, and some of his foot soldiers went into the town. Everyone came out to look at them, but in Zerewa they didn't see the European. Everyone at Karo ran away—"There's a European, there's a European!"

At that time Yusufu was the king of Karo. He did not like the Europeans, he did not wish them, he would not sign their treaty. Then he say that perforce he would have to agree, so he did. We Habe wanted them to come, it was the Fulani who did not like it. When the Europeans came the Habe saw that if you worked for them they paid you for it, they didn't say, like the Fulani, "Commoner, give me this!

Commoner, bring me that!" Yes, the Habe wanted them; they saw no harm in them.

The Europeans said that there were to be no more slaves; if someone said "Slave!" you could complain to the *alkali* who would punish the master who said it, the judge said, "That is what the Europeans have decreed." The first order said that any slave, if he was younger than you, was your younger brother, if he was older than you was your elder brother—they were all brothers of their master's family. No one used the word "slave" any more. When slavery was stopped, nothing much happened at our *rinji* except that some slaves whom we had bought in the market ran away. Our own father went to his farm and worked, he and his son took up their large hoes; they loaned out their spare farms. Tsoho our father and Kadiri my brother with whom I live now and Babambo worked, they farmed guineacorn and millet and groundnuts and everything; before this they had supervised the slaves' work—now they did their own.

In the old days if the chief liked the look of your daughter he would take her and put her in his house; you could do nothing about it. Now they don't do that.

Ilanga, a Congolese Woman, Recounts Her Capture by Agents of the Congo Free State

. . . we were all busy in the fields hoeing our plantations, for it was the rainy season, and the weeds sprang quickly up, when a runner came to the village saying that a large band of men was coming, that they all wore red caps and blue cloth, and carried guns and long knives, and that many white men were with them, the chief of whom was Kibalanga (Michaux). Niendo at once called all the chief men to his house, while the drums were beaten to summon the people to the village. A long consultation was held, and finally we were all told to go quietly to the fields and bring in ground-nuts, plantains, and cassava for the warriors who were coming, and goats and fowl for the white men. ➤

> The women all went with baskets and filled them, and put them in the road, which was blocked up, so many were there. Niendo then commanded everyone to go and sit quietly in the houses until he gave other orders. This we did, everyone remaining quietly seated while Niendo went up the road with the head men to meet the white chief. We did not know what to think, for most of us feared that so many armed men coming boded evil; but Niendo thought that, by giving presents of much food, he would induce the strangers to pass on without harming us. And so it proved, for the soldiers took the baskets, and were then ordered by the white men to move off through the village. Many of the soldiers looked into the houses and shouted at us words we did not understand. We were glad when they were all gone, for we were much in fear of the white men and the strange warriors, who are known to all the people as being great fighters, bringing war wherever they go. . . .

When the white men and their warriors had gone, we went again to our work, and were hoping that they would not return; but this they did in a very short time. As before, we brought in great heaps of food; but this time *Kibalanga* did not move away directly, but camped near our village, and his soldiers came and stole all our fowl and goats and tore up our cassava; but we did not mind as long as they did not harm us. The next morning it was reported that the white men were going away; but soon after the sun rose over the hill, a large band of soldiers came into the village, and we all went into the houses and sat down. We were not long seated when the soldiers came rushing in shouting, and threatening Niendo with their guns. They rushed into the houses and dragged the people out. Three or four came to our house and caught hold of me, also my husband Oleka and my sister Katinga. We were dragged into the road, and were tied together with cords about our necks, so that we could not escape. We were all crying, for now we knew that we were to be taken away to be slaves. The soldiers beat us with the iron sticks from their guns, and compelled us to march to the camp of *Kibalanga*, who ordered the women to be tied up separately, ten to each cord, and the men in the same way. When we were all collected—and there were many from other villages whom we now saw, and many from Waniendo—the soldiers brought baskets of food for us to carry, in some of which was smoked human flesh (*niama na nitu*).

We then set off marching very quickly. My sister Katinga had her baby in her arms, and was not compelled to carry a basket; but my husband Oleka was made to carry a goat. We marched until the afternoon, when we camped near a stream, where we were glad to drink, for we were much athirst. We had nothing to eat, for the soldiers would give us nothing, so we lay upon the ground, and at night went to sleep. The next day we continued the march, and when we camped at noon were given some maize and plantains, which were gathered near a village from which the people had run away. So it continued each day until the fifth day, when the soldiers took my sister's baby and threw it in the grass, leaving it to die, and made her carry some cooking pots which they found in the deserted village. On the sixth day we became very weak from lack of food and from constant marching and sleeping in the damp grass, and my husband, who marched behind us with the goat, could not stand up longer, and so he sat down beside the path and refused to walk more. The soldiers beat him, but still he refused to move. Then one of them struck him on the head with the end of his gun, and he fell upon the ground. One of the soldiers caught the goat, while two or three others stuck the long knives they put on the ends of their guns into my husband. I saw the blood spurt out, and then saw him no more, for we passed over the brow of a hill and he was out of sight. Many of the young men were killed the same way, and many babies thrown into the grass to die. A few escaped; but we were so well guarded that it was almost impossible.

QUESTIONS FOR ANALYSIS

1. How do Baba and Ilanga recall their existence before the Europeans came?
2. What did they expect when they first heard of the arrival of Europeans? Instead, what happened to them, their relatives, and their towns?
3. How do you explain the difference between these two accounts?

Sources: From M. F. Smith, ed., *Baba of Karo: A Woman of the Muslim Hausa* (New York: Philosophical Library, 1955), 66–68. Edgar Canisius, *A Campaign Amongst Cannibals* (London: R. A. Everett & Co., 1903), 250–256.

trade through naval patrols. This equaled the profits British slave traders had made in the fifty years before the trade was banned in 1807. Although British patrols captured 1,635 slave ships and liberated over 160,000 enslaved Africans, continued demand for slaves in Cuba and Brazil kept the trade going until 1867.

To satisfy their desire for cloth, metals, and other goods after slavery was outlawed, Africans expanded their **"legitimate" trade** (exports other than slaves). The most successful of the new exports from West Africa was palm oil, used by British manufacturers for soap, candles, and lubricants. Though still a major source of slaves until the mid-1830s, the trading states of the Niger Delta emerged as the premier exporters of palm oil. Coastal Africans grew rich and purchased large numbers of male slaves to paddle the giant dugout canoes that transported palm oil from inland markets along the narrow delta creeks to the trading ports.

Suppressing the slave trade helped spread Western cultural influences in West Africa. In 1808, the British had taken over the small colony of Sierra Leone (see-AIR-uh lee-OWN) as a base for their anti-slave trade naval squadron. In the following years, 130,000 men, women, and children taken from "captured" vessels were liberated in Sierra Leone. Christian missionaries helped settle these impoverished and dispirited **recaptives** in and around Freetown, the capital. In time, the mission churches and schools made many converts among such unfortunates.

Sierra Leone's schools also produced a number of distinguished graduates. Samuel Adjai Crowther (1808–1891), freed from a slave ship in 1821, became the first Anglican bishop in West Africa in 1864, administering a pioneering diocese along the lower Niger River. James Africanus Horton (1835–1882), the son of slaves liberated in Sierra Leone, became a doctor and the author of many studies of West Africa.

Other Western cultural influences came from people of African birth or descent returning to their ancestral homeland. In 1821, to the south of Sierra Leone, free black Americans founded a settlement that grew into the Republic of Liberia, a place of liberty at a time when slavery was legal and flourishing in the United States.

With the British patrolling West Africa, slavers moved southward and then around the tip of the continent to eastern Africa, where an existing trade

SECTION REVIEW

- In the south, Shaka established a Zulu kingdom that came in conflict with European settlers.
- Differences between the British and Dutch-descended Afrikaners led to the Boer War.
- In the west, Usuman dan Fodio conquered the former Hausa states and formed the Sokoto Caliphate.
- The Suez Canal conferred new economic and political importance on Egypt.
- The abolition of slavery had economic and political consequences.

in slaves to the Islamic world was expanding. Two-thirds of the 1.2 million slaves exported from eastern Africa in the nineteenth century went to markets in North Africa and the Middle East; the other third went to plantations in the Americas and the Indian Ocean.

Between 1800 and 1873 local Arab and Swahili (swah-HEE-lee) owners purchased some 700,000 slaves from inland eastern Africa to do the hard work of harvesting cloves on plantations on Zanzibar Island and the neighboring coast. These territories belonged to the sultanate of Oman, a realm in southeastern Arabia. The sultan had even moved his court to Zanzibar in 1840 to take advantage of the burgeoning trade in cloves. Zanzibar also exported ivory and slaves until British pressure induced the sultan to ban the export of slaves in 1857 and their import in 1873.

INDIA UNDER BRITISH RULE

■ *How did Britain secure its hold on India, and what colonial policies led to the beginnings of Indian nationalism?*

The people of South Asia felt the impact of European commercial, cultural, and colonial expansion more immediately and profoundly than did the Africans. Europeans laid claim to only small parts of Africa

"legitimate" trade Exports from Africa in the nineteenth century that did not include the newly outlawed slave trade.

recaptives Africans rescued by Britain's Royal Navy from the illegal slave trade of the nineteenth century and restored to free status.

between 1750 and 1870, but nearly all of India (with three times the population of Africa) came under Britain's direct or indirect rule. After the founding of the East India Company in 1600, it took British interests 250 years to commandeer the colonies and trade of the Dutch, fight off French and Indian challenges, and pick up the pieces of the decaying Mughal (MOO-guhl) Empire.

The might of the Mughal Empire had not lasted long after the reign of Aurangzeb, who died in 1707 (see Chapter 18). In 1739 Iranian invaders sacked Delhi and carried off vast amounts of booty. Indian states also took advantage of Mughal weakness to assert their independence. By midcentury, the Maratha (muh-RAH-tuh) Confederation, a coalition of states in central India, controlled more land than the Mughals did. Several **nawabs** (NAH-wab), a term used for Muslim princes who were nominally deputies of the Mughal emperor, carved out powerful states of their own. Ambitious young "company men" employed by British, French, and Dutch trading companies used hard bargaining, and hard fighting when necessary, to persuade these Indian rulers to allow them to establish coastal trading posts. To protect their fortified warehouses, the companies hired trained Indian troops known as **sepoys** (SEE-poy). In fragmented India, these private armies came to hold the balance of power.

In 1691, the East India Company (EIC) had persuaded the nawab of Bengal in northeast India to allow a company trading post at the fishing port of Calcutta. In 1756 a new nawab overran the post and imprisoned a group of EIC men in a cell so small that many died of suffocation. To avenge their deaths in this "Black Hole of Calcutta," a large EIC force from Madras overthrew the nawab. The weak Mughal emperor was persuaded to acknowledge the EIC's right to rule Bengal in 1765. By 1788 Calcutta had grown into a city of 250,000.

Along with Calcutta and Madras, the third major center of British power was Bombay, on the western coast. There, in 1818, the EIC annexed large territories to form the core of what was called the "Bombay Presidency." This gave the EIC an empire with fifty times the population of the colonies the British had lost in North America.

One goal of the **British raj** (reign) was to remake India on a British model through administrative measures, economic development, and modern technology. But the company men—like the Mughals before them—had to temper their interference with Indian social and religious customs lest they provoke rebellion or lose the support of their Indian princely allies.

The main policy was to create a powerful and efficient system of government. Another British policy was to substitute private property for India's complex and overlapping patterns of landholding. In Bengal this reform worked to the advantage of large landowners, but in Mysore the peasantry gained. Private ownership made it easier for the state to collect the taxes that were needed to pay for administration, the army, and economic reform.

Such policies of "westernization, Anglicization, and modernization," as they have been called, were only one side of British rule. The other side was the bolstering of "traditions"—both real and newly invented. In the name of tradition the Indian princes who ruled nearly half of British India were permitted to expand their power and splendor. The British rulers themselves invented many "traditions"—including elaborate parades and displays, called **durbars**, that were half borrowed from European royal pomp, half from Mughal ceremonies.

The British and Indian elites danced sometimes in close partnership, sometimes in apparent opposition. But the ordinary people of India—women of every status, members of subordinate Hindu castes, the "untouchables" and "tribals" outside the caste system, and the poor generally—found less benefit from the British reforms and much new oppression from the taxes and "traditions."

The transformation of British India's economy was also double-edged. On the one hand, the growth in internal and external trade created many new jobs, as did the expansion of farming: opium in Bengal,

nawab Technically, a semi-autonomous deputy of the Mughal emperor but often a Muslim prince allied to British India.

sepoy A soldier in colonial India, especially in the service of the British.

British raj The rule over much of South Asia between 1765 and 1947 by the East India Company and then by a British government.

durbar An elaborate display of political power and wealth in British India in the nineteenth century, ostensibly in imitation of the pageantry of the Mughal Empire.

Topham/The Image Works

Delhi Durbar, January 1, 1903 The parade of Indian princes on ornately decorated elephants and accompanied by retainers fostered their sense of belonging to the vast empire of India that British rule had created.

largely for export to China (see Chapter 22); coffee in Ceylon; and tea in Assam in northeastern India (ruled by Burma prior to EIC conquest in 1826). On the other hand, competition from cheap cotton goods produced in Britain's industrial mills drove many Indians out of the handicraft textile industry. In the eighteenth century India had been the world's greatest exporter of cotton textiles; in the nineteenth century India increasingly shipped raw cotton fiber to Britain.

Economic changes, including beneficial ones, caused disruption. Thus, local rebellions by displaced ruling elites, disgruntled religious traditionalists, and the economically dispossessed were almost constant during the first half of the nineteenth century. The greatest concern was over the loyalty of Indian sepoys in the EIC's army.

In the early decades of EIC rule, most sepoys came from Bengal. The Bengali sepoys resented the recruitment of other ethnic groups into the army after 1848, such as Sikhs (sicks) from Punjab and Gurkhas from Nepal. Many high-caste Hindus objected to a new law in 1856 requiring new recruits to be available for service overseas, for their religion prohibited ocean travel. Then in 1857 the replacement of the standard muskets by the more accurate Enfield rifles sparked outrage because they required soldiers to use their teeth to tear open the ammunition cartridges, which were greased with animal fat. Fat from cattle offended Hindus; fat from pigs offended Muslims.

A quick change in the cartridge-opening procedure could not forestall a rebellion by Hindu sepoys in May 1857. Muslim sepoys, peasants, and discontented elites joined in. The rebellion was put down ten months later, but it shook this empire to its core.

Historians have attached different names and meanings to the events of 1857 and 1858. Nineteenth-century British historians labeled it the **"Sepoy Rebellion"** or "Mutiny." Seeing in these events the beginnings of the later movement for independence, some modern Indian historians have termed it the "Revolution of 1857."

Political Reform and Industrial Impact

Regardless of label, the events of 1857–1858 marked a turning point in the history of modern India. In their wake Indians gained a new centralized government, entered a period of rapid economic growth, and began to develop a new national consciousness.

In 1858 Britain eliminated the last traces of Mughal and EIC rule. In their place, a new secretary of state for India in London oversaw Indian policy, and a new governor-general in Delhi acted as the British monarch's viceroy. In November 1858 Queen Victoria, who would assume the title Empress of India in 1877, guaranteed all Indians equal protection of the law and the freedom to practice their religions and social customs, but she also assured Indian princes that so long as they were loyal to the queen British India would respect their control of territories and "their rights, dignity and honour."[3]

Meanwhile, a powerful and efficient bureaucracy controlled India. Members of the elite **Indian Civil Service** (ICS), mostly graduates of Oxford and Cambridge University, held the senior administrative and judicial posts. Numbering only a thousand at the end of the nineteenth century, they visited the villages in their districts, heard lawsuits and complaints, and passed judgments. A far greater number of Indian officials and employees served beneath them. Recruitment into the ICS was by open examination given only in England and thus inaccessible to most Indians. In 1870 only one Indian was a member of the ICS. Subsequent reforms led to fifty-seven Indian appointments by 1887, but there the process stalled.

Beginning in the 1840s a railroad boom gave India its first national transportation network, followed by telegraph lines, and by 1870 India had the fifth largest rail network in the world. The government invested

millions of pounds sterling in other public works as well. Forests were felled to make way for tea plantations. Indian farmers were persuaded to grow cotton and jute for export. Engineers built great irrigation systems to alleviate the famines that periodically decimated whole provinces. As a result, India's trade expanded rapidly.

Most of the exports were agricultural commodities: cotton fiber, opium, tea, silk, and sugar. In return India imported manufactured goods from Britain, including machine-made cotton textiles that undercut Indian hand-loom weavers. Some women found jobs at very low pay on plantations or in the growing cities, where prostitution flourished. Everywhere in India poverty remained the norm.

Easier movement and urbanization promoted the spread of cholera (KAHL-uhr-uh), a disease transmitted through water contaminated by human feces. In 1867, officials demonstrated the close connection between cholera and pilgrims who bathed in and drank from sacred pools and rivers. The installation of a new sewerage system and a filtered water supply (1869) in Calcutta dramatically reduced cholera deaths there. Similar measures in Bombay and Madras also led to great reductions, but most Indians lived in small villages where famine and lack of sanitation kept cholera deaths high.

Indian Nationalism

Both the successes and failures of British rule stimulated Indian nationalism. The failure of the rebellion of 1857 led some thoughtful Indians to argue that the only way to regain control of their destiny was to reduce their country's social and ethnic divisions.

Individuals such as Rammohun Roy (1772–1833) had promoted development along these lines a generation earlier. A Western-educated Bengali from a Brahmin family, Roy was a successful administrator for the EIC and a student of comparative religion. His

---

[3]Quoted by Bernard S. Cohn, "Representing Authority in Victorian India," in *The Invention of Tradition*, ed. Eric Hobsbawm and Terence Ranger (Cambridge, England: Cambridge University Press, 1983), 165.

Sepoy Rebellion The revolt of Indian soldiers in 1857 against certain practices that violated religious customs; also known as the Sepoy Mutiny.

Indian Civil Service The elite professional class of officials who administered the government of British India. Originally composed exclusively of well-educated British men, it gradually added qualified Indians.

An Indian Railway Station, 1854 (engraving) (b/w photo), English School, (19th century)/The Illustrated London News Picture Library, London, UK/The Bridgeman Art Library

AN INDIAN RAILWAY STATION.— (SEE PRECEDING PAGE.)

Indian Railroad Station, 1866   British India built the largest network of railroads in Asia. People of every social class traveled by train.

Brahmo Samaj (BRAH-moh suh-MAHJ) (Divine Society), founded in 1828, attracted Indians who sought to reconcile the values of the West with the religious traditions of India. They backed the British outlawing of *sati* (suh-TEE) (widow burning) in 1829 and of slavery in 1834 and sought to correct other abuses of women and female infanticide. Roy and his followers advocated reforming the caste system and urged a

SECTION REVIEW

- Between 1757 and 1857, Britain gained nearly complete control of India.

- The British exploited local traditions and rulers and instituted a colonial government that conferred benefits on those Indians who governed on its behalf, while most of the population lived in worsening conditions.

- The Sepoy Rebellion of 1857–1858 prompted reforms and substantial investments in railroads and other public works.

- In response to modernization, Indian nationalism arose in the educated middle class.

return to the founding principles of the *Upanishads*, ancient sacred writings of Hinduism.

Although Brahmo Samaj remained influential after the rebellion of 1857, many Indian intellectuals turned to Western secular values and nationalism as the way to reclaim India, often aided by European and American missionaries. In 1870 there were 790,000 Indians in over 24,000 elementary and secondary schools, and India's three universities (established in 1857) awarded 345 degrees. Many new nationalists arose from the Indian middle class, and in 1885 nationalists convened the first **Indian National Congress**, which called for a larger Indian role in the civil service and for greater efforts to

Indian National Congress A movement and political party founded in 1885 to demand greater Indian participation in government. Its membership was middle class, and its demands were modest until World War I. Led after 1920 by Mohandas K. Gandhi, it appealed increasingly to the poor, and it organized mass protests demanding self-government and independence.

reduce poverty. But although the Indian National Congress promoted unity among the country's many religions and social groups, most early members were upper-caste Western-educated Hindus and Parsis. Until it attracted the support of the masses, it could not hope to challenge British rule.

SOUTHEAST ASIA AND THE PACIFIC

■ *What were the social and cultural effects of imperialism in Southeast Asia and the Pacific?*

The underlying goal of imperialism in the nineteenth century was not territory but trade. Southeast Asia and the Pacific have differing histories, yet all came under intense imperialist pressure. From the far corners of the world came coffee, cocoa, tea, and sugar for the tables of Western consumers, as well as indigo dyes and cotton fibers for the expanding textile factories. In return for the foodstuffs and industrial raw materials that flowed toward Europe and the United States, the factories of the industrialized nations supplied manufactured goods at very attractive prices. In most cases such trade benefited both sides, but there is no question that the industrial nations were the dominant partners.

Southeast Asia and Indonesia

Until the mid-nineteenth century, independent kingdoms had ruled most of the Southeast Asian peninsula and the Indonesian archipelago. Only Siam (now Thailand) would remain independent. Burma (now Myanmar), which had already lost several provinces to British India, went fully to Britain in a war ending in 1885. Malaya (now Malaysia)—with its Singapore port—also came under British rule. Indochina fell under French control. By the early 1900s, the Dutch has subdued northern Sumatra. (See Map 23.2.)

What all these regions had in common was fertile soil, constant warmth, and heavy rains, along with a long tradition of intensive gardening, irrigation, and terracing. The climate favored the transfer of commercially valuable plants from other parts of the world. Tobacco, cinchona (sin-CHO-nah) (an antimalarial drug), manioc (an edible root crop), maize (corn), and natural rubber came from the Americas; sugar from India; tea from China; and coffee and oil

A Rubber Plantation As bicycles and automobiles proliferated in the early twentieth century, the demand for rubber outstripped the supply available from wild rubber trees in the Amazon forest. Rubber grown on plantations in Southeast Asia came on the market from 1910 on. The rubber trees had to be tapped very carefully and on a regular schedule to obtain the latex or sap from which rubber was extracted. In this picture a woman and a boy perform this operation on a plantation in British Malaya.

palms from Africa. By 1914 much of the world's supply of these valuable products—in the case of rubber, almost all—came from Southeast Asia and Indonesia.

Colonialism and population growth spurred many social changes. Agricultural and commercial peoples gradually moved into mountainous and forested areas, displacing groups that practiced hunting and gathering or shifting agriculture and had not experienced as much population growth. Javanese migrating to Borneo and Sumatra are but one example. Immigrants from China and India changed the ethnic composition and culture of every country in

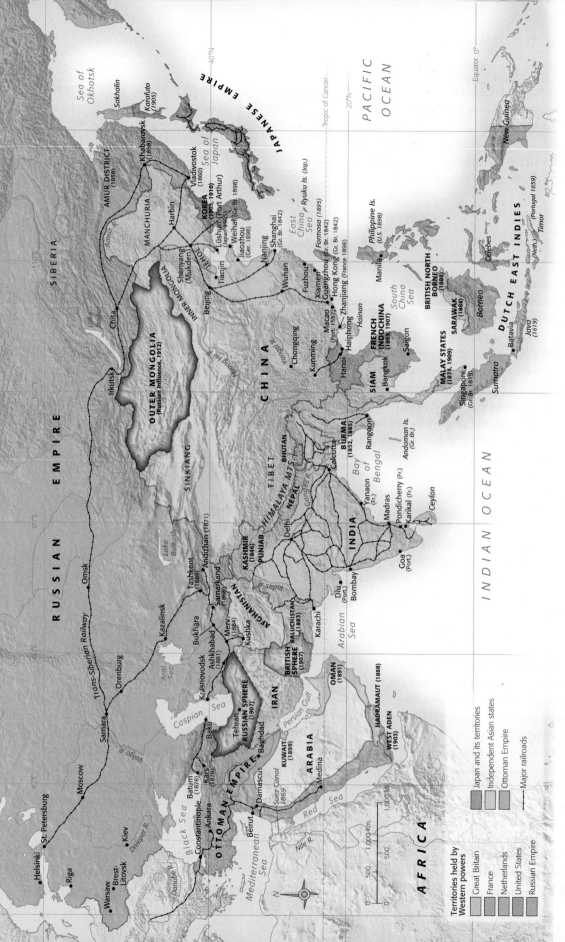

Map 23.2 Asia in 1914 By 1914, much of Asia was claimed by colonial powers. The southern rim, from the Persian Gulf to the Pacific, was occupied by Great Britain, France, the Netherlands, and the United States. © Cengage Learning

Territories held by Western powers
- Great Britain
- France
- Netherlands
- United States
- Russian Empire
- Japan and its territories
- Independent Asian states
- Ottoman Empire
- Major railroads

RUSSIAN EMPIRE

Sea of Okhotsk

Sakhalin
Karafuto (1905)

SIBERIA

JAPANESE EMPIRE

AMUR DISTRICT (1858)
Khabarovsk (1858)
Vladivostok (1860)
Sea of Japan
Japan

MANCHURIA
Harbin
KOREA (1905, 1910)
Lüshun (Port Arthur) (Japan 1905)
Ryukyu Is. (Jap.)

Shenyang (Mukden)
Beijing
Tianjin
Weihai (Gr. Br. 1898)
Jiaozhou (Ger. 1898)

INNER MONGOLIA
Nanjing
Shanghai (Gr. Br. 1842)
East China Sea
Formosa (Gr. Br. 1842)

OUTER MONGOLIA (Russian Influence, 1912)

Irkutsk
Chita

Lake Baikal

Wuhan
Fuzhou
Xiamen (Gr. Br. 1842)
Guangzhou (Gr. Br. 1842)
Hong Kong (Gr. Br. 1842)
Macao (Port. 1557)
Zhanjiang (France 1898)
Hainan

CHINA

Chongqing
Kunming

Philippine Is. (U.S. 1898)
Manila

Amur R.

Trans-Siberian Railway

Omsk
Orenburg
Samara
Moscow
St. Petersburg
Helsinki
Riga
Warsaw
Brest-Litovsk
Kiev

Kazalinsk
Aral Sea
Lake Balkash

SINKIANG
TIBET
HIMALAYA MTS.
BHUTAN
NEPAL

Tashkent (1865)
Samarkand (1868)
Bukhara
Andizhan (1871)
Merv (1884)
Kushka
AFGHANISTAN
KASHMIR (1846)
PUNJAB

BRITISH SPHERE (1907)
BALUCHISTAN (1883)

Ashkhabad (1881)
Krasnovodsk
Caspian Sea
Baku

IRAN

Tehran
RUSSIAN SPHERE (1907)

Kars (1878)
Batum (1878)
Ankara
Constantinople
Beirut
Damascus
Baghdad

OTTOMAN EMPIRE

KUWAIT (1899)

ARABIA
Medina

Delhi
INDIA
Calcutta
BURMA (1852, 1885)
Rangoon
Bay of Bengal
Andaman Is. (Gr. Br.)
Madras
Pondicherry (Fr.)
Karikal (Fr.)
Ceylon
Yanaon (Fr.)

Karachi
Bombay
Diu (Port.)
Goa (Port.)
Arabian Sea

Indus R.
Ganges R.
Huang He R.
Yangzi R.

SIAM
Bangkok
FRENCH INDOCHINA (1859, 1907)
Hanoi
Haiphong
Saigon

MALAY STATES (1874, 1909)
Singapore (Gr. Br. 1819)
Sumatra
Batavia
Java (1619)

BRITISH NORTH BORNEO (1888)
SARAWAK (1888)
Borneo
South China Sea

DUTCH EAST INDIES
Celebes

New Guinea
Timor (Neth.) (Portugal 1859)

OMAN (1891)
HADRAMAUT (1888)
WEST ADEN (1903)

Suez Canal (1869)
Red Sea
Mediterranean Sea
Black Sea
Danube R.
Dniepr R.
Volga R.
Persian Gulf

AFRICA
Nile R.

INDIAN OCEAN

PACIFIC OCEAN

Tropic of Cancer
20°N
40°N
Equator 0°

0   500   1,000 Mi.
0 500 1,000 Km.

N

the region. Thus the population of the Malay Peninsula became one-third Malay, one-third Chinese, and one-third Indian.

Australia and New Zealand

Rather than rule indigenous populations, as they had done in India, or set up commercial outposts, as they did in Singapore and Cape Town, British settlers displaced indigenous populations in the new colonies of Australia and New Zealand, just as they had done in North America.

Portuguese mariners had sighted Australia in the early seventeenth century, but it was too remote to be of interest. However, after the English captain James Cook explored New Zealand and the eastern coast of Australia between 1769 and 1778, expanding shipping networks brought in growing numbers of visitors and settlers.

The Australia Cook visited was the home of about 650,000 hunting-and-gathering people whose Melanesian (mel-uh-NEE-zhuhn) ancestors had arrived some forty thousand years earlier. About 250,000 Maori (MOW-ree [ow as in cow]) inhabited the two Islands of New Zealand, lying 1,000 miles (1,600 kilometers) southeast of Australia. They practiced hunting, fishing, and cultivation of root crops that their Polynesian ancestors had introduced around 1200. These two populations were as vulnerable as the Amerindians had been to unfamiliar diseases introduced by new overseas contacts. By the 1890s, only 93,000 aboriginal Australians and 42,000 Maori survived, and British settler populations both outnumbered and dominated them.

The first permanent British settlers in Australia were 736 convicts, of whom 188 were women, sent into exile in 1788. Australian penal colonies grew slowly and had only slight contact with the indigenous population, whom the British called "Aborigines." However, the discovery of gold in 1851 brought a flood of free European settlers (and some Chinese) and hastened the end of the penal colonies. When the gold rush subsided, government subsidies enabled tens of thousands of British settlers to settle "down under." Though it still took more than three months to reach Australia from Britain, by 1860 Australia had a million immigrants, and the settler population doubled during the next fifteen years.

British settlements in New Zealand proceeded more slowly. Initially a few temporary residents along the coast slaughtered seals and exported pelts to Western countries to be made into men's felt hats. A single ship in 1806 took away sixty thousand sealskins, and by the early 1820s overhunting had nearly exterminated the seal population. Sperm whales were also targeted; whalers hunted them near New Zealand for their oil, used for lubrication, soap, and lamps; ambergris (AM-ber-grees), an ingredient in perfume; and whalebone or baleen, a flexible substance used in women's corsets. Military suppression of Maori resistance, a brief gold rush, faster ships, and subsidized passages attracted more British immigrants after 1860. The colony especially courted women immigrants to offset the preponderance of single men. By the early 1880s the fertile agricultural lands of this most distant frontier of the British Empire had a settler population of 500,000.

Britain encouraged the settlers in Australia and New Zealand to become self-governing, following the 1867 model that had formed the Dominion of Canada out of the diverse and thinly settled colonies of British North America. In 1901, a unified Australia emerged from the federation of six separate colonies. New Zealand became a self-governing dominion in 1907.

By gradually turning over governing power to the colonies' inhabitants, Britain accomplished three things. It satisfied the settlers' desire for greater control; it muted demands for independence; and it made the colonial governments responsible for most of their own expenses. Indigenous peoples were outvoted by the settlers or even excluded from voting.

North American patterns also shaped the indigenous peoples' fate. An 1897 Australian law segregated the remaining Aborigines onto reservations, where they lacked the rights of Australian citizens. The requirement that voters had to be able to read and write English kept Maori from voting in early New Zealand elections, but four seats in the lower house of the legislature were reserved for Maori from 1867 on.

Hawaii and the Philippines, 1878–1902

By the 1890s the United States had a fast-growing population and industries that produced more manufactured goods than they could sell at home. Merchants and bankers began

Bettmann/CORBIS

Emilio Aguinaldo In 1896, a revolt led by Emilio Aguinaldo attempted to expel Spaniards from the Philippines. When the United States purchased the Philippines from Spain two years later, the Filipino people were not consulted. Aguinaldo continued his campaign, this time against the American occupation forces, until his capture in 1901. In this picture, he appears on horseback, surrounded by some of his troops.

to look for export markets. Guam, Hawaii, and the Philippines being naval stations on the route to China, the new expansionists looked in that direction. China was also in the sights of those who agreed with the naval strategist Alfred T. Mahan (mah-HAHN): "Whether they will or no, Americans must now begin to look outward. The growing production of the country requires it."

Some Americans had been looking outward for quite some time. In 1878 the United States obtained the harbor of Pago Pago in Samoa as a coaling and naval station, and in 1887 it secured the use of Pearl Harbor in Hawaii for the same purpose. By 1898 the United States under President William McKinley (1897–1901) had become openly imperialistic and annexed Hawaii as a steppingstone to Asia. As the United States became ever more involved in Asian affairs, Hawaii's strategic location brought an inflow of U.S. military personnel, and its fertile land caused planters to import laborers from Japan, China, and the Philippines. These immigrants soon outnumbered the native Hawaiians.

While large parts of Asia were falling under colonial domination, the people of the Philippines were chafing under Spanish rule. Emilio Aguinaldo, leader

of a secret society, rose in revolt. The revolutionaries had a good chance of winning independence, for Spain had its hands full with a revolution in Cuba. Unfortunately for Aguinaldo and his followers, the United States declared war against Spain in April 1898 and quickly overcame Spanish forces in the Philippines and Cuba. After the Spanish defeat, President McKinley realized that a weakened Spain might lose the islands to another imperialist power. Japan, having recently defeated China in the Sino-Japanese War (1894–1895) and annexed Taiwan (see Chapter 24), was eager to expand. So was Germany, which had taken over parts of New Guinea and Samoa and several Pacific archipelagoes during the 1880s. To forestall them, McKinley purchased the Philippines from Spain for $20 million.

The Filipinos were not eager to trade one master for another. For a while, Aguinaldo cooperated with the Americans in the hope of achieving full independence. When his plan was rejected, he rose up again in 1899 and proclaimed the independence of his country. In spite of protests by anti-imperialists in the United States, the U.S. government decided that its global interests outweighed the interests of the Filipino people. In rebel areas, a U.S. army of occupation tortured prisoners, burned villages and crops, and forced the inhabitants into "reconcentration camps." By the end of the insurrection in 1902, the war had cost the lives of 5,000 Americans and 200,000 Filipinos.

After the insurrection ended, the United States attempted to soften its rule with public works and economic development projects. New buildings went up in the city of Manila; roads, harbors, and railroads were built; and the Philippine economy was tied ever more closely to that of the United States. In 1907 Filipinos were allowed to elect representatives to a legislative assembly, but ultimate authority remained in the hands of a governor appointed by the president of the United States. In 1916 the Philippines were the first U.S. colony to be promised independence, a promise that remained unfulfilled for thirty years.

IMPERIALISM IN LATIN AMERICA

■ *Where were the economic motives behind imperialism in Latin America?*

The United States played a lesser role than Britain and other European countries in the economic dominance that characterized imperialism in Latin America, and business played a more important role than military intervention. But America's clash with Spain over control of the Philippines carried over into Spanish possessions closer to home.

American Expansionism and the Spanish-American War, 1898

The United States had long had interests in Cuba, the closest and richest of the Caribbean islands and a Spanish colony. American businesses had invested great sums of money in Cuba's sugar and tobacco industries, and

thousands of Cubans had migrated to the United States. In 1895 the Cuban nationalist José Martí started a revolution against Spanish rule. American newspapers thrilled readers with lurid stories of Spanish atrocities; businessmen worried about their investments; and politicians demanded that the U.S. government help liberate Cuba.

On February 15, 1898, the U.S. battleship *Maine* accidentally blew up in Havana harbor, killing 266 American sailors. The U.S. government immediately blamed Spain and issued an ultimatum that the Spanish evacuate Cuba. Spain agreed to the ultimatum, but the American press and Congress were eager for war, and President McKinley did not restrain them.

The **Spanish-American War** was over quickly. On May 1, 1898, U.S. warships destroyed the Spanish fleet at Manila in the Philippines. Two months later the U.S. Navy sank the Spanish Atlantic fleet off Santiago, Cuba, and by mid-August Spain was suing for peace. Secretary of State John Hay called it "a splendid little war." The United States purchased the Philippines from Spain but took over Puerto Rico and Guam as war booty. The two islands remain American possessions to this day. Cuba became an independent republic, subject to interference by the United States.

Economic Imperialism

Latin America achieved independence from Spain and Portugal in the nineteenth century (see Chapter 21), but it suffered from ideological divisions, unstable governments, and violent upheavals, and its societies remained deeply split between wealthy landowners and desperately poor peasants. But Latin America's economic potential was huge, for the region could produce many agricultural and mineral products that were needed by the industrial countries. Foreign merchants, bankers, and Latin American landowners embraced railroads as a means of opening the interior to development. Starting in the 1870s, almost every country in Latin America acquired railroads, usually connecting mines or agricultural regions

Spanish-American War U.S. war fought with Spanish in 1898 over control of Cuba, ostensibly because of the sinking of a U.S. ship and also after reports of Spanish atrocities had fanned flames of American popular opinion. Won handily in three months, the war unofficially made Cuba a protectorate of the United States.

with the nearest port rather than linking up the different parts of the interior. All the equipment and building material came from Britain or the United States. So did the money to build the networks, the engineers who designed and maintained them, and the managers who ran them. Latin American political elites encouraged foreign companies with generous concessions as the most rapid way to modernize their countries.

Mexico

At the beginning of the twentieth century Mexican society was divided into rich and poor and into persons of Spanish, Indian, and mixed ancestry. A few very wealthy families of Spanish origin, less than 1 percent of the population, owned 85 percent of Mexico's land, mostly in huge *haciendas* (estates). A handful of American and British companies controlled most of Mexico's railroads, silver mines, plantations, and other productive enterprises. At the other end of the social scale were Indians, many of whom did not speak Spanish. *Mestizos* (mess-TEE-so), people of mixed Indian and European ancestry, were only slightly better off; most of them were peasants who worked on the haciendas or farmed small communal plots near their ancestral villages.

After independence in 1821, wealthy Mexican families and American companies used bribery and force to acquire millions of acres of good agricultural land from villages in southern Mexico. Peasants lost not only their fields but also their access to firewood and pasture for their animals and had little choice but to work on haciendas. To survive, they had to buy food and other necessities on credit from the landowner's store; eventually, they fell permanently into debt.

Despite many upheavals, in 1910 the government seemed in control. For thirty-four years General Porfirio Díaz (DEE-as) (1830–1915) had ruled Mexico under the motto "Liberty, Order, Progress." To Díaz "liberty" meant freedom for rich hacienda owners and foreign investors to acquire more land. The government imposed "order" through rigged elections, bribes to Díaz's supporters, and summary justice for those who opposed him. "Progress" meant mainly the importing of foreign capital, machinery, and technicians to take advantage of Mexico's labor, soil, and natural resources.

During the Díaz years (1876–1910) Mexico City became a showplace with paved streets, streetcar lines, electric street lighting, and public parks. New telegraph and railroad lines connected cities and towns throughout Mexico. But this material progress benefited only a handful of well-connected businessmen and lowered the average Mexican's standard of living.

Though a mestizo himself, Díaz discriminated against the nonwhite majority of Mexicans. He and his supporters tried to eradicate what they saw as Mexico's rustic traditions. On many middle- and upper-class tables French cuisine replaced traditional Mexican dishes, and the wealthy traded sombreros and ponchos for European garments. To the educated middle class—the only group with a strong sense of Mexican nationhood—this devaluation of Mexican culture became a symbol of the Díaz regime's failure to defend national interests against foreign influences.

Revolution and Civil War in Mexico

The **Mexican Revolution** was a social revolution that developed haphazardly under ambitious but limited leaders, each representing a different segment of Mexican society. The first was American-educated Francisco I. Madero (1873–1913), the son of a wealthy landowning and mining family. Strongly opposed to Díaz, he called on his fellow citizens to oppose electing him for a sixth term. This sparked a revolution in 1910 and the election of Madero as Díaz's successor. But although the Madero presidency was welcomed in some quarters, it aroused opposition in others. He was assassinated two years into his presidency by a former supporter, General Victoriano Huerto, who had been encouraged by the American ambassador. U.S. president Woodrow Wilson (1856–1924) disavowed American support, recalled the ambassador, and, concerned about Mexican unrest, sent U.S. Marines to occupy Veracruz.

Angered by the inequities of Mexican society and foreign intervention in Mexico's affairs, Mexico's middle class and industrial workers found new leaders. Calling themselves *Constitutionalists*, Venustiano

---

Mexican Revolution A social revolution that developed haphazardly under ambitious but limited leaders, each representing a different segment of Mexican society. The revolution evolved into civil war for over ten years of armed struggle, but it established a constitution for Mexico.

Francisco "Pancho" Villa Francisco "Pancho" Villa led an army of cowboys and ranch hands in northern Mexico during the revolution. He became very popular by confiscating large haciendas and dividing them among the poor. In March 1916 he entered the United States with 500 soldiers and attacked the town of Columbus, New Mexico, provoking an American invasion of Mexico. He was assassinated in 1923.

Topical Press Agency/Getty Images

Carranza, a landowner, and Alvaro Obregón (oh-bray-GAWN), a schoolteacher, overthrew Huerta in 1914. By then, the revolution had spread to the countryside.

Emiliano Zapata (sah-PAH-tah) (1879–1919), himself an Indian farmer, led a revolt against the haciendas in the mountains of Morelos, south of Mexico City. For several years Zapata's supporters would periodically come down from the mountains, burn hacienda buildings, and return land to the Indian villages to which it had once belonged.

Another leader appeared in Chihuahua, a northern state where seventeen individuals owned two-fifths of the land and 95 percent of the people had no land at all. Starting in 1913, **Francisco "Pancho" Villa** (1877–1923), a former ranch hand, mule driver, and bandit, organized an army of three thousand men, most of them cowboys. They also seized land from the large haciendas, not to rebuild traditional communities as in southern Mexico but to create family ranches.

After Villa led a failed and unexplained attack on the town of Columbus, New Mexico, the U.S. Army sent General John Pershing on a nine-month mission to hunt him down. The mission was cut short by American entry into World War I, but, like the occupation of Veracruz, it demonstrated increasing American concern for protecting land and business interests in Mexico.

Zapata and Villa enjoyed tremendous popular support but could never rise above their regional and peasant origins to lead a national revolution. The Constitutionalists had fewer soldiers than Zapata and Villa, but they held the major cities, controlled the country's oil exports, and used the proceeds to buy modern weapons. Gradually the Constitutionalists took over most of Mexico. In 1919 they defeated and killed Zapata; Villa was assassinated four years later. An estimated 2 million people lost their lives in the civil war, and much of Mexico lay in ruins.

The Constitutionalists adopted many of their rivals' agrarian reforms, such as restoring communal lands to the Indians of Morelos. They also proposed social programs aimed at workers and the middle class. The Constitution of 1917 promised universal

Emiliano Zapata (1879–1919) Revolutionary and leader of peasants in the Mexican Revolution. He mobilized landless peasants in south-central Mexico in an attempt to seize and divide the lands of the wealthy landowners. Though successful for a time, he was ultimately defeated and assassinated.

Francisco "Pancho" Villa (1877–1923) A popular leader during the Mexican Revolution. An outlaw in his youth, when the revolution started he formed a cavalry army in the north of Mexico and fought for the rights of the landless in collaboration with Emiliano Zapata. He was assassinated in 1923.

suffrage and a one-term presidency, state-run education, the end of debt peonage, restrictions on foreign ownership of property, and laws specifying minimum wages and maximum hours to protect laborers. However, powerful Mexican forces and the United States sought to prevent full implementation.

In the early 1920s, after years of violence, the Mexican Revolution lost momentum. Only in Morelos did peasants receive land. Carranza, elected in 1917, was killed in an anti-Carranza plot organized by Obregón. In 1928, Obregón was assassinated.

The Caribbean and Central America, 1901–1914

American intervention in the Western Hemisphere was not limited to Mexico. The nations of the Caribbean and Central America were small and poor, and their governments were corrupt, unstable, and often bankrupt. They seemed to offer an open invitation to foreign interference. A government would borrow money to pay for railroads, harbors, electric power, and other symbols of modernity. When it could not repay the loan, the lending banks in Europe or the United States would ask for assistance from their home governments, which sometimes threatened to intervene. To ward off European intervention, the United States sent in the marines on more than one occasion.

Presidents Theodore Roosevelt (1901–1909), William Taft (1909–1913), and Woodrow Wilson (1913–1921) felt impelled to intervene in the region, though they differed sharply on the proper policy the United States should follow toward the small nations to the south. Roosevelt encouraged regimes friendly to the United States; Taft sought to influence them through loans from American banks; and the moralist Wilson tried to impose clean governments by military means.

Having "liberated" Cuba from Spain, in 1901 the United States forced the Cuban government to accept the Platt Amendment, which gave the United States the "right to intervene" to maintain order on the island. The United States used this excuse to occupy Cuba militarily from 1906 to 1909, in 1912, and again from 1917 to 1922. In all but name Cuba became an American protectorate. U.S. troops also occupied the Dominican Republic from 1904 to 1907 and again in 1916, Nicaragua and Honduras in 1912, and Haiti in

SECTION REVIEW

- After the Spanish-American War, Cuba nominally became an independent republic but was subject to constant interference by the United States, which had strong economic stakes in the country.

- U.S. and European countries invested in railroads and other industrial enterprises throughout Latin America.

- Strong economic and social divisions in Mexico contributed to a confused revolution led by various players.

- After a decade of violence Mexico gained a new constitution, but the revolution lost momentum after the 1920s.

- Repeated American interventions in the region peaked with the building of the Panama Canal.

1915. They brought sanitation and material progress but no political improvements.

The United States was especially forceful in Panama, which was a province of Colombia. Here the issue was not corruption or debts but a more vital interest. When the United States acquired Hawaii and the Philippines, it recognized the need for a canal that would allow warships to move quickly between the Atlantic and Pacific Oceans. The main obstacle was Colombia, which refused to give the United States a piece of its territory. In 1903 the U.S. government supported a Panamanian rebellion against Colombia and quickly recognized the independence of Panama. In exchange, it obtained the right to build a canal and to occupy a zone 5 miles (8 kilometers) wide on either side of it. Work began in 1904, and the **Panama Canal** opened on August 15, 1914.

THE WORLD ECONOMY AND THE GLOBAL ENVIRONMENT

■ *How did imperialism contribute to the growth and globalization of the world economy?*

The nineteenth-century imperialists were not traditional conquerors or empire builders like the Spanish conquistadors. They expressed their belief in

Panama Canal Ship canal cut across the Isthmus of Panama by U.S. Army engineers; it opened in 1914. It greatly shortened the sea voyage between the east and west coasts of North America. The United States turned the canal over to Panama on January 1, 2000.

progress and their good intentions in the clichés of the time: "the conquest of nature," "the annihilation of time and space," "the taming of the wilderness," and "our civilizing mission."

Expansion of the World Economy

For centuries Europe had been a ready market for spices, sugar, silk, and other imported products. The Industrial Revolution expanded this demand, especially for stimulants such as tea, coffee, and chocolate. Demand grew even faster for industrial raw materials: agricultural products like cotton, jute for bags, and palm oil for soap and lubricants, and minerals like diamonds, gold, and copper. Some wild forest products eventually came to be cultivated: timber for buildings and railroad ties, cinchona bark, rubber for rainwear and tires, and gutta-percha (gut-tah-PER-cha) (the sap of a Southeast Asian tree) to insulate electric cables.

Economic botany and agricultural science were applied to every promising plant species. European botanists had long collected and classified exotic plants from around the world. In the nineteenth century they founded botanical gardens in Java, India, Mauritius (maw-REE-shuss), Ceylon, Jamaica, and other tropical colonies. These gardens not only collected local plants but also transferred commercially valuable plant species from one tropical region to another. Tobacco, sugar, coffee, tea, and other crops were introduced, improved, and vastly expanded in the colonies of Southeast Asia and Indonesia, and oil-palm plantations were established in Nigeria and the Congo Basin.

Throughout the tropics, land once covered with forests or devoted to shifting slash-and-burn agriculture was transformed into permanent farms and plantations. Even in areas not developed to export crops, growing populations put pressure on the land. In Java and India farmers felled trees to obtain arable land and firewood, terraced hillsides, drained swamps, and dug wells.

New Labor Migrations

Between 1834 and 1870 many thousands of Indians, Chinese, and Africans went overseas to work, especially on sugar plantations. In the half century after 1870, tens of thousands of Asians and Pacific islanders made similar voyages.

In part these migrations were linked to the end of slavery. After their emancipation in British colonies in 1834, many slaves left the plantations. To compete with sugar plantations in Cuba, Brazil, and the French Caribbean that were still using slave labor, British colonies had to recruit new laborers.

India's impoverished people seemed one obvious alternative. After planters on Mauritius successfully introduced Indian laborers, the Indian labor trade moved to the British Caribbean in 1838. In 1841 the British government also allowed Caribbean planters to recruit Africans whom British patrols had rescued from slave ships and liberated in Sierra Leone and elsewhere. By 1870 nearly 40,000 Africans had settled in British colonies, along with over half a million Indians and over 18,000 Chinese. After the French and Dutch abolished slavery in 1848, their colonies also recruited new laborers from Asia and Africa.

Slavery continued in Cuba until 1886, but the rising cost of slaves led the sugar planters to recruit 138,000 new laborers from China between 1847 and 1873. Indentured labor recruits also became the mainstay of new sugar plantations in places that had never known slave labor. After 1850 American planters in Hawaii recruited labor from China and Japan; British planters in Natal (in South Africa) recruited from India; and those in Queensland (in northeastern Australia) relied on laborers from neighboring South Pacific islands.

Larger, faster ships made transporting laborers halfway around the world affordable. Nevertheless, crowded accommodations encouraged the spread of cholera and other contagious diseases. All of these laborers served under **contracts of indenture**, which bound them to work for a specified period (usually from five to seven years) in return for free passage to their overseas destination. They were paid a small salary and were provided with housing, clothing, and medical care. Indian indentured laborers also received the right to free passage home if they worked a second five-year contract. British Caribbean colonies required forty women to be recruited for every hundred men as

contract of indenture A voluntary agreement binding a person to work for a specified period of years in return for free passage to an overseas destination. Before 1800 most indentured servants were Europeans; after 1800 most indentured laborers were Asians.

a way to promote family life. So many Indians chose to stay in Mauritius, Trinidad, British Guiana, and Fiji that they constituted a third or more of the total population of these colonies by the early twentieth century.

The indentured labor trade reflected the unequal commercial and industrial power of the West, but it was not an entirely one-sided creation. The men and women who signed indentured contracts were trying to improve their lives by emigrating, and many succeeded. Whether for good or ill, more and more of the world's peoples saw their lives being influenced by the existence of Western colonies, Western ships, and Western markets.

CONCLUSION

What is the global significance of these complex political and economic changes in southern Asia, Africa, the South Pacific, and Latin America? One perspective stresses the continuing and growing imperialist exploitation of non-Europeans. From another perspective what was most important about this period was not the political and military strength of the Europeans but their growing domination of the world's commerce, especially their investment in plantations, railroads, mines, and long-distance ocean shipping. Motives differed somewhat from region to region. Imperialists were drawn to Africa and Southeast Asia by a desire for tropical foodstuffs and industrial raw materials. Land for settlement was the attraction in Australia, New Zealand, and South Africa, as it earlier had been for European settlers in the New World. India and Latin America, having more prosperous middle classes, provided markets for European and American manufactures.

The growing exchanges could be mutually beneficial. As in Europe itself, overseas consumers found industrially produced goods far cheaper and sometimes better than the handicrafts they replaced. Industrialization also created new markets for African and Asian goods, such as vegetable oil from West Africa or rubber from Malaya. There were also negative impacts, as in the case of weavers thrown out of work in India and the beginnings of deforestation in Southeast Asia.

Imperialist military and commercial strength did not reduce Africa, Asia, Latin America, and the Pacific to mere appendages of Europe. While the balance of power shifted in the Europeans' favor between 1750 and 1914, other cultures were still vibrant and local initiatives often dominant. Islamic reform movements, the rise of the Zulu nation, and the Mexican Revolution had as great significance for their respective regions as Western forces.

CHAPTER REVIEW

CHANGES AND EXCHANGES IN AFRICA

■ *Why were imperialists interested in conquering Africa, and how did their presence on that continent change the environment?* (page 539)

Imperialists were interested in conquering Africa because they wanted to extract its resources to further their own military and economic power. After the slave trade was abolished, vegetable oils, gold, ivory, diamonds, and rubber were major exports. Their production, such as deep mining for diamonds, transformed the environment, as did the railroads that were constructed to reach the interior. European companies invested in rubber and palm-oil plantations, gold and diamond mines, and other resources. Traditional land-use patterns were disrupted, and all Africans were affected by changes in social and cultural customs. The Suez Canal, a major alteration to the environment, supported much of this activity, and the British also constructed a dam across the Nile to help develop agriculture.

INDIA UNDER BRITISH RULE

■ *How did Britain secure its hold on India, and what colonial policies led to the beginnings of Indian nationalism?* (page 548)

The British East India Company, using negotiation and force in dealing with local princes, was able to secure control of the cities of Calcutta, Madras, and Bombay. The British instituted a powerful colonial government and skillfully exploited native traditions and local rulers. In 1857–1858 the Sepoy Rebellion prompted a wave of reforms: Queen Victoria promised all Indians freedom of religion and equal protection under the law, and great sums of money were invested in harbors, canals, railroads, and telegraph lines. The rebellion also began to stir feelings of nationalism in thoughtful Indians. In addition, the higher standard of living, missionary influences, and the Indian Civil Service helped form a more educated middle class that became interested in nationalist ideas.

SOUTHEAST ASIA AND THE PACIFIC

■ *What were the social and cultural effects of imperialism in Southeast Asia and the Pacific?* (page 553)

The effects of colonialism varied throughout Asia, although in all regions the economic profits benefited the Europeans rather than the indigenous peoples. Southeast Asia's fertile soil and heavy rains made farming of various crops, most importantly rubber, quite profitable. As laborers were brought in from overseas, they gradually displaced the earlier inhabitants. A similar situation occurred in Hawaii, where U.S. military personnel and foreign farm laborers eventually outnumbered native Hawaiians. After James Cook had explored New Zealand and eastern Australia, expanded shipping networks brought growing numbers of white settlers there, displacing the native Maori and Australian peoples. Europeans also brought new and devastating diseases, as they had to Amerindian peoples two centuries before: over 80 percent of native New Zealanders and Australians perished in just over a century.

IMPERIALISM IN LATIN AMERICA

■ *What were the economic motives behind imperialism in Latin America?* (page 557)

Latin America had great economic potential because of its wealth of agricultural and mineral products. The construction of railroads, using equipment, engineers, and funding from Britain and the United States, helped to connect the interior regions with the coastal ports. Americans also saw economic potential in Cuba and invested heavily in the sugar and tobacco industries there. After the Spanish-American War, they issued the Platt Amendment to maintain their influence in Cuba. The United States also supported the Panamanian secession from Colombia in 1903 in order to build the Panama Canal.

THE WORLD ECONOMY AND THE GLOBAL ENVIRONMENT

■ *How did imperialism contribute to the growth and globalization of the world economy?* (page 560)

Imperialism opened up the world to increased trade and communication. Shipping, canals, and railroads were the most visible means of globalization. Economically valuable plant species were transferred from region to region while the transformation of forests into working plantations and the end of slavery led to the migration of thousands of Indians, Chinese, Africans, and Pacific Islanders to British colonies, above all to the Caribbean, under contracts of indenture.

Key Terms

Zulu (p. 539)
Afrikaners (p. 540)
Cecil Rhodes (p. 541)
Sokoto Caliphate (p. 543)
King Leopold II (p. 544)
Berlin Conference (p. 544)
modernization (p. 544)
Suez Canal (p. 545)
"legitimate" trade (p. 548)
recaptives (p. 548)
nawab (p. 549)
sepoy (p. 549)
British raj (p. 549)

durbar (p. 549)
Sepoy Rebellion (p. 551)
Indian Civil Service (p. 551)
Indian National Congress (p. 552)
Spanish-American War (p. 557)
Mexican Revolution (p. 558)
Emiliano Zapata (p. 559)
Francisco "Pancho" Villa (p. 559)
Panama Canal (p. 560)
contract of indenture (p. 561)

The New Power Balance

© Cengage Learning

On July 8, 1853, four American warships, two of them steam-powered, appeared in Edo Bay, close to the capital of Japan. The commander of the fleet, **Commodore Matthew Perry**, delivered a letter from the president of the United States, demanding that Japan open its ports to foreign trade. Japan had had contact with Europe since the sixteenth century, when Portuguese mariners and Jesuit missionaries arrived. The Dutch followed in the seventeenth century. Worried by this Western presence, Japan suppressed Christianity and "excluded" European merchants in 1639, although limited contact was permitted at the port of Nagasaki (see Chapter 19).

While Japan had rejected a similar request delivered by a smaller U.S. naval force in 1845, the sight of Perry's modern, well-armed fleet made clear the dangers associated with refusing his demand. When he returned the following year, the Japanese agreed to end the exclusion policies. Perry's visit also introduced to Japan a compelling array of the Industrial Revolution's technological and scientific triumphs, including a miniature railroad, a short telegraph line, and other marvels. For the next twenty years, Japanese society was torn between those who wanted to retreat into isolation and those who wished to embrace Western ways. For it was now clear that only by industrializing could Japan escape the fate of weaker nations then being taken over by Europe and the United States.

In the late nineteenth century Japan joined the ranks of "great powers" that dominated the world. Great Britain and France had been recognized as great powers long before the industrial age. Russia achieved that status as an ally against Napoleon and began industrializing in the late nineteenth century, as did Germany, the United States, and now Japan. This handful of wealthy industrialized nations imposed on the other peoples of the world a domination more powerful than any experienced before or since.

TECHNOLOGY ALTERS THE WORLD ECONOMY

■ *What new technologies and industries appeared between 1850 and 1900, and how did they alter the world economy?*

The Industrial Revolution marked the beginning of a massive transformation of the world. Textile mills, railroads, steamships, the telegraph—all spread from Britain to other parts of the world in the nineteenth century (see Chapter 20). By 1890 Germany and the United States had surpassed Great Britain as the world's leading industrial powers. Industrialization also introduced entirely new technologies that revolutionized everyday life and transformed the world economy. Potent combinations of business, engineering, and science led to the institutionalization of engineering schools and research laboratories, which resulted in the discovery of electricity and new steel and chemical industries.

While industrialization brought vast amounts of wealth, it also caused considerable damage to nature and human health. Rapidly growing urban populations in industrializing Europe and America overwhelmed primitive sanitation systems until the last decades of the nineteenth century. In 1858, Londoners experienced *The Big Stink* due to vast quantities of untreated human and industrial waste dumped into the Thames. While coal-burning steam engines powered the new machine age, they also filled the skies of Manchester, England, and other manufacturing centers with dense smog. The coal smoke of railroad locomotives and other steam engines contributed to air pollution as well. More threatening still were pollution-related diseases like typhoid and cholera.

Railroads   By the mid-nineteenth century, steam engines had become the prime mover of industry and commerce. Nowhere was this more evident than in the spread of **railroads**. By 1850 the first railroads had proved so successful that every industrializing country, and many that aspired to become industrial, began to build lines. The next fifty years saw a tremendous expansion of the world's rail networks. After a rapid spurt of building new lines,

Commodore Matthew Perry A navy commander who, on July 8, 1853, became the first foreigner to break through the barriers that had kept Japan isolated from the rest of the world for 250 years.

railroads Networks of iron (later steel) rails on which steam (later electric or diesel) locomotives pulled long trains at high speeds. The first railroads were built in England in the 1830s. Their success caused a railroad-building boom throughout the world that lasted well into the twentieth century.

Arrivals from the East

In 1853, Commodore Matthew Perry's fleet sailed into Edo (now Tokyo) Bay. The first steam-powered warships to appear in Japanese waters caused a sensation among the Japanese. In this print done after the Meiji Restoration, the traditionally dressed local samurai go out to confront the mysterious "black ships."

Courtesy of the Trustees of the British Museum/The Art Archive

British railroad mileage leveled off in the 1870s at around 20,000 miles (over 32,000 kilometers). France and Germany built networks longer than Britain's, as did Canada and Russia. Already the nation with the largest railroad network in 1865, the United States increased its mileage eleven times by 1917.

Railroads benefited not only industrialized nations but also regions with abundant raw materials or agricultural products, like South Africa, Mexico, and Argentina, or densely populated countries like Egypt. The British built the fourth largest rail network in the world in their largest colony, India, to reinforce their presence and develop trade.

With one exception, European or American engineers built these railroads with equipment imported from the West. In 1855, barely a year after Commodore Perry's visit, the Japanese instrument maker Tanaka Hisashige built a model steam train that he demonstrated to an admiring audience. In the 1870s the Japanese government hired British engineers to build the first line from Tokyo to Yokohama and sent them home in the 1880s once they had trained Japanese engineers. Within a few years, Japan began manufacturing its own railroad equipment.

Railroads consumed huge amounts of land. Many old cities doubled in size to accommodate railroad stations, sidings, tracks, warehouses, and repair shops. In the countryside, railroads required bridges, tunnels, and embankments. Railroads also consumed vast quantities of timber, initially for fuel and then for ties to support the rails and for bridges. As railroads pushed across the landscape, they often left miles of deforested land on either side of their tracks. At the same time, railroads opened new land to agriculture, mining, and other exploitation of natural resources wherever they were built, becoming major engines of global economic development.

Steamships and Telegraph Cables

In the mid-nineteenth century, a series of developments radically transformed ocean shipping. First iron, then steel, replaced the wood that had been used for hulls since shipbuilding began. Paddle wheels replaced sails and then were replaced by propellers as engineers built more powerful and fuel-efficient engines. The average size of freighters increased from 200 tons in 1850 to 7,500 tons in 1900. Coaling stations and ports able to handle large ships were built around the world. The Suez Canal, which opened in 1869, shortened the distance between Europe and Asia and triggered a massive switch from sail power to steam (see Chapter 23).

Shipping lines offered fast, punctual, and reliable service for passengers, mail, and perishable freight as the world's merchant ships grew from 9 million tons in 1850 to 35 million tons in 1910. The result was

Chronology

	Political Events	Social, Cultural, and Technological Events
1850	**1853–1854** Commodore Matthew Perry visits Japan	**1850s** Laws abolished in Britain that prohibited worker strikes, workers form "friendly societies" **1851** Majority of British population living in cities **1856** First synthetic dye **1859** Charles Darwin, *On the Origin of Species*
1860	**1860–1870** Unification of Italy **1861–1865** American Civil War **1862–1908** Rule of Empress Dowager Cixi (China) **1868** Meiji Restoration begins modernization drive in Japan	**1861** Emancipation of serfs (Russia) **1866** Alfred Nobel develops dynamite **1866** First successful Transatlantic cable **1867** Karl Marx, *Das Kapital* **1868–1894** Japan undergoes Western-style industrialization and societal changes
1870	**1870–1871** Franco-Prussian War **1871** Unification of Germany	**1872** Anarchist Mikhail Bakunin expelled from the International Workingman's Association **1879** Thomas Edison develops incandescent lamp
1890	**1894** Sino-Japanese War	
1900	**1900** Boxer Uprising (China) **1904–1905** Russo-Japanese War **1905** Revolution in Russia **1910** Japan annexes Korea	**1914** Women win right to vote in 12 U.S. states; British women follow in 1918

falling freight costs and greater commercial integration, changes that benefited not only the exporters of industrial products in Europe and North America but also the Asian, African, and Latin American exporters of agricultural and mining products.

At the same time, shipping companies and commercial firms were able to use the new **submarine telegraph cables**—laid across the Atlantic in 1866—to communicate with distant colonies and markets. By the turn of the century, cables connected every country and almost every inhabited island. As they became the indispensable tools of modern shipping and business, the public and the press extolled the "annihilation of time and space."

The Steel and Chemical Industries

Steel, a special form of iron, was reserved for swords, knives, axes, and watch springs until a series of inventions made it the cheapest and most versatile metal ever known. As a result, world steel production rose from a half-million tons in 1870 to 28 million in 1900—10 million produced by the United States, 8 by Germany, and 4.9 by England. Steel became affordable and abundant enough to make rails, bridges, ships, and even "tin" cans meant to be used once and thrown away. But steel mills took as much space as whole towns, belched smoke, and left behind huge hills of waste, degrading the environment.

The chemical industry followed suit. The development of synthetic dyes starting in 1856 delighted consumers with their bright, long-lasting colors and were cheap to produce, but in the process the indigo

submarine telegraph cables Insulated copper cables laid along the bottom of a sea or ocean for telegraphic communication. The first short cable was laid under the Hooghly River in Calcutta in 1839; the first successful transatlantic cable was laid in 1866.

steel A form of iron that is both durable and flexible. It was first mass-produced in the 1860s and quickly became the most widely used metal in construction, machinery, and railroad equipment.

plantations of India and Latin America were ruined. Chemistry also advanced the manufacture of explosives. In 1866 the Swedish scientist Alfred Nobel found a way to turn nitroglycerin into a stable solid—dynamite. This and other new explosives were useful in mining and the construction of railroads and canals. They also enabled the armies and navies to arm themselves with increasingly accurate and powerful rifles and cannon.

The growing complexity of industrial chemistry made it one of the first fields where science and technology interacted on a daily basis. By the end of the nineteenth century, Germany had the most advanced engineering schools and scientific institutes and the government funded research that helped make it the world's leading producer of dyes, drugs, synthetic fertilizers, ammonia, and nitrates used in making explosives. However, chemical industries also produced tons of toxic effluents that were dumped into rivers.

Electricity

No innovation of the late nineteenth century changed people's lives as radically as **electricity**. At first, producing electric current was so costly that it was used only for electroplating and telegraphy. Then in 1831 the Englishman Michael Faraday showed that the motion of a copper wire through a magnetic field induced an electric current in the wire. Based on his discovery, inventors in the 1870s devised generators that turned mechanical energy into electric current. Electricity was more flexible and much easier to use than waterpower or the stationary steam engine, which had powered industrialization until then.

Electricity now had a host of new applications. Initially, arc lamps lit up public squares, theaters, and stores. For a while homes continued to rely on gas lamps, which produced a softer light, but in 1879 **Thomas Edison** developed an incandescent lamp well suited to lighting small rooms. In 1882 Edison created the world's first electrical distribution network in New York City. By the turn of the century electric lighting was rapidly replacing gas lamps in the cities of Europe and North America.

Other uses of electricity quickly appeared. Electric streetcars and subways transported people throughout the cities of Europe and North America.

Electric motors replaced steam engines and power belts, increasing productivity and improving workers' safety. Commonly dependent on coal-fired generators, electric energy production contributed to air pollution as well. As demand for electricity grew, engineers built hydroelectric plants. The plant at Niagara Falls, on the border between Ontario, Canada, and New York State, produced an incredible 11,000 horsepower when it opened in 1895. At the newly created Imperial College of Engineering in Japan, an Englishman, William Ayrton, became the first professor of electrical engineering anywhere in the world; his students later went on to found major corporations and government research institutes.

World Trade and Finance

World trade expanded tenfold between 1850 and 1913, transforming varied economies in different parts of the world. The capitalist economies of western Europe and North America, the prime beneficiaries, grew more diversified and prosperous. Industries mass-produced consumer goods for a growing number of middle-class and even working-class customers: soap, canned and packaged foods, ready-made clothes, household items, and small luxuries like cosmetics and engravings. Nonindustrial areas were more vulnerable, for many of them produced raw materials that could be replaced by synthetic substitutes. Nevertheless, the value of exports from tropical nations remained generally high until World War I.

German and American industries surpassed the British, but Great Britain continued to dominate the flow of trade, finance, and information. In 1900 two-thirds of the world's submarine cables were British or passed through Britain, and over half of the world's shipping was British owned. Britain invested one-fourth of its national wealth overseas, much of it in India, the United States, and Argentina, financing railroads, harbors, mines, and other big projects.

electricity A form of energy used in telegraphy from the 1840s on and for lighting, industrial motors, and railroads beginning in the 1880s.

Thomas Edison American inventor best known for inventing the electric light bulb, acoustic recording on wax cylinders, and motion pictures.

- Industrialization spread throughout the world through trade and new technologies.
- Railroads, almost always financed by Western nations, spread to all continents, changing and enlarging cities and facilitating economic growth.
- Steamships and telegraph cables connected continents and encouraged trade.
- In three new industries—steel, chemicals, and electricity—the United States and Germany surpassed Great Britain.
- World trade boomed in an age of globalization.

Despite global expansion, capitalist economies were prey to periodic depressions in which workers lost their jobs and investors their fortunes. Because of the close connection among the industrial economies, the collapse of a bank in Austria in 1873 triggered a depression that spread to the United States, causing mass unemployment. Worldwide recessions also occurred in the mid-1880s and mid-1890s. Fears that recession would result from industrial production growing faster than the capacity of traditional markets to consume goods helped justify new imperialist adventures by the United States and the European powers to expand markets and gain protected access to raw materials in Asia, Africa, and Latin America (see Chapter 23).

SOCIAL CHANGES

■ *How did the societies of the industrial countries change during this period?*

As industry and technology ensured steady food supplies, fast-growing populations swelled cities to unprecedented size. Millions of Europeans emigrated to the Americas, Australia, and New Zealand, and nonindustrial workers from Africa, China, India, the Pacific, and elsewhere were recruited to work on distant plantations, in mines, and on railroads (see Chapter 23). The roles of women and men also became more isolated, and women found their lives dramatically altered by economic and technological change, both in the home and in the public sphere.

Population Growth and Urbanization

The population of Europe grew faster from 1850 to 1914 than ever before or since, almost doubling from 265 million to 468 million. Much of the increase came from a drop in mortality, as epidemics and starvation became less common. The Irish famine of the 1840s was the last peacetime famine in European history. North American wheat supplemented Europe's food supplies, and new technologies like canning and refrigeration made food abundant year-round, permitting the export of Argentine beef and mutton to Europe. Meat, fruit, vegetables, and oils became part of the daily fare of city dwellers.

In 1851, Britain became the first nation with a majority of its population living in towns and cities. By 1914, 80 percent of Britain's population was urban, as was 60 percent of Germany's population and 45 percent of France's. London grew from 2.7 million in 1850 to 6.6 million in 1900. New York, expanded to include five boroughs, reached 3.4 million by 1900. In the English Midlands, in the German Ruhr, and around Tokyo Bay, fast-growing towns fused into one another, filling in the fields and woods that had once separated them.

In early industrial cities, the poor crowded together in unsanitary tenements. However, new urban technologies transformed city life for most residents. Pipes brought in clean water and carried away sewage. At the same time, gas and then electric lighting made cities safer at night. By the end of the century, municipal governments in Europe and North America provided police and fire protection, schools, parks, and other amenities unheard of a century earlier.

As sanitation improved, urban death rates fell below birthrates for the first time. Confident that their children would survive infancy, couples began to limit the number of children they had. To accommodate the growing population, urban planners laid out new cities on rectangular grids, and middle-class families moved to suburban developments on the edges of cities. In Paris older neighborhoods with narrow crooked streets and rickety tenements were replaced with broad boulevards and modern apartment buildings. Paris became the "city of lights," a model for city planners from New Delhi to Buenos

Paris Lit Up by Electricity, 1900   The electric light bulb was invented in the United States and Britain, but Paris made such extensive use of the new technology that it was nicknamed "city of lights." To mark the Paris Exposition of 1900, the Eiffel Tower and all the surrounding buildings were illuminated with strings of light bulbs while powerful spotlights swept the sky.

Aires. By 1900, electric streetcars and subways allowed working-class people to live miles from their workplaces.

In fast-growing cities such as London, New York, and Chicago, newcomers arrived so quickly that housing construction and municipal services could not keep up. Immigrants who saved money to reunite their families could not afford costly municipal services. As a result, the poorest neighborhoods remained as overcrowded, unhealthy, and dangerous as they had been since the early decades of industrialization.

While urban environments improved in many ways, air quality worsened. Coal, burned to power steam engines and heat buildings, polluted the air, coating everything with a film of grimy dust. And the thousands of horses that pulled carts and carriages covered the streets with their waste, causing a terrible stench.

Middle-Class Women's "Separate Sphere"

In English-speaking countries the period from about 1850 to 1901 is known as the **Victorian Age**. The expression refers not only to the reign of Queen Victoria of England (r. 1837–1901) but also to rules of behavior and to an ideology surrounding the family and the relations between men and women. The Victorians contrasted the masculine ideals of strength and courage with the feminine virtues of beauty and kindness, and they idealized the home as a peaceful and loving refuge from the dog-eat-dog world of competitive capitalism.

Victorian Age The reign of Queen Victoria of Great Britain (r. 1837–1901). The term is also used to describe late-nineteenth-century society, with its rigid moral standards and sharply differentiated roles for men and women and for middle-class and working-class people.

Separate Spheres in Great Britain In the Victorian Age, men and women of the middle and upper classes led largely separate lives. In *Aunt Emily's Visit* (1845), we see women and children at home, tended by a servant. *The Royal Exchange*, meanwhile, was a place for men to transact business.

Victorian morality claimed to be universal, yet it best fit upper- and middle-class European families. Men and women were thought to belong in **"separate spheres."** While successful businessmen worked or relaxed in men's clubs, their wives spent their time rearing children, running the household, and enhancing the family's social status. However, constant financial pressure caused many less privileged women to work outside the home for wages or take in laundry or low-wage piecework, like sewing for garment companies, to supplement household income.

Before electric appliances, maintaining a middle-class home involved enormous amounts of work. Families were larger, and middle-class couples entertained often and lavishly. Carrying out these tasks required servants. A family's status and the activities and lifestyle of the "mistress of the house" depended on the availability of servants to help with household tasks. Only families that employed at least one full-time servant were considered middle class.

Toward the turn of the century modern technology began to transform middle-class homes. Plumbing eliminated the pump and the outhouse. Central heating replaced fireplaces, stoves, and endless dusting. Gas and electricity lit houses and cooked food without soot, smoke, and ashes. But the vacuum cleaners and washing machines of the twentieth century did not mean less housework for women. As families acquired new household technologies, they raised their standards of cleanliness. Meanwhile, young working-class women increasingly preferred factory or office work to domestic service, and the burden of housework more often fell on the mistress of the house.

Unlike the rich of previous eras, who handed their children over to wet nurses and tutors, Victorian women nursed their own babies and supervised the education of their children, even if they employed governesses. Girls' education was very different from that of boys. While boys were being prepared for business or professional life, girls learned embroidery, drawing, and music—social graces that enhanced their marriage prospects.

Victorian morality frowned on middle-class women working. Young women could work until they got married, but only in genteel places like stores and offices, never in factories. When the typewriter and telephone entered the business world in the 1880s, businessmen turned to educated young women who worked for lower wages than men. Operating these machines was stereotyped as women's work.

"separate spheres" Nineteenth-century idea in Western societies that men and women, especially of the middle class, should have clearly differentiated roles in society: women as wives, mothers, and homemakers; men as breadwinners and participants in business and politics.

Jimmy Sime/Hulton Archive/Getty Images

Emmeline Pankhurst Under Arrest   The leader of the British women's suffrage movement frequently called attention to her cause by breaking the law to protest discrimination against women. Here she is being arrested and carried off to jail by the police.

Most professional careers were closed to women. Until late in the century, few universities granted women degrees. In the United States higher education was available to women only at elite colleges in the East and teachers' colleges in the Midwest. European women had fewer opportunities. Before 1914 very few women became doctors, lawyers, or professional musicians.

The first profession open to women was teaching, due to laws calling for universal compulsory education. By 1911, for instance, 73 percent of all teachers in England were women. They were considered well suited to teaching young children and girls—an extension of the duties of Victorian mothers—but only until marriage. When a woman married, she was expected to become pregnant right away and stay home to take care of her own children.

A home life, no matter how busy, did not satisfy all middle-class women. Some became volunteer nurses or social workers, receiving little or no pay. Others organized to fight prostitution, alcohol, and child labor. By the turn of the century a few chal-

lenged male domination of politics and the law. Suffragists, led in Britain by Emmeline Pankhurst and in the United States by Elizabeth Cady Stanton and Susan B. Anthony, demanded the right to vote. By 1914 U.S. women had won the vote in twelve states. British women won the vote in 1918.

Working-Class Women   In the new industrial cities, men and women no longer worked together at home or in the fields. The separation of work and home affected women even more than men. Women formed a majority of the workers in the textile industries and in domestic service. Yet working-class women needed to keep homes and raise children as well as earn their living. As a result, they led lives of toil and pain, considerably harder than the lives of their menfolk. In Japan, as in Ireland and New England, tenant farmers, squeezed by rising taxes and rents, were forced to send their daughters to work in textile mills. Others became domestic servants, commonly working sixteen or more hours a day, six and a half days a week, for little more than room and board, usually in attics or basements. Without appliances, much of their work was physically hard: hauling coal and water up stairs, washing laundry by hand. Female servants were also vulnerable to sexual abuse by their masters or their masters' sons, and the majority of families fired servants who got pregnant rather than embarrass the master of the house.

Young women often preferred factory work to domestic service. Here, too, Victorian society practiced a strict division of labor by gender. Men worked in construction, iron and steel, heavy machinery, or on railroads; women worked in textiles and the clothing trades, extensions of traditional women's household work (see Material Culture: Cotton Clothing). Appalled by the abuses of women and children in the early years of industrialization, most industrial countries passed protective legislation limiting the hours or forbidding the employment of women in the hardest and most dangerous occupations, such as mining and foundry work. Such legislation reinforced gender divisions in industry, keeping women in low-paid, subordinate positions. Female factory workers earned between one-third and two-thirds of men's wages.

Married women with children were expected to stay home, even if their husbands did not make enough to support the family. Yet they had to contribute to the family's income. Families who had room to spare, even a bed or a corner in the kitchen, took in boarders. Many women did piecework such as sewing dresses, making hats or gloves, or weaving baskets at home. The hardest and worst-paid work was washing other people's clothes. Overall, many poor women worked at home ten to twelve hours a day and

enlisted the help of their small children, perpetuating practices long outlawed in factories.

THE STRUGGLE BETWEEN CAPITAL AND LABOR

■ *How did industrialism contribute to the socialist and labor movements?*

Strained relations between industrial employers and workers spawned labor movements and new forms of radical politics. **Socialism** was an ideology developed by radical thinkers who questioned the sanctity of private property and argued in support of industrial workers against their employers. **Labor unions** were organizations formed by industrial workers to defend their interests in negotiations with employers. The socialist and labor movements were never identical. Most of the time they were allies; occasionally they competed for the support of workers.

The growing wealth and power of new industrial elites and the harsh living and working conditions experienced by industrial workers led to the formation of labor unions, the creation of the first social welfare policies, demands for voting rights, and, for some, the dream of revolutionary transformation. Those seeking a revolution were divided among numerous parties and factions. **Karl Marx** was a formidable theorist of revolution as well as a major contestant for power within the diverse and contentious world of left-leaning politics (see Chapter 20). Heir to the Enlightenment's enthusiasm for reason and logic, he identified his revolutionary ideal as "scientific socialism," although his adherents commonly called themselves communists. Marx believed that industrial capitalism would ultimately lead to a social order

SECTION REVIEW

- As European population grew, millions migrated to other continents.

- Cities grew to enormous size, changing in character and posing difficult housing, sanitation, and environmental problems.

- Middle-class women inhabited a "separate sphere" from men and devoted their lives to their homes and families, but a few fought for equal rights.

- Gender divisions widened between working-class men and women. Working-class women, who had to keep a home while earning a living, led hard lives.

socialism A political ideology that originated in Europe in the 1830s. Socialists advocated government protection of workers from exploitation by property owners and government ownership of industries. This ideology led to the founding of socialist or labor parties throughout Europe in the second half of the nineteenth century.

labor union An organization of workers in a particular industry or trade, created to defend the interests of members through strikes or negotiations with employers.

Karl Marx German journalist and philosopher, founder of the Marxist branch of socialism. He is known for two books: *Manifesto of the Communist Party* (1848) and *Das Kapital* (Vols. I–III, 1867–1894).

Material Culture

Cotton Clothing

Of all the things that bring us comfort, nothing compares to cotton. For clothes, sheets, and towels, it is the world's favorite textile. And no wonder: cotton is cool next to the skin, can be dyed in bright colors, absorbs moisture, and, unlike other fabrics such as wool, can be washed easily.

The use of cotton for clothing has a long history dating back to 3000 B.C.E., when it was grown in the Indus River Valley. Originally, the cotton plant was grown and the cloth woven only in India, Mexico, Peru, and a few other places in the tropics. The Maya wove fine textiles from cotton and traded them with other parts of Mesoamerica. Indian cottons were particularly fine and exported as luxury items to China and Rome. Cotton replaced hemp clothing in China in the time of the Mongols and was used extensively for turbans, pants, and other items of clothing. The Arabs spread cotton growing and weaving to the Middle East and Spain. By the tenth century, it was a major crop in Iran and elsewhere in the region. Many of our names for particular kinds of cotton fabric come from cities in India, like *calico* (from Calicut) or *madras*, or in the Middle East, like *damask* (from Damascus) or *muslin* (from Mosul in Iraq).

Around 800 C.E., Arab merchants brought cotton cloth to Europe, where it became as precious as silk. Five centuries later Italy borrowed Arab techniques to develop its own cotton industry. With the invention of machines like the spinning jenny and the water frame in the eighteenth century (see Chapter 20), cotton became less precious and more available. Cotton thread and cloth were the first items to be mass-produced in the Industrial Revolution, with important consequences for India, the American South, and other countries.

Mass production means mass consumption. In the nineteenth century, for the first time, the poor could afford to wear bright, colorful clothes and—even more important—to wash them. Wealthy European families hired seamstresses and tailors who came to the house, took measurements, and returned a few days later with finished clothes. Other women sewed clothes for themselves and their families.

Sewing by hand was time-consuming and increasingly costly compared to the declining price of cloth. By

The Sewing Machine *The Japanese imported many innovations from the West after the Meiji Restoration of 1868. Among the most popular were Western-style clothing and sewing machines.*
Image copyright © The Metropolitan Museum of Art. Image source: Art Resource, NY

the mid-nineteenth century, prosperity and a faster pace of life in Europe and America provided an incentive for inventors to devise a machine that could sew. In 1850, Isaac Singer manufactured the first practical machine for commercial use. A few years later, he designed the "Singer Family Sewing Machine" with an iron stand and a foot-treadle for home use. By 1891 Singer alone had manufactured 10 million machines in the United States and Europe. Some were industrial machines sold to makers of ready-to-wear clothes in the new garment districts. Others were home models, some inexpensive enough for the working class. There were even portable models that seamstresses could take with them to their clients' homes.

The combination of cotton cloth and sewing machines revolutionized clothing. A shirt that took fourteen and a half hours to sew by hand could be made in an hour and a quarter on a machine; an apron could be made in nine minutes instead of an hour and a half. Now the poor could afford to own several shirts, skirts, or pants, even underwear. Better-off homemakers subscribed to fashion magazines, bought patterns, and made blouses and dresses, even complicated items like crinolines and hoopskirts, which would once have been too tedious to sew by hand.

Today, the world uses more cotton than any other fiber. China is the largest producer (and consumer) of cotton, followed by the United States, India, and Pakistan. Almost all of the cotton clothing sold is produced on powerful computerized machines in the developing countries of Asia and Latin America.

divided between a wealthy powerful few and a mass of exploited and impoverished workers. This division, once in place, would lead to revolution. A dictatorship of the proletariat would then abolish private property, distribute the material benefits and scientific progress achieved by the Industrial Revolution to society in general, and end poverty and injustice.

Many of those committed to revolutionary change rejected Marx's insistence that revolution depended on the proletariat taking up arms. Others doubted that his imagined dictatorship of the proletariat, or, indeed, any government, could avoid recreating the inequality and injustice that already oppressed the poor. The Russian intellectual, Mikhail Bakunin (1814–1876), argued forcibly that peasants, displaced and unemployed artisans, and other exploited groups also had revolutionary potential and, consequently, that many parts of Europe were ready for revolution. He also dismissed as naive Marx's faith in a future workers' government.

Bakunin exercised a powerful influence over the development of **anarchism**, the chief revolutionary alternative to communism. Anarchists believed that revolution could be achieved through direct action by individuals and small groups, what they called *propaganda of the deed*. The result of this movement's development was a series of assassinations and bombings that shook the political structures of Europe and America. These attacks included the bombings of the opera (1893) and Corpus Christi celebration (1896) in Spain and the Haymarket bombing in Chicago (1896). They also included the assassinations of President Carnot of France (1894), Prime Minister Cánovas del Castillo of Spain (1897), Empress Elizabeth of Austria (1898), King Umberto of Italy (1900), and President McKinley of the United States (1901).

The conflict between Marx and Bakunin culminated in 1872 when Bakunin and his adherents were expelled from the revolutionary umbrella organization, the International Workingman's Association. While the followers of Marx forced Bakunin from the center of revolutionary activity, his followers remained a potent source of political violence and working-class mobilization in Italy, Spain, and Argentina well into the twentieth century.

Since the beginning of the nineteenth century, workers had united to create "friendly societies" for

SECTION REVIEW

• The plight of workers led Karl Marx to predict a future workers' revolution, while Mikhail Bakunin's anarchist ideas spawned acts of violence and rebellion in many countries.
• Labor movements and unions worked to improve workers' pay and working conditions.

mutual assistance in times of illness, unemployment, or disability. Laws that forbade workers to strike were abolished in Britain in the 1850s and in the rest of Europe soon thereafter. Labor unions sought not only better wages but also improved working conditions and insurance against illness, accidents, disability, and old age. They grew slowly because they required a permanent staff and a great deal of money to sustain their members during strikes. Still, by the end of the century British labor unions counted 2 million members, and German and American unions had 1 million members each. They also became a political force in democratic countries, advocating improved wages and working conditions.

NATIONALISM AND THE RISE OF ITALY, GERMANY, AND JAPAN

■ *How was nationalism transformed from a revolutionary to a conservative ideology?*

The most influential idea of the nineteenth century was **nationalism**. French revolutionaries defined people, previously considered the subjects of a sovereign, as the citizens of a *nation*—a concept identified with a territory, the state that ruled it, and the culture of its people.

anarchism Movement of revolutionaries who wanted to abolish all private property and governments, usually by violence, and replace them with free associations of groups.

nationalism A political ideology that stresses people's membership in a nation—a community defined by a common culture and history as well as by territory. In the late eighteenth and early nineteenth centuries, nationalism was a force for unity in western Europe. In the late nineteenth century it hastened the disintegration of the Austro-Hungarian and Ottoman Empires. In the twentieth century it provided the ideological foundation for scores of independent countries emerging from colonialism.

Language and National Identity in Europe Before 1871

Language was usually the crucial element in creating a feeling of national unity. It was important both as a way to unite the people of a nation and as the means of persuasion by which political leaders could inspire their followers. Yet language and citizenship seldom coincided.

The fit between France and the French language was closer than in most large countries, though some French-speakers lived outside of France and some French people spoke other languages. Italian- and German-speaking people, however, were divided among many small states. Living in the Austrian Empire were peoples who spoke German, Czech, Slovak, Hungarian, Polish, and other languages. Even where people spoke a common language, they could be divided by religion or institutions. The Irish, though English-speaking, were mostly Catholic, whereas the English were primarily Protestant.

The idea of redrawing the boundaries of states to accommodate linguistic, religious, or cultural differences was revolutionary. In Italy and Germany it led to the forging of large new states out of many small ones in 1871. In central and eastern Europe, nationalism threatened to break up large states into smaller ones.

Until the 1860s nationalism was associated with **liberalism**, the revolutionary middle-class ideology that emerged from the French Revolution; it asserted the sovereignty of the people and demanded constitutional government, a national parliament, and freedom of expression (see Chapter 21). The most famous nationalist of the early nineteenth century was the Italian liberal Giuseppe Mazzini (jew-SEP-pay mots-EE-nee) (1805–1872), who led a failed revolution in 1848 in Italy. Russia, Prussia, and Austria tried but could not quash Mazzini's idea of nationhood and liberty for peoples oppressed by tyrants and foreigners. The revolutions of 1848 convinced conservatives that governments could not keep citizens out of politics and that, if properly managed, they could strengthen rather than weaken the state (see Chapter 21). A new generation of conservative political leaders learned how to preserve the status quo through public education, universal military service, and colonial conquests, all of which built a sense of national unity.

The Unification of Italy, 1860–1870

By midcentury, popular sentiment was building throughout Italy for unification. Opposing it were Pope Pius IX, who abhorred everything modern, and Austria, which controlled two Italian provinces, Lombardy and Venetia. The prime minister of Piedmont-Sardinia, Count Camillo Benso di Cavour, saw the rivalry between France and Austria as an opportunity to unify Italy. He secretly formed an alliance with France, then instigated a war with Austria in 1858. The war triggered uprisings throughout northern and central Italy in favor of joining Piedmont-Sardinia, a moderate constitutional monarchy under King Victor Emmanuel.

If the conservative, top-down approach to unification prevailed in the north, a more radical approach was still possible in the south. In 1860 the fiery revolutionary **Giuseppe Garibaldi** (jew-SEP-pay gary-BAHL-dee) and a small band of followers landed in Sicily and then in southern Italy, overthrew the Kingdom of the Two Sicilies, and prepared to found a democratic republic. The royalist Cavour, however, took advantage of the unsettled situation to sideline Garibaldi and expand Piedmont-Sardinia into a new Kingdom of Italy. Unification was completed with the addition of Venetia in 1866 and the Papal States in 1870.

The process of Italian unification illustrates the shift of nationalism from a radical democratic idea to a conservative method of building popular support for a strong centralized government, even an aristocratic and monarchical one.

The Unification of Germany, 1866–1871

Some German nationalists wanted to unite all Germans under the Catholic Austrian throne. Others wanted to exclude Austria with its many non-Germanic peoples and unite all other German-speaking areas under Lutheran Prussia. The Prussian state had two

liberalism A political ideology that emphasizes the civil rights of citizens, representative government, and the protection of private property. This ideology, derived from the Enlightenment, was especially popular among the property-owning middle classes of Europe and North America.

Giuseppe Garibaldi Italian nationalist and revolutionary who conquered Sicily and Naples and added them to a unified Italy in 1860.

advantages: (1) the newly developed industries of the Rhineland, and (2) the first European army to make use of railroads, telegraphs, breech-loading rifles, steel artillery, and other products of modern industry.

The king of Prussia, Wilhelm I (r. 1861–1888), had entrusted the running of his government to his chancellor, the brilliant and authoritarian aristocrat **Otto von Bismarck** (UTT-oh von BIS-mark) (1815–1898), who was determined to use the Prussian military and German nationalism to advance the interests of the Prussian state. In 1866 Prussia attacked and defeated Austria. To everyone's surprise, Prussia took no Austrian territory. Instead, Prussia and some smaller states formed the North German Confederation, the nucleus of a future Germany. Then in 1870, Bismarck attacked France. In this "Franco-Prussian War," German armies used their superior firepower and tactics to achieve a quick victory.

The spoils of victory included a large indemnity and the two provinces of Alsace and Lorraine (see Map 24.1). To the Germans, this region was German because a majority of its inhabitants spoke German. To the French, it was French because most of its inhabitants considered themselves French. These two conflicting definitions of nationalism kept enmity between France and Germany smoldering for decades.

The West Challenges Japan

In Japan a completely different political organization was in place. The emperor was revered but had no power. Instead, Japan was governed by the Tokugawa Shogunate—a secular government under a military leader, or *shogun*, that had come to power in 1600 (see Chapter 19). Local lords, called *daimyo*, were permitted to control their lands and populations with very little interference from the shogunate.

Because this system did not permit the coordination of resources necessary to resist a major invasion, the shoguns attempted to minimize exposure to foreigners. In the early 1600s they prohibited foreigners from entering Japan and Japanese from going abroad. The most flagrant violators of these rules were powerful lords in southern Japan who ran large pirate or black-market operations. These lords benefited from the decentralization of the shogunal political system. But when a genuine foreign threat was suggested—as when, in 1792, Russian and British ships were spotted off the Japanese coast—the local lords realized that a decentralized Japan was perilously weak.

Some regional lords began to develop their own reformed armies, arsenals, and shipyards. By the 1800s Satsuma (SAT-soo-mah) and Choshu (CHOE-shoo), two large domains in southern Japan, had become wealthy and ambitious, enjoying high rates of revenue and population growth. Their remoteness from the capital Edo (now Tokyo) and their economic vigor also fostered a strong sense of local self-reliance.

This situation changed with the 1853 arrival of Commodore Matthew C. Perry's fleet (discussed at the beginning of this chapter). Perry demanded that Japan open its ports to trade and allow American ships to refuel and take on supplies during their voyages between China and California. His demands sparked a crisis in the shogunate. After consultation with the provincial daimyo, the shogun's advisers advocated capitulation to Perry, pointing to China's humiliating defeats in the Opium and Arrow Wars (see Chapter 22). In 1854, when Perry returned, representatives of the shogun indicated their willingness to sign the Treaty of Kanagawa (KAH-nah-GAH-wah), modeled on the unequal treaties between China and the Western powers. Angry and disappointed, some provincial governors began to encourage an underground movement calling for the destruction of the Tokugawa regime and the banning of foreigners from Japan.

Tensions between the shogunate and some provincial leaders, particularly in Choshu and Satsuma, increased in the early 1860s. When British and French ships shelled the southwestern coasts in 1864 to protest the treatment of foreigners, the action enraged the provincial samurai, who rejected the Treaty of Kanagawa. Young, ambitious, educated men who faced mediocre prospects under the rigid Tokugawa class system emerged as provincial leaders. In 1867 the Choshu leaders Yamagata Aritomo and Ito Hirobumi finally realized that they should stop warring with their rival province, Satsuma, and join forces to rebel against the shogunate.

Otto von Bismarck Chancellor (prime minister) of Prussia from 1862 until 1871, when he became chancellor of Germany. A conservative nationalist, he led Prussia to victory against Austria (1866) and France (1870) and was responsible for the creation of the German Empire in 1871.

Map 24.1 Unification of Germany, 1866–1871 Germany was united after a series of short, success-ful wars by the kingdom of Prussia against Austria in 1866 and against France in 1871. © Cengage Learning

The Meiji Restoration and the Modernization of Japan, 1868–1894

The civil war was intense but brief. In 1868 provincial rebels overthrew the Tokugawa Shogunate and declared young emperor Mutsuhito (moo-tsoo-HEE-toe) (r. 1868–1912) "restored." The new leaders called their regime the **Meiji** (MAY-gee) **Restoration** after Mutsuhito's reign name (*Meiji* means "enlightened rule"). The "Meiji oligarchs," as the new rulers were known, were extraordinarily talented and far-sighted. Though imposed from above, the Meiji Restoration marked as profound a change as the French Revolution (see Map 24.2).

The oligarchs knew they would have to transform their institutions and their society. In the Char-

Meiji Restoration The political program that followed the destruction of the Tokugawa Shogunate in 1868, in which a collection of young leaders set Japan on the path of centralization, industrialization, and imperialism.

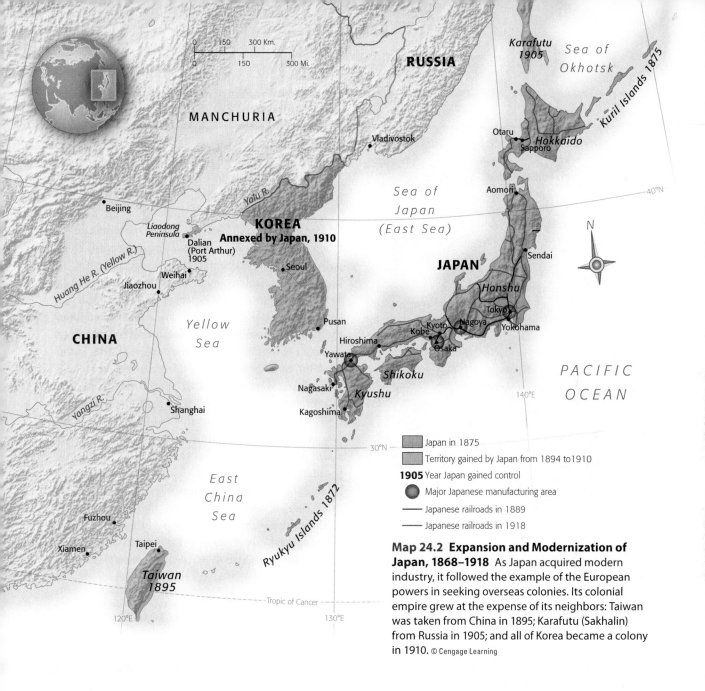

Map 24.2 Expansion and Modernization of Japan, 1868–1918

As Japan acquired modern industry, it followed the example of the European powers in seeking overseas colonies. Its colonial empire grew at the expense of its neighbors: Taiwan was taken from China in 1895; Karafutu (Sakhalin) from Russia in 1905; and all of Korea became a colony in 1910. © Cengage Learning

ter Oath issued in 1868, the young emperor included a prophetic phrase: "Knowledge shall be sought throughout the world and thus shall be strengthened the foundation of the imperial polity." It was to be the motto of a new Japan, which embraced all foreign ideas, institutions, and techniques that could strengthen the nation. The literacy rate in Japan was the highest in Asia at the time, and the oligarchs shrewdly exploited it in their introduction of new educational systems, a conscript army, and new communications. The government was able to establish heavy industry, without extensive foreign debt, thanks to decades of industrial development and financing in the provinces in the earlier 1800s.

The Meiji leaders copied the government structure of imperial Germany. They modeled the new Japanese navy on the British and the army on the Prussian. They introduced Western-style postal and telegraph services, railroads and harbors, banking, clocks, and calendars. To learn the secrets of Western strength, they sent hundreds of students to Britain, Germany, and the United States. Western-style clothing and hairstyles and garden parties and formal dances became popular.

The Granger Collection, NYC

Japan's New Army After the Meiji Restoration in 1868, the leaders of the new government set out to make Japan "a rich country with a strong army." They modeled the new army on the European armies of the time, with Western-style uniforms, rifles, cannon, and musical instruments.

Especially interested in Western technology, the government opened vocational, technical, and agricultural schools, founded four imperial universities, and brought in foreign experts to advise on medicine, science, and engineering. To encourage industrialization, the government set up state-owned enterprises to manufacture cloth and inexpensive consumer goods for sale abroad. The first Japanese industries exploited their workers ruthlessly, just as the first industries in Europe and America had done. In 1881 the government sold these enterprises to private investors, mainly large *zaibatsu* (zye-BOT-soo), or conglomerates, encouraging individual technological innovation. Thus the carpenter Toyoda Sakichi

founded the Toyoda Loom Works (now Toyota Motor Company) in 1906; ten years later he patented the world's most advanced automatic loom.

Nationalism and Social Darwinism

In many countries, the dominant group used nationalism to impose its language, religion, or customs on minority populations. The Russian Empire attempted to "Russify" its diverse ethnic populations. The Spanish government made Spanish compulsory in the schools, newspapers, and courts of its Basque- and Catalan-speaking provinces. Immigrants to the United States were expected to learn English.

Some people attempted to use science to support the harsh inequalities of gender, ethnicity, and class common across Europe and the Americas. One of the most influential scientists of the century, and the one whose ideas were most widely appropriated and misinterpreted, was the English biologist **Charles Darwin** (1809–1882), who based his theory of evolution on the observations he made during a research voyage in South America and while observing English livestock breeders. His famous book, *On the Origin of Species* (1859), argued that, over the course of hundreds of thousands of years, living beings had either evolved in the struggle for survival or become extinct. The philosopher Herbert Spencer (1820–1903) and others took up Darwin's idea of "natural selection" and coin-

Charles Darwin (1809–1882) Author of *On the Origin of Species* (1859), which developed the theory of evolution through natural selection.

SECTION REVIEW

- Nationalism, the most powerful new ideology of the nineteenth century, defined nations primarily on the basis of language.

- Cavour and Garibaldi helped unify Italy between 1860 and 1870, and Bismarck unified Germany from 1866 to 1871.

- In response to Western intrusion, provincial Japanese lords launched the Meiji Restoration and quickly transformed Japan into a modern industrial nation.

- During this era, Charles Darwin's theory of evolution was often misinterpreted to justify the power of the privileged few.

ing the phrase "survival of the fittest" applied it to human society. Extreme Social Darwinists developed elaborate pseudo-scientific theories of racial and ethnic differences, claiming that they were the result not of history but of biology. Although not based on any research, these ideas gave a scientific-sounding justification for the power of the privileged.

THE GREAT POWERS OF EUROPE, 1871–1900

■ *How did the forces of nationalism affect the major powers of Europe?*

After the middle of the century, politicians and journalists discovered how easily they could whip up popular frenzy against neighboring countries. Rivalries over colonial territories, ideological differences between liberal and conservative governments, and even minor border incidents or trade disagreements contributed to a growing international tension.

Germany at the Center of Europe

International relations revolved around Germany, because Germany was located in the center of Europe and had the most powerful army on the European continent. After creating a unified Germany in 1871, Bismarck worked to maintain the peace in Europe. To isolate France, he forged a loose coalition with Austria-Hungary and Russia that held for twenty years.

Bismarck proved equally adept at manipulating mass politics at home. To weaken the influence of middle-class liberals, he extended the vote to all adult men. By imposing high tariffs on manufactured goods and wheat, he gained the support of both the wealthy industrialists of the Rhineland and the great landowners of eastern Germany. He stole the thunder of the socialists by introducing social legislation—medical, unemployment, and disability insurance and old-age pensions—long before other industrial countries. Under his leadership, the German people developed a strong sense of national unity and pride in their industrial and military power.

In 1888 Wilhelm I was succeeded by his grandson Wilhelm II (r. 1888–1918), who dismissed Chancellor Bismarck. Wilhelm II talked about his "global policy" and demanded that Germany, with the mightiest army and the largest industrial economy in Europe, deserved a colonial empire, "a place in the sun."

France had difficulty reconciling itself to being second to Germany. Its population and its army lagged far behind Germany's, and its industry was growing more slowly, because it had lost the iron and coal mines of Lorraine in 1871. The French people were also deeply divided politically: some were monarchists and Catholics, but a growing number held republican and anticlerical views. Despite these problems, a long tradition of popular participation in politics and a strong sense of nationhood, reinforced by a fine system of public education, gave the French people a deeper cohesion than appeared on the surface.

Great Britain was the only other country in Europe with a democratic tradition. The British government alternated smoothly between the Liberal and Conservative Parties, and the income gap between rich and poor gradually narrowed. Nevertheless, Britain had problems. One was Irish resentment of English occupation and rule. Another was the British economy. Great Britain lagged behind the United States and Germany in such important industries as steel, chemicals, electricity, and textiles. Germany was even catching up in shipbuilding. Finally, Britain's far-flung empire was a constant drain on Britain's finances.

The Conservative Powers: Russia and Austria-Hungary

The forces of nationalism weakened rather than strengthened Russia and Austria-Hungary. Their populations were far more divided, socially and ethnically, than were the German, French, or British peoples.

Nationalism was most divisive in the Austrian Empire. The decision to rename itself the Austro-Hungarian Empire in 1867 appeased its Hungarian critics but alienated its Slavic-speaking minorities. The Austro-Hungarian Empire still considered itself a great power and attempted to dominate the Balkans. This strategy irritated Russia, which thought of itself as the protector of Slavic peoples everywhere, and it eventually led to war (see Chapter 25).

The Doss House, 1889 (oil on canvas), Makovsky, Vladimir Egorovic (1846–1920)/State Russian Museum, St. Petersburg, Russia/The Bridgeman Art Library

The Doss House Late-nineteenth-century cities showed more physical than social improvements. This painting by Makovsky of a street in St. Petersburg contrasts the broad avenue and impressive new buildings with the poverty of the crowd.

Russia was the most misunderstood country in Europe. Its enormous size and population led many Europeans to exaggerate its military potential, but it was weakened by national and social divisions. All in all, only 45 percent of the peoples of the tsarist empire spoke Russian. To strengthen the bonds between the monarchy and the Russian people and promote industrialization by enlarging the labor

SECTION REVIEW

- A united Germany, the most powerful state in Europe, became a threat to peace under Wilhelm II.

- France and Great Britain, though liberal democracies, faced difficulties at home and overseas.

- Russia and Austria-Hungary, two conservative empires, failed to adapt their politics to the modernization of their societies.

pool, the moderate conservative Tsar Alexander II (r. 1855–1881) emancipated the peasants from serfdom in 1861. That measure, however, did not create a modern society but only turned serfs into farm workers with few skills and little capital. Though "emancipated," the great majority of Russians had little education, few legal rights, and no say in the government.

After Alexander's assassination in 1881, his successors Alexander III (r. 1881–1894) and Nicholas II (r. 1894–1917) reluctantly permitted half-hearted attempts at social change. Industrialization consisted largely of state-sponsored projects, such as railroads, iron foundries, and armament factories, and led to social unrest among urban workers. Wealthy landowning aristocrats dominated the Russian court and administration and blocked most reforms.

The weaknesses in Russia's society and government became glaringly obvious after Russia's defeat in the Russo-Japanese War of 1904–1905 (discussed later in this chapter). The shock of defeat caused a revolution in 1905, forcing Tsar Nicholas II to grant a constitution and permit an elected Duma (parliament). But as soon as he was able to rebuild the army and the police, he reverted to the traditional despotism of his forefathers. Small groups of radical intellectuals, angered by the contrast between the wealth of the elite and the poverty of the common people, began plotting the violent overthrow of the tsarist autocracy.

CHINA, JAPAN, AND THE WESTERN POWERS

■ *How did Western pressure affect East Asia?*

After 1850 China and Japan—the two largest countries in East Asia—felt the influence of the Western powers as never before, but their responses were completely opposite. China resisted Western influence and became weaker, while Japan transformed itself into a major industrial and military power. One reason for this difference was the Western powers' heavy involvement in China. More important was the difference between the Chinese and Japanese elites' attitudes toward foreign cultures.

China in Turmoil

China had been devastated by the Taiping (tie-PING) Rebellion that raged from 1850 to 1864 (see Chapter 22). The French and British took advantage of China's weakness to demand treaty ports where they could trade at will and freely import opium.

China's attempts to resist these changes were ultimately self-defeating. A Chinese "self-strengthening movement" tried in vain to bring about reform by reducing government expenditures and eliminating corruption. The **Empress Dowager Cixi** (TSUH-shee) (r. 1862–1908), who had once encouraged the construction of shipyards, arsenals, and telegraph lines, opposed railways and other foreign technologies that could carry foreign influences to the interior. Government officials, who did not dare resist the Westerners outright, secretly encouraged crowds to attack and destroy the intrusive devices. They were able to slow the foreign intrusion, but in doing so, they denied themselves the best means of defense against foreign pressure.

Japan Confronts China

The motive for the transformation of Japan was defensive—to protect the nation from the Western powers—but the methods that protected Japan could also be used for Japanese conquest. Japan's path to imperialism was laid out by **Yamagata Aritomo**, a leader of the Meiji oligarchs. He believed that an independent Japan required a "sphere of influence" that included Korea, Manchuria, and part of China (see Map 24.2). If other countries controlled this sphere, Japan would be at risk. To protect this sphere of influence, Yamagata insisted, Japan must accelerate its military industrialization, culminating in the building of battleships.

As Japan grew stronger, China was growing weaker. In 1894 the two nations went to war over Korea. The Sino-Japanese War lasted less than six months, and it forced China to evacuate Korea, cede Taiwan and the Liaodong (li-AH-oh-dong) Peninsula, and pay a heavy indemnity. France, Germany, Britain, Russia, and the United States, upset at seeing a newcomer join the ranks of the imperialists, made Japan give up Liaodong in the name of the "territorial integrity" of China. In exchange for their "protection," the Western powers then made China grant them territorial and trade concessions, including ninety treaty ports.

In 1900 Chinese officials around the Empress Dowager Cixi encouraged a series of antiforeign riots known as the Boxer Uprising. Military forces from the European powers, Japan, and the United States put down the riots and occupied Beijing. Emboldened by China's obvious weakness, Japan and Russia competed for possession of the mineral-rich Chinese province of Manchuria.

Japan's participation in the suppression of the Boxer Uprising demonstrated its military power in

Empress Dowager Cixi Empress of China and mother of Emperor Guangxi. She put her son under house arrest, supported antiforeign movements, and resisted reforms of the Chinese government and armed forces.

Yamagata Aritomo One of the leaders of the Meiji Restoration.

East Asia. Then in 1905, Japan surprised the world by defeating Russia in the Russo-Japanese War. By the Treaty of Portsmouth that ended the war, Japan established a protectorate over Korea. In spite of Western attempts to restrict it to the role of junior partner, Japan continued to increase its influence. It gained control of southern Manchuria, with its industries and railroads, and in 1910 it finally annexed Korea, joining the ranks of the world's colonial powers.

CONCLUSION

The late nineteenth century witnessed the most rapid changes in technology, society, and politics that had ever taken place until that time. The changes were concentrated in a few regions of the world—Europe, the United States, and Japan—but would have repercussions everywhere.

Two primary causes—industrialization and nationalism—were responsible for the changes. Industrialization provided an abundance of goods as well as new and much better means of transportation and communication. After 1850, some of the worst abuses of industrialization that had characterized the previous age were attenuated, and new technologies promised to improve the lives of workers, city dwellers, and women.

Industrialization and the new politics of national identity increased the power of certain states but threatened others. States founded on a strong sense of national identity, such as France and Japan, found that the politics of nationalism benefited them and their citizens. But nationalism could also threaten the cohesion of multinational states like Russia and Austria-Hungary or weaken traditional states like China. The two great revolutions of the eighteenth and early nineteenth centuries—the industrial and the political—were about to destabilize the world, first in the nonindustrial regions, and then in the very heartland of the industrial world (see Chapter 25).

CHAPTER REVIEW

TECHNOLOGY ALTERS THE WORLD ECONOMY

■ *What new technologies and industries appeared between 1850 and 1900, and how did they alter the world economy?* (page 565)

After World War I broke out in 1914, many people, especially in Europe, looked back on the period from 1850 to 1914 as a golden age. For some, and in certain ways, it was. Industrialization was a powerful torrent changing Europe, North America, and East Asia. While shipping and railroads increased their global reach, new technologies—electricity, the steel and chemical industries, and the global telegraph network—contributed to the enrichment and empowerment of the industrial nations. World trade increased tenfold during this period, and many countries' economies were transformed.

SOCIAL CHANGES

■ *How did the societies of the industrial countries change during this period?* (page 569)

With these new technologies, memories of the great scourges—famines, wars, and epidemics—faded. Clean water, electric lights, and railways began to improve the lives of city dwellers, even the poor. Municipal services made city life less dangerous and chaotic. Goods from distant lands, even travel to other continents, came within the reach of millions. Middle-class women continued to focus on domestic pursuits and lived in a "separate sphere" from men. Many working-class women took jobs in the textile industry, yet their work outside the home did not lessen their domestic and child-rearing responsibilities. At the same time women mobilized in large numbers to demand political rights.

THE STRUGGLE BETWEEN CAPITAL AND LABOR

■ *How did industrialization contribute to socialist and labor movements?* (page 573)

Industrialization created a large class of factory and railroad workers, and Karl Marx predicted that a class struggle between industrial workers and employers would lead to revolution. Anarchism, a rival revolutionary philosophy, included all who were oppressed as potential revolutionary agents. Anarchism shook the political structures of Europe and America with terrorist attacks and remained a potent source of political violence and working-class mobilization in Italy, Spain, and Argentina well into the twentieth century. Socialism became more an intellectual current than a revolutionary movement. By the turn of the century, liberal political reforms had taken hold in western Europe. Through labor unions, workers did achieve some measure of recognition and security.

NATIONALISM AND THE RISE OF ITALY, GERMANY, AND JAPAN

■ *How was nationalism transformed from a revolutionary to a conservative ideology?* (page 575)

The framework for all these changes was the nation-state. Until the 1860s nationalism was associated with liberalism, but later generations of conservatives used public education, military service, and colonial conquests to build a sense of national unity. By 1871 both Italy and Germany had become unified states. In Japan, the Meiji Restoration restored power to the emperor and ushered in a period of Western influences.

THE GREAT POWERS OF EUROPE, 1871–1900

■ *How did the forces of nationalism affect the major powers of Europe?* (page 581)

The world economy, international politics, and even cultural and social issues revolved around a handful of countries—the great powers—that believed they controlled the destiny of the world. These included the most powerful European nations of the previous century, as well as three newcomers—Germany, the United States, and Japan—that were to play important roles in the future. Under the leadership of Bismarck, the German people developed a strong sense of national pride. Religious differences proved to be a hindrance to nationalism in France. Great Britain's problems were due to economic issues and Irish resentment of English rule.

CHINA, JAPAN, AND THE WESTERN POWERS

■ *How did Western pressure affect East Asia?* (page 583)

Japan responded to western pressure by imitating the industrialized countries and adopting many of their institutions and attitudes. Japan's efforts to acquire a European-style colonial empire led to successful wars with China and Russia. China's response to the west was much less successful, partly because of western intrusions into the chinese economy in the name of free trade and partly because of internal divisions.

Key Terms

Commodore Matthew Perry (p. 565)

railroads (p. 565)

submarine telegraph cables (p. 567)

steel (p. 567)

electricity (p. 568)

Thomas Edison (p. 568)

Victorian Age (p. 570)

"separate spheres" (p. 571)

socialism (p. 573)

labor union (p. 573)

Karl Marx (p. 573)

anarchism (p. 575)

nationalism (p. 575)

liberalism (p. 576)

Giuseppe Garibaldi (p. 576)

Otto von Bismarck (p. 577)

Meiji Restoration (p. 578)

Charles Darwin (p. 580)

Empress Dowager Cixi (p. 583)

Yamagata Aritomo (p. 583)

The Crisis of the Imperial Order

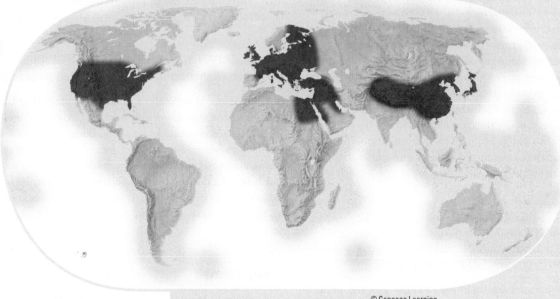

© Cengage Learning

On June 28, 1914, Archduke Franz Ferdinand, heir to the throne of Austria-Hungary, was riding in an open carriage through Sarajevo, a city Austria had annexed six years earlier. When the carriage stopped momentarily, Gavrilo Princip, a member of a pro-Serbian conspiracy, fired his pistol twice, killing the archduke and his wife.

Those shots ignited a global conflict. All previous wars had caused death and destruction, but they were also marked by heroism and glory. In this new war, four years of bitter fighting produced no victories, no gains, and no glory, only death for millions of soldiers. The war became global as the Ottoman Empire fought against Britain and Japan attacked German positions in China. France and Britain involved their empires in the war and brought Africans, Indians, Australians, and Canadians to Europe to fight and labor on the front lines. Finally, in 1917, the United States entered the fray.

In this chapter, we will look at the causes of war between the great powers, the consequences of that conflict in Europe, the Middle East, and Russia, and the upheavals in China and Japan.

ORIGINS OF THE CRISIS IN EUROPE AND THE MIDDLE EAST

■ *What led to the outbreak of the First World War?*

When the twentieth century opened, the world seemed firmly under the control of the great powers. Its first decade saw peace, economic growth, and the spread of new technologies: airplanes, automobiles, radio, and cinema. The only international war of the period, the Russo-Japanese War (1904–1905), ended quickly with a decisive Japanese victory.

However, two major changes undermined the apparent stability of the world. In Europe, Germany challenged Britain at sea and France in Morocco. The Ottoman Empire grew weaker, leaving a dangerous power vacuum. The resulting chaos in the Balkans gradually drew the European powers into a web of hostilities.

The Ottoman Empire and Balkans

By 1900, the once-great Ottoman Empire had become the "sick man of Europe" and began losing its outlying provinces. Between 1902 and 1913, Macedonia rebelled, Austro-Hungary annexed Bosnia, Crete merged with Greece, and Albania became independent. In 1912–1913 Serbia, Bulgaria, Romania, and Greece chased the Turks out of the Balkans. France and Britain controlled Ottoman finances, taxes, railroads, mines, and public utilities.

In reaction, the Turks began to assert themselves against rebellious minorities and meddling foreigners. Many officers in the army, the most Europeanized segment of Turkish society, blamed Sultan Abdul Hamid II (r. 1876–1909) for the decline of the empire. In 1908–1909, a revolutionary group known as "Young Turks" plotted to overthrow the sultan and reinstate a still-born constitution that he had suspended in 1876. The new regime reinvigorated the Tanzimat reform movement (see Chapter 22) that had begun in the early nineteenth century. At the same time, it cracked down on Greek and Armenian minorities. Galvanized by their defeat in the Balkan Wars, the Turks hired a German general to modernize their armed forces. The dangerous mixture of modern armies and nationalism was not limited to the Ottoman Empire, however.

Nationalism, Alliances, and Military Strategy

Nationalism united the citizens of France, Britain, Italy, and Germany behind their respective governments and gave them tremendous cohesion and strength of purpose. But nationalism could divide as well as unify. In the large but fragile multinational empires—Russia, Austria-Hungary, and the Ottoman Empire—ethnic and religious minorities were stirring. The easy victories in the colonial wars (see Chapter 23) had led some in power to believe that only war could heal the divisions in their societies.

What turned the assassination of Franz Ferdinand into a conflict involving all the great powers was the system of alliances that had accumulated over the previous decades. Germany stood at Europe's center as the most heavily industrialized country in Europe. Its army was the best trained and equipped, and its battleships were challenging Great Britain's naval supremacy. Germany joined Austria-Hungary and Italy in the Triple Alliance in 1882. When in 1907 Britain, France, and Russia formed an Entente (on-TONT) ("understanding"), Europe was divided into two blocs of roughly equal power (see Map 25.1).

The alliance system was cursed by inflexible military planning. Anticipating war, military planners in France and Germany had worked out elaborate railroad timetables to mobilize their respective armies in a few days. Other countries were less well prepared. Russia with its underdeveloped rail system needed several weeks. Britain, with a tiny volunteer army, had no mobilization plans. German generals, believing that the British would stay out of a European war, made plans to defeat France in a matter of days and then transport the entire army by train across Germany to the Russian border before Russia could fully mobilize.

On July 28, 1914, emboldened by the backing of Germany, Austria-Hungary declared war on Serbia, triggering mobilization plans in other countries. The next day, Russia ordered general mobilization to force Austria to back down. On August 1, France honored its treaty obligation to Russia and ordered general mobilization. Minutes later Germany did the same. War was now unavoidable.

The German General Staff expected France to capitulate before the British could get involved. But on August 3, when German troops entered Belgium, Britain demanded their withdrawal. When Germany refused, Britain declared war on Germany.

THE "GREAT WAR" AND THE RUSSIAN REVOLUTIONS, 1914–1918

■ *How did war lead to revolution in Russia?*

Throughout Europe, people greeted the outbreak of war with parades and flags, expecting a quick victory.

The German sociologist Max Weber wrote: "This war, with all its ghastliness, is nevertheless grand and wonderful. It is worth experiencing."[1] Very few imagined that their side might not win. No one foresaw that everyone would lose.

Stalemate, 1914–1917 The generals' carefully drawn plans went awry from the start. Believing that a spirited attack would always prevail, French generals hurled their troops against the well-defended German border and suffered a crushing defeat. By early September, the Germans held Belgium and northern France and were fast approaching Paris. German victory seemed assured. But when Russia attacked, German troops needed for the final push into France were shifted to the eastern front. A gap opened between two German armies along the Marne River, into which moved France's last reserves. At the Battle of the Marne, the Germans were thrown back several miles.

During the next month, both sides spread out until they formed an unbroken battlefront extending over 300 miles (some 500 kilometers) from the North Sea to the border of Switzerland. All along this **western front**, machine guns provided an almost impenetrable defense against advancing infantry but were useless for the offensive because they were too heavy for one man to carry and took too much time to set up. To escape the deadly streams of bullets, soldiers dug holes in the ground, connected the holes to form shallow trenches, and then dug communications trenches to the rear. Within weeks, the battlefields were scarred by lines of trenches several feet deep, their tops protected by sandbags and their floors covered with planks.

For four years, generals on each side again and again ordered their thousands of young men to climb out of their trenches, race across the open fields, and be mowed down by enemy machine-gun fire. Poison gas added to the horror of battle.

---

[1]Frank B. Tipton, *A History of Modern Germany since 1815* (Berkeley: University of California Press, 2003), 295.

western front A line of trenches and fortifications in World War I that stretched without a break from Switzerland to the North Sea. Scene of most of the fighting between Germany, on the one hand, and France and Britain, on the other.

Chronology

	Europe and North America	Middle East	East Asia
1900	**1907** British-Russian Entente	**1909** Young Turks overthrow Sultan Abdul Hamid	**1900** Boxer Uprising in China **1904–1905** Russo-Japanese War
1910	**1912–1913** Balkan Wars **1914** Assassination of Archduke Franz Ferdinand sparks World War I **1916** Battles of Verdun and the Somme **1917** Russian Revolutions; United States enters the war **1918** Armistice ends World War I **1918–1921** Civil war in Russia **1919** Treaty of Versailles	**1915** British defeat at Gallipoli **1916** Arab Revolt in Arabia **1917** Balfour Declaration **1919–1922** War between Turkey and Greece	**1911** Chinese revolutionaries led by Sun Yat-sen overthrow Qing dynasty **1915** Japan presents Twenty-One Demands to China **1919** May Fourth Movement in China
1920	**1923–1928** New Economic Policy in Russia	**1922** Egypt nominally independent **1923** Mustafa Kemal proclaims Turkey a republic **1932** Britain grants Iraq official independence	**1927** Guomindang forces occupy Shanghai and expel communists

The year 1916 saw the bloodiest and most futile battles of the war. The Germans attacked French forts at Verdun, losing 281,000 men and causing 315,000 French casualties. In retaliation, the British attacked the Germans at the Somme River and suffered 420,000 casualties—60,000 on the first day alone—while the Germans lost 450,000 and the French 200,000.

This was not warfare as it had ever been waged before; it was mass slaughter. Neither side could win, for the armies were stalemated by trenches and machine guns. During four years of the bloodiest fighting the world had ever seen, the western front moved no more than a few miles one way or another.

At sea, the war was just as inconclusive. As soon as war broke out, the British cut the German overseas telegraph cables, blockaded the coasts of Germany and Austria-Hungary, and set out to capture or sink all enemy ships still at sea. The German High Seas Fleet, built at enormous cost, seldom left port. Only once, in May 1916, did it confront the British Grand Fleet. At the Battle of Jutland, off the coast of Denmark, the two fleets lost roughly equal numbers of ships, and the Germans escaped back to their harbors.

In early 1915, in retaliation for the British naval blockade, Germany announced a blockade of Britain by submarines. German submarines attacked every vessel they could. One attack sank the British ocean liner *Lusitania*, killing 198 people, 139 of them Americans. When the United States protested, Germany ceased its submarine campaign, hoping to keep America neutral.

The Home Front and the War Economy

The war economy transformed civilian life. In France and Britain, food rations were allocated according to need, improving nutrition among the poor. Unemployment vanished, and thousands of Africans, Indians, and Chinese were recruited for heavy labor in Europe. Employers also hired women to fill jobs in steel mills, mines, and munitions plants. Women became streetcar drivers, mail carriers, and police officers or found work in the burgeoning government bureaucracies. Many

NORWAY
SWEDEN
FINLAND
Helsinki
Petrograd (St. Petersburg)
ESTONIA
LATVIA
Moscow
Riga
COURLAND
British blockade line
Jutland 1916
DENMARK
North Sea
Baltic Sea
LITHUANIA
Wilno (Vilnius)
Treaty of Brest-Litovsk, March 1918
Farthest Russian advance, 1914
Masurian Lakes 1914
E. PRUSSIA
BELARUS
RUSSIA
IRELAND
GREAT BRITAIN
London
NETHERLANDS
Kiel
Elbe R.
GERMANY
Berlin
Tannenberg 1914
Warsaw
KINGDOM OF POLAND (Russia)
Brest-Litovsk
Kiev
Armistice line, December 1917
Dnieper R.
Don R.
ATLANTIC OCEAN
Louvain
BELGIUM
Rhine R.
LUXEMBOURG
GALICIA
Dniester R.
MAY 1915
UKRAINE
Seine R.
Paris
ALSACE-LORRAINE
AUSTRIA-HUNGARY
Vienna
Budapest
Loire R.
Western front
SWITZERLAND
AUG. 1917
Caporetto 1917
MAR. 1918
TRANSYLVANIA
Bordeaux
FRANCE
Italian front
Po R.
ROMANIA
Bucharest
Danube R.
Black Sea
Garonne R.
Rhône R.
Sarajevo
SERBIA
BULGARIA
Adriatic Sea
MONTENEGRO
Ebro R.
SPAIN
Corsica
Elba
ITALY
Rome
Dardanelles
Constantinople
OTTOMAN EMPIRE
Gallipoli 1915
ALBANIA
1917–1918
1915
1916
GREECE
Sardinia
Balearic Is.
Balkan front
Triple Entente and its Allies
Central Powers
Neutral nations
Greatest extent of territory gained by Germany-Austria
Battle line
Sicily
Tunis
TUNISIA (France)
Malta
Mediterranean Sea
Crete
Cyprus
0 200 400 Km.
0 200 400 Mi.
N
0 25 50 Km.
0 25 50 Mi.
NETHERLANDS
Ruhr R.
Dover
Ostend
FLANDERS
Ghent
Antwerp
Rhine R.
Cologne
Calais
English Channel
Brussels
Scheldt R.
BELGIUM
Liège
Meuse R.
Coblenz
Arras
ARDENNES
Moselle R.
Somme R.
Somme
Amiens
St. Quentin
LUXEMBOURG
GERMANY
FRANCE
Aisne R.
Sedan
Saar R.
Compiègne
ARGONNE FOREST
Belleau Wood
Reims
LORRAINE
Marne I
Marne R.
Verdun
St. Mihiel
Seine R.
Paris
Châlons-sur-Marne
Marne II
Chateau-Thierry
Nancy
Strasbourg
ALSACE
Germany, 1914
German offensive, 1915
Greatest extent of territory gained by Germany, Sept. 1914
Front at beginning of 1915
German offensive, Summer 1918
Armistice line, November 1918
Major battle
Epinal
Mulhouse
Basel

Map 25.1 The First World War in Europe After an initial surge through Belgium into northern France, the German offensive bogged down for four years along the western front. To the east, the German armies conquered a large part of Russia during 1917 and early 1918. Despite spectacular victories in the east, Germany lost the war because its armies collapsed along the strategically important western front. © Cengage Learning

joined auxiliary military services as doctors, nurses, mechanics, and ambulance drivers. These positions gave thousands of women a sense of participation in the war effort and a taste of personal and financial independence.

The British naval blockade punished Germany's civilians. German chemists developed synthetic explosives and fuel, but not synthetic food. Wheat flour disappeared, replaced first by rye, then by potatoes and turnips, then by acorns and chestnuts, and finally by sawdust. After the failure of the potato crop in 1916 came the "turnip winter," when people had to survive on 1,000 calories per day, half the normal amount that an active adult needs. Women, children, and the elderly were especially hard hit. Even soldiers went hungry.

Abroad the British and French overran all of Germany's African colonies except German East Africa, which remained undefeated until the end of the war (see Map 25.1). In many African colonies, war policies imposed heavy taxes, low prices for requisitioned supplies, and military recruitment. Many Europeans stationed in Africa left to join the war, leaving areas with little or no European presence. Over a million Africans served in the various armies, and perhaps three times that number were drafted as porters to carry army equipment. In some places these impositions provoked African uprisings that lasted for years.

One country grew rich during the war: the United States, which for two and a half years stayed technically neutral while its companies did a roaring business supplying France and Britain with food and war materiel. After the United States entered the war in 1917, civilians were exhorted to help the war effort by investing their savings in war bonds and growing food in backyard "victory gardens." Employment created by the war opened up jobs for women and African Americans.

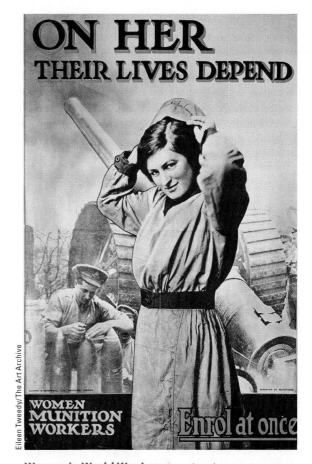

Women in World War I Women played a more important role in World War I than in previous wars. As the armies drafted millions of men, employers hired women for essential war work. This poster extols the importance of women workers in supplying munitions.

The Ottoman Empire at War

On August 2, 1914, the Turks signed a secret alliance with Germany. In November they joined the fighting, hoping to gain land at Russia's expense. But the campaign in the Caucasus proved disastrous for both sides. Suspecting the local Armenians of being pro-Russian, the Turks forced them to march from their homelands across the mountains in the winter, a trek during which hundreds of thousands died of hunger, exposure, and outright slaughter. Famine stalked the empire.

The Turks also closed the Dardanelles, the strait between the Mediterranean and Black Seas (see Map 25.1). When a British attack on the Dardanelles failed disastrously at the Battle of Gallipoli, they tried to subvert the Ottoman Empire from within by promising the emir (governor) of Mecca, Hussein ibn Ali, a kingdom of his own. In 1916 Hussein started an Arab revolt against the Turks. His son **Faisal I** (FIE-sahl) led an Arab army into Palestine and Syria in support of

Faisal I (1885–1933) Arab prince, leader of the Arab Revolt in World War I. The British made him king of Iraq in 1921, and he reigned under British protection until 1933.

the British advance from Egypt, thereby contributing to the Ottoman defeat.

The British made promises to Chaim Weizmann (hi-um VITES-mun), leader of the British Zionists, that a Jewish homeland in Palestine could be carved out of the Ottoman Empire and placed under British protection. In November 1917, as British armies were advancing on Jerusalem, Foreign Secretary Sir Arthur Balfour wrote:

> His Majesty's Government view with favor the establishment in Palestine of a national home for the Jewish people and will use their best endeavours to facilitate the achievement of that object, it being clearly understood that nothing shall be done which may prejudice the civil and religious rights of existing non-Jewish communities in Palestine.[2]

The British did not foresee that this statement, known as the **Balfour Declaration**, would lead to conflicts between Palestinians and Jewish settlers.

Double Revolution in Russia, 1917

Russia began the war with the largest army in the world, but its generals were incompetent, supplies were lacking, and soldiers were poorly trained and equipped. In August 1914 two Russian armies were thrown back in eastern Germany. Russia did better against the Austro-Hungarian army but again was defeated by the Germans. In 1916, after a string of defeats, the Russian army ran out of ammunition and other essential supplies. Soldiers were ordered into battle unarmed and told to pick up the rifles of fallen comrades.

With so many men in the army, railroads broke down for lack of fuel and parts, and crops rotted in the fields. Civilians faced shortages and widespread hunger. In the cities food and fuel became scarce. During the bitterly cold winter of 1916–1917, factory workers and housewives had to line up in front of grocery stores before dawn to get food. The court of Tsar Nicholas II, however, remained as extravagant and corrupt as ever.

When food ran out in Petrograd (St. Petersburg), the capital, in early March 1917, housewives and women factory workers staged mass demonstrations. Soldiers mutinied and joined striking workers to form *soviets* (councils) to take over factories and barracks. A few days later, the tsar abdicated, and leaders of the parliamentary parties, led by Alexander Kerensky, formed a Provisional Government. Thus began what Russians called the "February Revolution" because their calendar was two weeks behind the one in use elsewhere.

Revolutionary groups came out of hiding. Most numerous were the Social Revolutionaries, who advocated redistributing land to the peasants. The Social Democrats, a Marxist party, were divided. The Mensheviks, who advocated electoral politics and reform in the tradition of European socialists, had a large following among intellectuals and factory workers. The **Bolsheviks** were a small but tightly disciplined group dedicated to revolution. **Vladimir Lenin** (1870–1924), the Bolshevik leader, became a revolutionary in his teens when his older brother was executed for plotting to kill the tsar. His goal was to create a party that would lead the revolution rather than wait for it.

In early April 1917, the German government, hoping to destabilize Russia, allowed Lenin to travel from Switzerland to Russia in a sealed railway car. As soon as he arrived in Petrograd, he announced his program: immediate peace, all power to the soviets, and transfers of land to the peasants and factories to the workers. This plan proved immensely popular among soldiers and workers exhausted by the war.

When the Provisional Government ordered another offensive against the Germans, Russian soldiers deserted by the hundreds of thousands, throwing away their rifles and walking back to their villages. The Bolsheviks, meanwhile, were gaining support among the workers of Petrograd and the soldiers and sailors stationed there. On November 6,

Balfour Declaration Statement issued by Britain's foreign secretary Arthur Balfour in 1917 favoring the establishment of a Jewish national homeland in Palestine.

Bolsheviks Radical Marxist political party founded by Vladimir Lenin in 1903. Under Lenin's leadership, the Bolsheviks seized power in November 1917 during the Russian Revolution.

Vladimir Lenin (1870–1924) Leader of the Bolshevik (later Communist) Party. He lived in exile in Switzerland until 1917, then returned to Russia to lead the Bolsheviks to victory during the Russian Revolution and the civil war that followed.

---

[2]Walter Z. Laqueur and Barry Rubin, eds., *The Arab-Israeli Reader: A Documentary History of the Middle East Conflict*, 4th ed. (New York: Penguin Books, 1984), 18.

Lenin the Orator The leader of the Bolshevik revolutionaries was a spellbinding orator. Here Lenin is addressing Red Army soldiers in Sverdlov Square, Moscow, in 1920.

1917 (October 24 in the Russian calendar), they rose up and took over the city. This "October Revolution" overthrew the Provisional Government and the Bolsheviks arrested Mensheviks, Social Revolutionaries, and other rivals.

The Bolsheviks nationalized all private land and ordered the peasants to hand over their crops without compensation. The peasants, having seized their landlords' estates, resisted. In the cities the Bolsheviks took over the factories and drafted the workers into compulsory labor brigades. To enforce his rule, Lenin created the Cheka, a secret police force with powers to arrest and execute opponents. The Bolsheviks also sued for peace with Germany and Austria-Hungary. By the Treaty of Brest-Litovsk, signed on March 3, 1918, Russia lost territories containing a third of its population and wealth.

The End of the War in Western Europe, 1917–1918

Like many Americans, President **Woodrow Wilson** wanted to stay out of the European conflict. For nearly three years he kept the United States neutral and tried to persuade the belligerents to compromise. But in late 1916, Germany's decision to starve the British by using submarines to sink food ships risked bringing the United States into the war. Germany was willing to gamble that Britain and France would collapse before the United States could send a decisive number of troops.

The German gamble failed. The British organized their merchant ships into convoys protected by destroyers, and on April 6 President Wilson asked the United States Congress to declare war on Germany.

On the western front, the two sides were so evenly matched in 1917 that the war seemed unlikely to end until one side or the other ran out of young men. Losing hope of winning, soldiers began to mutiny. In May 1917, before the arrival of U.S. forces, fifty-four of one hundred French divisions along the western front refused to attack. At Caporetto, Italian troops were so demoralized that 275,000 were taken prisoner.

Between March and August 1918, German general Erich von Ludendorff launched a series of surprise attacks that pushed to within 40 miles

Woodrow Wilson (1856–1924) President of the United States (1913–1921) and a leading figure at the Paris Peace Conference of 1919. He was unable to persuade the U.S. Congress to ratify the Treaty of Versailles or join the League of Nations.

SECTION REVIEW

- Europeans greeted the outbreak of war with joy.

- Huge battles, often fought from trenches on the western front, cost hundreds of thousands of casualties but did not bring victory.

- On the home fronts, civilians suffered shortages and women entered the workforce, while the United States grew richer.

- Great Britain destabilized the Ottomans by supporting the Arab Revolt and backed the Balfour Declaration, which promised a Jewish homeland.

- In Russia, the February Revolution replaced the tsar with a Provisional Government, which later fell to the Bolshevik-led October Revolution.

- In 1917–1918, U.S. troops reinvigorated the Allies and the German offensives failed, forcing Germany to sign an armistice.

(64 kilometers) of Paris, but victory eluded him. Meanwhile, every month brought another 250,000 American troops to the front. In August the Allies counterattacked, and the Germans began a retreat that could not be halted, for German soldiers, many of them sick with the flu, had lost the will to fight.

In late October Ludendorff resigned, and sailors in the German fleet mutinied. Two weeks later, Kaiser Wilhelm fled to Holland as a new German government signed an armistice. At 11 A.M. on November 11, the guns on the western front went silent.

PEACE AND DISLOCATION IN EUROPE, 1919–1929

■ *What role did the war play in eroding European dominance in the world?*

The Great War lasted four years. It took almost twice as long for Europe to recover. Millions of people had died or been disabled; political tensions lingered; and national economies remained depressed until the mid-1920s. The return of peace and prosperity in the late 1920s soon proved illusory.

The Impact of the War

It is estimated that between 9 million and 10 million soldiers died, almost all of them young men. Perhaps twice that many returned home wounded, gassed, or shell-shocked, many of them disabled for life. In addition, the war created millions of refugees.

France welcomed 1.5 million refugees, but the preferred destination was the United States. About 800,000 immigrants succeeded in reaching it before immigration laws passed in 1921 and 1924 closed the door to eastern and southern Europeans. Canada, Australia, and New Zealand adopted similar restrictions on immigration. The Latin American republics welcomed European refugees, but their poverty discouraged potential immigrants.

One unexpected disaster was the great influenza epidemic of 1918–1919, which started among soldiers heading for the western front. This was no ordinary flu but a virulent strain that infected almost everyone on earth and killed one person in every forty. Half a million Americans perished in the epidemic—five times as many as died in the war. Worldwide, some 20 million people died.

The war also caused serious damage to the environment. No place on earth was ever so completely devastated as the scar across France and Belgium known as the western front. The fighting ravaged forests and demolished towns. The earth was gouged by trenches, pitted with craters, and littered with ammunition, broken weapons, chunks of concrete, and the bones of countless soldiers. After the war, it took a decade to clear away the debris, rebuild the towns, and create dozens of military cemeteries with neat rows of crosses stretching for miles.

The Peace Treaties

In early 1919 delegates of the victorious Allies met in Paris. The defeated powers were kept out until the treaties were ready for signing. Russia, in the throes of civil war, was not invited.

From the start, three men dominated the Paris Peace Conference: U.S. president Wilson, British prime minister David Lloyd George, and French premier Georges Clemenceau (zhorzh cluh-mon-SO). They ignored the Italians, who had joined the Allies in 1915, and paid even less attention to the smaller European nations. They rejected the Japanese proposal that all races be treated equally and ignored the call of the Pan-African Congress for attention to the concerns of Africans. They also ignored delegates who did not represent sovereign states—the Arab revolt leader Faisal, the Zionist Chaim Weizmann, and several Armenian delegations.

Each man had his agenda. Wilson wanted to apply the principle of self-determination, by which he meant creating nations that reflected ethnic or linguistic divisions. He proposed a **League of Nations**, a world organization to safeguard the peace and foster international cooperation. His idealism clashed with the more hardheaded and self-serving nationalism of the Europeans. Lloyd George insisted that Germany pay a heavy indemnity. Clemenceau wanted Germany to return Alsace and Lorraine, cede the industrial Saar region to France, and make the Rhineland a buffer state.

The result was a series of compromises that satisfied no one. The European powers formed a League of Nations, but the U.S. Congress refused to let the United States join. France recovered Alsace and Lorraine but was unable to detach the Rhineland and had to content itself with vague promises of British and American protection if Germany ever rebuilt its army. Britain acquired new territories in Africa and the Middle East but was greatly weakened by human losses and the disruption of its trade.

On June 28, 1919, the German delegates reluctantly signed the **Treaty of Versailles** (vuhr-SIGH). Germany was forbidden to have an air force and was permitted only a token army and navy. It also gave up large parts of its eastern territory to a newly reconstituted Poland. The Allies made Germany promise to pay reparations, but they did not set a figure or a period of time for payment. A "guilt clause," which was to rankle for years to come, obliged the Germans to accept "responsibility for causing all the loss and damage" of the war. The treaty left Germany humiliated but largely intact and potentially the most powerful nation in Europe. Establishing a peace neither of punishment nor of reconciliation, it was one of the great failures in history.

In eastern Europe, the Allies created new national states in the lands lost by the old Russian, German, and Austro-Hungarian Empires. Austria and Hungary became separate states; Poland was resurrected after over a century; Czechoslovakia and Yugoslavia were created from parts of Austria-Hungary. These small nations all contained disaffected minorities

and were safe only as long as Germany and Russia remained weak.

Russian Civil War and the New Economic Policy

Fighting continued in Russia for another three years after the end of the Great War. The Bolshevik Revolution had provoked Allied intervention, and, in December 1918, civil war broke out in Russia. The communists—as the Bolsheviks now called themselves—held central Russia, but all the surrounding provinces rose up against them. Counter-revolutionary armies led by former tsarist officers obtained weapons and supplies from the Allies. However, by 1921 the superior discipline of the Red Army, led by Leon Trotsky, gave the communists victory.

Gradually, the communists reunited the old Russian Empire. In 1920 Ukrainian communists declared the independence of a Soviet republic in the Ukraine; then in 1922, this merged with Russia to create the Union of Soviet Socialist Republics (USSR), or Soviet Union. In 1920–1921 the Red Army reconquered the oil-rich Caucasus and established Soviet control over Central Asia. In 1922 the new Soviet republics of Georgia, Armenia, and Azerbaijan joined the USSR.

By then, the Russian economy was in a state of ruin. Factories and railroads had shut down, and farmland had been devastated and livestock killed. Lenin decided to release the economy from party and government control. In 1923, he announced the **New Economic Policy** (NEP), which allowed peasants to own land and sell their crops, private merchants to trade, and private workshops to produce goods

League of Nations International organization founded in 1919 to promote world peace and cooperation but greatly weakened by the refusal of the United States to join. It proved ineffectual in stopping aggression by Italy, Japan, and Germany in the 1930s, and it was superseded by the United Nations in 1945.

Treaty of Versailles (1919) The treaty imposed on Germany by France, Great Britain, the United States, and other Allied powers after World War I. It demanded that Germany dismantle its military and give up some lands to Poland. It humiliated but did not weaken Germany.

New Economic Policy Policy proclaimed by Vladimir Lenin in 1923 to encourage the revival of the Soviet economy by allowing small private enterprises. Joseph Stalin ended the NEP in 1928 and replaced it with a series of Five-Year Plans.

and sell them on the free market. Only the biggest businesses, such as banks, railroads, and factories, remained under government ownership.

The relaxation of controls had an immediate effect. Production began to climb, and food and other goods became available. In the cities, food remained scarce because farmers used their crops to feed their livestock rather than sell them. But the NEP reflected no change in the communist goal of creating a modern industrial economy without private property. It merely provided breathing space—what Lenin called "one step back to advance two steps forward." This meant investing in heavy industry and electrification, moving farmers to the new industries, and providing food for the urban workers. In other words, it meant making the peasants, the great majority of the Soviet people, pay for the industrialization of Russia.

When Lenin died in January 1924, his associates jockeyed for power. Leon Trotsky, commander of the Red Army, had the support of many "Old Bolsheviks" who had joined the party before the Revolution, but Joseph Stalin, general secretary of the Communist Party, got the support of the majority and filled the party bureaucracy with individuals loyal to himself. In January 1929, he forced Trotsky to flee the country. Then, as absolute master of the party, he prepared to industrialize the Soviet Union at breakneck speed.

An Ephemeral Peace

After the war came five years of painful recovery and readjustment (1919–1923), followed by six years of growing peace and prosperity (1924–1929). In the first period, the German government had printed money recklessly to fund reparations payments, causing a devastating inflation. As Germany teetered on the brink of civil war, radical nationalists tried to overthrow the government. Finally, the German government issued a new currency and promised to resume reparations payments, and the French, who had occupied the Ruhr when reparation payments ceased, agreed to withdraw their troops.

Then in 1924 the vexed issue of reparations vanished as Germany borrowed money from New York banks to make its payments to France and Britain, which used the money to repay their wartime loans from the United States. This triangular flow of money stimulated the rapid recovery of the European econo-

SECTION REVIEW

- The Great War left millions dead or disabled and caused environmental devastation. The influenza epidemic of 1918–1919 killed millions more.
- France, Britain, and the United States dominated the Paris Peace Conference, refusing to listen to other voices, and humiliating but not weakening Germany with the Treaty of Versailles.
- When Austria-Hungary and Russia fell apart, several smaller nations arose in Europe, creating another source of potential conflict.
- After the Bolshevik victory in the Russian civil war, the Russian economy was in ruins, and Stalin took power.
- Prosperity returned in 1924–1929 when Germany resolved its reparations issues, primarily through U.S. bank loans that flowed from Germany through France and Britain and back to the United States.

mies. France began rebuilding its war-torn northern zone; Germany recovered from its hyperinflation and joined the League of Nations; and in the United States a boom began that was to last for over five years.

While their economies flourished, governments grew more cautious and businesslike. Yet Germany and the Soviet Union did not accept their borders with the small nations that had arisen between them. In 1922 they signed a secret pact allowing the German army to conduct maneuvers in Russia (in violation of the Versailles treaty) in exchange for German help in building up Russian industry.

For a time, the League of Nations proved adept at resolving issues pertaining to health, labor relations, and postal and telegraph communications. But without U.S. participation, sanctions against states that violated League rules carried little weight.

CHINA AND JAPAN: CONTRASTING DESTINIES

■ *Why did China and Japan follow such divergent paths in this period?*

China and Japan took different directions in the early twentieth century. Still in need of deep internal reform, giant China went through a revolution but soon collapsed into chaos. Japan's reforms before 1900 had gained it industry and a powerful military, which it used to take advantage of China's weakness.

The Bund in Shanghai On the Bund, the most important street in Shanghai, banks, corporate headquarters, and luxury hotels faced the waterfront where ships from around the world docked. Although Shanghai was China's industrial and commercial center, many of its workers loaded and unloaded ships by hand or pulled wealthy customers in rickshaws.

Bettmann/Corbis

Revolution in China

China's population—about 400 million in 1900—was the largest of any country in the world and growing fast. Most Chinese worked incessantly, survived on a diet of grain and vegetables, and spent their lives in fear of floods, bandits, and tax collectors. Peasant plots averaged half what they had been two generations earlier. Meanwhile, landowners lived off the rents of their tenants. Officials, chosen through an elaborate examination system, enriched themselves from taxes and the government's monopolies on salt, iron, and other products. Wealthy merchants handled China's growing import-export trade in collaboration with foreign companies. The contrast between the squalor in which most urban residents lived and the luxury of the foreigners' enclaves in the treaty ports sharpened the resentment of educated Chinese.

When China's Empress Dowager Cixi (TSUH-shee) died in 1908, eight years after the Boxer Uprising that she had encouraged (see Chapter 24), the Revolutionary Alliance led by **Sun Yat-sen** (soon yot-SEN) (Sun Zhongshan, 1867–1925) prepared to take over. Sun had spent much of his life in Japan, Eng-

land, and the United States, plotting the overthrow of the Qing dynasty. His tenacious spirit and his ideas, a mixture of nationalism, socialism, and Confucian philosophy, attracted a large following. A revolutionary assembly elected Sun president of China in December 1911, and the last Qing ruler, the boy-emperor Puyi, abdicated the throne. But Sun had no military forces at his command. To avoid a clash with the army, he resigned after a few weeks, and a new national assembly elected **Yuan Shikai** (you-AHN she-KIE), the most powerful of the regional generals, president of the new Chinese republic.

Yuan was an able military leader, but he had no political program. When Sun reorganized his followers into a political party called the **Guomindang**

Sun Yat-sen (1867–1925) Chinese nationalist revolutionary, founder and leader of the Guomindang until his death. He attempted to create a liberal democratic political movement in China but was thwarted by military leaders.

Yuan Shikai (1859–1916) Chinese general and first president of the Chinese Republic (1912–1916). He stood in the way of the democratic movement led by Sun Yat-sen.

(gwo-min-dong) (National People's Party), Yuan quashed every attempt at creating a Western-style government and harassed Sun's followers.

Japan and World War I

Japan's population reached 60 million in 1925 and was increasing by a million a year. The crash program of industrialization begun in 1868 by the Meiji oligarchs (see Chapter 24) accelerated during the First World War when the Japanese suddenly found their textiles, consumer goods, and munitions in great demand.

The Japanese economy grew four times faster than western Europe's and eight times faster than China's. Blessed with a rainy climate and many fast-flowing rivers, Japan expanded its hydroelectric capacity. By the mid-1930s, 89 percent of Japanese households had electric lights, compared with 44 percent of British households.

The *zaibatsu* (zie-BOT-soo), four giant corporations—Mitsubishi, Sumitomo, Yasuda, and Mitsui—that controlled most of Japan's industry and commerce profited the most. Farmers, who constituted half of the population, remained poor; some, in desperation, sold their daughters to textile mills or into domestic service, where young women formed the bulk of the labor force. Labor unions were weak and repressed by the police.

Japan was quick to join the Allied side in World War I. Japanese forces soon conquered the German colonies in the northern Pacific and on the coast of China, and then turned their attention to the rest of China. In 1915, Japan presented China with Twenty-One Demands, which would have turned it into a virtual protectorate. Britain and the United States persuaded Japan to soften the demands but could not prevent it from keeping the German coastal enclaves and extracting railroad and mining concessions at China's expense. Thus began a bitter struggle between the two countries that was to last for thirty years.

China in the 1920s

To many educated Chinese, the Western powers' decision at the Paris Peace Conference to agree to Japan's seizure of the German enclaves in China was a cruel insult. On May 4, 1919, students demonstrated

in front of the Forbidden City of Beijing. Despite a government ban, the May Fourth Movement spread to other parts of China.

China's regional generals—the warlords—still supported their armies through plunder and arbitrary taxation, frightening off trade and investment. While neglecting the dikes and canals on which Chinese farmers depended, they fought one another and protected the gangsters who ran the opium trade. During the warlord era, China grew poorer. Only the treaty ports prospered.

Sun Yat-sen tried to make a comeback in Guangzhou (Canton) in the early 1920s. Though not a communist, he was impressed with the efficiency of Lenin's revolutionary tactics and let a Soviet adviser reorganize the Guomindang along Leninist lines. He also welcomed members of the newly created Chinese Communist Party into the Guomindang.

When Sun died in 1925, the leadership of his party passed to Chiang Kai-shek (chang kie-shek) (1887–1975). An officer and director of the military academy, Chiang trained several hundred young officers who remained loyal to him thereafter. In 1927 he determined to defeat the regional warlords. Moving north from his base in Canton, he briefly formed an alliance with the communists. Once Shanghai was occupied, however, he allied himself with local gangsters to crush the labor unions and decimate the communists, whom he considered a threat. He then defeated or co-opted most of the other warlords and established a dictatorship.

Chiang's government issued ambitious plans to revitalize the economy, but his administrators were neither competent like the Japanese officials of the Meiji Restoration nor ruthless like the Russian Bolshevik modernizers. Instead, the government attracted thousands of opportunists whose goals were to "become officials and get rich" by taxing and plundering businesses. In the countryside tax collectors and landowners squeezed the peasants ever harder.

Guomindang Nationalist political party founded on democratic principles by Sun Yat-sen in 1912. After 1925, the party was headed by Chiang Kai-shek, who turned it into an increasingly authoritarian movement.

- Japan prospered during the war and quickly modernized; it also began preying on China.
- When the Qing dynasty ended in 1911, the regional general Yuan Shikai took over China and repressed Sun Yat-sen's party, the Guomindang.
- After Sun Yat-sen's death, Chiang Kai-shek established a corrupt military dictatorship.

THE NEW MIDDLE EAST

■ *How did the Middle East change as a result of the war?*

At the Paris Peace Conference, France, Britain, and Italy proposed to divide the territories of the Ottoman Empire among themselves, but their ambitions clashed with President Wilson's ideal of national self-determination. While Turkish nationalists fought for and achieved independence, the Arab-speaking territories of the old Ottoman Empire became part of the League of Nations' new **mandate system**, run by French and British administrations charged with promoting "the material and moral well-being and the social progress of the inhabitants." In Palestine, Zionists accelerated Jewish immigration (see Map 25.2).

The Rise of Modern Turkey

At the end of the war, Allied forces occupied the Ottoman Empire and made the sultan give up most of his lands. But they had to reckon with Mustafa Kemal, a war hero who formed a nationalist government in central Anatolia with the backing of fellow army officers. His armies defeated a Greek army of occupation in western Anatolia in 1922. An ensuing population exchange moved hundreds of thousands of Greeks to Greece and brought Muslims from that country to Turkey.

As a war hero and proclaimed savior of his country, Mustafa Kemal was able to impose wrenching changes on his people. An outspoken modernizer, he was eager to bring Turkey closer to Europe as quickly as possible. He abolished the sultanate, declared Turkey a secular republic in 1923, and introduced European laws. In a radical break with Islamic tradition, he suppressed Muslim courts, schools, and religious orders and replaced the Arabic alphabet with the Latin alphabet.

Women received civil equality, including the right to vote and to be elected to the national assembly. Kemal forbade polygamy and instituted civil marriage and divorce. He even changed people's clothing, strongly discouraging women from veiling their faces, and ordering Turkish men to wear European brimmed hats instead of the fez. He ordered everyone to take a family name, choosing the name **Atatürk** ("father of the Turks") for himself.

Arab Lands and the Question of Palestine

Among the Arab people, the thinly disguised colonialism of the mandate system set off protests and rebellions. Arabs viewed the European presence not as liberation from Ottoman oppression, but as foreign occupation.

The British attempted to control the Middle East with a mixture of bribery and intimidation. They made Faisal, leader of the Arab Revolt, the first king of Iraq and used aerial bombing of rebellious nomads to quell opposition. In 1931 they reached an agreement with King Faisal's government. A year later Britain granted Iraq official independence in exchange for a military alliance, the right to keep two air bases, and an assured flow of petroleum. France, meanwhile, sent thousands of troops to Syria and Lebanon to crush nationalist uprisings.

In Egypt, as in Iraq, the British substituted a phony independence for official colonialism. They declared Egypt independent in 1922 but reserved the right to station troops in the Suez Canal zone to secure their link with India. Despite nationalist opposition, Britain was successful in keeping Egypt in limbo—neither independent nor a colony—thanks to an alliance with King Fuad (sultan, 1917–1922; king 1922–1936) and conservative Egyptian politicians who feared both secular and religious radicalism.

mandate system Allocation of former German colonies and Ottoman possessions to the victorious powers after World War I, to be administered under League of Nations supervision.

Atatürk (1881–1938) The founder of modern Turkey. He distinguished himself as a war hero in World War I and expelled a Greek expeditionary army from Anatolia in 1921–1922. He replaced the Ottoman Empire with the Turkish Republic in 1923. As president, he pushed through a radical westernization and reform of Turkish society.

Diversity & Dominance

The Middle East After World War I

During the First World War, Entente forces invaded and occupied Palestine, Mesopotamia, and Syria. This raised the question of what to do with these territories after the war. Would they be returned to the Ottoman Empire? Would they simply be added to the colonial empires of Britain and France? Or would they become independent Arab states?

The following documents illustrate the diversity of opinions among various groups planning the postwar settlement: Great Britain, concerned with defeating Germany and maintaining its empire; the United States, basing its policies on lofty principles; and Arab delegates from the Middle East, seeking self-determination.

In the early twentieth century, in response to the rise of anti-Semitism in Europe, a movement called Zionism had arisen among European Jews. Zionists, led by Theodore Herzl, hoped for a return to Israel, the ancestral homeland of the Jewish people. For two thousand years this land had been a province of various empires—Roman, Byzantine, Arab, and Ottoman—and was inhabited by Arabic-speaking people, most of whom practiced the Islamic religion.

During the war the British government was receptive to the idea of establishing a Jewish homeland in Palestine. It was motivated by the need to win the war, but it also considered the more distant future. The result was a policy statement, sent by Foreign Secretary Arthur James Balfour to Baron Rothschild, a prominent supporter of the Zionist movement in England. This statement, called the "Balfour Declaration," has haunted the Middle East ever since.

The Balfour Declaration of 1917

Foreign Office
November 2nd, 1917

Dear Lord Rothschild:

I have much pleasure in conveying to you, on behalf of His Majesty's Government, the following declaration of sympathy with Jewish Zionist aspirations which have been submitted to, and approved by, the Cabinet:

His Majesty's Government view with favor the establishment in Palestine of a national home for the Jewish people, and will use their best endeavors to facilitate the achievement of this object, it being clearly understood that nothing shall be done which may prejudice the civil and religious rights of existing non-Jewish communities in Palestine, or the rights and political status enjoyed by Jews in any other country.

I should be grateful if you would bring this declaration to the knowledge of the Zionist Federation.

Yours,
Arthur James Balfour

On January 8, 1918, the American president Woodrow Wilson issued his famous Fourteen Points proposal to end the war. Much of his speech was devoted to European affairs or to international relations in general, but one of his fourteen points referred to the Arab world.

Woodrow Wilson's Fourteen Points

What we demand in this war . . . is that the world be made fit and safe to live in; and particularly that it be made safe for every peace-loving nation which, like our own, wishes to live its own life, determine its own institutions, be assured of justice and fair dealing by the other peoples of the world as against force and selfish aggression. All the peoples of the world are in effect partners in this interest, and for our own part we see very clearly that unless justice be done to others it will not be done to us. The programme of the world's peace, therefore, is our programme; and that programme, the only possible programme, as we see it, is this:

XII. The Turkish portions of the present Ottoman Empire should be assured a secure sovereignty, but the other nationalities which are now under Turkish rule should be assured an undoubted security ▶

> of life and an absolutely unmolested opportunity of autonomous development. . . .

When the war ended, the victorious Allies assembled in Paris to determine, among other things, the fate of the former Arab provinces of the Ottoman Empire. Arab leaders had reason to doubt the intentions of the great powers, especially Britain and France. When the Allies decided to create mandates in the Arab territories on the grounds that the Arab peoples were not ready for independence, Arab leaders expressed their misgivings, as in the following statement:

Memorandum of the General Syrian Congress, July 2, 1919

We the undersigned members of the General Syrian Congress, meeting in Damascus on Wednesday, July 2nd, 1919, made up of representatives from the three Zones, viz., The Southern, Eastern, and Western, provided with credentials and authorizations by the inhabitants of our various districts, Moslems, Christians, and Jews, have agreed upon the following statement of the desires of the people of the country who have elected us. . . .

1. We ask absolutely complete political independence for Syria. . . .
3. Considering the fact that the Arabs inhabiting the Syrian area are not naturally less gifted than other more advanced races and that they are by no means less developed than the Bulgarians, Serbians, Greeks, and Roumanians at the beginning of their independence, we protest against Article 22 of the Covenant of the League of Nations, placing us among the nations in their middle stage of development which stand in need of a mandatory power.
4. . . . . relying on the declarations of President Wilson that his object in waging war was to put an end to the ambition of conquest and colonization, . . . and believing that the American Nation is furthest from any thought of colonization and has no political ambition in our country, we will seek the technical and economic assistance from the United States of America, provided that such assistance does not exceed 20 years.

5. In the event of America not finding herself in a position to accept our desire for assistance, we will seek this assistance from Great Britain, also provided that such does not prejudice our complete independence and unity of our country and that the duration of such assistance does not exceed that mentioned in the previous article.
6. We do not acknowledge any right claimed by the French Government in any part whatever of our Syrian country and refuse that she should assist us or have a hand in our country under any circumstances and in any place.
7. We opposed the pretensions of the Zionists to create a Jewish commonwealth in the southern part of Syria, known as Palestine, and oppose Zionist migration to any part of our country; for we do not acknowledge their title but consider them a grave peril to our people from the national, economical, and political points of view. Our Jewish compatriots shall enjoy our common rights and assume our common responsibilities.

QUESTIONS FOR ANALYSIS

1. Was there a contradiction between Balfour's proposal to establish "a national home for the Jewish people" and the promise "that nothing shall be done which may prejudice the civil and religious rights of existing non-Jewish communities in Palestine"? If so, why did he make two contradictory promises?
2. How would Woodrow Wilson's statements about "an absolutely unmolested opportunity of autonomous development" apply to Palestine?
3. Why did the delegates to the General Syrian Congress object to the plan to create mandates in the former Ottoman provinces? What alternatives did they offer?
4. Why did the delegates object to the creation of a Jewish commonwealth?

Sources: The Balfour Declaration, *The Times* (London), November 9, 1917. Memorandum of the General Syrian Congress, *Foreign Relations of the United States: Paris Peace Conference,* vol. 12 (Washington, DC: Government Printing Office, 1919), 780–781.

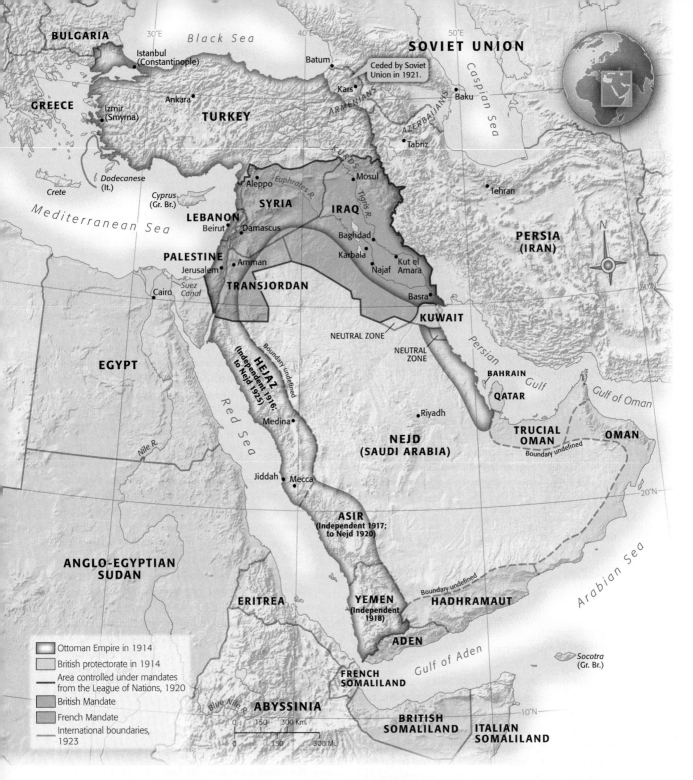

Map 25.2 Territorial Changes in the Middle East After World War I The defeat and dismemberment of the Ottoman Empire at the end of World War I resulted in an entirely new political map of the region. The Turkish Republic inherited Anatolia and a small piece of Europe, while the Ottoman Empire's Arab provinces were divided between France and Great Britain. Only Iran and Egypt did not change. © Cengage Learning

The Jewish Settlement of Palestine Thousands of Jews fleeing persecution and discrimination in Europe settled on the land and founded *kibbutzim*, or collective farms. In this picture taken in 1912, an eighty-four-year-old immigrant from Russia plows the land.

As soon as Palestine became a British mandate in 1920, Jewish immigrants, encouraged by the Balfour Declaration of 1917, arrived to join the small community that had immigrated in the nineteenth century. Most settled in the cities, but those supporting a socialist version of Zionism established *kibbutzim*, or communal farms. The purchases of land by Jewish agencies angered the indigenous Arabs, especially tenant farmers who were evicted to make room for settlers. In 1920–1921 riots erupted between Jews and Arabs. When far more Jewish immigrants arrived than they had anticipated, the British tried to limit immigration, thereby alienating the Jews without mollifying the Arabs. Increasingly, Jews arrived without papers, smuggled in by militant Zionist organizations. In the 1930s the country was torn by

strikes and guerrilla warfare that the British could not control. In the process, Britain earned the hatred of both sides.

SECTION REVIEW

- Former Arab provinces of the Ottoman Empire became "mandates" under French or British control.

- Mustafa Kemal (Atatürk) expelled the Greek minority from Anatolia and founded the Turkish Republic, then pushed it toward secular reform.

- As Middle Eastern society modernized, the Arabs became more politically active but had to endure the mandate system.

- Jewish immigration to Palestine caused growing tensions between Jews, Arabs, and the British.

CONCLUSION

In the late 1920s it seemed that the victors in the Great War might reestablish the prewar prosperity and European dominance of the globe. But the spirit of the 1920s was not real peace; instead it was the eye of a hurricane. The Great Depression and World War II were in the offing.

The Great War caused a major realignment among the nations of the world. France and Britain, the two leading colonial powers, emerged economically weakened despite their victory. The war brought defeat and humiliation to Germany but did not reduce its military or industrial potential. It destroyed the old regime of Russia, leading to civil war and revolution from which the victorious powers sought to isolate themselves.

Two other old empires—the Austro-Hungarian and the Ottoman—were divided into many smaller and weaker nations.

Japan took advantage of the European conflict to develop its industries and press its demands on a China weakened by domestic turmoil and social unrest. The United States emerged as the most prosperous and potentially most powerful nation, restrained only by the isolationist sentiments of many Americans.

In the Middle East, the fall of the Ottoman Empire awakened aspirations of nationhood among the Turkish and Arab inhabitants and Jewish immigrants. These aspirations were thwarted when france and Great Britain tried to impose their rule upon the former Ottoman lands, causing conflicts and bitter enmities.

CHAPTER REVIEW

ORIGINS OF THE CRISIS IN EUROPE AND THE MIDDLE EAST

■ *What led to the outbreak of the First World War?* (page 587)

In 1914 the great powers of Europe had not had a major conflict in decades and believed a war would be quick and victorious. The two alliances they formed—the Central Powers and the Entente—were locked into a rigid timetable of mobilizations and railroad schedules. When competing nationalist movements in the Balkans triggered a conflict between Serbia and Austria-Hungary, the alliances quickly drew Russia, Germany, France, and Britain into this conflict.

THE "GREAT WAR" AND THE RUSSIAN REVOLUTIONS, 1914–1918

■ *How did war lead to revolution in Russia?* (page 588)

Russia was the least prepared for war. Chaotic mobilization and a string of defeats disrupted the economy, causing severe shortages. As the war progressed, soldiers began to desert, and the government lost control of the army and the population. The moderate government that replaced the tsar in March 1917 could neither satisfy the people nor pursue the war. Its failure allowed the Bolsheviks to overthrow it in a second revolution.

PEACE AND DISLOCATION IN EUROPE, 1919–1929

■ *What role did the war play in eroding European dominance in the world?* (page 594)

France, Great Britain, and Italy expected to reap the benefits of victory and expand their empires at the expense of the defeated powers. However, with the exception of the United States, which withdrew to the Western Hemisphere, the victors were exhausted and impoverished and had lost the will to fight in colonial wars. Meanwhile, the idea of self-determination had spread to the Middle East and Asia, where nationalist politicians and their followers were determined to resist European dominance.

CHINA AND JAPAN: CONTRASTING DESTINIES

■ *Why did China and Japan follow such divergent paths in this period?* (page 596)

After 1868, Japan established a strong government and built an industrial economy comparable to those of Europe. Meanwhile, China, long ruled by the Qing dynasty, erupted after 1911 in civil wars in which warlords and political factions vied for power. The Japanese military and major industries seized the opportunity of Europe's involvement in the Great War to build up Japan's economy at China's expense.

THE NEW MIDDLE EAST

■ *How did the Middle East change as a result of the war?* (page 599)

In Anatolia, the heartland of the Ottoman Empire, a movement for national unity led by Kemal Atatürk fought for and achieved Turkish independence. In the predominantly Arab lands, nationalist leaders decried European domination. Jewish immigration into Palestine provoked a violent reaction from the Arabs, which their British overlords found hard to control.

Key Terms

western front (p. 588)	Treaty of Versailles (p. 595)
Faisal I (p. 591)	New Economic Policy (p. 595)
Balfour Declaration (p. 592)	Sun Yat-sen (p. 597)
Bolsheviks (p. 592)	Yuan Shikai (p. 597)
Vladimir Lenin (p. 592)	Guomindang (p. 598)
Woodrow Wilson (p. 593)	mandate system (p. 599)
League of Nations (p. 595)	Atatürk (p. 599)

CHAPTER 26

1900–1950

Revolutions in Living

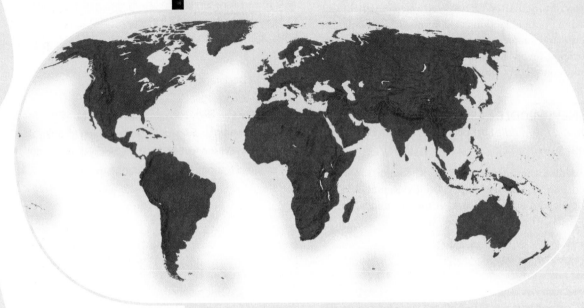

© Cengage Learning

In 1869 three Japanese businessmen, an entrepreneurial former cook, a green grocer, and a wagon builder, responded to government concerns about urban congestion and applied for a license to build a *jinriksha* ("man-power-vehicle"). They described it as "a little seat in the Western style, mounted on wheels so that it can be pulled about. It does not shake as much as the usual cart, and it is easy to turn round. It will not hinder other traffic, and since it can be pulled by one person, it is very cheap."[1] Their first vehicles, which quickly came to be called rickshaws, appeared a year later. A year after that, in 1871, Japan enacted its first patent law, and the three applied for exclusive manufacturing rights. However, so many workshops were by then turning out rickshaws that their application was denied.

An alternative claim of invention arose when an irascible American Baptist missionary named Jonathan Goble petitioned the Tokyo Metropolitan Government to grant him a share of the tax levied on the thirty thousand rickshaws then officially registered. He claimed to be the inventor, and a number of Westerners living in Japan supported him, some stating that Goble had built the first rickshaw for his ailing wife, and others that he had designed it at the request of a Japanese officer for use in the "imperial pleasure gardens."

The Japanese version of the story, which was reinforced in 1900 by government cash awards to the three businessmen, is highly credible since two-wheeled carts with a similar arrangement of shafts for pulling were in use on Japanese farms and for transporting loads well before European carriages came to be known through the "opening of Japan" in the 1850s (see Chapter 24). Moreover, Japan became the export source for rickshaws throughout Asia and the Indian Ocean region. The Goble story, however, made better sense to Westerners, who had a hard time crediting non-Europeans with inventiveness.

---

[1]F. Calvin Parker, *Jonathan Goble of Japan: Marine, Missionary, Maverick* (Lanham, MD: University Press of America, 1990), 222.

People today often look back and marvel at the changes their parents and grandparents lived through in the twentieth century. Movies, radio, television, telephones, automobiles, and airplanes all developed during the first half of the century. Familiar patterns of daily life gave way to new assumptions about many aspects of human life, with important differences according to what part of the world a person lived in.

NEW TECHNOLOGY OUTSIDE THE INDUSTRIALIZED WORLD

■ *How were Asians and Africans impacted by technology and innovation differently from Europeans and Americans?*

Before we discuss changes in the way people lived in the West between 1900 and 1950, we will consider how other parts of the world adapted local cultural traditions to the changing times and thereby took their societies in distinctive directions. A new technology could originate in the West or the East, but the point of origin did not determine its impact.

The rickshaw discussed at the beginning of this chapter provides a rare example of an Asian invention transforming urban life in ways unfamiliar to Europeans and Americans. The rickshaw stimulated the growth of Asian cities like Shanghai, Beijing, Singapore, Calcutta, and Bombay and reached across the Indian Ocean to Madagascar and South Africa. Much like European villagers entered the urban economy by way of unskilled manufacturing jobs, tens of thousands of unskilled Asian workers flocked to these cities to become rickshaw pullers, and eventually to stimulate a labor movement. Since a rickshaw puller usually ran rather than walked, the rickshaw cut the expense of personal transport in half while doubling its speed—and did not bury the streets under horse manure, the plague of Western cities. In Asia the rickshaw effectively enlarged the area of cities that had previously been scaled for pedestrians, transforming urban life in the Eastern Hemisphere just as streetcars had earlier done in Europe and America.

Some Western technologies were influentially adapted in the non-Western world. Photography and film contributed to feelings of national identity and common experience even in lands that were internally divided by language and ethnicity. In India, the first full-length feature screening occurred in 1912 two years after **Auguste and Louis Lumière**, who had premiered the first motion pictures in Paris in 1895, held motion picture demonstrations all over the world. Movies also caught on quickly in Japan. Not just for entertainment, newsreels and documentaries became major sources of information throughout the world, especially after the advent of sound in the late 1920s.

Practical photography began in Europe in 1839, and forty years later an efficient way was developed for printing photographs in newspapers. Photographic images soon became common throughout the world, often as picture postcards. European photographers, however, tended to look upon Asians and Africans, particularly seminude women, as exotic subjects and thereby catered to common European assumptions about racial superiority.

Non-European photographers rarely became known outside their home countries. Chinese newspapers and magazines usually published images without naming the photographers. A dozen early photographers became famous in Japan, however, possibly because popular woodblock prints had created an audience. In Iran, despite Muslim clerical disapproval of making images of human beings, the ruler Naser al-Din Shah (r. 1848–1896) shot some forty-eight thousand pictures, including members of his own family and even nudes and prisoners.

Photography enabled newspapers, magazines, and advertisements to inform even illiterate people about what their country and their fellow citizens

Hung Chung Chih/Shutterstock.com

Rickshaw Traffic Invented in 1869, the rickshaw transformed urban life in East Asia and the lands bordering on the Indian Ocean.

looked like, who was ruling them, and how traditional elites and prosperous Europeanized families lived. Thus photography contributed to feelings of national identity and common experience even in lands that were internally divided by language and ethnicity.

From the 1890s onward, electricity transformed home life in Europe and North America by attracting private customers. Outside Europe and North America, however, the small size of the middle class limited private subscription. Electricity might be supplied to streetlights, tramways, and factories, but an appliance-oriented lifestyle was slow to develop. By contrast, the foot-operated sewing machine and manually wound phonograph found wider global acceptance than any other appliances before World War II.

Radio development was uneven. Outside of North America, where 600 stations were broadcasting by 1924, the new medium was often limited by governments. Radio developed vigorously in Japan, Shanghai, and most Latin American countries and became an outlet for local cultural and political programming. In India and Africa, on the other hand, British and French colonial authorities imposed strict controls on radio transmissions and programming.

SECTION REVIEW

- Rickshaws contributed to urbanization, making transport in cities easier and faster and bringing rickshaw pullers to the city for employment.

- Technologies such as movies and photography were embraced and adapted in non-Western countries creating cultural cohesion and informing illiterate populations.

- The electrical appliance culture of the West spread slowly in parts of the world with small middle class populations.

Auguste (1862–1954) and Louis (1864–1948) Lumière French inventors of motion pictures whose equipment demonstrations abroad stimulated the growth of cinema around the world.

Chronology

	Technology	India	Africa	Latin America
1900	**1903** Wright brothers fly first airplane	**1905** Viceroy Curzon splits Bengal; mass demonstrations **1906** Muslims found All-India Muslim League **1911** British transfer capital from Calcutta to Delhi	**1900s** Railroads connect ports to the interior **1912** African National Congress founded	**1876–1910** Porfirio Diaz, dictator of Mexico **1911–1919** Mexican Revolution **1917** New constitution proclaimed in Mexico
	1912 First feature-length movie in India **1913** Henry Ford introduces assembly-line production **1915–1920** Women gain vote in Norway, Russia, Canada, Germany, Britain, and United States			
1920	**1920** Commercial radio begins in United States **1923** Magaret Sanger opens first birth control clinic **1925** Commercial radio begins in Japan	**1919** Amritsar Massacre **1929** Gandhi leads Walk to the Sea	**1920s** J. E. Casely Hayford organizes political movement in British West Africa	**1928** Plutarco Elías Calles founds Mexico's National Revolutionary Party
1930	**1932** Empire State Building opens	**1930s** Gandhi calls for independence; he is repeatedly arrested **1939** British bring India into World War II	**1939–1945** A million Africans serve in World War II	**1930–1945** Getulio Vargas, dictator of Brazil **1934–1940** Lázaro Cárdenas, president of Mexico **1938** Cárdenas nationalizes Mexican oil industry; Vargas proclaims Estado Novo in Brazil
1940		**1940** Muhammad Ali Jinnah demands a separate nation for Muslims **1947** Partition and independence of India and Pakistan		**1943** Juan Perón leads military coup in Argentina **1946** Perón elected president of Argentina

NEW WAYS OF LIVING IN THE INDUSTRIALIZED WORLD

■ *How did daily life and thought change in early-twentieth-century industrialized countries?*

World War I left a deep imprint on European society and culture. The centuries-old European distinction between aristocrats and commoners faded. Advances in science offered astonishing new insights into the mysteries of nature and the universe. New technologies, many of them pioneered in the United States, promised to change the daily lives of millions of people (see Environment and Technology: New Materials). At the same time, new cultural trends developed that had profound effects.

Class and Gender So many European aristocrats died on the battlefields that with them went their class's long domination of the army, the diplomatic corps, and other elite sectors of society. On both sides of the Atlantic, engineers, businessmen, lawyers, and other professionals rose to prominence, increasing the relative importance of the middle class.

At the same time, governments had expanded during the war and continued to grow, providing housing, highways, schools, public health, broadcasting, and other services. The ambitions and tastes of the rapidly expanding middle class became increasingly evident in the postwar period, while the role of the working class remained about the same.

Women's lives changed more rapidly in the 1920s than ever before. Although the end of the war marked a retreat from wartime job opportunities, some women remained in the workforce. The young and wealthy enjoyed more personal freedoms; they drove cars, played sports, traveled alone, and smoked in public. For others, the upheavals of war brought more suffering than liberation. Millions of women had lost their male kin in the war or in the great influenza epidemic. After the war many single women led lives of loneliness and destitution.

In Europe and North America, advocates of women's rights had been demanding the vote for women since the 1890s. New Zealand was the only nation to grant women the vote before the twentieth century. Norway followed in 1915, Russia in 1917, and Canadians and Germans in 1918. Britain gave women over thirty the vote in 1918 and later extended it to younger women. The Nineteenth Amendment to the U.S. Constitution granted suffrage to American women in 1920. Women in Turkey began voting in 1934. Everywhere, their influence on politics was less radical than feminists had hoped and conservatives had feared. Even when it did not transform politics and government, however, the right to vote was a potent symbol.

On both sides of the Atlantic, women participated in social reform movements to prevent mistreatment of women and children and industrial workers. In the United States such reforms were championed by progressives like Jane Addams (1860–1935), who founded a settlement house in a poor neighborhood and received the Nobel Peace Prize in 1931. In Europe reformers were generally aligned with Socialist or Labor Parties.

Among the most controversial, and eventually most effective, of the reformers were those who advocated contraception, such as the American **Margaret Sanger** (1883–1966). Her campaign brought her into conflict with many authorities, who equated birth control with pornography. Finally, in 1923 she was able to found a birth control clinic in New York. In France, the government prohibited contraception and abortion in 1920 in an effort to increase the birthrate and make up for the loss of so many young men in the war.

Revolution in the Sciences At the end of the nineteenth century, a revolution in physics undermined the old certainties about nature. Physicists discovered that atoms, the building blocks of matter, are not indivisible, but consisted of far smaller subatomic particles. In 1900 the German physicist **Max Planck** (1858–1947) found that atoms emit or absorb energy in discrete amounts called *quanta*. Few people understood these findings at the time, much less **Albert Einstein**'s (1879–1955) pronouncement in 1916 that time, space, energy, and mass are not fixed but are relative to one another. But the new physics promised to unlock the secrets of matter and provide humans with plentiful—and potentially dangerous—new sources of energy.

The new social sciences were more understandable, and thus more unsettling, for they challenged Victorian morality and middle-class values. **Sigmund Freud** (1856–1939), a Viennese physician, developed the technique of psychoanalysis to probe the minds of his patients. His technique uncovered hidden layers of emotion and desire repressed by social restraints.

Margaret Sanger (1883–1966) American nurse and author; pioneer in the movement for family planning; organized conferences and established birth control clinics.

Max Planck (1858–1947) German physicist who developed quantum theory and was awarded the Nobel Prize for physics in 1918.

Albert Einstein (1879–1955) German physicist who developed the theory of relativity, which states that time, space, and mass are relative to each other and not fixed.

Sigmund Freud (1856–1939) Austrian psychiatrist, founder of psychoanalysis. He argued that psychological problems were caused by traumas, especially sexual experiences in early childhood, that were repressed in later life. His ideas caused considerable controversy among psychologists and in the general public. Although his views on repressed sexuality are no longer widely accepted, his psychoanalytic methods are still very influential.

Rural Japan Before World War I This village scene from Japan reflects the taste for landscapes and ordinary life typical of the earliest photographers in Japan, both European and Japanese. The popularity of such scenes in earlier colored woodcuts may have influenced the choice of such subjects.

SSPL/Getty Images

just as advanced, and public fascination with the latest inventions—the cult of the modern—was just as strong.

No innovation attracted more public interest more than airplanes. In 1903, two young American mechanics, **Wilbur and Orville Wright**, built the first aircraft that was heavier than air and could be maneuvered in flight. From that moment on airplanes fascinated people. During the Great War, the exploits of air aces relieved the tedium of news from the front.

The first flight of **KLM Royal Dutch Airlines**, the oldest continuously operating airline, took off in 1920. That year it carried 440 passengers and 22 tons of cargo. Its most important service as an air link to the Dutch East Indies (now Indonesia) began in 1929. Every country with imperial possessions saw international air service as a political necessity.

Electricity's impact on home life was more sweeping. The first home use of electricity was for lighting, thanks to the economical and long-lasting incandescent bulb (see Chapter 24). Then electrical utilities joined manufacturers in advertising electric irons, fans, washing machines, hot plates, radios, and other electrical appliances. After the war, radio moved from the battlefield into the home. The first commercial station began broadcasting in Pittsburgh in 1920. By 1930, hundreds of stations were broadcasting news, sports, soap operas, and advertisements to 12 million homes in North America. Another medium that spread explosively in the 1920s was film. Motion pictures had begun in France in 1895 and flourished in Europe. In the United States, filmmaking started at almost the same time, but American filmmakers saw the medium's potential to entertain audiences rather than preserve outstanding theatrical performances. After World War I, filmmaking took root and flourished in

"The primitive, savage and evil impulses have not vanished from any individual, but continue their existence, although in a repressed state,"[2] he warned. Meanwhile, sociologists and anthropologists had begun the empirical study of societies, both Western and non-Western. Before the war the French sociologist Emile Durkheim (1858–1917) had come to the then shocking conclusion that "there are no religions that are false. All are true after their own fashion."[3]

If the words *primitive* and *savage* applied to Europeans as well as to other peoples, and if religions were all equally "true," then what remained of the superiority of Western civilization? Cultural relativism, as the new approach to human societies was called, could be as unnerving as relativity in physics.

The New Technologies of Modernity

In North America, even working-class people could afford some of the new products of inventors' ingenuity. Mass consumption lagged in Europe, but science and technology were

[2]Ragnhild Fiebig von Hase and Ursula Lehmkuhl, *Enemy Images in American History* (Oxford: Berghahn Books, 1997), 5.

[3]Sigmund Freud, *Three Contributions to the Theory of Sex*, tran. A. A. Brill, 2 ed. (Washington: Nervous and Mental Health Disease Publishing Company, 1920), 40.

Wilbur (1867–1912) and Orville (1871–1948) Wright American bicycle mechanics; the first to build and fly an airplane, at Kitty Hawk, North Carolina, December 7, 1903.

KLM Royal Dutch Airlines Oldest major airline, operating since 1920 in Europe and connecting to the Dutch East Indies in 1929.

New Materials

Nineteenth-century commerce brought many raw materials from European colonies and other far-away places into industrial use. Examples include rubber, a Southeast Asian tree sap called gutta-percha used for electrical insulation, Central Asian camel's hair used for transmission belts, and whale oil for lighting. These exotic materials were valuable, but they did not change the age-old pattern of almost every useful item being manufactured from natural substances.

The first half of the twentieth century saw a revolutionary change in this pattern. Metallurgists and chemists led the way in creating new materials that wrought permanent changes in the look and feel of everyday life. Materials science would go on to become one of the most important areas of technical innovation in later decades.

Though aluminum follows oxygen and silicon as the third most abundant element, it combines so readily with other elements that it was not discovered until 1827. Initially as precious as silver, a 2.4-kilogram piece was installed as the capstone of the Washington Monument in 1884. Four years later, however, almost simultaneously in the United States and France, an inexpensive electrolytic method of extracting the metal from bauxite ore was discovered. The lightweight, noncorrosive metal now became available for all manner of uses, from airplanes, beginning with a design by the German Hugo Junkers in 1917, to aluminum foil, which was invented in 1910.

Stainless steel, made by combining noncorrosive chromium with steel, was invented in 1912, and its many uses accustomed people to thinking of metal products as shiny. Electroplating with chromium came into use in 1924 in Germany and two years later in the United States. The shiny, rust-free metal, which could be deposited as a thin film on either a metallic or plastic base, found numerous uses from musical instruments to automobiles.

Plastics were invented at about the same time. Alexander Parkes invented celluloid, a stable form of explosive guncotton—itself made by soaking fine cotton in sulfuric and nitric acids—and exhibited it at London's Great Exhibition in 1862. The first thermoplastic, it could be molded above a certain temperature but became solid when it cooled. It was used for detachable men's shirt collars,

imagebroker/Alamy

Bakelite Jewelry *This pioneering plastic was so attractive that it was made into jewelry. However, its ease of manufacture, hardness, and resistance to electricity, heat, and chemicals suited it to thousands of other uses from clarinets to wire insulation to kitchenware. During World War II it was even considered as a replacement for the copper penny.*

ping-pong balls, and photographic film, but it was both fragile and flammable.

Belgian-born Leo Hendrik Baekeland invented Bakelite, a more durable plastic that was also attractive enough to be used for jewelry in 1907. Five years later the Swiss chemist Jacques E. Brandenberger, trying to discover a way of waterproofing cloth, experimented with a cellulose-based coating that failed to stick to the cloth and instead peeled off in a clear sheet. Thus was cellophane invented. In the 1930s an American, Richard Drew, coated cellophane with adhesive and Scotch tape was born.

And there were others. Silklike rayon, 1904; isoprene synthetic rubber, 1909; vinyl, 1926; neoprene synthetic rubber, 1931; plexiglass, 1933; nylon, 1935; Lucite, 1936; fiberglass, 1938—the list goes on, with even more new materials being developed in the later decades of the century.

QUESTIONS FOR ANALYSIS

1. Why do we take for granted a material environment constructed from manufactured substances that did not even exist before 1900?
2. What are the objects we use every day made of?
3. Why did new materials find such broad acceptance?

Japan, India, Turkey, Egypt, and a suburb of Los Angeles, California, called Hollywood. American and European movie studios were both successful in exporting films, since silent movies presented no language problems. Then in 1927 the United States introduced the first "talking" motion picture, *The Jazz Singer*, which changed all the rules. Hollywood studios began the diffusion of American culture that has continued to this day.

Advances in medicine—some achieved in the war—saved many lives. Wounds were regularly disinfected, and **Marie Curie** (1867–1934), the French discoverer of x-rays, organized radiology vans to help army doctors diagnose fractures during the Great War. Cities built costly water supply and sewage treatment systems. By the 1920s indoor plumbing and flush toilets were becoming common even in working-class neighborhoods. Interest in cleanliness entered private life. Doctors and home economists bombarded women with warnings and advice on how to banish germs. Soap and appliance manufacturers filled women's magazines with advertisements for products to help keep homes and clothing spotless and meals fresh and wholesome. The decline in infant mortality and improvements in general health and life expectancy in this period owe as much to the cult of cleanliness as to advances in medicine.

Museum of Flight/Corbis

First Aluminum Airplane From the Wright Brothers' first aircraft in 1903 down to the air battles of World War I, wood, cloth, and wire made up the wings and bodies of airplanes. Metals were too heavy for anything but engines and weapons until the German manufacturer Hugo Junkers designed the first aluminum flying machine, shown here, in 1917.

Technology and the Environment

Two new technologies—the skyscraper and the automobile—transformed the urban environment even more radically than the railroad had done. At the end of the nineteenth century architects had begun to design ever-higher buildings using load-bearing steel frames and elevators. Major corporations in Chicago and New York competed to build the most daring buildings in the world, such as New York's fifty-five-story Woolworth Building (1912). A building boom in the late 1920s produced dozens of skyscrapers, culminating with the eighty-six-story Empire State Building in New York in 1932. In the 1920s the Swiss **Le Corbusier** (luh corbooz-YEH) (1887–1965) outlined a new approach to architecture that featured simplicity of form, absence of surface ornamentation, easy manufacture, and inexpensive materials such as concrete and glass in what came to be known as the International Style.

Meanwhile, instead of being blamed for their exhaust emissions, automobiles were praised as the solution to urban pollution: as they replaced horse-drawn carts and carriages, tons of manure disappeared from city streets. The assembly line pioneered by Henry Ford in 1913 mass-produced vehicles in ever-greater volume and at falling prices. By 1929 the

Marie Curie (1867–1934) Twice winner of the Nobel Prize, the Polish Maria (Marie, in French) Sklodowska worked in Paris and, with her husband Pierre Curie, discovered the element radium and radioactivity, changing the knowledge of matter and the treatment of many diseases. In World War I, she convinced wealthy patrons to donate vehicles for use as X-Ray centers and traveled to aid doctors in detecting fractures and shrapnel in wounded soldiers.

Le Corbusier (1887–1965) Professional name of architect Charles-Éduard Jeanneret who led a modernist movement away from surface decoration and toward form following function.

United States had one car for every five people. The most important environmental effect of automobiles was suburban sprawl. Middle-class families could now live in single-family homes too far apart to be served by public transportation, and cities acquired rings of automobile suburbs. It was less common for Europeans to own automobiles; their premodern narrow streets adapted less easily to passenger automobiles. In the countryside outside European cities, however, high-speed expressways—*autostrada* in Italy and *autobahn* in Germany—became sources of national pride.

Technological advances also transformed rural economies. In 1915 Ford introduced a gasoline-powered tractor, and by the mid-1920s these versatile machines began replacing horses. Larger farms profited most from this innovation, while small farmers sold their land and moved to the cities. Tractors and other expensive equipment hastened the transformation of agriculture from family enterprises to larger businesses, or in the USSR to collective farms with state-owned tractor stations (see Chapter 27).

In India, Australia, Latin America, and the western United States, engineers built dams and canals to generate electricity, control floods, and irrigate dry lands. The immediate benefits of dams and irrigation far outweighed such distant consequences as salt deposits on irrigated lands and harm to fishing industries.

SECTION REVIEW

- Government bureaucracies and the middle class grew after the war, but not the working class.

- In many countries, women gained the right to vote and led reform movements.

- Max Planck and Albert Einstein led a revolution in physics.

- Social scientists like Sigmund Freud undermined the old certainties of European culture by revealing a dark side to human nature.

- After the Wright brothers' first flight, other aviation pioneers set flying records.

- Electricity, radio, and cinema changed lifestyles and cultures, and the cult of cleanliness improved health.

- American cities were transformed by skyscrapers, and the automobile led to the creation of suburbs.

A NEW INDIA, 1905–1947

■ *Why did the educated elites of India want independence? What were ordinary Indians hoping for?*

Some parts of the world, such as India, became much more involved in the emerging technologically oriented culture than others, such as sub-Saharan Africa (discussed later in this chapter). The consequences of this inequality of access to "modern" developments are still felt today.

Under British rule India acquired railroads, harbors, modern cities, and cotton and steel mills, as well as an active and worldly middle class. The economic transformation of the region awakened in this educated middle class a sense of national dignity that demanded political fulfillment. In response, the British gradually granted India limited political autonomy while maintaining overall control. Religious and communal tensions among the Indian peoples were carefully papered over, and when the British, exhausted by World War II (see Chapter 27), withdrew in 1947, violent conflicts tore India apart (see Map 26.1).

The Land and the People

Despite periodic famines, notably between 1896 to 1900, when 2 million people died of starvation, the Indian population grew from 250 million in 1900 to 319 million in 1921 and 389 million in 1941. This growth caused landless young men to converge on the cities, exceeding the number of jobs available in the slowly expanding industries. Many of them entered the urban economy as rickshaw pullers. To produce timber for construction and railroad ties and to clear land for tea and rubber plantations, foresters cut down most of the tropical hardwood forests that had covered the subcontinent in the nineteenth century. In spite of deforestation and extensive irrigation, the amount of land available to peasant families shrank with each successive generation.

Economic development hardly benefited the average Indian. After paying rent to landowners, interest to village moneylenders, and taxes to the government, peasants—always the great majority—had little left to improve their land or raise their standard of living. The government protected property owners, from village moneylenders all the way up to the maharajahs (mah-huh-RAH-juh) or ruling princes, who

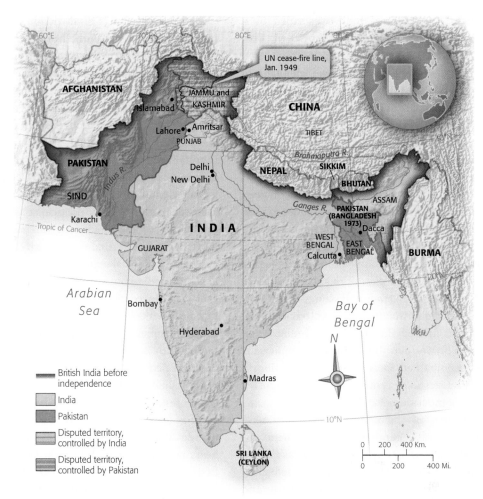

Map 26.1 The Partition of India, 1947 Before the British, India was divided among many states, ethnic groups, and religions. When the British left in 1947, the subcontinent split along religious lines. The predominantly Muslim regions in the northwest and East Bengal in the east formed the new nation of Pakistan. The predominantly Hindu center became the Republic of India. Jammu and Kashmir remained disputed territories and poisoned relations between the two new countries. © Cengage Learning

owned huge tracts of land. The cities were crowded with craftsmen, traders, and workers of all sorts, most very poor. Although the British had banned the burning of widows on their husbands' funeral pyres, in other respects women's lives changed little under British rule.

Indians also spoke many different languages. As a result of British rule, increasing trade and travel, and newspapers like *The Times of India*, established under that name in 1861, English became the common medium of communication for the Western-educated middle class. This new class of English-speaking bureaucrats, professionals, and

merchants was to play a leading role in the independence movement.

The majority of Indians practiced Hinduism and were subdivided into hundreds of castes (*jati*), each affiliated with a particular occupation. Hinduism discouraged intermarriage and other social interactions among the castes and with non-Hindus. Until displaced by the British in the eighteenth century, Muslim rulers had dominated northern and central India, and Muslims now constituted one-quarter of the Indian population but formed a majority in the northwest and in eastern Bengal. They felt discriminated against by both British and Hindus.

British Rule and Indian Nationalism

Colonial India was ruled by a viceroy appointed by the British government and administered by a few thousand members of the Indian Civil Service. Drawn mostly from the English gentry, they liked to think of India as a land of lords and peasants. They believed it was their duty to protect the Indian people from the dangers of industrialization, while defending their own positions from Indian nationalists.

As Europeans they admired modern technology but tried to control its introduction into India so as to maximize the benefits to Britain and to themselves. For example, they encouraged railroads, harbors, telegraphs, and other communications technologies, as well as irrigation and plantations, because these increased India's foreign trade and strengthened British control. Yet, they discouraged the cotton and steel industries and limited the training of Indian engineers, ostensibly to spare India the social upheavals that had accompanied the Industrial Revolution in Europe, while actually protecting British industry from Indian competition.

At the turn of the century most Indians—especially peasants, landowners, and princes—accepted British rule. But the Europeans' racist attitude toward dark-skinned people increasingly offended Indians who had learned English and absorbed English ideas of freedom and representative government, only to discover that racial quotas excluded them from the Indian Civil Service, the officer corps, and prestigious country clubs.

In 1885 a small group of English-speaking Hindu professionals founded a political organization called the **Indian National Congress**. For twenty years its members respectfully petitioned the government for access to higher administrative positions and for a voice in official decisions, but they had little influence. Then, in 1905, Viceroy Lord Curzon divided the province of **Bengal** in two to improve the efficiency of its administration. This decision, made without consulting anyone, angered not only educated Indians, who saw it as a way to lessen their influence, but also millions of uneducated Hindu Bengalis, who found themselves outnumbered by Muslims in East Bengal. Soon Bengal was the scene of demonstrations, boycotts of British goods, and even incidents of anti-British violence.

Muslims, fearful of Hindu dominance elsewhere in India, founded the **All-India Muslim League** in 1906. The government responded by granting Indians a limited franchise based on wealth. Muslims, however, were on average poorer than Hindus, possibly because many poor and low-caste Hindus had converted to Islam to escape caste discrimination. Accordingly, the British instituted separate representation and different voting qualifications. Then, in 1911, the British transferred the capital of India from Calcutta to Delhi (DEL-ee), the former capital of the Mughal (MOO-guhl) emperors. These changes raised the political consciousness of all Indian classes and religions, giving rise to two mass movements: one by Hindus and one by Muslims.

Fearful of social upheavals, the British resisted the idea that India could, or should, industrialize. Their geologists looked for minerals like coal and manganese that British industry required. However, when the only Indian member of the Indian Geological Service, Pramatha Nath Bose, wanted to prospect for iron ore, he had to resign because the government wanted no part of an Indian steel industry that might compete with that of Britain. Bose joined forces with Jamsetji Tata, a Bombay textile magnate who decided to produce steel anyway. With the help of German and American engineers and equipment, Tata's son Dorabji opened the first steel mill in India in 1911, in a town called Jamshedpur in honor of his father. Although it produced only a fraction of the steel that India required, Jamshedpur became a powerful symbol of Indian national pride.

Indian National Congress A movement and political party founded in 1885 to demand greater Indian participation in government. Its membership was middle class, and its demands were modest until World War I. Led after 1920 by Mohandas K. Gandhi, it appealed increasingly to the poor and organized mass protests demanding self-government and independence.

Bengal Region of northeastern India. It was the first part of India to be conquered by the British in the eighteenth century and remained the political and economic center of British India throughout the nineteenth century. The 1905 split of the province into predominantly Hindu West Bengal and predominantly Muslim East Bengal (now Bangladesh) sparked anti-British riots.

All-India Muslim League Political organization founded in India in 1906 to defend the interests of India's Muslim minority. Led by Muhammad Ali Jinnah, it attempted to negotiate with the Indian National Congress. In 1940, the League began demanding a separate state for Muslims, to be called Pakistan.

During World War I Indians supported Britain enthusiastically; 1.2 million men volunteered for the army, and millions more voluntarily contributed money to the government. Many expected the British to reward their loyalty with political concessions. Others organized to demand a voice in the government. Responding to the agitation, the British government announced in 1917 "the gradual development of self-governing institutions with a view to the progressive realization of responsible government in India as an integral part of the British Empire." This sounded like a promise of self-government, but the timetable was so vague that nationalists denounced it as a devious maneuver to postpone India's independence.

On April 13, 1919, in the city of Amritsar, General Reginald Dyer ordered his troops to fire into a peaceful crowd of some 10,000 demonstrators, killing at least 379 and wounding 1,200. While waves of angry demonstrations swept over India, the British House of Lords voted to approve Dyer's actions, and a fund was raised in appreciation of his services. Indians interpreted these gestures as showing British contempt for their colonial subjects, effectively bringing to a close the period of gradual accommodation.

Mahatma Gandhi and Militant Nonviolence

For the next twenty years, violent uprisings and harsh repression, possibly even war, seemed imminent. That the worst did not come to pass was due to **Mohandas K. Gandhi** (GAHN-dee) (1869–1948), a man known to his followers as "Mahatma," the "great soul."

Gandhi began life with every advantage. His wealthy family sent him to England for his education. After his studies he lived in South Africa and practiced law for the small Indian community there. During World War I he returned to India and was one of many Western-educated Hindu intellectuals who joined the Indian National Congress.

Unlike many radical political thinkers of his time, Gandhi denounced the popular ideals of power, struggle, and combat. Instead, inspired by both Hindu and Christian ideals, he preached the saintly virtues of *ahimsa* (uh-HIM-sah) (nonviolence) and *satyagraha* (suh-TYAH-gruh-huh) (the search for truth). He refused to countenance violence among his

followers and called off several demonstrations when they turned violent.

In 1921 Gandhi gave up the Western-style suits worn by lawyers and the fine raiment of wealthy Indians and henceforth wore simple peasant garb: a length of homespun cloth below his waist (*dhoti*) and a shawl to cover his torso. He spoke for the farmers and the outcasts, whom he called *harijan* (HAH-ree-jahn), "children of God." He attracted ever-larger numbers of followers among the poor and the illiterate, who soon began to revere him; and he transformed the cause of Indian independence from an elite movement of the educated into a mass movement with a quasi-religious aura.

Gandhi was a brilliant political tactician and a master of public relations gestures; he also knew how to use the new media. In 1929, for instance, he led a few followers on an 80-mile (129-kilometer) walk, camped on a beach, and gathered salt from the sea in a blatant and well-publicized act of civil disregard for the government's monopoly on salt. But he discovered that unleashing the power of popular participation was one thing and controlling its direction was quite another. Within days of his "Walk to the Sea," demonstrations of support broke out all over India, in which the police killed a hundred demonstrators and arrested over sixty thousand.

Many times during the 1930s Gandhi threatened to fast "unto death," and several times he came close to death, to protest the violence of both the police and his followers and to demand independence. He was repeatedly arrested and spent a total of six years in jail. But every arrest made him more popular. He became an iconic figure not only in his own country but also in the Western media. In the words of historian Percival Spear, he made the British "uncomfortable in their cherished field of moral rectitude," and he gave Indians the feeling that theirs was the ethically superior cause.

Mohandas K. Gandhi (1869–1948) Leader of the Indian independence movement and advocate of nonviolent resistance. After being educated as a lawyer in England, he returned to India and became leader of the Indian National Congress in 1920. He appealed to the poor, led nonviolent demonstrations against British colonial rule, and was jailed many times. Soon after independence he was assassinated for attempting to stop Hindu-Muslim rioting.

Gandhi's Salt March to the Sea Mohandas Gandhi, bareheaded and more simply dressed than his followers, led a march of 80 miles to collect sea salt in an act of civil disobedience. News photographs like this played a key role in popularizing his cause and displaying his saintly habits. To his left one man carries a sitar and another has a drum hanging from his shoulder.

India Moves Toward Independence

In the 1920s, slowly and reluctantly, the British handed over control of "national" areas such as education, the economy, and public works to Indians. They also gradually admitted more Indians into the Civil Service and the officer corps. Economically, Indian politicians obtained the right to erect high tariff barriers against imports to protect India's infant industries. Behind these barriers, Indian entrepreneurs built plants to manufacture iron and steel, cement, paper, textiles, sugar, and other products. While early industrialization did not improve the lives of the Indian peasants or urban poor, it created a class of wealthy Indian businessmen who supported the Indian National Congress and its demands for independence. Though paying homage to Gandhi, they preferred his designated successor as leader of the Indian National Congress, **Jawaharlal Nehru** (NAY-roo) (1889–1964).

Unlike Gandhi, Nehru looked forward to creating a modern industrial India.

Congress politicians won regional elections but continued to be excluded from the viceroy's cabinet, the true center of power. When World War II began (see Chapter 27), Viceroy Lord Linlithgow declared war without consulting a single Indian. The Congress-dominated provincial governments resigned in protest and found that boycotting government offices increased their popular support. When the British offered to give India its independence once the war ended, Gandhi demanded full independence immediately. His "Quit India" campaign aroused popular

Jawaharlal Nehru (1889–1964) Indian statesman who succeeded Mohandas K. Gandhi as leader of the Indian National Congress. He negotiated the end of British colonial rule in India and became India's first prime minister (1947–1964).

demonstrations against the British and provoked a wave of arrests, including his own.

Most Indian soldiers felt they were fighting to defend their country rather than to support the British Empire. As in World War I, Indians contributed heavily to the Allied war effort, supplying 2 million soldiers and enormous amounts of resources, especially the timber needed for emergency construction. A small number of Indians were so anti-British that they joined the Japanese side.

Partition and Independence

When the war ended, Britain's new Labor Party government prepared for Indian independence, but deep suspicions between Hindus and Muslims complicated the process. The break between the two communities had started in 1937, when the Indian National Congress won provincial elections and refused to share power with the Muslim League. In 1940 the leader of the League, **Muhammad Ali Jinnah** (JIH-nah) (1876–1948), demanded what many Muslims had been dreaming of for years: a country of their own, to be called Pakistan.

As independence approached, talks between Jinnah and Nehru broke down and violent rioting between Hindus and Muslims broke out. Gandhi's appeals for tolerance and cooperation fell on deaf ears. The British made frantic proposals to keep India united, but their authority was waning fast.

In early 1947 the Indian National Congress accepted the partition of India into two states, one secular but dominated by Hindus, the other Muslim. On August 15 British India gave way to a new India and Pakistan. The Indian National Congress, led by Nehru, formed the first government of India; Jinnah and the Muslim League established a government for the provinces that made up Pakistan.

Violent clashes between Muslims and Hindus marred any celebration of independence. Throughout the land, Muslim and Hindu neighbors turned on one another, and armed members of one faith hunted down people of the other faith. For centuries Hindus and Muslims had intermingled throughout most of India. Now, leaving most of their possessions behind, Hindus fled from predominantly Muslim areas, and Muslims fled from Hindu areas. Trainloads of desperate refugees

were attacked and massacred by members of the opposite faith. Within a few months some 12 million people had abandoned their ancestral homes and a half-million lay dead. In January 1948 Gandhi died too, gunned down by an angry Hindu refugee.

When the dust cleared, few Hindus remained in Pakistan, and Muslims were a minority in all but one state of India. That state was Kashmir, a strategically important region in the foothills of the Himalayas. India annexed Kashmir because the local maharajah was Hindu and because the state held the headwaters of the rivers that irrigated millions of acres of Indian farmland. The majority of the inhabitants of Kashmir were Muslims, however, and would have joined Pakistan if they had been allowed to choose. The annexation of Kashmir turned India and Pakistan into bitter enemies that fought several wars over the next half century.

SECTION REVIEW

- The inequities of British rule caused the rising class of English-speaking Indian professionals to create an independence movement.
- Changes in colonial administration and voting rights played upon religious divisions and created parallel Hindu and Muslim political movements.
- World War I and its aftermath stimulated nationalist agitation, which turned violent after the Amritsar Massacre.
- Employing militant nonviolence, Gandhi built a morally charged mass independence movement.
- Under Nehru's leadership, Indians pushed for greater independence, but World War II subordinated India to British interests.
- After gaining independence, India split into two states, and violence erupted between Hindus and Muslims.

Muhammad Ali Jinnah (1876–1948) Indian Muslim politician who founded the state of Pakistan. A lawyer by training, he joined the All-India Muslim League in 1913. As leader of the League from the 1920s on, he negotiated with the British and the Indian National Congress for Muslim participation in Indian politics. From 1940 on, he led the movement for the independence of India's Muslims in a separate state of Pakistan, founded in 1947.

MEXICO, ARGENTINA, AND BRAZIL, 1917–1949

■ How did the most powerful Latin American economies and political cultures change in the aftermath of World War I?

Though some parts of the world, notably Latin America, were untouched by the fighting, they were still struck by the disruptions of the postwar period. After a decade of violence that saw revolutionaries turn into political leaders only to be assassinated in the new Republic of Mexico (see Chapter 23), former general and interior minister Plutarco Elías Calles (KAH-yace) was elected president and served from 1924 to 1928. Calles reinvigorated the revolutionary principles of an exhausted country. He founded the National Revolutionary Party, or PNR (the abbreviation of its name in Spanish), which governed the country from 1929 to 2000, becoming a symbol for populist reform and a forum where all the pressure groups and vested interests—labor, peasants, businessmen, landowners, the military, and others—worked out compromises.

Lázaro Cárdenas (LAH-sah-roe KAHR-dih-nahs), chosen by Calles to be president in 1934, brought peasants' and workers' organizations into the party, removed generals from government positions, and implemented the reforms promised in the constitution. Cárdenas redistributed 44 million acres (17.6 million hectares) to peasant communes, replaced church-run schools with government schools, and nationalized the railroads and other businesses.

Most dramatic was the expropriation of foreign-owned oil companies. In the early 1920s Mexico was the world's leading producer of oil, but a handful of American and British companies exported almost all of it. In 1938 Cárdenas seized the foreign-owned oil industry, which had gained importance with the wartime recognition that modern armies ran on gasoline. The American and British oil companies expected their governments to come to their rescue, perhaps with military force. But Mexico and the United States chose to resolve the issue through negotiation, and Mexico retained control of its oil.

The Royal Navy was now set to continue its rule of the seas undaunted by supply problems, but Britain's strategic security had become dependent on control of Iran, a nominally independent country, and of Iraq, a part of the Ottoman Empire. Oil supplies had become an essential feature of world military calculations, and with the accelerating spread of motorized land transport after World War I, the civilian economies of the industrialized world became equally dependent.

This dependency lies behind a myriad of military and political decisions made over the subsequent decades, making the division between producing countries with surplus oil to sell and consuming countries reliant on a steady supply of imported fuel a crucial factor in world affairs.

When Cárdenas's term ended in 1940, Mexico was still a land of poor farmers with a small industrial base, but the political system was free of both chaos and dictatorships. The wealthy few no longer monopolized land and resources; the military was tamed; the Catholic Church no longer controlled education; and the nationalization of oil had demonstrated Mexico's independence.

The Transformation of Argentina

Most of Argentina consists of *pampas* (POM-pus), flat, fertile land that is easy to till, much like the prairies of the midwestern United States and Canada. Throughout the nineteenth century, Argentina's economy was based on two exports, the hides of longhorn creole cattle and the wool of merino sheep, which roamed the pampas in huge herds. At the end of the nineteenth century railroads and refrigerator ships that transported meat safely changed not only the composition of Argentina's exports but also the way they were produced. European consumers preferred the soft flesh of Lincoln sheep and Hereford cattle to the tough, sinewy meat of creole cattle and marino sheep. The valuable Lincolns and Herefords, however, had to be carefully bred and receive a diet of alfalfa and oats. To safeguard them, the pampas had to be divided, cultivated, and fenced with barbed wire. Once fenced, the

Lázaro Cárdenas (1895–1970) President of Mexico (1934–1940). He brought major changes to Mexican life by distributing millions of acres of land to the peasants, bringing representatives of workers and farmers into the inner circles of politics, and nationalizing the oil industry.

land could be used to produce wheat as well as beef and mutton. Within a few years grasslands that had stretched to the horizon were transformed into farmland. Like the North American Midwest, the pampas became one of the world's great producers of wheat and meat.

Argentina's government represented the interests of the *oligarquía* (oh-lee-gar-KEE-ah), a very small group of wealthy landowners. They also owned fine homes in Buenos Aires (BWAY-nos EYE-res), a city that was built to resemble Paris, traveled frequently to Europe, and spent so lavishly the French coined the superlative "rich as an Argentine." Focused on producing wheat and meat, they were content to let British companies build Argentina's railroads, processing plants, and public utilities. In exchange for its agricultural exports, Argentina imported almost all its manufactured goods from Europe and the United States. So important were British interests in the Argentinean economy that English, not Spanish, was used on the railroads.

Brazil and Argentina, to 1929

Before the First World War, Brazil produced most of the world's coffee and cacao, grown on vast estates, and natural rubber, gathered by Indians from rubber trees growing wild in the Amazon rain forest. Planters and rubber exporters made up Brazil's elite. Like their Argentinean counterparts, they spent extravagantly, building palaces in Rio de Janeiro (REE-oh day zhuh-NAIR-oh) and one of the world's most beautiful opera houses in Manaus (meh-NOWSE), deep in the Amazon. As in Argentina, British companies built railroads, harbors, and other infrastructure and imported most manufactured goods.

Both Argentina and Brazil had small but outspoken middle classes that demanded a share in government and looked to European models. The poor, at the bottom of the social pyramid, were mainly Spanish and Italian immigrants turned landless laborers and meat processors in Argentina and sharecroppers and plantation workers in Brazil, many descended from slaves.

Rubber exports collapsed after 1912, replaced by cheaper plantation rubber from Southeast Asia. The outbreak of war put an end to imports from Europe

as Britain and France focused all their industries on war production and Germany was cut off entirely. These disruptions weakened the landowning class. In Argentina the urban middle class obtained the secret ballot and universal male suffrage in 1916 and elected a liberal politician, **Hipólito Irigoyen** (ee-POH-lee-toe ee-ree-GO-yen), as president. To a certain extent, the United States replaced the European countries as suppliers of machinery and consumers of coffee. European immigrants built factories to manufacture textiles and household goods. Desperate for money to pay for the war, Great Britain sold many of its railroad, streetcar, and other companies to the governments of Argentina and Brazil.

South America prospered during the postwar years. Trade with Europe resumed; export prices for agricultural exports remained high; and both Argentina and Brazil used accumulated profits to industrialize and improve their transportation systems and public utilities. Nevertheless, workers and middle-class professionals demanded social reforms and a larger voice in politics. In Argentina, students' and workers' demonstrations were brutally crushed. In Brazil junior officers rebelled several times, calling for universal suffrage, social reforms, and freedom for labor unions. Though they accomplished little, these demonstrations laid the groundwork for later reformist movements. In neither country did the urban middle class take power away from the wealthy landowners. Instead, the two shared power at the expense of both landless peasants and urban workers.

Though Argentina and Brazil moved forward, new technologies again left them dependent on the advanced industrial countries. Brazilians are justly proud that the first person to fly an airplane outside the United States was Alberto Santos-Dumont, a Brazilian. But he did so in 1906 in France, where he lived most of his life and had access to engine manufacturers and technical assistance. Aviation reached Latin America after World War I, when European and American companies such as Aéropostale and

Hipólito Irigoyen (1850–1933) Argentine politician, president of Argentina from 1916 to 1922 and 1928 to 1930. The first president elected by universal male suffrage, he began his presidency as a reformer but later became conservative.

Pan American Airways introduced airmail service between cities and linked Latin America with the United States and Europe.

Before and during World War I, radio was used only for point-to-point communications. Transmitters powerful enough to send messages across oceans or continents were complex and expensive with antennas covering many acres. They used as much electricity as a small town.

Right after the war, the major powers scrambled to build powerful transmitters on every continent to take advantage of the boom in international business and news reporting. However, no Latin American country possessed the knowledge or funds to build its own transmitters. Four powerful radio companies—one British, one French, one German, and one American—formed a cartel to control all radio communications in Latin America. Thus, even as Brazil and Argentina were asserting state control over their railroads and older industries, as Mexico had done with its oil industry, the major industrial countries controlled the diffusion of the newer aviation and radio technologies.

The Depression and the Vargas Regime in Brazil

The Depression hit Latin America as hard as Europe and the United States and was in many ways a more important turning point for the region than either world war. As long-term customers cut back their orders, the value of agricultural and mineral exports fell by two-thirds between 1929 and 1932. Argentina and Brazil could no longer afford imported manufactured goods. An imploding economy also undermined their shaky political systems. Like European countries, Argentina and Brazil veered toward authoritarianism.

In 1930 **Getulio Vargas** (jay-TOO-lee-oh VAR-gus) (1883–1954), a state governor, staged a coup and proclaimed himself president of Brazil. He proved to be a masterful politician. He wrote a new constitution that broadened the franchise and limited the president to one term. He also raised import duties and promoted national firms and state-owned enterprises, culminating in the construction of the Volta Redonda steel mill in the 1930s. By 1936 industrial

production had doubled, especially in textiles and small manufactures. Brazil was on its way to becoming an industrial country. Vargas's policy, called **import-substitution industrialization**, became a model for other Latin American countries attempting to break away from neocolonial dependency.

The industrialization of Brazil brought all the familiar environmental consequences. Powerful new machines allowed the reopening of old mines and the digging of new ones. Cities grew as poor peasants looking for work arrived from the countryside. In Rio de Janeiro and São Paulo (sow PAL-oh), the poor turned steep hillsides and vacant lands into immense *favelas* (feh-VEL-luhs) (slums) of makeshift shacks.

The countryside also was transformed. Scrubland was turned into pasture or planted in wheat, corn, and sugar cane. Even the Amazon rain forest—half of the land area of Brazil—was affected. In 1930 American industrialist Henry Ford invested $8 million to clear land along the Tapajós River and prepare it to become the site of the world's largest rubber plantation. Ford encountered opposition from Brazilian workers and politicians; the rubber trees proved vulnerable to diseases; and he had to abandon the project—but not before leaving 3 million acres (1.2 million hectares) denuded of trees.

Although Vargas instituted many reforms favorable to urban workers, he refused to take measures to help the millions of landless peasants or challenge the great landowners. Prohibited by his own constitution from being reelected in 1938, Vargas staged another coup, abolished the constitution, and instituted the

Getulio Vargas (1883–1954) Dictator of Brazil from 1930 to 1945 and from 1951 to 1954. Constitutionally barred from another term in 1938 and fearful of a military takeover, he suspended elections and created Estado Novo ("New State"), a dictatorship that emphasized industrialization and helped the urban poor but did little to alleviate the problems of the peasants.

import-substitution industrialization An economic system aimed at building a country's industry by restricting foreign trade. It was especially popular in Latin American countries such as Mexico, Argentina, and Brazil in the mid-twentieth century. It proved successful for a time but could not keep up with technological advances in Europe and North America.

Estado Novo (esh-TAH-doe NO-vo), or "New State," with himself as supreme leader. He abolished political parties, jailed opposition leaders, and turned Brazil into a fascist state, though one that contributed troops and ships to the Allied war effort once the Second World War broke out.

Argentina After 1930

Economically, the Depression hurt Argentina badly. Politically, however, the consequences were delayed. In 1930 General José Uriburu (hoe-SAY oo-ree-BOO-roo) overthrew the popularly elected President Irigoyen. For thirteen years the generals and the oligarchy ruled, doing nothing to lessen the poverty of the workers or the frustrations of the middle class. When World War II broke out, Argentina remained officially neutral.

In 1943 another military revolt flared, this one among junior officers led by Colonel **Juan Perón** (hoo-AHN pair-OWN) (1895–1974). The intentions of the rebels were clear:

> Civilians will never understand the greatness of our ideal; we shall therefore have to eliminate them from the government and give them the only mission which corresponds to them: work and obedience.[4]

Once in power the officers took over the highest positions in government and business and began to lavish money on military equipment and their own salaries. Their goal, inspired by Nazi victories, was nothing less than the conquest of South America.

As the war turned against the Nazis, the officers saw their popularity collapse. Perón, however, had other plans. Inspired by his charismatic wife **Eva Duarte Perón** (AY-vuy doo-AR-tay pair-OWN) (1919–1952), he appealed to the urban workers. Eva became the champion of the *descamisados* (des-cah-mee-SAH-dohs), or "shirtless ones," and campaigned tirelessly for social

[4]George Blankenstein, *Perón's Argentina* (Chicago: Unversity of Chicago Press, 1953), 37.

Bettmann/Corbis

Juan and Eva Perón Juan Perón's presidency of Argentina (1946–1955) relied on his, and especially on his wife Eva's, popularity with the working class. To sustain their popularity, they often organized parades and demonstrations in imitation of the fascist dictators of Europe. This picture shows them riding in a procession in Buenos Aires in 1952.

Juan Perón (1895–1974) President of Argentina (1946–1955, 1973–1974). As a military officer, he championed the rights of labor. Aided by his wife Eva Duarte Perón, he was elected president in 1946. He built up Argentinean industry, became very popular among the urban poor, but harmed the economy.

Eva Duarte Perón (1919–1952) Wife of Juan Perón and champion of the poor in Argentina. She was a gifted speaker and popular political leader who campaigned to improve the life of the urban poor by founding schools and hospitals and providing other social benefits.

SECTION REVIEW

- Wealthy elites dominated small middle classes and large working classes composed mainly of agricultural laborers.

- Mexico's Cárdenas and the PRM expanded party representation, implemented reforms, and nationalized foreign-owned oil companies.

- World War I prompted economic and political changes, especially in Argentina.

- The hardships of the Depression caused political instability from which emerged authoritarian regimes devoted to rapid industrialization.

benefits and for the cause of women and children. With his wife's help, Perón won the presidency in 1946 and created a populist dictatorship in imitation of the Vargas regime in Brazil.

Like Brazil and Mexico, Argentina industrialized rapidly under state sponsorship. Perón spent lavishly on social welfare projects as well as on the military, depleting the capital that Argentina had earned during the war. Though a skillful demagogue who played off the army against the navy and both against the labor unions, Perón could not create a stable government. When Eva died in 1952, he lost his political skills (or perhaps they were hers) and soon thereafter was overthrown in yet another military coup.

SUB-SAHARAN AFRICA, 1900–1945

■ *Why was Africa so little involved in the transformations of that era?*

When nationalist movements threatened European rule in Asia in the early twentieth century, Africa was still being subjected to the economic and political forces of imperialism, but it would be a mistake to conclude that developments in Africa would have resembled those in India or China if imperialism had started sooner. Affected by a long history of racism, Europeans maintained that people who were accustomed to bare subsistence would work fewer hours if their pay was raised rather than strive to better their standard of living (the way European workers theoretically would). This theory stigmatized African labor and justified paying subsistence wages.

Colonial Africa: Economic and Social Changes

Outside of Algeria, Kenya, and South Africa, few Europeans lived in Africa. In 1930 Nigeria, with a population of 20 million, was ruled by 386 British officials and by 8,000 policemen and military personnel, of whom 150 were European. Yet even such a small presence stimulated deep social and economic changes.

Since the turn of the century, the colonial powers had built railroads from coastal cities to mines and plantations in the interior to transport raw materials. But few Africans benefited from these changes. Colonial governments took lands from Africans and sold or leased them to European companies or to white settlers. Large European companies dominated wholesale commerce, while Indians, Greeks, and Syrians handled much of the retail trade.

Where land was divided into small farms, some Africans benefited from the boom. Farmers in the Gold Coast (now Ghana [GAH-nuh]) profited from the high price of cacao, as did palm-oil producers in Nigeria and coffee growers in East Africa. In most of Africa women played a major role in the retail trades, selling cloth, food, pots and pans, and other items in the markets. Many maintained their economic independence and kept their household finances separate from those of their husbands, following a custom that predated the colonial period.

For many Africans, however, economic development meant working in European-owned mines and plantations, often under compulsion. Colonial governments were eager to develop the resources of their territories but would not pay wages high enough to attract workers. Instead, they used their police powers to force Africans to work under harsh conditions for little or no pay. In the 1920s, when the government of French Equatorial Africa decided to build a railroad from Brazzaville to the Atlantic coast, a distance of 312 miles (502 kilometers), it drafted 127,000 men to carve a roadbed across mountains and through rain forests. Lacking adequate food, clothing, and medical care, 20,000 of them died, an average of 64 deaths per mile of track.

Making Palm Oil Oil palms produce two products, a red palm oil squeezed from the pulpy fruit and a yellow palm kernel oil extracted from the fruit's seeds with a simple press. Because it stands up well to heat, it is widely used as a cooking oil and is a major export crop in West Africa and other tropical regions.

Europeans prided themselves on bringing modern health care to Africa; yet before the 1930s there was too little of it to help the majority of Africans, and other aspects of colonialism actually worsened public health. Migrants and soldiers spread syphilis, gonorrhea, tuberculosis, and malaria. Sleeping sickness and smallpox epidemics raged throughout Central Africa. In recruiting men to work, colonial governments also depleted rural areas of farmers needed to plant and harvest crops. Forced requisitions of food to feed the workers left the remaining populations undernourished and vulnerable to diseases. Not until the 1930s did colonial governments realize the negative consequences of their labor policies and begin to invest in agricultural development and health care for Africans.

In 1900 Ibadan (ee-BAH-dahn) in Nigeria was the only city in sub-Saharan Africa with more than 100,000 inhabitants; fifty years later, dozens of cities had reached that size. Africans migrated to cities because they offered hope of jobs and excitement and, for a few, the chance to become wealthy.

However, migrations damaged family life, for almost all the migrants were men leaving women in the countryside to farm and raise children. Cities built during the colonial period had racially segregated housing, clubs, restaurants, hospitals, and other institutions. Racial discrimination was most rigid in the white-settler colonies of eastern and southern Africa.

Religious and Political Changes

Traditional religious belief could not explain the dislocations that foreign rule, migrations, and sudden economic changes brought to the lives of Africans. Many therefore turned to Christianity or Islam for guidance.

Christianity, introduced into Africa by Western missionaries (except in Ethiopia, where it was indigenous), was most successful in West and South Africa, where the European influence was strongest. Mission schools, which taught both craft skills and basic literacy, provided access to employment as minor functionaries, teachers, and shopkeepers. These schools

A Quranic School In Muslim countries, religious education is centered on learning to read, write, and recite the Quran, the sacred book of the Islamic religion, in the original Arabic. This picture shows boys in a Libyan madrasa (Quranic school) studying writing and religion.

also imparted Western political ideas to a new educated elite. Many Africans read the suffering of their own peoples into the biblical stories of Moses and the parables of Jesus. The churches trained some pupils to become catechists, teachers, and clergymen. Independent Christian churches associated Christian beliefs with radical ideas of racial equality and political participation.

Islam spread inland from the East African coast and southward from the Sahel (SAH-hel) through the influence and example of Arab and African merchants. Islam also emphasized literacy—in Arabic rather than a European language—and was less disruptive of traditional African customs such as polygamy.

In a few places, such as Dakar in Senegal and Cape Town in South Africa, small numbers of Africans could obtain secondary education. Even smaller numbers went on to college in Europe or America. Though few in number, they became the leaders of political movements. The contrast between the liberal ideas imparted by Western education and the

realities of racial discrimination under colonial rule contributed to the rise of nationalism among educated Africans. In Senegal **Blaise Diagne** (dee-AHN-yuh) agitated for African participation in politics and fair treatment in the French army. In the 1920s J. E. Casely Hayford began organizing a movement for greater autonomy in British West Africa. In South Africa, Western-educated lawyers and journalists founded the **African National Congress** in 1912 to

Blaise Diagne (1872–1934)   Senegalese political leader. He was the first African elected to the French National Assembly. During World War I, in exchange for promises to give French citizenship to Senegalese, he helped recruit Africans to serve in the French army. After the war, he led a movement to abolish forced labor in Africa.

African National Congress   An organization dedicated to obtaining equal voting and civil rights for black inhabitants of South Africa. Founded in 1912 as the South African Native National Congress, it changed its name in 1923. Though it was banned and its leaders were jailed for many years, it eventually helped bring majority rule to South Africa.

defend the interests of Africans. These nationalist movements were partly inspired by the ideas of Pan-Africanists from America such as W. E. B. Du Bois and Marcus Garvey, who advocated the unity of African peoples around the world. Before World War II, however, they were small and had little influence.

The new media of cinema and radio had little impact on Africa. The first attempts at radio broadcasting occurred in South Africa in 1924, and down to World War II, the South African Broadcasting Corporation established a monopoly over the medium and broadcast only in English and Afrikaans. Efforts in other colonies likewise targeted European listeners, with the exception of British West Africa—Sierra Leone, Ghana, and Nigeria—where African languages were utilized. After 1936 the British authorities began to see radio as a medium for reaching Africans who did not understand English. Africa also had almost no cinematic presence prior to World War II, apart from fourteen Tarzan films made in Hollywood between 1918 and 1949. A few films were made for British and Afrikaner audiences in South Africa, but the French issued a decree in 1934 prohibiting the shooting of movies.

During the Second World War (see Chapter 27) increased forced labor, inflation, and requisitions of raw materials had a profound effect even on Africans who were far removed from the theaters of war. Yet the war also brought hope. During the campaign to oust the Italians from Ethiopia, Emperor **Haile Selassie** (HI-lee seh-LASS-ee) (r. 1930–1974) led his own troops into Addis Ababa, his capital, and reclaimed his title. A million Africans served as soldiers and carriers in Burma, North Africa, and Europe. They listened to Allied propaganda in favor of European liberation movements and against Nazi racism and returned to their countries with new and radical ideas.

CONCLUSION

The narratives of world war, global depression, and varying regional development do not incorporate the profound change in ways of living that affected most parts of the world, to a greater or lesser degree, between 1900 and 1950. Europe's colonies, and the nonindustrialized world in general, witnessed increases in political awareness and contact with the world at large that stemmed in large part from the adoption of new technologies like electricity and airplanes, but also from media technologies. The latter incorporated themes and images from local cultural sources and helped mold national consciousness.

The industrialized world experienced the same flood of new inventions but was more strongly affected at a popular level. Respect for science grew along with an expectation that science would continue indefinitely to improve human lives. This was the cult of the modern. Social science and a concern for social welfare, health, and the rights of women were part of this trend.

Imperialism being focused as always on benefits for the home country, colonial administrators in different parts of the world tried to control the flow of global technological and ideological changes. Having a larger and better-educated middle class than many other non-European lands, India entered more fully into the new ways of living than did sub-Saharan Africa. Political and cultural independence became a realizable goal in the former, where Mahatma Gandhi's nonviolent movement pioneered an entirely new form of political activism. In the latter region, however, European racism and the unwavering favoritism shown to European settlers stifled almost all attempts at change. In Latin America, economic imperialism similarly guaranteed that most benefits of the new revolutions in living would go to the wealthiest people.

Haile Selassie (1892–1975) Emperor of Ethiopia (r. 1930–1974) and symbol of African independence. He fought the Italian invasion of his country in 1935 and regained his throne during World War II, when British forces expelled the Italians. He ruled Ethiopia as a traditional autocracy until he was overthrown in 1974.

CHAPTER REVIEW

NEW TECHNOLOGY OUTSIDE THE INDUSTRIALIZED WORLD

■ *How were Asians and Africans impacted by technology and innovation differently from Europeans and Americans?* (page 607)

Outside the United States and Europe, innovations were adapted to local cultural conditions. India and Japan, for example, spawned their own film industries that reflected their own aesthetic traditions, while newsreels and photography were used to inform illiterate populations. These new media helped create a culturally cohesive identity. The rickshaw contributed to urbanization from Asia to Africa. These technologies were able to thrive locally because they were less expensive than technologies like railroads and steelmills.

NEW WAYS OF LIVING IN THE INDUSTRIALIZED WORLD

■ *How did daily life and thought change in early-twentieth-century industrialized countries?* (page 609)

Many women who had participated in the war effort remained in the workforce and demanded voting and other rights. Governments took on new responsibilities for education, public health, and social welfare. Automobiles, movies, and radio broadcasts were eagerly adopted. Advances in the sciences, especially in physics and psychology, undermined the old cultural certainties, while birth control and family planning provoked considerable opposition from traditionalists.

A NEW INDIA, 1905–1947

■ *Why did the educated elites of India want independence? What were ordinary Indians hoping for?* (page 614)

In the late nineteenth century, educated Indians began to resent the racist condescension with which they were treated by their colonial overlords. They believed that they could govern India and develop its economy better than the British could. Mahatma Gandhi's leadership of a powerful but non-violent independence movement galvanized both Hindus and Muslims. However, as British withdrawal neared, other political leaders played on religious identity and brought about a partition of the country.

MEXICO, ARGENTINA, AND BRAZIL, 1917–1949

■ *How did the most powerful Latin American economies and political cultures change in the aftermath of World War I?* (page 620)

Three countries, Mexico, Brazil, and Argentina, contained well over half of Latin America's land, population, and wealth. Their societies remained deeply split between wealthy landowners and desperately poor peasants even after independence, and their economies remained dependent on foreign investment and the exchange of raw materials and agricultural products for foreign manufactured goods. World War I disrupted this trade, weakening the landowning classes, and workers and the middle class demanded reforms. However, the Depression, more than the war, brought about the most dramatic changes in Latin America. Dependence on foreign investment had made economic growth difficult to achieve, and democracy was fragile. Authoritarian leaders emerged who attempted to make Latin American countries more independent and to industrialize Latin American economies.

SUB-SAHARAN AFRICA, 1900–1945

■ *Why was Africa so little involved in the transformations of that era?* (page 624)

Sub-Saharan Africa was still under colonial rule when the Northern Hemisphere was engulfed in the First and Second World Wars. Colonial powers built cities, railroads, harbors, mines, and plantations. But the new media was monopolized by Europeans or white settlers or prohibited altogether, while Africans were forced to provide labor at subsistence wages that kept workers from accruing the benefits of industrialization. Many turned to Christianity or Islam for spiritual guidance during these upheavals.

Key Terms

Auguste (1862–1954) and Louis (1864–1948) Lumière (p. 608)

Margaret Sanger (p. 610)

Max Plank (p. 610)

Albert Einstein (p. 610)

Sigmund Freud (p. 610)

Wilbur and Orville Wright (p. 611)

KLM Royal Dutch Airlines (p. 611)

Marie Curie (p. 613)

Le Corbusier (p. 613)

Indian National Conference (p. 616)

Bengal (p. 616)

All-India Muslim League (p. 616)

Mohandas K. Gandhi (p. 617)

Jawaharlal Nehru (p. 618)

Muhammad Ali Jinnah (p. 619)

Lázaro Cárdenas (p. 620)

Hipólito Irigoyen (p. 621)

Getulio Vargas (p. 622)

import-substitution industrialization (p. 622)

Juan Perón (p. 623)

Eva Duarte Perón (p. 623)

Blaise Diagne (p. 626)

African National Congress (p. 626)

Haile Selassie (p. 627)

The Collapse of the Old Order

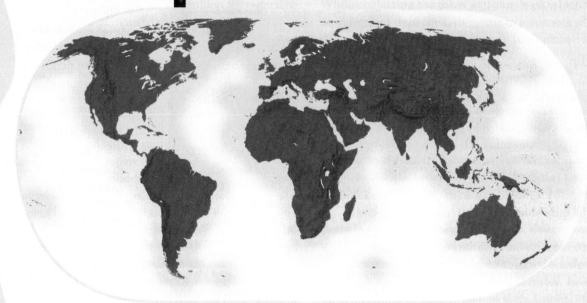

© Cengage Learning

CHAPTER PREVIEW

THE STALIN REVOLUTION
■ *How did the Soviet Union change under Stalin?*

THE DEPRESSION
■ *What caused the Depression, and what effects did it have on the world?*

THE RISE OF FASCISM
■ *How did fascism in Italy and Germany lead to the Second World War?*

EAST ASIA, 1931–1945
■ *Why did Japan invade Manchuria?*

THE SECOND WORLD WAR
■ *How was the war fought, and why did Japan and Germany lose?*

THE CHARACTER OF WARFARE
■ *How did science and technology change the nature of warfare?*

Conclusion

DIVERSITY & DOMINANCE: Women, Family Values, and the Russian Revolution

they could no longer prevent their Asian and African subjects from demanding independence.

THE STALIN REVOLUTION

■ *How did the Soviet Union change under Stalin?*

After **Joseph Stalin** (1879–1953) achieved total mastery over the USSR in 1929 (see Chapter 25), he led it through an economic and social transformation that turned it into a great industrial and military power and intensified both admiration for and fear of communism throughout the world.

Five-Year Plans

Stalin's ambition to turn the USSR into an industrial nation was not intended initially to produce consumer goods for a mass market or enrich individuals. Instead, his aim was to increase the power of the Communist Party domestically and that of the Soviet Union in relation to other countries. By building up Russia's industry, Stalin was determined to prevent a repetition of the humiliating defeat Russia had suffered at the hands of Germany in 1917.

Stalin encouraged rapid industrialization through a series of **Five-Year Plans**, a system of centralized control copied from the German experience or World War 1. The goal of the first Five-Year Plan was to quintuple the output of electricity and double that of heavy industry: iron, steel, coal, and machinery. Beginning in October 1928, the Communist government created whole industries and cities from scratch, then trained millions of peasants to work in the new factories, mines, and offices. In every way except actual fighting, Stalin's Russia resembled a nation at war.

Rapid industrialization hastened environmental changes. Hydroelectric dams turned rivers into

B efore the First World War the Italian poet Filippo Marinetti exalted violence as noble and manly: "We want to glorify war, the world's only hygiene—militarism, deed, destroyer of anarchisms, the beautiful ideas that are death-bringing, and the subordination of women."[1] His friend Gabriele d'Annunzio added: "If it is a crime to incite citizens to violence, I shall boast of this crime."[2] Poets are sometimes more prescient than they imagine.

Most survivors of World War I had learned to abhor violence, and after the trauma of World War I, the world seemed to return to what U.S. president Warren Harding called "normalcy": prosperity in Europe and America, European colonialism in Asia and Africa, U.S. domination of Latin America, and peace almost everywhere. But in 1929 normalcy vanished. The Great Depression spread around the world, and for a few, war and domination became a creed, a goal, and a solution to their problems. Governments turned against one another in desperate attempts to protect their people's livelihood.

The Japanese military tried to save their country from the Depression by conquering China, which erupted in revolution. In Germany many blamed their troubles on communists and Jews and turned to the Nazis, who promised to save German society by crushing others. In the Soviet Union, Stalin used energetic and murderous means to force his country into a communist version of the Industrial Revolution.

As the old order collapsed, the world was engulfed by a second Great War, one far more global and destructive than World War I. In World War II, entire countries were conquered in a matter of weeks, fighter planes and bombers targeted civilians, and, finally, atomic bombs obliterated entire cities.

At the end of World War II much of Europe and East Asia lay in ruins, and millions of destitute refugees sought safety in other lands. The European colonial powers were either defeated or so weakened that

[1]Apollonio Umbro, ed., *Documents of Twentieth Century Art: Futurist Manifestos* (New York: Viking Press, 1973), 23.
[2]Richard F. Hamilton and Holger H. Herwig, *Decisions for War, 1914–1917* (Cambridge: Cambridge University Press, 2004), 199.

Joseph Stalin (1879–1953) Bolshevik revolutionary, head of the Soviet Communist Party after 1924, and dictator of the Soviet Union from 1928 to 1953. He led the Soviet Union with an iron fist, using Five-Year Plans to increase industrial production and terror to crush all opposition.

Five-Year Plans Plans that Joseph Stalin introduced to industrialize the Soviet Union rapidly, beginning in 1928. They set goals for the output of steel, electricity, machinery, and most other products and were enforced by the police powers of the state. They succeeded in making the Soviet Union a major industrial power before World War II.

strings of reservoirs. Roads, canals, and railroad tracks cut the landscape. Forests and grassland were turned into farmland. From an environmental perspective, the Five-Year Plans resembled the transformation that had occurred in the United States and Canada a few decades earlier.

Collectivization of Agriculture

Since the Soviet Union was still a predominantly agrarian country, the only way to pay for these massive investments, provide the labor, and feed the millions of new industrial workers was to squeeze the peasantry. Stalin therefore proceeded with the most radical social experiment conceived up to that time: the collectivization of agriculture.

Collectivization meant consolidating small private farms into vast collectives and making the farmers work together in commonly owned fields. Each collective was expected to supply the government with a fixed amount of food and distribute what was left among its members. Collectives were to become outdoor factories through the techniques of mass production and the use of machinery. Collectivization was expected to bring the peasants once and for all under government control so they never again could withhold food supplies, as they had done during the period of Lenin's New Economic Policy (see Chapter 25).

The government mounted a massive propaganda campaign to enlist the farmers' support. At first all seemed to go well, but soon *kulaks* (COO-lock) ("fists"), the better-off peasants, began to resist giving up all their property. When soldiers came to force them into collectives at gunpoint, they burned their crops, smashed their equipment, and slaughtered their livestock. Within a few months they slaughtered half of the Soviet Union's horses and cattle and two-thirds of the sheep and goats. In retaliation, Stalin ruthlessly ordered the "liquidation of kulaks as a class" and incited the poor peasants to attack their wealthier neighbors. Over 8 million kulaks were arrested. Many were executed, and the rest were sent to slave labor camps, where most starved to death.

The peasants who were left had been the least successful before collectivization and proved to be the least competent after. Many were sent to work in factories. The rest were forbidden to leave their

Poster concerning the 1st 5 Year Plan with a photograph of Joseph Stalin 1879-1953), 'At the end of the Plan, the basis of collectivization must be completed', 1932 (colour litho), Klutchis (fl.1932)/Deutsches Plakat Museum, Essen, Germany/Archives Charmet/The Bridgeman Art Library

The Collectivization of Soviet Agriculture One of the goals of collectivization was to introduce modern farm machinery. This poster highlights Josef Stalin's personal connection with mechanization. The tractors and operators were assigned to tractor stations, which then supplied them to individual collective farms.

farms. With half of their draft animals gone, they could not plant or harvest enough to meet the swelling demands of the cities. Yet government agents took whatever they could find, leaving little or nothing for the farmers themselves. After bad harvests in 1933 and 1934, a famine swept through the countryside, killing some 5 million people, about one in every twenty farmers.

Stalin's second Five-Year Plan, designed to run from 1933 to 1937, was originally intended to produce consumer goods. But when the Nazis took over Germany in 1933 (discussed later in this chapter), Stalin changed the plan to emphasize heavy industries that could produce armaments. Between 1927 and 1937, the Soviet output of metals and machines increased fourteen-fold while consumer goods became scarce and food was rationed. After a decade of Stalinism, the Soviet people were more poorly clothed, fed, and

Chronology

	United States, Europe, and North Africa	Asia and the Pacific
1920	**1928** Stalin introduces Five-Year Plans and the collectivization of agriculture **1929** Great Depression begins in United States	
1930	**1931** Great Depression reaches Europe **1933** Hitler comes to power in Germany	**1931** Japanese forces occupy Manchuria **1934–1935** Mao leads communists on Long March
1935		**1937** Japanese troops invade China, conquer coastal provinces; Chiang Kai-shek flees to Sichuan **1937–1938** Japanese troops take Nanjing
	1939 (Sept. 1) German forces invade Poland	
1940	**1940** (March–April) German forces conquer Denmark, Norway, the Netherlands, and Belgium **1940** (May–June) German forces conquer France **1940** (June–Sept.) Battle of Britain **1941** (June 21) German forces invade USSR	**1941** (Dec. 7) Japanese aircraft bomb Pearl Harbor **1942** (Jan.–March) Japanese conquer Thailand, Philippines, Malaya **1942** (June) U.S. Navy defeats Japan at Battle of Midway
	1942–1943 Allies and Germany battle for control of North Africa **1943** Soviet victory in Battle of Stalingrad **1943–1944** Red Army slowly pushes Wehrmacht back to Germany **1944** (June 6) D-day: U.S., British, and Canadian troops land in Normandy	
1945	**1945** (May 7) Germany surrenders	**1945** (Aug. 6) United States drops atomic bomb on Hiroshima **1945** (Aug. 14) Japan surrenders **1945–1949** Civil war in China **1949** (Oct. 1) Communists defeat Guomindang; Mao proclaims People's Republic of China

housed than they had been before Lenin's New Economic Policy.

Terror and Opportunities

The 1930s brought both terror and opportunities to the Soviet people. The forced pace of industrialization, the collectivization of agriculture, and the uprooting of millions of people could be accomplished only under duress. To prevent any possible resistance or rebellion, Stalin's secret police force created a climate of suspicion and fear.

First "Old Bolsheviks" and high officials were put on trial; then the terror spread steadily downward. The government regularly made demands that people could not meet, so everyone was guilty of breaking some regulation. People from all walks of life were arrested, some on mere suspicion or because of a false accusation by a jealous coworker or neighbor, some for expressing a doubt or working too hard or not hard enough, some for being related to someone previously arrested, some for no reason at all. Millions of people were sentenced without trials. At the height of the terror, some 8 million were sent to *gulags* (GOO-log) (labor camps), where perhaps a million died each year of exposure or malnutrition. To its victims the terror seemed capricious and random.

Yet Stalin's regime received the support of many Soviet citizens. Suddenly, with so many people gone and new industries and cities being built everywhere, there were opportunities for those who remained, especially the poor and the young. Women entered careers and jobs previously closed to them, becoming steelworkers, physicians, and office managers; but they retained their household and child-rearing duties, receiving little help from men (see Diversity and Dominance: Women, Family Values, and the Russian Revolution). People who moved to the cities, worked enthusiastically, and asked no questions could hope to rise into the upper ranks of the Communist Party, the military, the government, or the professions—where the privileges and rewards were many.

Stalin's brutal methods helped the Soviet Union industrialize faster than any country had ever done. By the late 1930s the USSR was the world's third largest industrial power, after the United States and Germany. To foreign observers it seemed to be booming with construction projects and labor shortages. Even anti-Communist observers admitted that government planning worked. To millions of Soviet citizens who took pride in the new strength of their country, and to many foreigners who contrasted conditions in the Soviet Union with the unemployment and despair in the West, Stalin's achievement seemed worth any price.

THE DEPRESSION

■ *What caused the Depression, and what effects did it have on the world?*

On October 24, 1929—"Black Thursday"—the New York stock market went into a dive. Within days stocks had lost half their value. Their value continued to fall for three years. Thousands of banks and businesses collapsed. Millions of workers lost their jobs. The stock market crash started the deepest and most widespread depression in history.

Economic Crisis As consumers reduced their purchases, businesses cut production, laying off thousands of workers. Female employees were the first laid off on the grounds that men had to support families while women worked only for "pin money." Jobless men deserted their families. Small farmers went bankrupt and lost their land. By mid-1932 the American economy had shrunk by half, and 25 percent of the workforce was unemployed. Many observers thought that free-enterprise capitalism was doomed.

In 1930 the U.S. government, hoping to protect American industries from foreign competition, imposed the highest import duty in American history. In retaliation, other countries also raised their tariffs. As a result, global industrial production declined by 36 percent between 1929 and 1932, while world trade dropped by a breathtaking 62 percent.

Depression in Industrial Nations This massive economic upheaval had profound political repercussions. In the United States, Franklin D. Roosevelt was elected president in 1932 on a "New Deal" platform of government programs to stimulate and revitalize the economy. British and French governments also intervened in their economies, and they remained democratic. In Germany and Japan, as economic grievances worsened long-festering political resentments, radical leaders came to power and turned their nations into military machines, hoping to acquire, by war if necessary, empires large enough to support self-sufficient economies.

Depression in Nonindustrial Regions The Depression affected Asia, Africa, and Latin America, but very unevenly. Because a wall of new import duties protected India's infant industries from foreign competition, living standards stagnated but did not drop. The Depression added little to China's problems, which were more political than economic.

However, countries that depended on exports were hard hit by the Depression. When automobile production dropped by half in the United States and Europe, so did imports of rubber, devastating the economies of Southeast Asia. Egypt, dependent on cotton exports, was also affected, and in the resulting political strife, the government became autocratic and unpopular. The industrialization of Argentina and Brazil was set back a decade or more by the loss of export markets, and in response, military officers seized power in several Latin American countries, consciously imitating dictatorships emerging in Europe (see Chapter 26).

Southern and Central Africa recovered from the Depression quickly because falling prices made their gold and other minerals more valuable. But this mining boom benefited only a small number of mine owners and investors. For Africans, it was a mixed blessing, for mining provided men with jobs and cash wages, while women stayed behind in the villages to manage without their husbands' help.

SECTION REVIEW

- The New York stock market crash of 1929 caused business and bank failures and massive unemployment.
- The Depression soon spread to all industrial nations, especially Germany and Japan.
- Nonindustrial countries, especially those that depended on exports to industrial countries, were also hard hit; only southern and central Africa were spared.
- In the face of this threat, some countries turned to dictatorship to save their economies.

THE RISE OF FASCISM

■ *How did fascism in Italy and Germany lead to the Second World War?*

The Russian Revolution and its Stalinist aftermath frightened property owners in Europe and North America. In western Europe and North America, middle- and upper-income voters took refuge in conservative politics. In southern and central Europe,

Two Views of the American Way In this classic photograph, *Life* magazine photographer Margaret Bourke-White captured the contrast between advertisers' view of the ideal American family and the reality of bread lines for the poor.

Women, Family Values, and the Russian Revolution

The Bolsheviks were of two minds on the subject of women. They were opposed to bourgeois morality and to the oppression of women, especially working-class women, under capitalism. But what to put in its place?

Alexandra Kollontai was the most outspoken of the Bolsheviks on the subject of women's rights. She advocated the liberation of women, the replacement of housework by communal kitchens and laundries, and divorce on demand. Under socialism, love, sex, and marriage would be entirely equal, reciprocal, and free of economic obligations. Childbearing would be encouraged, but children would be raised communally: "The worker mother . . . must remember that there are henceforth only our children, those of the communist state, the common possession of all workers."

In a lecture she gave at Sverdlov University in 1921, Kollontai declared:

. . . it is important to preserve not only the interests of the woman but also the life of the child, and this is to be done by giving the woman the opportunity to combine labour and maternity. Soviet power tries to create a situation where a woman does not have to cling to a man she has learned to loathe only because she has nowhere else to go with her children, and where a woman alone does not have to fear for her life and the life of her child. In the labour republic it is not the philanthropists with their humiliating charity but the workers and peasants, fellow-creators of the new society, who hasten to help the working woman and strive to lighten the burden of motherhood. . . . I would like to say a few words about a question which is closely connected with the problem of maternity—the question of abortion, and Soviet Russia's attitude toward it. On 20 November 1920 the labour republic issued a law abolishing the penalties that had been attached to abortion. What is the reason behind this new attitude? Russia after all suffers not from an overproduction of living labour but rather from a lack of it. Russia is thinly, not densely populated. Every unit of labour power is precious. Why then have we declared abortion to be no longer a criminal offence? . . .

Abortion exists and flourishes everywhere, and no laws or punitive measures have succeeded in rooting it out. A way round the law is always found. But "secret help" only cripples women; they become a burden on the labour government, and the size of the labour force is reduced. Abortion, when carried out under proper medical conditions, is less harmful and dangerous, and the woman can get back to work quicker. Soviet power realizes that the need for abortion will only disappear on the one hand when Russia has a broad and developed network of institutions protecting motherhood and providing social education, and on the other hand when women understand that *childbirth is a social obligation*; Soviet power has therefore allowed abortion to be performed openly and in clinical conditions.

Besides the large-scale development of motherhood protection, the task of labour Russia is to strengthen in women the healthy instinct of motherhood, to make motherhood and labour for the collective compatible and thus do away with the need for abortion. This is the approach of the labour republic to the question of abortion, which still faces women in the bourgeois countries in all its magnitude. In these countries women are exhausted by the dual burden of hired labour for capital and motherhood. In Soviet Russia the working woman and peasant woman are helping the Communist Party to build a new society and to undermine the old way of life that has enslaved women. As soon as woman is viewed as being essentially a labour unit, the key to the solution of the complex question ➤

➤ of maternity can be found. . . . The emancipation of women can only be completed when a fundamental transformation of living is effected; and life-styles will change only with the fundamental transformation of all production and the establishment of a communist economy. The revolution in everyday life is unfolding before our very eyes, and in this process the liberation of women is being introduced in practice.

Fifteen years later Joseph Stalin reversed the Soviet policy on abortion.

The published draft of the law prohibiting abortion and providing material assistance to mothers has provoked a lively reaction throughout the country. It is being heatedly discussed by tens of millions of people and there is no doubt that it will serve as a further strengthening of the Soviet family. . . .

When we speak of strengthening the Soviet family, we are speaking precisely of the struggle against the survivals of a bourgeois attitude towards marriage, women, and children. So-called "free love" and all disorderly sex life are bourgeois through and through, and have nothing to do with either socialist principles or the ethics and standards of conduct of the Soviet citizens. Socialist doctrine shows this, and it is proved by life itself.

The elite of our country, the best of the Soviet youth, are as a rule also excellent family men who dearly love their children. And vice versa: the man who does not take marriage seriously, and abandons his children to the whims of fate, is usually also a bad worker and a poor member of society. . . .

It is impossible even to compare the present state of the family with that which obtained before the Soviet regime—so great has been the improvement towards greater stability and, above all, greater humanity and goodness. The single fact that millions of women have become economically independent and are no longer at the mercy of men's whims, speaks volumes. Compare, for instance, the modern woman collective farmer who sometimes earns more than her husband, with the pre-revolutionary peasant woman who completely depended on her husband and was a slave in the household. Has not this fundamentally changed family relations, has it not rationalized and strengthened the family? The very motives for setting up a family, for getting married, have changed for the better, have been cleansed of atavistic and barbaric elements. Marriage has ceased to be a matter of sell-and-buy. Nowadays a girl from a collective farm is not given away (or should we say "sold away"?) by her father, for now she is her own mistress, and no one can give her away. She will marry the man she loves. . . .

We alone have all the conditions under which a working woman can fulfill her duties as a citizen and as a mother responsible for the birth and early upbringing of her children.

A woman without children merits our pity, for she does not know the full joy of life. Our Soviet women, full-blooded citizens of the freest country in the world, have been given the bliss of motherhood. We must safeguard the family and raise and rear healthy Soviet heroes!

QUESTIONS FOR ANALYSIS

1. How does Kollontai expect women to be both workers and mothers without depending on a man? How would Soviet society make this possible?
2. Why does Alexandra Kollontai advocate the legalization of abortion in Soviet Russia? Does she view abortion as a permanent right or as a temporary necessity?
3. Why does Stalin characterize a "lighthearted, negligent attitude toward marriage" and "all disorderly sex life" as "bourgeois through and through"?
4. How does Stalin's image of the Soviet family differ from Kollontai's? Are his views a variation of her views, or the opposite?

Sources: First selection from Alexandra Kollontai, "The Labour of Women in the Revolution of the Economy," in *Selected Writings of Alexandra Kollontai*, translated by Alix Holt (Lawrence Hill & Company, 1978), pp. 148–149. Second selection from *Discussion of the Law on Abolition of Legal Abortion*, Pravda, Editorials of May 28 and June 9, 1936. English translation in Rudolf Schlesinger, ed., *Changing Attitudes in Soviet Russia: The Family in the USSR*, London, Routledge & Kegan Paul, 1949, pp. 251–54, 268–69.

the war had turned people's hopes of victory to bitter disappointment. Radical politicians quickly became adept at appealing to people's fears. They promised to bring back full employment, stop the spread of communism, and achieve the territorial conquests that World War I had denied them.

Mussolini's Italy

The first country to seek radical answers was Italy. World War I, which had never been popular, left thousands of veterans who found neither pride in their victory nor jobs in the postwar economy. Unemployed veterans and violent youths banded together into *fasci di combattimento* (fighting units) to demand action and intimidate politicians. When workers threatened to strike, factory and property owners hired gangs of these *fascisti* to defend them.

Benito Mussolini (1883–1945), a spellbinding orator, quickly became the leader of the **Fascist Party**, which glorified warfare and the Italian nation. By 1921 the party had 300,000 members, many of whom used violent methods to repress strikes, intimidate voters, and seize municipal governments. A year later Mussolini threatened to march on Rome if he was not appointed prime minister. The government gave in.

Mussolini then proceeded to install Fascist Party members in all government jobs, crush all opposition parties, and jail anyone who criticized him. The party took over the press, public education, and youth activities and gave employers control over their workers. The Fascists lowered living standards but reduced unemployment and provided social security and public services. They proved to be neither ruthless radicals nor competent administrators.

What Mussolini and the Fascist movement really excelled at was bombastic speeches, spectacular parades, and signs everywhere proclaiming "Il Duce (eel DOO-chay) [the Leader] is always right!" Mussolini's genius was to apply the techniques of modern mass communications and advertisement to political life. Billboards, movie footage, and radio news bulletins galvanized the masses in ways never before done in peacetime. His techniques of whipping up public enthusiasm were not lost on other radicals. By the 1930s fascist movements had appeared in most European countries, as well as in Latin America, China, and Japan.

Hitler's Germany

Like Mussolini, **Adolf Hitler** (1889–1945) had served in World War I and looked back fondly on the clear lines of authority and the camaraderie he had experienced in battle. After the war, he used his gifts as orator to appeal to Germans disappointed at their country's humiliation and formed the National Socialist German Workers' Party—**Nazis** for short. While serving a brief jail sentence he wrote *Mein Kampf* (mine kompf) (*My Struggle*), in which he outlined his goals and beliefs, but when it was published in 1925, almost no one took seriously its intense hatred for Jews, on whom he blamed every disaster that had befallen Germany, or its ideas of a "master race" of Aryans (he meant Germans, Scandinavians, and Britons), a degenerate "Alpine" race of French and Italians, and an inferior race of Russian and eastern European Slavs, fit only to be slaves of the master race. He glorified violence, which would enable the "master race" to defeat and subjugate all others.

But when the Depression hit, the Nazis gained supporters among the unemployed, who believed Nazi promises of jobs for all, and among property owners frightened by the growing popularity of communists. In March 1933, as leader of the largest party in Germany, Hitler became chancellor.

Once in office, he quickly assumed dictatorial power, just as Mussolini had done. He put Nazis in charge of all government agencies, educational

Benito Mussolini (1883–1945)   Fascist dictator of Italy (1922–1943). He led Italy to conquer Ethiopia (1935), joined Germany in the Axis pact (1936), and allied Italy with Germany in World War II. He was overthrown in 1943 when the Allies invaded Italy.

Fascist Party   Italian political party created by Benito Mussolini during World War I. It emphasized aggressive nationalism and was Mussolini's instrument for the creation of a dictatorship in Italy from 1922 to 1943.

Adolf Hitler (1889–1945)   Born in Austria, Hitler became a radical German nationalist during World War I. He led the National Socialist German Workers' Party—the Nazis—in the 1920s and became dictator of Germany in 1933. He led Europe into World War II.

Nazis   German political party led by Adolf Hitler, emphasizing nationalism, racism, and war. When Hitler became chancellor of Germany in 1933, the Nazis became the only legal party and an instrument of Hitler's absolute rule. The party's formal name was National Socialist German Workers' Party.

A Nazi Rally Hitler organized mass rallies at Nuremberg to whip up popular support for his regime and to indoctrinate young Germans with a martial spirit. Thousands of men in uniform marched in torch-lit parades before Hitler and his top officials.

institutions, and professional organizations; banned all other political parties; and threw their leaders into concentration camps. The Nazis deprived Jews of their citizenship and civil rights, prohibited them from marrying "Aryans," ousted them from the professions, and confiscated their property. In August 1934 Hitler proclaimed himself *Führer* (FEW-rer) ("leader") and called Germany the "Third Reich," the third German empire after the Holy Roman Empire of medieval times and the German Empire of 1871 to 1918.

The Nazis' economic and social policies were spectacularly effective. The government undertook massive public works projects and gave contracts to businesses to manufacture weapons. Women who had entered the workforce during and after World War I were urged to concentrate on *"Kinder, Kirche, Kuche"* (children, church, kitchen), releasing jobs for men. By 1936, business was booming, unemployment was at its lowest level since the 1920s, and living standards were rising. Hitler's popularity soared because most Germans believed their economic well-being outweighed the loss of liberty.

The Road to War, 1933–1939

What Hitler really wanted was not prosperity or popularity, but conquest. As soon as he came to office, he began to build up the armed forces. Meanwhile, he tested the reactions of the other powers through a series of surprise moves followed by protestations of peaceful intent.

In 1933, when Hitler withdrew Germany from the League of Nations, France and Britain hesitated to retaliate by blockading or invading Germany. Two years later, he announced that Germany was going to introduce conscription, build up its army, and create an air force—in violation of the Versailles treaty. Instead of protesting, Britain signed a naval agreement with Germany. The message was clear: neither

Britain nor France was willing to risk war by standing up to Germany. The United States, absorbed in its own domestic economic problems, had reverted to isolationism.

By 1938 Hitler decided that his rearmament plans were far enough advanced that he could afford to escalate his demands. In March, Germany invaded Austria, without protest from its German-speaking citizens. Then came Czechoslovakia. Hitler first demanded autonomy for its German-speaking borderlands, then their annexation to Germany. At the Munich Conference of September 1938, the leaders of France, Britain, and Italy gave him everything he wanted to keep him from starting a war. Hitler learned that aggression paid off.

The democracies' policy of "appeasement" ran counter to the European balance-of-power tradition for three reasons. The first was the deep-seated fear of war among people who had lived through World War I. The second was fear of communism. The conservative politicians who ruled France and Britain were more afraid of Stalin than of Hitler, for Hitler claimed to respect Christianity and private property. The third cause was the very novelty of fascist tactics. Britain's prime minister, Neville Chamberlain, assumed that political leaders (other than the Bolsheviks) were honorable men and that an agreement was as valid as a business contract. Thus, when Hitler promised "no further territorial demands," Chamberlain believed him.

After Munich, it was too late to stop Hitler, short of war. Germany and Italy were now united in an alliance

called the Axis. In March 1939, Germany invaded what was left of Czechoslovakia. Belatedly realizing that Hitler could not be trusted, France and Britain sought Soviet help. Stalin, however, distrusted the "capitalists" as much as they distrusted him. When Hitler offered to divide Poland between Germany and the Soviet Union, Stalin accepted. The Nazi-Soviet Pact of August 23, 1939, freed Hitler from the fear of a two-front war and gave Stalin time to build up his armies. One week later, on September 1, German forces swept into Poland, and the war was on.

EAST ASIA, 1931–1945

■ *Why did Japan invade Manchuria?*

When the Depression ruined Japan's export trade, especially in silk and rice, ultranationalists, including young army officers, resented their country's dependence on foreign trade and what they believed was unnecessary party politics that sullied the righteousness of the divine imperial will. If only Japan had a colonial empire, they thought, it would not be beholden to the rest of the world. But Europeans and Americans had already taken most potential colonies in Asia. Japanese nationalists saw the conquest of China, with its vast population and resources, as the solution to their country's problems.

Meanwhile, in China the Guomindang (see Chapter 25) was becoming stronger and preparing to challenge the Japanese presence in Manchuria, a province rich in coal and iron ore. Junior officers in the Japanese army, frustrated by the caution of their superiors, took action. In September 1931 they blew apart railroad track as a pretext for invading Manchuria (*Manchukuo*) (man-CHEW-coo-oh) and recognizing its "independence," while in reality putting Manchukuo under Japanese control. Those in Tokyo who disapproved of the attack were persuaded by the overwhelmingly positive reaction expressed by the public, press, and even leftist critics.

The U.S. government condemned the Japanese conquest, and the League of Nations refused to recognize Manchukuo and urged the Japanese to remove their troops from China. Persuaded that the Western powers would not fight, Japan resigned from the League.

During the next few years, the Japanese built railways and heavy industries in Manchuria and northeastern China and sped up their rearmament. The government grew more authoritarian, jailing thousands of dissidents. On several occasions, ultranationalists, many of them junior officers, mutinied or assassinated leading political figures, receiving only mild punishments, and generals and admirals sympathetic to their views replaced more moderate civilian politicians.

The Long March

Until the Japanese seized Manchuria, the Chinese government seemed to be creating conditions for a national recovery. The main challenge to the government of **Chiang Kai-shek** (chang kie-shek) came from the Chinese communists, who were industrial workers and who worked in alliance with the nationalists until 1927, when Chiang Kai-shek arrested and executed communists and labor leaders alike (see Chapter 25).

The few communists who escaped the mass arrests fled to the remote mountains of Jiangxi (jang-she), in southeastern China. Among them was **Mao Zedong** (ma-oh zay-dong) (1893–1976), a farmer's son who had left home to study philosophy.

In the early 1920s Mao discovered the works of Karl Marx, joined the Communist Party, and soon became one of its leaders. In Jiangxi, Mao began studying conditions among the peasants, in whom communists had previously shown no interest. He planned to redistribute land from the wealthier to the poorer peasants, thereby gaining adherents for the coming struggle with the Guomindang army.

Mao's reliance on the peasantry was a radical departure from Marxist-Leninist ideology, which stressed the backwardness of the peasants and pinned its hopes on industrial workers. Mao was also an advocate of women's equality. Before 1927 the communists had organized the women who worked in Shanghai's textile mills, the most exploited of all Chinese workers. Later, in their mountain stronghold in Jiangxi, they organized women farmers, allowed divorce, and banned arranged marriages and footbinding.

The Guomindang army pursued the communists into the mountains, building small forts throughout the countryside. Rather than risk direct confrontations, Mao responded with guerrilla warfare. Whereas government troops often mistreated civilians, Mao insisted that his soldiers help the peasants, pay a fair price for food and supplies, and treat women with respect. In spite of their good relations with the peasants of Jiangxi, the communists decided to break out of the southern mountains and trek to Shaanxi (SHAWN-she), an even more remote province in northwestern China. The so-called **Long March** took them 6,000 miles (nearly 9,700 kilometers) in one year, 17 miles a day over desolate mountains and through swamps and deserts, pursued by the army and bombed by Chiang's aircraft. Of the 100,000 communists who left Jiangxi in October 1934, only 4,000 reached Shaanxi a year later.

The Sino-Japanese War, 1937–1945

On July 7, 1937, Japanese troops attacked Chinese forces near Beijing. As in 1931, the junior officers who ordered the attack quickly obtained the support of their commanders and then, reluctantly, of the government. By November, Japanese troops had seized Beijing, Tianjin, Shanghai, and other coastal cities, and the Japanese navy blockaded the entire coast of China.

Once again, the United States and the League of Nations denounced the Japanese atrocities. Yet the Western powers were too preoccupied with events in Europe and with their own economic problems to risk a military confrontation in Asia. When the Japanese sank a U.S. gunboat and shelled a British ship on the Yangzi River, the U.S. and British governments

Chiang Kai-shek (1886–1975) Chinese military and political leader. Succeeded Sun Yat-sen as head of the Guomindang in 1925; headed the Chinese government from 1928 to 1948; fought against the Chinese communists and Japanese invaders. After 1949 he headed the Chinese nationalist government in Taiwan.

Mao Zedong (1893–1976) Leader of the Chinese Communist Party (1927–1976). He led the communists on the Long March (1934–1935) and rebuilt the Communist Party and Red Army during the Japanese occupation of China (1937–1945). After World War II, he led the communists to victory over the Guomindang.

Long March (1934–1935) The 6,000-mile flight of Chinese communists from southeastern to northwestern China. The communists, led by Mao Zedong, were pursued by the Chinese army under orders from Chiang Kai-shek. The four thousand survivors of the march formed the nucleus of a revived communist movement that defeated the Guomindang after World War II.

responded only with righteous indignation and pious resolutions.

The large Chinese armies were poorly led and armed and lost every battle. Within a year Japan controlled the coastal provinces of China and the lower Yangzi and Yellow River Valleys, China's richest and most populated regions, but the Chinese people continued to resist, either in the army or with the communist guerrilla forces. Japan's periodic attempts to turn the tide by conquering one more piece of China only pushed it deeper into the quagmire.

Warfare between the Chinese and Japanese was incredibly violent. In the winter of 1937–1938 Japanese troops took Nanjing, raped 20,000 women, killed roughly 200,000 prisoners and civilians, and looted and burned the city. To slow them down, Chiang ordered the Yellow River dikes blasted open, causing a flood that destroyed four thousand villages, killed 890,000 people, and made millions homeless. Two years later, when the communists ordered a massive offensive, the Japanese retaliated with a "kill all, burn all, loot all" campaign, destroying hundreds of villages down to the last person, building, and farm animal.

The Chinese government, led by Chiang Kai-shek, escaped to the mountains of Sichuan in the center of the country. There Chiang built up a huge army, not to fight Japan but to prepare for a future confrontation with the communists. The army drafted over 3 million men, even though it had only a million rifles and could not provide food or clothing for all its soldiers. The Guomindang raised farmers' taxes, even when famine forced farmers to eat the bark of trees. Such taxes were not enough to support both a large army and the thousands of government officials and hangers-on who had fled to Sichuan. To avoid taxing its wealthy supporters the government printed money, causing inflation, hoarding, and corruption.

From his capital of Yan'an in Shaanxi province, Mao also built up his army and formed a government. Unlike the Guomindang, the communists listened to the grievances of the peasants, especially the poor, to whom they distributed land confiscated from wealthy landowners. Because they presented themselves as the only group in China that was serious about fighting the Japanese, they obtained support and intelligence from farmers in Japanese-occupied territory, turning military reversals into propaganda victories.

SECTION REVIEW

- Seeing conquest as a solution to its economic problems, in 1931 Japan conquered Manchuria.

- The Chinese government under Chiang Kai-shek fought both the Japanese and the communists led by Mao Zedong, who fled into the mountains of northern China.

- The communists supported both peasants and women, while Chiang Kai-shek taxed farmers, printed money, and diverted war efforts to prepare to fight the communists.

- In 1937, Japanese forces conquered the coastal provinces of China; in the ensuing violent war, the Chinese communists offered the most effective resistance and Japan gained few real advantages.

THE SECOND WORLD WAR

■ *How was the war fought, and why did Japan and Germany lose?*

The Second World War was much bigger and deadlier than the first in every way. It was fought around the world, from Norway to New Guinea and from Hawaii to Egypt, and on every ocean. It was a total war that showed how effectively industry, science, and nationalism could be channeled into mass destruction.

The War of Movement

In World War II motorized weapons gave back the advantage to the offensive. Opposing forces moved fast, their victories hinging as much on the aggressive spirit of their commanders and the military intelligence they obtained as on numbers of troops and firepower.

The Wehrmacht (VAIR-mokt), or German army, was the first to learn this lesson. It not only had tanks, trucks, and fighter planes, but also had perfected their combined use in a tactic called *Blitzkrieg* (BLITS-creeg) (lightning war): fighter planes scattered enemy troops and disrupted communications, tanks punctured the enemy's defenses, and then, with the help of the infantry, they encircled and captured enemy troops. At sea, both Japan and the United States had developed aircraft carriers that could launch planes against targets hundreds of miles away.

Armies ranged over vast theaters of operation, and countries were conquered in days or weeks. The

TASS-Sovfoto

Soviet Tanks at Stalingrad In the winter of 1942–1943, the Red Army encircled a German army at Stalingrad, a strategic city in southern Russia that marked the furthest eastward advance of the Wehrmacht. The Soviets deployed their new T-34s, the best tanks in the world at the time. Unlike the Germans, Soviet soldiers were equipped with warm winter uniforms with a white outer layer for camouflage in the snow.

belligerents mobilized the economies of entire continents, squeezing them for every possible resource. They tried not only to defeat their enemies' armed forces but—by blockades, submarine attacks, and bombing raids—to damage the economies that supported those armed forces. They thought of civilians as legitimate targets and, later, as vermin to be exterminated.

War in Europe and North Africa

It took less than a month for the Wehrmacht to conquer Poland. Britain and France declared war on Germany but took no military action. Meanwhile, the Soviet Union invaded eastern Poland and the Baltic republics. Although the Poles fought bravely, their infantry and cavalry were no match for German and Russian tanks. During the winter of 1939–1940, Germany and the Western democracies faced each other in what soldiers called a "phony war."

In March 1940 Hitler went on the offensive again, conquering Denmark, Norway, the Netherlands, and Belgium in less than two months. In May he attacked France. Although the French army had as many soldiers, tanks, and aircraft as the Wehrmacht, its morale was low and it quickly collapsed. By the end of June Hitler was master of all of Europe between Russia and Spain.

Germany still had to face Britain. The British had no army to speak of, but they had other assets: the English Channel, the Royal Navy and Air Force, and a tough new prime minister, Winston Churchill. The Germans knew they could invade Britain only by gaining control of the airspace over the Channel, so they launched a massive air attack—the Battle of Britain—lasting from June through September. The attack failed because the Royal Air Force used radar and code-breaking to detect approaching German planes.

Frustrated in the west, Hitler turned his attention eastward. In June 1941, the Wehrmacht invaded the Soviet Union. In five months it conquered the Baltic states, Ukraine, and half of European Russia, captured a million prisoners of war, and stood at the very gates of Moscow and Leningrad (now St. Petersburg). The USSR seemed on the verge of collapse when suddenly the weather turned cold, machines froze, and the fighting came to a halt. Like Napoleon, Hitler had ignored the climate of Russia at his peril.

The next spring the Wehrmacht renewed its offensive and surrounded Leningrad in a siege that was to cost a million lives. Leaving Moscow aside, it turned toward the Caucasus and its oil wells. In August the Germans attacked **Stalingrad** (now Volgograd), the key to the Volga River and the supply of oil. For months, German and Soviet soldiers fought over every street and every house. When winter came, the Red Army counterattacked and encircled the city, and in February 1943, the remnants of the German army in Stalingrad surrendered. Hitler had lost his greatest gamble (see Map 27.1).

From Europe the war spread to Africa. During 1941 British forces conquered Italian East Africa and invaded Libya as well. The Italian rout in North Africa brought the Germans to the rescue. During 1942, the German army and the forces of the British Commonwealth seesawed back and forth across the deserts of Libya and Egypt. Because the British could decode German messages and had more weapons and supplies, they were finally able to expel the Germans from Africa in May 1943.

War in Asia and the Pacific

The war presented Japan with the opportunity to take over European colonies in Southeast Asia, with their abundant oil, rubber, and other strategic materials. After Japanese forces occupied Indochina in September 1940, the United States stopped shipments of steel, scrap iron, oil, and other products that Japan desperately needed. This left Japan with three alternatives: give up its conquests, as the Americans insisted; face economic ruin; or widen the war. Japan chose war. On December 7, 1941, Japanese planes bombed the U.S. naval base at **Pearl Harbor**, sinking or damaging scores of warships but missing the aircraft carriers, which were at sea. Then, in early 1942, the Japanese conquered all of Southeast Asia and the Dutch East Indies. They soon began to confiscate food and raw materials and demand heavy labor from the inhabitants.

Japan's dream of an East Asian empire seemed within reach, but the Pearl Harbor attack had finally mobilized the United States. In April 1942 American planes bombed Tokyo. In May the U.S. Navy defeated a Japanese fleet in the Coral Sea, ending Japanese plans to conquer Australia. A month later, at the **Battle of Midway**, Japan lost four of its six largest aircraft carriers. Without them, Japan faced a long and hopeless war (see Map 27.2).

The End of War

America's entry into the war also helped the Soviet Union capitalize on the advantage it had won in the Battle of Stalingrad. Aided by a growing stream of supplies from the United States, the Red Army began pushing the Wehrmacht back toward Germany. The Western powers, meanwhile, staged two invasions of Europe. Beginning in July 1943, they captured Sicily and invaded Italy. Italy signed an armistice, but German troops held off the Allied advance for two years. Then on D-day (June 6, 1944), 156,000 British, American, and Canadian troops landed on the coast of Normandy in western France. Within a week, the Allies had more troops in France than Germany did. To meet this growing force, Hitler had to transfer part of the Wehrmacht from the eastern front. Despite advancing armies on three sides, Germany held out for almost a year. On May 7, 1945, a week after Hitler committed suicide, German military leaders surrendered.

By June 1944, U.S. bombers were also attacking Japan from newly captured island bases in the Pacific, and U.S. submarines were sinking large numbers of Japanese merchant ships, cutting Japan off from its sources of oil and other raw materials. After May 1945, with Japanese fighters grounded for lack of fuel, U.S. planes began destroying Japanese shipping, industries, and cities at will.

Stalingrad City in Russia, site of a Red Army victory over the German army in 1942–1943. The Battle of Stalingrad was the turning point in the war between Germany and the Soviet Union. Today Volgograd.

Pearl Harbor Naval base in Hawaii attacked by Japanese aircraft on December 7, 1941. The sinking of much of the U.S. Pacific Fleet brought the United States into World War II.

Battle of Midway U.S. naval victory over the Japanese fleet in June 1942, in which the Japanese lost four of their best aircraft carriers. It marked a turning point in World War II.

Hiroshima City in Japan, the first to be destroyed by an atomic bomb, on August 6, 1945. The bombing hastened the end of World War II.

On August 6, 1945, the United States dropped an atomic bomb on **Hiroshima**, killing some 80,000 people in a flash and leaving about 120,000 more to die from burns and radiation. Three days later another atomic bomb destroyed Nagasaki. On August 14 Emperor Hirohito gave the order to lay down arms. Two weeks later Japanese leaders signed the terms of surrender. The war was officially over.

Collapse of the Guomindang and Communist Victory

The Japanese surrender meant the end of Japanese occupation for much of China. The United States gave millions of dollars in aid and weapons to the Guomindang, all the while urging "national unity" and a "coalition government" with the communists. But Chiang used all means available to prepare for a

Map 27.1 World War II in Europe and North Africa In a series of quick and decisive campaigns from September 1939 to December 1941, German forces overran much of Europe and North Africa. There followed three years of bitter fighting as the Allies slowly pushed the Germans back. © Cengage Learning

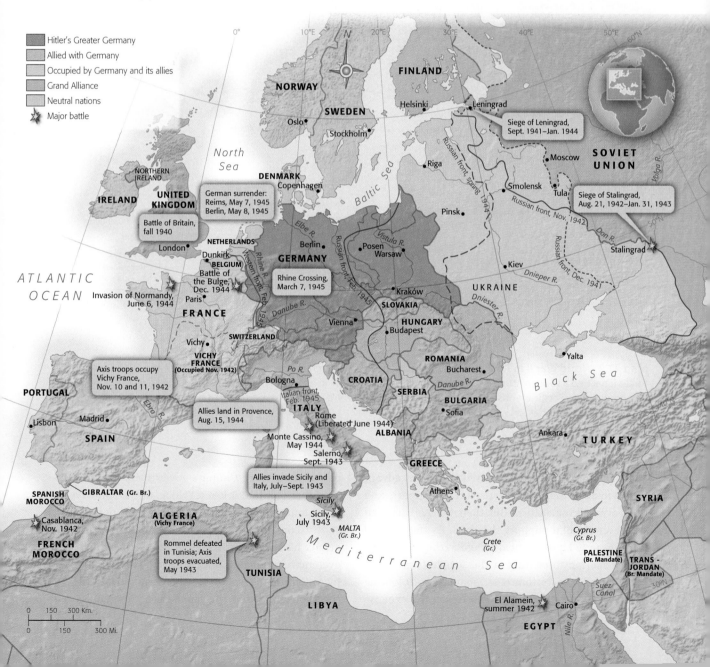

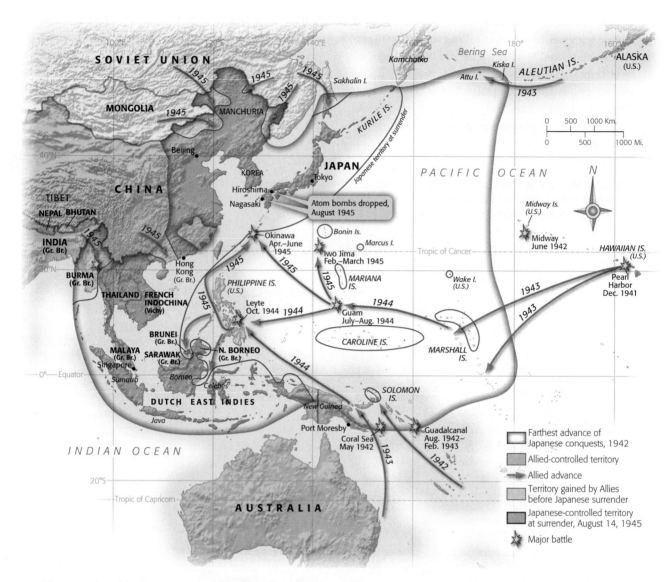

Map 27.2 World War II in Asia and the Pacific Having conquered much of China between 1937 and 1941, Japanese forces launched a sudden attack on Southeast Asia and the Pacific in late 1941 and early 1942. American forces slowly reconquered the Pacific islands and the Philippines. In August 1945, the atomic bombing of Hiroshima and Nagasaki forced Japan's surrender. © Cengage Learning

civil war. The Guomindang started with many advantages, more troops and weapons, U.S. support, and control of China's cities. But their behavior eroded whatever popular support they had. As they moved into formerly Japanese-held territory, they acted like an occupation force, taxing the people they "liberated" more heavily than the Japanese had, looting businesses, and enriching themselves at the expense of the population. Chiang's government had printed money so fast that it lost all value. In the countryside the Guomindang's brutality alienated the peasants.

In contrast, the communists' land reform programs had won them popular support, which was even more important than the weapons brought over by Guomindang soldiers, who began deserting by the thousands, and the Japanese equipment seized

Bettmann/CORBIS

Hiroshima After the Atomic Bomb On August 6, 1945, an atomic bomb destroyed the city, killing some eighty thousand people. This fire truck, stationed at the Hiroshima Fire Department, is one of the few identifiable objects in the photo. It was located 4,000 feet from ground zero.

by the Soviets in the last weeks of the war. By 1949, the Guomindang armies were collapsing everywhere, defeated more by their own greed and ineptness than by the communists. As the communists advanced,

high-ranking members of the Guomindang fled to Taiwan, protected from the mainland by the U.S. Navy. On October 1, 1949, Mao Zedong announced the founding of the People's Republic of China.

SECTION REVIEW

- World War II was a war of machines and movement covering entire continents and oceans.

- Germany quickly conquered most of continental Europe but failed to subdue Britain.

- Soviet troops halted Germany's invasion at Stalingrad, and Britain drove German forces from North Africa.

- Despite initial successes, Japan lost critical battles, particularly Midway, and never could match U.S. war production.

- With the help of vital U.S. resources, the Western powers defeated Germany, while the United States pressed Japan, dropping two atomic bombs to force its surrender.

- In China, Mao's communists won the civil war with the Guomindang by gaining support from the people.

THE CHARACTER OF WARFARE

■ *How did science and technology change the nature of warfare?*

The war left an enormous death toll. Recent estimates place the figure at close to 60 million deaths, six to eight times more than in World War I. Over half of the dead were civilian victims of massacres, famines, and bombs. The Soviet Union lost between 20 and 25 million people, more than any other country. China suffered 15 million deaths; Poland lost some 6 million, of whom half were Jewish; the Jewish people lost another 3 million outside Poland. Over 4 million Germans and over 2 million Japanese died. Great Britain lost 400,000 people, and the United States 300,000.

One reason for the terrible toll in human lives and suffering was a change in moral values, as belligerents identified not just soldiers but entire peoples as enemies. Some even labeled their own ethnic minorities as "enemies." Another reason for the devastation was the appearance of new technologies that carried destruction deep into enemy territory, far beyond the traditional battlefields.

The Science and Technology of War

Scientists made many contributions to the technology of warfare. Chemists found ways to make synthetic rubber from coal or oil. Physicists perfected radar, which warned of approaching enemy aircraft and submarines. Others broke enemy codes and developed antibiotics that saved the lives of countless wounded soldiers.

Aircraft development was especially striking. As war approached, German, British, and Japanese aircraft manufacturers developed fast, maneuverable fighter planes. U.S. industry produced aircraft of every sort but was especially noted for heavy bombers designed to fly in huge formations and drop tons of bombs on enemy cities. Germany responded with radically new designs, including the first jet fighters, low-flying pilotless buzz bombs, and long-range V-2 missiles.

In October 1939, President Roosevelt received a letter from physicist Albert Einstein, a Jewish refugee from Nazism, warning of the dangers of nuclear power. Fearing that Germany might develop a nuclear bomb first, Roosevelt placed the vast resources of the U.S. government at the disposal of physicists and engineers. By 1945 they had built two atomic bombs, each one powerful enough to annihilate an entire city.

Bombing Raids

The Germans began the war from the air, but it was the British and Americans who excelled at large-scale urban bombardment. Since it was very hard to pinpoint individual buildings, especially at night, air raids were aimed at weakening the morale of civilian populations.

In May 1942, 1,000 British planes dropped incendiary bombs on Cologne, setting fire to the old city. Between July 24 and August 2, 1943, 3,330 British and American bombers set fire to Hamburg, killing 50,000 people. Later raids destroyed Berlin, Dresden, and other German cities. The bombing raids against Germany killed 600,000 people—more than half of them women and children—and injured 800,000, but they failed to break the morale of the German people. The only effective bombing raids were those directed against oil depots and synthetic fuel plants; by early 1945, they had almost brought the German war effort to a standstill.

American bombing raids on Japanese cities were even more devastating that the fire-bombing of German cities, for Japanese cities were built of wood. In March 1945, a large raid set Tokyo ablaze, killing 80,000 people and leaving a million homeless. Five months later, each atomic bomb did as much damage as a thousand-plane raid.

The Holocaust

The Nazis killed defenseless civilians on an even larger scale. Their murders were not the byproducts of some military goal but a calculated policy of extermination.

Their first targets were Jews. Soon after Hitler came to power, he deprived German Jews of their citizenship and legal rights. When eastern Europe fell under Nazi rule, the Nazis herded its large Jewish population into ghettos in the major cities, where many died of starvation and disease. Then, in early 1942, the Nazis decided to carry out Hitler's "final solution to the Jewish problem" by applying modern industrial methods to the slaughter of human beings. German companies built huge extermination camps in eastern Europe. Every day, trainloads of cattle cars arrived at the camps and disgorged thousands of captives and the corpses of those who had died of starvation or asphyxiation along the way. The strongest survivors were put to work and fed almost nothing until they died. Women, children, the elderly, and the sick were shoved into gas chambers and asphyxiated with poison gas. **Auschwitz**, the biggest camp, was a giant industrial complex designed to kill up to twelve thousand people a day. This mass extermination, now called the **Holocaust** ("burning"), claimed some 6 million Jewish lives.

Auschwitz Nazi extermination camp in Poland, the largest center of mass murder during the Holocaust. Close to a million Jews, Gypsies, communists, and others were killed there.

Holocaust Nazis' program during World War II to kill people they considered undesirable. Some 6 million Jews perished during the Holocaust, along with millions of Poles, Gypsies, communists, socialists, and others.

Hulton Deutsch Collection/Corbis

U.S. Army Medics and Holocaust Victims When Allied troops entered the Nazi concentration camps, they found the bodies of thousands of victims of the Holocaust. In Dachau in southern Germany, two U.S. Army medics are overseeing a truckload of corpses to be taken to a burial site.

The Home Front

Rapid military movements and air power carried the war into people's homes in China, Japan, Southeast Asia, and Europe. Armies swept through the land, confiscating food, fuel, and anything else of value. Bombers and heavy artillery pounded cities into rubble, leaving only the skeletons of buildings, while survivors cowered in cellars. Air-raid sirens awakened people throughout the night. Millions fled their homes in terror. Of all the major belligerents, only Americans escaped such nightmares, and war production ended the joblessness of the Depression years.

The war demanded an enormous production effort from civilians. In the face of advancing Germans in 1941, the Soviets dismantled over fifteen hundred factories and rebuilt them in the Ural Mountains and Siberia, where workers soon turned out more tanks and artillery than the Axis. American factories produced an unending supply of ships, aircraft, trucks, tanks, and other materiel for the Allied effort. The Axis powers could not compete with the vast outpouring.

With so many men mobilized for war, women were responsible for much of this production. Six million American women entered the labor force, 2.5 million of them in manufacturing jobs previously considered "men's work." Soviet women took over half of all industrial and three-quarters of all agricultural jobs. In other belligerent countries, women also played major roles in the war effort, replacing men in fields, factories, and offices. The Nazis, in contrast, believed that German women should stay home and bear children, and they imported 7 million "guest workers"—a euphemism for captured foreigners.

Besides the Jews, the Nazis killed 3 million Polish Catholics—especially professionals, army officers, and the educated—in an effort to reduce the Polish people to slavery. They also exterminated homosexuals, Jehovah's Witnesses, Gypsies, the disabled, and the mentally ill—all in the interests of "racial purity." Whenever a German was killed in an occupied country, the Nazis retaliated by burning a village and all its inhabitants. After the invasion of Russia the Wehrmacht was given orders to execute all captured communists, government employees, and officers. They also worked millions of prisoners of war to death or let them die of starvation.

War and the Environment

As in World War I, battles scarred the landscape, leaving behind spent ammunition and damaged equipment. Retreating armies flooded large areas of China and the Netherlands. The bombing of cities left ruins that remained visible for a generation

- World War II caused 60 million deaths, most of them civilians, as well as many refugees.

- Scientific technology, especially aircraft design and nuclear weapons, contributed to the mobility and destruction of warfare.

- Allied bombing raids set fire to entire cities in both Europe and Japan.

- In the Holocaust, the Nazis murdered millions of Jews, Poles, Gypsies, and other minorities.

- Environments in war zones were badly damaged, and construction for the war transformed the environments of many countries.

or more. The main cause of environmental stress, however, was not the fighting but the economic development that sustained it.

As war industries boomed—the United States increased its industrial production fourfold during the war—so did the demand for raw materials. Mining companies opened new mines and towns in Central Africa to supply strategic minerals. Latin American countries deprived of manufactured imports began building their own steel mills, factories, and shipyards. In India, China, and Europe, timber felling accelerated far beyond forest regrowth. Yet, the environmental impact of the war was quite

modest compared to the damage inflicted on the earth by the long consumer boom that began after World War II.

CONCLUSION

During the two decades from 1929 to 1949, industrialization and nationalism led to Depression, political violence, and war. In the Soviet Union, Joseph Stalin used terror to turn his country into a modern industrial state prepared for war. In the United States and western Europe, a shaky economy based on credit and speculation collapsed, throwing millions out of work and causing worldwide misery. France and Britain survived by making their colonial empires purchase their products. In Italy, Germany, and Japan the economic turmoil, the disillusionment with liberal parliamentary politics, and nationalist resentments played into the hands of extremists who believed that war offered solutions to their nations' problems.

The Second World War was not just another war between states and armed forces, but a war against peoples. Of the roughly 60 million people who died in the war, most were civilians. Modern industrial technologies like aviation that had been developed for peaceful purposes, as well as new scientific breakthroughs like nuclear physics, were turned into engines of destruction. The war that resulted was by far the most violent and deadly in the history of humanity.

CHAPTER REVIEW

THE STALIN REVOLUTION
■ *How did the Soviet Union change under Stalin?* (page 631)

After the Great War ended, the world seemed to return to its prewar state, but it was an illusion. In the Soviet Union, Joseph Stalin was determined to turn his country into a modern industrial sate at breakneck speed, regardless of the human cost. Several million people—most of them peasants—died, and millions more were enslaved during the Five-Year Plans and the collectivization of agriculture. By 1914 Soviet industry was much better prepared for a war with Germany than it had been in 1914–1917.

THE DEPRESSION
■ *What caused the Depression, and what effects did it have on the world?* (page 634)

In 1929, after a few years of prosperity, excessive speculation based on shaky loans caused the New York stock market to collapse. Within a few months, the world economy fell into the Great Depression, which threw millions out of work, not only in the industrial nations but also throughout the world. Countries such as France and Britain survived the Depression by making their colonial empires purchase their products. Countries that were dependent on exports, such as Germany and Japan, suffered more. Only the USSR and southern

Africa, where gold became more valuable, booming during the 1930s.

THE RISE OF FASCISM
■ *How did fascism in Italy and Germany lead to the Second World War?* (page 635)

In Italy, the government that was already fascist became more tyrannical. Mussolini installed Fascist Party members in all government jobs and jailed anyone who criticized him. In Germany, economic collapse led people to entrust their government to Adolf Hitler and his Nazi followers, who quickly set to work establishing a totalitarian government. Nazi Germany's rebuilding of its military and its invasion of Austria and Czechoslovakia were greeted with a policy of appeasement by Western democracies, until finally they could no longer overlook Germany's intentions.

EAST ASIA, 1931–1945
■ *Why did Japan invade Manchuria?* (page 640)

The Depression hit Japan hard because the worldwide demand for silk and rice collapsed. Japan saw China as a potential new colony with a vast population and resources to help solve its economic problems. In 1931, Japan conquered Manchuria and proceeded to build railways and heavy industries there. The United States and the League of Nations protested but did little else. The Sino-Japanese War, which began with the Japanese invasion of Beijing in 1937, was a long and brutal war that became a drain on the Japanese economy and resources. Meanwhile, the communists, led by Mao Zedong, were slowly gaining support in the Chinese countryside.

THE SECOND WORLD WAR
■ *How was the war fought, and why did Japan and Germany lose?* (page 642)

Italy conquered Ethiopia in 1935, and Japan attacked China in 1937, while the Western democracies disapproved but took no action. War began in Europe in 1939 when Germany conquered Poland and thenk, in

the following Spring, Denmark, Norway, the low countries and France. The war turned global when Germany invaded the Soviet Union and Japan attacked the United States in 1941. The Allies won because of Russia's hard fighting and victory at Stalingrad; the Allies' overwhelming materiel resources, especially those of the United States; the invasion of D-day, which put enough men on the European continent to finally drive Germany back; and U.S. naval victories in the Pacific and the use of atomic weapons against Japan.

THE CHARACTER OF WARFARE
■ *How did science and technology change the nature of warfare?* (page 647)

The Second World War was by far the deadliest and most horrific in history. Modern mechanized forces swept across entire nations and oceans. Their targets were not only each other's armed forces, but their civilian populations as well. Though Germany had considerable scientific and technical talent, the war favored the nations with the most heavy industries, namely, the United States and the Soviet Union. The Allies destroyed German and Japanese cities with fire-bombs, and the United States dropped atomic bombs on Hiroshima and Nagasaki. Of the roughly 60 million people who died in the war, most were civilians.

Key Terms

Joseph Stalin (p. 631)
Five-Year Plans (p. 631)
Benito Mussolini (p. 638)
Fascist Party (p. 638)
Adolf Hitler (p. 638)
Nazis (p. 638)
Chiang Kai-shek (p. 641)
Mao Zedong (p. 641)
Long March (p. 641)
Stalingrad (p. 644)
Pearl Harbor (p. 644)
Battle of Midway (p. 644)
Hiroshima (p. 644)
Auschwitz (p. 648)
Holocaust (p. 648)

Famines and Politics

Human history is filled with tales of famines—times when crops failed, food supplies ran out, and people starved.

Natural Famines

India, dependent on the monsoon rains, has been particularly prone to such calamities, with famines striking two to four times a century, whenever the rains fail for several years in succession. Three times in the eighteenth century famines killed several million people. The nineteenth century was worse, with famines in 1803–1804, 1837–1838, 1868–1870, and 1876–1878. The famine of 1876–1878 also afflicted northern China, causing between 9 and 13 million deaths from hunger and from the diseases of malnutrition. There were even incidents of cannibalism, as starving adults ate starving children.

When drought hit a region, it decimated not only the human population but also the animals they relied on to transport crops or plow the land. When water levels dropped in rivers and canals, food could not be transported by boat to areas where people were starving.

Commercial Famines

That all changed in the nineteenth century. Railroads and steamships could transport foodstuffs quickly across great distances, regardless of the weather. Great Britain became dependent on imports of wheat and beef. Yet the global death toll from starvation has been far higher since the mid-nineteenth century than ever before. Why?

Consider Ireland. By the early nineteenth century the potato had become the main source of nutrition for the Irish people. Potatoes grew abundantly and produced more calories per acre than any other crop, allowing the population to increase dramatically.

In 1845 a blight turned the potatoes in the fields black, mushy, and inedible. The harvest was ruined the following year as well. It recovered slightly in 1847 but was bad again in 1848. Tens of thousands died of starvation, while hundreds of thousands died from the diseases that strike malnourished people, especially dysentery, typhus, or cholera. Travelers saw corpses rotting in their hovels or on the sides of roads. Altogether, a million or more people died, while another million emigrated, reducing the population of Ireland by half.

Throughout those years, Ireland exported wheat to England, where people had money to pay for it. Food cost money, and the Irish, poor even before the famines, could not afford to buy the wheat. The British government was convinced that interfering with the free market would only make things worse. Relief efforts were half-hearted at best; the official responsible for Irish affairs preferred to leave the situation to "the operation of natural causes."

The same held true in India, like Ireland a colony of Great Britain. The drought of 1876–1878 killed over 5 million Indians in the Deccan region, while British officials were helpless or indifferent. Part of the problem was transportation. In the 1870s most goods were still transported in bullock carts, but the bullocks also starved during the drought. Another obstacle was political. The idea that governments should be responsible for feeding the population was unthinkable at the time. So millions starved in the Deccan, while the Punjab exported wheat to Britain.

Over the next twenty years, so-called famine railways were built in the regions historically most affected by the failures of the monsoon. When drought struck again at the end of the century, the railways were ready to transport food to areas that had previously been accessible only by bullock carts. However, the inhabitants of the affected regions were too poor to buy what little food there was, so grain merchants bought all the stocks, hoarded them until the price rose, and then used the railways to transport them to regions where people had more money. The government was still reluctant to interfere with free enterprise.

In the twentieth century, governments do take responsibility for their own people as well as for people in other countries, but commercial famines still exist. When a catastrophic flood covered half of Bangladesh in 1974, its disorganized government sold its stocks of rice to merchants (who exported it to India) rather than distributing it. Thousands died. Survival depended on food shipped from donor countries.

Political Famines

In the twentieth century global food supplies were always adequate for the population of the world, and transportation was seldom a problem. Yet the century witnessed the most murderous famines ever recorded.

In 1942 the Japanese army had conquered Burma, a rich rice-producing colony. Food supplies in Bengal, which imported rice from Burma, dropped by 5 percent. As prices began to rise, merchants bought stocks of rice and held them, hoping that prices would continue to increase. Sharecroppers sold their stocks to pay off their debts. Meanwhile, the railroads that in peacetime would have carried food from other parts of India were fully occupied with military traffic. By the time Viceroy Lord Wavell ordered the army to transport food to Bengal in October 1943, between 1.5 and 2 million Bengalis had died.

Worst of all were the famines caused by deliberate government policies. The most famous was the famine of 1932–1933 caused by Stalin's collectivization of agriculture. The Communists tried to force the peasants to give up their land and livestock and join collectives, where they could be made to work harder and provide food for the growing cities and industries. When the peasants resisted, their crops were seized. Millions were sent to prison camps, and millions of others died of starvation.

An even worse famine took place in China from 1958 to 1961 during the "Great Leap Forward" (see Chapter 28). Communist Party chairman Mao Zedong decided to hasten the transformation of China into a communist state by relying not on the expertise of economists and technocrats but on the enthusiasm of the masses. Farms were consolidated into huge communes. Peasants were told to make steel out of household utensils in backyard furnaces. The harvest of 1959 was poor, and later ones were even worse. The amount of grain per person declined from 452 pounds (205 kilograms) in 1957 to 340 pounds (154 kilograms) in 1961. Since the Central Statistical Bureau had been shut down, the central government was unaware of the shortages and demanded ever higher requisitions of food to feed the army and urban and industrial workers and to export to the Soviet Union to pay off China's debts. The amount of food left to the farmers was between one-fifth and one-half of their usual subsistence diet. From 1958 to 1961 between 20 and 30 million Chinese are estimated to have starved or died of the diseases of malnutrition. It was the worst famine in the history of the world. Mao denied its existence.

The destruction or requisitioning of crops also caused famines in the Russian civil war of 1921–1922, the Japanese occupation of Indochina in 1942–1945, and the Great Leap Forward. In the 1970s and 1980s, droughts in Africa were used to crush rebellions: the governments of Ethiopia and Sudan denied that their people were hungry and prevented food shipments from reaching drought victims.

In the world today, natural disasters are as frequent as ever, and many countries are vulnerable to food shortages. No one now claims that governments have no business providing food to the starving. However, humanitarian feelings compete with other political agendas, and the specter of politically motivated famines still stalks the world.

Part Eight

Perils and Promises of a Global Community, 1945 to the Present

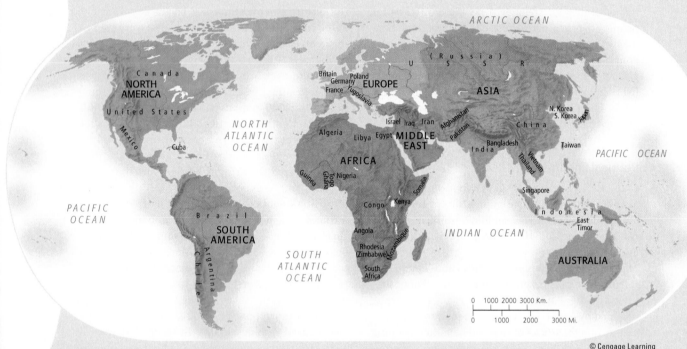

© Cengage Learning

	1950	1960	1970
AMERICAS	• **1945** United Nations charter signed in San Francisco • **1946** International Monetary Fund and World Bank founded • **1952** U.S. tests first hydrogen bomb	Military takes power in Brazil **1964** • Cuban Revolution **1959** • • **1962** Cuban missile crisis Neil Armstrong walks on moon **1969** •	Military coup overthrows Allende in Chile **1973** •
EUROPE	**1948–1952** Marshall Plan helps rebuild western Europe • **1949** NATO founded • **1955** Warsaw Pact formed Soviet troops crush revolt in Hungary **1956** • • **1957** Common Market founded	• **1961** Berlin Wall built	• **1968** Student uprising in France
AFRICA	Apartheid becomes official in South Africa **1948** • Guinea wins independence from France **1958** • Ghana first British colony in West Africa to win independence **1957** •	• **1960** Nigeria, Congo, Somalia, Togo win independence • **1963** Kenya independent	**1970–1980** White domination of Rhodesia yields to international pressure
MIDDLE EAST	• **1948** State of Israel founded; first Arab-Israeli War • **1956** Suez crisis **1954–1962** Algerian war for Independence	• **1960** Organization of Petroleum Exporting Countries founded	• **1967** Six Day Arab- Israeli War October Arab-Israeli War leads to oil embargo, price hikes **1973** •
ASIA AND OCEANIA	Communist Revolution in China **1949** • • **1949** Indonesia wins independence from Netherlands **1951–1953** Korean War **1954–1975** Vietnam War	Japan becomes world economic power **1970s** •	**1966–1969** Cultural Revolution in China • **1971** Independence of Bangladesh

After World War II an increasingly interconnected world faced new hopes and fears. The United Nations promoted peace, international cooperation, and human rights. Colonized peoples gained independence, and global trade expanded. At the same time the United States and the Soviet Union, victorious former allies in the war against the Axis, mobilized every resource in a global contest for economic and political influence. This "Cold War" led to nuclear stalemate as well as a new round of warfare, dispelling dreams of world peace. Wars in Korea and Vietnam, as well as proxy conflicts—local or regional wars in which the superpowers armed, trained, and financed the combatants—pitted the United States against communist regimes.

Following the Cold War nuclear proliferation and terrorism became top concerns. The 9/11 attacks by Muslim extremists on the World Trade Center and the Pentagon triggered an American-led "global war on terrorism." The ensuing invasions of Afghanistan and Iraq made the Middle East a top danger spot.

The industrialized nations, including Germany and Japan, recovered quickly from World War II. Elsewhere economic development came slowly, except in a handful of countries: South Korea, Taiwan, Brazil, Argentina, and, after 2000, China and India. In Africa and other poor regions, population growth usually offset economic gains.

Although the Green Revolution of the 1960s and the fruits of genetic engineering thirty years later alleviated much world hunger, industrial growth and automobile use increased pollution and competition for petroleum supplies. Global warming became an international concern, along with overfishing, deforestation, and endangerment of wild species.

Globalization affected culture as well. Transnational corporations selling uniform products threatened localized economic enterprises, and Western popular culture aroused fears of cultural imperialism, fear offset in part by the rise of Asian economic powers. The Internet and the emergence of English as the global language improved international communication but also stimulated fears that cultural diversity would be lost.

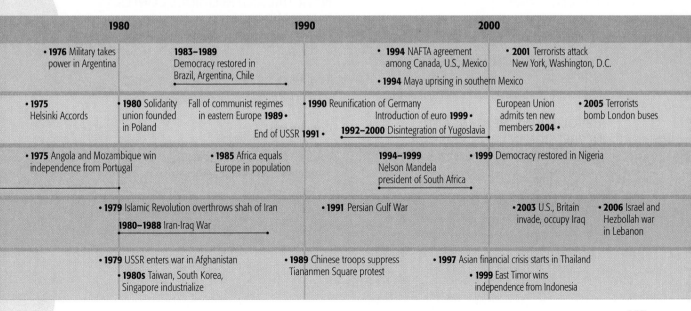

1980	1990	2000
• **1976** Military takes power in Argentina	**1983–1989** Democracy restored in Brazil, Argentina, Chile	• **1994** NAFTA agreement among Canada, U.S., Mexico • **2001** Terrorists attack New York, Washington, D.C.
		• **1994** Maya uprising in southern Mexico
• **1975** Helsinki Accords	• **1980** Solidarity union founded in Poland Fall of communist regimes in eastern Europe **1989** • End of USSR **1991** •	• **1990** Reunification of Germany Introduction of euro **1999** • European Union admits ten new members **2004** • • **2005** Terrorists bomb London buses
		1992–2000 Disintegration of Yugoslavia
• **1975** Angola and Mozambique win independence from Portugal	• **1985** Africa equals Europe in population	**1994–1999** Nelson Mandela president of South Africa • **1999** Democracy restored in Nigeria
	• **1979** Islamic Revolution overthrows shah of Iran **1980–1988** Iran-Iraq War	• **1991** Persian Gulf War • **2003** U.S., Britain invade, occupy Iraq • **2006** Israel and Hezbollah war in Lebanon
	• **1979** USSR enters war in Afghanistan • **1980s** Taiwan, South Korea, Singapore industrialize	• **1989** Chinese troops suppress Tiananmen Square protest • **1997** Asian financial crisis starts in Thailand • **1999** East Timor wins independence from Indonesia

The Cold War and Decolonization

© Cengage Learning

On January 1, 1959, the thirty-two-year-old Fidel Castro entered Havana, Cuba, after having successfully defeated the dictatorship of Fulgencio Batista (ful-HEHN-see-oh bah-TEES-tah). Castro had initiated his revolution in 1953 with an attack on a military barracks, but the attack failed. At his trial, Castro proclaimed that his objectives were the restoration of Cuban democracy and the institution of reforms designed to ameliorate the effects of underdevelopment.

In his September 26, 1960, United Nations address, Castro offered a broad internationalist and anti-imperialist criticism of the world's developed nations and of the United Nations. Claiming that the United States had supported the Batista dictatorship to protect American investors, he outlined an ambitious program of new revolutionary reforms in Cuba, which included concentrating power in the hands of its closest allies and nationalizing most American investments.

The Cuban government and the United States were already heading for confrontation because of Castro's policies when Cuba became a flash point in the Cold War. In 1961 the United States tried and failed to overthrow Castro. Castro retaliated by declaring himself a socialist and forging an economic and military alliance with the Soviet Union that led in 1962 to the Cuban Missile Crisis.

The intensity of the Cold War, with its accompanying threat of nuclear destruction, obscured a postwar phenomenon of more enduring importance: the colonial empires were overthrown, and Western influence declined in Asia, Africa, and Latin America. The leaders who headed these new nations were sometimes able to use Cold War antagonism to their own advantage when they sought economic or military assistance. Some, like Castro, became frontline participants in this struggle.

THE COLD WAR

■ *What were the major threats to world peace during the Cold War?*

The wartime alliance between the United States, Great Britain, and the Soviet Union had been an uneasy one. Political and economic leaders in the industrialized West had viewed socialism as a threat to free markets and private property. With the defeat of Germany, growing Soviet assertiveness in Europe and communist insurgencies in China and elsewhere seemed to confirm the threat of worldwide revolution.

Each side viewed every action by its rival as a direct threat. Fearful of growing Soviet power, the United States and the nations of western Europe established a military alliance in 1949, the **North Atlantic Treaty Organization (NATO)**. Soviet leaders, struggling to recover from their terrible war losses and feeling themselves surrounded by hostile nations, responded by creating their own military alliance, the **Warsaw Pact**, in 1955. The **Cold War** of suspicion and distrust between these two alliances would now play out on a worldwide stage.

The United Nations

Founded on October 1945, the **United Nations** had two main bodies: the General Assembly, with representatives from all fifty-one member states; and the Security Council, with five permanent members—China (until 1971 the anticommunist Chinese government based in Taiwan), France, Great Britain, the United States, and the Soviet Union—and seven rotating members. The United Nations operated by majority vote, except that the five permanent members of the Security Council had veto power in that chamber. All signatories to the United Nations Charter renounced war and territorial conquest. Yet the permanent members often exercised their vetoes to protect their allies and interests. From time to time the United Nations

North Atlantic Treaty Organization (NATO) Organization formed in 1949 as a military alliance of western European and North American states against the Soviet Union and its east European allies.

Warsaw Pact The 1955 treaty binding the Soviet Union and countries of eastern Europe in an alliance against the North Atlantic Treaty Organization.

Cold War The ideological struggle between communism (Soviet Union) and capitalism (United States) for world influence. The Cold War came to an end when the Soviet Union dissolved in 1991.

United Nations International organization founded in 1945 to promote world peace and cooperation. It replaced the League of Nations.

sent observers or peacekeeping forces to monitor truces or other international agreements.

The decolonization of Africa and Asia greatly swelled the size of the General Assembly. As many newly independent countries looked to the United Nations for material assistance and access to a wider political world, the General Assembly became an arena for debates over issues like decolonization and development.

In the early years of the United Nations, General Assembly resolutions carried great weight. An example is a 1947 resolution that sought to divide Palestine into sovereign Jewish and Arab states. Gradually, though, the flood of new members produced a voting majority concerned more with poverty, racial discrimination, and the struggle against imperialism than with the Cold War. As a result, Western powers increasingly disregarded the General Assembly, allowing new countries to have their say but not to act collectively.

May Day Parade in Red Square, 9th May 1967 (colour photo)/Moscow, Russia/© Mirrorpix/The Bridgeman Art Library

May Day Parade 1967   At the height of the Cold War the annual May Day celebration in Moscow became a demonstration of Soviet military might.

Capitalism and Communism

In July 1944, economic specialists representing over forty countries met at Bretton Woods, a New Hampshire resort, to devise a new international monetary system. The signatories eventually agreed to fix exchange rates. They also created the International Monetary Fund (IMF) and **World Bank** to provide funds for reconstructing Europe and helping needy countries.

The Soviet Union attended the Bretton Woods Conference and signed the agreements, but by 1946 suspicion between the Soviet Union and the West undermined cooperation. While the United States held reserves of gold and the rest of the world held reserves of dollars to maintain the stability of the monetary system, the Soviet Union established a closed monetary system for itself and for allied communist regimes in eastern Europe. In Western countries, supply and demand determined prices; in the Soviet command economy, government agencies allocated resources, labor, and goods and set prices, irrespective of market forces.

Many leaders of newly independent states preferred the Soviet Union's socialist example to the capitalism of their former colonizers. Thus, the relative success of economies patterned on Eastern or Western models became an element in the Cold War. Each side trumpeted economic successes measured by industrial output, changes in per capita income, and productivity gains.

After World War II, the United States enjoyed prosperity and an international competitive advantage, while European economies were still heavily damaged from the war. To support European reconstruction, the American **Marshall Plan** provided more than $20 billion to Europe by 1961. In 1948, European nations also promoted economic cooperation and

World Bank A specialized agency of the United Nations that makes loans to countries for economic development, trade promotion, and debt consolidation. Its formal name is the International Bank for Reconstruction and Development.

Marshall Plan U.S. program to support the reconstruction of western Europe after World War II. By 1961 more than $20 billion in economic aid had been dispersed.

Chronology

	International Crises	Decolonization
1945	1947–1948 Soviet blockade of Berlin 1949 NATO formed	1947 Partition of India 1949 Dutch withdraw from Indonesia
1950	1950–1953 Korean War 1952 United States detonates first hydrogen bomb 1954 Jacobo Arbenz overthrown in Guatemala, supported by CIA	1954 CIA intervention in Guatemala; defeat at Dienbienphu ends French hold on Vietnam
1955	1955 Warsaw Pact created 1956 Soviet Union suppresses Hungarian revolt; Suez War pits Israel, England, and France against Egypt 1957 Soviet Union launches first artificial satellite into earth orbit	1955 Bandung Conference 1957 Ghana becomes first British colony in Africa to gain independence 1959 Triumph of Fidel Castro's revolution in Cuba
1960	1961 East Germany builds Berlin Wall 1961 Bay of Pigs (Cuba) 1962 Cuban Missile Crisis 1967 Six-Day War between Israel and Arab neighbors 1968 Nuclear Non-Proliferation Treaty	1960 Shootings in Sharpeville intensify South African struggle against apartheid; Nigeria becomes independent 1962 Algeria wins independence
1970	1973 Yom Kippur War between Israel and Egypt 1974 OPEC raises world oil prices 1975 End of Vietnam War 1979 Shah of Iran overthrown in Islamic Revolution	1971 Bangladesh secedes from Pakistan
1980	1980–88 Iran-Iraq War 1989 Berlin Wall falls	1983 United States invades Grenada 1989 United States arrests president of Panama
1990	1991 Disintegration of Soviet Union	1990 Nelson Mandela released from prison in South Africa 1994 Nelson Mandela elected president of South Africa 1997 Hong Kong passes from British control to become part of the People's Republic of China 1999 United States cedes Panama Canal to Panama

integration with the creation of the Organization of European Economic Cooperation (OEEC). After cooperative policies on coal and steel proved successful, some OEEC countries lowered tariffs to encourage trade. In 1957 France, West Germany, Italy, the Netherlands, Belgium, and Luxembourg signed a treaty creating the **European Economic Community (EC)**, also known as the **Common Market**. By 1963, a resurgent European economy had doubled 1940 output, and by the 1970s the EC nations had nearly overtaken

the United States in industrial production. The economic alliance expanded after 1970 as Great Britain, Denmark, Greece, Ireland, Spain, Portugal, Finland, Sweden, and Austria joined.

European Economic Community (Common Market)
An organization promoting economic unity in Europe, formed in 1957 by consolidation of earlier, more limited, agreements. With the addition of many new nations it became the European Union (EU) in 1993.

Prosperity brought dramatic changes to western Europe. Wages increased and social welfare benefits expanded. Governments increased spending on health care, unemployment benefits, old-age pensions, public housing, and grants to poor families. Richer nations subsidized poorer nations, and the combination of economic growth and income redistribution raised living standards and fueled demand for consumer goods.

The Soviet experience was dramatically different. Even though the Soviet Union was more devastated than western Europe at the end of the Second World War, it also had enormous natural resources, a large population, and abundant energy—all of which initially contributed to its recovery. Moreover, Soviet planners had made large investments in technical and scientific education, and the Soviet state had developed heavy industry in the 1930s and war years. But as the postwar period progressed, the inefficiencies of bureaucratic control became obvious. By the 1970s the economic gap with the West had widened. Soviet industry failed to meet domestic demand for clothing, housing, food, automobiles, and consumer electronics. In addition, agricultural production failed to meet even domestic needs. More significant still, the Soviet Union fell behind the West in civilian-sector technological innovation.

West Versus East

For Germany, Austria, and Japan, peace brought foreign military occupation and governments controlled by the victors. The Soviet Union initially seemed willing to accept governments in neighboring states that included a mix of parties as long as they were not hostile to local communist groups or to the Soviets. Many were willing to embrace the communists as a hedge against those who had supported fascism or cooperated with the Germans. As relations between the Soviets and the West worsened in the late 1940s, communists gained a series of political victories across eastern Europe. Western leaders saw the emergence of communist regimes in Poland, Czechoslovakia, Hungary, Bulgaria, Romania, Yugoslavia, and Albania as a threat.

In 1946 Great Britain's wartime leader, Winston Churchill, said in a speech in Missouri, "From Stettin in the Baltic to Trieste in the Adriatic, an iron curtain has descended across the Continent. . . . I am convinced there is nothing they [the communists] so much admire as strength, and there is nothing for which they have less respect than weakness, especially military weakness." The phrase **iron curtain** became a watchword of the Cold War.

Increased hostility did not lead to a direct military confrontation between the two powerful alliances, however. In the waning days of World War II, the United States had seemed amenable to the Soviet desire for access to the Mediterranean through the Turkish straits. But in July 1947, the U.S. **Truman Doctrine** offered military aid to strengthen Turkish and Greek resistance to Soviet military pressure and subversion. In 1951, Turkey and Greece were admitted to NATO.

The West tested Eastern resolve by encouraging divisions within the Warsaw Pact, contributing to armed uprisings in Hungary and peaceful reform efforts in Czechoslovakia. Both were crushed by Soviet troops—Hungary in 1956 and Czechoslovakia in 1968—while the West stood by.

The East tested Western resolve as well. In 1947–1948, the Soviet Union blockaded the British, French, and American zones of Berlin (located in Soviet-controlled East Germany) and in 1961 built the Berlin Wall to prevent East Germans from fleeing to West Berlin. The political and ideological boundaries of the Cold War were established by these events.

A more explosive crisis erupted in Korea. At the end of World War II, Soviet troops were left in control north of the thirty-eighth parallel, while American troops controlled the south. When no agreement could be reached on holding countrywide elections, communist North Korea and a noncommunist South Korea became independent states in 1948. Two years later, North Korea invaded South Korea. In the absence of the Soviet delegation, the UN Security Council condemned the invasion and called on its members to come to the defense of South Korea.

iron curtain Winston Churchill's term for the Cold War division between the Soviet-dominated East and the U.S.-dominated West.

Truman Doctrine Foreign policy initiated by U.S. president Harry Truman in 1947. It offered military aid to help Turkey and Greece resist Soviet military pressure and subversion.

In the ensuing **Korean War**, which lasted until 1953, the United States was the primary military ally of South Korea. Military progress by American and South Korean forces stalled when the People's Republic of China entered the war in support of North Korea's communist regime. The United States feared that launching attacks into China might prompt China's ally, the Soviet Union, to retaliate. The contending armies eventually reached a stalemate along the thirty-eighth parallel. The two sides agreed to a truce but not a formal peace treaty. As a result, fear of renewed warfare has lingered until the present.

The United States and Vietnam

The most important postwar communist movement arose in French Indochina in Southeast Asia. The Vietnamese leader Ho Chi Minh (hoe chee min) (1890–1969) had spent several years in France during World War I and helped form the French Communist Party. After training in Moscow, he returned to Vietnam to found the Indochina Communist Party in 1930. Ho Chi Minh's nationalist coalition, called the Viet Minh, fought the French with help from the People's Republic of China. Under President Dwight D. Eisenhower (1953–1961), the United States provided limited support to the French but ultimately decided not to prop up French colonial rule in Vietnam, perceiving that the European colonial empires were doomed. After a brutal struggle, the French stronghold of Dienbienphu (dee-yen-bee-yen-FOO) fell in 1954, marking the end of France's colonial enterprise. Ho's Viet Minh government took over in the north, and a noncommunist nationalist government ruled in the south.

After winning independence, communist North Vietnam supported a communist guerrilla movement—the Viet Cong—against the noncommunist government of South Vietnam. When President John F. Kennedy (served 1961–1963) changed American policy to support the South Vietnamese government of President Ngo Dinh Diem (dee-YEM), North Vietnam committed its military forces more directly to the war with support from the Soviet Union and the Republic of China. Although Kennedy knew that the Diem government was corrupt and unpopular, he feared that a communist victory would encourage communist movements throughout Southeast Asia

and alter the Cold War balance of power. Kennedy increased the number of American military advisers while hoping that a more popular and honest government would come to power. But Diem's overthrow and execution only brought new rulers just as corrupt and unpopular, resulting in some popular South Vietnamese support for the Viet Cong and Hanoi's drive for national reunification.

Lyndon Johnson (served 1963–1969), who became president after Kennedy was assassinated, gained congressional support for an unlimited U.S. military deployment that eventually reached 500,000 troops. Despite battlefield success in the **Vietnam War**, the United States failed to achieve a comprehensive victory. In the massive 1968 Tet Offensive, the Viet Cong guerrillas and their North Vietnamese allies suffered significant losses but gained military credibility.

With a clear victory now unlikely, the antiwar movement in the United States grew in strength. President Johnson, having begun his administration committed to a broad program of social reforms and civil rights initiatives called the Great Society, was instrumental in passing major civil rights legislation that responded to the heroic campaign for voting rights and integration led by Martin Luther King, Jr. As the commitment of U.S. troops in Vietnam grew, a massive antiwar movement applied the tactics of the civil rights movement to end the war. Growing economic problems and a rising tide of antiwar rallies, soon acquiring an international character, undermined support for Johnson, who declined to seek reelection.

In 1973 a treaty between North Vietnam and the United States ended U.S. involvement in the war and promised future elections. Two years later, in violation of the treaty, Viet Cong and North Vietnamese troops overran the South Vietnamese army and captured the southern capital of Saigon, renaming it Ho

Korean War (1950–1953) Conflict that began with North Korea's invasion of South Korea and that came to involve the United Nations (primarily the United States) allying with South Korea and the People's Republic of China allying with North Korea.

Vietnam War (1954–1975) Conflict pitting North Vietnam and South Vietnamese communist guerrillas against the South Vietnamese government, aided after 1961 by the United States.

Dana Stone/Black Star

The Vietnamese People at War American and South Vietnamese troops burned many villages to deprive the enemy of civilian refuges. This policy undermined support for the South Vietnamese government in the countryside.

Chi Minh City. They then united the two Vietnams in a single state ruled from the north. Over a million Vietnamese and 58,000 Americans had died during the war. As the victors imposed a new economic and political order, hundreds of thousands of refugees from South Vietnam left for the United States and other Western nations.

While the United States had justified its military involvement in South Vietnam as an effort to defend against the spread of communism in the region, the communist-led government of a newly reunited Vietnam soon found itself at war with its communist neighbors. In 1975 communist revolutionaries (the Khmer Rouge) gained power in Cambodia, Vietnam's western neighbor. Not only did this brutal regime led by Pol Pot execute more than 1 million of their fellow

citizens, but they also provoked a war with the communist government of Vietnam in 1978. A Vietnamese force of more than 150,000 defeated the Khmer Rouge and set up an occupation government, but a resilient guerrilla force drove the Vietnamese out after a decade of war. The Vietnamese invasion of Cambodia also led to a two-month-long war with the Republic of China, which favored the Cambodians.

The Race for Nuclear Supremacy

The terrible devastation of Hiroshima and Nagasaki by atomic weapons (see Chapter 27) framed the strategic decisions in the Korean and Vietnamese wars. The Soviet Union had exploded its first nuclear device in 1949. The United States exploded a far more powerful hydrogen bomb in 1952, but the Soviet Union followed suit less than a year later. As a result, the United States took care not to directly challenge the Soviet Union or China (a nuclear power from 1964) during the Korean or Vietnamese conflicts. But the threat of superpowers willing to use nuclear weapons to protect their vital interests spread fear around the world.

Everyone's worst fears seemed about to be realized in the **Cuban Missile Crisis** of 1962. When the Soviet Union deployed nuclear-tipped missiles in Cuba in response to the U.S. missiles in Turkey, the world held its breath. Confronted by unyielding, diplomatic pressure and military threats from President Kennedy, the Soviet Union backed down and pulled the missiles from Cuba. Subsequently, the United States removed its missiles from Turkey.

Arms limitations also saw progress. In 1963 Great Britain, the United States, and the Soviet Union agreed to ban the testing of nuclear weapons in the atmosphere, in space, and under water, thus reducing the danger of radioactive fallout. In 1968 the United States and the Soviet Union together proposed the Nuclear Non-Proliferation Treaty (NPT) signed by 137 countries.

Space exploration was another offshoot of the nuclear arms race. The contest to build larger and more accurate missiles prompted the superpowers

Cuban Missile Crisis (1962) Brink-of-war confrontation between the United States and the Soviet Union over the latter's placement of nuclear-armed missiles in Cuba.

- The United Nations was created to manage international disputes and facilitate decolonization and development.

- The United States developed the Marshall Plan to aid European recovery from the devastation of World War II.

- The Cold War was a confrontation between two military alliances, NATO and the Warsaw Pact, and two distinct economic systems, capitalism and communism.

- The United States and the Soviet Union avoid a direct conflict, but the Cold War led to wars in Korea and Vietnam.

- The development of nuclear weapons made the Cold War a threat to the survival of the human race and led to nonproliferation treaties.

to prove their skills in rocketry by launching space satellites. The Soviet Union placed a small *Sputnik* satellite into orbit around the earth in October 1957, thereby administering a deep shock to American pride and confidence. The United States responded with its own satellite three months later. In 1969, two Americans, Neil A. Armstrong and Edwin E. ("Buzz") Aldrin, became the first humans to walk on the moon.

DECOLONIZATION AND NATION BUILDING

■ *What problems did less developed nations face?*

Whereas the losing countries in World War I were stripped of colonies, it was primarily countries on the winning side in World War II that ended up losing their colonies (see Map 28.1). Circumstances differed profoundly from place to place. In some Asian countries, where colonial rule was of long standing, new states possessed viable industries, communications networks, and education systems. In other countries, notably in Africa, decolonized nations faced dire economic problems and internal disunity.

Despite their differences, a sense of kinship arose among the nations of Latin America, Africa, and Asia. All shared feelings of excitement and rebirth. As North Americans, Europeans, and the Chinese settled into the exhausting deadlock of the Cold War, visions of independence and national development captivated the rest of the world.

Challenges of Nation Building

Each former colony had its own history and followed its own route to independence. Fifty-one nations signed the United Nations Charter in the closing months of 1948. During the United Nations' first decade, twenty-five new members joined, a third of them upon gaining independence. During the next decade, forty-six more new members were admitted, nearly all of them former colonial territories.

All spoke with one voice about their need for economic and technical assistance and the obligation of the wealthy nations to satisfy those needs. However, these new nations had difficulty finding a collective voice in a world increasingly oriented toward two superpowers. Antagonistic ethnic, religious, and linguistic groups strained the stability of fledgling governments trying to build an infrastructure.

Though some developing nations—particularly in Asia—attained substantial benefits from rapid technological change and world economic integration, many new nations faced basic problems of educating their citizens, nurturing industry, and escaping the economic constraints imposed by former imperialist masters that often maintained ownership of key resources. Wrenching social change accompanied the opening of markets to foreign investment and competition. The environment suffered severe pressures from oil exploration and transport to support the growing economies of the wealthy nations and from deforestation and urbanization in poor regions. Increased globalization coincided with increased inequality in many nations.

The Superpowers and the Nonaligned Movement

Although the East-West superpower rivalry dominated world affairs, newly independent nations had concerns that were primarily domestic and regional. Their challenge was to pursue their ends within the bipolar structure of the Cold War—and when possible to take advantage of the East-West rivalry. In short, the superpowers dominated the world but did not control it. As time progressed, they dominated it less and less.

As one of the most successful leaders of the decolonization movement, Indonesia's President Sukarno

Map 28.1 Decolonization, 1947–1990 Independence was achieved a decade or so earlier in South and Southeast Asia than in Africa. © Cengage Learning

Former ruler

1960 Year independence achieved

Great Britain	Belgium
France	Portugal
Netherlands	United States
Italy	Other

ATLANTIC OCEAN

PACIFIC OCEAN

INDIAN OCEAN

Mediterranean Sea

Black Sea

Caspian Sea

Arabian Sea

Bay of Bengal

GREAT BRITAIN

FRANCE

NETHERLANDS

BELGIUM

ITALY

SPAIN

PORTUGAL

JAPAN

20°W · 0° · 20°E · 40°E · 60°E · 80°E · 100°E · 120°E

40°N · 20°N · Tropic of Cancer · Equator 0° · 20°S · Tropic of Capricorn

WESTERN SAHARA 1975 (Morocco) (From Spain)
CAPE VERDE 1975 (From Port.)
MOROCCO 1956
MAURITANIA 1960
SENEGAL 1960
GAMBIA 1965
GUINEA-BISSAU 1974
GUINEA 1958
SIERRA LEONE 1961
LIBERIA 1820s
CÔTE D'IVOIRE 1960
GHANA 1957
BURKINA FASO 1960
MALI 1960
ALGERIA 1962
TUNISIA 1957
LIBYA 1951
NIGER 1960
BENIN 1960
TOGO 1960
NIGERIA 1960
EQUATORIAL GUINEA 1968 (From Spain)
SÃO TOMÉ AND PRÍNCIPE 1975 (From Port.)
GABON 1960
CAMEROON 1960
CENTRAL AFRICAN REPUBLIC 1960
CHAD 1960
EGYPT 1922
SUDAN 1956
ERITREA 1993 (From Ethiopia)
DJIBOUTI 1977
ETHIOPIA
SOMALIA 1960
REPUBLIC OF CONGO 1960
DEM. REP. OF CONGO 1960
UGANDA 1962
RWANDA 1962
BURUNDI 1962
KENYA 1963
TANZANIA 1964
ANGOLA 1975
ZAMBIA 1964
MALAWI 1964
MOZAMBIQUE 1974
ZIMBABWE 1980
NAMIBIA 1990 (From South Africa)
BOTSWANA 1966
SOUTH AFRICA (Republic 1961)
SWAZILAND 1968
LESOTHO 1966
MADAGASCAR 1960

SEYCHELLES 1976 (From Gr. Br.)
COMOROS 1975 (From France)
MAURITIUS 1968 (From Gr. Br.)

CYPRUS 1960
MALTA 1964 (From Gr. Br.)
SYRIA 1944
LEBANON 1944
ISRAEL 1948
IRAQ 1932
JORDAN 1946
KUWAIT 1961
BAHRAIN 1971
QATAR 1971
UNITED ARAB EMIRATES 1971
OMAN 1971
P.D.R. OF YEMEN 1967 (Unified 1990) YEMEN

INDIA 1947
PAKISTAN 1947
PAKISTAN 1947, BANGLADESH 1973
SRI LANKA (CEYLON) 1948
MALDIVES 1975 (From Gr. Br.)

MYANMAR (BURMA) 1947
LAOS 1949
NORTH VIETNAM 1954 (Unified 1975)
SOUTH VIETNAM 1954
CAMBODIA 1953
MALAYSIA 1963
SINGAPORE 1965 (From Malaysia)
BRUNEI 1984 (From Gr. Br.)
PHILIPPINES 1946
INDONESIA 1949
TIMOR-LESTE 1999 (From Indonesia)

NORTH KOREA 1948
SOUTH KOREA 1948 (From Japan)

PAPUA NEW GUINEA 1975 (From Australia)

N

0 · 1,000 · 2,000 Km.
0 · 1,000 · 2,000 Mi.

AP Photo/George Sweers

Bandung Conference, 1955 India's Jawaharlal Nehru (in white hat) was a central figure at the conference held in Indonesia to promote solidarity among nonaligned developing nations.

was an appropriate figure to host a 1955 meeting of twenty-nine African and Asian countries at Bandung, Indonesia, that proclaimed solidarity among those fighting against colonial rule. This conference marked the beginning of an effort by the many new, poor, mostly non-European nations emerging from colonialism to gain more influence in world affairs. The terms **nonaligned nations** and **Third World**, which became commonplace in the following years, signaled these countries' collective stance toward the rival sides in the Cold War. If the West, led by the United States, and the East, led by the Soviet Union, represented two worlds locked in mortal struggle, the Third World consisted of everyone else.

Leaders of so-called Third World countries preferred the label *nonaligned*, which signaled their independence from Soviet or U.S. control. However, because the Soviet Union supported national liberation movements and the nonaligned movement

included communist countries such as China, Western leaders did not take the term *nonaligned* seriously. They saw Sukarno, Nehru, Nkrumah, and Egypt's Gamal Abd al-Nasser (gah-MAHL AHB-d al–NAH-suhr) as stalking horses for a global campaign to extend Soviet influence. This may have also been the hope of some Soviet leaders, who were quick to offer military and financial aid to many nonaligned countries.

For the movement's leaders, however, nonalignment was primarily a way to extract money and support from one or both superpowers. By flirting with the Soviet Union or its ally, the People's Republic of China, some skilled nonaligned leaders were able to

nonaligned nations Developing countries that announced their neutrality in the Cold War.

Third World Term applied to a group of developing countries who professed nonalignment during the Cold War.

gain from both sides. Nasser, who had led a military coup against the Egyptian monarchy in 1952, and his successor Anwar al-Sadat (al-seh-DAT) played this game well. The United States offered to build a dam at Aswan (AS-wahn), on the Nile River, to increase Egypt's electrical generating and irrigation capacity, but it withdrew the offer when Egypt turned to the Soviet Union for armaments in 1956. The Soviet Union then committed to building the dam.

Later that same year Israel, Great Britain, and France conspired to invade Egypt, aiming to overthrow Nasser, regain the Suez Canal that had recently been nationalized, and secure Israel from any Egyptian threat. The invasion succeeded militarily, but both the United States and the Soviet Union pressured the invaders to withdraw, thus saving Nasser's government. In 1972 Sadat evicted Soviet military advisers, but a year later he used his Soviet weapons to attack Israel. After he lost that war, he disengaged from the Soviets and sought increased aid from the United States.

Numerous other countries adopted similar balancing strategies. In each case, local leaders sought to develop their nations' economies and assert or preserve their nations' interests. Manipulating the superpowers was a means toward those ends and implied very little about true ideological orientation.

New Nations in South and Southeast Asia

After partition in 1947 the independent states of India and Pakistan were strikingly dissimilar (see Chapter 26). Muslim Pakistan defined itself according to religion and quickly fell under the control of military leaders. Though 90 percent of India's population was Hindu, this much larger republic was secular. It inherited most of the considerable industrial and educational resources the British had developed, along with the larger share of trained civil servants and military officers.

The decision of the Hindu ruler of the northwestern state Jammu and Kashmir to join India without consulting his overwhelmingly Muslim subjects led to a war between India and Pakistan in 1947 that ended with an uneasy truce. Pakistan and India have since fought two wars: a brief one in 1965 over Kashmir, and another in 1971 when East Bengal, with India's help, seceded from Pakistan to form the new nation of Bangladesh. Despite the truce between the two nations, Kashmir remained a flash point, with new clashes in 1999 and 2000. India, Pakistan, and Bangladesh have found cooperation difficult and have pursued markedly different economic, political, religious, and social paths.

Elsewhere in the region, nationalist movements won independence as well. Britain granted independence to Burma (now Myanmar [my-ahn-MAHR]) in 1948 and established the Malay Federation that year. Singapore, once a member of the federation, became an independent city-state itself in 1965. In 1946, the United States kept its promise of postwar independence for the Philippine Islands but retained close economic ties and leases on military bases. In the Dutch East Indies, a military confrontation resulted in Dutch withdrawal in 1949, and an architect and nationalist named Sukarno (1901–1970) became dictator of the resource-rich but underdeveloped nation of Indonesia. He ruled until 1965, when a military coup ousted him, eliminated the powerful Communist Party, and targeted the large Chinese ethnic community in an attempt to force assimilation.

The Struggle for Independence in Africa

In the quarter-century between 1955 and 1980, African nationalists succeeded in ending European colonial rule. Mostly they gained independence peacefully, but where European settlers were numerous, violence became the norm.

In 1954, the Muslim people of Algeria rebelled against France. Having lost Indochina, France was determined to hold on to Algeria because 10 percent of the Algerian population was European and Algeria's economy was strongly oriented toward France. Both sides fought with great brutality. When Algeria finally won independence in 1962, the departure of the colonists undermined Algeria's economy, since few Arabs had received technical training or had management experience. None of the other African independence movements matched the Algerian struggle in scale or brutality.

Many African leaders dedicated their lives to winning independence. Kwame Nkrumah (KWAH-mee nn-KROO-muh) (1909–1972), for example, spent

Jomo Kenyatta Kenya's newly elected premier, Jomo Kenyatta, cheered by crowds in Nairobi in 1963. Kenyatta (waving ceremonial "whisk") had led the struggle to end British colonial rule in Kenya.

a decade studying philosophy and theology in the United States, where he absorbed ideas about black pride and independence propounded by W. E. B. Du Bois and Marcus Garvey. When he returned to the Gold Coast in 1947 to work for independence, Great Britain had already freed its Asian colonies. Nkrumah quickly united the people of Ghana behind him and won independence without bloodshed. He became prime minister of Ghana (formerly the Gold Coast) in 1957, the first British colony in West Africa to achieve independence. However, Nkrumah proved more effective as an international spokesman than as an administrator, and he was overthrown in 1966 by a disaffected group of army officers.

Jomo Kenyatta (ca. 1894–1978) traveled a more difficult road in Kenya, where a substantial number of European coffee planters strengthened British desire to retain control. A protest movement among the Kikuyu (kih-KOO-you) people, which settlers called the "Mau Mau," became violent. After 1952, British troops hunted down movement leaders and resettled the Kikuyu. The British charged Kenyatta with being a Mau Mau leader, imprisoned him, and then put him in internal exile for eight years during a declared state of emergency. Released in 1961, Kenyatta negotiated with the British to write a constitution for an independent Kenya, and in 1964 he was elected the nation's first president. Kenyatta proved to be an effective, though autocratic, ruler.

In contrast, African leaders in the French colonies of sub-Saharan Africa were slow to call for full independence. They believed in the promises of political and civil rights made in 1944 by General Charles de Gaulle at a conference in Brazzaville. This Brazzaville conference also promised to expand French education at the village level, to improve health services, and to open more lower-level administrative positions to Africans, but the word *independence* was never mentioned.

African leaders also realized that some French colonies—such as Ivory Coast, with coffee and cacao exports, fishing, and hardwood forests—had good economic prospects, while others, such as landlocked, desert Niger, did not. Furthermore, they recognized the importance of French investment. Ultimately, however, African patriotism prevailed everywhere. Guinea, under the dynamic leadership of Sékou Touré (SAY-koo too-RAY), gained full independence in 1958, and the others did the same in 1960.

In southern Africa, European settlers fought hard to hold on. The African struggle against Portuguese rule in Angola and Mozambique dragged on until the overthrow of the antidemocratic government of Portugal in 1974; independence was granted the following year. After a ten-year fight, European settlers in the British colony of Southern Rhodesia accepted African majority rule in 1980. The new government renamed the country Zimbabwe, the name of a great city built long before the arrival of Europeans.

Only South Africa and neighboring Namibia remained in the hands of European minorities much longer. After World War II, the white minority government of South Africa achieved effective independence in 1961 but imposed a system of extreme racial segregation called *apartheid* (a-PART-hite) in which the cities, best jobs, and most of the land were reserved for Europeans. Africans and others classified as "nonwhites" were subjected to strict limitations on place of residence, right to travel, and access to jobs and public facilities.

The African National Congress (ANC), formed in 1912, led opposition to apartheid (see Diversity and Dominance: Race and the Struggle for Justice in South Africa). After police fired on demonstrators in the African town of Sharpeville in 1960 and banned all peaceful political protest by Africans, a lawyer named Nelson Mandela (b. 1918) organized guerrilla resistance by the ANC. Mandela was sentenced to life in prison in 1964 and the government persecuted the ANC, but it was unable to defeat the movement. Facing growing opposition internationally, South Africa freed Mandela from prison in 1990 and began the transition to majority rule.

SECTION REVIEW

- Newly independent nations faced the challenge of developing their economies and educating their peoples.
- Some new nations aligned themselves with the United States or with the Soviet Union, but many referred to themselves as nonaligned.
- Independence in India and Pakistan led to war over Kashmir, which has continued to cause conflict.
- Algeria gained independence from France after a long and violent revolution.
- West African colonies eventually gained independence from Great Britain and France through negotiation.
- In southern African colonies, large white populations resisted independence, and whites in South Africa instituted the system of segregation called apartheid.

REVOLUTIONS, REFORM, AND REPRESSION IN LATIN AMERICA

■ *How did U.S. policies during the Cold War affect Latin America?*

Although Latin America had achieved independence from colonial rule more than a hundred years earlier, it struggled in the postwar decades over foreign ownership and social inequality. European and American companies dominated the economies of the region, creating a semicolonial order (see Chapters 21 and 23). Foreigners controlled Chile's copper, Cuba's sugar, Colombia's coffee, Guatemala's bananas, and the communication networks of several countries. Even in a country like Mexico, where the ruling Institutional Revolutionary Party, or PRI, was committed to revolutionary independence and economic development, a yawning gulf between rich and poor persisted. According to one estimate from the mid-1960s, some three hundred foreign and eight hundred Mexican companies dominated the country, and some two thousand families controlled much of the nation's wealth. At the other end of the economic scale were the millions of poor Mexicans struggling to survive. Thwarted by limited opportunities at home, millions of Mexicans migrated to the United States.

Guatemala and the CIA Jacobo Arbenz Guzmán, elected president of Guatemala in 1951, was typical of Latin American leaders like Perón of Argentina and Vargas of Brazil (see Chapter 25), who confronted powerful foreign interests. His expropriation of large estates angered the United Fruit Company, a U.S. corporation that dominated banana exports and held vast tracts of land in reserve. Reacting to reports that Arbenz was becoming friendly toward communism, the U.S. Central Intelligence Agency (CIA) sponsored a takeover by the Guatemalan military in 1954. CIA intervention removed Arbenz, but it also condemned Guatemala to decades of governmental instability and violence.

The Cuban Revolution

In Cuba, U.S. companies owned 40 percent of raw sugar production, 23 percent of nonsugar industry, 90 percent of telephone and electrical services, and 50 percent of public service railways. The needs of the U.S. economy largely determined Cuban foreign trade and held back development. Profits went north to the United States or to a small class of wealthy Cubans, many of foreign origin. Cuba's ruler during that period, Fulgencio Batista, became a symbol of corruption, repression, and foreign economic domination.

In 1959, a popular rebellion forced Batista to flee the country (see the discussion at the beginning of this chapter). Fidel Castro, the leader of the rebels, his brother Raul Castro, and Ernesto ("Che") Guevara (CHAY guh-VAHR-uh), the main theorist of communist revolution in Latin America, created a new regime. Within a year, Castro's government had redistributed land, lowered urban rents, and raised wages, effectively transferring 15 percent of the national income from the rich to the poor. Within two years the Castro government had nationalized the property of almost all U.S. corporations in Cuba as well as the wealth of Cuba's elite. This action resulted in a blockade by the United States, the flight of middle-class and technically trained Cubans, a drop in foreign investment, and the beginning of chronic food shortages.

Little evidence supports the view that Castro was committed to communism before the revolution, but his commitment to break the economic and political power of the United States in Cuba led him to turn

Bettmann/Corbis

Fidel Castro Arrives in Havana Castro and his supporters overthrew a brutal dictatorship and began the revolutionary transformation of Cuba that led to a confrontation with the United States.

to the Soviet Union for economic aid. In doing so, he unwittingly committed his nation to economic stagnation and dependence on a foreign power as damaging as the previous relationship with the United States had been.

In April 1961, some fifteen hundred Cuban exiles trained and armed by the CIA landed at the Bay of Pigs in an effort to overthrow Castro. The Cuban army defeated the attempted invasion in a matter of days, partly because the new U.S. president, John F. Kennedy, decided not to provide all the air support that the plan (drawn up by the previous Eisenhower administration) originally called for. The failure of the Bay of Pigs invasion tarnished the reputation of the United States and the CIA and helped precipitate the Cuban Missile Crisis. Fearful of a new invasion, Castro placed Soviet nuclear weapons as well as missiles and bombers in Cuba.

Armed revolutionary movements that imitated the tactics and objectives of Cuba's bearded revolutionaries experienced little success. Among the thousands to lose their lives was Che Guevara, captured and executed in 1967 by Bolivian troops trained by the United States. Nevertheless, Castro had demonstrated that revolutionaries could successfully challenge American

Race and the Struggle for Justice in South Africa

One of South Africa's martyrs in the struggle against apartheid was the thinker and activist Steve Biko (1946–1977). Biko was one of the founders of the Black Consciousness Movement, which focused on the ways in which white settlers had stripped Africans of their freedom. Between 1975 and 1977 police arrested and interrogated him four times. After his arrest in August 1977, the police severely beat him and denied him medical care. His death in police custody caused worldwide outrage.

[T]hese are not the people we are concerned with [those who support apartheid]. We are concerned with that curious bunch of nonconformists who explain their participation in negative terms: that bunch of do-gooders that goes under all sorts of names—liberals, leftists etc. These are the people who argue that they are not responsible for white racism and the country's "inhumanity to the black man." These are the people who claim that they too feel the oppression just as acutely as the blacks and therefore should be jointly involved in the black man's struggle for a place under the sun. In short, these are the people who say that they have black souls wrapped up in white skins.

The role of the white liberal in the black man's history in South Africa is a curious one. Very few black organisations were not under white direction. True to their image, the white liberals always knew what was good for the blacks and told them so. The wonder of it all is that the black people have believed in them for so long. It was only at the end of the 50s that the blacks started demanding to be their own guardians.

Nowhere is the arrogance of the liberal ideology demonstrated so well as in their insistence that the problems of the country can only be solved by a bilateral approach involving both black and white.... Hence the multiracial political organisations and parties and the "nonracial" student organisations, all of which insist on integration not only as an end goal but also as a means.

The integration they talk about is first of all artificial in that it is a response to conscious manoeuvre rather than to the dictates of the inner soul. In other words the people forming the integrated complex have been extracted from various segregated societies with their in built [sic] complexes of superiority and inferiority and these continue to manifest themselves even in the "nonracial" setup of the integrated complex. As a result the integration so achieved is a one-way course, with the whites doing all the talking and the blacks the listening....

. . .

It will not sound anachronistic to anybody genuinely interested in real integration to learn that blacks are asserting themselves in a society where they are being treated as perpetual under-16s. One does not need to plan for or actively encourage real integration. Once the various groups within a given community have asserted themselves to the point that mutual respect has to be shown then you have the ingredients for a true and meaningful integration. At the heart of true integration is the provision for each man, each group to rise and attain the envisioned self. Each group must be able to attain its style of existence without encroaching on or being thwarted by another. Out of this mutual respect for each other and complete freedom of self-determination there will obviously arise a genuine fusion of the life-styles of the various groups. This is true integration.

From this it becomes clear that as long as blacks are suffering from [an] inferiority complex—a result of 300 years of deliberate oppression, denigration and derision—they will be useless as co-architects of a normal society where man is nothing else but man for his own sake. Hence what is necessary as a prelude to anything else that may come is a very strong grassroots build-up of black consciousness such that blacks can learn to assert themselves and stake their rightful claim.

Thus in adopting the line of a nonracial approach, the liberals are playing their old game. They are claiming a "monopoly on intelligence and moral judgement" and setting the pattern and pace for the realisation of the black man's aspirations. They want to remain in good books ➤

with both the black and white worlds. They want to shy away from all forms of "extremisms," condemning "white supremacy" as being just as bad as "Black Power!" They vacillate between the two worlds, verbalising all the complaints of the blacks beautifully while skillfully extracting what suits them from the exclusive pool of white privileges. But ask them for a moment to give a concrete meaningful programme that they intend adopting, then you will see on whose side they really are. Their protests are directed at and appeal to white conscience, everything they do is directed at finally convincing the white electorate that the black man is also a man and that at some future date he should be given a place at the white man's table.

In the following selection Anglican bishop Desmond Tutu (b. 1931) expressed his personal anguish at the death of Steve Biko, summarizing Biko's contributions to the struggle for justice in South Africa. Tutu won the Noble Peace Prize in 1984 and was named archbishop in 1988. From 1995 to 1998 he chaired the Truth and Reconciliation Commission, which investigated atrocities in South Africa during the years of apartheid. He stated that his objective was to create "a democratic and just society without racial divisions."

When we heard the news "Steve Biko is dead" we were struck numb with disbelief.... But no, dear friends, he is dead and we are still numb with grief, and groan with anguish....

It all seems such a senseless waste of a wonderfully gifted person, struck down in the bloom of youth, a youthful bloom that some wanted to see blighted. What can be the purpose of such wanton destruction? . . . How long can we go on appealing for a more just ordering of society where we all, black and white together, count not because of some accident of birth or a biological irrelevance—where all of us black and white count because we are human persons, human persons created in your own image.

God called Steve Biko to be his servant in South Africa—to speak up on behalf of God, declaring what the will of this God must be in a situation such as ours, a situation of evil, injustice, oppression and exploitation. God called him to be the founder father of the Black Consciousness Movement against which we have had tirades and fulminations. It is a movement by which God, through Steve, sought to awaken in the Black person a sense of

his intrinsic value and worth as a child of God, not needing to apologise for his existential condition as a black person, calling on blacks to glorify and praise God that he had created them black. Steve, with his brilliant mind that always saw to the heart of things, realised that until blacks asserted their humanity and their personhood, there was not the remotest chance for reconciliation in South Africa. For true reconciliation is a deeply personal matter. It can happen only between persons who assert their own personhood, and who acknowledge and respect that of others. You don't get reconciled to your dog, do you? Steve knew and believed fervently that being pro-black was not the same thing as being anti-white. The Black Consciousness Movement is not a "hate white movement," despite all you may have heard to the contrary. He had a far too profound respect for persons as persons, to want to deal with them under readymade, shopsoiled [sic] categories.

All who met him had this tremendous sense of a warm-hearted man, and as a notable acquaintance of his told me, a man who was utterly indestructible, of massive intellect and yet reticent; quite unshakeable in his commitment to principle and to radical change in South Africa by peaceful means; a man of real reconciliation, truly an instrument of God's peace, unshakeable in his commitment to the liberation of all South Africans, black and white, striving for a more just and more open South Africa.

QUESTIONS FOR ANALYSIS

1. What are Steve Biko's charges against white liberals in South Africa?
2. What was the proper role for whites in the anti-apartheid movement according to Biko?
3. How does Bishop Tutu's eulogy differ from the political spirit and point of view expressed in Biko's 1970 essay?
4. According to Bishop Tutu, what were Biko's strongest characteristics? Were these characteristics demonstrated in Biko's essay?

Sources: First selection from Steve Biko, *I Write What I Like*, ed. by Aelred Stubbs C.R., Bowerdean Publishing Co., Ltd.; second selection from Bishop Desmond Tutu, *Crying in the Wilderness: The Struggle for Justice in South Africa*, ed. John Webster (William B. Eerdmans Publishing Co., 1982), pp. 61–63.

power and put in place a radical program of economic and social reform in the Western Hemisphere.

The Era of Violence and Repression

In the 1970s Latin America entered a dark era of political violence. Revolutionary movements challenged the established order, and democratic governments were overturned by military revolts. A region of weak democracies in 1960 became a region of military dictatorships with little patience for civil liberties and human rights fifteen years later.

The ongoing confrontation between Fidel Castro and the United States contributed to regional crisis. The fact that the Cuban communist government survived opposition from the United States energized the revolutionary left throughout Latin America. In response, the United States increased support for its political and military allies, training many of the military leaders who led coups during this period.

Brazil was the first nation to experience the conservative reaction to the Cuban Revolution. Claiming that Brazil's civilian political leaders could not protect the nation from communist subversion, the army overthrew the government of President João Goulart (ju-wow go-LARHT) in 1964. Once in power, the military suspended the constitution, outlawed political parties, and exiled former presidents and opposition leaders. Death squads—illegal paramilitary organizations sanctioned by the government—detained, tortured, and executed thousands of citizens. The dictatorship also undertook an ambitious economic program that promoted industrialization through import substitution (see Chapter 25). Using tax and tariff policies, the Brazilian dictatorship successfully compelled foreign-owned companies to increase investment in manufacturing, especially the auto industry.

This combination of dictatorship, violent repression, and government promotion of industrialization came to be called the "Brazilian Solution." Elements of this "solution" spread across much of the region. In 1970 Chile's newly elected president, **Salvador Allende** (sal-VAH-dor ah-YEHN-day), undertook an ambitious program of socialist reforms and nationalized Chile's heavy industry and mines, including the American-owned copper companies that domi-

nated the economy. From the beginning of Allende's presidency, the administration of President Richard Nixon (served 1969–1973) opposed the Allende reforms. Supported by the United States, General Augusto Pinochet (ah-GOOS-toh pin-oh-CHET) led a military uprising that overthrew Allende in 1973. President Allende and thousands of Chileans died in the uprising, and thousands more were jailed, tortured, and imprisoned without trial. Pinochet rolled back Allende's socialist innovations, reduced state participation in the economy, and encouraged foreign investment.

In 1976 Argentina followed Brazil and Chile into dictatorship. Juan Perón (see Chapter 26) had been exiled in 1955 after a military uprising, but with Argentina torn by political violence he was allowed to return and was then elected president in 1973. Perón insisted that his third wife, Isabel Martínez de Perón (EES-ah-bell mar-TEEN-ehz deh pair-OWN), be his vice president, and she inherited the presidency after his death in 1974, but Argentina suffered during her weak administration, wracked by inflation, terrorism, and labor protests. Impatient with her policies, the military seized power and suspended the constitution in 1976. During the next seven years it fought what it called the **Dirty War** against terrorism. More than nine thousand Argentines lost their lives; thousands of others endured arrest and torture before democracy was restored.

Yet some revolutionary movements persisted, reaching a peak in 1979 in Nicaragua with the overthrow of the corrupt dictatorship of Anastasio Somoza. This broad alliance of revolutionaries and reformers called themselves **Sandinistas** (sahn-din-EES-tahs), from Augusto César Sandino, who had led Nicaraguan opposition to U.S. military intervention

Salvador Allende (1908–1973) Socialist president of Chile who was elected in 1970 and overthrown and killed by the military in 1973.

Dirty War Suppression of leftist groups by the Argentine military (1976–1983) characterized by the use of illegal imprisonment, torture, and executions.

Sandinistas Members of a leftist coalition that overthrew the Nicaraguan dictator Anastosio Somoza in 1979 and attempted to install a socialist economy. The United States financed an armed uprising against the Sandinista government. In 1990 the Sandinistas lost power after a national election.

The Nicaraguan Revolution Overturns Somoza A revolutionary coalition that included Marxists drove the dictator Anastasio Somoza from power in 1979. The Somoza family had ruled Nicaragua since the 1930s and maintained a close relationship with the United States.

between 1927 and 1932. The Sandinistas sought to imitate the Soviet-style economy of Cuba, nationalizing the properties of the Nicaraguan elite and U.S. companies.

U.S. president Jimmy Carter (served 1977–1980) stopped the flow of U.S. arms to regimes with the worst records of human rights violations and reestablished Panamanian sovereignty of the Panama Canal in 1999, but he failed to find common ground with the intransigent Sandinistas. Ronald Reagan (served 1981–1989), who succeeded Carter as president, vigorously opposed both the Nicaraguan Revolution and a revolutionary movement in neighboring El Salvador. When the U.S. Congress would not support U.S. military intervention, Reagan turned to a proxy force of anti-Sandinista Nicaraguans, called *Contras* (counter-revolutionaries). Overconfident Sandinistas responded by calling for free elections in 1990, but they badly miscalculated. Exhausted

by more than a decade of violence, Nicaraguans rejected the Sandinistas and elected a middle-of-the-road coalition led by Violeta Chamorro (vee-oh-LET-ah cha-MOR-roe).

The Reagan administration also thwarted the FMLN (Farabundo Martí [fah-rah-BOON-doh mar-TEE] National Liberation Front) guerrilla movement in El Salvador by training the Salvadoran army and providing hundreds of millions of dollars in military assistance. Chastened by the Sandinista defeat, the FMLN negotiated for peace with the brutal dictatorship that had been responsible for the deaths of critics, even those in the Catholic clergy, and transformed themselves into a civilian political party.

Violence also abated when right-wing military dictatorships in Brazil, Chile, and Argentina came to an end between 1983 and 1990, brought down by their own excesses and by popular desires for a return to constitutional democratic government. But the U.S.

Susan Meiselas/Magnum Photos, Inc.

SECTION REVIEW

- The CIA interfered forcefully in Guatemala, and its attempt to do the same in Cuba helped lead to the Cuban Missile Crisis; meanwhile, Castro created a socialist economy.

- In Brazil, Argentina, Chile, and elsewhere, military dictatorship crushed revolutionary and reform movements.

- During the 1970s and 1980s, political violence grew in Latin America, sponsored in part by U.S. fears of communist subversion.

- The United States opposed revolutionary movements in Nicaragua and El Salvador.

- In the 1990s the United States pushed Latin American nations to introduce neoliberal reforms that opened economies to greater foreign investment.

invasion of the tiny Caribbean nation of Grenada in 1983 and the arrest of Panamanian dictator General Manuel Noriega (MAN-wel no-ree-EGG-ah) in 1989 were powerful reminders of American power in the region, and the United States pushed Latin American nations to remove limitations on foreign investment, eliminate many social welfare programs, and reduce public-sector employment.

JAPAN, CHINA, AND THE FOUR TIGERS

■ *Why were developments in China so different from those in other parts of East Asia?*

East Asia had suffered as much as Europe from the Second World War. Eastern China had been invaded and occupied by Japanese forces from 1937 to 1945, and the rest of China had been the scene of a long and bitter civil war (1934–1949) between the nationalist (or Guomindang) army supported by the United States and the communist People's Liberation Army (see Chapter 27). War continued on the Korean peninsula until 1953. After that, it took several decades before prosperity came to East Asia.

The Japanese Economic Miracle

Japan signed a peace treaty with most of its former enemies in 1951 and regained independence from American occupation the following year. Renouncing militarism and its imperialist past, Japan remained on the sidelines throughout the Korean War. Its new constitution, written under American supervision in 1946, allowed only a limited self-defense force, banned the deployment of Japanese troops abroad, and gave the vote to women.

With peace restored, the Japanese focused their resources on rebuilding industries and expanding trade. During the U.S. occupation, Japan became closely tied to the West by trade and soon benefited from the postwar recovery. At the same time, controls placed on Japan by peace conditions kept its military expenditures low during the Cold War, providing an exceptional environment to invest in economic development and infrastructure.

Three industries that took advantage of government aid and new technologies were key to Japan's emergence as an economic superpower after 1975. Electricity was in short supply in 1950, and Tokyo suffered from chronic power outages. Japan responded by constructing a power grid between 1951 and 1970 that produced 60 million kilowatts of electricity. Most of this new capacity came from hydroelectric sources. At the same time steel production and shipbuilding developed rapidly, placing Japan among world leaders in both industries.

The Japanese industrial model differed from the American and European models. During the American occupation, Japanese industrial conglomerates known as *zaibatsu* were broken up. Although ownership of major industries became less concentrated, new industrial alliances appeared. These formed six major **keiretsu** (kay-REHT-soo), each of which included a major bank as well as firms in industry, commerce, and construction tied together in an interlocking ownership structure. Minor keiretsu could also form around a corporation, like Toyota, and its major suppliers. These industrial combinations developed close relationships with the government, which imposed tariffs and import regulations to inhibit foreign competition. Such support was crucial in fostering the development of Japan's major industries.

Through the 1970s and 1980s, the Japanese superiority in manufactured goods produced huge trade surpluses. Attempts by the United States and the

keiretsu Alliances of corporations and banks that dominate the Japanese economy.

European Community to pry open the Japanese market through negotiation had only limited success. In 1990, Japan's trade surplus with the rest of the world was double that of 1985. Many experts assumed that Japan's competitive advantages would propel it past the United States as the world's preeminent industrial economy. But its economy began to stall at the end of the decade when Japanese real estate and stock markets became overvalued and prices collapsed. By the end of the 1990s Japan's GDP had suffered a loss greater than that suffered by the United States in the Great Depression.

Mao's Zedong's Many Revolutions

While Japan benefited from being outside the Cold War, China was deeply involved in Cold War politics. When Mao Zedong (maow dzuh-dong) and the communists defeated the nationalists in 1949 and established the People's Republic of China (PRC) (see Chapter 27), their main ally and arms supplier was the Soviet Union, although by 1956 the PRC and the Soviet Union had diverged politically. Mao had his own notions of communism that focused strongly on the peasantry, which the Soviets had ignored in favor of the industrial working class.

Mao's Great Leap Forward in 1958 was intended to propel China into the ranks of world industrial powers. His plan relied on maximizing the output of small-scale, village-level industries and instituting mass collectivization in agriculture. It took over a decade for this small-scale industrialization to result in record levels of agricultural and industrial production, but these policies demonstrated Mao's willingness to carry out massive economic and social experiments of his own devising.

In 1966, in another nationwide radical program called the **Cultural Revolution**, Mao ordered the mass mobilization of Chinese youth into Red Guard units to ward off the stagnation and bureaucratization he saw in the Soviet Union. To this end, Red Guard units criticized and purged teachers, party officials, and intellectuals for "bourgeois values." Internal party conflict continued until 1971, when Mao admitted that attacks on individuals had gotten out of hand. The last years of the Cultural Revolution were dominated by radicals led by Mao's wife, Jiang Qing (jyahn ching), who restricted artistic and intellectual activity.

The rift between the PRC and the Soviet Union allowed U.S. president Richard Nixon (served 1969–1974) to revive relations with China. In 1971 the United States agreed to allow the PRC to join the United Nations and occupy China's permanent seat on the Security Council, displacing the Chinese nationalist government on Taiwan. The following year, Nixon visited Beijing, initiating a new era of cooperation between the People's Republic of China and the United States.

The Four Tigers

A few other Asian states imitated the Japanese model of close cooperation between government and industry. South Korea overcame the devastation of the Korean War in little more than a decade through a combination of inexpensive labor, strong technical education, and sustained domestic capital reserves. It developed heavy industries like steel and shipbuilding, as well as consumer industries like automobiles and consumer electronics. Japanese investment and technology transfers accelerated this process.

Taiwan, Hong Kong, and Singapore moved so rapidly in the same direction that these three nations and South Korea were called the **Asian Tigers**. Taiwan suffered a number of political reverses, including the loss of its United Nations seat to the People's Republic of China in 1971 and the withdrawal of diplomatic recognition by the United States. Nevertheless, it achieved remarkable economic progress, based on smaller, more specialized companies and investment in the People's Republic of China.

Hong Kong and Singapore were former British colonies with limited resources. Singapore's economy rested on its busy port and on banking and commercial services. After separating from Malaysia in 1965, this society of around 4 million people diversified by building textile and electronics industries. Hong Kong's economic prosperity, based on its ports as well as its banking and commercial services, was increasingly

Cultural Revolution (China) Campaign in China ordered by Mao Zedong to purge the Communist Party of his opponents and instill revolutionary values in the younger generation.

Asian Tigers South Korea, Taiwan, Hong Kong, and Singapore, so called because their economies expanded so fast.

tied to China's growing economy. Worried about Hong Kong's reintegration into the People's Republic of China in 1997, local capitalists moved significant amounts of capital to safe havens like the United States and Canada, but in recent years Hong Kong has regained its dynamism and is now even more closely tied to the rapidly developing Chinese economy.

These **newly industrialized economies (NIEs)** all had disciplined and hardworking labor forces, and all invested heavily in education. As early as 1980 Korea had as many engineering graduates as Germany, Britain, and Sweden combined. These countries also emphasized outward-looking export strategies and had high rates of personal saving—about 35 percent of GDP—that allowed them to fund investment in new technology. Like Japan, they practiced government sponsorship and protection. Despite this momentum, the region was deeply shaken by a financial crisis that began in 1997. Like the recession that afflicted Japan in 1990, a combination of bad loans, weak banks, and the international effects of currency speculation led to a deep regional crisis that was stabilized only by the efforts of the United States, Japan, and international institutions like the International Monetary Fund.

NATIONAL AND RELIGIOUS CONFLICTS IN THE MIDDLE EAST

■ *What roles did nationalism and religious identity play in Middle Eastern politics?*

Independence came gradually to the Arab countries of the Middle East. Syria and Lebanon gained independence when the League of Nations mandate system ended after World War II. Iraq, Egypt, and Jordan enjoyed nominal independence between the two world wars but remained under indirect British control until the 1950s.

The Arab-Israeli Conflict

Overshadowing all Arab politics, however, was the struggle with Israel. British policy on Palestine between the wars oscillated between favoring Zionist Jewish immigrants and the indigenous Palestinian Arabs. After the war, under intense pressure to resettle European Jewish refugees, Britain turned the Palestine problem over to the United Nations. In November 1947 the General Assembly voted in favor of partitioning Palestine into two states, one Jewish and one Arab. The Jewish community made plans to declare independence, while the Palestinians, who felt the proposed land division was unfair, reacted in horror and took up arms. When Israel declared its independence in May 1948, neighboring Arab countries sent armies to help the Palestinians crush the newborn state.

Israel prevailed and some 700,000 Palestinians became refugees, finding shelter in United Nations refugee camps in Jordan, Syria, Lebanon, and the Gaza Strip (a bit of coastal land on the Egyptian-Israeli border). The right of these refugees to return home remains a focal point of Arab politics today. In 1967, Israel responded to threatening military moves by Egypt's Nasser by preemptively attacking Egyptian and Syrian air bases. In six days, Israel won a smashing victory. It also won control of Jerusalem (previously split with Jordan), the West Bank, the Gaza Strip, the strategic Golan Heights in southern Syria, and the entire Sinai Peninsula (see Map 28.2). Acquiring all of Jerusalem satisfied Jews' deep longing to return to their holiest city, but Palestinians continued to regard Jerusalem as their destined capital, and Muslims in many countries protested Israeli control of the Dome of the Rock, a revered Islamic shrine located in the city. These acquisitions resulted in a new wave of Palestinian refugees.

The rival claims to Palestine continued to plague Middle Eastern politics. The Palestine Liberation Organization (PLO), headed by Yasir Arafat (AR-uh-fat),

newly industrialized economies (NIEs) Rapidly growing new industrializing nations of the late twentieth century, including the Asian Tigers.

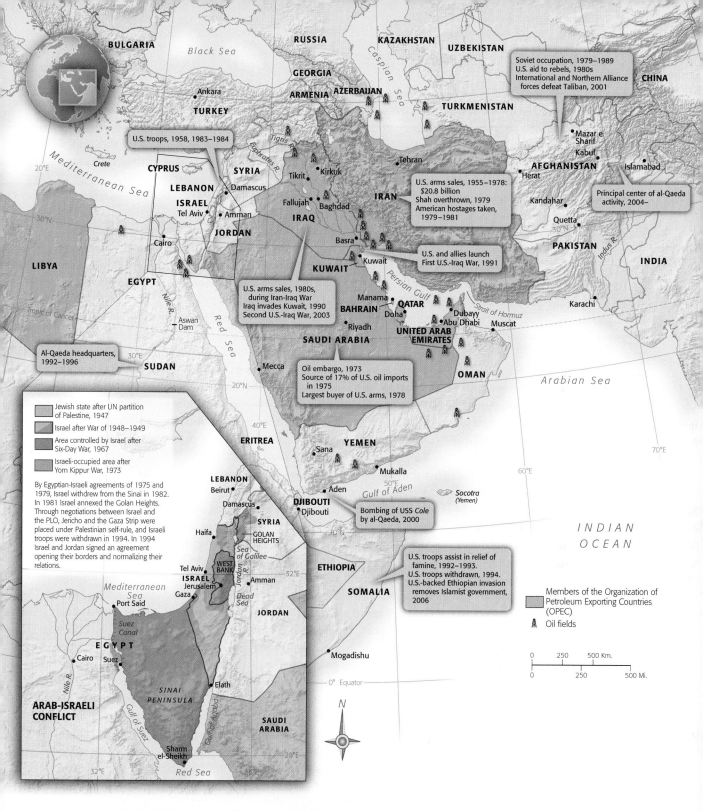

Map 28.2 Middle East Oil and the Arab-Israeli Conflict, 1947–1973 Private European and American companies had long controlled oil resources. In the 1960s OPEC negotiated agreements for sharing control and eventually establishing national ownership. This set the stage for the use of oil as a weapon in the 1973 Arab-Israeli war as well as for subsequent price increases. © Cengage Learning

677

waged guerrilla war against Israel, frequently engaging in acts of terrorism. The militarized Israelis were able to blunt or absorb these attacks and launch counterstrikes that involved assassinations and bombings. Though the United States proved a firm friend to Israel and the Soviet Union armed the Arab states, neither superpower saw the struggle between Zionism and Palestinian nationalism as a vital concern—until oil became a political issue.

The Oil Crisis of 1973

The phenomenal concentration of oil wealth in the Middle East—Saudi Arabia, Iran, Iraq, Kuwait, Libya, Qatar, Bahrain, and the United Arab Emirates—was not fully realized until after World War II, when demand for oil rose sharply as civilian economies recovered. In 1960, as world demand rose, oil-producing states formed the **Organization of Petroleum Exporting Countries (OPEC)** to promote their collective interest in higher revenues.

Oil politics and the Arab-Israeli conflict intersected in October 1973 during the Yom Kippur War. Surprise attacks by Syria and Egypt threw the Israelis into temporary disarray, but Israel won a clear military victory in the end. Supported by military supplies from the United States, it drove back Syrian forces and trapped an Egyptian army at the Suez Canal's southern end. The United States then arranged a cease-fire and the disengagement of forces. But before that could happen, the Arab oil-producing countries voted to embargo oil shipments to the United States and the Netherlands as punishment for their support of Israel.

The implications of using oil as an economic weapon profoundly disturbed the worldwide oil industry. Prices rose—along with feelings of insecurity. In 1974 OPEC responded to the turmoil in the oil market by quadrupling prices, setting the stage for massive transfers of wealth to the producing countries and provoking a feeling of crisis throughout the consuming countries.

Islamic Revolutions in Iran and Afghanistan

Although the Arab-Israel conflict and the oil crisis concerned both superpowers, the prospect of direct military involvement remained remote. When unexpected crises developed in Iran and Afghanistan, however, significant strategic issues came to the foreground. Both countries adjoined Soviet territory. Exercising post–Vietnam War caution, the United States reacted with restraint. The Soviet Union chose a bolder and ultimately disastrous course.

Muhammad Reza Pahlavi (REH-zah PAH-lah-vee) succeeded his father as shah of Iran in 1941. In 1953, covert intervention by the U.S. Central Intelligence Agency (CIA) helped the shah retain his throne in the face of a movement to overturn royal power. Even after nationalizing the foreign-owned oil industry, the shah continued to enjoy American support. When oil income mushroomed following the price increases of the 1970s, the United States encouraged the shah to spend his nation's growing wealth on advanced American weaponry. By the 1970s popular resentment against the shah's dependence on the United States, the ballooning wealth of the elite families that supported him, and the brutality, inefficiency, malfeasance, and corruption of his government led to mass opposition.

Ayatollah Ruhollah Khomeini (A-yat-ol-LAH ROOH-ol-LAH ko-MAY-nee), a Shi'ite (SHE-ite) philosopher-cleric who had spent most of his eighty-plus years in religious and academic pursuits, became the voice and symbolic leader of the opposition. Massive protests forced the shah to flee Iran and ended the monarchy in 1979. In the Islamic Republic of Iran, which replaced the monarchy, Ayatollah Khomeini was supreme arbiter of disputes and guarantor of the religious legitimacy. Elections were held, but monarchists, communists, and other groups opposed to the idea of an Islamic Republic were barred from office. Shi'ite clerics with little training for government service emerged in many of the highest posts, and stringent measures were taken to replace Western styles and culture with Islamic norms. Universities temporarily closed as their faculties were purged of secularists and monarchists.

Organization of Petroleum Exporting Countries (OPEC) Organization formed in 1960 by oil-producing states to promote their collective interest in generating revenue from oil.

Ayatollah Ruhollah Khomeini (1902–1989) Shi'ite philosopher and cleric who led the overthrow of the shah of Iran in 1979 and created an Islamic republic.

James Pozarik/Getty Images

Shortage at the Pumps As prices rose in the late 1970s, consumers tried to hoard supplies by filling gas cans at neighborhood stations. For the first time gas prices exceeded $1 a gallon.

Women were compelled to wear modest Islamic garments outside the house, while semi-official vigilante committees policed public morals and cast a pall over entertainment and social life.

The United States under President Carter had criticized the shah's repression, but the overthrow of a long-standing ally and the creation of the Islamic Republic were blows to American prestige. Khomeini saw the United States as a "Great Satan" and encouraged Islamic revolutionary movements elsewhere, to the distress of both the United States and Israel. In November 1979, Iranian radicals seized the U.S. embassy in Tehran and then held fifty-two diplomats hostage for 444 days. Americans felt humiliated by their inability to rescue the hostages or negotiate their release.

In the fall of 1980, shortly after negotiations for the release of the hostages began, **Saddam Husain** (sah-DAHM hoo-SANE), the ruler of neighboring Iraq, invaded Iran to topple the Islamic Republic. His own dictatorial rule rested on a secular Arab-nationalist philosophy and long-standing friendship with the Soviet Union, which supplied his army. He feared that Iran's revolutionary fervor would infect his own country's Shi'ite majority and threaten his power. While the war pitted American weapons in Iranian hands against Soviet weapons in Iraqi hands, the superpowers avoided overt involvement. Covertly, however, the Reagan administration sent arms via Israel to Iran, hoping to gain the release of other American hostages held by Muslim radicals in Lebanon and to secretly finance the Contra war against the Sandinista government of Nicaragua. When this deal came to light in 1986, the resulting political scandal intensified American hostility toward Iran. Openly tilting toward Iraq, President Reagan sent the U.S. Navy to the Persian Gulf, ostensibly to protect nonbelligerent shipping. This threatening move helped persuade Iran to accept a cease-fire in 1988.

While the United States experienced anguish and frustration in Iran, the Soviet Union found itself

Saddam Husain (1937–2006) President of Iraq from 1979 until overthrown by the American invasion in 2003. Waged war on Iran from 1980 to 1988. His invasion of Kuwait was repulsed in the Persian Gulf War of 1991.

- The politics of the postwar Middle East came to be dominated by the Arab-Israeli conflict.
- In response to an Arab-Israeli war, the Arab nations cut off oil exports, causing a severe economic crisis.
- In Iran, a radical anti-American Islamic revolution led by Ayatollah Khomeini overthrew the shah and established an anti-Western Shi'ite republic in 1979, after which Sunni Iraq attacked Iran.
- The Soviets intervened in Afghanistan in 1979 but failed to defeat religiously inspired Afghan guerrilla forces backed by the United States and Pakistan.

facing even more serious problems in neighboring Afghanistan. In 1978 a Marxist party with a secular reform agenda seized power in Afghanistan. Offended by these efforts to reform education and grant rights to women, traditional ethnic and religious leaders led a successful rebellion. In 1979, the Soviet Union responded by sending its army to Afghanistan to bolster communist rule.

With the United States, Saudi Arabia, and Pakistan paying, equipping, and training Afghan rebels, the Soviet Union found itself in the same kind of unwinnable war the United States had stumbled into in Vietnam. Unable to justify the continuing drain on manpower, morale, and economic resources and facing widespread domestic discontent, Soviet leaders finally withdrew their troops in 1989. The Afghan communists held on for another three years, and then rebel groups took control of the entire country and began to fight among themselves over who should rule.

In this chaotic situation a radical Islamic party with close ties to Pakistan, the Taliban, took power in 1996. They installed a harsh religious regime and soon faced armed opposition. The Taliban had received financial support from the Saudi Arabian Osama bin Laden during their rise to power and later provided him with protection as he organized al-Qaeda (discussed in Chapter 29).

THE END OF THE BIPOLAR WORLD

■ *What led to the collapse of the Soviet bloc?*

Few in 1980 predicted the startling collapse of the Soviet Union and the socialist nations of the Warsaw Pact. The once-independent nations and ethnic groups brought within the Soviet Union and the eastern European nations seemed securely transformed by the experiences and institutions of communism. But this arrangement was nearly finished.

Crisis in the Soviet Union

Under U.S. president Ronald Reagan and the Soviet Union's general secretary Leonid Brezhnev (leh-oh-NEED BREZ-nef), the rhetoric of the Cold War remained intense. Massive new U.S. investments in armaments placed heavy burdens on a Soviet economy already suffering from shortages and mismanagement. Obsolete industrial plants and centralized planning stifled initiative and led to a declining standard of living relative to the West, while the arbitrariness of the bureaucracy, the manipulation of information, and deprivations created a crisis in morale.

Despite the growing discontent, Brezhnev refused to modify his unsuccessful policies. But he could not escape criticism. In a series of powerful books, the writer Alexander Solzhenitzyn (sol-zhuh-NEET-sin) castigated the Soviet system and particularly the Soviet prison camps. He won a Nobel Prize in literature but was charged him with treason and expelled from the country in 1974. *Samizdat* (sah-meez-DAHT), self-published underground writings by critics of the regime, circulated widely despite government efforts to suppress them.

By the time **Mikhail Gorbachev** (GORE-beh-CHOF) took up the reins of the Soviet government in 1985, war weariness, economic decay, and vocal protest had reached critical levels. Casting aside Brezhnev's hard line, Gorbachev authorized major reforms in an attempt to stave off total collapse. His policy of political openness (*glasnost*) permitted criticism of the government and the Communist Party. His policy of *perestroika* (per-ih-STROY-kuh) ("restructuring") was an attempt to address long-suppressed economic problems by moving away from central state

Mikhail Gorbachev (b. 1931) Head of the Soviet Union from 1985 to 1991. His liberalization effort improved relations with the West, but he lost power after his reforms led to the collapse of the communist governments in eastern Europe.

perestroika Policy of "restructuring" that was the centerpiece of Mikhail Gorbachev's efforts to liberalize communism in the Soviet Union.

planning and toward a more open economic system. In 1989 he ended the unpopular war in Afghanistan.

The Collapse of the Socialist Bloc

Events in eastern Europe were very important in forcing change on the Soviet Union. In 1980 protests by Polish shipyard workers in the city of Gdansk led to the formation of **Solidarity**, a labor union that grew to 9 million members. The Roman Catholic Church in Poland, strengthened by the elevation of a Pole, Karol Wojtyla (KAH-rol voy-TIL-ah), to the papacy as John Paul II in 1978, gave strong moral support to the protest movement. As Gorbachev loosened political controls in the Soviet Union after 1985, communist leaders elsewhere lost confidence in Soviet resolve, and critics and reformers in Poland and throughout eastern Europe were emboldened.

Beleaguered Warsaw Pact governments vacillated between relaxation of control and suppression of dissent. As the Catholic clergy in Poland had supported Solidarity, Protestant and Orthodox religious leaders aided the rise of opposition groups elsewhere. This combination of nationalism and religion provided a powerful base for opponents of the communist regimes. Threatened by these forces, communist governments sought to quiet the opposition by seeking solutions to their severe economic problems. They turned to the West for trade and financial assistance and opened their nations to travelers, ideas, styles, and money from Western countries, all of which accelerated the demand for change.

By the end of 1989, communist governments across eastern Europe had fallen. The dismantling of the Berlin Wall, the symbol of a divided Europe and the bipolar world, vividly represented this transformation. In Poland, Hungary, Czechoslovakia, and Bulgaria, communist leaders decided that change was inevitable and initiated political reforms. When Romanian dictator Nicolae Ceausescu (nehk-oh-LIE chow-SHES-koo) refused to surrender power, he provoked a rebellion that ended with his arrest and execution. The comprehensiveness of these changes became clear in 1990, when Solidarity leader Lech Walesa (leck wah-LEN-sah) was elected president of Poland and dissident playwright Vaclav Havel (vah-SLAV hah-VEL) was elected president of Czechoslovakia. That same year, East and West Germany were reunited, and the

The Fall of the Berlin Wall The Berlin Wall was the most important symbol of the Cold War. Constructed to keep residents of East Germany from fleeing to the West and defended by armed guards and barbed wire, it was the public face of communism. As the Soviet system fell apart, the residents of East and West Berlin broke down sections of the wall.

eastern Baltic states of Lithuania, Estonia, and Latvia declared independence from the Soviet Union.

The end of the Soviet Union then came suddenly in 1991. Gorbachev's efforts to transform the Soviet system could not keep up with the tide of change sweeping through the region. After communist hardliners botched a poorly conceived coup against Gorbachev, disgust with communism boiled over. Boris Yeltsin, the president of the Russian Republic and a long-time member of the Communist Party, led popular resistance to the coup in Moscow and emerged as the most powerful leader in the country. Russia, the largest republic in the Soviet Union, was effectively

Solidarity Polish trade union created in 1980 to protest working conditions and political repression. It began the nationalist opposition in eastern Europe.

- A faltering economy and defeat in Afghanistan undermined the communist government of the Soviet Union.
- While unrest in eastern Europe increased, Mikhail Gorbachev instituted reform policies that accelerated the process of change.
- The Soviet Union collapsed in 1991, leaving behind sixteen independent nations.

taking the place of the disintegrating USSR. In September 1991, as the sixteen smaller republics of the Soviet Union declared their independence, the Congress of People's Deputies voted to dissolve the union. Mikhail Gorbachev went into retirement.

CONCLUSION

Shortly after World War II, the Soviet Union and the Western democracies led by the United States began to prepare for a new round of hostilities, establishing competing military alliances and attempting to influence the new governments of nations formerly occupied by the Axis. Each side portrayed this tension as a struggle between irreconcilably different social and economic systems. The boundary that separated the United States and its allies and the Soviet Union and its allies, and that Churchill called an "iron curtain," was soon defended by massive armies and powerful nuclear weapons.

This Cold War quickly became global in character as distant civil wars, regional conflicts, and nationalist revolutions were transformed by support provided by these rivals for global ascendancy. Many of the flash points in this war were provided by the desire of colonized peoples to establish independent nations. The most powerful force in the postwar era was nationalism, the desire of peoples to control their own destinies. This reality was obscured by the global contest of the Cold War.

In Africa, the Middle East, South Asia, and Latin America, this desire to throw off foreign controls led to the creation of scores of new nations by the 1970s. Each nation's struggle had its own character. While in India these passions led to a partition into two states, similar sentiments led in China to the overthrow of a weak pro-Western government and the creation of a communist dictatorship. In much of Africa, the Middle East, and the Caribbean, nationalism overturned colonial rule. In the Middle East the desire for self-government was complicated by the creation of the state of Israel. In Latin America, where most nations had been independent for well over a century, nationalist passions focused on a desire for economic independence and an end to foreign military interventions. For this reason Castro found it easy to connect his revolutionary ambitions to anticolonial movements elsewhere.

The end of Japanese control in Korea and Vietnam led to territorial partitions that separated Soviet-leaning and Western-allied polities. Civil war and foreign interventions soon followed. In both cases the Soviet Union and China supported communist forces. The United States committed large military forces to protect the anticommunist governments, gaining a stalemate in Korea and eventually losing in Vietnam. While these outcomes were mixed for the superpowers, the wars were contained and managed so as to prevent direct engagement and nuclear conflict.

CHAPTER REVIEW

THE COLD WAR

■ *What were the major threats to world peace during the Cold War?* (page 657)

The arms race associated with the rivalry between the West and the Soviets produced the largest peacetime militaries in world history. The reliance of both sides on nuclear weapons meant that any direct conflict had the potential to escalate into a global holocaust. For more than fifty years massed armies faced each other across Europe. This confrontation was projected into space, as each side sought to advertise its technological capacity through satellite launches and finally a moon landing. During the Cold War, leaders of the opposing alliances viewed their struggle as a global conflict between irreconcilable systems. This meant that every popular movement, revolution, or civil war was strategically important and could involve the superpowers or their allies. Because fighting each other directly would have risked escalation to the level of nuclear exchange, they carefully avoided crises that might provoke such confrontations. Nevertheless, the antagonism led to protracted and costly wars in Korea and especially Vietnam.

DECOLONIZATION AND NATION BUILDING

■ *What problems did less developed nations face?* (page 663)

Decolonization occurred on a vast scale. Each nation had to organize and institute some form of government, but few were able to do so without experiencing coups, rewritten constitutions, or regional rebellions. Most of the new nations, while trying to establish political stability, also faced severe economic challenges. Some new governments openly sided with one superpower of the other, and skilled leaders in the nonaligned countries could play the powers off each other and extract money and support from both.

REVOLUTIONS, REFORM, AND REPRESSION IN LATIN AMERICA

■ *How did U.S. policies during the Cold War affect Latin America?* (page 668)

Latin American nationalists aimed for economic independence and an end to foreign intervention. Fidel Castro identified these goals with those of countries struggling for independence in Asia and Africa. However, fear of communist revolution led the United States to support counter-revolutionary uprisings, coups, and military dictatorships in several Latin American countries, often causing disruption and hardship.

JAPAN, CHINA, AND THE FOUR TIGERS

■ *Why were developments in China so different from those in other parts of East Asia?* (page 674)

Protected by the American strategic umbrella, Japan turned its energies to building the world's second largest capitalist economy, and it was quickly followed by the four Asian Tigers. In China, in contrast, the victory of the communists over the nationalists and Cold War hostility toward the United States and its allies allowed Mae Zedong to instigate social revolutions along communist lines.

NATIONAL AND RELIGIOUS CONFLICTS IN THE MIDDLE EAST

■ *What roles did nationalism and religious identity play in Middle Eastern politics?* (page 676)

In the Middle East, nationalist movements were directed not just at former colonial powers but also at Israel and its allies in the West. The nationalist desire of Israelis to have their own country was partly inspired by religious feelings and came in direct conflict with the identical desire of Palestinians. In Iran, nationalists rejected Western and communist dominance, while in Afghanistan, a communist coup aroused opposition. In both areas nationalism found expression in a revival of Islamic identity.

THE END OF THE BIPOLAR WORLD

■ *What led to the collapse of the Soviet bloc?* (page 680)

Economic decline caused by inefficiencies in the communist system, as well as defeat in Afghanistan, weakened the hold of the Communist Party on the Soviet people and of the USSR on the nations of eastern Europe. As communists lost control, first the eastern European nations and then the smaller republics of the Soviet Union declared their independence.

Key Terms

North Atlantic Treaty Organization (NATO) (p. 657)

Warsaw Pact (p. 657)

Cold War (p. 657)

United Nations (p. 657)

World Bank (p. 658)

Marshall Plan (p. 658)

European Economic Community (Common Market) (p. 659)

iron curtain (p. 660)

Truman Doctrine (p. 660)

Korean War (p. 661)

Vietnam War (p. 661)

Cuban Missile Crisis (p. 662)

nonaligned nations (p. 665)

Third World (p. 665)

Salvador Allende (p. 672)

Dirty War (p. 672)

Sandinistas (p. 672)

keiretsu (p. 674)

Cultural Revolution (China) (p. 675)

Asian Tigers (p. 675)

newly industrialized economies (NIEs) (p. 676)

Organization of Petroleum Exporting Countries (OPEC) (p. 678)

Ayatollah Ruhollah Khomeini (p. 678)

Saddam Husain (p. 679)

Mikhail Gorbachev (p. 680)

perestroika (p. 680)

Solidarity (p. 681)

CHAPTER 29

New Challenges in a New Millennium

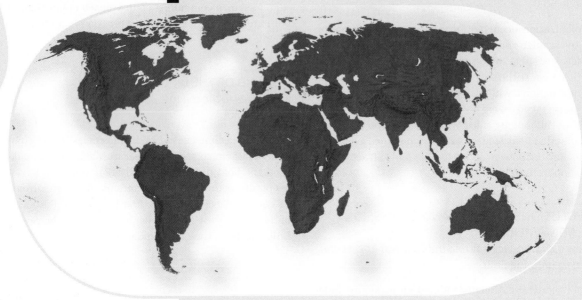

© Cengage Learning

The workday began normally at the World Trade Center in lower Manhattan on the morning of September 11, 2001. The fifty thousand people who worked there were making their way to the two 110-story towers. Suddenly, at 8:46 A.M., an American Airlines Boeing 767 with 92 people on board, traveling at a speed of 470 miles per hour (756 kilometers per hour), crashed into floors 94 to 98 of the north tower, igniting the 10,000 gallons (38,000 liters) of fuel in its tanks. Just before 9:03 A.M. a United Airlines flight with 65 people on board and a similar fuel load hit floors 78 to 84 of the south tower.

As the burning jet fuel engulfed the collision areas, the buildings' occupants struggled through smoke-filled corridors and down dozens of flights of stairs. Many of those trapped above the crash sites used cell phones to say good-bye to loved ones. Rather than endure the flames and fumes, a few jumped to their deaths.

Just before 10 o'clock, temperatures had risen to the point that the steel girders in the impacted area of the south tower suddenly gave way. The collapsing upper floors crushed the floors underneath one by one, engulfing lower Manhattan in a dense cloud of dust. Twenty-eight minutes later the north tower pancaked in a similar manner. Miraculously, most of the buildings' occupants had escaped before the towers collapsed. Besides the people on the planes, nearly 2,600 lost their lives, including some 400 police officers and firefighters helping in the evacuation.

That same morning another American Airlines jet crashed into the Pentagon, killing all 64 people on board and 125 others inside the military complex near Washington, D.C. Passengers on a fourth plane managed to overpower their hijackers, and the plane crashed in rural Pennsylvania, killing all 45 on board.

The four planes had been hijacked by teams of Middle Eastern men who slit the throats of service and flight personnel and seized control. Of the nineteen hijackers, fifteen were from Saudi Arabia. All had links to an extremist Islamic organization, al-Qaeda (ahl–KAW-eh-duh) (the base or foundation), commanded by a rich Saudi named Usama bin Laden (oo-SAH-mah bin LAH-din) who was incensed with

American political, military, and cultural influence in the Middle East. The men were educated and well traveled, had lived in the United States, and spoke English. Some had trained as pilots so that they could fly the hijacked aircraft.

The hijackers left few records of their motives, but the acts spoke for themselves. The World Trade Center was a focal point of international business, the Pentagon the headquarters of the American military. The fourth plane was probably meant to hit the Capitol or the White House, the legislative and executive centers of the world's only superpower.

The events of September 11, which became commonly referred to as 9/11, can be understood on many levels. The hijackers and those who sympathized with them saw themselves as engaged in a holy struggle against economic, political, and military institutions they believed to be evil. People directly affected, political leaders around the world, and most television watchers described the attacks as evil deeds against innocent victims.

To understand why the nineteen attackers were heroes to some and terrorists to others, one needs to explore the historical context of global changes at the turn of the millennium and the ideological tensions they have generated. The unique prominence of the United States in every major aspect of global integration, as well as its support for pro-American governments overseas, also elicits sharply divergent views.

GLOBALIZATION AND THE WORLD ECONOMY

■ *What are the main benefits and dangers of growing political, economic, and cultural integration?*

The turn of the millennium saw the intensification of **globalization** trends that had been building since the 1970s. Growing trade and travel and new technologies were bringing all parts of the world into closer economic, political, and cultural interdependence. The collapse of the Soviet Union had completed the dissolution of territorial empires that had been under

globalization The economic, political, and cultural integration and interaction of all parts of the world brought about by increasing trade, travel, and technology.

way throughout the twentieth century. In their place were some two hundred independent nations, a growing number of which embraced democratic institutions. However, increasing interdependency also facilitated a global economic crisis that exploded in 2008 when the massive accumulation of debt at the financial institutions in the gigantic U.S. economy (larger than the economies of the next five countries combined—Japan, Germany, Great Britain, China (including Hong Kong), and France—became unsustainable.

New Technologies and the World Economy

Since 1945 the global economy has expanded more rapidly than at any time in the past. Wave after wave of technological innovations have led to faster, cheaper communications and transportation as well as improvements in industrial and agricultural technologies. The material abundance would have amazed those who experienced the first Industrial Revolution (see Chapter 20). Improvements in existing technologies accounted for much of the developed world's productivity during the 1950s and 1960s, with both capitalist and socialist governments expanding highway systems, improving railroads, and constructing airports and nuclear plants. But new technologies played a role, too—none more so than the computer.

Few had anticipated that a silicon chip containing the computer's brains would lead to smaller, faster computers and now tablets and smart phones that when combined with the Internet would create a communication revolution. Access to a vast international database of research, opinion, entertainment, and commerce brought peoples and markets closer, and computer innovation also improved efficiency and product quality by allowing most modern industries to rely on small dedicated computers to control and monitor machines or, following Japan's early lead, incorporate robots into manufacturing and mining.

In the post–World War II years, many companies with multinational ownership and management invested in and marketed products throughout the world. These transnational corporations became the primary agents for technological change. By the end of the twentieth century the growing economic power of corporations in industrialized nations allowed them to invest directly in the mines, plantations, and public utilities of less developed regions. International trade agreements and open markets furthered the process. Not only did Ford, Nissan, BMW, and other car companies produce and sell cars internationally, but their shareholders, workers, and managers also came from numerous nations.

The location of manufacturing plants overseas and the acquisition of corporate operations by foreign buyers rendered such global firms as transnational as the products they sold. In the 1970s and 1980s American brand names like Levi's, Coca-Cola, Marlboro, Gillette, McDonald's, and Kentucky Fried Chicken were global phenomena. But in time Asian names—Honda, Hitachi, Sony, Sanyo, and Mitsubishi—were blazoned in neon and on giant video screens on the sides of skyscrapers, along with European brands such as Nestlé, Mercedes, Pirelli, and Benetton. Since 1979, China's emergence as a global industrial power has accelerated this process of integration and diffusion.

As transnational manufacturers, agricultural conglomerates, and financial giants became wealthier and more powerful, they increasingly escaped the controls imposed by national governments. If labor costs were too high in Japan, antipollution measures too intrusive in the United States, or taxes too high in Great Britain, transnational companies relocated—or threatened to do so. In 1945, for example, the U.S. textile industry was located in low-wage southern states, dominating the American market and exporting to the world. As wages in the American South rose and global competition increased, producers began relocating plants to Puerto Rico in the 1980s and to Mexico after NAFTA went into effect in 1994 (discussed later in this chapter). Now China is the primary manufacturer of textiles.

Globalization and Economic Crisis

The expansion of global trade and communications and the privatization of government enterprises fueled an economic boom in the 1990s that cooled abruptly in the wake of 9/11. The rate of growth in world trade fell from 13 percent in 2000 to only 1 percent in 2001.

However, growth in China and India resumed quickly, and the very large populations of these two

Chronology

	Politics	Economics and Society
2000	**2000** Al-Qaeda attacks American destroyer USS *Cole* in Yemen	
2001	**2001** Terrorists destroy the World Trade Center and damage the Pentagon on September 11 **2001** United States armed forces overthrow Taliban regime in Afghanistan	**2001–2003** Terrorist attacks trigger global recession **2001** Shanghai Cooperation Organization formed **2001** United Statess withdraws from Kyoto Protocol on global warming
2002		**2002** Euro currency adopted in twenty-seven European countries
2003	**2003** United States and allies invade Iraq	
2004	**2004** Terrorists bomb Spanish trains **2004–2009** Genocidal conflict ongoing in Darfur region of Sudan	**2004** Ten new members admitted to European Union
2005	**2005** Terrorists bomb London transit system	
2006	**2006** Israel attacks Hezbollah in Lebanon in response to its seizure of Israeli soldiers	
2007	**2007** Assassination of Benazir Bhutto deepens political crisis in Pakistan	
2008		**2008** Collapse of mortgage debt bubble in United States triggers global recession
2010		**2010** China becomes world's second largest economy
2011	**2011** Usama bin Laden killed by American raiders in Pakistan **2011** Arab Spring uprisings force government change in Egypt, Tunisia, Libya, and Yemen	

countries marked them as future world economic powers. Their growth increased pressure on world energy supplies; however, the United States continued to consume a quarter of the world's petroleum production and by 2013 had resumed its position as the world's largest producer through the production of oil derived from shale deposits. OPEC's manipulation of world oil prices, combined with political instability in the Middle East, had caused crude oil prices to soar between 1973 and 1985. But aside from those years, the average price of oil remained consistently below $20 per barrel (adjusted for inflation) throughout the second half of the twentieth century. In the year 2000, however, oil prices began to rise again because of confidence in world economic expansion. By 2008 a barrel of crude had spiked to $145, fueling ambitious economic programs in major oil producers like Russia, Venezuela, Iran, Saudi Arabia, and the small sheikhdoms of the Persian Gulf, as well as in the newer OPEC states Ecuador, Nigeria, and Angola. With the economic crisis of 2008, prices fell abruptly, but by 2013 the price per barrel was back in the $90–$100 range.

Regional trade associations came into being to promote growth, reduce the economic vulnerability of member states, and, less explicitly, balance American economic dominance. The twenty-seven-member European Union (EU) was the most successful (see Map 29.1), adopting in 2002 a new common currency, the euro, that competed with the U.S. dollar for investment and banking. However, unequal levels of development among members became a source of crisis in 2009 when an economic downturn devastated European stock markets, increasing unemployment.

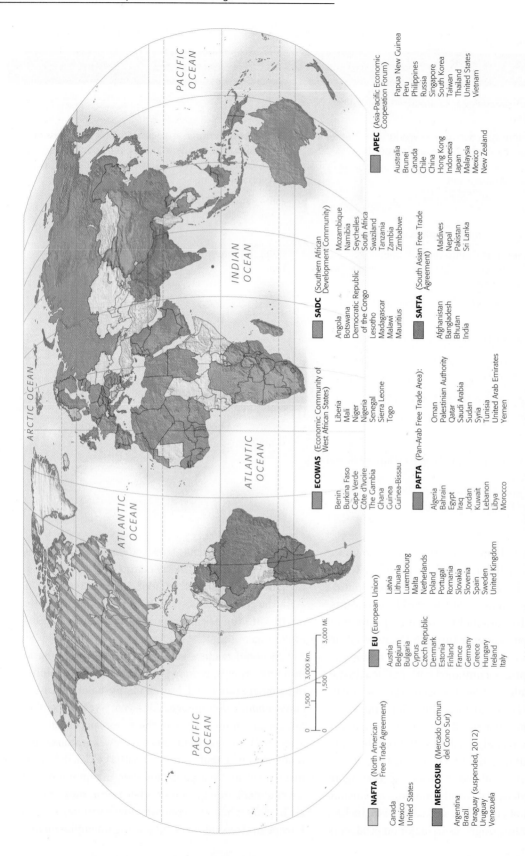

NAFTA (North American Free Trade Agreement)

Canada
Mexico
United States

MERCOSUR (Mercado Comun del Cono Sur)

Argentina
Brazil
Paraguay (suspended, 2012)
Uruguay
Venezuela

EU (European Union)

Austria
Belgium
Bulgaria
Cyprus
Czech Republic
Denmark
Estonia
Finland
France
Germany
Greece
Hungary
Ireland
Italy
Latvia
Lithuania
Luxembourg
Malta
Netherlands
Poland
Portugal
Romania
Slovakia
Slovenia
Spain
Sweden
United Kingdom

ECOWAS (Economic Community of West African States)

Benin
Burkina Faso
Cape Verde
Côte d'Ivoire
Ghana
Guinea
Guinea-Bissau
Liberia
Mali
Niger
Nigeria
Senegal
Sierra Leone
Togo

PAFTA (Pan-Arab Free Trade Area):

Algeria
Bahrain
Egypt
Iraq
Jordan
Kuwait
Lebanon
Libya
Morocco
Oman
Palestinian Authority
Qatar
Saudi Arabia
Sudan
Syria
Tunisia
United Arab Emirates
Yemen

SADC (Southern African Development Community)

Angola
Botswana
Democratic Republic of the Congo
Lesotho
Madagascar
Malawi
Mauritius
Mozambique
Namibia
Seychelles
South Africa
Swaziland
Tanzania
Zambia
Zimbabwe

SAFTA (South Asian Free Trade Agreement)

Afghanistan
Bangladesh
Bhutan
India
Maldives
Nepal
Pakistan
Sri Lanka

APEC (Asia-Pacific Economic Cooperation Forum)

Australia
Brunei
Canada
Chile
China
Hong Kong
Indonesia
Japan
Malaysia
Mexico
New Zealand
Papua New Guinea
Peru
Philippines
Russia
Singapore
South Korea
Taiwan
Thailand
United States
Vietnam

Map 29.1 Regional Trade Associations, 2004 International trade and development are major concerns of governments in developed and developing countries. NAFTA, Mercosur, and the EU are free-trade areas. The other associations promote trade and development. © Cengage Learning

With this crisis, the idea of the euro, a common currency that symbolized Europe's progress toward unity, came into question because some member states like Greece were not at liberty to devalue their currency to reduce the debt they could no longer cover with their shrunken economies. Wealthier countries, led by Germany, urged austerity over investment and thereby further increased unemployment and discontent. In an increasingly globalized network of financial markets and institutions, Europe's debt crisis generated economic anxiety from Japan to New York City.

Despite the EU's expansion, the North American Free Trade Agreement (NAFTA), which eliminated tariffs among the United States, Canada, and Mexico in 1994, governed the world's largest free-trade zone. Yet heated debate in the United States over illegal immigration across the Mexican border limited popular enthusiasm for the agreement. The third largest free-trade zone, Mercosur, created by Argentina, Brazil, Paraguay (now suspended), and Uruguay in 1991 and subsequently expanded to include five associate members, visualized a parliament consisting of eighteen representatives from each member state. Other free-trade associations operated in West Africa, southern Africa, Southeast Asia, Central America, the Pacific Basin, and the Caribbean.

The Shanghai Cooperation Organization (SCO), formed in 2001 with China, Russia, and four former Soviet Central Asian republics (Kazakhstan, Kyrgystan, Tajikistan, and Uzbekistan), originally pursued common security interests, such as combating separatist movements and terrorism. But the organization's five observer members—Iran, India, Pakistan, Afghanistan, and Mongolia—the first a major oil exporter and the latter two possessing rich unexploited mineral deposits, lent credence to its twenty-year plan for reducing barriers to trade and population movement. Iran, which formally applied for full membership in 2008, posed a special problem insofar as U.S.-led international pressures to curb its nuclear program encountered resistance from both Russia and China.

Because of the inequalities and downturns that are intrinsic to free economic markets, the global bodies that tried to manage world trade and finance found it hard to convince poorer nations that they were not concerned only with the welfare of richer countries. In 1995 the world's major traders established the **World Trade Organization (WTO)** to encourage reduced barriers and enforce international agreements. When Russia became the 157th member in 2012, the largest economy not to be included was Iran. The WTO has had many critics and has regularly encountered street protests during its ministerial meetings. Some protesters have claimed that the organization's idea of free trade enables low-cost foreign manufacturers to attract business and shrink the job opportunities in richer states; others have demanded continuing tariff protection for local farmers.

The International Monetary Fund (IMF) and the World Bank (see Chapter 28), established to help economically troubled nations, have also been criticized for giving conditional assistance and mandating such unpopular economic reforms as terminating government subsidies for basic foodstuffs, cutting social programs, and liberalizing investment. A 2002 United Nations meeting in Monterrey, Mexico, pledged increased attention to the problem of economic despair, especially in Africa, though these commitments have seldom resulted in increased support.

The global financial crisis that began in 2008 had complicated roots. In 1997 the investment boom in Asian markets burst and investment shifted to the United States, where now massive growth in imported goods and unprecedented increases in housing prices spurred a rapid increase in the U.S. stock market. At the same time, money from overseas was invested in the U.S. treasury, which helped fund the wars in Afghanistan and Iraq while lowering taxes. The American national debt climbed dramatically.

When housing prices collapsed in 2008, many homeowners who had borrowed money using their homes as collateral (at these higher values) found themselves so deeply in debt on their mortgages that they lost their homes. New and risky lending techniques spread these bad debts throughout the banking system. Stock prices fell, banks teetered on the brink of collapse, and employers laid off workers they could no longer afford or did not need as consumer demand plummeted. The effects spread worldwide.

World Trade Organization (WTO) An international body established in 1995 to foster and bring order to international trade.

Justin Lane/epa/Corbis

Watching Financial Markets Fall After years of economic boom, much of it fueled by inflated housing prices in the United States and ingenious new financial instruments that concealed risk, the world's stock markets fell drastically in 2008–2009. American stocks lost approximately one-third of their value. The banking crisis and resulting unemployment reminded economists of the Great Depression of the 1930s. People in all walks of life—from heads of state, to retirees, to ordinary workers—were forced to reappraise their financial situations.

Economists proclaimed it the worst economic crisis since the Great Depression of the 1930s.

In President Barack Obama's first weeks in office in January 2009, he proposed a series of steps, including massive increases in government spending, to jolt the economy back to health. Some of the plans yielded fruit, such as a rescue of the American automobile industry. Others were stymied after 2010 by partisan debate in the House of Representatives about whether the national debt or unemployment took precedence. Economic recovery remained slow and fragile in both the United States and the European Union. The trade expansion that had signaled the promise of globalization at the beginning of the century faded from memory, and the interdependence that had bound the world's economies in a cycle of growth became a dead weight that dragged many countries down.

China Rejoins the World Economy

After Mao Zedong's death in 1976, the Chinese communist leadership began economic reforms that relaxed state control, allowing more initiative and permitting individuals to accumulate wealth. Under China's leader **Deng Xiaoping** (dung shee-yao-ping), China permitted foreign investment for the first time since the communists came to power in 1949. Between 1979 and 2005 foreign direct investment in China grew to more than $600 billion as McDonald's, General Motors, Coca-Cola, Airbus, Toyota, and many other foreign companies began doing business. As a result,

Deng Xiaoping (1904–1997) Communist Party leader who forced Chinese economic reforms after the death of Mao Zedong.

Shanghai—Old Meets New The city of Shanghai is one of the great success stories in a rapidly growing Chinese economy, but its prosperity has left many behind. In this photo a poor man crosses a street in Shanghai's rich, modern commercial district carrying goods in hand-woven baskets balanced on a neck yoke, a technology thousands of years old.

by 2010 China had become a major industrial power and the world's most important exporting nation. But state-owned enterprises still employed more than 100 million workers, and most foreign-owned companies were limited to special economic zones. The result was a dual industrial sector—one modern, efficient, and connected to international markets, the other directed by political decisions. In 2010 China became the world's second largest economy, surpassing Japan.

Despite this enormous achievement, the Chinese people remain substantially poorer than people in mature industrial economies. Per capita GDP (GDP divided by population) has reached only $5,413.57, whereas advanced industrial economies have a per capita GDP of $42,063. However, China is now richer than much of the developing world. Latin America has a per capita GDP of $4,299, the Middle East $2,329, and sub-Saharan Africa $940.

SECTION REVIEW

- Improvements in existing technology and new technologies such as the computer have improved manufacturing efficiency and connections among producers and consumers from different regions and nations.

- Globalization has created a more integrated world economy, reducing the ability of a single nation to escape the effects of distant events.

- Global interdependence and rapid economic expansion and speculation led to a global financial crisis in 2008 that plunged the world into the worst economic slowdown since the Great Depression of the 1930s.

- China experienced three decades of rapid growth after Deng Xiaoping reformed and modernized its economy, and thus far it has weathered the worldwide financial crisis.

China's expansion has depended heavily on exports. While the Chinese economy continued to grow during the worldwide 2008 recession, some economists wonder if a deep contraction will hit the Chinese economy as it has others after a period of speculation-fueled investment.

THE QUESTION OF VALUES

■ *What roles do religious beliefs and secular ideologies play in the contemporary world?*

As people around the world first faced the opportunities of globalization and then the fear of global recession, they tried to make sense of these changes in terms of their own value systems. With 6 billion people, the world was big enough to include many different approaches, whether religious or secular, local or international, traditional or visionary. In some cases, however, conflicting visions fed violence.

Faith and Politics Religious beliefs increasingly inspired political actions during the second half of the twentieth century, and the trend intensified in the new century. Though for Americans this change reversed two centuries of growing secularism, Western analysts did not agree on the cause of the religious revival.

Evangelical Protestants became a powerful conservative political force in the United States, and

Catholic opposition to abortion, homosexuality, marriage of priests, and admission of women to the priesthood characterized conservative belief worldwide. In Israel, ultra-orthodox Jews played a leading role in settling the West Bank and Gaza, the Palestinian territories captured by Israel in 1967, and vehemently resisted both Israel's unilateral withdrawal from Gaza in 2005 and subsequent plans for withdrawal from the West Bank. And in India, Hindu zealots made the BJP party a powerful political force.

Yet Islam became the focus of most discussions of faith and politics (see Diversity and Dominance: Conflict and Civilization). The birth of the Islamic Republic of Iran in the revolution of 1979 made visible a current of Muslim political assertiveness that had been building in several Muslim countries for twenty years. But by the year 2000 acts of **terrorism** perpetrated by non-Iranian Muslim groups claiming to be acting for religious reasons were capturing the headlines.

Terrorism is a political tactic by which comparatively weak militants use violent acts against civilians to convince a frightened public that danger is everywhere and the government is incapable of protecting them. Though terrorism has a long history, the instantaneous communications and the tradition in the news business of publicizing violence increased its effectiveness from the 1980s onward.

Bombings, kidnappings, and assassinations made political sense to all sorts of political groups: Palestinians confronting Israel; national separatists like the Tamils in Sri Lanka, Basques in Spain; Chechens in Russia; Catholic and Protestant extremists in Northern Ireland; and racial militias in Rwanda and Darfur, to name a few. But al-Qaeda gained the lion's share of attention because it targeted the United States and Europe, concentrated on spectacular attacks, drew from Muslims all over the world, and made effective use of news coverage and audiovisual communications.

Their media star and ideological spokesman, **Usama bin Laden**, was born into a wealthy Saudi family and educated as an engineer. He fought against the Soviet Union in Afghanistan and trained a core group of fighters called al-Qaeda. Though his family disowned him and Saudi Arabia stripped him of his citizenship, his calls for holy war (*jihad*) and his

portrayal of the United States as a puppet-master collaborating with Israel to murder innocent Muslims and supporting the suppression of Muslim political movements by authoritarian Muslim governments made sense to millions of Muslims, even if only a very few committed themselves to follow him into battle.

Al-Qaeda blew up American embassies in Kenya and Tanzania in 1998, crippled the U.S. Navy destroyer *Cole* during a port call in Yemen in 2000, and then capped everything by attacking the World Trade Center and the Pentagon on 9/11. When the "global war on terrorism" declared by President George Bush (served 2001–2008) failed to eliminate bin Laden, his mystique grew; and the American toppling in 2001 of the Taliban regime in Afghanistan, which had sheltered Bin Laden, and invasion of Iraq in 2003 convinced many Muslims that Bin Laden was right. Further terrorist attacks—by Indonesians on tourists on the island of Bali in 2002, by North Africans on commuter trains servicing Madrid in 2004, by English-born Muslims on the London transit system in 2005, and by Pakistanis on luxury hotels in Mumbai, India, in 2008—made it clear that the violence unleashed by al-Qaeda had become decentralized and that recruits and cells might no longer be taking orders from bin Laden. Even after an American commando operation killed bin Laden in his hideout in Pakistan in 2011, groups affiliated with al-Qaeda continued to operate in Yemen, Libya, and Mali.

In trying to explain a current of violence that seemed to be centered on Muslims, some analysts argued that Islam itself encouraged violence against non-Muslims and that conservative Muslims like Usama bin Laden were opposed to freedom and modernity. The counterargument pointed out that the vast majority of Muslims saw their religion as one of peace, that al-Qaeda used modern military and

terrorism Political belief that extreme and seemingly random violence will destabilize a government and permit the terrorists to gain political advantage. Though an old technique, terrorism gained prominence in the late twentieth century with the growth of worldwide mass media that, through their news coverage, amplified public fears of terrorist acts.

Usama bin Laden (1957–2011) Saudi-born Muslim extremist who funded the al-Qaeda organization that was responsible for several terrorist attacks, including those on the World Trade Center and the Pentagon in 2001.

propaganda techniques, and that many of its operatives, like bin Laden himself, graduated from modern technical programs. To those who argued that the United States instigated al-Qaeda's wrath by supporting Israel and stationing troops in Saudi Arabia, others pointed out that the United States had championed the Muslim cause in Bosnia in 1992–1995, drove the secular dictator Saddam Husain out of Kuwait in 1991, and supported the popular uprisings of the Arab Spring in 2011.

Universal Rights and Values

Alongside the growing influence of religion on politics, efforts to promote adherence to universal human rights also expanded. The modern human rights movement grew out of the French Declaration of the Rights of Man (1789) and the U.S. Constitution (1787) and Bill of Rights (1791). Over the next century, the logic of universal rights moved Westerners to undertake international campaigns to end slave trading and slavery throughout the world and to secure equal rights for women.

International organizations in the twentieth century secured agreement on labor standards, the rules of war, and the rights of refugees. The pinnacle of those efforts was the **Universal Declaration of Human Rights**, passed by the United Nations General Assembly in 1948, which proclaimed itself "a common standard of achievement for all peoples and nations." Its thirty articles condemned slavery, torture, cruel and inhuman punishment, and arbitrary arrest, detention, and exile. The Declaration called for freedom of movement, assembly, and thought. It asserted rights to life, liberty, and security of person; to impartial public trials; and to education, employment, and leisure. The principle of equality was most fully articulated in Article 2:

> Everyone is entitled to all the rights and freedoms set forth in this Declaration, without distinction of any kind, such as race, color, sex, language, religion, or political or other opinion, national or social origin, property, birth or other status.[1]

This passage reflected an international consensus against racism and imperialism and a growing acceptance of the importance of social and economic equality. Most newly independent countries joining the United Nations willingly signed the Declaration because it implicitly condemned European colonial regimes.

Besides the official actions of the United Nations and various national governments, **nongovernmental organizations (NGOs)** have been important forces promoting human rights. Amnesty International, founded in 1961, concentrates on gaining the freedom of people who have been tortured or imprisoned without trial and campaigns against summary execution by government death squads or other gross violations of rights. Other NGOs have devoted themselves to famine relief, refugee assistance, and health care around the world. Médecins Sans Frontières (Doctors Without Borders), founded in 1971, was awarded the Nobel Peace Prize in 1999 for offering medical assistance in scores of crises.

While NGOs often worked on individual situations in specific countries, other universal goals became enshrined in international agreements. Such agreements made genocide a crime and promoted environmental protection of the seas, of Antarctica, and of the atmosphere. However, the United States and a few other nations were greatly concerned that such treaties would unduly limit their sovereignty or threaten their national interests. For this reason the U.S. Congress delayed ratifying the 1949 convention on genocide until 1986. More recently the United States demanded exemption for Americans from the jurisdiction of the International Criminal Court, created in 2002 to try international criminals, declaring that "enemy combatants" taken prisoner during the "global war on terrorism" should not be treated in accordance with the Third Geneva

Universal Declaration of Human Rights A 1948 United Nations covenant binding signatory nations to the observance of specified rights.

nongovernmental organizations (NGOs) Nonprofit international organizations devoted to investigating human rights abuses and providing humanitarian relief. Two NGOs won the Nobel Peace Prize in the 1990s: International Campaign to Ban Landmines (1997) and Doctors Without Borders (1999).

[1]"Universal Declaration of Human Rights," in *Twenty-five Human Rights Documents* (New York: Center for the Study of Human Rights, Columbia University, 1994), 6.

Diversity & Dominance

Conflict and Civilization

In 1993 Samuel P. Huntington, a professor of government at Harvard University, published "The Clash of Civilizations?" in the journal Foreign Affairs. This article provoked extraordinary debate, particularly after the 9/11 attacks on the World Trade Center and the Pentagon. Some readers deemed it an accurate description of a post–Cold War world in which Islamic countries were destined to conflict violently with the countries of Europe and North America. Others saw it as imprecise in its failure to clarify what a "civilization" is, imperialistic in its unquestioning assumption of Western superiority, and encouraging of anti-Muslim prejudice.

The interactions between civilizations vary greatly in the extent to which they are likely to be characterized by violence. Economic competition clearly predominates between the American and European subcivilizations of the West and between both of them and Japan. On the Eurasian continent, however, the proliferation of ethnic conflict, epitomized at the extreme in "ethnic cleansing," has not been totally random. It has been most frequent and most violent between groups belonging to different civilizations. In Eurasia the great historic fault lines between civilizations are once more aflame. This is particularly true along the boundaries of the crescent-shaped Islamic bloc of nations from the bulge of Africa to central Asia. Violence also occurs between Muslims, on the one hand, and Orthodox Serbs in the Balkans, Jews in Israel, Hindus in India, Buddhists in Burma and Catholics in the Philippines. Islam has bloody borders.

Rejoinders to Huntington's thesis saw it as a cornerstone of the aggressive policies adopted by the Bush administration after 9/11. As an alternative, they stressed the common values held by peaceful societies and the need for intercultural understanding. Mohammed Khatami, the president of the Islamic Republic of Iran, found support for a more positive framing of the matter when the United Nations, following his proposal, declared 2001 the year of "Dialogue Among Civilizations." Almost simultaneously, the Organization of the Islamic Conference (now called the Organization of Islamic Cooperation), a fifty-seven-member international body headquartered in Saudi Arabia and composed of states with large Muslim populations, elaborated upon this concept in the "Tehran Declaration on Dialogue Among Civilizations."

Tehran Declaration on Dialogue Among Civilizations

Praise be to Allah and peace and blessing be upon His prophet and kin and companion.

The representatives of Heads of State and Government of OIC member states . . . [recognizing] the United Nations General Assembly resolution 53/22, designating the year 2001 as the United Nations year of Dialogue among Civilizations;

Guided by the noble Islamic teachings and values [each of the following principles is accompanied by reference to a verse in the Quran] on human dignity and equality, tolerance, peace and justice for humankind, and promotion of virtues and proscription of vice and evil;

Drawing upon the Islamic principles of celebration of human diversity, recognition of diversified sources of knowledge, promotion of dialogue and mutual understanding, genuine mutual respect in human interchanges, and encouragement of courteous and civilized discourse based on reason and logic;

Reaffirming the commitment of their Governments to promote dialogue and understanding among various cultures and civilizations, aimed at reaching a global consensus to build a new order for the next millennium founded in faith as well as common moral and ethical values of contemporary civilizations;

Requests the Secretary-General of the OIC to submit this declaration for endorsement to the Chairman of the Eighth Islamic Summit and the 26th Islamic Conference of Foreign Ministers for appropriate action:

A) General principles of dialogue among civilizations
1. Respect for the dignity and equality of all human beings without distinctions of any kind and of nations large and small;
2. Genuine acceptance of cultural diversity as a permanent [quality] of human society and a cherished asset for the advancement and welfare of humanity at large;
3. Mutual respect and tolerance for the views and values of various cultures and civilizations, as well as the right of members of all civilizations to preserve their cultural heritage and values, and rejection of desecration of moral, religious or cultural values, sanctities and sanctuaries;

> 4. Recognition of diversified sources of knowledge throughout time and space, and the imperative of drawing upon the areas of strengths, richness and wisdom of each civilization in a genuine process of mutual enrichment;
> 5. Rejection of attempts for cultural domination and imposition as well as doctrines and practices promoting confrontation and clash between civilizations;
> 6. Search for common grounds between and within various civilizations in order to face common global challenges;
>   Acceptance of cooperation and search for understanding as the appropriate mechanism for the promotion of common universal values as well as for the suppression of global threats;
> 7. Commitment to participation of all peoples and nations, without any discrimination, in their own domestic as well as global decision-making and value distribution processes;
> 8. Compliance with principles of justice, equity, peace and solidarity as well as fundamental principles of international law and the United Nations Charter....

A few years later, a joint proposal by the governments of Spain and Turkey received a similar endorsement by the United Nations. This led to the creation of the Alliance of Civilizations. The underlying principles of this organization were expressed in the 2006 report of its "High-Level Group," a body of eminent political, intellectual, and spiritual figures from around the world.

Alliance of Civilizations Report of the High-Level Group

I. Bridging the World's Divides

1.1 Our world is alarmingly out of balance. For many, the last century brought unprecedented progress, prosperity, and freedom. For others, it marked an era of subjugation, humiliation and dispossession. Ours is a world of great inequalities and paradoxes: a world where the income of the planet's three richest people is greater than the combined income of the world's least developed countries; where modern medicine performs daily miracles and yet 3 million people die every year of preventable diseases; where we know more about distant universes than ever before, yet 130 million children have no access to education; where despite the existence of multilateral covenants and institutions, the international community often seems helpless in the face of conflict and genocide. For most of humanity, freedom from want and freedom from fear appear as elusive as ever.

1.2 We also live in an increasingly complex world, where polarized perceptions, fueled by injustice and inequality, often lead to violence and conflict, threatening international stability. Over the past few years, wars, occupation and acts of terror have exacerbated mutual suspicion and fear within and among societies. Some political leaders and sectors of the media, as well as radical groups have exploited this environment, painting mirror images of a world made up of mutually exclusive cultures, religions, or civilizations, historically distinct and destined for confrontation.

1.3 The anxiety and confusion caused by the "clash of civilizations" theory regrettably has distorted the terms of the discourse on the real nature of the predicament the world is facing. The history of relations between cultures is not only one of wars and confrontation. It is also based on centuries of constructive exchanges, cross-fertilization, and peaceful coexistence. Moreover, classifying internally fluid and diverse societies along hard-and-fast lines of civilizations interferes with more illuminating ways of understanding questions of identity, motivation and behavior. Rifts between the powerful and the powerless or the rich and the poor or between different political groups, classes, occupations and nationalities have greater explanatory power than such cultural categories. Indeed, the latter stereotypes only serve to entrench already polarized opinions. Worse, by promoting the misguided view that cultures are set on an unavoidable collision course, they help turn negotiable disputes into seemingly intractable identity-based conflicts that take hold of the popular imagination. It is essential, therefore, to counter the stereotypes and misconceptions that deepen patterns of hostility and mistrust among societies.

QUESTIONS FOR ANALYSIS

1. How important are culture and religion, as opposed to governing ideology or economic inequality, in explaining current world conflicts?
2. Can idealistic statements by governments be effective in curbing acts of violence carried out by individual zealots or terrorist groups?
3. Should general statements about culture play a role at the level of personal relations in the neighborhood, the workplace, or the classroom?

Sources: Samuel P. Huntington, "The Clash of Civilizations?," *Foreign Affairs* 72, no. 3 (Summer 1993). "The Tehran Declaration on Dialogue Among Civilizations," Organization of the Islamic Conference, *www.isesco.org.ma/english/publications/dig/CH11.php*; "High-Level Group Report," Alliance of Civilizations, available online at *www.unaoc.org/content/view/64/94/lang,english/*.

Convention (1950) on humane treatment of prisoners of war.

Women's Rights

The women's rights movement, which began on both sides of the North Atlantic in the nineteenth century, became an important human rights issue in the twentieth century. Rights for women became accepted in Western countries and were enshrined in the constitutions of many nations newly freed from colonial rule. In 1979 the United Nations General Assembly adopted the Convention on the Elimination of All Forms of Discrimination Against Women, and in 1985 the first international conference on the status of women, sponsored by the United Nations Division for the Advancement of Women, was held in Nairobi, Kenya. A second conference in Beijing ten years later added momentum to the movement. By 2012, all but seven UN member countries—Iran, Palau, Somalia, Sudan, South Sudan, Tonga, and the United States—had ratified the convention, though the United States and Palau had signed it without ratification.

Besides highlighting the similarity of the problems women face around the world, international conferences have also revealed great variety in the views and concerns of women. Feminists from the West, who had been accustomed to dictating the agenda and who had pushed for the liberation of women in other parts of the world, sometimes found themselves accused of having narrow concerns and condescending attitudes. Some non-Western women complained about Western feminists' endorsement of sexual liberation and about the deterioration of family life in the West. While agreeing with Western feminists' concerns about female circumcision, a form of genital mutilation that can cause chronic infections or permanently impair sexual enjoyment, some non-Western feminists found the issue less important than poverty, rape, and AIDS.

The conferences were more important for the attention they focused on women's issues than for the solutions they generated. The search for a universally accepted women's rights agenda proved elusive because of local concerns and strong disagreement on abortion and other issues. Nevertheless, increases in women's education, access to employment, political participation, and control of

---

SECTION REVIEW

- The second half of the twentieth century has seen an increase in political action inspired by religious belief.
- Militant Islam has risen in response to the claim that the United States supports such authoritarianism in many Muslim countries.
- Universal standards of human rights have gained wider acceptance and underlie the work of the United Nations, individual states, and NGOs.
- Concepts of human rights have expanded to address genocide and environmental protection.
- Global debates on women's rights have addressed a variety of economic, political, and social problems but have also involved clashes over cultural values.

---

fertility augured well for the eventual achievement of gender equality.

Such efforts raised the prominence of human rights as a global concern and put pressure on governments to consider human rights when making foreign policy decisions. Skeptics observed, however, that a Western country might successfully prod a non-Western country to improve its human rights performance—for example, by granting women better access to education and careers—but that reverse criticism of a Western country often fell on deaf ears—for example, condemnation of the death penalty in the United States. For such critics the human rights movement was seen not as an effort to make the world more humane but as another form of Western cultural imperialism. Still, support for universal rights has grown, especially because increasing globalization has made common standards of behavior more important.

THE CHALLENGE OF POPULATION GROWTH

■ *What explains differences in the rate of population growth among the world's regions?*

The empowerment of women and deep ideological divisions concerning abortion contributed to a wide-ranging debate over population growth. For most of human history, population growth was viewed as beneficial, and human beings were seen as a source of wealth. Since the late eighteenth century, however, population growth has been viewed with increasing alarm. Some feared that food supplies could not keep up with population growth. Others foresaw class and ethnic struggle as numbers overwhelmed resources. By the second half of the twentieth century, population growth was increasingly seen as a threat to the environment.

The Industrialized Nations

From the late eighteenth to the early twentieth centuries, educated Europeans were ambivalent about the rapid increase in human population. Some saw it as a blessing that would promote economic well-being. Others warned that the seemingly relentless increase would bring disaster. The best-known pessimist was the English cleric **Thomas Malthus**, who in 1798 argued that unchecked population growth would outstrip food production. To terrify his European readers, he claimed that a visitor to China "will not be surprised that mothers destroy or expose many of their children; that parents sell their daughters for a trifle; . . . and that there should be such a number of robbers. The surprise is that nothing still more dreadful should happen."[2]

The population of Europe almost doubled between 1850 and 1914, putting enormous pressure on rural land and urban housing and overwhelming fragile public institutions. This dramatic growth forced a large wave of immigration across the Atlantic, helping to develop the Western Hemisphere and invigorating the Atlantic economy. Population growth also contributed to Europe's Industrial Revolution by lowering labor costs and increasing consumer demand.

In the generation that came of age after World War II, the views of Malthus were casually dismissed as industrial and agricultural productivity multiplied supplies of food and other necessities while expanded female employment, older age at marriage, and more effective family planning slowed the birthrate. By the 1960s Europe and other industrial societies had made the **demographic transition** to lower fertility rates (average number of births per woman) and reduced mortality. This meant that the median age in the world's most developed nations rose from twenty-nine years in 1950 to thirty-seven years by 2000.

In much of Europe and Japan, fertility levels are so low that population would fall without immigration. Japanese women have an average of 1.4 children, while Italian women have 1.2. Although Sweden tries to promote fertility with cash payments, tax incentives, and job leaves to families with children, the average number of births per woman is 1.4. By comparison, the average African woman now has 4.6 children. Higher levels of female education and employment, the material values of consumer culture, and access to contraception and abortion explain the low fertility of mature industrial nations.

As fertility has declined in the industrialized nations of western Europe, the combination of abundant food, improved hygiene, and more effective medicines and medical care has lengthened human lives. In 2000 about 20 percent of the population in Europe was sixty-five or over. By 2050 this proportion will rise to over one-third. Italy soon will have more than twenty adults fifty years old or over for each five-year-old child. Because of higher fertility and greater levels of immigration, the United States is moving in this direction more slowly than western Europe; by 2050 the median age in Europe will be fifty-two, while it will be thirty-nine in the United States. The combination of falling fertility and rising life expectancy in the industrialized nations presents a challenge very different from the one foreseen by Malthus. As the

[2]Quoted in Antony Flew, "Introduction," in Thomas Robert Malthus, *An Essay on the Principle of Population and a Summary View of the Principle of Population* (New York: Penguin Books, 1970), 30.

Thomas Malthus (1766–1834) Eighteenth-century English intellectual who warned that population growth threatened the future generations because, in his view, it would always outstrip increases in agricultural production.

demographic transition A change in the rates of population growth. Before the transition, both birthrates and death rates are high, resulting in a slowly growing population; then the death rate drops but the birthrate remains high, causing a population explosion; finally the birthrate drops and the population growth slows down. This transition took place in Europe in the late nineteenth and early twentieth centuries, in North America and East Asia in the mid-twentieth century, and, most recently, in Latin America and South Asia.

| TABLE 29.1 | Population for World and Major Areas, 1750–2050 |

Population Size (Millions)

Major Area	1750	1800	1850	1900	1950	2000	2050*
World	791	978	1,262	1,650	2,521	6,122	8,909
Africa	106	107	111	133	221	796	1,803
Asia	502	635	809	947	1,399	3,680	5,222
Europe	163	203	276	408	547	728	632
Latin America and the Caribbean	16	24	38	74	167	520	768
North America	2	7	26	82	172	316	448
Oceania	2	2	2	6	13	31	46

Percentage Distribution

Major Area	1750	1800	1850	1900	1950	2000	2050*
World	100	100	100	100	100	100	100
Africa	13.4	10.9	8.8	8.1	8.8	13.1	20.2
Asia	63.5	64.9	64.1	57.4	55.5	60.6	58.6
Europe	20.6	20.8	21.9	24.7	21.7	12.0	7.1
Latin America and the Caribbean	2.0	2.5	3.0	4.5	6.6	8.6	8.6
North America	0.3	0.7	2.1	5.0	6.8	5.2	5.0
Oceania	0.3	0.2	0.2	0.4	0.5	0.5	0.5

* Estimated.

Source: J. D. Durand, "Historical Estimates of World Population: An Evaluation" (Philadelphia: University of Pennsylvania, Population Studies Center, 1974, mimeographed); United Nations, *The Determinants and Consequences of Population Trends*, vol. 1 (New York: United Nations, 1973); United Nations, *World Population Prospects as Assessed in 1963* (New York: United Nations, 1966); United Nations, *World Population Prospects: The 1998 Revision* (New York: United Nations, forthcoming); United Nations Population Division, Department of Economic and Social Affairs, *World Population to 2300*. 2004. http://www.un.org/esa/population/publications/longrange2/WorldPop2300final.pdf.
© Cengage Learning

number of retirees increases relative to the number of employed people, the cost of a broad array of social services, including retirement income, medical services, and housing supplements for the elderly, may become unsustainable.

The Developing Nations

At current rates, 95 percent of all future population growth will be in developing nations (see Table 29.1). A comparison between Europe and Africa illustrates these changes. In 1950 Europe had more than twice the population of Africa. By 1985 Africa's population had drawn even. According to projections, its population will be three times larger than Europe's by 2050.

By the late 1970s, the demographic transition had not occurred in the poorer countries, and the issue of population growth became politicized. Leaders in some developing nations argued that larger populations would increase national power. Industrialized, mostly white, nations raised concerns about rapid population growth in Asia, Africa, and Latin America. Populist political leaders in these regions asked whether these concerns were racist. The question temporarily disarmed Western advocates of birth control.

However, once the economic shocks of the 1970s and 1980s revealed the vulnerability of poor nations, governments in the developing world jettisoned policies that promoted population growth. In the 1970s the government of Mexico had encouraged high fertility, and population rose to 3 percent per year. In the 1980s Mexico rejected these policies and began to promote birth control, leading by the 1990s to an annual population growth of 1.7.

Mortality rates have also increased in some areas as improved transportation facilitates the transmission of disease. The rapid spread of HIV/AIDS is an

Chinese Family-Planning Campaign To slow population growth, the Chinese government has sought to limit parents to a single child. Billboards and other forms of mass advertising have been an essential part of the campaign.

example of this phenomenon. Less developed regions with poorly funded public health institutions and with few resources to invest in prevention and treatment experience the highest rates of infection and the greatest mortality. Of the countries with the highest HIV/AIDS rates in 2010, thirty-seven are in Africa, three in Asia, and six in Latin America and the Caribbean. These countries are home to 87 percent of all HIV/AIDS infections. By 2007 approximately 25 million people had died of AIDS and another 33 million were infected worldwide. Prevention programs and improved drug therapies have slowed both mortality and infection rates, with the greatest successes registered in rich countries with the greatest medical resources.

After 2000, rapid population growth continued in the developing world even as birthrates fell. Birthrates fell most steeply in countries experiencing the most rapid economic development. In China the birthrate fell from 42 births per thousand in 1950 to a First World level of 13 today. In this same period birthrates declined from 43 per thousand to 23 in India, another fast-growing economy. Latin America's

birthrate declined from 43 per thousand in 1950 to 19 in 2010. Birthrates fell more slowly in sub-Saharan Africa and in Muslim countries like Pakistan and Afghanistan. Regardless of these changes, birthrates remain more than twice as high in the developing world as in the mature industrial nations, with the highest levels in the poorest countries.

Old and Young Populations

Population pyramids generated by demographers clearly illustrate the profound transformation in human reproductive patterns and life expectancy since World War II. Figure 29.1 shows the 2001 age distributions in Pakistan, South Korea, and Sweden—nations at three different stages of economic development. Sweden is a mature industrial nation. South Korea is rapidly industrializing and has surpassed many European nations in both industrial output and per capita wealth. Pakistan is a poor, traditional Muslim nation with rudimentary industrialization, low educational levels, and little effective family planning.

Figure 29.1 Age Structure Comparison Islamic Nation (Pakistan), Non-Islamic Developing Nation (South Korea), and Developed Nation (Sweden), 2001.

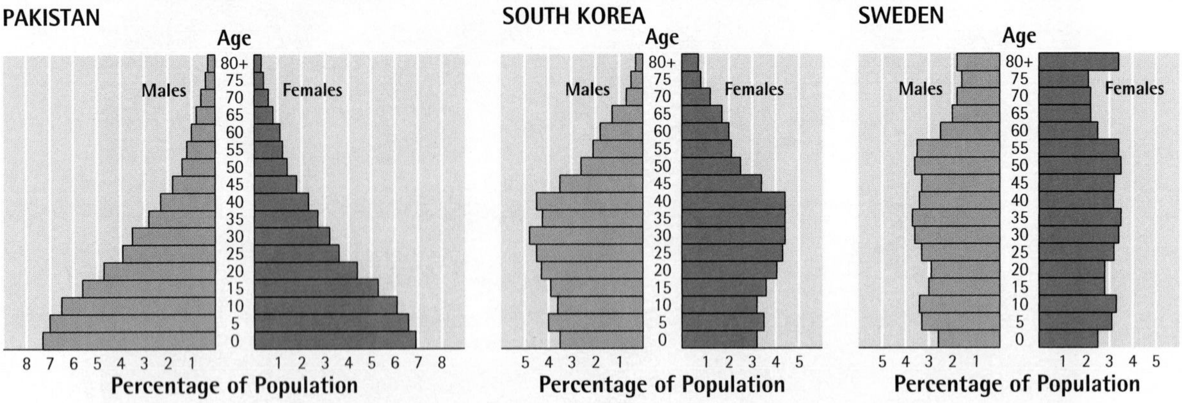

PAKISTAN

SOUTH KOREA

SWEDEN

Source: U.S. Bureau of the Census, *International Database*, 2001.

In 2001 nearly 50 percent of Pakistan's population was under age sixteen. The resulting pressures on the economy have been extraordinary. Every year approximately 150,000 men reach age sixty-five—and another 1.2 million turn sixteen. Pakistan, therefore, has to create more than a million new jobs a year or face growing unemployment and declining wages. Sweden confronts a different problem. Sweden's aging population, growing demand for social welfare benefits, and declining labor pool mean that its industries may become less competitive and living standards may decline. In South Korea, a decline in fertility dramatically altered the ratio of children to adults, creating an age distribution similar to that of western Europe.

SECTION REVIEW

- In the twentieth century the developed nations made the demographic transition to low birthrates, while the developing nations began by stressing higher birthrates.

- World population more than doubled between 1950 and 2000.

- In developed nations, falling birthrates and longer life expectancy will strain the ability of governments to care for an older population.

- Developing nations will contribute most of the world's future population growth, despite changing economies and population-planning efforts.

UNEQUAL DEVELOPMENT AND THE MOVEMENT OF PEOPLES

■ *How have differences in wealth between nations influenced global migration patterns?*

Two characteristics of the postwar world should now be clear. First, world population has increased to startlingly high levels, and much of the increase has been, and will continue to be, in the poorest nations. Second, despite decades of experimentation with state-directed economic development, most nations that were poor in 1960 are still poor today. There are notable exceptions. In Asia, first Japan, then the Asian Tigers (Taiwan, Singapore, South Korea, and Hong Kong), and more recently China have generated high rates of growth and are now among the world's most competitive industrial powers. In recent years Brazil, Mexico, India, and Turkey have also experienced significant growth. This industrial transformation has increased a world demand for raw materials that has enriched a small number of oil-exporting nations.

The Problem of Inequality

The persistence of poverty despite the global economic expansion has led to deepening inequality. The industrialized nations of the Northern Hemisphere now enjoy a larger share of the world's wealth than they did a century ago. As a result, the gap between rich and poor nations has grown

Eco Images/Universal Images Group/Getty Images

Garbage Dump in Manila, Philippines In Third World nations thousands of poor families live by sorting and selling bottles, aluminum cans, plastic, and newspapers in urban landfills.

wider. China's spectacular rise as an industrial power since 1980 is a strong indicator that some once-poor countries can become competitive. Nevertheless, the vast majority of the world's population continues to live in poverty.

There are many measures of the comparative relative wealth of nations; GDP (gross domestic product) per capita measured in U.S. dollars is among the most common. In 2010 the per capita GDP of Luxembourg was the highest in the world, $104,512; the U.S. figure was $46,702 and the Japanese figure $43,063. The countries of the European Union were generally rich, but some of the former Soviet satellites admitted to the EU recently have the GDP per capita of developing nations. France and Germany have per capita GDPs of $39,170 and $39,852, respectively. The poorest countries in the European Union, Bulgaria and Romania, have per capita GDPs similar to Russia's: $6,335, $7,539, and $10,481, respectively.

Many countries in the developing world now approach the poorest tier of European countries in

per capita GDP: Mexico, $9,133; Brazil, $10,993; Chile, $12,640; South Africa, $7,272; and Gabon, $8,768. But many more countries, especially in Asia and Africa, remain very poor: the Philippines, $2,140; India, $1,375; Pakistan, $1,019; Nigeria, $1,242; and Sudan, $1,538. The poorest, like Haiti, Kenya, and Bangladesh, have per capita GDP levels under $1,000.

International and Internal Migration

The combination of intractable poverty and growing population has generated a surge in international immigration. With the exception of Japan, large numbers of legal and illegal immigrants from poor nations with growing populations are entering the developed industrial nations. Few issues have stirred more controversy. Even moderate voices sometimes frame this discussion as a competition among peoples.

When an expanding European economy first confronted labor shortages in the 1960s, nations promoted guest worker programs and other inducements

TABLE 29.2		The World's Metropolitan Areas (population of 10 million or more)							
City	1970	City	1990	City	2011	City	2025
1 Tokyo	23.3	1 Tokyo	32.5	1 Tokyo	37.2	1 Tokyo	38.7
2 New York	16.2	2 New York	16.1	2 Delhi	22.7	2 Delhi	32.9
		3 Mexico City	15.3	3 Mexico City	20.4	3 Shanghai	28.4
		4 São Paulo	14.8	4 New York	20.4	4 Mumbai	26.6
		5 Mumbai	12.4	5 Shanghai	20.2	5 Mexico City	24.6
		6 Osaka-Kobe	11.0	6 São Paulo	19.9	6 New York	23.6
		7 Calcutta	10.9	7 Mumbai	19.7	7 São Paulo	23.2
		8 Los Angeles	10.9	8 Beijing	15.6	8 Dhaka	22.9
		9 Seoul	10.5	9 Dhaka	15.4	9 Beijing	22.6
		10 Buenos Aires	10.5	10 Calcutta	14.4	10 Karachi	20.2
				11 Karachi	13.9	11 Lagos	18.9
				12 Buenos Aires	13.5	12 Calcutta	18.7
				13 Los Angeles	13.4	13 Manila	16.3
						14 Los Angeles	15.7
						15 Shenzhen	15.5
						16 Buenos Aires	15.5
						17 Guangzhou	15.5
						18 Istanbul	14.9
						19 Cairo	14.7
						20 Kinshasa	14.5
						21 Chongqing	13.6
						22 Rio de Janeiro	13.6
						23 Bangalore	13.2

Source: International Migration Report 2002, United Nations, Department of Economic and Social Affairs, Population Division, "World Urbanization Prospects: The 1999 Revision," p. 6. The United Nations is the author of the original material. Reprinted by permission of United Nations Publications. © Cengage Learning

to immigration. However, attitudes toward immigrants changed as the size of immigrant populations grew, particularly during periods of economic contraction like the 2008 recession. Facing higher levels of unemployment, native-born workers see immigrants as competitors willing to work for lower wages and less likely to support labor unions.

Immigrants' native cultures in Latin America, Africa, and the Middle East also encourage early marriage and large families, and these high fertility rates among immigrants contribute to tensions. For example, Spain briefly became the major immigrant-receiving nation in the EU, and the immigrant component of Spain's population rose from 2.1 to 14.1 percent between 1990 and 2010, with foreign-born mothers accounting for 10 percent of all births. Since

the beginning of the recession in 2008, immigration to Spain has slowed and birthrates of both native-born and foreign-born have fallen. But even in this altered context, immigrant populations have increased in Europe and the United States, and the resulting cultural conflicts have tested definitions of citizenship and nationality.

Large-scale migrations within developing countries are a related phenomenon. Migration from rural areas to urban centers increased threefold between 1925 and 1950; the pace of migration then accelerated (see Table 29.2). While slums around the major cities of developing nations are seen as signs of social breakdown and economic failure, life in these urban slums was generally better than life in the countryside. A World Bank study estimated that three out of

- Despite rapid postwar economic growth, most of the world remains impoverished.
- Wealth inequality between industrialized and developing nations has grown.
- The resulting migration from developing to industrial nations has created growing social and cultural tensions in host countries.
- Internal migration from rural to urban areas has also rapidly increased the size of cities in developing nations since World War II.
- Migrants initially made economic gains, but the numbers are overwhelming limited urban resources.

four rural-to-urban migrants made economic gains. Residents of cities in sub-Saharan Africa, for example, were six times more likely than rural residents to have safe water. An unskilled migrant from the depressed northeast of Brazil could triple his or her income by moving to Rio de Janeiro.

As the scale of rural-to-urban migration grew, these benefits became more elusive. In the cities of the developing world, basic services have been crumbling under the pressure of rapid population growth. In Mexico City and Manila, among the world's largest cities, tens of thousands live in garbage dumps, scavenging for food. In Rio de Janeiro alone an estimated 350,000 abandoned children live in the streets and parks, begging, selling drugs, stealing, and engaging in prostitution to survive. Some nations have tried to relocate migrants back to the countryside. Indonesia, for example, has relocated more than a half-million urban residents since 1969.

TECHNOLOGICAL AND ENVIRONMENTAL CHANGE

■ *How has technological change affected the global environment in the recent past?*

Technological innovation powered the economic expansion that began after World War II. New technologies increased productivity and disseminated human creativity. They also altered the way people lived, worked, and played. Because most of the economic benefits were initially concentrated in the advanced industrialized nations, technology

increased the power of those nations relative to the developing world. This has changed in the last decade with globalization and the rising industrial role of China. Even within developed nations, postwar technological innovations did not benefit all classes, industries, and regions equally. There were losers as well as winners. Governments in the developing world were often hard-pressed to control the actions of powerful transnational corporations, for example. As a result, the worst abuses of labor or the environment usually occurred in poor nations.

Population growth and increased levels of migration and urbanization multiplied the numbers of acres farmed and the number of factories, intensifying environmental threats. In the early twenty-first century, loss of rain forest, soil erosion, global warming, air and water pollution, and extinction of species threatened the quality of life and the survival of human societies. Environmental protection, like the acquisition of new technology, has progressed most in societies with the greatest economic resources.

Conserving and Sharing Resources

In the 1960s environmental activists and political leaders began warning about the devastating environmental consequences of population growth, industrialization, and the expansion of agriculture onto marginal lands. Assaults on rain forests, the disappearance of species, and the poisoning of streams and rivers raised public consciousness. Environmental damage occurred in the advanced industrial economies and in the poorest of the developing nations. Perhaps the worst environmental record was achieved in the former Soviet Union, where industrial and nuclear wastes were routinely dumped with little concern for environmental consequences.

The expanding global population required increasing quantities of food, housing, energy, and other resources as the twentieth century ended (see Map 29.2). In the developed world, the consumer-driven economic expansion of the post–World War II years became an obstacle to addressing environmental problems, since modern economies depend on a profligate consumption of goods and resources. When consumption slows, industrial nations enter a recession, as recently demonstrated in 2008. How

Stephanie Maze/CORBIS

Loss of Brazilian Rain Forest   The destruction of large portions of Brazil's virgin rain forest has come to symbolize the growing threat to the environment caused by population growth and economic development. In this photograph we see the scale of environmental destruction.

could the United States, Germany, Japan, or China change consumption patterns to protect the environment without endangering corporate profits, wages, and employment levels?

Environmental pressures have also been extreme in the developing countries where population growth has been most dramatic. In Brazil, India, and China, for example, the need to expand food production led to rapid deforestation and the extension of farming and grazing onto marginal lands. The results were predictable—erosion and pollution—but many developing countries saw exploitation of their environmental resources and industrialization as the solution to their rapidly growing populations. Their argument was compelling: Why should Indians or Brazilians remain poor while Americans, Europeans, and Japanese grew rich?

Responding to Environmental Threats

Despite the gravity of environmental threats, there were many successful efforts to preserve and protect the environment. The Clean Air Act, the Clean Water Act, and the Endangered Species Act were passed in the United States in the 1970s as part of an environmental effort that included the nations of the European Community and Japan. Environmental awareness spread by means of the media and grassroots political movements, and most nations in the developed world enforced strict antipollution laws and sponsored massive recycling efforts. Many also encouraged resource conservation by rewarding energy-efficient factories and manufacturers of fuel-efficient cars and by promoting the use of alternative energy sources such as solar and wind power.

Environmental efforts produced significant results. In western Europe and the United States, air quality improved dramatically. In the United States, smog levels fell nearly a third from 1970 to 2000, even though the number of automobiles increased more than 80 percent. Emissions of lead and sulfur dioxide were down as well. The Great Lakes, Long Island Sound, and Chesapeake Bay were all much cleaner at the end of the century than they had been in 1970. The rivers of North American and Europe also improved.

New technologies made much of the improvement possible. Pollution controls on automobiles, planes, and factory smokestacks reduced harmful emissions. Similar progress was made in the chemical industry. Scientists identified the chemicals that threaten the ozone layer, and the phase-out of their use in new appliances and cars began.

Clearly the desire to preserve the natural environment was growing around the world. In the developed nations, continued political organization and enhanced awareness of environmental issues seemed likely to lead to step-by-step improvements in environmental policy. In the developing world and most of the former Soviet bloc, however, population pressures and weak governments were major obstacles to effective environmental policies. Since the 1990s the rapid expansion of China's industrial sector has put additional pressure on the environment. In China, for example, respiratory disease caused by pollution is the leading cause of death. It now seems likely that industrialized nations will have to fund global improvements and that the cost will be high.

Global Warming

Until the 1980s environmental alarms focused mainly on localized episodes of air and water pollution, exposure to toxic substances, waste management, and the disappearance of wilderness. The development of increasingly powerful computers and complex models of ecological interactions in the 1990s, however, made people aware of the global scope of certain environmental problems.

Many scientists and policymakers came to perceive global warming, the slow increase of the temperature of the earth's lower atmosphere, as an environmental threat requiring preventive action on an international scale. The warming is caused by a layer of atmospheric gases (carbon dioxide, methane, nitrous oxide, and ozone) that allow solar radiation to reach earth and warm it but that keep infrared energy (heat) from radiating from earth's surface back into space. Called the *greenhouse effect*, this process normally keeps the earth's temperature at a level suitable for life. However, increases in greenhouse-gas emissions—particularly from the burning of fossil fuels in industry and transportation—have added to this insulating atmospheric layer.

Flooding in Bangladesh
Typhoon-driven floods submerge the low-lying farmlands of Bangladesh with tragic regularity. Any significant rise in the sea level will make parts of the country nearly uninhabitable.

David Greedy/Getty Images

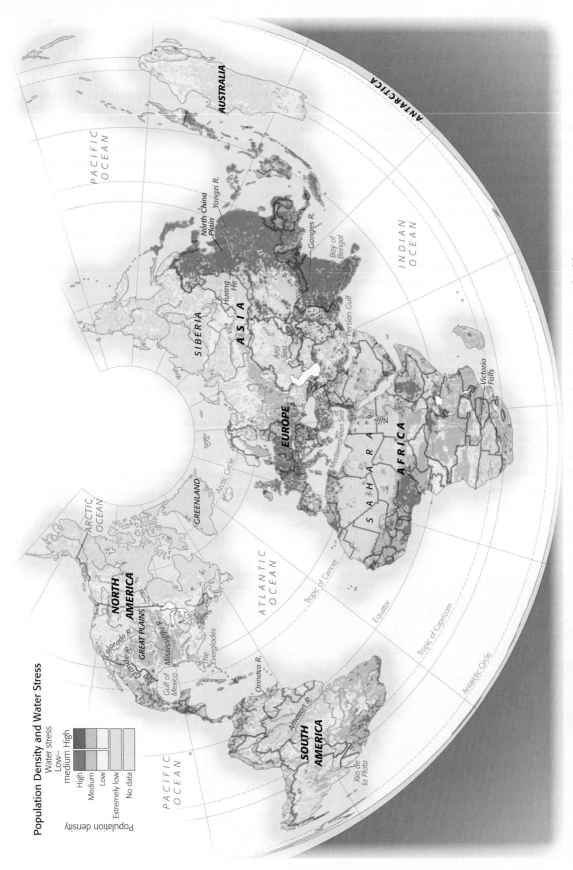

Population Density and Water Stress

Water stress

Low–
medium High

High	
Medium	
Low	
Extremely low	
No data	

Population density

PACIFIC OCEAN

ARCTIC OCEAN

GREENLAND

NORTH AMERICA

Colorado R.

Grande R.

GREAT PLAINS

Mississippi R.

The Everglades

Gulf of Mexico

Orinoco R.

SOUTH AMERICA

Amazon R.

Rio de la Plata

ATLANTIC OCEAN

Tropic of Cancer

Equator

Tropic of Capricorn

Antarctic Circle

EUROPE

Mediterranean Sea

Nile R.

SAHARA

AFRICA

Victoria Falls

INDIAN OCEAN

ASIA

SIBERIA

Huang He

Aral Sea

Persian Gulf

North China Plain

Yangzi R.

Ganges R.

Bay of Bengal

Arctic Circle

PACIFIC OCEAN

AUSTRALIA

ANTARCTICA

Map 29.2 Fresh Water Resources This map links population density and the availability of water. Red areas are highly stressed environments where populations use at least 40 percent or more of available water. Less stressed environments are blue. The deeper the shade of red or blue, the greater the environmental stress.? *Source:* From "Global Water Stress," *National Geographic,* September 2002, pp. 14–16. Reprinted by permission of the National Geographic Society. © Cengage Learning

706

Recent events have confirmed predictions of global temperature increases and melting glaciers and icecaps. Record heat hit northern Europe in the summer of 2003. Greenland glaciers and Arctic Ocean sea ice are melting at record rates, and a huge section of the Antarctic ice shelf broke up and floated away. Andean glaciers are shrinking so fast they could disappear in a decade, imperiling water supplies for drinking, irrigation, and hydroelectric production. Drought has affected much of the United States in recent years, and in 2002 Australia experienced the "Big Dry," its worst drought in a century.

Despite this evidence, governments of the industrialized countries that produce the most greenhouse gases have been slow to adopt measures stringent enough to reduce emissions because of the negative effects they believe this could have on their economies. Fearing limits on gas emissions could cripple their plans for industrial and economic expansion, many nations hesitated to sign the 1997 Kyoto Protocol, the first international agreement to impose penalties on countries that failed to cut greenhouse-gas emissions. It was a major environmental victory when Japan added its signature in March 2001, but to the consternation of many world leaders, President George W. Bush rejected the agreement, reluctant to burden American business. Shortly after being elected in 2008, President Barack Obama declared that "the United States will once again . . . lead the world toward a new era of global cooperation on climate change"; however, the issue of global warming played no role during the presidential election of 2012 until the tropical superstorm Sandy dealt a devastating blow to New York and New Jersey, vindicating

the prediction that the increased energy in the atmosphere caused by global warming would produce severe weather anomalies around the world.

GLOBAL CULTURE

■ *How has technology contributed to the process of global interaction?*

Because of changes in electronic technology, today political and economic events have almost instantaneous impact in all parts of the world. A global language, a global educational system, and global forms of artistic expression have all come into being. Trade, travel, and migration have made a common popular culture unavoidable. These changes have delighted and enriched some but angered others.

The Media and the Message

The fact that the most pervasive elements of global culture have their origins in the West has raised concerns in many quarters about **cultural imperialism**. Critics complain that entertainment conglomerates are flooding the world's movie theaters and television screens with Western images and that goods catering to Western tastes but manufactured in countries with low labor costs, like China and Indonesia, are flooding world markets. In this view, global marketing is especially insidious in trying to shape a world with a Western outlook based on capitalist ideology, while suppressing or devaluing traditional cultures and alternative ideologies. As the leader of the capitalist world, the United States is seen as the primary culprit.

But in truth, technology plays a more central role than ideology in spreading Western culture. Even though imperialist forces old and new shape choices, democratic forces are also at work as people around the world make their selections in the cultural marketplace. Thus a diversity of voices is more characteristic of cultural globalization than the cultural imperialism thesis maintains.

cultural imperialism Domination of one culture over another by a deliberate policy or by economic or technological superiority.

SECTION REVIEW

- Population growth and urbanization have led to deforestation and water and air pollution.
- Poorer countries feel their resources are being exploited by richer countries.
- Government measures and new technologies are reducing air and water pollution.
- Global warming caused by the accumulation of greenhouse gases will continue to affect the planet in coming decades.

Technological Innovations

The pace of cultural globalization began to quicken during the economic recovery after World War II. The Hollywood films and American jazz recordings that had become popular in Europe and parts of Asia continued to spread. The birth of electronic technology opened contacts with large numbers of people who could never have afforded to go to a movie or buy a record.

The first step was the development of cheap transistor radios that could run on a couple of small batteries. Perfected by American scientists in 1948, transistors replaced power-hungry tubes in radios and other devices. Small portable transistor radios, most made in Asia, spread rapidly in parts of the world where homes lacked electricity.

Television, which became widely available to Western consumers in the 1950s, spread to poorer parts of the world in the 1980s and 1990s after mass production and cheap transistors made sets more affordable. Outside the United States, television broadcasting was usually a government monopoly at first, following the pattern of telegraph and postal service and radio broadcasting. Governments expected news reports and other programming to disseminate a unified national viewpoint.

Government monopolies eroded as the high cost of television production opened up global markets for American soap operas, adventure series, and situation comedies. By the 1990s a global network of satellites brought privately owned television broadcasting to even remote areas of the world, and first the VCR (videocassette recorder), followed by DVD players, provided an even greater variety of programs to people everywhere.

As a result of wider circulation of programming, people often became familiar with different dialects and languages. People in Portugal have become avid fans of Brazilian soap operas, and immigrants from Albania and North Africa often arrive in Italy with a command of Italian learned from Italian stations whose signals they could pick up at home. CNN (Cable News Network) expanded its international market after becoming the most-viewed and informative news source during the 1991 Persian Gulf War, when it broadcast live from Baghdad. CNN's fundamentally American viewpoints stimulated broadcasters in other countries to develop their own round-the-clock coverage. Al-Jazeera, based in the Persian Gulf emirate of Qatar, offered video footage and interpretation that differed greatly from American coverage of the war in Iraq in 2003.

The Internet's linkage of academic, government, and business networks began to transform world culture in the early twenty-first century. With the easy-to-use graphic interface of the World Wide Web in 1994, the number of users skyrocketed, with myriad users of "e-commerce" sites and blogs (Web logs), easy access to entertainment as well as information, and social media sites, including Facebook (2004) and Twitter (2006). Smart phones, connected to the Web, were initially used to transmit pictures and keep in touch with friends, but the Arab Spring of 2011 saw them develop as tools for communication among antiregime protesters as well.

As had happened so often throughout history, technological developments had unanticipated consequences. Although the new telecommunications and entertainment technologies derived disproportionately from American inventions, Japan and other East Asian nations came to dominate the manufacture and refinement of electronic devices. Non-Western countries that had adopted telephones late and had limited networks of copper wire benefited most from the improved communication. In 2012 the United States ranked 114th in per capita cellular phone use, sandwiched between the Congo Republic and the Dominican Republic. Qatar topped the list as the country with the highest per capita use.

Lawren Lu/Photodisc/Getty Images

Always Connected Two students simultaneously apply the power of smartphone, tablet, and laptop to a project.

Japanese Comic Books
After World War II comic magazines emerged as a major form of publication and a distinctive product of culture in Japan. Different series are directed to different age and gender groups. Issued weekly and running to some three hundred pages in black and white, the most popular magazines sell as many copies as do major newsmagazines in the United States.

Eye Ubiquitous/Photoshot

The Spread of Pop Culture

For most of history, popular culture consisted of folk tales and highly localized styles of dress, cooking, music, and visual expression. Only the literate few had full access to the riches of a broader "great tradition," such as Confucianism, Islam, or Buddhism. In modern times, government school systems increased literacy rates but also promoted specifically national values and cultural tastes. Prescribed languages of instruction eroded the use and memory of local languages and traditions. In their place there arose **global pop culture**.

Initially, the content was heavily American. Singer Michael Jackson was almost as well known to the youth of Tanzania and Thailand as to American fans. Businesses sought out basketball star Michael Jordan and championship golfer Tiger Woods to endorse their products. American television programs, following in the path of American movies, acquired immense followings and inspired local imitations.

But the United States had no monopoly on global pop culture. Latin American soap operas, *telenovelas*, had a vast following in the Americas, eastern Europe, and elsewhere. Mumbai, India, long the world's largest producer of films, made or inspired more films for international audiences, like the 2009 Academy Award–winning *Slumdog Millionaire*. And the martial arts filmmakers of Hong Kong saw their style flourish in high-budget international spectaculars like director Ang Lee's *Crouching Tiger, Hidden Dragon* (2000) and the *Matrix* trilogy (1999–2003), which relied heavily on Hong Kong fight choreographers.

Emerging Global Culture

While the globalization of popular culture has been criticized, cultural links across national and ethnic boundaries at a more elite level have generated little controversy. The end of the Cold War reopened intellectual and cultural contacts between former adversaries, making possible such things as Russian-American collaboration on space missions and extensive business contacts among former rivals. The English language, modern science, and higher education became the key elements of this **global elite culture**.

The emergence of English as the first global language began with the British Empire's introduction of the language to far-flung colonies. After achieving

global pop culture Popular cultural practices and institutions that have been adopted internationally, such as music, the Internet, television, food, and fashion.

global elite culture At the beginning of the twenty-first century, the attitudes and outlook of well-educated, prosperous, Western-oriented people around the world, largely expressed in European languages, especially English.

independence in the wake of World War II, most for-mer colonies continued using English as an official language because it provided national unity and a link to the outside world that local languages could not. Countries that chose instead to make a local language official often found the decision counter-productive. Indian nationalists who had pushed Hindi to be India's official language found that stu-dents taught in Hindi were unable to compete inter-nationally because of poor knowledge of English. Sri Lanka, which had made Sinhala its official language in 1956, reversed itself in 1989 after reports that prominent officials were sending their children to private English-language schools.

The use of English as a second language was greatly stimulated by the importance of the United States in postwar world affairs. Individuals recog-nized the importance of mastering English for suc-cessful business, diplomatic, and military careers. After the collapse of Soviet domination, students in eastern Europe flocked to study English instead of Russian. Ninety percent of students in Cambodia (a former French colony) chose to study English, even though a Canadian agency offered a sizable cash bonus if they would study French. In the 1990s China made the study of English as a second language nearly universal from junior high school onwards.

English has become the language of choice for most international academic conferences, business meetings, and diplomatic gatherings. International organizations that provide equal status to many lan-guages, such as the United Nations and the European Union, often conduct informal committee meetings in English. In cities throughout the world, signs and notices are commonly posted in the local language and English. Writers from Africa and India have received high honors for novels written in English, as have Arab and Caribbean authors for works writ-ten in French. Nevertheless, world literature remains highly diverse in form and language.

By contrast, science and technology have become standardized components of global cul-ture. Though imperialism helped spread the West-ern disciplines of biology, chemistry, and physics around the world, their importance expanded even

further after decolonization as students from newly independent nations sought to compete at an inter-national level. Standardization of scientific terms, weights and measures, and computer codes underlay the worldwide expansion of commerce.

The third pillar of global elite culture is the uni-versity. The structure and curricula of modern uni-versities are nearly indistinguishable around the world, permitting students today to cross national boundaries as freely as medieval students in the European mainland (see Chapter 13) or the Muslim world (see Chapter 9). Instruction in the pure sciences varies little from place to place, and standardization is nearly as common in applied sciences such as engi-neering and medicine and only slightly less so in the social sciences.

While university subjects are taught in many lan-guages, instruction in English is spreading rapidly. Because discoveries are often first published in Eng-lish, advanced students in science, business, and inter-national relations need to know that language to keep up with the latest developments. Many courses in northern European countries have long been offered in English, and elsewhere in Europe courses taught in English have facilitated the EU's efforts to encourage students to study outside their home countries.

Enduring Cultural Diversity

Although protesters regularly denounce the "Americanization" of the world, a closer look suggests that cultural globalization is more complex. Although English has spread widely as a second language, global culture is primarily a second culture that dominates some contexts but does not dis-place other traditions. From this perspective, Ameri-can music, fast food, and fashions are more likely to add to a society's options than to displace local culture.

Japan first demonstrated that a country with a non-Western culture could industrialize effectively. Individuality was less valued in Japan than the abil-ity of each person to fit into a group, whether as an employee, a member of an athletic team, or a stu-dent in a class. Moreover, the Japanese considered it unmannerly to directly contradict, correct, or refuse the request of another person. From a Western point of view, these Japanese customs seemed to discourage individual initiative and personality development and to preserve traditional hierarchies. Even though Japanese women often worked outside the home, they responded only slowly to the American and European feminist advocacy of gender equality. However, the Japanese approach to social relations was well suited to an industrial economy. The efficiency, pride in workmanship, and group solidarity of Japanese workers played a major role in transforming Japan into an economic power by the 1980s, although it proved less well adapted to the severe economic slowdown that began in the 1990s.

As awareness of the economic impact of Japanese culture and society began to spread, it became apparent that Taiwan and South Korea, along with Singapore and Hong Kong (a British colony before being reunited with China in 1997), were developing dynamic industrial economies of their own. Today India and the People's Republic of China are following the same path without forsaking their national tastes and heritages.

This does not mean that the world's cultural diversity is secure. Every decade a number of minority languages cease to be spoken. Televised national ceremonies or performances for tourists may prevent folk customs and costumes from dying out, but they

SECTION REVIEW

- The global pervasiveness of Western culture has provoked charges of U.S. cultural imperialism.
- Technology such as radio, television, and the Internet has played a major role in the spread of Western culture since World War II.
- Technology has also contributed to the emergence of a global pop culture that blends a variety of cultural elements from different countries.
- A global elite culture has also developed combining the English language, science, and higher education.
- Despite globalizing forces, cultural diversity remains strong, if not completely secure.

also tend to devitalize rituals that once had many local variations. While a century ago it was possible to recognize the nationality of people from their clothing and grooming, today most urban men dress the same the world over, although women's clothing shows greater variety. As much as one may regret the disappearance or commercialization of some folkways, most anthropologists would agree that change is characteristic of all healthy cultures. What doesn't change risks extinction.

CHAPTER REVIEW

GLOBALIZATION AND THE WORLD ECONOMY
■ *What are the main benefits and dangers of growing political, economic, and cultural integration?*
(page 685)

Dramatic changes in technology—especially in computers, communication networks, and the media—have helped integrate national and regional economies into a global economy that has benefited from improved efficiencies and a growing demand. The expansion of global trade and communications and the privatization of government enterprises fueled an

economic boom in the 1990s that cooled abruptly in the wake of 9/11. Many nations joined a variety of trade organizations to promote growth and reduce the vulnerability created by American economic dominance. Global interdependence and rapid economic expansion and speculation led to a global financial crisis in 2008 that plunged the world into the worst economic slowdown since the Great Depression of the 1930s. The spectacular growth in the economy of China, fueled by the world's insatiable demand for its products, has been the most impressive change in the global economy.

THE QUESTION OF VALUES

■ *What roles do religious beliefs and secular ideologies play in the contemporary world?* (page 691)

In much of the world, religious movements are gaining adherents. The growing influence of Islam has been particularly important, in part as a reaction to Western values and Western imperialism. Extremists have used religion as an excuse to commit acts of terrorism. Meanwhile, certain universal values are also gaining ground. Among the most important are human rights and the rights of women.

THE CHALLENGE OF POPULATION GROWTH

■ *What explains differences in the rate of population growth among the world's regions?* (page 696)

Population changes mean that the richer nations have an aging population and growth has slowed. The populations of Latin America and Asia have also slowed, but not as fast as they did in the mid-twentieth century. Per capita income and industrialization play key roles in differences between countries. Countries with higher wages and educational levels generally have smaller families. Meanwhile, despite severe health problems such as HIV/AIDS, especially in the poorest regions, such as sub-Saharan Africa, the population is still growing fast and therefore consists predominantly of young people.

UNEQUAL DEVELOPMENT AND THE MOVEMENT OF PEOPLES

■ *How have differences in wealth between nations influenced global migration patterns?* (page 700)

The poor, particularly those living in rural areas, are leaving their homes in search of better opportunities. Most migrate to cities in their home countries, in numbers that far outstrip the ability of cities to provide jobs, housing, education, water, and sanitation. Many others cross continents and seas at great expense and risk to reach the richer countries of Europe and North America. Though they are willing to work hard for little pay, their presence is often resented by the native inhabitants, who fear the changes in culture and customs that immigrants bring.

TECHNOLOGICAL AND ENVIRONMENTAL CHANGE

■ *How has technological change affected the global environment in the recent past?* (page 703)

A growing economy has had profound effects on the global environment. The burning of fossil fuels and the release of other chemical emissions have caused the earth's climate to warm considerably since the mid-twentieth century. Technology has reduced polluting emissions, and advances in chemistry have helped protect the ozone layer as well. More warming is yet to come, however, which will cause changes in the weather and a rise in sea levels. International efforts to alleviate these problems have begun, but so far they have been insufficient to curb pollution and to slow down global warming.

GLOBAL CULTURE

■ *How has technology contributed to the process of global interaction?* (page 707)

Global communications have encouraged the rise of two common global cultures. Popular culture, especially in dress, food, and entertainment, initially reflected Western tastes and commercial interests but now includes many elements from other cultures. The parallel growth of a global elite culture has resulted from the spread of the English language, modern science, and increasingly uniform university curricula.

Key Terms

globalization (p. 685)

World Trade Organization (WTO) (p. 689)

Deng Xiaoping (p. 690)

terrorism (p. 692)

Usama bin Laden (p. 692)

Universal Declaration of Human Rights (p. 693)

nongovernmental organizations (NGOs) (p. 693)

Thomas Malthus (p. 697)

demographic transition (p. 697)

cultural imperialism (p. 707)

global pop culture (p. 709)

global elite culture (p. 709)

Abbasid Caliphate Descendants of the Prophet Muhammad's uncle, al-Abbas, the Abbasids overthrew the Umayyad Caliphate and ruled an Islamic empire from their capital in Baghdad (founded 762) from 750 to 1258. (p. 215)

abolitionists Men and women who agitated for a complete end to slavery. Abolitionist pressure ended the British transatlantic slave trade in 1808 and slavery in British colonies in 1834. In the United States the activities of abolitionists were one factor leading to the Civil War (1861–1865). (p. 506)

Acheh Sultanate Muslim kingdom in northern Sumatra. Main center of Islamic expansion in Southeast Asia in the early seventeenth century, it declined after the Dutch seized Malacca from Portugal in 1641. (p. 443)

Aden Port city in the modern south Arabian country of Yemen. It has been a major trading center in the Indian Ocean since ancient times. (p. 340)

Adolf Hitler (1889–1945) Born in Austria, Hitler became a radical German nationalist during World War I. He led the National Socialist German Workers' Party—the Nazis—in the 1920s and became dictator of Germany in 1933. He led Europe into World War II. (p. 638)

African National Congress An organization dedicated to obtaining equal voting and civil rights for black inhabitants of South Africa. Founded in 1912 as the South African Native National Congress, it changed its name in 1923. Though it was banned and its leaders were jailed for many years, it eventually helped bring majority rule to South Africa. (p. 626)

Afrikaners South Africans descended from Dutch and French settlers of the seventeenth century. Their Great Trek founded new settler colonies in the nineteenth century. Though a minority among South Africans, they held political power after 1910, imposing a system of racial segregation called apartheid after 1949. (p. 540)

Agricultural Revolutions The change from food gathering to food production that occurred between ca. 8000 and 2000 B.C.E. Also known as the Neolithic Revolution. (p. 10)

agricultural revolution The transformation of farming that resulted in the eighteenth century from the spread of new crops, improvements in cultivation techniques and livestock breeding, and the consolidation of small holdings into large farms from which tenants and sharecroppers were forcibly expelled. (p. 472)

Akbar Most illustrious sultan of the Mughal Empire in India (r. 1556–1605). He expanded the empire and pursued a policy of conciliation with Hindus. (p. 438)

Akhenaten Egyptian pharaoh (r. 1353–1335 B.C.E.). He built a new capital at Amarna, fostered a new style of naturalistic art, and created a religious revolution by imposing worship of the sun-disk. (p. 34)

Albert Einstein (1879–1955) German physicist who developed the theory of relativity, which states that time, space, and mass are relative to each other and not fixed. (p. 610)

Alexander King of Macedonia in northern Greece. Between 334 and 323 B.C.E. he conquered the Persian Empire, reached the Indus Valley, founded many Greek-style cities, and spread Greek culture across the Middle East. Later known as Alexander the Great. (p. 100)

Alexander Nevskii Prince of Novgorod (r. 1236–1263). He submitted to the invading Mongols in 1240 and received recognition as the leader of the Russian princes under the Golden Horde. (p. 291)

Alexandria City on the Mediterranean coast of Egypt founded by Alexander. It became the capital of the Hellenistic kingdom of the Ptolemies. It contained the famous Library and the Museum, a center for leading scientific and literary figures. Its merchants engaged in trade with areas bordering the Mediterranean and the Indian Ocean. (p. 102)

All-India Muslim League Political organization founded in India in 1906 to defend the interests of India's Muslim minority. Led by Muhammad Ali Jinnah, it attempted to negotiate with the Indian National Congress. In 1940, the League began demanding a separate state for Muslims, to be called Pakistan. (p. 616)

altepetl An ethnic state in ancient Mesoamerica, the common political building block of that region. (p. 346)

amulet Small charm meant to protect the bearer from evil. Found frequently in archaeological excavations in Mesopotamia and Egypt, amulets reflect the religious practices of the common people. (p. 16)

Amur River This river valley was a contested frontier between northern China and eastern Russia until the settlement arranged in the Treaty of Nerchinsk (1689). (p. 459)

anarchism Movement of revolutionaries who wanted to abolish all private property and governments, usually by violence, and replace them with free associations of groups. (p. 575)

Anasazi Important culture of what is now the southwest United States (700–1300 C.E.). Centered on Chaco Canyon in New Mexico and Mesa Verde in Colorado, the Anasazi culture built multistory residences and worshiped in subterranean buildings called kivas. (p. 170)

aqueduct A conduit, either elevated or underground, that used gravity to carry water from a source to a location—usually a city—that needed it. The Romans built many aqueducts in a period of substantial urbanization. (p. 119)

Arawak Amerindian peoples who inhabited the Greater Antilles of the Caribbean at the time of Columbus. (p. 359)

Armenia One of the earliest Christian kingdoms, situated in eastern Anatolia and the western Caucasus and occupied by speakers of the Armenian language. (p. 204)

Ashikaga Shogunate The second of Japan's military governments headed by a shogun (a military ruler). Sometimes called the Muromachi Shogunate. (p. 302)

Ashoka Third ruler of the Mauryan Empire in India (r. 273–232 B.C.E.). He converted to Buddhism and broadcast his precepts on inscribed stones and pillars, the earliest surviving Indian writing. (p. 145)

Asian Tigers South Korea, Taiwan, Hong Kong, and Singapore, so called because their economies expanded so fast. (p. 675)

Atahuallpa Last ruling Inka emperor of Peru. He was executed by the Spanish. (p. 372)

Atatürk (1881–1938) The founder of modern Turkey. He distinguished himself as a war hero in World War I and expelled a Greek expeditionary army from Anatolia in 1921–1922. He replaced the Ottoman Empire with the Turkish Republic in 1923. As president, he pushed through a radical westernization and reform of Turkish society. (p. 599)

Atlantic system The network of trading links after 1500 that moved goods, wealth, people, and cultures around the Atlantic Basin. (p. 403)

Auguste (1862–1954) and Louis (1864–1948) Lumière French inventors of motion pictures whose equipment demonstrations abroad stimulated the growth of cinema around the world.   (p. 608)

Augustus Honorific name of Octavian, founder of the Roman Principate, the military dictatorship that replaced the failing rule of the Roman Senate. After defeating all rivals, between 31 B.C.E. and 14 C.E. he laid the groundwork for several centuries of stability and prosperity in the Roman Empire.   (p. 112)

Auschwitz Nazi extermination camp in Poland, the largest center of mass murder during the Holocaust. Close to a million Jews, Gypsies, communists, and others were killed there.   (p. 648)

australopithecines The several extinct species of humanlike primates that existed from about 4.5 million years ago to 1.4 million years ago (genus *Australopithecus*).   (p. 6)

Ayatollah Ruhollah Khomeini (1902–1989) Shi'ite philosopher and cleric who led the overthrow of the shah of Iran in 1979 and created an Islamic republic.   (p. 678)

ayllu Andean lineage group or kin-based community.   (p. 173)

Aztec The Mexica-dominated alliance that created a powerful empire in central Mexico (1325–1521).   (p. 346)

Babylon The largest and most important city in Mesopotamia. It achieved particular eminence as the capital of the Amorite king Hammurabi in the eighteenth century B.C.E.   (p. 13)

balance of power The policy in international relations by which, beginning in the eighteenth century, the major European states acted together to prevent any one of them from becoming too powerful.   (p. 397)

Balfour Declaration Statement issued by Britain's foreign secretary Arthur Balfour in 1917 favoring the establishment of a Jewish national homeland in Palestine.   (p. 592)

Bannermen Hereditary military servants of the Qing Empire, in large part descendants of peoples of various origins who had fought for the founders of the empire.   (p. 526)

Bantu Collective name of a large group of sub-Saharan African languages and of the peoples speaking these languages.   (p. 201)

Bartolomé de Las Casas First bishop of Chiapas, in southern Mexico. He devoted most of his life to protecting Amerindian peoples from exploitation. His major achievement was the New Laws of 1542, which limited the ability of Spanish settlers to compel Amerindians to labor for them.   (p. 404)

Bartolomeu Dias Portuguese explorer who in 1488 led the first expedition to sail around the southern tip of Africa from the Atlantic and sight the Indian Ocean.   (p. 363)

Batavia Fort established around 1619 as headquarters of Dutch East India Company operations in Indonesia; today the city of Jakarta.   (p. 446)

Battle of Midway U.S. naval victory over the Japanese fleet in June 1942, in which the Japanese lost four of their best aircraft carriers. It marked a turning point in World War II.   (p. 644)

Beijing China's northern capital, first used as an imperial capital in 906 and now the capital of the People's Republic of China.   (p. 294)

Bengal Region of northeastern India. It was the first part of India to be conquered by the British in the eighteenth century and remained the political and economic center of British India throughout the nineteenth century. The 1905 split of the province into predominantly Hindu West Bengal and predominantly Muslim East Bengal (now Bangladesh) sparked anti-British riots.   (p. 616)

Benito Mussolini (1883–1945) Fascist dictator of Italy (1922–1943). He led Italy to conquer Ethiopia (1935), joined Germany in the Axis pact (1936), and allied Italy with Germany in World War II. He was overthrown in 1943 when the Allies invaded Italy.   (p. 638)

Berlin Conference (1884–1885) Conference that German chancellor Otto von Bismarck called to set rules for the partition of Africa. It led to the creation of the Congo Free State under King Leopold II of Belgium.   (p. 544)

Bhagavad-Gita The most important work of Indian sacred literature, a dialogue between the great warrior Arjuna and the god Krishna on duty and the fate of the spirit.   (p. 146)

bipedalism The ability to walk upright on two legs, characteristic of hominids.   (p. 6)

Black Death An outbreak of bubonic plague that spread across Asia, North Africa, and Europe in the mid-fourteenth century, carrying off vast numbers of persons.   (p. 309)

Blaise Diagne (1872–1934) Senegalese political leader. He was the first African elected to the French National Assembly. During World War I, in exchange for promises to give French citizenship to Senegalese, he helped recruit Africans to serve in the French army. After the war, he led a movement to abolish forced labor in Africa.   (p. 626)

Bolsheviks Radical Marxist political party founded by Vladimir Lenin in 1903. Under Lenin's leadership, the Bolsheviks seized power in November 1917 during the Russian Revolution.   (p. 592)

Borobodur A massive stone monument on the Indonesian island of Java, erected by the Sailendra kings around 800 C.E. The winding ascent through ten levels, decorated with rich relief carving, is a Buddhist allegory for the progressive stages of enlightenment.   (p. 152)

bourgeoisie In early modern Europe, the class of well-off town dwellers whose wealth came from manufacturing, finance, commerce, and allied professions.   (p. 388)

British raj The rule over much of South Asia between 1765 and 1947 by the East India Company and then by a British government.   (p. 549)

bronze An alloy of copper with a small amount of tin (or sometimes arsenic), which is harder and more durable than copper alone. The term *Bronze Age* is applied to the era—the dates of which vary in different parts of the world—when bronze was the primary metal for tools and weapons.   (p. 19)

bubonic plague A bacterial disease of fleas that can be transmitted by flea bites to rodents and humans; humans in late stages of the illness can spread the bacteria by coughing. Because of its very high mortality rate and the difficulty of preventing its spread, major outbreaks have created crises in many parts of the world.   (p. 285)

Buddha An Indian prince named Siddhartha Gautama, who renounced his wealth and social position. After becoming "enlightened" (the meaning of *Buddha*), he enunciated the principles of Buddhism. This doctrine evolved and spread throughout India and to Southeast, East, and Central Asia.   (p. 140)

Byzantine Empire Historians' name for the eastern portion of the Roman Empire from the fourth century onward, taken from *Byzantion*, an early name for Constantinople, the Byzantine capital city. The empire fell to the Ottomans in 1453.   (p. 229)

caliphate Office established in succession to the Prophet Muhammad, to rule the Islamic empire; also the name of that empire.   (p. 213)

calpolli A group of up to a hundred families that served as a social building block of an altepetl in ancient Mesoamerica.   (p. 346)

capitalism The economic system of large financial institutions—banks, stock exchanges, investment companies—that first developed in early modern Europe. *Commercial capitalism,* the trading system of the early modern economy, is often distinguished from *industrial capitalism*, the system based on machine production.   (p. 418)

caravel A small, highly maneuverable three-masted ship used by the Portuguese and Spanish in the exploration of the Atlantic.   (p. 361)

Carthage City located in present-day Tunisia, founded by Phoenicians around 800 B.C.E. It became a major commercial center and naval power in the western Mediterranean until defeated by Rome in the third century B.C.E.   (p. 49)

Catholic Reformation Religious reform movement within the Latin Christian Church, begun in response to the Protestant Reformation. It clarified Catholic theology and reformed clerical training and discipline.   (p. 383)

Cecil Rhodes (1853–1902) British entrepreneur and politician involved in the expansion of the British Empire from South Africa into Central Africa. The colonies of Southern Rhodesia (now Zimbabwe) and Northern Rhodesia (now Zambia) were named after him.   (p. 541)

Celts Peoples sharing common linguistic and cultural features that originated in Central Europe in the first half of the first millennium B.C.E.   (p. 73)

Champa rice Quick-maturing rice that can allow two harvests in one growing season. Originally introduced into Champa from India, it was later sent to China as a tribute gift by the Champa state.   (p. 273)

Chang'an City in the Wei River Valley in eastern China. It became the capital of the early Han Empire. Its main features were imitated in the cities and towns that sprang up throughout the Han Empire.   (p. 127)

Charlemagne King of the Franks (r. 768–814); emperor (r. 800–814). Through a series of military conquests he established the Carolingian Empire, which encompassed all of Gaul and parts of Germany and Italy. Though illiterate himself, he sponsored a brief intellectual revival.   (p. 229)

Charles Darwin (1809–1882) Author of *On the Origin of Species* (1859), which developed the theory of evolution through natural selection.   (p. 580)

chartered companies Groups of private investors who paid an annual fee to France and England in exchange for a monopoly over trade to the West Indies colonies.   (p. 419)

Chavín The first major urban civilization in South America (900–200 B.C.E.). Its capital, Chavín de Huántar, was located high in the Andes Mountains of Peru. Chavín became politically and economically dominant in a densely populated region that included two distinct ecological zones, the Peruvian coastal plain and the Andean foothills.   (p. 161)

Chiang Kai-shek (1886–1975) Chinese military and political leader. Succeeded Sun Yat-sen as head of the Guomindang in 1925; headed the Chinese government from 1928 to 1948; fought against the Chinese communists and Japanese invaders. After 1949 he headed the Chinese nationalist government in Taiwan.   (p. 641)

chiefdom Form of political organization with rule by a hereditary leader who held power over a collection of villages and towns. Less powerful than kingdoms and empires, chiefdoms were based on gift giving and commercial links.   (p. 172)

Chimú Powerful Peruvian civilization based on conquest. Located in the region earlier dominated by Moche. Conquered by Inka in 1465.   (p. 178)

chinampas Raised fields constructed along lakeshores in central Mexico to increase agricultural yields.   (p. 164, 347)

Chinggis Khan The title of Temüjin when he ruled the Mongols (1206–1227). It means the "oceanic" or "universal leader." Chinggis Khan was the founder of the Mongol Empire.   (p. 281)

Choson The Choson dynasty ruled Korea from the fall of the Koryo kingdom to the colonization of Korea by Japan.   (p. 300)

Christopher Columbus Genoese mariner who in the service of Spain led expeditions across the Atlantic, reestablishing contact between the peoples of the Americas and the Old World and opening the way to Spanish conquest and colonization.   (p. 363)

city-state A small independent state consisting of an urban center and the surrounding agricultural territory. A characteristic political form in early Mesopotamia, Archaic and Classical Greece, Phoenicia, and early Italy.   (p. 16)

civilization An ambiguous term often used to denote more complex societies but sometimes used by anthropologists to describe any group of people sharing a set of cultural traits.   (p. 15)

Cold War The ideological struggle between communism (Soviet Union) and capitalism (United States) for world influence. The Cold War came to an end when the Soviet Union dissolved in 1991.   (p. 657)

Commodore Matthew Perry A navy commander who, on July 8, 1853, became the first foreigner to break through the barriers that had kept Japan isolated from the rest of the world for 250 years.   (p. 565)

Confucius Western name for the Chinese philosopher Kongzi (551–479 B.C.E.). His doctrine of duty and public service had a great influence on subsequent Chinese thought and served as a code of conduct for government officials.   (p. 63)

Congress of Vienna Meeting of representatives of European monarchs called to reestablish the old order after the defeat of Napoleon I.   (p. 500)

conquistadors Early-sixteenth-century Spanish adventurers who conquered Mexico, Central America, and Peru.   (p. 371)

Constantine Roman emperor (r. 312–337). After reuniting the Roman Empire, he moved the capital to Constantinople and made Christianity a favored religion.   (p. 120)

Constitutional Convention Meeting in 1787 of the elected representatives of the thirteen original states to write the Constitution of the United States.   (p. 495)

contract of indenture A voluntary agreement binding a person to work for a specified period of years in return for free passage to an overseas destination. Before 1800 most indentured servants were Europeans; after 1800 most indentured laborers were Asians.   (p. 561)

Cossacks Peoples of the Russian Empire who lived outside the farming villages, often as herders, mercenaries, or outlaws. Cossacks led the expansion into Siberia in the sixteenth and seventeenth centuries.   (p. 440)

creoles In colonial Spanish America, the term used to describe someone of European descent born in the New World. Elsewhere in the Americas, the term is used to describe all nonnative peoples.   (p. 408)

Crimean War Conflict between the Russian and Ottoman Empires fought primarily in the Crimean peninsula. To prevent Russian expansion, Britain and France sent troops to support the Ottomans.   (p. 519)

Crusades (1095–1204) Armed pilgrimages to the Holy Land by Christians determined to recover Jerusalem from Muslim rule. The Crusades brought an end to western Europe's centuries of intellectual and cultural isolation.   (p. 250)

Crystal Palace Building erected in Hyde Park, London, for the Great Exhibition of 1851. Made of iron and glass, like a gigantic greenhouse, it was a symbol of the industrial age.   (p. 479)

Cuban Missile Crisis (1962) Brink-of-war confrontation between the United States and the Soviet Union over the latter's placement of nuclear-armed missiles in Cuba.   (p. 662)

Culhuacán Multiethnic Mesoamerican state south of and historically connected with Teotihuacan.   (p. 168)

cultural imperialism Domination of one culture over another by a deliberate policy or by economic or technological superiority.   (p. 707)

Cultural Revolution (China) Campaign in China ordered by Mao Zedong to purge the Communist Party of his opponents and instill revolutionary values in the younger generation.   (p. 675)

culture Socially transmitted patterns of action and expression. *Material culture* refers to physical objects such as dwellings, clothing, tools, and crafts. Culture also includes arts, beliefs, knowledge, and technology.   (p. 5)

cuneiform A system of writing in which wedge-shaped symbols represented words or syllables. It originated in Mesopotamia and was used initially for Sumerian and Akkadian but later was adapted to represent other languages of western Asia. Literacy was confined to a relatively small group of administrators and scribes.   (p. 15)

Cyrus Founder of the Achaemenid Persian Empire. Between 550 and 530 B.C.E. he conquered Media, Lydia, and Babylon. Revered in the traditions of both Iran and the subject peoples, he employed Persians and Medes in his administration and respected the institutions and beliefs of subject peoples.   (p. 84)

daimyo Literally, "great name(s)." Japanese warlords and great landowners, whose armed samurai gave them control of the Japanese islands from the eighth to the later nineteenth century. Under the Tokugawa Shogunate they were subordinated to the imperial government.   (p. 451)

Daoism Chinese school of thought, originating in the Warring States Period with Laozi. Daoism offered an alternative to the Confucian emphasis on hierarchy and duty, emphasizing instead understanding the "path" of nature.   (p. 63)

Darius I Third ruler of the Persian Empire (r. 521–486 B.C.E.). He crushed the widespread initial resistance to his rule and gave major government posts to Persians rather than to Medes. He established a system of provinces and tribute, began construction of Persepolis, and expanded Persian control in the east (Pakistan) and west (northern Greece).   (p. 85)

Decembrist revolt Abortive attempt by army officers to take control of the Russian government upon the death of Tsar Alexander I in 1825.   (p. 523)

Declaration of the Rights of Man and of the Citizen Statement of fundamental political rights adopted by the French National Assembly at the beginning of the French Revolution.   (p. 498)

deforestation The removal of trees faster than forests can replace themselves.   (p. 392)

Delhi Sultanate Centralized Indian empire of varying extent, created by Muslim invaders.   (p. 332)

democracy System of government in which all "citizens" (however defined) have equal political and legal rights, privileges, and protections, as in the Greek city-state of Athens in the fifth and fourth centuries B.C.E.   (p. 90)

demographic transition A change in the rates of population growth. Before the transition, both birthrates and death rates are high, resulting in a slowly growing population; then the death rate drops but the birthrate remains high, causing a population explosion; finally the birthrate drops and the population growth slows down. This transition took place in Europe in the late nineteenth and early twentieth centuries, in North America and East Asia in the mid-twentieth century, and, most recently, in Latin America and South Asia.   (p. 697)

Deng Xiaoping (1904–1997) Communist Party leader who forced Chinese economic reforms after the death of Mao Zedong.   (p. 690)

dhows Characteristic cargo and passenger ships of the Arabian Sea.   (p. 338)

Diaspora Greek word meaning "dispersal," used to describe the communities of a given ethnic group living outside their homeland. Jews, for example, spread from Israel to western Asia and Mediterranean lands in antiquity and today can be found throughout the world.   (p. 46)

Dirty War Suppression of leftist groups by the Argentine military (1976–1983) characterized by the use of illegal imprisonment, torture, and executions.   (p. 672)

division of labor A manufacturing technique that breaks down a craft into many simple and repetitive tasks that can be performed by unskilled workers. Pioneered in the manufacture of pottery and in other eighteenth-century factories, it greatly increased the productivity of labor and lowered the cost of manufactured goods.   (p. 476)

driver A privileged male slave whose job was to ensure that a slave gang did its work on a plantation.   (p. 417)

Druids The class of religious experts who conducted rituals and preserved sacred lore among some ancient Celtic peoples.   (p. 74)

durbar An elaborate display of political power and wealth in British India in the nineteenth century, ostensibly in imitation of the pageantry of the Mughal Empire.   (p. 549)

Dutch West India Company Trading company chartered by the Dutch government to conduct its merchants' trade in the Americas and Africa.   (p. 419)

electricity A form of energy used in telegraphy from the 1840s on and for lighting, industrial motors, and railroads beginning in the 1880s.   (p. 568)

electric telegraph A device for rapid, long-distance transmission of information over an electric wire. It was introduced in England and North America in the 1830s and 1840s and replaced telegraph systems that utilized visual signals such as semaphores.   (p. 481)

Emiliano Zapata (1879–1919) Revolutionary and leader of peasants in the Mexican Revolution. He mobilized landless peasants in south-central Mexico in an attempt to seize and divide the lands of the wealthy landowners. Though successful for a time, he was ultimately defeated and assassinated.   (p. 559)

Empress Dowager Cixi Empress of China and mother of Emperor Guangxi. She put her son under house arrest, supported antiforeign movements, and resisted reforms of the Chinese government and armed forces.   (p. 583)

encomienda A grant of authority over a population of Amerindians in the Spanish colonies. It provided the grant holder with a supply of cheap labor and periodic payments of goods by the Amerindians. It obliged the grant holder to Christianize the Amerindians.   (p. 405)

English Civil War (1642–1649) A conflict over royal versus parliamentary rights, caused by King Charles I's arrest of his parliamentary critics and ending with his execution. Its outcome checked the growth of royal absolutism and, with the Glorious Revolution of 1688 and the English Bill of Rights of 1689, ensured that England would be a constitutional monarchy.   (p. 395)

Enlightenment A philosophical movement in eighteenth-century Europe that fostered the belief that one could reform society by discovering rational laws that governed social behavior and were just as scientific as the laws of physics.   (p. 387, 491)

equites In ancient Italy, prosperous landowners second in wealth and status to the senatorial aristocracy. The Roman emperors allied with this group to counterbalance the influence of the old aristocracy and used the equites to staff the imperial civil service. (p. 112)

Estates General France's traditional national assembly with representatives of the three estates, or classes, in French society: the clergy, nobility, and commoners. The calling of the Estates General in 1789 led to the French Revolution. (p. 497)

Ethiopia East African highland nation lying east of the Nile River. (p. 204)

European Economic Community (Common Market) An organization promoting economic unity in Europe, formed in 1957 by consolidation of earlier, more limited, agreements. With the addition of many new nations it became the European Union (EU) in 1993. (p. 659)

Eva Duarte Perón (1919–1952) Wife of Juan Perón and champion of the poor in Argentina. She was a gifted speaker and popular political leader who campaigned to improve the life of the urban poor by founding schools and hospitals and providing other social benefits. (p. 623)

evolution The biological theory that, over time, changes occurring in plants and animals, mainly as a result of natural selection and genetic mutation, result in new species. (p. 5)

extraterritoriality The right of foreign residents in a country to live under the laws of their native country and disregard the laws of the host country. In the nineteenth and early twentieth centuries, European and American nationals living in certain areas of Chinese and Ottoman cities were granted this right. (p. 519)

Faisal I (1885–1933) Arab prince, leader of the Arab Revolt in World War I. The British made him king of Iraq in 1921, and he reigned under British protection until 1933. (p. 591)

Fascist Party Italian political party created by Benito Mussolini during World War I. It emphasized aggressive nationalism and was Mussolini's instrument for the creation of a dictatorship in Italy from 1922 to 1943. (p. 638)

Ferdinand Magellan Portuguese navigator who led the Spanish expedition of 1519–1522 that was the first to sail around the world. (p. 364)

fief In medieval Europe, land granted in return for a sworn oath to provide specified military service. (p. 238)

First Temple A monumental sanctuary built in Jerusalem by King Solomon in the tenth century B.C.E. to be the religious center for the Israelite god Yahweh. The Temple priesthood conducted sacrifices, received a tithe or percentage of agricultural revenues, and became economically and politically powerful. (p. 45)

Five-Year Plans Plans that Joseph Stalin introduced to industrialize the Soviet Union rapidly, beginning in 1928. They set goals for the output of steel, electricity, machinery, and most other products and were enforced by the police powers of the state. They succeeded in making the Soviet Union a major industrial power before World War II. (p. 631)

foragers People who support themselves by hunting wild animals and gathering wild edible plants and insects. (p. 8)

Francisco "Pancho" Villa (1877–1923) A popular leader during the Mexican Revolution. An outlaw in his youth, when the revolution started he formed a cavalry army in the north of Mexico and fought for the rights of the landless in collaboration with Emiliano Zapata. He was assassinated in 1923. (p. 559)

Francisco Pizarro Spanish explorer who led the conquest of the Inka Empire of Peru in 1531–1533. (p. 372)

Fujiwara Aristocratic family that dominated the Japanese imperial court between the ninth and twelfth centuries. (p. 272)

Funan An early complex society in Southeast Asia between the first and sixth centuries C.E. It was centered in the rich rice-growing region of southern Vietnam, and it controlled the passage of trade across the Malaysian isthmus. (p. 151)

gens de couleur Free men and women of color in Haiti. They sought greater political rights and later supported the Haitian Revolution. (p. 502)

gentry In China, the class of prosperous families, next in wealth below the rural aristocrats, from which the emperors drew their administrative personnel. Respected for their education and expertise, these officials became a privileged group and made the government more efficient and responsive than in the past. (p. 127)

gentry In England, the class of landholding families below the aristocracy. (p. 391)

George Washington Military commander of the American Revolution. He was the first elected president of the United States (1789–1797). (p. 495)

Getulio Vargas (1883–1954) Dictator of Brazil from 1930 to 1945 and from 1951 to 1954. Constitutionally barred from another term in 1938 and fearful of a military takeover, he suspended elections and created Estado Novo ("New State"), a dictatorship that emphasized industrialization and helped the urban poor but did little to alleviate the problems of the peasants. (p. 622)

Ghana First known kingdom in sub-Saharan West Africa between the sixth and thirteenth centuries C.E. Also the modern West African country once known as the Gold Coast. (p. 216)

Giuseppe Garibaldi Italian nationalist and revolutionary who conquered Sicily and Naples and added them to a unified Italy in 1860. (p. 576)

global elite culture At the beginning of the twenty-first century, the attitudes and outlook of well-educated, prosperous, Western-oriented people around the world, largely expressed in European languages, especially English. (p. 709)

globalization The economic, political, and cultural integration and interaction of all parts of the world brought about by increasing trade, travel, and technology. (p. 685)

global pop culture Popular cultural practices and institutions that have been adopted internationally, such as music, the Internet, television, food, and fashion. (p. 709)

Gold Coast Region of the Atlantic coast of West Africa occupied by modern Ghana; named for its gold exports to Europe from the 1470s onward. (p. 363)

Golden Horde Mongol khanate founded by Chinggis Khan's grandson Batu. It was based in southern Russia and quickly adopted both the Turkish language and Islam. Also known as the Kipchak Horde. (p. 288)

Gothic cathedrals Large churches originating in twelfth-century France; built in an architectural style featuring pointed arches, tall vaults and spires, flying buttresses, and large stained-glass windows. (p. 315)

Grand Canal The 1,100-mile (1,771-kilometer) waterway linking the Yellow and the Yangzi Rivers. It was begun in the Han period and completed during the Sui Empire. (p. 255)

Great Ice Age Geological era that occurred between ca. 2 million and 11,000 years ago. (p. 6)

"great traditions" Historians' term for a literate, well-institutionalized complex of religious and social beliefs and practices adhered to by diverse societies over a broad geographical area. (p. 199)

Great Western Schism A division in the Latin (Western) Christian Church between 1378 and 1415, when rival claimants to the papacy existed in Rome and Avignon. (p. 323)

Great Zimbabwe City, now in ruins (in the modern African country of Zimbabwe), whose many stone structures were built between about 1250 and 1450, when it was a trading center and the capital of a large state. (p. 340)

guild In medieval Europe, an association of men (rarely women), such as merchants, artisans, or professors, who worked in a particular trade and banded together to promote their economic and political interests. Guilds were also important in other societies, such as the Ottoman and Safavid Empires. (p. 314)

Gujarat Region of western India famous for trade and manufacturing; the inhabitants are called Gujaratis. (p. 336)

gunpowder A mixture of saltpeter, sulfur, and charcoal, in various proportions. The formula, brought to China in the 400s or 500s, was first used to make fumigators to keep away insect pests and evil spirits. In later centuries it was used to make explosives and grenades and to propel cannonballs, shot, and bullets. (p. 265)

Guomindang Nationalist political party founded on democratic principles by Sun Yat-sen in 1912. After 1925, the party was headed by Chiang Kai-shek, who turned it into an increasingly authoritarian movement. (p. 598)

Gupta Empire A powerful Indian state based, like its Mauryan predecessor, on a capital at Pataliputra in the Ganges Valley. It controlled most of the Indian subcontinent through a combination of military force and its prestige as a center of sophisticated culture. (p. 146)

Habsburg A powerful European family that provided many Holy Roman Emperors, founded the Austrian (later Austro-Hungarian) Empire, and ruled sixteenth- and seventeenth-century Spain. (p. 394)

hadith A tradition relating the words or deeds of the Prophet Muhammad; next to the Quran, the most important basis for Islamic law. (p. 221)

Haile Selassie (1892–1975) Emperor of Ethiopia (r. 1930–1974) and symbol of African independence. He fought the Italian invasion of his country in 1935 and regained his throne during World War II, when British forces expelled the Italians. He ruled Ethiopia as a traditional autocracy until he was overthrown in 1974. (p. 627)

Hammurabi Amorite ruler of Babylon (r. 1792–1750 B.C.E.). He conquered many city-states in southern and northern Mesopotamia and is best known for a code of laws, inscribed on a black stone pillar, illustrating the principles to be used in legal cases. (p. 17)

Han A term used to designate (1) the ethnic Chinese people who originated in the Yellow River Valley and spread throughout regions of China suitable for agriculture and (2) the dynasty of emperors who ruled from 206 B.C.E. to 220 C.E. (p. 126)

Hanseatic League An economic and defensive alliance of the free towns in northern Germany, founded about 1241 and most powerful in the fourteenth century. (p. 313)

Harappa Site of one of the great cities of the Indus Valley civilization of the third millennium B.C.E. It was located on the northwest frontier of the zone of cultivation (in modern Pakistan). (p. 134)

Hatshepsut Queen of Egypt (r. 1473–1458 B.C.E.). She dispatched a naval expedition to Punt (possibly northeast Sudan or Eritrea), the faraway source of myrrh. There is evidence of opposition to a woman as ruler, and after her death her name and image were frequently defaced. (p. 33)

Hebrew Bible A collection of sacred books containing diverse materials concerning the origins, experiences, beliefs, and practices of the Israelites. Most of the extant text was compiled by members of the priestly class in the fifth century B.C.E. and reflects the concerns and views of this group. (p. 43)

Hellenistic Age Historians' term for the era, usually dated 323–30 B.C.E., in which Greek culture spread across western Asia and northeastern Africa after the conquests of Alexander the Great. The period ended with the fall of the last major Hellenistic kingdom to Rome, but Greek cultural influence persisted until the spread of Islam in the seventh century C.E. (p. 101)

Henry the Navigator Portuguese prince who promoted the study of navigation and directed voyages of exploration down the western coast of Africa in the fifteenth century. (p. 361)

Hernán Cortés Spanish explorer and conquistador who led the conquest of Aztec Mexico in 1519–1521 for Spain. (p. 371)

Herodotus Heir to the technique of *historia* ("investigation/research") developed by Greeks in the late Archaic period. He came from a Greek community in Anatolia and traveled extensively, collecting information in western Asia and the Mediterranean lands. He traced the antecedents and chronicled the wars between the Greek city-states and the Persian Empire, thus originating the Western tradition of historical writing. (p. 92)

Hidden Imam Last in a series of twelve descendants of Muhammad's son-in-law Ali, whom Shi'ites consider divinely appointed leaders of the Muslim community. In occlusion since around 873, he is expected to return as a messiah at the end of time. (p. 434)

hieroglyphics A system of writing in which pictorial symbols represented sounds, syllables, or concepts. It was used for official and monumental inscriptions in ancient Egypt. Because of the long period of study required to master this system, literacy in hieroglyphics was confined to a relatively small group of scribes and administrators. (p. 23)

Hinduism A general term for a wide variety of beliefs and ritual practices that have developed in the Indian subcontinent since antiquity. Hinduism has roots in ancient Vedic, Buddhist, and south Indian religious concepts and practices. It spread along the trade routes to Southeast Asia. (p. 141)

Hipólito Irigoyen (1850–1933) Argentine politician, president of Argentina from 1916 to 1922 and 1928 to 1930. The first president elected by universal male suffrage, he began his presidency as a reformer but later became conservative. (p. 621)

Hiroshima City in Japan, the first to be destroyed by an atomic bomb, on August 6, 1945. The bombing hastened the end of World War II. (p. 644)

history The study of past events and changes in the development, transmission, and transformation of cultural practices. (p. 5)

Hittites A people from central Anatolia who established an empire in Anatolia and Syria in the Late Bronze Age. With wealth from the trade in metals and military power based on chariot forces, the Hittites vied with New Kingdom Egypt for control of Syria-Palestine before falling to unidentified attackers around 1200 B.C.E. (p. 32)

Holocaust Nazis' program during World War II to kill people they considered undesirable. Some 6 million Jews perished during the Holocaust, along with millions of Poles, Gypsies, communists, socialists, and others. (p. 648)

Holy Roman Empire Loose federation of mostly German states and principalities, headed by an emperor elected by the princes. It lasted from 962 to 1806. (p. 240, 394)

hominid The biological family that includes humans and humanlike primates. (p. 6)

Homo erectus An extinct human species. It evolved in Africa about 1.8 million years ago. (p. 7)

Homo habilis The first human species (now extinct). It evolved in Africa about 2.3 million years ago.   (p. 6)

Homo sapiens The current human species. It evolved in Africa sometime between 400,000 and 100,000 years ago.   (p. 8)

hoplite A heavily armored Greek infantryman of the Archaic and Classical periods who fought in the close-packed phalanx formation. Hoplite armies—militias composed of middle- and upper-class citizens supplying their own equipment—were for centuries superior to all other military forces.   (p. 89)

horse collar Harnessing method that increased the efficiency of horses by shifting the point of traction from the animal's throat to the shoulders; its adoption favors the spread of horse-drawn plows and vehicles.   (p. 248)

House of Burgesses Elected assembly in colonial Virginia, created in 1618.   (p. 410)

humanists (Renaissance) European scholars, writers, and teachers associated with the study of the humanities (grammar, rhetoric, poetry, history, languages, and moral philosophy), influential in the fifteenth century and later.   (p. 319)

Hundred Years' War (1337–1453) Series of campaigns over control of the throne of France, involving English and French royal families and French noble families.   (p. 323)

Ibn Battuta Moroccan Muslim scholar, the most widely traveled individual of his time. He wrote a detailed account of his visits to Islamic lands from China to Spain and the western Sudan. (p. 329)

Il-khan A "secondary" or "peripheral" khan based in Persia. The Il-khans' khanate was founded by Hülegü, a grandson of Chinggis Khan, and was based at Tabriz in the Iranian province of Azerbaijan. It controlled much of Iran and Iraq.   (p. 288)

import-substitution industrialization An economic system aimed at building a country's industry by restricting foreign trade. It was especially popular in Latin American countries such as Mexico, Argentina, and Brazil in the mid-twentieth century. It proved successful for a time but could not keep up with technological advances in Europe and North America. (p. 622)

indentured servant A migrant to British colonies in the Americas who paid for passage by agreeing to work for a set term ranging from four to seven years.   (p. 410)

Indian Civil Service The elite professional class of officials who administered the government of British India. Originally composed exclusively of well-educated British men, it gradually added qualified Indians.   (p. 551)

Indian National Congress A movement and political party founded in 1885 to demand greater Indian participation in government. Its membership was middle class, and its demands were modest until World War I. Led after 1920 by Mohandas K. Gandhi, it appealed increasingly to the poor, and it organized mass protests demanding self-government and independence. (p. 552)

Indian National Congress A movement and political party founded in 1885 to demand greater Indian participation in government. Its membership was middle class, and its demands were modest until World War I. Led after 1920 by Mohandas K. Gandhi, it appealed increasingly to the poor and organized mass protests demanding self-government and independence. (p. 616)

Indian Ocean Maritime System In premodern times, a network of seaports, trade routes, and maritime culture linking countries on the rim of the Indian Ocean from Africa to Indonesia. (p. 191)

indulgence The forgiveness of the punishment due for past sins, granted by the Catholic Church authorities as a reward for a pious act. Martin Luther's protest against the sale of indulgences is often seen as touching off the Protestant Reformation. (p. 382)

Industrial Revolution The transformation of the economy, the environment, and living conditions, occurring first in England in the eighteenth century, that resulted from the use of steam engines, the mechanization of manufacturing in factories, and innovations in transportation and communication.   (p. 471)

Inka Largest and most powerful Andean empire. Controlled the Pacific coast of South America from Ecuador to Chile from its capital of Cuzco. (p. 348)

investiture controversy Dispute between the popes and the Holy Roman Emperors over who held ultimate authority over bishops in imperial lands.   (p. 241)

Iron Age Historians' term for the period during which iron was the primary metal for tools and weapons. The advent of iron technology began at different times in different parts of the world. (p. 30)

iron curtain Winston Churchill's term for the Cold War division between the Soviet-dominated East and the U.S.-dominated West. (p. 660)

Iroquois Confederacy An alliance of five northeastern Amerindian peoples (six after 1722) that made decisions on military and diplomatic issues through a council of representatives. Allied first with the Dutch and later with the English, the Confederacy dominated the area from western New England to the Great Lakes. (p. 411)

Islam Religion expounded by the Prophet Muhammad on the basis of his reception of divine revelations, which were collected after his death into the Quran. In the tradition of Judaism and Christianity, and sharing much of their lore, Islam calls on all people to recognize one creator god—Allah—who rewards or punishes believers after death according to how they led their lives.   (p. 211)

Israel In antiquity, the land between the eastern shore of the Mediterranean and the Jordan River, occupied by the Israelites from the early second millennium B.C.E. The modern state of Israel was founded in 1948. (p. 43)

James Watt Scot who invented the condenser and other improvements that made the steam engine a practical source of power for industry and transportation. The watt, an electrical measurement, is named after him.   (p. 480)

Janissaries Infantry, originally of slave origin, armed with firearms and constituting the elite of the Ottoman army from the fifteenth century until the corps was abolished in 1826. (p. 429)

Jawaharlal Nehru (1889–1964) Indian statesman who succeeded Mohandas K. Gandhi as leader of the Indian National Congress. He negotiated the end of British colonial rule in India and became India's first prime minister (1947–1964).   (p. 618)

Jesus A Jew from Galilee in northern Israel who sought to reform Jewish beliefs and practices. He was executed as a revolutionary by the Romans. Hailed as the Messiah and son of God by his followers, he became the central figure in Christianity, a belief system that developed in the centuries after his death.   (p. 118)

joint-stock company A business, often backed by a government charter, that sold shares to individuals to raise money for its trading enterprises and to spread the risks (and profits) among many investors. (p. 391)

Joseph Stalin (1879–1953) Bolshevik revolutionary, head of the Soviet Communist Party after 1924, and dictator of the Soviet Union from 1928 to 1953. He led the Soviet Union with an iron fist, using Five-Year Plans to increase industrial production and terror to crush all opposition. (p. 631)

Josiah Wedgwood English industrialist whose pottery works were the first to produce fine-quality pottery by industrial methods.   (p. 476)

Juan Perón (1895–1974) President of Argentina (1946–1955, 1973–1974). As a military officer, he championed the rights of labor. Aided by his wife Eva Duarte Perón, he was elected president in 1946. He built up Argentinean industry, became very popular among the urban poor, but harmed the economy.   (p. 623)

junk A very large flatbottom sailing ship produced in the Tang, Song, and Ming Empires, specially designed for long-distance commercial travel.   (p. 264)

Kamakura Shogunate The first of Japan's decentralized military governments (1185–1333).   (p. 273)

kamikaze The "divine wind," which the Japanese credited with blowing Mongol invaders away from their shores in 1281.   (p. 302)

Kangxi Qing emperor (r. 1662–1722). He oversaw the greatest expansion of the Qing Empire.   (p. 458)

Karl Marx German journalist and philosopher, founder of the Marxist branch of socialism. He is known for two books: *Manifesto of the Communist Party* (1848) and *Das Kapital* (Vols. I–III, 1867–1894).   (p. 573)

karma In Indian tradition, the residue of deeds performed in past and present lives that adheres to a "spirit" and determines what form it will assume in its next life cycle. The doctrines of karma and reincarnation were used by the elite in ancient India to encourage people to accept their social position and do their duty.   (p. 139)

keiretsu Alliances of corporations and banks that dominate the Japanese economy.   (p. 674)

khipus System of knotted colored cords used by preliterate Andean peoples to record information.   (p. 173, 349)

Khubilai Khan Last of the Mongol Great Khans (r. 1260–1294) and founder of the Yuan Empire.   (p. 294)

Kievan Russia State established at Kiev in Ukraine around 880 by Scandinavian adventurers asserting authority over a mostly Slavic farming population.   (p. 229)

King Leopold II (1835–1909) King of Belgium (r. 1865–1909). He was active in encouraging the exploration of Central Africa and became the ruler of the Congo Free State (to 1908).   (p. 544)

KLM Royal Dutch Airlines Oldest major airline, operating since 1920 in Europe and connecting to the Dutch East Indies in 1929.   (p. 611)

Korean War (1950–1953) Conflict that began with North Korea's invasion of South Korea and that came to involve the United Nations (primarily the United States) allying with South Korea and the People's Republic of China allying with North Korea.   (p. 661)

Koryo Korean kingdom founded in 918 and destroyed by a Mongol invasion in 1259.   (p. 270)

Kush An Egyptian name for Nubia, the region alongside the Nile River south of Egypt, where an indigenous kingdom with its own distinctive institutions and cultural traditions arose beginning in the early second millennium B.C.E.   (p. 68)

labor union An organization of workers in a particular industry or trade, created to defend the interests of members through strikes or negotiations with employers.   (p. 573)

laissez faire The idea that government should refrain from interfering in economic affairs. The classic exposition of laissez-faire principles is Adam Smith's *Wealth of Nations* (1776).   (p. 485)

lama In Tibetan Buddhism, a teacher.   (p. 294)

Lázaro Cárdenas (1895–1970) President of Mexico (1934–1940). He brought major changes to Mexican life by distributing millions of acres of land to the peasants, bringing representatives of workers and farmers into the inner circles of politics, and nationalizing the oil industry.   (p. 620)

League of Nations International organization founded in 1919 to promote world peace and cooperation but greatly weakened by the refusal of the United States to join. It proved ineffectual in stopping aggression by Italy, Japan, and Germany in the 1930s, and it was superseded by the United Nations in 1945.   (p. 595)

Le Corbusier (1887–1965) Professional name of architect Charles-Éduard Jeanneret who led a modernist movement away from surface decoration and toward form following function.   (p. 613)

Legalism In China, a political philosophy that emphasized the unruliness of human nature and justified state coercion and control. The ruling class invoked it to validate the authoritarian nature of the regime and its profligate expenditure of subjects' lives and labor. It was later superseded by a more benevolent Confucian doctrine of governmental moderation.   (p. 62)

"legitimate" trade Exports from Africa in the nineteenth century that did not include the newly outlawed slave trade.   (p. 548)

liberalism A political ideology that emphasizes the civil rights of citizens, representative government, and the protection of private property. This ideology, derived from the Enlightenment, was especially popular among the property-owning middle classes of Europe and North America.   (p. 576)

Library of Ashurbanipal A large collection of writings drawn from the ancient literary, religious, and scientific traditions of Mesopotamia. It was assembled by the seventh-century B.C.E. Assyrian ruler Ashurbanipal. The many tablets unearthed by archaeologists constitute one of the most important sources of present-day knowledge of the long literary tradition of Mesopotamia.   (p. 42)

Linear B A set of syllabic symbols, derived from the writing system of Minoan Crete, used in the Mycenaean palaces of the Late Bronze Age to write an early form of Greek. It was used primarily for palace records, and the surviving Linear B tablets provide substantial information about the economic organization of Mycenaean society and tantalizing clues about political, social, and religious institutions.   (p. 37)

Li Shimin One of the founders of the Tang Empire and its second emperor (r. 626–649). He led the expansion of the empire into Inner Asia.   (p. 256)

Little Ice Age A century-long period of cool climate that began in the 1590s. Its ill effects on agriculture in northern Europe were notable.   (p. 391)

llama A hoofed animal indigenous to the Andes Mountains. It was the only domesticated beast of burden in the Americas before the arrival of Europeans. The use of llamas to transport goods made possible specialized production and trade among people living in different ecological zones and fostered the integration of these zones by Chavín and later Andean states.   (p. 162)

loess A fine, light silt deposited by wind and water. It constitutes the fertile soil of the Yellow River Valley in northern China.   (p. 58)

Long March (1934–1935) The 6,000-mile flight of Chinese communists from southeastern to northwestern China. The communists, led by Mao Zedong, were pursued by the Chinese army under orders from Chiang Kai-shek. The four thousand survivors of the march formed the nucleus of a revived communist movement that defeated the Guomindang after World War II.   (p. 641)

ma'at Egyptian term for the concept of divinely created and maintained order in the universe. The divine ruler was the earthly guarantor of this order. (p. 22)

Macartney mission The unsuccessful attempt by the British Empire to establish diplomatic relations with the Qing Empire. (p. 462)

Mahabharata A vast epic chronicling the events leading up to a cataclysmic battle between related kinship groups in early India. It includes the Bhagavad-Gita. (p. 146)

Mahayana Buddhism "Great Vehicle" branch of Buddhism followed in China, Japan, and Central Asia. The focus is on reverence for Buddha and for bodhisattvas, enlightened persons who have postponed nirvana to help others attain enlightenment. (p. 141)

Malacca Port city in the modern Southeast Asian country of Malaysia, founded about 1400 as a trading center on the Strait of Malacca. (p. 342)

Mali Empire created by indigenous Muslims in western Sudan of West Africa from the thirteenth to fifteenth century. It was famous for its role in the trans-Saharan gold trade. (p. 333)

mamluks Under the Islamic system of military slavery, Turkish military slaves formed an important part of the armed forces of the Abbasid Caliphate of the ninth and tenth centuries. Mamluks eventually founded their own state, ruling Egypt and Syria (1250–1517). (p. 216)

Manchu Federation of Northeast Asian peoples who founded the Qing Empire. (p. 449)

Mandate of Heaven Chinese religious and political ideology developed by the Zhou, according to which it was the prerogative of Heaven, the chief deity, to grant power to the ruler of China and to take away that power if the ruler failed to conduct himself justly and in the best interests of his subjects. (p. 62)

mandate system Allocation of former German colonies and Ottoman possessions to the victorious powers after World War I, to be administered under League of Nations supervision. (p. 599)

manor In medieval Europe, a large, self-sufficient landholding consisting of the lord's residence (manor house), outbuildings, peasant village, and surrounding land. (p. 237)

mansabs In India, grants of land given in return for service by rulers of the Mughal Empire. (p. 438)

Mansa Kankan Musa Ruler of Mali (r. 1312–1337). His pilgrimage through Egypt to Mecca in 1324–1325 established the empire's reputation for wealth in the Mediterranean world. (p. 335)

Mao Zedong (1893–1976) Leader of the Chinese Communist Party (1927–1976). He led the communists on the Long March (1934–1935) and rebuilt the Communist Party and Red Army during the Japanese occupation of China (1937–1945). After World War II, he led the communists to victory over the Guomindang. (p. 641)

Margaret Sanger (1883–1966) American nurse and author; pioneer in the movement for family planning; organized conferences and established birth control clinics. (p. 610)

Marie Curie (1867–1934) Twice winner of the Nobel Prize, the Polish Maria (Marie, in French) Sklodowska worked in Paris and, with her husband Pierre Curie, discovered the element radium and radioactivity, changing the knowledge of matter and the treatment of many diseases. In World War I, she convinced wealthy patrons to donate vehicles for use as X-Ray centers and traveled to aid doctors in detecting fractures and shrapnel in wounded soldiers. (p. 613)

maroon A slave who ran away from his or her master. Often a member of a community of runaway slaves in the West Indies and South America. (p. 418)

Marshall Plan U.S. program to support the reconstruction of western Europe after World War II. By 1961 more than $20 billion in economic aid had been dispersed. (p. 658)

mass deportation The forcible removal and relocation of large numbers of people or entire populations. The mass deportations practiced by the Assyrian and Persian Empires were meant as a terrifying warning of the consequences of rebellion. They also brought skilled and unskilled labor to the imperial center. (p. 41)

mass production The manufacture of many identical products by the division of labor into many small repetitive tasks. This method was introduced into the manufacture of pottery and into the spinning of cotton thread. (p. 476)

Mauryan Empire The first state to unify most of the Indian subcontinent. It was founded by Chandragupta Maurya in 324 B.C.E. and survived until 184 B.C.E. From its capital at Pataliputra in the Ganges Valley it grew wealthy from taxes on agriculture, iron mining, and control of trade routes. (p. 144)

Max Planck (1858–1947) German physicist who developed quantum theory and was awarded the Nobel Prize for physics in 1918. (p. 610)

Maya Mesoamerican civilization concentrated in Mexico's Yucatán Peninsula and in Guatemala and Honduras but never unified into a single empire. Major contributions were in mathematics, astronomy, and development of the calendar. (p. 165)

Mecca City in western Arabia; birthplace of the Prophet Muhammad and ritual center of the Islamic religion. (p. 211)

mechanization The application of machinery to manufacturing and other activities. Among the first processes to be mechanized were the spinning of cotton thread and the weaving of cloth in late-eighteenth- and early-nineteenth-century England. (p. 477)

medieval Literally "middle age," a term that historians of Europe use for the period from roughly 500 to 1300, signifying its intermediate point between Greco-Roman antiquity and the Renaissance. (p. 229)

Medina City in western Arabia to which the Prophet Muhammad and his followers emigrated in 622 to escape persecution in Mecca. (p. 212)

megaliths Structures and complexes of very large stones constructed for ceremonial and religious purposes in Neolithic times. (p. 12)

Meiji Restoration The political program that followed the destruction of the Tokugawa Shogunate in 1868, in which a collection of young leaders set Japan on the path of centralization, industrialization, and imperialism. (p. 578)

Memphis The capital of Old Kingdom Egypt, near the head of the Nile Delta. Early rulers were interred in the nearby pyramids. (p. 23)

mercantilism European government policies of the sixteenth, seventeenth, and eighteenth centuries designed to promote overseas trade between a country and its colonies and accumulate precious metals by requiring colonies to trade only with their motherland country. The British system was defined by the Navigation Acts, the French system by laws known as the *Exclusif.* (p. 418)

Meroë Capital of a flourishing kingdom in southern Nubia from the fourth century B.C.E. to the fourth century C.E. In this period Nubian culture shows more independence from Egypt and the influence of sub-Saharan Africa. (p. 68)

Mexican Revolution A social revolution that developed haphazardly under ambitious but limited leaders, each representing a different segment of Mexican society. The revolution evolved into civil war for over ten years of armed struggle, but it established a constitution for Mexico. (p. 558)

Miguel Hidalgo y Costilla Mexican priest who led the first stage of the Mexican independence war in 1810. He was captured and executed in 1811. (p. 504)

Mikhail Gorbachev (b. 1931) Head of the Soviet Union from 1985 to 1991. His liberalization effort improved relations with the West, but he lost power after his reforms led to the collapse of the communist governments in eastern Europe. (p. 680)

Ming Empire Empire based in China that Zhu Yuanzhang established after the overthrow of the Yuan Empire. The Ming emperor Yongle sponsored the building of the Forbidden City and the voyages of Zheng He. The later years of the Ming saw a slowdown in technological development and economic decline. (p. 296)

Minoan Prosperous civilization on the Aegean island of Crete in the second millennium B.C.E. The Minoans engaged in far-flung commerce around the Mediterranean and exerted powerful cultural influences on the early Greeks. (p. 36)

mita Andean labor system based on shared obligations to help kinsmen and work on behalf of the ruler and religious organizations. (p. 173)

Moche Civilization of north coast of Peru (200–700 C.E.). An important Andean civilization that built extensive irrigation networks as well as impressive urban centers dominated by brick temples. (p. 174)

Moctezuma II Aztec emperor who died while in custody of the Spanish conquistador Hernán Cortés. (p. 371)

modernization The process of reforming political, military, economic, social, and cultural traditions in imitation of the early success of Western societies, often with little regard for accommodating local traditions in non-Western societies. (p. 544)

Mohandas K. Gandhi (1869–1948) Leader of the Indian independence movement and advocate of nonviolent resistance. After being educated as a lawyer in England, he returned to India and became leader of the Indian National Congress in 1920. He appealed to the poor, led nonviolent demonstrations against British colonial rule, and was jailed many times. Soon after independence he was assassinated for attempting to stop Hindu-Muslim rioting. (p. 617)

Mohenjo-Daro Largest of the cities of the Indus Valley civilization, centrally located in the extensive floodplain of the Indus River in contemporary Pakistan. (p. 134)

moksha The Hindu concept of the spirit's "liberation" from the endless cycle of rebirths. There are various avenues—such as physical discipline, meditation, and acts of devotion to the gods—by which the spirit can distance itself from desire for the things of this world and be merged with the divine force that animates the universe. (p. 139)

monasticism Living in a religious community apart from secular society and adhering to a rule stipulating chastity, obedience, and poverty. It was a prominent element of medieval Christianity and Buddhism. Monasteries were the primary centers of learning and literacy in medieval Europe. (p. 241)

Mongols A people of this name is mentioned as early as the records of the Tang Empire, living as nomads in northern Eurasia. After 1206 they established an enormous empire under Chinggis Khan, linking western and eastern Eurasia. (p. 281)

monotheism Belief in the existence of a single divine entity. Some scholars cite the devotion of the Egyptian pharaoh Akhenaten to Aten (sun-disk) and his suppression of traditional gods as the earliest instance. The Israelite worship of Yahweh developed into an exclusive belief in one god, and this concept passed into Christianity and Islam. (p. 46)

monsoon Seasonal winds in the Indian Ocean caused by the differences in temperature between the rapidly heating and cooling landmasses of Africa and Asia and the slowly changing ocean waters. These strong and predictable winds have long been ridden across the open sea by sailors, and the large amounts of rainfall that they deposit on parts of India, Southeast Asia, and China allow for the cultivation of several crops a year. (p. 137)

monsoon Seasonal winds in the Indian Ocean caused by the differences in temperature between the rapidly heating and cooling landmasses of Africa and Asia and the slowly changing ocean waters. These strong and predictable winds have long been ridden across the open sea by sailors, and the large amounts of rainfall that they deposit on parts of India, Southeast Asia, and China allow for the cultivation of several crops a year. (p. 330)

most-favored-nation status A clause in a commercial treaty that awards to any later signatories all the privileges previously granted to the original signatories. (p. 528)

movable type Type in which each individual character is cast on a separate piece of metal. It replaced woodblock printing, allowing for the arrangement of individual letters and other characters on a page, rather than requiring the carving of entire pages at a time. It may have been invented in Korea in the thirteenth century. (p. 266)

Mughal Empire Muslim state (1526–1857) exercising dominion over most of India in the sixteenth and seventeenth centuries. Fragmentation of power and growth of English imperial strength marked the subsequent period. (p. 437)

Muhammad Ali Jinnah (1876–1948) Indian Muslim politician who founded the state of Pakistan. A lawyer by training, he joined the All-India Muslim League in 1913. As leader of the League from the 1920s on, he negotiated with the British and the Indian National Congress for Muslim participation in Indian politics. From 1940 on, he led the movement for the independence of India's Muslims in a separate state of Pakistan, founded in 1947. (p. 619)

Muhammad Ali Leader of Egyptian modernization in the early nineteenth century. He ruled Egypt as an Ottoman governor but had imperial ambitions. His descendants ruled Egypt until overthrown in 1952. (p. 513)

Muhammad Arab prophet (570–632 C.E.); founder of religion of Islam. (p. 211)

mummy A body preserved by chemical processes or special natural circumstances, often in the belief that the deceased will need it again in the afterlife. (p. 26)

Muscovy The Russian principality that emerged gradually during the era of Mongol domination. The muscovite dynasty ruled without interruption from 1276 to 1598. (p. 440)

Muslim An adherent of the Islamic religion; a person who "submits" (in Arabic, *Islam* means "submission") to the will of God. (p. 211)

Mycenae Site of a fortified palace complex in southern Greece that controlled a Late Bronze Age kingdom. In ancient epic poems, Mycenae was the base of King Agamemnon, who commanded the Greeks besieging Troy. Contemporary archaeologists call the complex Greek society of the second millennium B.C.E. "Mycenaean." (p. 37)

Napoleon Bonaparte General who overthrew the French Directory in 1799 and became emperor of the French in 1804. Failed to defeat Great Britain and abdicated in 1814. Returned to power briefly in 1815 but was defeated and died in exile. (p. 500)

Nasir al-Din Tusi Persian mathematician and cosmologist whose academy near Tabriz provided a model for heavenly motions that helped to inspire the Copernican model of the solar system. (p. 290)

National Assembly French Revolutionary assembly (1789–1791). The Estates General gave itself this title when it came together and demanded radical change. In 1789 it passed the Declaration of the Rights of Man and of the Citizen. (p. 497)

nationalism A political ideology that stresses people's membership in a nation—a community defined by a common culture and history as well as by territory. In the late eighteenth and early nineteenth centuries, nationalism was a force for unity in western Europe. In the late nineteenth century it hastened the disintegration of the Austro-Hungarian and Ottoman Empires. In the twentieth century it provided the ideological foundation for scores of independent countries emerging from colonialism. (p. 575)

nawab Technically, a semi-autonomous deputy of the Mughal emperor but often a Muslim prince allied to British India. (p. 549)

Nazis German political party led by Adolf Hitler, emphasizing nationalism, racism, and war. When Hitler became chancellor of Germany in 1933, the Nazis became the only legal party and an instrument of Hitler's absolute rule. The party's formal name was National Socialist German Workers' Party. (p. 638)

Neo-Assyrian Empire An empire extending from western Iran to Syria-Palestine, conquered by the Assyrians of northern Mesopotamia between the tenth and seventh centuries B.C.E. They used force and terror and exploited the wealth and labor of their subjects. They also preserved and continued the cultural and scientific developments of Mesopotamian civilization. (p. 40)

Neo-Babylonian kingdom Under the Chaldaeans (nomadic kinship groups that settled in southern Mesopotamia in the early first millennium B.C.E.), Babylon again became a major political and cultural center in the seventh and sixth centuries B.C.E. After participating in the destruction of Assyrian power, the monarchs Nabopolassar and Nebuchadnezzar took over the southern portion of the Assyrian domains. (p. 53)

neo-Confucianism Term used to describe new approaches to understanding classic Confucian texts that became the basic ruling philosophy of China from the Song period to the twentieth century. (p. 265)

Neolithic The period of the Stone Age associated with the ancient Agricultural Revolution(s). (p. 10)

New Economic Policy Policy proclaimed by Vladimir Lenin in 1923 to encourage the revival of the Soviet economy by allowing small private enterprises. Joseph Stalin ended the NEP in 1928 and replaced it with a series of Five-Year Plans. (p. 595)

New France French colony in North America, with a capital in Quebec, founded in 1608. New France fell to the British in 1763. (p. 412)

newly industrialized economies (NIEs) Rapidly growing new industrializing nations of the late twentieth century, including the Asian Tigers. (p. 676)

new monarchies Historians' term for the monarchies in France, England, and Spain from 1450 to 1600. The centralization of royal power was increasing within more or less fixed territorial limits. (p. 324)

nomads People without permanent, fixed places of residence, whose way of life and means of subsistence require them to periodically migrate, often with their herds of domesticated animals, to a familiar series of temporary seasonal encampments. (p. 70)

nonaligned nations Developing countries that announced their neutrality in the Cold War. (p. 665)

nongovernmental organizations (NGOs) Nonprofit international organizations devoted to investigating human rights abuses and providing humanitarian relief. Two NGOs won the Nobel Peace Prize in the 1990s: International Campaign to Ban Landmines (1997) and Doctors Without Borders (1999). (p. 693)

North Atlantic Treaty Organization (NATO) Organization formed in 1949 as a military alliance of western European and North American states against the Soviet Union and its east European allies. (p. 657)

Olmec The first Mesoamerican civilization. Between about 1200 and 400 B.C.E., the Olmec people of central Mexico created a vibrant civilization that included intensive agriculture, wide-ranging trade, ceremonial centers, and monumental construction. The Olmec had great cultural influence on later Mesoamerican societies. (p. 158)

Oman Arab state based in Musqat, the main port in the southeast region of the Arabian peninsula. Oman succeeded Portugal as a power in the western Indian Ocean in the eighteenth century. (p. 445)

Opium War War between Britain and the Qing Empire that was, in the British view, occasioned by the Qing government's refusal to permit the importation of opium into its territories. The victorious British imposed the one-sided Treaty of Nanking on China. (p. 526)

Organization of Petroleum Exporting Countries (OPEC) Organization formed in 1960 by oil-producing states to promote their collective interest in generating revenue from oil. (p. 678)

Ottoman Empire Islamic state founded by Osman in northwestern Anatolia around 1300. After the fall of the Byzantine Empire, the Ottoman Empire was based at Istanbul (formerly Constantinople) from 1453 to 1922. It encompassed lands in the Middle East, North Africa, the Caucasus, and eastern Europe. (p. 293, 427)

Otto von Bismarck Chancellor (prime minister) of Prussia from 1862 until 1871, when he became chancellor of Germany. A conservative nationalist, he led Prussia to victory against Austria (1866) and France (1870) and was responsible for the creation of the German Empire in 1871. (p. 577)

Paleolithic The period of the Stone Age associated with the evolution of humans. (p. 7)

Panama Canal Ship canal cut across the Isthmus of Panama by U.S. Army engineers; it opened in 1914. It greatly shortened the sea voyage between the east and west coasts of North America. The United States turned the canal over to Panama on January 1, 2000. (p. 560)

Pan-Slavism Movement among Russian intellectuals in the second half of the nineteenth century to identify culturally and politically with the Slavic peoples of eastern Europe. (p. 522)

papacy The central administration of the Roman Catholic Church, of which the pope is the head. (p. 240, 381)

papyrus A reed that grows along the banks of the Nile River in Egypt. From it was produced a coarse, paperlike writing medium used by the Egyptians and many other peoples in the ancient Mediterranean and Middle East. (p. 23)

Parthians Iranian ruling dynasty between ca. 250 B.C.E. and 226 C.E. (p. 189)

pastoralism A way of life dependent on moving large herds of small and large stock to new pastures and watering places throughout the year. (p. 11)

patron/client relationship In ancient Rome, a fundamental social relationship in which the patron—a wealthy and powerful individual—provided legal and economic protection and assistance to clients, men of lesser status and means, and in return the clients supported the political careers and economic interests of their patron. (p. 109)

Paul A Jew from the Greek city of Tarsus in Anatolia, he initially persecuted the followers of Jesus but, after receiving a revelation on the road to Syrian Damascus, became a Christian.

Taking advantage of his Hellenized background and Roman citizenship, he traveled throughout Syria-Palestine, Anatolia, and Greece, preaching the new religion and establishing churches. Finding his greatest success among pagans ("gentiles"), he began the process by which Christianity separated from Judaism.   (p. 118)

pax Romana Literally, "Roman peace," it connoted the stability and prosperity that Roman rule brought to the lands of the Roman Empire in the first two centuries C.E. The movement of people and trade goods along Roman roads and safe seas allowed for the spread of cultural practices, technologies, and religious ideas.   (p. 117)

Pearl Harbor Naval base in Hawaii attacked by Japanese aircraft on December 7, 1941. The sinking of much of the U.S. Pacific Fleet brought the United States into World War II.   (p. 644)

Peloponnesian War A protracted (431–404 B.C.E.) and costly conflict between the Athenian and Spartan alliance systems that convulsed most of the Greek world. The war was largely a consequence of Athenian imperialism. Possession of a naval empire allowed Athens to fight a war of attrition. Ultimately, Sparta prevailed because of Athenian errors and Persian financial support.   (p. 100)

perestroika Policy of "restructuring" that was the centerpiece of Mikhail Gorbachev's efforts to liberalize communism in the Soviet Union.   (p. 680)

Pericles Aristocratic leader who guided the Athenian state through the transformation to full participatory democracy for all male citizens, supervised construction of the Acropolis, and pursued a policy of imperial expansion that led to the Peloponnesian War. He formulated a strategy of attrition but died from the plague early in the war.   (p. 93)

Persepolis A complex of palaces, reception halls, and treasury buildings erected by the Persian kings Darius I and Xerxes in the Persian homeland. It is believed that the New Year's festival was celebrated here, as well as the coronations, weddings, and funerals of the Persian kings, who were buried in cliff-tombs nearby.   (p. 86)

Persian Wars Conflicts between Greek city-states and the Persian Empire, ranging from the Ionian Revolt (499–494 B.C.E.) through Darius's punitive expedition that failed at Marathon (490 B.C.E.) and the defeat of Xerxes's massive invasion of Greece by the Spartan-led Hellenic League (480–479 B.C.E.). This first major setback for Persian arms launched the Greeks into their period of greatest cultural productivity. Herodotus chronicled these events in the first "history" in the Western tradition.   (p. 94)

Peter the Great Russian tsar (r. 1689–1725). He enthusiastically introduced Western languages and technologies to the Russian elite and moved the capital from Moscow to the new city of St. Petersburg.   (p. 441)

pharaoh The central figure in the ancient Egyptian state. Believed to be an earthly manifestation of the gods, he used his absolute power to maintain the safety and prosperity of Egypt.   (p. 22)

Phoenicians Canaanites living on the coast of modern Lebanon and Syria in the first millennium B.C.E. From major cities such as Tyre and Sidon, Phoenician merchants and sailors explored the Mediterranean, engaged in widespread commerce, and founded Carthage and other colonies in the western Mediterranean.   (p. 47)

pilgrimage Journey to a sacred shrine by Christians seeking to show their piety, fulfill vows, or gain absolution for sins. Other religions also have pilgrimage traditions, such as the Muslim pilgrimage to Mecca and the pilgrimages made by early Chinese Buddhists to India in search of sacred Buddhist writings.   (p. 250)

Pilgrims Group of English Protestant dissenters who established Plymouth Colony in Massachusetts in 1620 to seek religious freedom after having lived briefly in the Netherlands.   (p. 411)

polis The Greek term for a city-state, an urban center and the agricultural territory under its control. It was the characteristic form of political organization in southern and central Greece in the Archaic and Classical periods. Of the hundreds of city-states in the Mediterranean and Black Sea regions settled by Greeks, some were oligarchic, others democratic, depending on the powers delegated to the Council and the Assembly.   (p. 89)

positivism A philosophy developed by the French Count of Saint-Simon. Positivists believed that social and economic problems could be solved by application of the scientific method, leading to continuous progress. Their ideas became popular in France and Latin America in the nineteenth century.   (p. 485)

Potosí Located in Bolivia, one of the richest silver mining centers and most populous cities in colonial Spanish America.   (p. 405)

printing press A mechanical device for transferring text or graphics from a woodblock or type to paper using ink. Presses using movable type first appeared in Europe in about 1450.   (p. 321)

proletariat Industrial workers whose oppression was an example of how, according to *The Communist Manifesto*, history was dominated by class struggle between the workers who sold their labor for survival and those who owned the mills, factories, mines, or other means of industrial production and wealth (the bourgeoisie).   (p. 485)

Protestant Reformation Religious reform movement within the Latin Christian Church beginning in 1519. It resulted in the "protesters" forming several new Christian denominations, including the Lutheran and Reformed Churches and the Church of England.   (p. 382)

Ptolemies The Macedonian dynasty, descended from one of Alexander the Great's officers, that ruled Egypt for three centuries (323–30 B.C.E.). From their magnificent capital at Alexandria on the Mediterranean coast, the Ptolemies largely took over the system created by Egyptian pharaohs to extract the wealth of the land, rewarding Greeks and Hellenized non-Greeks serving in the military and administration.   (p. 102)

Puritans English Protestant dissenters who believed that God predestined souls to Heaven or Hell before birth. They founded Massachusetts Bay Colony in 1629.   (p. 411)

pyramid A large, triangular stone monument, used in Egypt and Nubia as a burial place for the king. The largest pyramids, erected during the Old Kingdom near Memphis, reflect the Egyptian belief that the proper and spectacular burial of the divine ruler would guarantee the continued prosperity of the land.   (p. 22)

Qin A people and state in the Wei River Valley of eastern China that conquered rival states and created the first Chinese empire (221–206 B.C.E.). The Qin ruler, Shi Huangdi, standardized many features of Chinese society and ruthlessly marshaled subjects for military and construction projects, engendering hostility that led to the fall of his dynasty shortly after his death. The Qin framework was largely taken over by the succeeding Han dynasty.   (p. 125)

Qing Empire Empire established in China by Manchus who overthrew the Ming Empire in 1644. At various times the Qing also controlled Manchuria, Mongolia, Turkestan, and Tibet. The last Qing emperor was overthrown in 1911.   (p. 457)

Quran Book composed of divine revelations made to the Prophet Muhammad between roughly 610 and his death in 632; the sacred text of the religion of Islam.   (p. 213)

railroads Networks of iron (later steel) rails on which steam (later electric or diesel) locomotives pulled long trains at high speeds. The first railroads were built in England in the 1830s. Their success caused a railroad-building boom throughout the world that lasted well into the twentieth century. (p. 565)

Rajputs Members of a mainly Hindu warrior caste from northwest India. The Mughal emperors drew most of their Hindu officials from this caste, and Akbar married a Rajput princess. (p. 438)

Ramesses II A long-lived ruler of New Kingdom Egypt (r. 1290–1224 B.C.E.). He reached an accommodation with the Hittites of Anatolia after a standoff in battle at Kadesh in Syria. He built on a grand scale throughout Egypt. (p. 35)

Rashid al-Din Adviser to the Il-khan ruler Ghazan, who converted to Islam on Rashid's advice. (p. 289)

recaptives Africans rescued by Britain's Royal Navy from the illegal slave trade of the nineteenth century and restored to free status. (p. 548)

reconquest of Iberia Beginning in the eleventh century, military campaigns by various Iberian Christian states to recapture territory taken by Muslims. In 1492 the last Muslim ruler was defeated, and Spain and Portugal emerged as united kingdoms. (p. 324)

Renaissance (European) A period of intense artistic and intellectual activity, said to be a "rebirth" of Greco-Roman culture. Usually divided into an Italian Renaissance, from roughly the mid-fourteenth to mid-fifteenth century, and a Northern (trans-Alpine) Renaissance, from roughly the early fifteenth to early seventeenth century. (p. 318)

Revolutions of 1848 Democratic and nationalist revolutions that swept across Europe. The monarchy in France was briefly overthrown. In Germany, Austria, Italy, and Hungary the revolutions failed. (p. 502)

Romanization The process by which the Latin language and Roman culture became dominant in the western provinces. Indigenous peoples in the provinces often chose to Romanize because of the political and economic advantages that it brought, as well as the allure of Roman success. (p. 117)

Roman Principate A term used to characterize Roman government in the first three centuries C.E., based on the ambiguous title *princeps* ("first citizen") adopted by Augustus to conceal his military dictatorship. (p. 112)

Roman Republic The period from 507 to 31 B.C.E., during which Rome was largely governed by the aristocratic Roman Senate. (p. 109)

Roman Senate A council whose members were the heads of wealthy, landowning families. Originally an advisory body to the early kings, in the era of the Roman Republic the Senate effectively governed the Roman state and the growing empire. Under Senate leadership, Rome conquered an empire of unprecedented extent in the lands surrounding the Mediterranean Sea. (p. 109)

Royal African Company A trading company chartered by the English government in 1672 to conduct its merchants' trade on the Atlantic coast of Africa. (p. 419)

sacrifice A gift given to a deity, often with the aim of creating a relationship, gaining favor, and obligating the god to provide some benefit to the sacrificer, sometimes in order to sustain the deity and thereby guarantee the continuing vitality of the natural world. (p. 91)

Saddam Husain (1937–2006) President of Iraq from 1979 until overthrown by the American invasion in 2003. Waged war on Iran from 1980 to 1988. His invasion of Kuwait was repulsed in the Persian Gulf War of 1991. (p. 679)

Safavid Empire Iranian kingdom (1502–1722) established by Ismail Safavi, who declared Iran a Shi'ite state. (p. 434)

Sahel Belt south of the Sahara; literally "coastland" in Arabic. (p. 198)

Salvador Allende (1908–1973) Socialist president of Chile who was elected in 1970 and overthrown and killed by the military in 1973. (p. 672)

samurai Literally "those who serve," the hereditary military elite of the Tokugawa Shogunate. (p. 453)

Sandinistas Members of a leftist coalition that overthrew the Nicaraguan dictator Anastosio Somoza in 1979 and attempted to install a socialist economy. The United States financed an armed uprising against the Sandinista government. In 1990 the Sandinistas lost power after a national election. (p. 672)

Sasanid Empire Iranian empire, established around 224, with a capital in Ctesiphon, Mesopotamia. The Sasanid emperors established Zoroastrianism as the state religion. Islamic Arab armies overthrew the empire around 651. (p. 208)

satrap The governor of a province in the Achaemenid Persian Empire, often a relative of the king. He was responsible for protection of the province and for forwarding tribute to the central administration. Satraps in outlying provinces enjoyed considerable autonomy. (p. 85)

savanna Tropical or subtropical grassland, either treeless or with occasional clumps of trees. Most extensive in sub-Saharan Africa but also present in South America. (p. 199)

schism A formal split within a religious community. (p. 232)

scholasticism A philosophical and theological system, associated with Thomas Aquinas, devised to reconcile Aristotelian philosophy and Roman Catholic theology in the thirteenth century. (p. 319)

Scientific Revolution The intellectual movement in Europe, initially associated with planetary motion and other aspects of physics, that by the seventeenth century had laid the groundwork for modern science. (p. 386)

scribe In the governments of many ancient societies, a professional position reserved for men who had undergone the lengthy training required to be able to read and write using cuneiform, hieroglyphics, or other early, cumbersome writing systems. (p. 18)

Scythians Term used by the ancient Greeks for the nomadic peoples living on the steppe north of the Black and Caspian Seas. (p. 71)

seasoning An often difficult period of adjustment to new climates, disease environments, and work routines, such as that experienced by slaves newly arrived in the Americas. (p. 417)

"separate spheres" Nineteenth-century idea in Western societies that men and women, especially of the middle class, should have clearly differentiated roles in society: women as wives, mothers, and homemakers; men as breadwinners and participants in business and politics. (p. 571)

sepoy A soldier in colonial India, especially in the service of the British. (p. 549)

Sepoy Rebellion The revolt of Indian soldiers in 1857 against certain practices that violated religious customs; also known as the Sepoy Mutiny. (p. 551)

Serbia The Ottoman province in the Balkans that rose up against Janissary control in the early 1800s. After World War II the central province of Yugoslavia. (p. 514)

serf In medieval Europe, an agricultural laborer legally bound to a lord's property and obligated to perform set services for the lord. In Russia, later, some serfs worked as artisans and in factories; serfdom was not abolished there until 1861. (p. 237, 441)

shaft graves A term used for the burial sites of elite members of Mycenaean Greek society in the mid-second millennium B.C.E. At the bottom of deep shafts lined with stone slabs, the bodies were laid out along with gold and bronze jewelry, implements, weapons, and masks. (p. 37)

Shah Abbas I The fifth and most renowned ruler of the Safavid dynasty in Iran (r. 1587–1629). Abbas moved the royal capital to Isfahan in 1598. (p. 435)

shamanism The practice of identifying special individuals (shamans) who will interact with spirits for the benefit of the community. Characteristic of the Korean kingdoms of the early medieval period and of early societies of Central Asia. (p. 270)

Shang The dominant people in the earliest Chinese dynasty for which we have written records (ca. 1750–1045 B.C.E.). (p. 60)

Shi Huangdi Founder of the short-lived Qin dynasty and creator of the Chinese Empire (r. 221–210 B.C.E.). He is remembered for his ruthless conquests of rival states, standardization of practices, and forcible organization of labor for military and engineering tasks. His tomb, with its army of life-size terracotta soldiers, has been partially excavated. (p. 125)

Shi'ites Muslims belonging to the branch of Islam believing that God vests leadership of the community in a descendant of Muhammad's son-in-law Ali. Shi'ism is the state religion of Iran. (p. 213)

Shi'ites Muslims belonging to the branch of Islam believing that God vests leadership of the community in a descendant of Muhammad's son-in-law Ali. Shi'ism is the state religion of Iran. (p. 434)

Siberia The extreme northeastern sector of Asia, including the Kamchatka Peninsula and the present Russian coast of the Arctic Ocean, the Bering Strait, and the Sea of Okhotsk. (p. 440)

Sigmund Freud (1856–1939) Austrian psychiatrist, founder of psychoanalysis. He argued that psychological problems were caused by traumas, especially sexual experiences in early childhood, that were repressed in later life. His ideas caused considerable controversy among psychologists and in the general public. Although his views on repressed sexuality are no longer widely accepted, his psychoanalytic methods are still very influential. (p. 610)

Silk Road Caravan routes connecting China and the Middle East across Central Asia and Iran. (p. 187)

Simón Bolívar The most important military leader in the struggle for independence in South America. Born in Venezuela, he led military forces there and in Colombia, Ecuador, Peru, and Bolivia. (p. 504)

Slavophiles Russian intellectuals in the early nineteenth century who favored resisting western European influences and taking pride in the traditional peasant values and institutions of the Slavic peoples. (p. 522)

"small traditions" Historians' term for a localized, usually nonliterate, set of customs and beliefs adhered to by a single society, often in conjunction with a "great tradition." (p. 199)

socialism A political ideology that originated in Europe in the 1830s. Socialists advocated government protection of workers from exploitation by property owners and government ownership of industries. This ideology led to the founding of socialist or labor parties throughout Europe in the second half of the nineteenth century. (p. 573)

Socrates Athenian philosopher (ca. 470–399 B.C.E.) who shifted the emphasis of philosophical investigation from questions of natural science to ethics and human behavior. He attracted young disciples from elite families but made enemies by revealing the ignorance and pretensions of others, culminating in his trial and execution by the Athenian state. (p. 96)

Sokoto Caliphate A large Muslim state founded in 1809 in what is now northern Nigeria. (p. 543)

Solidarity Polish trade union created in 1980 to protest working conditions and political repression. It began the nationalist opposition in eastern Europe. (p. 681)

Song Empire Empire in central and southern China (960–1126) while the Liao people controlled the north. Empire in southern China (1127–1279; the "Southern Song") while the Jin people controlled the north. Distinguished for its advances in technology, medicine, astronomy, and mathematics. (p. 263)

Spanish-American War U.S. war fought with Spanish in 1898 over control of Cuba, ostensibly because of the sinking of a U.S. ship and also after reports of Spanish atrocities had fanned flames of American popular opinion. Won handily in three months, the war unofficially made Cuba a protectorate of the United States. (p. 557)

Srivijaya A state based on the Indonesian island of Sumatra between the seventh and eleventh centuries C.E. It amassed wealth and power by a combination of selective adaptation of Indian technologies and concepts, control of the lucrative trade routes between India and China, and skillful showmanship and diplomacy in holding together a disparate realm of inland and coastal territories. (p. 151)

Stalingrad City in Russia, site of a Red Army victory over the German army in 1942–1943. The Battle of Stalingrad was the turning point in the war between Germany and the Soviet Union. Today Volgograd. (p. 644)

steam engine A machine that turns the energy released by burning fuel into motion. Thomas Newcomen built the first crude but workable steam engine in 1712. James Watt vastly improved his device in the 1760s and 1770s. Steam power was later applied to operating machinery in factories and to propelling ships and locomotives. (p. 479)

steel A form of iron that is both durable and flexible. It was first mass-produced in the 1860s and quickly became the most widely used metal in construction, machinery, and railroad equipment. (p. 567)

steppe An ecological region of grass- and shrub-covered plains that is treeless and too arid for agriculture. (p. 70, 199)

stock exchange A place where shares in a company or business enterprise are bought and sold. (p. 391)

Stone Age The historical period characterized by the production of tools from stone and other nonmetallic substances. (p. 7)

submarine telegraph cables Insulated copper cables laid along the bottom of a sea or ocean for telegraphic communication. The first short cable was laid under the Hooghly River in Calcutta in 1839; the first successful transatlantic cable was laid in 1866. (p. 567)

sub-Saharan Africa Portion of the African continent lying south of the Sahara. (p. 195)

Suez Canal Ship canal dug across the Isthmus of Suez in Egypt, designed by Ferdinand de Lesseps. It opened to shipping in 1869 and shortened the sea voyage between Europe and Asia. Its strategic importance led to the British occupation of Egypt in 1882. (p. 545)

Suleiman the Magnificent The most illustrious sultan of the Ottoman Empire (r. 1520–1566); also known as Suleiman Kanuni, "The Lawgiver." He significantly expanded the empire in the Balkans and eastern Mediterranean. (p. 428)

Sumerians The people who dominated southern Mesopotamia through the end of the third millennium B.C.E.   (p. 15)

Sunnis Muslims belonging to branch of Islam believing that the community should select its own leadership. The majority religion in most Islamic countries.   (p. 214)

Sun Yat-sen (1867–1925) Chinese nationalist revolutionary, founder and leader of the Guomindang until his death. He attempted to create a liberal democratic political movement in China but was thwarted by military leaders.   (p. 597)

Swahili Bantu language with Arabic loanwords spoken in coastal regions of East Africa.   (p. 445)

Swahili Coast East African shores of the Indian Ocean between the Horn of Africa and the Zambezi River; from the Arabic *sawahil*, meaning "shores."   (p. 339)

Taiping Rebellion A Christian-inspired rural rebellion that threatened to topple the Qing Empire.   (p. 528)

Tamil kingdoms The kingdoms of southern India, inhabited primarily by speakers of Dravidian languages, which developed in partial isolation, and somewhat differently, from the Arya north. They produced epics, poetry, and performance arts. Elements of Tamil religious beliefs were merged into the Hindu synthesis.   (p. 146)

Tang Empire Empire unifying China and part of Inner Asia (618–907). The Tang emperors presided over a magnificent court at their capital, Chang'an.   (p. 256)

Tanzimat Restructuring reforms by the nineteenth-century Ottoman rulers, intended to move civil law away from the control of religious elites and make the military and the bureaucracy more efficient.   (p. 515)

tax farmers Private individuals or small partnerships who were given contracts to collect taxes for the government. In return tax farmers could keep whatever money they were able to collect above their tax obligation to the government.   (p. 397)

Tenochtitlan Capital of the Aztec Empire, located on an island in Lake Texcoco. Its population was above 150,000 on the eve of the Spanish conquest. Mexico City was constructed on its ruins.   (p. 346)

Teotihuacan A powerful city-state in central Mexico (100 B.C.E.–750 C.E.). Its population was about 150,000 at its peak in 600.   (p. 163)

terrorism Political belief that extreme and seemingly random violence will destabilize a government and permit the terrorists to gain political advantage. Though an old technique, terrorism gained prominence in the late twentieth century with the growth of worldwide mass media that, through their news coverage, amplified public fears of terrorist acts.   (p. 692)

theater-state Historians' term for a state that acquires prestige and power by developing attractive cultural forms and staging elaborate public ceremonies (as well as redistributing valuable resources) to attract and bind subjects to the center. Examples include the Gupta Empire in India and Srivijaya in Southeast Asia.   (p. 147)

Thebes Capital city of Egypt and home of the ruling dynasties during the Middle and New Kingdoms. Monarchs were buried across the river in the Valley of the Kings.   (p. 23)

Theravada Buddhism "Way of the Elders" branch of Buddhism followed in Sri Lanka and much of Southeast Asia. Theravada remains close to the original principles set forth by the Buddha; it downplays the importance of gods and emphasizes austerity and the individual's search for enlightenment.   (p. 141)

third-century crisis Historians' term for the political, military, and economic turmoil that beset the Roman Empire during much of the third century C.E.: frequent changes of ruler, civil wars, barbarian invasions, decline of urban centers, and near-destruction of long-distance commerce and the monetary economy. After 284 C.E. Diocletian restored order by making fundamental changes.   (p. 120)

Third World Term applied to a group of developing countries who professed nonalignment during the Cold War.   (p. 665)

Thomas Edison American inventor best known for inventing the electric light bulb, acoustic recording on wax cylinders, and motion pictures.   (p. 568)

Thomas Malthus (1766–1834) Eighteenth-century English intellectual who warned that population growth threatened the future generations because, in his view, it would always outstrip increases in agricultural production.   (p. 697)

three-field system A rotational system for agriculture in which two fields grow food crops and one lies fallow. It gradually replaced the two-field system in medieval Europe.   (p. 308)

Tibet Country centered on the high, mountain-bounded plateau north of India. Tibetan political power occasionally extended farther to the north and west between the seventh and thirteenth centuries.   (p. 259)

Timbuktu City on the Niger River in the modern country of Mali. It was founded by the Tuareg as a seasonal camp sometime after 1000. As part of the Mali Empire, Timbuktu became a major terminus of the trans-Saharan trade and a center of Islamic learning.   (p. 343)

Timur Member of a prominent family of the Mongols' Chagatai Khanate, Timur through conquest gained control over much of Central Asia and Iran. He consolidated the status of Sunni Islam as orthodox, and his descendants, the Timurids, maintained his empire for nearly a century and founded the Mughal Empire in India.   (p. 289)

Tiwanaku Name of capital city and empire centered on the region near Lake Titicaca in modern Bolivia (375–1000 C.E.).   (p. 175)

Tokugawa Shogunate The last of the three shogunates of Japan.   (p. 454)

Toltecs Powerful postclassic empire in central Mexico (900–1175 C.E.). It influenced much of Mesoamerica. Aztecs claimed ties to this earlier civilization.   (p. 168)

Toussaint L'Ouverture Leader of the Haitian Revolution. He freed the slaves and gained effective independence for Haiti despite military interventions by the British and French.   (p. 503)

trans-Saharan caravan routes Trading network linking North Africa with sub-Saharan Africa across the Sahara.   (p. 195)

Treaty of Nanking The treaty that concluded the Opium War. It awarded Britain a large indemnity from the Qing Empire, denied the Qing government tariff control over some of its own borders, opened additional ports of residence to Britons, and ceded the island of Hong Kong to Britain.   (p. 528)

Treaty of Versailles (1919) The treaty imposed on Germany by France, Great Britain, the United States, and other Allied powers after World War I. It demanded that Germany dismantle its military and give up some lands to Poland. It humiliated but did not weaken Germany.   (p. 595)

treaty ports Cities opened to foreign residents as a result of the forced treaties between the Qing Empire and foreign signatories. In the treaty ports, foreigners enjoyed extraterritoriality.   (p. 528)

tributary system A system in which, from the time of the Han Empire, countries in East and Southeast Asia not under the direct control of empires based in China nevertheless enrolled as tributary states, acknowledging the superiority of the emperors in China in exchange for trading rights or strategic alliances.   (p. 257)

tribute system A system in which defeated peoples were forced to pay a tax in the form of goods and labor. The forced transfer of food, cloth, and other goods subsidized the development of large cities. An important component of the Aztec and Inka economies.   (p. 347)

trireme Greek and Phoenician warship of the fifth and fourth centuries B.C.E. It was sleek and light, powered by 170 oars arranged in three vertical tiers. Manned by skilled sailors, it was capable of short bursts of speed and complex maneuvers.   (p. 95)

tropical rain forest High-precipitation forest zones of the Americas, Africa, and Asia lying between the Tropic of Cancer and the Tropic of Capricorn.   (p. 199)

tropics Equatorial region between the Tropic of Cancer and the Tropic of Capricorn. It is characterized by generally warm or hot temperatures year-round, though much variation exists due to altitude and other factors. Temperate zones north and south of the tropics generally have a winter season.   (p. 329)

Truman Doctrine Foreign policy initiated by U.S. president Harry Truman in 1947. It offered military aid to help Turkey and Greece resist Soviet military pressure and subversion.   (p. 660)

tsar (czar) From Latin *caesar*, this Russian title for a monarch was first used in reference to a Russian ruler by Ivan III (r. 1462–1505).   (p. 292, 440)

Tulip Period Last years of the reign of Ottoman sultan Ahmed III (1718–1730), during which European styles and attitudes became briefly popular in Istanbul.   (p. 432)

tyrant The term the Greeks used to describe someone who seized and held power in violation of the normal procedures and traditions of the community. Tyrants appeared in many Greek city-states in the seventh and sixth centuries B.C.E., often taking advantage of the disaffection of the emerging middle class and, by weakening the old elite, unwittingly contributing to the evolution of democracy.   (p. 90)

tzompantli Images of impaled skulls in scenes of human sacrifice included in the decoration of a prominent public buildings and temples in Tula.   (p. 168)

Uighurs A group of Turkish-speakers who controlled their own centralized empire from 744 to 840 in Mongolia and Central Asia.   (p. 259)

ulama Muslim religious scholars. From the ninth century onward, the primary interpreters of Islamic law and the social core of Muslim urban societies.   (p. 219)

Umayyad Caliphate First hereditary dynasty of Muslim caliphs (661 to 750). From their capital at Damascus, the Umayyads ruled an empire that extended from Spain to India. Overthrown by the Abbasid Caliphate.   (p. 213)

umma The community of all Muslims. A major innovation against the background of seventh-century Arabia, where traditionally kinship rather than faith had determined membership in a community.   (p. 212)

United Nations International organization founded in 1945 to promote world peace and cooperation. It replaced the League of Nations.   (p. 657)

Universal Declaration of Human Rights A 1948 United Nations covenant binding signatory nations to the observance of specified rights.   (p. 693)

universities Degree-granting institutions of higher learning. Those that appeared in the countries of western Europe from about 1200 onward became the model of all modern universities.   (p. 318)

Urdu A Persian-influenced literary form of Hindi written in Arabic characters and used as a literary language since the 1300s.   (p. 343)

Usama bin Laden (1957–2011) Saudi-born Muslim extremist who funded the al-Qaeda organization that was responsible for several terrorist attacks, including those on the World Trade Center and the Pentagon in 2001.   (p. 692)

varna/jati Two categories of social identity of great importance in Indian history. Varnas are the four major social divisions: the Brahmin priest class, the Kshatriya warrior/administrator class, the Vaishya merchant/farmer class, and the Shudra laborer class. Within the system of varnas are many jatis, regional groups of people who have a common occupational sphere and who marry, eat, and generally interact with other members of their group.   (p. 138)

Vasco da Gama Portuguese explorer. In 1497–1498 he led the first naval expedition from Europe to sail to India, opening an important commercial sea route.   (p. 363)

vassal In medieval Europe, a sworn supporter of a king or lord committed to rendering specified military service to that king or lord.   (p. 238)

Vedas Early Indian sacred "knowledge"—the literal meaning of the term—long preserved and communicated orally by Brahmin priests and eventually written down. These religious texts, including the thousand poetic hymns to various deities contained in the *Rig Veda*, are our main source of information about the Vedic period (ca. 1500–500 B.C.E.).   (p. 138)

Versailles The huge palace built for French king Louis XIV south of Paris. The palace symbolized both French power and the triumph of royal authority over the French nobility.   (p. 396)

Victorian Age The reign of Queen Victoria of Great Britain (r. 1837–1901). The term is also used to describe late-nineteenth-century society, with its rigid moral standards and sharply differentiated roles for men and women and for middle-class and working-class people.   (p. 570)

Vietnam War (1954–1975) Conflict pitting North Vietnam and South Vietnamese communist guerrillas against the South Vietnamese government, aided after 1961 by the United States.   (p. 661)

Vladimir Lenin (1870–1924) Leader of the Bolshevik (later Communist) Party. He lived in exile in Switzerland until 1917, then returned to Russia to lead the Bolsheviks to victory during the Russian Revolution and the civil war that followed.   (p. 592)

Wari Andean civilization culturally linked to Tiwanaku, perhaps beginning as a colony of Tiwanaku.   (p. 175)

Warsaw Pact The 1955 treaty binding the Soviet Union and countries of eastern Europe in an alliance against the North Atlantic Treaty Organization.   (p. 657)

western front A line of trenches and fortifications in World War I that stretched without a break from Switzerland to the North Sea. Scene of most of the fighting between Germany, on the one hand, and France and Britain, on the other.   (p. 588)

Wilbur (1867–1912) and Orville (1871–1948) Wright American bicycle mechanics; the first to build and fly an airplane, at Kitty Hawk, North Carolina, December 7, 1903.   (p. 611)

witch-hunt The pursuit of people suspected of witchcraft, especially in northern Europe in the late sixteenth and seventeenth centuries.   (p. 385)

Women's Rights Convention An 1848 gathering of women angered by their exclusion from an international antislavery meeting. They met at Seneca Falls, New York, to discuss women's rights.   (p. 507)

Woodrow Wilson (1856–1924) President of the United States (1913–1921) and a leading figure at the Paris Peace Conference of 1919. He was unable to persuade the U.S. Congress to ratify the Treaty of Versailles or join the League of Nations.   (p. 593)

World Bank A specialized agency of the United Nations that makes loans to countries for economic development, trade promotion, and debt consolidation. Its formal name is the International Bank for Reconstruction and Development.   (p. 658)

World Trade Organization (WTO) An international body established in 1995 to foster and bring order to international trade.   (p. 689)

Xiongnu A confederation of nomadic peoples living beyond the northwest frontier of ancient China. Chinese rulers tried a variety of defenses and stratagems to ward off these "barbarians," as they called them, and finally succeeded in dispersing the Xiongnu in the first century C.E.   (p. 129)

Yamagata Aritomo One of the leaders of the Meiji Restoration.   (p. 583)

yin/yang In Chinese belief, complementary factors that help to maintain the equilibrium of the world. Yang is associated with masculine, light, and active qualities; yin with feminine, dark, and passive qualities.   (p. 66)

Yongle The third emperor of the Ming Empire (r. 1403–1424). He sponsored the building of the Forbidden City, a huge encyclopedia project, the expeditions of Zheng He, and the reopening of China's borders to trade and travel.   (p. 296)

Young Ottomans Movement of young intellectuals to institute liberal reforms and build a feeling of national identity in the Ottoman Empire in the second half of the nineteenth century.   (p. 521)

Yuan Empire Empire created in China and Siberia by Khubilai Khan.   (p. 282)

Yuan Shikai (1859–1916) Chinese general and first president of the Chinese Republic (1912–1916). He stood in the way of the democratic movement led by Sun Yat-sen.   (p. 597)

Zen The Japanese word for a branch of Mahayana Buddhism based on highly disciplined meditation. It is known in Sanskrit as *dhyana*, in Chinese as *chan*, and in Korean as *son*.   (p. 265)

Zheng He An imperial eunuch and Muslim, entrusted by the Ming emperor Yongle with a series of state voyages that took his gigantic ships through the Indian Ocean, from Southeast Asia to Africa.   (p. 297)

Zhou The people and dynasty that took over the dominant position in north China from the Shang and created the concept of the Mandate of Heaven to justify their rule. The Zhou era, particularly the vigorous early period (1045–771 B.C.E.), was remembered in Chinese tradition as a time of prosperity and benevolent rule.   (p. 61)

ziggurat A massive pyramidal stepped tower made of mud bricks. It is associated with religious complexes in ancient Mesopotamian cities, but its function is unknown.   (p. 16)

Zoroastrianism A religion originating in ancient Iran that became the official religion of the Achaemenids. It centered on a single benevolent deity, Ahuramazda, who engaged in a struggle with demonic forces before prevailing and restoring a pristine world. It emphasized truth-telling, purity, and reverence for nature.   (p. 87)

Zulu A people of modern South Africa whom King Shaka united in 1818.   (p. 539)

INDEX